ANCIENT INDIAN POLITICAL THOUGHT AND INSTITUTIONS

ANCIENT INDIAN POLITICAL THOUGHT AND INSTITUTIONS

BHASKER ANAND SALETORE

GYAN

Published by

GYAN

Gyan Publishing House
5, Ansari Road
Daryaganj, New Delhi-110002
Phone: 011-47034999, 9811692060
E-mail: books@gyanbooks.com

Distribution Network
gyanbooks.com
India, USA, Canada, UK, Australia

ISBN: 978-93-6920-082-5 (HB)

First Published, 1963

2nd Impression 2025

Printed at: Gyan Press, Delhi.

ANCIENT INDIAN POLITICAL THOUGHT AND INSTITUTIONS
Author: BHASKER ANAND SALETORE

ANCIENT INDIAN POLITICAL THOUGHT AND INSTITUTIONS

ANCIENT INDIAN POLITICAL THOUGHT AND INSTITUTIONS

BHASKER ANAND SALETORE
M.A., PH.D. (LOND.), D.PHIL. (GIESSEN)
Director of National Archives (Retired)
Government of India

To My Wife

KAMALA SALETORE

PREFACE

THE SUBJECT matter of this book is fortunately receiving now a wider recognition at the hands of the Indian Universities than before. This is but natural when it is realized that the political thought and institutions of the ancient Indians are best studied along with the facts of their history. Indeed, State action in the past is understood and appreciated only on the background of political thought. Those like me engaged in teaching this subject to the Post-Graduate classes, have, however, felt a need of a work which would give in one compass materials that are spread over a number of books. I have attempted, therefore, in this work to present the political theories and institutions of the ancients in a manner which, I hope, will be serviceable to the students as well as to laymen interested in this important subject.

In one particular detail, this book is a departure from others dealing with the same topic. I have ventured to assess the relative work of four great political thinkers of the ancient times—Manu, Hammurabi, Aristotle, and Kauṭilya—in the field of ancient political thought. I am not aware of any scholar who has undertaken a comparative study of the four great minds in the manner I have done. As to how far my method has been successful is left to the reader to judge.

It will be noticed in the following pages that I have taken my stand by a few well-known names in the history of ancient political thought. This is inevitable, especially when we remember that we know more about them than about many others, whose works are either lost to us, or are known to us only as intelligent abridgements of the *dharmaśāstras* and the *arthaśāstras* mentioned in these pages. And if in the course of this study, heavy weightage has been put on the side of Kauṭilya, it is because he, more than any one else, epitomized in himself the fundamental ideas that were agitating the minds of the ancients in the most formative period of their history.

My obligations are due to all the previous authors on the subject, whom I have mentioned at every step, and whose works have made it possible for me to write this book. If I have taken the liberty of differing from them in some essentials, it is because I feel that we are all engaged in the eternal task of laying "bare the grain of truth which exists at the core of every political practice and belief".

Bombay B. A. SALETORE

CONTENTS

PART ONE

INTRODUCTORY

PART TWO

THE MAIN SCHOOLS OF POLITICAL THOUGHT

PART FIVE

POLITICAL INSTITUTIONS (ELEMENTS OF THE STATE)

PART SIX

THEORY IN PRACTICE

Part One

INTRODUCTORY

CHAPTER I

MAIN CHARACTERISTICS OF OUR STUDY

A. A STUDY OF GREAT MINDS AND ENDEAVOURS

THE HISTORY of ancient Indian political thought is the story of great minds that evolved political institutions and guided Hindu society for nearly three millenniums. Its significance lies also in the fact that it deals with a vast country which has had a civilization that goes back to at least 5,000 years from now, and which witnessed the rise and fall of many kingdoms and empires in the course of its long and eventful history. Our study takes us to a literature of considerable antiquity in which the roots of Indian political thought and institutions may be said to have been laid. Because of their practical utility and service to the community, the ancient Indian political institutions were carefully fostered and maintained for well-nigh three thousand years. This by itself entitles our study to considerable respect at our hands, especially when we compare the longevity and stability of our institutions with those of the great countries of antiquity like Babylonia and Egypt. Unlike the political institutions of those ancient countries which, to some extent in the earliest ages, were contemporaneous with those of this land, these latter survived the shocks of Time, and were handed down almost intact till our own days.

B. ITS CONTINUITY

In this sense our study is marked by a continuity which is its next significant feature. Superficially it might seem that later political thinkers merely reproduced the theories of earlier writers. This view might receive some support when, for instance, we come across a statement of the great lawgiver Manu who, while describing the duties of the priestly class relating to education, enjoins that neither the *śruti* (sacred knowledge, the *Veda*) nor the *smṛiti* (knowledge delivered by human authors, civil and religious law) could be opposed by heterodox arguments, since from the two proceed the whole system of duties ; and that men of the three highest classes in society, who treat with contempt these two roots of *dharma,* should be driven out as atheists from the company of the virtuous.[1] This referred to the rejection of the ancient doctrines, and not to their criticism or modification. The ancients were too generous and tolerant to disarm legitimate criticism. It is this which explains why, in the purely speculative fields of religious thought, they had room for such agnostic teachers like Bṛihaspati, whose school came to be called Cārvāka or Lokāyata;[2] and why in the purely practical side of life, they had, as we shall see presently, in the fourth century B.C., a great statesman and thinker, who not only mentioned the prominent theorists preceding him, but criticized them, including his own unnamed teacher, in the most unequivocal terms. It would, therefore, be incorrect to maintain that the ancient theorists merely echoed one another; on the other hand, they carefully maintained what their predecessors had said in regard to political thought, recorded wherever necessary divergent opinions, and thereby added to the totality and continuity of the subject. Their conservatism was by itself one of the factors which enabled our subject to possess a continuity of its own. It is this sequence which, to use the language of a well-known modern British historian—who writes, no doubt, in a different context,—is noticeable between the successive chapters or periods in the history of one and the same society.[3] Herein lies a special feature of our study which marks it as being peculiarly interesting in the field of Eastern Political Thought and Institutions.

C. AN INTELLIGIBLE FIELD OF STUDY

The above is related to another important aspect of our study. The continuity of ancient Indian political thought and institutions makes it an intelligible field of enquiry. This is particularly noticeable when we take into account the genesis of ancient political thought, the institutions which it brought into existence, the factors which helped their growth from their primitive stage to, for instance, the age of the great lawgiver Manu, when they received to a great extent their general form, and their final crystallization in the later age of Kauṭilya, after which they remained practically unchanged for centuries. Indeed, it may legitimately be maintained that there was progress in political thought from the earliest times till those of Kauṭilya after whose days "the conditions were, in a sense", as the late Professor K. V. Rangaswamy Aiyangar rightly affirmed, "unfavourable to the advance of political speculation".[4]

D. SUBJECT COMPLETE IN ITSELF

From this point of view, our subject is not only continuous but complete in itself, carrying with it the characteristics of an ancient beginning, an enduring growth through centuries, and a long fulfilment and flowering which invest it with an abiding interest and fascination that are unique in the wide field of historical studies. To the moderners the study has a special appeal in the sense that, as we shall see later on in this book, some of the fundamental problems which were tackled by the ancient Indian theorists and statesmen, have a striking resemblance to those which confront the modern State. In this sense, the ancient Indians traversed much ground which, inspite of centuries of turmoil, transformation, and travail, seems to present problems of perplexity, although of a slightly different hue and texture, to the present-day statesmen.

CHAPTER II

LIMITATIONS OF OUR STUDY

A. CHRONOLOGICAL DIFFICULTY

A STUDY like ours that covers centuries of thought and action naturally is beset with certain limitations. The first is the want of chronological data which could have made it more precise and accurate. The chronological difficulty centers round the ancient literature upon which is based our knowledge of the most ancient Indian thinkers, the great theorists themselves, and the ages that intervened between them. Not only are the ages in which the earliest literature, like the *Vedas,* the *Āraṇyakas,* and the *Samhitas* which give us a glimpse of the ancient Indian political thought, still subject to speculation, but the periods separating them and the writings of great thinkers like Manu are also a matter of uncertainty.

Add to this difficulty is the one which surrounds that great lawgiver himself and others who came after him. The problem is made more complicated by the wide divergence of opinion among scholars as to the existence of one or more Manus, and by the views postulated by some that Manu was of a comparatively later date.[5] We shall refer again to the problem of Manu in a later context in this work.

B. RELATIONSHIP BETWEEN DIFFERENT SCHOOLS UNCERTAIN

The complications are made worse when we note the names of political thinkers after Manu and before Kauṭilya, the ages in which they lived, and the relationship between the different schools founded by them. There is nothing that could enable us to establish any connection between the many schools of political thought in the ages ranging from that of Manu down to that of Kāmandaka, excepting the fact that the theorists who came later mention those who lived earlier, agreeing with the latter in many, and differing from them in some, details. This by itself does not enable us to postulate anything beyond the generalization that there were schools of political thought that succeeded one another. We shall see below that the succession of those schools rest more on speculation than on fact.

C. RECURRENCE OF IDENTICAL NAMES

The difficulty of fixing chronologically the ages of the great political thinkers, and the uncertainty of deciding the relationship between their schools of thought are made worse by the next obstacle which comes in our way. This relates to the recurrence of identical names of political theorists. We may take the greatest among them mentioned above, Manu. In the *Rig Veda*, the *Atharva Veda*, and the *Taittirīya Samhita*, he appears to be only a legendary person, the first man, the father of the race, "with no claim to historical reality".[6] It would mean that Manu, in the pre-Vedic and Vedic ages, was not a sovereign. But in some passages in the *Yajur Samhitas* and in the *Brāhmaṇas*, he is described as the first consecrated man—a view which is repeated in the Epics.[7] This fact that in some of the earlier Vedic texts there is no reference to Manu as the first sovereign ruler, is to be borne in mind when we shall describe and comment below on the antiquity of the ancient Indian political thought and institutions.

The difficulties centering round Manu are increased when we come to the *Dharmaśāstra* attributed to him. In that work Manu explicitly refers to the *Vedas* as being the root of *dharma*, and states that whatever *dharma* was ordained by him, had been fully declared in the *Veda*.[8] The same work clearly states that he was the first sovereign ruler, the supreme ruler, who appraised mankind of the sacred laws in their order, as they were to be followed by all the four classes, and by each of them in their several degrees, together with the duties of every mixed class.[9] These statements seem to indicate that, as is generally assumed by scholars, Manu, the supreme ruler, came after the *Vedas* ; and that he is to be distinguished from his namesake, the father of the human race, who was evidently a figure of great antiquity.

The post-Vedic age to which Manu, the first sovereign ruler and the great lawgiver, may be assigned has an important bearing on our subject. If in the times of those ancient texts called the *Vedas*, there was no great consecreated sovereign like Manu, then, it is obvious that in the Vedic age the ancient Indians did not develop a polity that had a centralized government with all its constituent elements which, in the later ages, came to be associated with it. In other words, the existence of an elaborate machinery of government centering round a monarch which, as will be shown later on in this work, some modern Indian scholars have so enthusiastically pictured as having existed in the Vedic age, becomes extremely doubtful. if not fanciful.

But the above does not mean that we could agree to the other view that Manu was posterior to Kauṭilya. The agreement between the views of Manu and those of Kauṭilya on some important questions, which we shall dilate at length below, was very pronounced ; and it is clear that Kauṭilya was himself aware of a great thinker called Manu, who preceded him, and to whom he refers on several occasions. The point to be borne in mind, so far as the present context is concerned. is that there was a Manu who preceded Kauṭilya by centuries ; and that that earlier Manu was undoubtedly a lawgiver and a political thinker. Without going further into this complicated problem, it may merely be noted that the evidence of the *Arthaśāstra* itself seems to support the view that there was an earlier *Mānavadharma-sūtra* as distinct from the later *Manusmṛiti* or Code of Manu,[10] thereby proving our statement that the same name was sometimes borne by more than one ancient political thinker.

Other examples may be given of the same name being borne by two or more thinkers. These are the following: Bṛihaspati, Parāśara, and Yājñavalkya. There was a Vedic and a post-Vedic Bṛihaspati.[11] In the world of political thought, an ancient teacher of this name attained wide celebrity, as is proved by the fact that in the *Mahābhārata,* he is represented as having summarized an earlier work on *daṇḍanīti.* It is this which has prompted some modern scholars, like the late Professor Keith, to affirm that Bṛihaspati was the founder of the science of the *daṇḍanīti.* But the same eminent scholar admitted that the text of the *Bārhaspatya Arthaśāstra,* as it has come down to us, "is a modern production of uncertain but late date, which contains little if anything of the old doctrines of the school even as we know them from *Kauṭilīya Arthaśāstra".*[12] Professor Keith's statements help us only to maintain the possibility of there having been two Bṛihaspatis but not to trace the antiquity of the science of the *daṇḍanīti,* much less to decide the date of either the *Arthaśāstra* of Bṛihaspati or that of Kauṭilya. The later Bṛihaspati, we may incidentally note, has been assigned to the sixth or seventh century A.D. by Professors Bühler and Jolly ; and to the period ranging from A.D. 200 to A.D. 400 by Dr. P. V. Kane.[13]

A similar difficulty exists in the case of Parāśara. There was one thinker of that name who preceded Kauṭilya ; and a later one of that name who, according to Professor Macdonell, was anterior to A.D. 1300.[14] The indefiniteness among scholars in regard to the chronology of most of the early authors is seen when we note that, according to Dr. Kane, Parāśara lived in an age ranging from A.D. 100 to A.D. 500![15]

The repetition of names is likewise illustrated in the case of Yājñavalkya. This celebrated name appears often in the *Bṛihadāraṇyaka Upaniṣad* as that of a teacher, whose pupil was Āsuri. Yājñavalkya himself is said to have been the pupil of the famous teacher Śvetaketu, who was the son of Uddālaka Āruṇi, one of the most prominent teachers of the Vedic period.[16] The relationship between the three great teachers Uddālaka Āruṇi, Śvetaketu, and Yājñavalkya is of significance in the sense that the last named teacher can be assigned to a very ancient period of antiquity. He is to be distinguished from a later Yājñavalkya, who was the author of a *Dharmaśāstra.* About the latter thinker, too, there is no unanimity among scholars as regards his age. Professors Macdonell, Aiyangar, and Jolly would assign him to the fourth century A.D. ; but Dr. Kane would date him not later than the third century A.D. The last named authority would even mention three Yājñavalkyas—Vṛiddhayājñavalkya, Yogayājñavalkya, and Bṛihadyājñavalkya,[17] thereby adding to the complexity of the whole problem.

The chronological indefiniteness which marks the ancient period of Indian history is seen also in the case of Kauṭilya, the great Mauryan statesman, whom some would assign to a period before A.D. 300, but who may with some definiteness, as will be shown in the last Part of this work, be dated to the fourth century B.C.[18]

The same chronological vagueness pervades the figures of later writers on the *Dharmaśāstras* like Gautama, Vasiṣṭha, Viṣṇu, Nārada, and even Kāmandaka. Thus, Gautama's *Dharmaśāstra*, according to Professor Macdonell, although "it does not form part of a Kalpa Sūtra, it must at one time have been connected with a Vedic school". But the same authority affirms that Gautama's is "the oldest Dharma Śāstra that has been presented, or at least published, and can hardly date from later than about 500 B.C."[19] Professor Aiyangar is inclined to assign Gautama's *Dharmaśāstra* to about the sixth century B.C., although he has adduced no reasons in support of his view.[20] But Professors Meyer and Baṭa Krishna Ghosh would assign Gautama to a later date.[21] Vasiṣṭha, who was a well-known writer on the *Dharmaśāstra*, and who may not be confounded with his namesake, the rival of Viśvāmitra, has been assigned to about the second century B.C. by Professor Aiyangar ;[22] but Professor Keith dated him to the fourth century B.C.[23] About the age of Viṣṇu, too, there is no agreement among scholars. Professor Jolly maintained that the *Dharmaśāstra* attributed to Viṣṇu, also called *Vaiṣṇava-dharmaśāstra*, or *Viṣṇu-smṛiti*, which is said to be closely connected with the *Kāṭhaka-gṛihya-sūtras*, was not earlier than A.D. 200 ;[24] while Professor Aiyangar would date the work of Viṣṇu to *circa* A.D. 100.[25] Professors Macdonell and Aiyangar seem to agree in assigning Nārada to about the sixth century A.D. ;[26] while other scholars refer to the *Nāradasmṛiti* without enlightening us on its date.[27]

Of the later writers who come within the limits of our study are Kāmandaka, the author of the well-known *Nītisāra*, and Somadeva, the author of *Nītivākyāmṛita*. Kāmandaka has been considered by some scholars as the contemporary of Varāhamihira (who began his astronomical calculations in about A.D. 505, and died, according to one of his commentators, in A.D. 587) ;[28] while others would assign him to the age of Kālidāsa and Daṇḍin, and even to about A.D. 700.[29]

We reach firmer ground when we come to the last great name in the list of the ancient Indian political writers falling within the period of our study. This was Somadeva Sūri, the author of *Nītivākyāmṛita* and *Yaśastilaka*. His date is determined by the latter work at the end of which he says that he finished it on the 13th of the month of Caitra when 881 years of the Śaka king had elapsed, the cyclic year being Siddhārtin, during the time of the feudatory prince Yaśodhara when the latter's suzerain, the

Rāṣṭrakūṭa monarch Kṛṣṇa III (A.D. 939-68) reigned. This would correspond to A.D. 959-60.[30] Since Somedeva also wrote the *Nītivākyāmṛita* ("Nectar of Political Maxims"), under the same feudatory Yaśodhara, he has to be assigned to the second half of the tenth century A.D.[31]

D. DIVERGENCE AMONG MODERN SCHOLARS IN REGARD TO TERMS

The above discussion will have made it clear to the reader that, so far as the chronological data are concerned, there is nothing definite about the ancient Indian political writers until we come to Somadeva Sūri. The uncertainty about the names of the early writers on polity is as much a hindrance to our study as the want of unanimity among modern scholars on the exact connotation of some of the fundamental terms in our study, like *dharma, daṇḍa,* and *nīti,* and on the relationship between the *dharmaśāstras,* on the one hand, and the *daṇḍanīti,* on the other. We shall first deal with the technical terms, and, then, with the important question of the relationship between the two branches of our study—the *dharmaśāstras* and the *daṇḍanīti* or *nītiśāstra.*

CHAPTER III

MEANING OF THE TERM DHARMA

A. EARLIER DEFINITIONS

IN THE early stages of Indological studies (1879), Professor Heinrich Zimmer interpreted the term *dharman* (*dharma*) to mean the fixed order of heaven and earth.[32] This erroneous definition found favour with some later scholars.[33] No fact or argument is needed to discard this fantastic interpretation of *dharma* which the later Western Indologists themselves have refused to accept. The ancient Indians were not so unrealistic as to invent a term which was to cover the entire world or the earth and heaven together! One may venture to think that Professor Zimmer was misled in his interpretation of *dharma* perhaps because the word *dharman* was read in the ancient texts in conjunction with the term *ṛita,* meaning "eternal order".[34] While discussing the concept of *daṇḍa,* the same eminent scholar said *daṇḍa,* or the rod, was "corrective", that it symbolized justice, and that it was connected with *drupada,* or the wooden pillar, or the stake, to which the criminal was, according to him, bound, there being no imprisonment in those ancient times.[35] This view is likewise untenable, since the wooden pillar, which is referred to in the *Rig Veda* and in the later works, was used more for sacrificial purposes than for punishing criminals, although, as in the case of Śunaḥśepa (lit., "Dog's Tail", i.e. a man named Ājīgarti), it was used for binding a person.[36] Professor Zimmer, one cannot help feeling, unduly magnified a detail which his follower Professor Jhering took to be the "corrective" and "penal" aspects of the stake,[37] without grasping the meaning of *daṇḍa,* and particularly its relationship with *dharma.* This was due perhaps to the fact that both those distinguished German Indologists were more eager to describe what they imagined to be the "very inadequate" nature of the ancient Indian law, when compared with the later Roman law, rather than to deal with the question of the origin and significance of both *dharma* and *daṇḍa* in the context of ancient Indian political thought and institutions.

The baneful influence of the early Western Indologists manifested itself so late as this century when, for instance, another eminent German Indologist, Professor M. Winternitz, went to the extent of asserting that the *dharmaśāstras* and the *arthaśāstras*, were nothing but mere didactic poetry in which *dharma* and *artha* were taught as subjects in the curricula of study meant for the education of a prince![38]

B. LATER DEFINITIONS

That the above and other equally erroneous notions of *dharma* and *daṇḍa* are incorrect and inadequate has been amply demonstrated both by Western and Indian scholars. Professor Macdonell, for instance, interpreted *dharma* or *dharman* in the sense of law or custom covering both criminal and civil law and morality.[39] That this learned Indologist was not quite sure of the interpretation given by him is evident when in another context he maintains that *dharma* is religion and morality.[40]

A more accurate definition of the term *dharman* is that given by Professor Keith who equated it with custom, law, and righteous conduct.[41] This definition contains the essentials of *dharma,* as will be evident when we shall discuss the contents of the *dharmaśāstras* and the *nītiśāstras* below. But even Professor Keith could not escape the uncertainty which has enveloped the Western minds in regard to this detail, as is clear from his statement made in a later content in his *History of Sanskrit Literature* to the effect that the *dharmaśāstras* "deal after all with duty and morality as the basis of law".[42] As against this indefiniteness we may note the opinion of another eminent Western Indologist, Professor F. Kielhorn, who wrote thus: "I find no English word by which I can fully express all the meanings of the Sanskrit *dharma.*"[43] Dr. Kane not only shares this view but affirms that its exact meaning is uncertain.[44]

That there is a genuine difficulty about the exact connotation of that word will be evident when we follow Indian historians, who are likewise not quite clear about its meaning. Professor Rangaswami Aiyangar in one context maintains that *dharma* means virtue or precepts ; in a later context suggests that that term means canonical law ; and in a still later passage in the same work, affirms that *dharma* is of various kinds, constantly growing and "never very definite". This learned historian would, therefore, differentiate between the various kinds of *dharma,* thus: *saddharma* or ordinary equity and morality ; *asādhāraṇa dharma* or *dharma* of a special character which comprised *varṇa dharma* (or the obligation of castes), *āśrama dharma* (regulations relating to the orders or stages in life) ; *varṇāśrama dharma* (rules about both castes and orders and their interrelations) ; *guṇa dharma* ; and *naimittika dharma.* The eminent Professor would further analyse *dharma* into cross-sections thus—*ācāra dharma* (valid usage), *vyavahāra dharma* (rules about affairs), and *prāyascitta dharma* (rules of penance).[45]

While the above account of the different types of *dharma*—which, no doubt, is based on the ancient texts and on Vijñāneśvara, the famous commentator on *Yājñavalkyasmṛiti,*[46]—helps us to understand how *dharma* was applied to various types of human conduct, it does not enlighten us on the main problem before us, namely, the content of *dharma* and its relation to the science of *daṇḍanīti* or *nītiśāstra*. Indeed, Professor Aiyangar himself seems to be aware of this difficulty which he partially explains when he states that the term *dharma* may connote such different things like law proper, virtue, religion, duty, piety, justice, innate property, or quality; and that it was in this general sense that it was used in the ancient times when it was maintained by the lawgivers that the State had to maintain *dharma*.[47] We shall see below that the above will help us to arrive at a plausible explanation of the term *dharma*.

Turning to *daṇḍa*, the same authority maintains that that term meant "an institution of correction to restrain the natural turbulence and depravity of men, which led them to violate the regulations of the different castes and orders of life (*varṇāśrama dharma*), and of the divine creation of such a power of chastisement or *Daṇḍa*".[48] Professor Aiyangar, we may venture to remark, approaches in this definition the stand taken by Professors Zimmer and Jhering who, as stated earlier, had interpreted *daṇḍa* as a penal and corrective stake. But we shall see below that a wider, a more comprehensive, and a more rational definition of *daṇḍa* is possible. This will be evident when we shall discuss below the connotation of *dharma* and the relationship between the *dharmaśāstras* and the *daṇḍanīti*.

C. CONNOTATION OF THE TERM DHARMA

Notwithstanding the uncertainty prevailing among Indologists in regard to the meaning of *dharma*, it is clear that, barring scholars like Professors Zimmer, Jhering, and Winternitz, most of the Indologists are unanimous about the comprehensive nature of the term *dharma*, under which they group diverse subjects like law, custom, usage, morality, virtue, religion, duty, piety, justice and righteous conduct. Since these are related essentially to human beings living in society, it is evident that *dharma* in its wider sense comprised rules and principles of conduct relating to men, and not, as Professor Zimmer had unjustifiably assumed, to heavenly creatures as well. We know from the ancient texts that the authors of the *dharmaśāstras* did not confine these principles only to a particular class of people but made them cover all sections, that is, those who came within the denomination of *varṇas* (castes) and *āsramas* (orders), and those who were grouped under the general categories of offsprings born out of regular and irregular unions (*anuloma* and *pratiloma* castes), as well as those who were living outside the pale of the Hindu society.[49] We have, therefore, to assume that the rules of conduct, etc., embodied in the *dharmaśāstras* were meant for the entire range of Hindu society which extended its sphere with the widening of the frontiers of the ancient Indian kingdoms, and with the gradual absorption of foreign peoples into its variegated folds.[50]

From the wide range of subjects covered by the term *dharma* given above, which stretched from law to piety, it is obvious that the *dharmaśāstras* regulated not, as Professor Aiyangar maintains, "certain matters of conduct",[51] but practically all matters of public behaviour which had a vital bearing on the progress of society. These considerations would justify our assumption that the *dharmaśāstras* formed essentially a universal code of righteous conduct for all castes and classes.[52]

CHAPTER IV

RELATIONSHIP BETWEEN THE DHARMAŚĀSTRAS AND THE DAṆḌANĪTI

A. SIGNIFICANCE OF THE STUDY

THE QUESTION of the relationship between the *dharmaśāstras* and the *daṇḍanīti* or the *nītiśāstras* is of particular significance to our study. It will help us to understand, firstly, in what manner the two branches of knowledge were connected with each other. Secondly, it will enable us to know the main schools of ancient Indian political thought, and the contribution to the science of government by some of the great political thinkers of the ancient times. And, thirdly, it will take us to the problem of the analysis of ancient political thought and to the concept of the State as it existed in ancient India. When we shall have elucidated these problems, we shall be in a position to see how far the greatest of the Indian thinkers could be compared with their contemporaries in the West ; and to describe the different political institutions of the ancient times.

B. CONNOTATION OF THE TERM DAṆḌA

Before we do so, however, it is necessary to understand as to what the ancients meant by the term *daṇḍanīti*. The vagueness which surrounds the term *dharma* is not seen in the case of the *daṇḍanīti*. At the outset it may be observed that *daṇḍa, daṇḍanīti, arthaśāstra, nītiśāstra, rājaśāstra, rājanīti* and *rājadharma* are more or less synonyms signifying, in general, the rules of conduct of kings, regulations relating to the production and acquisition of wealth, and ideals of administration which came within the purview of the science of government.[53] The term *daṇḍa* appears to have been used in different periods of antiquity for a staff that was meant to ward off demons, who came to disturb a sacrifice, or for driving away cattle, or for signifying the attainment of manhood by a youth on the completion of his initiation (*upanayanam*), or for the handle of a ladle, or a similar implement used in a sacrifice, or, as in most cases, for a weapon.[54] This last meaning ultimately prevailed over all the rest, and, because of the nature of the factors that brought the ancient Indian State into existence, came to be finally and irrevocably identified with the science of government. We shall have to revert to the theory of *daṇḍa* later on when we shall discuss the justification of the State in the ancient times.

C. THEORIES RELATING TO THE RELATIONSHIP BETWEEN THE DHARMAŚĀSTRAS AND THE DAṆḌANĪTI

1. INTRODUCTION

There are three theories relating to the above problem—the first which maintains that the *daṇḍanīti* was evolved from the *dharmaśāstras* ; the second which affirms that it did not come out of the latter but that both developed on parallel lines ; and the third which states that it was opposed to the *dharmaśāstras*. A discussion of these theories will bring us to the question of the probable period when the *daṇḍanīti* originated, and when it was reduced to a systematized body of knowledge.

2. THE DANDANITI WAS EVOLVED FROM THE DHARMASASTRAS

The advocates of this theory are Professor Winternitz and Dr. Kane.

(a) *Professor Winternitz's Theory*

Professor Winternitz's arguments may be summarized thus: the *arthaśāstra* was originally taught in the schools of the *dharmaśāstras* among the duties of the king ; but, at some time, it branched off from the *dharmaśāstras* and was taught in separate schools of the *arthaśāstra*, the reason being that the same teachers appear in the *Mahābhārata* and elsewhere as authors of both the *dharmaśāstras* and the *arthaśāstras*.[55]

Professor Winternitz seems to maintain in the above theory that the *daṇḍanīti* was originally included in the *dharmaśāstras* but that it branched off from the latter in the course of ages, having an independent existence of its own. This is not, as we shall see presently, unreasonable, but his other statement relating to the similarity in the names of the teachers, who appear in the *Mahābhārata* and in other works as authors of both the *dharmaśāstras* and the *arthaśāstras*, is more superficial than convincing.

(b) *Dr. Kane's Theory*

Dr. Kane's elucidation of this theory is clearer and more rational. This eminent authority on the *dharmaśāstras* writes thus: "Though Arthaśāstra and Dharmaśāstra are often contradistinguished on account of the difference of the two Śāstras in ideals and in the methods adopted to reach them,

Arthaśāstra is really a branch of the Dharmaśāstra as the former deals with the responsibilities of the kings for whom rules are laid down in many treatises on *dharma*." In an earlier context he states that *rājadharma* is a very important subject of the *dharmaśāstras* ; and that the *arthaśāstra*, which is principally connected with the rights, privileges, and responsibilities of the ruler is, therefore, properly speaking a part of the *dharmaśāstra*.[56]

Dr. Kane has given us a clue to the solution of the problem relating to the relationship between the two branches of knowledge, but has not elaborated it. His exposition of the theory is decidedly more reasonable than that of Professor Winternitz, but it will have to be explained more fully in order to understand in what manner the *daṇḍanīti* was related to the *dharmaśāstras*.

3. THE DANDANITI WAS NOT BORN OUT OF THE DHARMASASTRAS BUT WAS EVOLVED ON INDEPENDENT LINES

This theory has been maintained by Dr. Narendra Nath Law and Professor Rangaswami Aiyangar.

(a) *Dr. Law's Theory*

Dr. Law subjected the theory of Professor Winternitz to a searching criticism, and came to the conclusion that the *dharmaśāstras* and the *arthaśāstras* developed on parallel lines. ". . . Just as the *Dharmaśāstras* had a *sūtra* period, so also the branches of learning, *vārttā* and *daṇḍanīti*, utilized by the *Arthaśāstras*, passed through a similar *sūtra* period, and could well have been contemporaneous with the works of the corresponding stages of development of the *dharmaśāstras*."[57]

Evaluation of Dr. Law's Theory. Dr. Law's argument relating to the existence of the *sūtra* period in the history of the *daṇḍanīti*, is plausible, although it is doubtful if we have to agree to the other view that the *sūtra* period of the *daṇḍanīti* also passed through the identically corresponding stages of development which the *dharmaśāstras* underwent.[58] Until sufficient proof is available in the *sūtra* literature itself that, along with the main topics dealt with in it, namely, those relating to domestic ritual of all kinds, there were other subjects relating to administration and government,[59] it is difficult to accept the hypothesis that the different stages in the history of the *daṇḍanīti* were contemporaneous with those in the history of the *dharmaśāstras*.

A significant point in this connection is that relating to the chronology of the *dharmaśāstras* and of the *daṇḍanīti*. It is true that there is no definite chronological data that could help us to settle this point beyond dispute. But the evidence of Yāska, and of the authors of the *dharmaśāstras* themselves. Gautama. Baudhāyana, and Āpastamba, conclusively proves that the *dharmaśāstra* literature, as Dr. Kane has amply shown, existed prior to the age of Yāska (sixth century B.C.); while the *sūtra* literature, according to the same authority, cannot go beyond 600 B.C.[60] A further point which militates against the theory that the *daṇḍanīti* literature might have passed through stages of development corresponding to those of the *dharmaśāstras* is that such a parallel development in the *daṇḍanīti* literature is not visible even if we compare it with the *sūtra* literature itself. For instance, all the Vedic *Samhitas*, according to Professor Julius Eggeling, came to be collected in digests called the *Brāhmaṇas*; which, because of their diversity in arrangement and treatment of materials, came to be treated, in their turn, in concise manuals of ceremonial rules called the *Kalpa Sūtras.*[61] Here we have a clue to the rejection of the theory of Dr. Law. It relates to the fact that what were originally, as in the case of the Vedic *Samhitas,* ancient texts of an elaborate nature, came to be condensed into a form of digests like the *Brāhmaṇas* which, in their turn, came to be treated in the shape of more concise manuals like the *Kalpa Sūtras*. In other words, this process points to a gradual reduction in size of the original texts with a view to bringing them into a form that could meet with the practical needs of the later ages.

One wonders whether one could come across this process of gradual reduction in size in the case of the *daṇḍanīti.* No doubt, as mentioned below, the reduction of the original size of the *arthaśāstra* from 100,000 stanzas attributed to Brahmā, to 10,000 stanzas by Śiva as Viśālākṣa, then, to 5,000 by Indra, then, to 3,000 by Bṛihaspati, and again, to 1,000 by Uśanas, undoubtedly points to a reduction in size of the earlier versions of the *arthaśāstra.* But there are two objections against the assumption that the above necessarily corresponded to the stages of development through which the *Samhitas* passed. First, according to the *Mahābhārata,* the whole literature described in it represents the three topics of *dharma, artha,* and *kāma,*[62] and not *artha* alone. This would preclude the *arthaśāstra's* or *daṇḍanīti's* possessing an individuality of its own—a consideration which would rob the strength of the main argument relating to the existence of the *daṇḍanīti* as a separate body of literature. And, secondly, admitting that there was a gradual reduction in size of the *arthaśāstra,* it cannot be understood why a further reduction was not attempted, especially after the age of Uśanas, so as to make it truly concise in the manner of the *Kalpa Sūtras.* On the other hand, we have the fact that Kauṭilya's *Arthaśāstra* was made up of 6,000 stanzas, 180 sections, 150 chapters, and 15 books, as Kauṭilya himself informs us.[63] That Mauryan Prime Minister, therefore, not only did not observe the main characteristic of the *sūtra* literature, namely, the reduction in size of the earlier manuals on statecraft, but raised it to a size higher than that attributed to Indra himself, viz., 5,000 *ślokas*! Here is a fact which seems to violate any assumption that the *daṇḍanīti* literature could be made to agree with the *dharmaśāstra* literature in the matter of a parallel development.

Indeed, there is good ground to assume that till a certain period, concerning which we have no definite chronological data, the *daṇḍanīti* was a part of the *dharmaśāstras*. What makes it difficult for us to accept the view relating to the parallel development of the *dharmaśāstras* and the *daṇḍanīti*, as given by Dr. Law, is that there is no indication anywhere that the *daṇḍanīti* literature passed through even such stages which, for instance, Dr. Kane would ascribe to the *dharmaśāstras*. These were, according to the latter scholar, the first stage of the *dharmasūtras* and of *Manusmṛiti* dating "from at least the 6th century B.C. to the beginning of the Christian era" ; the second stage when most of the versified *smṛitis* were composed, ranging from the early centuries of the Christian era to about A.D. 800 ; and the third stage of the commentators and writers on digests, covering over a thousand years from about the seventh century A.D. to A.D. 1800.[64] Granting for argument's sake, that the chronological division of the above three periods which, as Dr. Kane admits, although well-marked somewhat overlap each other, is correct, it cannot be said that the different stages in the development of the *daṇḍanīti* literature were contemporaneous with the periods of the *dharmaśāstras*. What supports this assumption is that even in the age of the *Manusmṛiti* itself, the *daṇḍanīti* had no separate existence, although Manu undoubtedly refers to the great antiquity of the *daṇḍanīti* thus: "For the king's sake, the Lord formerly created after his own son, Punishment, the protector of all creatures, (an incarnation of) the law, formed of Brahman's glory."[65] This proves that the science of punishment, or *daṇḍanīti*, was of great antiquity ; and that it is not improbable that it might have been, as Dr. Law affirms, in existence along with the *dharmaśāstras* from the most ancient times. But the silence of the author of the *Manusmṛiti* in regard to the individual existence of the *daṇḍanīti* prevents us from maintaining that that branch of knowledge, granting its antiquity, necessarily evolved its existence parallel to that of the *dharmaśāstras*. We shall see below that we could within bounds of probability indicate the age when the *daṇḍanīti* originated. But, we may repeat, until more definite evidence is found to the contrary, it is difficult to subscribe to the view that the *dharmaśāstras* and the *daṇḍanīti* had a parallel course of development.[66]

(b) *Professor Aiyangar's Theory*

Professor Aiyangar is also of the opinion that the *daṇḍanīti* was not born out of the *dharmaśāstra* but was developed on independent lines. While dealing with the *dharmaśāstras* and the *arthaśāstras*, this eminent historian writes thus: "In the Nītiśāstras we have, on the other hand, an independent body of literature, whose origin, standpoint, outlook, and standards differ from those of the canonical lawbooks (i.e. those on the *dharmaśāstras*)." Later on in the same work, while elucidating the practical side of the *arthaśāstras*, and the difference between the canonical law books and those on polity, Professor Aiyangar writes thus: "It is hardly necessary to enlarge further on this difference between the canonical law books and the books on polity. It should suffice to say that it is on this ground that a canonical law book would claim to supersede a mere work on polity." He then cites the opinion of Yājñavalkya that the "Dharmaśāstra is stronger than Arthaśāstra", and adds the testimony of Kauṭilya in regard to the superiority of the *dharmaśāstras* over the *daṇḍanīti*[67] about which there is hardly any dispute.

Evaluation of Professor Aiyangar's Theory. It has to be admitted that, in regard to the outlook and standards, the two branches of literature differ considerably. But beyond explaining the point that the *nītiśāstras* reflect the actual political conditions as prevailing in ancient India,[68] the learned Professor has not elucidated his main theory that the *daṇḍanīti* did not originate from the *dharmaśāstras,* and that the two developed on independent lines. He has further not explained a significant point in the comparison between the two branches of study—that relating to the origin of the *daṇḍanīti.* We shall see that it is this that will enable us to maintain that the theory relating to the so-called independent origin of the *daṇḍanīti* is hardly tenable ; and that, therefore, the exposition of this theory by Dr. Law and Professor Aiyangar does not rest on cogent grounds.

4. DANDANITI WAS OPPOSED TO THE DHARMASASTRAS

The advocate of this theory was Professor A. B. Keith who, while admitting that the *arthaśāstras* or the *nītiśāstras* or the *rājanīti* or the *daṇḍanīti* were one and the same, viz., the science of conduct, or the conduct of kings,[69] affirmed that the *arthaśāstra* and the *nitiśāstra* were opposed to the *dharmaśāstra* inasmuch as they are "not codes of morals but deal with man's action in practical politics and conduct of the ordinary affairs of every day life and intercourse".[70]

Evaluation of Professor Keith's Theory. While dwelling on the difference in the outlook of the two branches of study, which is not denied by any one, Professor Keith does not explain the origin of the *daṇḍanīti,* although he certainly mentions the redactions of the *arthaśāstras* from the time of the *Mahābhārata* and in particular by Bṛihaspati.[71] We shall revert to this point later on. But Professor Keith's theory relating to the opposition between the outlook of the *daṇḍanīti* and that of the *dharmaśāstras* does not help us to solve the question as to which of the two branches was earlier. Indeed, he admits the antiquity of the concept of *dharma* and *artha* by citing the *Hiraṇyakeśi Gṛihyasūtra* which knows the three objects in life—*dharma, artha,* and *kāma.*[72] But neither this nor the learned Indologist's reference to the existence of a collection of 100,000 sections of the *arthaśāstra* in the *Mahābhārata,*[73] helps us to understand the main point concerning the precedence of one branch of knowledge over the other. We cannot escape the conclusion that the eminent British Professor has failed to establish his theory relating to the opposition of the *daṇḍanīti* to the *dharmaśāstras.* The indecision on his part is apparent where we note what he says about the relationship between the *daṇḍanīti* and the *dharmaśāstras.* While commenting on poetics, he writes thus:

> Poetics, on the other hand, was hardly in any sense Vedic, and represents an independent secular science. Largely the same remark may be applied to the Arthaśāstra, or Nītiśāstra, but there is some connection between it and the Dharmaśāstra, even when both were distinctly developed, and we may quite legitimately suppose that the original schools of Dharmaśāstra included in their scope the matters which later became specifically the objects of Arthaśāstra, politics, practical knowledge, technique in matters not primarily sacrificial.[74]

It appears as if Professor Keith got himself involved in a number of presumptions only the last of which is acceptable. If we agree with him in his comparison of Sanskrit poetics with the *arthaśāstra,* it is evident that, like poetics, the *arthaśāstra* "represents an independent secular science". This point he does not seem to have elaborated either here or elsewhere in his well-known book. All that he has stated is, as remarked above, that the *daṇḍanīti* or the *arthaśāstra* was opposed to *dharmaśāstra* inasmuch as the former was not a code of moral conduct but a code of practical behaviour. This is not equal to stating that the *daṇḍanīti* represents an independent secular science. But Professor Keith almost came to the point when he stated that there is some connection between the *daṇḍanīti* and the *dharmaśāstra* ;and that the original schools of the latter included within their scope matters which later on became the specific objects of the *arthaśāstra,* viz., politics, practical knowledge, and techniques in matters not primarily sacrificial. In the last detail, Professor Keith does not seem to be quite correct, since the *dharmaśāstras* did not deal so much with sacrificial matters or domestic ritual which, as we have seen above, formed the subject matter of the *dharmasūtras,* as with the universal code of righteous conduct. Professor Keith, on the whole, therefore, does not enlighten us on the exact relationship between the *dharmaśāstras* and the *daṇḍanīti,* although in his statement that the original schools of the *dharmaśāstras* included within their scope the matters which were specialized in the *arthaśāstra,* he approaches nearest the first theory mentioned above.

5. CONCLUSION

Of the three theories discussed above, the most plausible appears to be the first one which would trace the evolution of the *daṇḍanīti* from the *dharmaśāstras.* In order to understand this point we may note the source of all knowledge, according to the ancients ; the relationship of the *dharmaśāstras* to it, and the connection between the *dharmaśāstras* and the *daṇḍanīti* as given in the *Manusmṛiti.* All knowledge, according to the ancients, flowed from the *Vedas*. In fact, as is well-known, the word *Veda* itself connotes knowledge (from *vid*, "to know"). It signifies the sacred lore of the ancients.[75] The *Vedas* are styled *śruti*, or revelation, and as such were earlier than the *smṛiti*, or tradition. The relative importance of these two has been given by Professor Macdonell thus: "Works of Vedic 'revelation' were deemed of higher authority in case of doubt than the later works on religious and civil usage, called *smṛiti* or memory, as embodying only the tradition derived from the ancient sages."[76] This is in regard to the source of all knowledge.

Now we come to the next two points—the relationship between the *dharmaśāstras* and the *Vedas*. This point is clarified in the *Manusmṛiti* thus: "The whole Veda is the source of the sacred law (*dharma*), next the tradition and the virtuous conduct of those who know (the Veda further), also the customs of holy men, and (finally) self-satisfaction. Whatever law has been ordained for any (person) by Manu, that has been fully declared in the Veda: for that (sage was) omniscient." Then, again: "For that man obeys the law prescribed in the revealed texts and in the sacred tradition, gains fame in this (world) and after death unsurpassable bliss." Further, Manu states: "The Veda (i.e. the *śruti*, or revelation), the sacred tradition (the *smṛiti*), the customs of virtuous men, and one's own pleasure, they declare to be visibly the fourfold means of defining the sacred law (*dharma*)."[77]

The relationship between the *dharmaśāstras* and the *daṇḍanīti* is given thus by Manu: "From those versed in the three Vedas let him (the king) learn the threefold (sacred science), the primeval science of government, the science of dialectics, and the knowledge of the (supreme) soul; from the people (the theory of) the (various) trades and professions."[78] The position which the State, as typified by the king, occupied in the ancient times will be further clarified, when we shall discuss below its origin. Here it may be observed that the relative importance of the *daṇḍanīti* and the *dharmaśāstras* is further clarified by Manu, who justifies the *daṇḍanīti* thus: "Punishment alone governs all created beings, punishment alone protects them, punishment watches them where they sleep; the wise declare punishment (to be identical with) law."[79]

In the above passages Manu lays stress on the supreme importance of the *daṇḍanīti*, although in the statement that "the wise declare Punishment to be identical with the law", he seems to imply that the *daṇḍanīti* was equal in importance to the *dharmaśāstras*, and was perhaps co-existent with the latter. This would appear to lend support to the view that the *daṇḍanīti* passed through the stages of development similar to those which the *dharmaśāstras* passed through; and that it had the same status as the *dharmaśāstras*. But as against this it may be argued that the ancients did not seem to have considered the *daṇḍanīti* as having precedence over the *dharmaśāstra*. On the other hand, the *dharmaśāstra* was definitely superior to the *daṇḍanīti*. This is admitted even by

Kauṭilya, who writes thus: "Righteous and unrighteous conduct (*dharmā-dharmau*) are learnt from the triple Vedas; wealth and non-wealth from Vārtā; the expedient and the inexpedient (*nayānayau*), as well as potency and impotency (*balābale*) from the science of government."[80] The explicit statement in Kauṭilya that "righteous and unrighteous conduct are learnt from the triple Vedas", and that only "potency and impotency (are learnt) from the science of government" (*daṇḍanīti*), is enough to prove that the ancients clearly demarcated the wide range of righteous and unrighteous conduct from the limited objective of maintaining strength or of losing it, so far as the State was concerned.

That Kauṭilya definitely assigned to the *dharmaśāstras* the right of precedence over the *daṇḍanīti,* or, over all matters of the State, is further suggested by the following statement in the *Arthaśāstra*: "Whenever there is disagreement between history (*caritra*) and sacred law (*dharma*), or between evidence (*vyavahāra*) and sacred law, then, the matter shall be settled in accordance with sacred law" (*saṁsthāyā dharmaśāstreṇa śāstraṁ vā vyāvahārikaṁ yasmin-arthe virudhyet dharmeṇārthaṁ vinascayet*).[81] We shall see below that Kauṭilya will clarify his position still further in regard to the subordinate position of the *daṇḍanīti,* when compared to the *dharmaśāstras.* Yājñavalkya is even more emphatic on this point. He states: "*Dharmaśāstra* is stronger than the *arthaśāstra* (*arthaśāstrāt-tu balavat-dharmaśāstraṁ iti sthitaḥ*); and that when the former and the latter are in conflict, the *dharmaśāstra* will prevail."[82] It is clear from this that the *arthaśāstra* or the *daṇḍanīti* occupied a subordinate position in regard to the *dharmaśāstras.*

CHAPTER V

WHEN DID THE DAṆḌANĪTI SECURE AN INDIVIDUALITY OF ITS OWN?

A. INTRODUCTION

NEITHER THE statement of Manu that the science of government was primeval, and that "the wise will declare Punishment to be identical with the law", nor that of Yājñavalkya that the *dharmaśāstra* will prevail in a conflict with the *arthaśāstra*, will help us to understand as to when the *daṇḍanīti* branched off from the universal code of righteous conduct, and came to have an individuality of its own. In other words, we have to find out from the ancient texts the probable period when the *daṇḍanīti* was separated from the *dharmaśāstra* as a kind of an independent branch of knowledge.

B. THE EVIDENCE OF THE ŚATAPATHA BRĀHMAṆA

The answer to the above question is found in the *Śatapatha Brāhmaṇa* ("The Brāhmaṇa of the Hundred Paths", so called because it consists of one hundred lectures or *adhyāyās*), in which the king is represented as the wielder of the *daṇḍa* or the rod of punishment, while he was at the same time himself immune from punishment. The passage in question is the following:

> They (the *adhvaryu* or sacrificial priest and his assistants) then silently strike him (the king who is being consecrated) with sticks (*daṇḍa*), they guide him safely over judicial punishment (*daṇḍabadha*): whence the king is exempt from punishment (*a-daṇḍya*), because they guide him safely over judicial punishment.[83]

Here we have in the above passage the clearest proof of the *dharmaśāstras* preceding the *daṇḍanīti* in the sense that the consecration of the king, according to the former, takes place first, while his association with the sticks (*daṇḍa*) comes afterwards. Before we discuss further the significance of the above, it is necessary to observe as to what were the texts called the *Brāhmaṇas*, and how the above could be utilized to substantiate a statement made in the *Manusmṛiti* in regard to the antiquity of the *daṇḍanīti*. The *Brāhmaṇas* were theological treatises dealing with devotion or prayer, and written mostly in prose. They grew up amidst a sacredotal tradition long after the Vedic hymns had been composed.[84] There is no chronological indication in regard to the *Śatapatha Brāhmaṇa*. But this work is considered "next to the Rig Veda, the most important production in the whole range of Vedic literature".[85] "The internal evidence of the *Śatapatha Brāhmaṇa*", according to Professor Macdonell, "belongs to a later period of the *Brāhmaṇa* age".[86] Since that eminent Indologist would assign the *Brāhmaṇas* to the period ranging from *circa* 800 B.C. to 500 B.C.,[87] and since, according to the same authority, the *Śatapatha Brāhmaṇa* belonged to a later period of the *Brāhmaṇa* age, it would not be wrong to assign it to about 700 B.C. For our purpose, we may observe that the definite association of the sticks or *daṇḍa* with the king during the latter's consecration (*abhiṣeka*), as given in the *Śatapatha Brāhmaṇa*, seems to justify the statement made in the *Manusmṛiti* about the primeval nature of the science of punishment while, at the same time, clearly pointing to the precedence of the *dharmaśāstras* over the *daṇḍanīti*.

C. THE REDUCTIONS OF THE ARTHAŚĀSTRA

The antiquity of the *daṇḍanīti* suggested above may not be confounded with the question of the reduction of that science to some definite form to which we have referred in a previous context. The traditional account of this process as given in the *Mahābhārata* may be repeated thus: Brahmā, the Creator, was the author of a work in 100,000 sections on the topics of *dharma*, *artha*, and *kāma*. God Śiva as Viśālākṣa reduced it to 10,000 sections in consideration of the brevity of human life. Indra brought it down to 5,000 ; and, finally, Indra's work called *Bāhudantaka*, called so after one of his epithets, was reduced by Bṛihaspati to 3,000, and by Uśanas still further to 1,000 sections.[88] The mythological account of the reduction of the earlier versions of the *arthaśāstra*, which were written or composed along with the other topics of *dharma* and *kāma*, thus given in that epic, may be understood in the sense that in some period before its age, attempts had already been made to reduce into some shape the concept of the *daṇḍanīti* or *arthaśāstra*. The antiquity of the science of polity is suggested not only by the account given in the *Mahābhārata* but also by the opening sentence in the *Arthaśāstra* of Kauṭilya to the following effect: "This Arthaśāstra is made as a compendium of almost all the Arthaśāstras which, in view of the acquisition and maintenance of the earth, have been composed by ancient teachers."[89] Kauṭilya will, as will be narrated below, give the names of most of the ancient teachers.

D. CONCLUSION

The above traditional account, it may be added, which mentions the three branches of study—*dharma, artha,* and *kāma*—does not, however, explicitly prove that the *daṇḍanīti* had branched off from the parent body of the *dharmaśāstras* but it points to the fact that, along with the two other subjects, it had been reduced to writing. It may be presumed that, since the beginning of a clear concept of the *daṇḍanīti,* in the shape of *daṇḍa,* is found only in the *Śatapatha Brāhmaṇa,* and since its reduction to some order is mentioned in the *Mahābhārata,* it is not improbable that from the age of the *Śatapatha Brāhmaṇa* to that of that epic, the science of *daṇḍanīti* had not emerged in its final form. Indeed, the absence of a definite body of rules embodying the *daṇḍanīti* in the earlier epic *Rāmāyana,* suggests that this supposition of ours is not without some foundation. It seems as if the *arthaśāstra* as a distinct branch of study received recognition only in the age of the *Mahābhārata.*

CHAPTER VI

SOME REMARKS ON THE DAṆḌANĪTI IN GENERAL

A. THE STATUS OF THE AUTHORS OF THE DAṆḌANĪTI

A FEW more considerations about the *dadṇanīti* in general may be made before we pass on to the next major topic of the schools of ancient political thought. The first point relates to the status of the authors of the *daṇḍanīti*. The statements in the ancient texts that all knowledge, including that of the *daṇḍanīti*, is to be traced to the *Vedas*, and that *dharma* was superior to the State, do not mean, as Professor Macdonell maintained, that "even in the first Vedic period" the priesthood "had occupied an influential position", and that the priests "secured for themselves the dominant power which they have maintained ever since".[90] The proper appreciation of the position of *dharma* is given thus in the *Bṛihadāraṇyaka Upaniṣad*: "Brahmā (the Supreme Being) created the most excellent Dharma. Dharma is the king of kings (*kṣatrasya-kṣtraṁ*). Therefore, there is nothing higher than Dharma. Henceforth, even a weak man rules with the help of the Dharma as with the help of a king."[91] When the ancients had thus immortalized *dharma*, and raised it above the State, they gave expression to an idea which far transcended that of Pindar, who said that "Law (was) the king of all, both mortals and immortals".[92] This is because the *dharma* of the ancients connoted far more subjects than the law of Pindar.

B. THE DAṆḌANĪTI WAS NOT THE PRODUCT OF IDLE AND MISCHIEVOUS BRAINS

The next point to be borne in mind is that the concept of *daṇḍa* was not the work of idle brains, who invented it to enslave and to maintain in perpetual political servitude the Indian population. Nor does that concept reflect a philosophical outlook unrelated to practical life. Both these views are erroneous estimates of the theory of *daṇḍanīti*. Instead of holding the population in eternal bondage, the ancient State which was based on the *daṇḍanīti*, created an atmosphere in which the aspirations and feelings which sprang from the unrepressed activities of all sections of Society, were allowed to grow adding thereby to the general well-being of the social order. While the *daṇḍanīti* restrained the unruly, it helped the bulk of the society to release the responsive talents inherent in men. Along with *dharma,* it brought into existence social instincts which were latent in the varoius sections of the people, and which could grow only with the assurance born out of protection. The ancients learnt to depend upon society and to protect it because of the opportunities which the *daṇḍanīti* provided them. The *daṇḍanīti* was not a code of profitless and relentless precepts. It reflected the actual conditions in which men lived ;[93] and it was directed to the maintenance of the material side of society which needed vigilance and guidance. While the *dharmaśāstras* embodied the universal code of righteous conduct, the *daṇḍanīti* touched a specific aspect of that code which referred to the State. When the ancients acknowledged the superiority of the *dharmaśāstras* over the *daṇḍanīti,* they gave expression to an eternal truth which was as much valid then as it is today, namely, that the specific behaviour of the State can be understood only in terms of the general behaviour of society. The goal of the *dharmaśāstras* was the fulfilment of the lives of all sections and classes of the people, each class according to the duties and rights assigned to it by ancient usage and convention. The *daṇḍanīti* made it possible for that ideal to be realized through the instrumentality of the State. It is only in this way that we can appreciate the dictum of the ancients that the State had to maintain *dharma.*

Part Two

THE MAIN SCHOOLS OF POLITICAL THOUGHT

CHAPTER I

SOURCES OF INFORMATION

A. INTRODUCTION

THE HISTORIAN who attempts to describe the main schools of ancient Indian political thought performs an apparently impossible task. He is not only confronted with the difficulties relating to the limitations of the entire study of ancient political thought but faced with the problem of looking for in vain for materials in the alluring lists of teachers mentioned in the ancient texts. These are the genealogical lists of teachers called the *vaṁśa* (lit., bamboo, in the sense of spiritual descent). The *Vaṁśa Brāhmaṇa* of the *Sāma Veda,* for instance, has a long list of teachers of that *Veda.* Then, there is the *vaṁśa* of the *Śankhyāyana Āraṇyaka* and the *vaṁśa* in the *Śatapatha Brāhmaṇa.*[1] These refer more to teachers of the theological subjects and sacrificial ceremonies than to those who were concerned with the problems of the State.[2] They may not be of much use to us in the elucidation of our subject. We have to fall back upon the *arthaśāstras* themselves in order to find out some clues regarding the names of great teachers and their schools in the field of the *daṇḍanīti.* While some illustrious names of teachers and their schools are available in the ancient texts, it is only in the comprehensive work of Kauṭilya that we have some details about the teachers and schools that preceded him. We have, therefore, to turn to the *Arthaśāstra* of that Mauryan Prime Minister.

B. KAUṬILYA'S STATEMENTS ANALYSED

Kauṭilya clearly states, we may repeat, at the beginning and end of his book that his work was "a compendium of all the Arthaśāstras, which, in view of acquisition and maintenance of the earth, have been composed by ancient teachers".[3] This settles beyond doubt that many authors on Politics had preceded him. On two occasions he refers to them vaguely as ancient teachers ;[4] but in fourteen different contexts, as will be clear from the accompanying Table A, he mentions them by name. But his own teacher, who is referred to on many occasions, he never calls him by his name! The question now arises: how shall we find out the different schools from the time of Kauṭilya backwards?

To the above question there is no definite answer, especially in view of the limitations to our study which have already been explained earlier. In the absence of any positive data relating to this side of the question, we can only work on a hypothetical basis, keeping in view the statements of Kauṭilya. When we analyse his references to the various teachers who preceded him, we find the following:

1. That, on some occasions he mentions consecutively certain teachers, as if they formed one category ;
2. That, on other occasions, he mentions some other teachers likewise in a way to suggest that they formed another category ; and
3. That, on still some other occasions, he mentions in disorder the names of teachers, as if to create the impression that no order in their enumeration was ever intended by him at all!

If we try to analyse the various contexts in which the different teachers are mentioned, we arrive at the following categories:

Category A of Table B comprising four lists in which Manu, Bṛihaspati, Parāśara and Uśanas are mentioned in succession, without any mention being made of Kauṭilya's teacher, although in all cases Kauṭilya himself is mentioned!
Category B of Table B comprising five lists in which the following two sets of teachers are mentioned one after another—one set consisting of Bharadvāja, Viśālākṣa, Parāśara, Piśuna, Kauṇapadanta, Vātavyādhi, Bāhudantīputra, and Kauṭilya, the school of Āmbhiyas being mentioned separately ; and the other set comprising Kātyāyana, Kaṇinka Bharadvāja, Carāyaṇa, Ghotamukha, Kiñjalka, Piśuna and Piśuna's son, without mention being made either of Kauṭilya's teacher or of Kauṭilya himself.
Category C comprising all the above teachers, excepting those beginning with Kātyayana, all being mentioned in utter confusion. The unnamed teacher of Kauṭilya is always mentioned excepting on three occasions (Category A of Table B, list III ; Category C of Table B, lists II and IV).

C. THE POLITICAL PREDECESSORS OF KAUṬILYA ENUMERATED (THE MAIN SCHOOLS OF POLITICAL THOUGHT)

From the careful manner in which Kauṭilya mentions the various teachers and their schools, it is apparent that, not withstanding the confusion in Category C, he considered certain teachers to be distinct from the rest. This is clear from the way he mentions the earliest of them—Manu, Bṛihaspati, and Uśanas. He does not confound them with the next set of eight teachers beginning with Bharadvāja and ending with Bāhudantīputra—Bhāradvāja, Viśālākṣa, Parāśara, Piśuna, Kauṇapadanta, Vātavyādhi, and Bāhudantīputra. The consistent manner in which Parāśara is mentioned in the first three lists of Category B, proves that we have to assign that teacher to an age after Viśālākṣa and before Piśuna, and not to an age prior to that of Bṛihaspati, as given in list II of Category A.

In Category B there is another distinct set of seven teachers mentioned in list IV. They were, in succession, Kātyāyana, Kaṇinka Bharadvāja, Carāyana, Ghotamukha, Kiñjalka, Piśuna, and Piśuna's unnamed son. The occurrence of Piśuna in this list is rather inexplicable, since he has been consistently mentioned in the same Category B in lists I, II, and III, as coming after Parāśara and before Kauṇapadanta. That this relative position of the three teachers—Parāśara, Piśuna, and Kauṇapadanta—is correct is proved even by referring to lists V and VI of Category C, where the teachers are mentioned in disorder. In these last two lists, if we omit the many references to Kauṭilya and to his teacher, we arrive at a succession list which is identical to that given in Category B, lists I, II, and III.

It must be confessed that there is nothing to indicate the source upon which Kauṭilya based his succession lists. Neither his own work nor that of any other thinker helps us in this matter. We have to fall back upon a hypothetical explanation that Kauṭilya seems to have had four distinct categories of teachers in his mind—the first comprising three teachers; the second, seven; the third, again seven; and the fourth, two (Kauṭilya's teacher and himself). The succession lists, arranged on mere supposition, may be grouped thus:

1. Manu
2. Bṛihaspati
3. Uśanas (Śukrācārya?)

4. Bharadvāja
5. Viśālakāṣa
6. Parāśara
7. Piśuna
8. Kauṇapadanta
9. Vātavyādhi
10. Bāhudantīpura

11. Kātyāna
12. Kaṇinka Bharadvāja
13. Carāyaṇa
14. Ghotamukha
15. Kiñjalka
16. Piśuna's son
17. Āmbhiyas (intervening somewhere in the above list)

18. The unnamed teacher
19. Kauṭilya

The above list mentions, therefore, nineteen schools of political thought from the age of Manu till that of Kauṭilya.[5] If we accept it as valid, it appears that from Manu till Kauṭilya, the number of authors on the *arthaśāstra* was smaller than the number of teachers given in the *vaṁśa* of the *Brāhmaṇas* mentioned in an earlier context. There is another detail which we may keep in mind. It may not be necessary to agree with Dr. Kane that, because Kauṭilya mentions, for instance, the schools of Manu, Bṛihaspati, Uśanas, Parāśara, and the Āmbhiyas in some contexts, and the individual teachers in some other contexts,[5a] they are to be classified

TABLE A

Sr. No.	Context : Subject matter	Names of Teachers	Their number	Ref. to the Arthaśāstra	Remarks
1.	Number of Sciences: the place of *Anvikṣaki*.	Manu, Bṛihaspati, Uśanas	Three	Page 5	The schools of the three mentioned.
2.	Creation of Ministers	Bharadvāja, Viśālākṣa, Parāśara, Piśuna, Kauṇapadanta, Vātavyādhi, Bāhudantīputra.	Seven	Pages 12-14	
3.	Business of Council Meeting	Manu, Bṛhaspati, Uśanas, Bharadvāja, Viśālākṣa, Parāśara, Piśuna.	Seven	Pages 27-28	The schools of Manu, Bṛihaspati and Uśanas mentioned.
4.	Protection of Princes	Bharadvāja, Viśālākṣa, Parāśara, Piśuna, Kauṇapadanta, Vātāvyādhi, the Āmbhiyas.	Seven	Pages 32-33	The school of Parāśara. Perhaps the Āmbhīyas formed a school.
5.	Accountant-General's routine work of maintaining accounts.	Manu, Parāśara, Bṛihaspati, Uśanas.	Four	Pages 62-63	The schools of the four are metioned.
6.	Taking of oaths	Uśanas, Manu, Bṛihaspati	Three	Page 201	
7.	Robbery	Manu, Uśanas, Bṛihaspati	Three	Page 216	The schools of the three are mentioned.
8.	Time-serving	Kātyāyana, Kaṇiṅka Bharadvāja, Carāyaṇa, Ghotamukha, Kiñjalka, Piśuna.	Six	Page 282	
9.	The Consolidation of Sovereignty	Bharadvāja	One	Page 284	
10.	Six-fold policy	Vātavyādhi	One	Page 293	
11.	Calamities befalling sovereignty	Bharadvāja, Viśālākṣa, Parāśara, Piśuna, Kauṇapadanta, Vātavyādhi.	Six	Pages 349-52	
12.	Aggregate troubles of men	Bharadvāja, Viśālaksa, Parāśara, Piśuna, Kauṇapadanta, Vātavyādhi.	Six	Pages 354-56	
13.	Duties of royal messengers	Bharadvāja, Viśālāksa	Two	Page 411	The schools of the three mentioned.
14.	Paragraphical Divisions of the Arthaśāstra.	Manu, Bṛihaspati, Uśanas	Three	Pages 460-61	
15.	Different contexts	Kautilya's unnamed teacher	Many times	Pages 8, 69 ff.	

TABLE B

(Categories A, B, C, D)

Category A. Names of Teachers in Some Order. (Four lists).

List I	List II	List III	List IV
1. Manu 2. Bṛihaspati 3. Uśanas 4. Kauṭilya	1. Manu 2. Parāśāra 3. Bṛihaspati 4. Uśanas 5. Kauṭilya	1. Manu 2. Uśanas 3. Kauṭilya	1. Manu 2. Bṛihaspati 3. Uśanas 4. Kauṭilya
(The teacher of Kauṭilya not mentioned) (Ref. Kauṭilya, pp. 5, 28)	(The teacher of Kauṭilya not mentioned) (Ref. Kauṭilya, pp. 62, 63)	(Later on the teacher is mentioned, and then Bṛihaspati) (Ref. Kauṭilya, p. 217)	(The teacher not mentioned) (Ref. Kauṭilya, p. 460)

Category B. Names of Teachers in Some Order. (Five lists).

List I	List II	List III	List IV	List V
1. Bharadvāja 2. Viśālākṣa 3. Parāśara 4. Piśuna 5. Kauṇapadanta 6. Vātavyādhi 7. Bāhudantīputra 8. Kauṭilya	1. Bharadvāja 2. Viśālākṣa 3. Parāśara 4. Piśuna 5. Kauṭilya	1. Bharadvāja 2. Viśālākṣa 3. Parāśara 4. Piśuna 5. Kauṇapadanta 6. Vātavyādhi 7. Kauṭilya Āmbhīyas mentioned separately 8. Kauṭilya (again)	1. Kātyāyana 2. Kaṇinka Bharadvāja 3. Carāyaṇa 4. Ghotamukha 5. Kiñjalka 6. Piśuna 7. Piśuna's son	1. Bharadvāja 2. Viśālākṣa 3. Kauṭilya
(The teacher not mentioned) (Ref.: Kauṭilya, pp. 12-14)	(No teacher mentioned) (Ref.: Kauṭilya, pp. 27-28)	(No teacher mentoined) (Ref.: Kauṭilya, pp. 32-33)	(No teacher mentioned) (Ref.: Kauṭilya, p. 282)	(The teacher not mentioned) (Ref.: Kauṭilya p. 411)

TABLE B—(*Contd.*)

Category C. Names of Teachers mentioned in complete disorder (Six lists).

LIST I	LIST II	LIST III	LIST IV	LIST V	LIST VI
1. Uśanas 2. Manu 3. Bṛihaspati 4. Kauṭilya	1. Manu 2. Uśanas 3. Kauṭilya Then at some interval. 4. Bṛihaspati	1. Kauṭilya 2. Bharadvāja 3. Kauṭilya (again)	1. Teacher 2. Vātavyādhi 3. Kauṭilya	1. Bharadvāja 2. Kauṭilya 3. Viśālākṣa 4. Kauṭilya (again) 5. Parāśara 6. Kauṭilya (again) 7. Piśuna 8. Kauṭilya (again) 9. Kauṇapadanta 10. Kauṭilya (again) 11. Vātavyādhi 12. Kauṭilya (again)	1. Teacher 2. Bharadvāja 3. Kauṭilya 4. Viśālāksa 5. Kauṭilya (again) 6. Parāśara 7. Kauṭilya (again) 8. Piśuna 9. Kauṭilya (again) 10. Kauṇapadanta 11. Kauṭilya (again) 12. Vātavyādhi 13. Kauṭilya (again)
(No teacher mentioned) (Ref.: Kauṭilya, p. 201)	(Teacher mentioned after Kauṭilya and before Bṛihaspati) (Ref.: Kauṭilya, pp. 216, 217)	(No teacher mentioned) (Ref.: Kauṭilya, p. 411)	(Teacher mentioned) (Ref.: Kauṭilya, p. 293)	(Ref. Kauṭilya, pp. 354-57)	(Ref. Kauṭilya, pp. 349-57)

Category D. Kauṭilya's unnamed Teacher.

Mentioned once in list III of Category A; and twice in list II and list IV of Category C. The teacher is mentioned on many occasions. See Kauṭilya, pp. 8, 69, 183, 186, 209. 217, 221-23, 293, 294, 302, 304, (twice), 311, 319, (many times), 320, 321, 322, 324, 326, 327, 328, 331. 332, 341, 349, 353, 354, 357, 358, 359, 360, 367, 368, 369 and 373.

apart from the individual teachers mentioned by Kauṭilya. Unless proved to the contrary, the assumption that every one of those ancient teachers had a school of his own may be entertained. This alone explains why Kauṭilya mentions the six schools on some, and the teachers on many, occasions.

CHAPTER II

THE SCHOOLS DISCUSSED

A. THE HISTORICITY OF THE TEACHERS MENTIONED BY KAUṬILYA

ARE THE names of the exponents of the theory of statecraft mentioned in the *Arthaśāstra* of Kauṭilya imaginary or were they historical? An answer to this question will lead us to an inquiry whether any of the names mentioned by Kauṭilya are identical to those mentioned by other authors. We have in the *Mahābhārata* the names of teachers of statecraft mentioned on two occasions—once in the *Anuśāsanaparva,* and then, in the *Śāntiparva.* In the former, *rājadharma* is said to have been composed by Bṛihaspati and Uśanas; while in the latter, the expounders of the *rājaśāstra* (which is another name of *arthaśāstra*) are given thus: Bṛihaspati, Bharadvāja, Gauraśiras, Kāvya, Mahendra, Manu Prācetasa, and Viśālākṣa. These were the *ācāryas,* or professors, whose views were opposed to those of Śambara.[6]

Some considerations emerge from the above—first, that Bṛihaspati preceded Uśanas, who came earlier than Bharadvāja, thus agreeing with the succession of those two teachers as given later by Kauṭilya. Secondly, the figure of Viśālākṣa appears to have been real, although the same epic gives that name as an attribute of god Indra.[7] And, thirdly, the *Mahābhārata* mentions five theorists, all of whom are not mentioned by Kauṭilya, namely, Gauraśiras, Kāvya, Mahendra, Manu Prācetasa and Śambara. It cannot be made out why Kauṭilya excluded some of them from his lists. If we take them into consideration, it would mean that they have to be added to the names of teachers as given by Kauṭilya, in order to form a complete account of the ancient teachers. The total number of exponents of the *rājadharma* would then be twenty-four.[8] We have to leave this question of the historicity of the ancient authors on the *arthaśāstra* here for want of further evidence. But there seems to be hardly any doubt that the nineteen names must have referred to historical personages, otherwise they would not have merited recognition at the hands of Kauṭilya, the most practical of all authors on statecraft.

B. ON THEIR NAMES

The question of the historicity of the ancient teachers mentioned by Kauṭilya leads us to another consideration—that relating to some of their names.

They are so queer that one may wonder whether they ever stood for any historical personages at all! Thus, Vātavyādhi meant "one who suffered from gout" ; Kauṇapadanta, "he who has teeth like a demon" ; and Piśuna, "a spy". In the *Rig Veda,* and occasionally in later literature, the last name meant "a traitor".[9] These names might be compared with others found in the ancient texts. Thus, for instance, Kutsa meant "one of the seven Sages" ; "Śunaḥṣepa", "one like a dog's tail" ; Divodāsa, "one who was a time-server" ; and Carmaśiraḥ, "one with the leather head". The metronymic "Bāhudantīputra", which meant "one who was the son of a woman whose teeth were as long as the arm", may be compared with similar names occurring in the *Brāhmaṇas* like Bhāradvājīputra, "son of a female descendant of Bhāradvāja", Gautamīputra, "son of a female descendant of Gotama", Bhālukīputra, "son of Bhālukī", etc. Some of these names are also met with in the *Bṛihadāraṇyaka Upaniṣad.* As was pointed out by Professor J. Jolly long ago, "this mode of bestowing names throws a peculiar light on the literary etiquette of that time the traces of which are to be more discovered in the Upanishads."[10] We have seen above that, as is related in the *Mahābhārata,* Indra's recension of the *arthaśāstra* was called *Bāhudantaka* ; while Viśālaksa was another form of the name of Śiva.[11] As to whether we have to agree with Mādhavayajvan, the commentator on Kauṭilya's *Arthaśāstra,* that the names Piśuna, Bhāradvāja, Kauṇapadanta, and Vātavyādhi stood for Narada, Droṇācarya, Bhīśma, and Uddhava respectively,[12] cannot be made out, since we do not know on what sources the commentator based his identification. So far as the names occurring in Kauṭilya's *Arthaśāstra* are concerned, there seems no valid reason for rejecting them as being unhistorical merely because they sound queer. It would be as incorrect to reject them as it would be, for instance, to reject the name Kauṭilya itself. For tradition seems to connect it with Kuṭila, "crooked". But, as Dr. Ganapati Śāstri has shown, the correct form of that name seems to be Kauṭilya, "born in Kuṭala gotra", the term Kuṭala being interpreted by Keśavasvamin in his *Nānārthārṇavasaṁkṣepa,* as meaning both *gotrarṣī* and an ornament.[13].

The unnamed teacher of Kauṭilya deserves a passing note. True to the traditional convention of merely referring respectfully to his teacher but without calling him by his name, Kauṭilya never gives any indication of the identity of his illustrious teacher. But that did not prevent Kauṭilya from differing from his teacher on various fundamental issues. The only plausible explanation as to why the teacher was not mentioned by Kauṭilya is that, perhaps, in addition to the above reason, the teacher stood by himself in the field of Politics. It may as well be that the teacher was as little as possible influenced by the earlier schools of thought. This explains why the teacher is not mentioned by Kauṭilya, along with the other ancient authorities, excepting in list III of Category A and in lists II and IV of Category C.

CHAPTER III

A TENTATIVE CHRONOLOGY OF THE SCHOOLS

A. INTRODUCTION: PRINCIPLES ON WHICH THE CHRONOLOGY IS BASED

ANY DISCUSSION of the probable ages in which the great exponents of the ancient theory of Politics lived, can only be hypothetical, since, excepting their names as given in some order and disorder in Kauṭilya, and to some extent in the *Mahābhārata,* there is no indication anywhere as to the criteria by which we could arrive even at a semblance of a solution. Nevertheless it is worth while to attempt such a task, even if it were to give us an indication of their probable chronology the verification of which we may leave to future research.

Before we undertake the above task, it is desirable to see if there are any principles by which we could understand Kauṭilya's classification of the ancient schools. Here it is necessary to repeat a few considerations which have already been mentioned earlier. Kauṭilya mentions three sets of teachers—the one beginning with Manu ; the second, with Bharadvāja ; and the third, with Kātyāyana—in a manner to suggest that they were not contemporaries but that they followed one another at some distant intervals. This would mean that we have to consider the three sets of teachers as belonging to different ages. Secondly, in these classifications Kauṭilya always gives the place of precedence, in each of these three classifications, consistently to three great names—the earliest of them being that of Manu, the next in point of sequence, that of Bharadvāja, and the third, of Kātyāyana. In classifying his groups, Kauṭilya never mentions Manu excepting in lists Nos. I, II, III and IV of Category A. This would justify our assumption that the most ancient name in the list of teachers was undoubtedly that of Manu. And, thirdly, Kauṭilya differentiates between the other teachers and Manu, whom he places earlier than Bṛihaspati, and whom, for want of a more definite standard, we might style Manu, the lawgiver, as distinct from Manu Vaivasvata, whom Kauṭilya refers in one definite context when he makes a spy say the following in regard to the justification of the king's authority: "People suffering from anarchy, as illustrated by the proverbial tendency of a large fish swallowing a small one (*mātsyanyāyābhibhūtaḥ prajāḥ*) first elected Manu, the Vaivasvata, to be king."[14] But Kauṭilya mentions Manu, the lawgiver, in various other contexts,[15] and does not confound him with Manu Vaivasvata. This enables us to presume that the two were not identical.

B. MANU VAIVASVATA NOT THE SAME AS MANU, THE LAWGIVER

1. THE LEGEND OF MANU OF THE DELUGE

A brief examination of the ancient texts reveals that the above conclusion in regard to the difference between Manu Vaivasvata and Manu, the lawgiver, is justifiable. The story of Manu of the Deluge, or of the fish legend, is given in the *Śatapatha Braāmaṇa* thus:

> The Adhvaryu (sacrificial priest) brought one morning water to Manu for washing his hands. When he was washing himself, a fish came into his hands. It said—'Rear me, I will save thee!' Manu asked the fish, 'Wherefrom wilt thou save me?' It replied, 'A flood will carry away all these creatures: from that I will save thee!' Then Manu asked—'How am I to rear thee?' It said, 'As long as we are small, there is great destruction for us: fish devour fish. Thou wilt first keep me in a jar. When I outgrow that, thou wilt dig a pit and keep me in it. When I outgrow that, thou wilt take me down to the sea, for then I shall be beyond destruction.' It soon became a *jhāṣa* (a large fish); and it said—'In such and such a year that flood will come. Thou shalt then attend to me (i.e. to my advice) by preparing a ship, and when the flood has risen thou shalt enter into the ship, and I will save thee from it.' And it happened as the fish prophesied; in the same year in which the fish had indicated him, Manu prepared a ship; and when the flood had arisen, he entered the ship. The fish then swam up to him, and to its horn he tied the rope of the ship, and by that means he passed up to the northern mountain which came to be called the slope of the northern mountain or Manu's descent.[16]

2. MANU OF THE DELUGE NOT THE SAME AS MANU VAIVASVATA

There is nothing to indicate in the above legend that Manu, who is thus associated with the Deluge, was the same as Manu Vaivasvata. On the other hand, the latter seems to have been a later personage far removed from the former. In the first place, the entire legend refers to a period of destruction and subsequent creation of mankind, when the question of ruling over men did not arise. Secondly, the latter part of the legend in which occurs the story of the procreation of the human race by Manu, who had been saved by the fish, clearly points to a period of antiquity when there could not have been even a tribal polity or the semblance of a monarchical organization which could be associated with Manu Vaivasvata.[17]

3. MANU VAIVASVATA IN THE SATAPATHA BRAHMANA

And, thirdly, the *Śatapatha Brāhmaṇa* itself refers to Manu Vaivasvata in a later context, while describing the Pāriplava Āhyāyana or the Revolving Legend, during the performance of the *aśvamedha* or the horse sacrifice ritual. When the Adhvaryu (sacrificial priest) sits on a golden stool, in the company of the Hotṛi, the sacrificer, the Brāhmaṇa, and the Udgātṛi, he calls upon the Hotri to recount the beings, when the latter being about to tell the Pāriplava legend (so called because it was renewed every ten days during the year), addressed the Adhvaryu, thus: "King Manu Vaivasvata, his people are Men, and they are staying here."[18] Evidently these men represented a stage of life far removed from the desolate one of destruction and the subsequent creation of mankind. We have to imagine a great interval between the age of Manu of the Deluge and that associated with Manu Vaivasvata. It is only when we come to the latter that we have evidence of government, since Manu Vaivasvata is explicitly called king Manu Vaivasvata in the *Śatapatha Brāhmaṇa.* Since Manu of the Deluge was called "Our Father", was considered as the ancestor of the human race, and looked upon as the most important of the ancient priests and heroes in the *Rig Veda* ; and since the latter work cannot be assigned to an age lower than 2500 B.C., it appears as if we have to place Manu of the Deluge in an age much earlier than that *Veda.* Hypothetically he may be assigned to about 3500 B.C. or earlier.[19]

4. THE AGE OF MANU VAIVASVATA

Having thus seen that Manu Vaivasvata was later than Manu of the Deluge, the next point is: to what age could the former be assigned? The fact that he is mentioned in the *Śatapatha Brāhmaṇa* proves that he was prior to the age of that *Brāhmaṇa.* This presumption is borne out by another consideration relating to Nābhā-Nediṣṭa Mānava, whose story is mentioned in the *Taittirīya Samhita* and in the *Āitareya Brāhmaṇa.*[20] As his name suggests, he was nearest in descent to Manu. He has become famous in the later *Samhitas* and the *Brāhmaṇas,* for the way he was treated when his father Manu divided his property amongst his sons. Manu referred to here was evidently Manu Vaivasvata, and not Manu of the Deluge, since the latter was amidst too primitive and forlorn a condition to think of dividing property among his sons. We are to infer from the story of Nābhā-Nediṣṭa Mānava that he was earlier than the age of those texts. It would not be too much to presume that he belonged to the slightly developed period in which Manu Vaivasvata himself lived. The reference to the legacy of cows, which Nābhā-Nediṣṭa Mānava received from the

Āngīrasas,[21] points to a stage of primitive development which cannot be associated with Manu of the Deluge. Manu Vaivasvata may be assigned to *circa* 2500 B.C., again, on purely hypothetical grounds.

5. RELATIONSHIP BETWEEN MANU VAIVASVATA AND MANU, THE LAWGIVER

Manu Vaivasvata's relaionship with Manu, the lawgiver, may now be discussed. Here we are again confronted with the same difficulty we have mentioned above, namely, that there is no clue in the ancient texts that could help us to arrive at a tangible conclusion. We have to depend upon the statements of the *Manusmṛiti* in which it is stated that in the process of creation, Brahmā created seven great sages (named) among whom was Bhṛigu; and that "they created seven other Manus possessing great brilliancy, gods, and classes of gods and great sages of measureless power".[22] In a later context in the same work, Bhṛigu being addressed by Manu, relates thus:

> Listen! Six other high-minded, very powerful Manus, who belong to the race of this Manu, the descendant of the Self-Existent (Svayambhū, and who having severally produced created beings (are) Svārociṣa, Auttami, Tāmasa, Raivata, Cākṣuṣa, possessing great lustre, and the son of Vivasvat. These seven great glorious Manus, the first among whom was Svayambhū, produced and protected this whole moveable and immoveable (creation) each during the period allotted to him.[23]

It was seen above that Bhrigu was one of the ten great sages created by Brahmā; and that, along with the other sages, he had created seven other Manus. This suggests that the last of the seven Manus, the son of Vivasvat, or Vaivasvata, could not have been the lawgiver, since he belonged to an age immediately following that of Bhṛigu himself. It must be admitted that this is only a surmise, and that neither the *Manusmṛiti* nor any ancient text is clear on the above point. The absence of the names of the six Manus in the *Śatapatha Brāhmaṇa,* points to their having been later than the age of the *Brāhmaṇa*. We may leave this question unsolved, and merely observe that the statement that "the six other high-minded, very powerful Manus, who belong to the race of this Manu", as given in the *Manusmṛiti,* is to be perhaps understood in the sense that Manu Vaivasvata preceded Manu, the lawgiver, by some centuries. The absence of the name Vaivasvata while referring to the "Wise Manu", who composed "these Institutes of the Sacred Law", as given in the *Manusmṛiti,*[24] seems to support the assumption made above.[25]

6. THE PROBABLE AGE OF MANU, THE LAWGIVER

If we agree to the above supposition that Manu Vaivasvata was not the same as Manu, the lawgiver, it follows that there was a considerable interval after the former and before the latter. We cannot make out what exactly was the age that intervened between the two great figures. Neither is there any clue as to how many teachers flourished between them. Assuming for argument's sake, that there might have been about six teachers from the time of Manu Vaivasvata to that of Manu, the lawgiver, and allotting a span of one hundred years to every one of them, on the basis of the statement in the *Manusmṛiti* that "men are free from disease, accomplish all their aims, and live four hundred years in the Kṛita age, but in the Tretā and (in each of) the succeeding (ages) their life is lessened by one quarter",[26] we arrive at the probable age of Manu, the lawgiver, thus:

Manu Vaivasvata: *circa* 2500 B.C.
Intervening six sages,
everyone of whom
living one hundred years: (years) 600
Manu, the lawgiver: 1900-1800 B.C.

An objection to the above calculation may be raised by saying that there is nothing to suggest that there were six other teachers intervening between Manu Vaivasvata and Manu, the lawgiver. This is a valid objection which cannot be satisfactorily explained. But the date 1900-1800 B.C. which has been thus hypothetically arrived at for Manu, the lawgiver, will enable us to reach the probable dates of the various teachers from that celebrated figure till Kauṭilya.

C. THE POST-MANU SCHOOLS

1. CATEGORY FIRST

The two important schools after Manu, the lawgiver, according to Kauṭilya, were those of Bṛihaspati and Uśanas. We have to recount the version of the different editions of the *arthaśāstra* as given in the *Mahābhārata* which was cited in an earlier context. Brahmā, the creator, had originally written a work on *dharma, artha,* and *kāma* in 100,000 verses ; Śiva Viśālākṣa had reduced it to 10,000 in consideration of the brevity of human life ; Indra brought it down to 5,000 *ślokas* in the shape of *Bāhudantaka* ; Bṛihaspati still reduced it to 3,000 ; and, finally, Uśanas still further reduced it to 1,000 verses.[27] From this it may be inferred that Bṛihaspati preceded Uśanas, and the latter, the author of the *Mahābhārata*. There is no justification to accept the opinion of the late Professor Keith that we have to doubt the authenticity of the works attributed to Bṛihaspati and Uśanas.[28]

On the other hand, we may agree to the view of Dr. Kane that the work of Uśanas was certainly an historical work, since it is referred to and cited in the *Mahābhārata*, the *Mudrārākṣasa*, the *Tāṇḍya-Mahābrāhmaṇa*, and by Viśvarūpa in his commentary on *Yājñavalkya*.[29] The schools of Bṛihaspati and Uśanas, therefore, have to be assigned to a period after Manu and before the age of the *Mahābhārata*. It is true that there is nothing to indicate that Manu, Bṛihaspati, and Uśanas followed one another in rapid succession. But there should be no objection to our reckoning them as having followed one another with probably a gap intervening between Manu and Bṛihaspati. Since we have assigned Manu to *circa* 1900-1800 B.C., we may allot Bṛihaspati and Uśanas to the age ranging from *circa* 1700 B.C. to 1500 B.C.

2. THE SCHOOLS OF CATEGORY SECOND

In our lists described above, the three names of Manu, Bṛihaspati, and Uśanas are always mentioned in a manner to suggest that all the three were apart from those appearing in the next list beginning with Bharadvāja, who was followed by Viśālākṣa and Parāśara. These three thinkers may be assigned to the age ranging from *circa* 1500 B.C. to 1200 B.C.

3. THE SCHOOLS OF CATEGORY THIRD

The third category of teachers, as given by Kauṭilya, begins with Kātyāyana and ends with Vātavyādhi. We may assign these ten or eleven thinkers, if we include in this list the Āmbhiyas, to the period ranging from *circa* 1200 B.C. to 400 B.C., with an average of about seventy-five years to each thinker. It is not improbable that they were the predecessors of the unnamed teacher of Kauṭilya, whom we have to assign to the earlier part of the same age to which Kauṭilya belonged (fourth century B.C.).

D. THE PROBABLE CHRONOLOGY OF ALL THE SCHOOLS

The chronology we have arrived at, on purely hypothetical grounds, for all the thinkers from Manu, the lawgiver, till Kauṭilya, may now be stated as follows:

1. Manu, the lawgiver	*circa* 1900-1800 B.C.
2. Bṛihaspati 3. Uśanas	*circa* 1700-1500 B.C.
4. Bharadvāja 5. Viśālakṣa 6. Parāśara	*circa* 1500-1200 B.C.

7.	Kātyāyana	circa 1200-400 B.C.
8.	Kaṇinka Bharadvāja	
9.	Carāyana	
10.	Gotamukha	
11.	Kiñjalka	
12.	Piśuna	
13.	Piśuna's son	
14.	Kauṇapadanta	
15.	Vātavyādhi	
16.	Bāhudantīputra	
17.	The Āmbhiyas	
18.	The unnamed teacher of Kauṭilya	400-320 B.C.
19.	Kauṭilya	

E. OBJECTIONS AGAINST THE ABOVE CHRONOLOGY

1. THE AGE OF THE SATAPATHA BRAHMANA

The above chronological classification has certain objections against it. Leaving aside the innumerable objections centering round the names of Manu Vaivasvata and Manu, the lawgiver, which are met with in ancient literature, we may confine ourselves to three major objections which are as follows: first, since in the *Śatapatha Brāhmaṇa* Manu, the lawgiver, is not mentioned, it would mean that we have to assign that great lawgiver to a period later than that *Brāhmaṇa.* If, according to scholars like Professor Macdonell, the *Śatapatha Brāhmaṇa* (along with the other *Brāhmaṇas*) is to be assigned to a period ranging from *circa* 800 B.C. to 500 B.C.,[30] it follows that Manu, the lawgiver, cannot be assigned to an age earlier than *circa* 800 B.C.

But this objection does not carry much weight. In the first place, the fact that the author (or authors) of the *Śatapatha Brhāhmaṇa* does (do) not mention Manu, the lawgiver, need not necessarily be interpreted to mean that that lawgiver was posterior to the above work. One could as well argue that because Manu, the lawgiver, is not mentioned in the Buddhist canonical texts, he is to be assigned to an age later than that of those texts! Further, the age of the *Śatapatha Brāhmaṇa* itself is based on speculation. There is nothing to prevent us from assigning that work to an age earlier than the date assigned to it by Professor Macdonell. Moreover, it is evident from Kauṭilya's *Arthaśāstra* that between him and Manu, the lawgiver, there were, as shown above, at least eighteen schools of political thought. They could not have been the result of the imagination of Kauṭilya. Now if Kauṭilya, as is rightly maintained by some scholars, is said to have lived in the fourth century B.C., it cannot be that we have to assign Manu, the lawgiver, to the period ranging from *circa* 800 B.C. to 500 B.C. which is the age of the *Brāhmaṇas*, according to Professor Macdonell. We have no other alternative but to assign Manu, the lawgiver, to a much earlier age, so as to make provision for all the thinkers mentioned after him and before Kauṭilya. The age suggested above for Manu, viz., *circa* 1900 B.C. to 1800 B.C., alone helps us to fix chronologically all the schools coming after him in a satisfactory manner.

But assigning Manu, the lawgiver, to that age, lands us amidst certain difficulties relating to the nature of the language used in the *Manusmṛiti*, to its internal evidence, and to the relationship of that work to the other *dharmaśāstras*, all of which form a subject that is outside the scope of this book. We may only mention this difficulty without attempting to solve it.

2. MANU, THE LAWGIVER, AND THE MAHABHARATA

There is, moreover, an equally insurmountable difficulty about the chronological arrangement of the schools proposed above. If Manu, the lawgiver, is to be assigned to *circa* 1900-1800 B.C., it would run counter to the date of the *Mahābhārata* which, as some scholars maintain, has to be assigned to *circa* 3102-1 B.C.[30a] If in that epic, as related already, Bṛihaspati and Uśanas are mentioned as having abridged the *arthaśāstra*, then, we have to assign these two teachers to an age previous to that of the *Mahābhārata*, Manu himself coming earlier than Bṛihaspati. There should be no objection to our assigning to him to an age earlier than that of Bṛihaspati, according to this criterion, provided it is presumed that all the three thinkers lived a life much longer than the span of one hundred years given to them above, or that there were other teachers intervening between Manu and Uśanas about whom we know nothing for the present. This is, however, only a supposition which cannot be substantiated by proof.

3. THE PROBLEM OF KATYAYANA

Finally, another objection may be raised against the chronological calculation made above. It may be argued, for instance, that the dates given for Kātyāyana are inadmisible, because he has been assigned to *circa* fourth century B.C. Here it may be observed that that name was borne by many persons, and that it was more a surname than the name of a particular individual. The ancient texts mention the names of Kātyāyanī, a woman, Kātyāyana Dakṣa Atreya, a teacher, and Kātyāyanīputra, also a teacher.[31] An index of the *White Yajur Veda* is attributed to a Kātyāyana, who is also credited with the authorship of the *Śrauta Sūtras*.[32] His age is uncertain. Then, there is Kātyāyana, the author of the *Vārtikas* or notes on Pāṇini's *Grammar*, whom Professor Macdonell assigned to about the third century B.C., but whom Professor R. G. Bhandarkar dated in the fourth century B.C. in the age of the Nandas.[33] Kātyāyana mentioned by Kauṭilya cannot be identified with any one of the above, since he was more concerned with the exposition of the *arthaśāstra* than with the *Śrauta Sūtras* or with grammar. Dr. Kane rightly differentiated between Kātyāyana, the author of a *smṛiti,* Kātyāyana, the author of the *Śrauta Sūtra,* Kātyāyana, the author of the *Vārtikas,* and Kātyāyana, the author of the *arthaśāstra.*[34] But the date he has proposed for the last named Kātyāyana, viz., *circa* third or fourth century A.D.,[35] is, in our opinion, far too late to be accepted. If it is agreed that Kātyāyana mentioned by Kauṭilya was an historical figure—about which there can be hardly any doubt—then, we have to assign him to an age earlier than the fourth century B.C. which is the date usually given to Kauṭilya, that is, the age that has been suggested to the latter in this work. Kātyāyana's version of the *arthaśāstra,* as in the case of others mentioned by Kauṭilya, has been lost to us.

CHAPTER IV

IMPORTANCE OF THE SCHOOLS OF POLITICAL THOUGHT

A. THE SCHOOLS REPRESENT DEFINITE STAGES OF GROWTH

WHATEVER MAY be the scepticism with which the above assumptions in regard to the chronology of the political predecessors of Kauṭilya are viewed, it is clear that their schools represent definite stages in the history of the development of ancient Indian political thought. The fact that most of their works have been lost need not come in our way of appreciating their contribution to the subject under discussion. The importance of the teachers and of their schools lies in the fact that they take us to a period of considerable antiquity, thereby suggesting that *daṇḍanīti* or *arthaśāstra* or the science of government had already attracted the attention of ancient thinkers long before the days of Kauṭilya. The discussion of the various schools, particularly those of Manu, Bṛihaspati, and Ūsanas before the age of the *Mahābhārata,* would have convinced the reader that we have to refer to the pre-Mahābhāratan times for the beginnings of the formative period in the development of the ancient Indian political thought. The existence of various schools at different times suggests that the discussion of the theories was not confined to a single person or to a particular age but was spread over hundreds of years.

B. THE ANCIENTS TACKLED PRACTICAL PROBLEMS OF THE STATE

The numerous points of difference between Kauṭilya and his predecessors, some of which are on questions of fundamental importance, undoubtedly suggest that the ancient Indian mind was as intensely engaged in ascertaining the truth and excellence of political ideals as it was concerned with the subtle controversies in the spheres of metaphysics, ethics and religion.[36] When we realize that these discussions are to be dated to the ages corresponding, and perhaps anterior, to those of Plato and Aristotle,[37] we may venture to say that those times were, indeed, of intellectual fermentation that had for their object the material well-being of society. The nineteen schools of political thought ending with Kauṭilya definitely prove that the ancients were not given to a mechanical repetition of each other's views but to ceaseless endeavours to ascertain how far the end of the State could best be realized within the ambit of the ancient *dharma*. They reveal, further, that the ancient Indian State was not in a moribund condition but was actuated by ideas which were modified by the political thinkers to suit the needs of the changing times. We shall see towards the end of this book that the principles enunciated by the ancient teachers, and as collated and edited by Kauṭilya, far from representing an idyllic picture of the State, were theories that actually governed the Indian States for centuries after his time.

C. KAUṬILYA'S IMPORTANCE

1. THE ARTHASASTRA: A WORK FOR ALL TIME

Of all the schools of ancient Indian political thought, the most noteworthy is that of Kauṭilya. Professor Keith's judgment that the *Arthaśāstra* of Kauṭilya did not represent the fine flower of Indian political thought,[38] does as much injustice to the Mauryan Prime Minister as to the learned Professor himself. We shall see below in Part Four that Kauṭilya admits of an admirable comparison with Aristotle; and to that extent represents as fine a flower of Indian thought as that celebrated Greek political thinker does of the Western mind. Professor Keith passed a hasty judgment on Kauṭilya before undertaking a comparative study of this nature. That eminent Indologist's other remark, given in the same context, that Kauṭilya, although the minister of an Emperor, confined his remarks to a moderate-sized kingdom; and that he did not "by word or allusion betray the name of the country for which and in which he was writing",[39] shows a woeful lack of appreciation of the *Arthaśāstra* which, as we shall mention in detail below, definitely refers to the vast country over which his royal patron reigned; and, what is likewise interesting, alludes to the latter in unmistakable terms. There is reason to believe that Kauṭilya, who was a thorough matter-of-fact statesman, promulgated regulations which were designed to meet the needs of a State; and that his State was not of the impracticable and universal type as conceived of by Alexander the Great, or of an ideal condition like that visualized by Plato, but was exclusively meant for the people amidst whom he lived. It should not be forgotten that his *Arthaśāstra*, in addition to its being a book of guidance for his royal master, was a manual on statecraft for the whole country and for all time.[40]

2. KAUTILYA'S ROYAL PATRON

We may now take up the next point whether he mentions or at least alludes to his royal patron. Even granting that Kauṭilya does not mention by name his suzerain, it need not come in our way of appreciating the importance of the *Arthaśāstra*. It is a matter of common knowledge that very many ancient Indian texts do not contain either the names of their authors or of the regions whose products they were. This has not prevented Indologists, including Professor Keith, from assessing their worth. Neither has it made such works less historical or less significant. What is of material consequence for our purpose is that Kauṭilya, following the ancient Indian tradition, did not mention either his own teacher's or his royal patron's name. But this shortcoming, if ever it was from the standards of those ages, Kauṭilya compensated for by informing his readers that he wrote his work for the King of Men (*Kauṭilyena Narendrārthe sāsanasya vidhiḥ kṛitaḥ*). The Narendra referred to here could have been no other than Candragupta Maurya himself.[41]

3. HIS REFERENCE TO THE COUNTRY AND THE TIMES IN WHICH HE LIVED

As for Kauṭilya's explicit reference to the country in which he lived, we shall discuss it in detail in our comparative study of Kauṭilya and Aristotle below. The critics of Kauṭilya, who have found fault with him because of his alleged unscrupulous teachings, have failed to note the nature of the times in which he lived. It was an age when the ancient culture appeared to be crumbling; when the monarchs whom Kauṭilya helped to overthrow, namely, the Nandas, had proved utterly worthless in the matter of preserving the scriptures; when after their overthrow the country was still filled with their adherents, who were a source of great anxiety to the new Mauryan government; when, to add to the difficulties of the latter, there were the foreigners in the Punjab and the adjoining regions, whose loyalty to the new government set up in Pāṭaliputra was doubtful; when in the sphere of international politics a dangerous example of insecurity, perfidy, and opportunism had already been set in by the greatest of the Western conquerors, Alexander the Great, who had annexed a great part of the north-western regions,[42] and whose most trusted lieutenant had, on the death of the great Conqueror, assumed an independent status as a monarch; and when amidst all these internal and external dangers there was the dire need of setting up a State which, while being able to withstand any possible attack on it by the erstwhile royal family that had been overthrown in Magadha, and by the still powerful foreigners in the Punjab, had to devise ways and means of creating an environment that would maintain the ancient *dharma*, fulfil its obligations to the various sections of the people, and demand from them the utmost loyalty and service which only a stern and benevolent government could expect from its citizens. Kauṭilya has in his usual cryptic manner given the object of his great work in the last verse of the same thus: "This science has been made by him who from intolerance (of misrule) quickly rescued the scriptures and the science of weapons and the earth which had passed to the

Nanda king" (*yena śāstraṁ ca śastraṁ ca Nandarājagatā ca bhūḥ amarṣeṇodhritānyāśu tena śāstram idam kṛitam*).[43]

4. KAUTILYA'S TITLE TO GREATNESS

(*a*) *His Work a Compendium*

Kauṭilya's title to greatness consists in having written a compendium of almost all the *arthaśāstras* existing till his time, as he states in the opening sentence of his great work, and again in the last Book XV: "This Arthaśāstra is made as a compendium of almost all the Arthaśāstras, which, in view of acquisition and maintenance of the earth, have been composed by ancient teachers" (*purvācāryaiḥ prasthāpitāni prāyaśasthāni*).[44] Its object was entirely practical as is proved not only from the above but also from the concluding verses of the work:

> Thus this Śāstra, conforming to those paragraphic divisions, is composed as a guide to acquire and secure this and the other world. In the light of this Śāstra one can not only set on foot righteous, economical, and aesthetical acts and maintain them, but also put down unrighteous, uneconomical, and displeasing acts.[45]

In the light of these statements it might be justifiably maintained that Kauṭilya's work was not only based on the *arthaśāstras* extant till his days but was meant for the practical guidance of statesmen. It might be objected that the words "this and the other world" (*lokasya asya parasya ca*) reveal the author's predilection to a metaphysical belief in the utility of the *Arthaśāstra*. Such an objection is invalidated by the opening sentence of the same Book XV in which he defines the term *arthaśāstra* thus:

> The substance of mankind is termed *artha*, wealth ; the earth which contains mankind is termed *artha*, wealth ; that science which treats of the means of acquiring and maintaining the earth is the Arthaśāstra, Science of Polity (*manuṣyāṇāṁ vṛittiḥ-arthaḥ manuṣyavatī bhūmiḥ-iti-arthaḥ tasyāḥ prithivyā lābhapālanopāyaḥ Śāstraṁ-arthaśāstraṁ-iti*).[46]

(*b*) *Kauṭilya a Realist*

The above helps us to give his next title to greatness. He was essentially a realist who dealt with the problems confronting men in this world. In his *Arthaśāstra* he has given to the country a practical manual on statecraft which no other author before him or after him has given. With a grim reality that would have done credit to a believer in the modern totalitarian tendencies of the State, Kauṭilya analyses and solves the many complicated questions facing the government of his day in a most practical and, perhaps, in a ruthless manner.[47] In this connection it is necessary to note and reject a view which maintains that Kauṭilya was only an idealist, because his statements are not corroborated by the account of the foreign witness, Megasthenes. This view is erroneous not only because it does not take into account the nature of the narrative of Megasthenes but also because it ignores the many points of similarity between it and the *Arthaśāstra*. In the last Part of this book dealing with Theory in Practice, it will be shown that there is agreement between Kauṭilya and Megasthenes. If the latter differs from the former, the error is entirely on his part. Megasthenes' account of the Mauryan Empire, and especially of Pāṭaliputra, was based more on hearsay than on personal observation ;[48] and as such cannot be said to possess the details of a work written in Sanskrit of which language that Greek ambassador was perfectly ignorant. Indeed, that foreign ambassador, inspite of having visited Pāṭaliputra twice,[49] does not seem to have acquainted himself with the actual conditions prevailing in the land some parts of which he has attempted to describe in his *Indika*. But what little information he has given in his work, which has come down to us in fragments, only helps to confirm the opinion we have expressed above relating to the realistic approach of Kauṭlya to the many complicated problems of the State.

(c) *Treats Politics by Itself*

There is a third claim of that Mauryan Prime Minister to greatness. Of all the great teachers and writers on Polity, he was perhaps the only one who treated Politics by itself and distinct from Religion. His reference to the "other world", which occurs once or twice in his work, should not blind us to the fact that he does not treat political problems in terms of either ethical standards or of religious dogmas. No doubt, he was, like all great writers on Polity, aware of the larger concept of *dharma*. This was in perfect accordance with the standards set up by his predecessors. But nowhere in his book does Kauṭilya evaluate political action in terms of religious thought. His work, indeed, was a daring attempt at divesting Politics of Religion[50]—an attempt which is unparallelled in the entire field of ancient Indian political thought, because he based the whole treatment of the subject on *ānvikṣakī* or reasoning. It is true that, towards the end of his work, he introduced a stratum of supernaturalism in the handling of important problems like the protection of the institution of the four castes ;[51] but even here he does not lose sight of the practical ends of the State which he kept before him, and which are evident throughout his great work. The supernatural bias bordering on the superstitious, on the part of Kauṭilya, may not be mistaken for his predilection for religion to solve some of the fundamental problems facing the State.[51a] He was as much superstitious as any of the modern statesmen who, faced with the crisis of a war and of a doubtful victory, have recourse to mass prayers to realize their ends. Kauṭilya's treatment of Politics by itself and independent of Religion is one of the most conspicuous features of his work.[52]

(d) *His Contribution in General*

Finally, Kauṭilya's greatness consists in giving to the country a strong and centralized government which was perhaps unknown before him, which was administered by a bureaucratic machinery of a vast and complicated type, and which, among other things, laid great stress on the importance of local usage and customs of tribes, communities, and corporations. We shall analyse in detail the government as described in the *Arthaśāstra* in Parts Four and Five below. Here it is enough to say that statements like the following, the "portion of inheritance shall be made in accordance with the customs prevalent in the country, caste, guild (*sangha*), or the village of the inheritors", and that "the acquisition of the help of corporations is better than the acquisition of an army, a friend, or profits",[53] clearly point to the importance which Kauṭilya attached to the recognition of what may be called the Common law of the country, even when, as we shall see below, he had unequivocally declared the commands of the king, or, in modern language, the statutes enacted by the monarch, to be binding on all. In thus upholding the local customs and usage, he had more than justified the injunction of Manu, who had ordained that immemorial custom was transcendent law, that it was, indeed, a source of law, and that the king should settle the problems relating to the different castes, districts, guilds, and families after ascertaining the laws of every one of them.[54]

D. POST-KAUṬILYAN SCHOOLS

The post-Kauṭilyan Schools of political thought which fall within the period of our study ending with A.D. 1000, were confined mainly to the following: that of Viṣṇu, (before A.D. 200) ; Yājñavalkya, (*circa* A.D. 350) ; Nārada (*circa* A.D. 500) ; Kāmandaka (*circa* A.D. 700) ; and Somadeva Sūri (A.D. 959).[55] Of these the last two based their works on that of Kauṭilya with this difference that Kāmandaka does not give any tinge of his own to the views which he borrowed from Kauṭilya ; while Somadeva Sūri, like a devout Jaina, modified the views of the Mauryan Prime Minister, especially when they came into conflict with the religion which he professed.[56] As to what extent he and the other Jaina author before him, Jinasena, the author of *Ādipurāṇa* (A.D. 783-84),[57] contributed to the totality of ancient Indian political thought will be discussed in Part Five below under the chapter on Kingship in Jaina Thought.

Part Three

POLITICAL THOUGHT ANALYSED

CHAPTER I

INTRODUCTION

A. MODERN THEORIES IN RELATION TO ANCIENT CONCEPTS

WHILE ATTEMPTING to analyse the political thought of the ancients, we are faced with the problem of our modern concepts intruding into the ancient theories with the result that we seem to justify the latter only in the context of the former. A common method of approach in this direction is the one adopted by some Indian scholars, who seem to see many modern political ideas in the ancient mind. It is true that, as we shall see, some aspects of the ancient theories may appear to be of interest to us in the modern times. But the proper way of judging the ancient theories is to study and appreciate them on the background of the past; and, if necessary, to see how far they could be comparable with those expounded by contemporary thinkers in the West. Indeed, we shall devote a considerable part of our study to a comparative estimate of the political ideas of the greatest thinkers of India, Babylonia, and Greece. But the allurement of grafting modern ideas on the ancient soil is so great that the most serious attempts have been made in India to explain the ancient theories in terms of the modern trends of political thought. One of them refers to the concept of the State in the elucidation of which we are confronted with some difficulties.

B. DID THE MODERN CONCEPTS EXIST IN THE PAST?

The modern concepts of the State and government have cast such a spell on scholars as to make some of them maintain that the idea of the State, as it is now understood, existed in the past. There seems to be no justification for such a view. The theoretical concept of the State, as we now understand it, was non-existent in the past; and the ancients do not seem to have endeavoured to differentiate between the State and government as has been done in the modern times.

It is well-known to students of Political Science that by the term State is meant a numerous assemblage of human beings generally occupying a certain territory, independent of external control and possessing an organized government to which the greater body of citizens render habitual obedience.[1] The main factors that go to form a modern State are the following: territory, population, unity, and organization. Three of these, as we shall see below, are also visible in the ancient Indian State. But they did not include the concept of government which has both a broad and a narrow meaning. In its broad aspect government means the sum total of those organizations that exercise or may exercise the sovereign powers of the State ; and in its narrow sense, the person or group of persons (who in a modern community may be numerous) in whose hands the organization of the State places for the time being the function of political control. In the latter sense government is the machinery of the State which includes within it all the persons who express or administer the will of the State. It follows, therefore, that the idea of the State is theoretical, and that of government, practical.[2] In terms of sovereign power, the State is the ultimate sovereign underneath which lies the agreement of the general will of the bulk of the people ; while govrnment is only the legislative sovereign which, during the term assigned to it by the ultimate sovereign, makes laws of universal validity within its own competence, and possesses the right to exercise force in the maintenance of such laws and to maintain its own authority. "Any body which exercises those rights constitutes a government."[3] Government, therefore, is the legal aspect of the ultimate sovereign, which cannot arrogate to itself the substance of the latter. As the history of many modern countries has shown, governments may fall without disturbing either the strength or dignity of the State.

The above concept of the ultimate sovereign called the State and of the legal sovereign called the government is the result of the endeavours of modern Western political thinkers, who have thus not only distinguished between the two ideas mentioned above but have introduced a third one which is intimately connected with one of them. This is the concept of the general will which, as is well-known, was first enunciated by Rousseau in the age of the French Revolution. It lies at the basis of the modern democratic State. Without entering further into this intricate and interesting question, it may be said that when we speak of the general will, we refer to the will of the people to maintain the State, and to their general acquiescence in the decisions of government, even when they may not approve of them or be convinced of their righteousness. The general will is unformulated but real in the sense that it lies at the back of the State. It is the will of the community which upholds the unity of the State. The relative position of the three fundamental concepts of the general will, the State, and government may be summarized thus: if the general will sustains the State, the latter in its turn guarantees to government, during a specific period, the exercise of the right of making laws and of the use of coercive power for maintaining such laws.[4]

Did the Ancients entertain the Above Ideas? It is futile to expect that the ancient Indians ever made such a fine distinction between the three main concepts of the State, government, and the general will, although they undoubtedly were aware of the concepts of the State, government, and to some extent of even the general will, the last one in the sense of being the will of the people to overthrow wicked monarchs. In the following pages we shall use the term State in the sense defined above, and also in that of organized government expressing the will of the monarch. On the subjects of the State, government, as well as on other topics there was complete agreement among the ancient authors, particularly on questions like the need of the State, the justification of the State, the functions of the State, and the elements of the State,[5] all of which we shall discuss at great length in the following pages. But in order to understand them as well as the fundamental concepts of the State and government, it is necessary to see how and when they originated. This brings us to the problem of their origin and antiquity.

CHAPTER II

THE ANTIQUITY OF THE STATE—ORIGIN OF SOME IMPORTANT CONCEPTS

A. CHARACTERISTICS OF THE PAST

When we attempt to find the antiquity of the State in India, we have to realize that we are referring to a very distant age when the Aryan settlers had first come to India, bringing along with them the ideas of a social and political life which in a still earlier period they had in common with a larger Aryan population to which not only they but others had belonged. We should also note that when they came to the north-western regions of India, they were confronted with a civilization which was more advanced than their own, and which had spread far and wide in Sind and the Punjab, and perhaps along the coast of Surāṣṭra and North Gujarat. Nothing is known of the impact of this earlier and perhaps indigenous civilization on the Aryan people. The only sources of information about the earliest socio-political organization of the Aryans are the *Vedas* which enable us to form a fairly comprehensive picture of their political and socio-religious existence. We do not come across in the Vedic age of any centralized imperial power like that of either the Mauryas or of the Imperial Guptas of the later ages. There is no evidence in that early age of a concerted territorial expansion, nor of large scale economic enterprise which we see, for instance, in the fourth and fifth centuries after Christ. But there were germs of the future State, vague as they were both in their meaning and content, in the Vedic age. The whole atmosphere, particularly in the Rig Vedic times, was one of righteous religious living; and some of the ideas which came later on to have a profound political significance, were nothing but concepts couched in a religious mould. This was because in ancient India, as elsewhere in ancient Egypt, Greece, and Rome, there was religion long before the State.[6] It was an age of an undifferentiated religio-political society, when the authority of the priest and of the king was one; and when the power of the former was greater than that of the latter, because the priest was the undisputed interpreter of the unknown forces of nature, while the king, who could not divine into them, occupied a relatively subordinate position in society. We have to traverse many centuries before we come across the separation of the religious from the political officialdom, and before the authority of the king came to have a decisive influence in society.

B. ORIGIN OF SOME CONCEPTS: EVIDENCE OF THE ŚATAPATHA BRĀHMAṆA

Inter-twined to a great extent as the religious and political duties of the leaders were in the dim past, we may nevertheless endeavour to see to what extent there was any indication in the ancient texts of the future concepts which were to play an important part in the political life of the people. That the ancient Indians, even in those early days of the *Vedas,* the *Samhitas,* and the *Brāhmaṇas,* were aware of important concepts relating to their socio-political life is proved by the existence of such terms like *rājya, svarājya, sāmrājya, bhaujya, vairājya, mahārājya,* and *ādhipatya* which are met with, especially in the ancient texts like the *Atharva Veda,* the *Taittirīya Samhita,* the *Aitareya Brāhmaṇa,* and the *Jaiminīya Upaniṣad Brāhmaṇa.*[7] Of these terms the first is taken to mean "sovereign power", which when coupled with another term *āsandi* (sitting on the throne) came to be one of the characteristics of the *sāmrājya.*[8]

C. CONCLUSIONS FROM A STUDY OF THE ABOVE SOURCE

The above mentioned texts help us to arrive at certain conclusions. The first is that, so early as the age of the *Śatapatha Brāhmaṇa,* the Brahman or priest was excluded from exercising sovereign power as implied in the term *rājya.* In this connection we are informed of the following in that work:

> To the king (*rājan*) doubtless belongs the *rājasūya* ; for by offering the *rājasūya* he becomes king ; and unsuited for kingship is the Brāhmaṇa. And, moreover, the *rājasūya* is the lower, and the *vājapeya* the higher (sacrifice). For by offering the *rājasūya* he becomes king, and by the *vājapeya* (he becomes) emperor (*sāmrāj*) ; and the office of the king is lower, and that of the emperor the higher. . . . Thus, that (king) who, by performing the *vājapeya,* becomes emperor, possesses himself of everything here.[9]

From the above it is clear that in order to attain the position of a king, a Kṣatriya had to perform a *rājasūya* sacrifice, and to become an emperor, a *vājapeya* sacrifice ; that sovereign power was associated with the term *rājya;* and that kingship was unsuited to the priest or the Brahman.

D. THE IDEA OF SOVEREIGNTY: ITS RELIGIOUS COLOURING

When the *Śatapatha Brāhmaṇa* was composed, the idea of sovereignty as well as of overlordship was already in the minds of men, more stress being laid on its religious than on its political aspect. Further proof of this is available in the same *Brāhmaṇa* which, while dealing with the question of political power (*Kṣātra*), says the following, the context being the ceremony of *dīksā* when the *iṣṭi* (offerings) have come to an end:

> Some, however, say, Let him offer (them) on the fires of his Purohita. But why should one who is initiated make offering? There are twelve *dīkṣā* (days), twelve *upaṣad* days, and three *sutyās* (soma-days), that amount to three-nine fold (*stoma*), but the three-nine fold, indeed, is a thunderbolt, and horse is the nobility (*kṣātra*), and the *rājānya* is the nobility; and political power (*kṣātra*) is won by the thunderbolt: thus he wins political power by means of the thunderbolt.[10]

E. THE SIGNIFICANCE OF THE AŚVAMEDHA

In a later passage in the same *Brāhmaṇa*, we have not only the *mahārāja* or *sāmrāja* Janaka of Videha mentioned, but an elaborate account of another sacrifice which came later on to be exclusively associated with the universal dominion of kings. This was the *aśvamedha* or the horse sacrifice concerning which the same *Brāhmaṇa* gives a detailed account. Notwithstanding the fact that the performance of the horse sacrifice was "a great function in which the religious and the sacrificial element is closely and deftly interwoven with a varied programme of secular ceremonies"; and that it involved "an assertion of power and a display of political authority such as only a monarch of undisputed authority could have ventured upon without courting humiliation",[11] yet the fact remains that, as is proved by the *Taittirīya Brāhmaṇa* and the *Āpastamba Sūtra*, the performance of that sacrifice was not necessarily tantamount to the actual wielding of imperial power. The *Taittirīya Brāhmaṇa* speaks of a weak king performing the horse sacrifice; while the *Āpastamba Sūtra* admits that that sacrifice could be performed by a king ruling the whole land (*sārvabhauma*) as well as by a king who did not rule over the whole land.[12]

Even on the strength of the *Śatapatha Brāhmaṇa* itself, it might be maintained that no imperial significance was exclusively attached to the performance of the horse sacrifice. Indeed, the concept of the *aśvamedha* seems to have remained almost unchanged till the days of the *Rāmāyaṇa*. The *Śatapatha Brāhmaṇa* relates that from old a hero was born to him who had performed the (*aśvamedha*) sacrifice; and the epic informs us that king Daśaratha performed the same sacrifice in order to obtain the birth of a son.[13] These considerations suggest that the performance of the *aśvamedha*, whether in the age of the *Śatapatha Brāhmaṇa* or after, was not always indicative of the existence of large empires in the early ages. It would be more reasonable to suppose that in the age of that *Brāhmaṇa*, the *aśvamedha* sacrifice had not yet got out of the cosmogonic setting in which it had originated in the earlier days. That it continued to be so till the days of the *Rāmāyaṇa* is proved not only by the reference to king Daśaratha's performance of that sacrifice in order to obtain a son, as stated above, but also by the other significant fact that, although that monarch called himself a sovereign of the east, west, north, and south,[14] yet it appears that he never subjugated equally powerful kings like himself, namely, those of Mithila, Kekaya, Kāśi, Sindhu, Sauvīra, Surāṣṭra, Viśāla, Samkāśi, and Vanga, all of whom were independent rulers.[15]

F. THE GROWING IMPORTANCE OF SOVEREIGN POWER

From the above discussion it may be inferred that, while the germs of sovereign power are seen in the age of the *Śatapatha Brāhmaṇa*, there is nothing to indicate that the concept of sovereignty, especially as it was understood in later times, had taken a concrete political shape in that age. There were, of course, kings like Janaka of Videha in those and earlier times. In the Vedic period we come across many names of kings, but none of them can be considered as exercising the sovereign power of an imperial monarch.[16] Perhaps of all the ancient works, it is the *Śatapatha Brāhmaṇa* alone that helps us to understand the growing importance of sovereign power in the secular sphere, although even in that work, as stated above, it was not divested of a spiritual colouring. The use of the title *rājādhirāja* in the *Taittirīya Āraṇyaka*, as a divine epithet,[17] only confirms the statement made above that some of the important concepts, which were to have in later ages a political significance attached to them, were in the earlier times invested with a non-secular connotation. We may conclude this section by observing that, whereas there is evidence of the concept of sovereign power, and of the existence of kings, in the Vedic and post-Vedic periods, there is nothing to suggest that in those ancient times, there prevailed the idea of a strong, unified, and centralized State that wielded power over a large territory. It cannot be made out how long it took the ancients to evolve such a State but it appears that many centuries must have elapsed before it was brought into existence.

CHAPTER III

THE NEED OF THE STATE

A. INDEFINITENESS CENTERING ROUND THIS PROBLEM

We shall now be concerned with the next question: how did the State in ancient India arise? To this question there is no definite answer, since the beginnings of ancient Indian society cannot easily be determined. But it seems that here in India as elsewhere the State emerged within the society; and that the ties of kinship, religion, and economic needs were primarily responsible for the formation of the rudiments of the State. In addition to these factors there must have been the tendency to subordinate individuals to an authority which looked to the interests of the larger group, and which tried to unite all the groups within it.[18] These factors, however, do not help us in solving the question posed above. In this connection the remarks made in Part One above concerning the relationship of the *dharmaśāstras* and the *nītiśāstras* or the *arthaśāstras*, may be recalled along with the observations made in regard to the religious colouring of some of the most important political concepts. Inspite of the indefiniteness surrounding the above question, it is worth while investigating it.

B. PRIMARY NEED OF THE STATE: PROTECTION

The primary justification of the State was protection. The *Manusmṛiti* relates the following: "For, when these creatures (created by Prajāpati), being without a king, through fear, dispersed in all directions, the Lord created a king for the protection of this whole (creation)."[19] In a later context in the same work the following is stated: "Through fear of him (the king) all created beings, both the immovable and the movable, allowed themselves to be enjoyed and swerve not from their duties."[20] And, finally, in the same chapter later on we have the following:

> If the king did not, without tiring, inflict punishment on those worthy to be punished, the stronger would roast the weaker, like fish on a spit; the crow would eat the sacrificial cake and the dog would lick the sacrificial viands, and ownership would not remain with any one, the lower ones would (usurp the place of) the higher ones.[21]

The conclusions that may be deduced from the above are the following: firstly, there existed a society prior to the formation of the State ; secondly, the members of that society were afraid of the strong coercing the weak ; and, thirdly, in order to protect the latter, the king, whose punitive power had a divine sanctity about it, inflicted punishment compelling the turbulent members of society to acknowledge his authority. Here was, therefore, the supreme need of a State. The simile of the stronger fish eating the smaller fish as given in the *Manusmṛiti* is to be traced to the statement in the *Śatapatha Brāhmaṇa* wherein the following is stated: "... wherever there is drought, then the stronger seizes upon the weaker."[22] That this was the greatest justification for the creation of the State is also evident from the graphic description of a kingless State, as given in the *Rāmāyaṇa,* which will be cited in full below ; and from Kauṭilya, who writes that when the law of punishment is kept in abeyance, it gives rise to such disorder as is implied in the proverb of fishes, for, in the absence of a magistrate, the strong will swallow the weak, but under his protection, the weak will resist the strong.[23] Although Kauṭilya improves upon the concept of Manu by saying that with the help of the magistrate, i.e. by the exercise of punishment, the weaker will resist the stronger, yet he admits that the need of the State as given by Manu was valid in his own age.

C. THE ANCIENT ESTIMATE OF HUMAN NATURE

It appears that we have to construe from the above that the authors of the *Śatapatha Brāhmaṇa,* Manu, and Kauṭilya had little faith in the ultimate goodness of human nature ; and that they believed that the ordinary men were so depraved that they could be kept on the proper path only by the fear of punishment. Manu plainly stated the following in this connection: "The whole race of men is kept in order by punishment, for a guiltless man is hard to find: through fear of punishment, indeed, this universe is called to enjoy its blessings."[24] This want of faith in man is echoed in the later works like the *Mahābhārata,* and those of Yājñavalkya, and Kāmandaka, and in the *Śukranīti.*[25]

Before we see how the above estimate of human nature by the ancients is visible also in the writings of modern Western political thinkers, it is necessary to complete the answer to the main question with which we opened this section as to how the ancient Indian State arose. The use of punishment being thus an accepted principle with the ancient Indian political philosophers for justifying the creation of the State, we have now to see to what end it was directed. In other words, the question may be put thus: what was the object of inflicting punishment? This leads us to the antiquity of the idea of protection.

D. ANTIQUITY OF THE CONCEPT OF PROTECTION

The concept of protection was a very ancient one. Professors Macdonell and Keith have shown that in the Vedic literature, it was connoted by the term *nātha,* which appears in the neuter, and which was a word of rare occurrence. But in the post-Vedic literature, it was used in the masculine, meaning "protection", and is very common.[26] This elucidation is of interest to us inasmuch as it enables us to postulate the theory that in the early ages of the *Vedas,* perhaps the Aryan society was not only small and compact but that it did not have any complex social problems that required a continual use of punishment. It does not preclude the idea of protection which, even in those early ages, was certainly in the minds of men. Thus, for instance, when in the *Aitareya Brāhmaṇa,* the king, while performing the rite of the *rājasūya* (or the ceremony of the royal consecration) is given, among other titles, that of *rāja-piṭri,* it did not indicate, as Professors Macdonell and Keith have maintained, the hereditary character of the monarchy,[27] but it may have conveyed the idea of the king's being the protector of his people. A king to be called "Father of the people" or, as Professor Hopkins suggested, "having a king as a Father", was not altogether meaningless; but it is more reasonable to suppose that the king was considered a father, since in all early societies, it was the father who alone was entitled to protect his children and dependants.

The Vedic literature does not enable us to understand fully the problem of protection, although it is not improbable that in some of the attributes of Varuṇa, like the one referring to his being the "Punisher of the Wicked",[28] we see the germs of the later idea. A comparison need not necessarily be drawn from this, as the learned authors of the *Vedic Index* have done, that "generally, too, very little appears in Vedic literature of practices such as those which produced Anglo-Saxon society or the Roman *patronatus*".[29] The criterion is unsound in the sense that the practices of the Aryans in a remote period of antiquity like that of the *Vedas,* are likened to those of a comparatively recent society like that of the Romans and the Anglo-Saxons. This method of judging the past cannot be maintained. It is forgotten by the advocates of such a standard that, when a part of the early Aryans had branched off in the direction of the West, it had encountered a physical and political environment which was different to the one which the Aryans, who had come to India, had met with in the north-western regions of India. The political institutions of the two great sections of the Aryan people—that which came to India, and that which migrated to Europe—necessarily had to be different in some respects, although their Aryan framework probably remained practically the same. We are thus constrained to see in the ancient Indian texts themselves a clue to the solution of the problem of protection.

E. OBJECT OF PROTECTION

We have to come to the age of Manu in order to see the different aspects of the question. The following is given in the *Manusmṛiti*: "The king has been created (to be) the protector of the castes (*varṇa*) and orders, who, all according to their rank, discharge their several duties."[30] In a later context in the same chapter, it is stated that the king should behave like a father towards all men.[31] That the State should protect the weak against the strong, and prevent social confusion, is clear from the injunction in the same work to the following effect: "By taking his due, by preventing the confusion of the castes (*varṇa*), and by protecting the weak, the power of the king grows, and he prospers in this (world) and after death."[32] Only if the king protected his subjects was he entitled to receive all the sixth-part of their spiritual merit.[33]

When we reach the times of Kauṭilya, we find a longer and more detailed list of duties of the king who, as in the earlier ages of Manu, represented the State. We shall have to revert to some of these duties while explaining the concept of the State as described in the *Arthaśāstra*. Here we may merely mention that the State was not only to prevent the weak from being devoured by the strong but to protect all against the eight kinds of providential visitations like fire, floods, pestilences, diseases, famines, rats, tigers, serpents, and demons. The State was likewise to afford protection to all sections of the people against artisans, merchants, and all kinds of governmental departments.[34] The object of protection is given thus by Kauṭilya:

> This people (*loka*) consisting of four castes and four orders of religious life, when governed by the king with his sceptre, will keep to their respective paths, even devotedly adhering to their respective duties and occupations (*caturvarṇāśramo loko rājñā daṇḍena pālitaḥ svadharma-karmābhirato vartate sveṣu vartmasu*).[35]

Kauṭilya here merely echoed the earlier injunctions of Manu and the *dharmaśāstras*.[36]

F. UNANIMITY AMONGST ANCIENT AND LATER WRITERS ON THE IMPORTANCE OF PROTECTION

That the duty of protection was the foremost function of the king, which justified the existence of the State, is proved by the later political thinkers like Somedeva Sūri, who wrote thus in his work styled *Nītivākyāmrita*: "How can he be a king, who does not protect the subjects?" In the tenth century A.D. the people ascribed the greatest importance to the duty of protection, as is further proved by the same Jaina author, who asserts that "the protection of the subjects is the king's sacrifice", and that when the king protects his people in just ways, the skies pour forth all desires.[37] We shall have to discuss Somadeva Sūri's theory in detail later on in these pages.[38]

G. HOW THE ANCIENT CONCEPTS INTEREST THE MODERNERS

It will be seen from the above that there was complete unanimity amongst the ancient political theorists in regard to the supreme importance of the duty of protection on the part of the State ; and that it was directed not only to strengthening the power of the monarch but also to maintaining and preserving the social order which comprised the *varṇāśrama-dharmas,* and even those who were outside the pale of the orthodox Aryan society. We have already dealt with this side of the problem in Part One above, while describing the inter-relationship between the *dharmaśāstras* and the *arthaśāstras.*[39] Here it may only be observed that the ancient Indian concept of punishment with a view to affording protection is of interest to us in the modern times in three ways: we could understand it in terms of force as a primary cause of the origin of the State ; secondly, as an incidental factor in the origin of the State ; and, thirdly, as a justification for the maintenance of social good.

1. FORCE AS A PRIMARY CAUSE OF THE ORIGIN OF THE STATE

Let us take the first point relating to the importance of force as the *ultima ratio* of the State. The ancient Indian idea of this aspect of the question presupposes an inherent propensity of man to encroach on his weaker neighbour, and to be prone to commit acts of disorder and aggression. We have to read the writings of modern Western thinkers in order to see the universal applicability of the truth enunciated by the ancients. Professor Salmond in his well-known work on *Jurisprudence* wrote that "man is by nature a fighting animal ; and force is the *ultima ratio* not of all kings alone but of all mankind".[40] Another distinguished Western writer Jeremy Taylor, wrote that "a herd of wolves is quieter and more at one than so many men unless they all had one reason in them or have one power over them".[41] The same opinion about the pugnacious and selfish nature of man is confirmed by Machiavelli, who wrote in his *Discourses,* thus:

> Those who have discussed the problems of civic life demonstrate—and history is full of examples to confirm the fact—that whoever organizes a state and arranges laws for the government of it must presuppose that all men are wicked, and that they will not fail to show their natural

depravity whenever they have a clear opportunity, though possibly it may be concealed for a while.[42]

The reader will be convinced from the above that the appraisal of human nature by the ancients was not fantastic but reasonable ; and that their concept of force as being the primary cause of the origin of the State is justifiable even from the point of view of modern Western political thinkers.

2. FORCE AS AN INCIDENTAL FACTOR IN THE ORIGIN OF THE STATE

According to some modern Western political thinkers like Professor MacIver, "the emergence of the state was not due to force, although in the process of expansion force undoubtedly played a part".[43] We have in this statement a tacit admission that, in the evolution of the State, force was a contributory factor. If it is only recalled here that in ancient India, as elsewhere, society had existed prior to the State, as has been proved by the statements of Manu cited above, and amplified by the description of the origin of the State as given in the *Mahābhārata* ;[44] and that, according to the ancients, the *nītiśāstras,* which lay much stress on force, originated from the *dharmaśāstras,* which emphasized the social aspect of the State, it is not impossible to see how the ancient Indian concept of the origin of the State is intelligible even from the modern standpoint that restricts force to its contributory nature.

3. FORCE AS A FACTOR FOR MAINTAINING SOCIAL GOOD

Turning to the third aspect of the question, it may be noted that, again, according to the modified view of the theory of force as propounded by modern Western political theorists, it is possible to appreciate the ancient Indian idea of force in relation to protection and social progress. It is well-known to students of Politics that the theory of force has been considered as one of the fallacious theories along with the Divine Right, Utilitarian, and Social Contract theories. We shall not examine the arguments on which the rejection of the theory of force by modern political thinkers rests. It is enough to observe that, according to some modern authors, coercion does not help us to understand the origin of the State. Coercion is not the essence but the criterion of the State.[45] When all has been said against force being the main cause of the origin of the State, the incontrovertible fact remains that to the State alone, admitting that it is only one, and the most powerful, of all the social institutions within society, belongs the exclusive right of force ; that this power is over the life and property of all the other associations and persons within society ; that the State settles by force all disputes, including political, between the members and associations which comprise society; that the visible expressions and embodiments of force in the State are the armed forces, the police, the legislative authority, and various other coercive agencies which it brings into existence; and that the State uses all these and similar facets of force for the maintenance of the community of purpose and social good through an array of corresponding institutions within the limits of society.[46]

4. WHERE THE ANCIENT CONCEPT IS LINKED UP WITH THE MODERN ONE

The last idea affords a connecting link between the modern concept and the ancient Indian one. We have seen above, and we shall have to refer to it again, on the basis of the many statements of Manu and Kauṭilya, that the sceptre of *daṇḍa* was to be used by the king as typifying the State, not for his personal profit but for the furtherance of the social good of all sections of the people—that of the *varṇas, āśramas,* and even the wild tribes, foreigners, and offsprings of mixed races. In this connection we may well appreciate the statement of Kauṭilya who, while commenting on *daṇḍa* or punishment or force, wrote thus: "That sceptre on which the well-being and progress of the sciences of Ānvikṣakī (which comprised the philosophy of Sāṅkhya, Yoga, and Lokāyata), the triple Vedas, and Vārtā (agriculture, cattle-breeding and trade) depend is known as *daṇḍa*", and more particularly, that upon *daṇḍa* "the course of the progress of the world depends".[47]

CHAPTER IV

THE NATURE OF THE STATE

IN ORDER to understand the nature of the ancient Indian State, it is necessary to examine some fallacious theories which are the following.

A. FALLACIOUS THEORIES

1. THE STATE AN IRRESPONSIBLE TAX-COLLECTING MACHINERY

Sir Henry Maine, followed by Professor T. H. Green, maintained the theory that the ancient Indian State was nothing but an irresponsible tax-collecting machinery. Professor Green elaborated the observations of Sir Henry Maine, when he wrote in his classical book on *The Principles of Political Obligation,* thus:

> The great empires of the East were, in the main, tax-collecting institutions. They exercised coercive force on their subjects of the most violent kind, for certain purposes, and at certain times, but they do not impose laws as distinct from particular and occasional commands. Nor do they judicially administer and enforce customary law. In a certain sense the subjects render them habitual obedience, that is, they habitually submit when the agents of the empire descend on them for taxes and recruits, but the general tenor of their lives, their actions, and forbearances are regulated by authorities with which the empire never interferes, with which it probably could not interfere without destroying itself. These authorities can scarcely be said to reside in any determinate person or persons, but so far as they do, they reside mixedly in priests as exponents of customary religion, in heads of families acting within the family, and in some village councils acting beyond the limits of the family.[48]

Whatever may be the truth of the above observations relating to the conditions prevailing in ancient Persia and Mesopotamia which have been described by Sir Henry Maine in his work styled *Early Law and Customs,*[49] they are erroneous so far as ancient India is concerned. Professor Rangaswami Aiyangar has rightly rejected the statements of Professor Green as possessing obvious inconsistencies which do not need serious refutation.[50]

The above judgment on the Eastern governments in general, and on the Indian State in particular, was partly the result of an incomplete, superficial, and biassed study of the ancient texts, and partly of the confused political condition in the latter half of the eighteenth century in India, when the exigencies of the times threatened to submerge the ancient ideals of government in some parts of India. Critics like Sir Henry Maine were obviously inclined to look at the past from the standpoint of the times in which they lived. But there is no evidence, either in the writings of the ancient Indian thinkers or in the available historical accounts, of rapacious governments in ancient India which lived a life of perpetual extortion, unmindful of their own duties and obligations to their subjects. Even in the confused conditions prevailing in the eighteenth century, it should be remembered that, inspite of the onrush of new ideas, the Indian States, on the whole, continued to maintain and foster some of the ideals of ancient Hindu monarchy.[51] The above estimate of the ancient Indian State as given by Sir Henry Maine, and as generalized by Professor Green, may be rejected as being biassed and without any foundation.

2. THE STATE WAS SACREDOTAL IN NATURE

This is the second fallacious theory in regard to the nature of the Indian State. This theory considers the ancient State as being entirely under the influence of priests and of their writings. Superficially it may seem that we have to give credence to this theory when it is realized that religion in India, as elsewhere in the contemporary world, played a vital part in the lives of the ancient peoples ; and that the priestly class, as custodians of learninng and as interpreters of the *dharmaśāstras,* necessarily wielded great influence over the monarchs. To this consideration we have to add another one relating to the immunities which they enjoyed and which are described in the *Manusmṛiti.*[52]

The sacredotal theory of the nature of the ancient Indian State is as much one sided as it is unhistorical. The priests were undoubtedly an important factor in society but they were not the only people whose rôle was considered as being indispensable for the progress of society. Making all allowance for the uncommonly high position which the learned priests occupied in early society, it cannot be ignored that the Kṣatriyas and the Vaiśayas were also weighty factors in society. There is ample evidence in the *Manusmṛiti* to prove their importance.[53] While it is true that the priests were the custodians and interpreters of the *dharmaśāstras,* they were not promulgators of laws.[54] Moreover, the Brahmans were not completely exempted from punishemnt, as is proved both by Manu and Kauṭilya. The many immunities which they enjoyed did not save them from law, if they violated it. Manu would banish a Brahman if the latter gave false evidence, or subject him to heavy fines, thus: if the Brahman defamed a Kṣatriya, he was fined fifty *paṇas* ; and if he committed certain specified immoral acts, he was fined 500 or 1,000 *paṇas*.[55]

Kauṭilya was more pronounced in his punishment of the Brahmans, although he himself belonged to the priestly class. He laid it down that if the Brahmans sold or mortgaged their *Brahmadeya* lands, that is, lands which they had received as free gifts, excepting those who were endowed with such lands, they were liable to be punished with the first amercement, that is, a fine ranging from forty-eight to ninety-six *paṇas*.[56] If a Brahman or a person superior to a Brahman disobeyed an order "of any person attempting to do a work beneficial to all" in a village of which he was a resident, he was to be punished with a fine of twelve *paṇas*. If a Brahman did not take part in the combined performance of any sacrifice of his village, and thereby violated the State regulations relating to the performance of agreements by joint effort, he was not to be violated but was to be persuaded to pay his share.[57] Kauṭilya's impartial attitude towards the Brahmans is seen in his regulation that "persons learned in the Vedas", who could, as a rule, only have belonged to the priestly class, were declared to be legally unfit to carry on transactions, and were prohibited from being cited as witnesses in cases of transactions in one's own community.[58] Since this rule is included in the chapter on the recovery of debts and the levying of interest on loans, it is evident that it referred to transactions between creditors and debtors. In regard to certain miscellaneous offences, which are described in detail by Kauṭilya, the transactions involving the Brahmans were to be settled by the judges themselves.[59] This clearly demonstrates that even in judicial matters, which involved the interpretation of the *dharmaśāstras,* the Brahmans could claim no immunity, being subject, like all the other citizens, to the law of the land. In the case of remarriage of women, no distinction was made by Kauṭilya between the wives of the Śūdras, the Vaiśyas, the Kṣatriyas, and the Brahmans—the same rule which required a wife to wait for a specified period (ranging from ten to twelve years) before remarriage was applicable to them.[60] Kauṭilya would not exempt a Brahman from a fine of twelve *paṇas* if, under the pretext of being a member of the priestly class, he evaded the payment of the dues while passing military stations, or crossing rivers, or bawled out, or invited others to fight against his neighbours.[61] Although the Mauryan Prime Minister clearly stated that "whatever may be the nature of the crime, no Brahman offender shall be tortured", yet he ordered that the face of a Brahman convict was to be branded with the sign of the social crime committed by him ; and after being publicly proclaimed, was to be banished by the king, and sent to the mines for life.[62] If a Brahman committed treason, he was drowned (*Brāhmaṇam tamapaḥ praveśayat*).[63]

Conclusions from the Above. These injunctions of Kauṭilya, which do not exhaust the list, enable us to arrive at two important conclusions. In the first place, the members of the sacredotal class were by no means immune from the ordinary law of the land, although in the case of one or two offences, they were exempted from torture and corporal punishment. But this was more than compensated for by the stigma of social odium which attended the alternate punishments given to them. And, secondly, they were, along with the king, subject to the *dharmaśāstras* which were higher than the king himself. Herein lies an essential point of difference between the priestly class in India and its counterpart in Egypt and elsewhere. Whereas in that country it remained dominant overruling even the monarch, here in India it was, along with the ruler, subordinate to the *dharmaśāstras.* This alone is enough to demolish any theory that the Brahmans in ancient India were the controlling factor in the State. It also helps to dismiss as altogether fallacious the alleged sacredotal nature of the Indian State.

3. THE DIVINE RIGHT THEORY

Four versions of this theory have been advocated by Indian historians, which may first be given before we see how far they are in agreement with the divine right theory as it is commonly understood by Western scholars.

(*a*) *The First Version*

It is the one adumbrated by Dr. N. C. Bandopadhyaya which refers to the existence in Vedic literature of traditions relating to Manu and to Pṛithu Vainya, to the recognition of the earliest king as the greatest benefactor, and to his evolution from a military chieftain. This theory is untenable because the Vedas do not refer to Manu or Pṛithu Vainya as the first king, although some passages in the *Yajus Samhita* and the *Brāhmaṇas* certainly refer to Manu as "the first consecrated man". There is no evidence to substantiate the other statement relating to the evolution of the king from a successful military chieftain.[64]

(*b*) *The Second Version*

It is advocated by Professor Radha Kumud Mookerjee, who distinguishes between *dharma,* which he interprets as the State, and *daṇḍa,* as the king. The learned Professor states the following:

> Hindu thought counts *Dharma* as the true Sovereign of the State, as the Rule of the Law. The King is the executive called the *Daṇḍa* to uphold and enforce the decrees of the *Dharma* as the spiritual sovereign . . . . In this way democracy descends to the villages and the lowest strata of the social structure and operated as the most potent agency of uplifting the masses. Thus ancient Hindu monarchy was a limited monarchy under the very constitution of the State.[65]

The above theory is both confused and misleading. It is true that *dharma* reigned supreme in the public and private life of the ancients but to equate it with the Rule of Law is not to understand both *dharma* as well as the Rule of the Law. The Rule of the Law, which refers to the rights and duties of citizens, is best understood from its working in the British constitution where it means that no man is punished, or can be made lawfully to suffer in body or goods, except for a distinct breach of the law established in the ordinary manner before the ordinary courts of the land. Secondly, it means not only that no man is above the law but that every man, whatever his rank or condition, is subject to the ordinary law of the realm, and within the jurisdiction of the ordinary tribunals. And, thirdly, it means that the general principles of the constitution (e.g., the right to personal liberty, or the right to public meeting) are the result of judicial decisions determining the rights of private persons in particular cases brought before the ordinary courts, as in England, and as distinct from the conditions "where the security (such as it is) given to the rights of individuals results or appears to result from the general principles of the constitution".[66]

Now it is extremely doubtful if any one of the above principles could be found in any ancient Indian text relating to the rights of the individuals resulting from the general principles of the constitution. We shall see below that the only "right", if it ever could be called by that name, that was tacitly admitted by Manu and Kauṭilya was the one of deposing and even killing a ruler, who had persistently violated the injunctions of the *dharmaśāstras,* and who continued to rule tyrannically over his people. But this was more of a concession than a right, since it was to be made use of only in cases of extreme provocation. No doubt, as will be pointed out later on, Kauṭilya explicitly mentions civil, economic, and legal rights which protected the citizens even against the State itself. But this is not equal to saying that they possessed political rights, or that the economic, legal, and civil rights of the people resulted from the general principles of the constitution, or that the latter were the source of the judicial decisions. These ideas of distinct breaches of constitutional law and of constitutional principles guiding judicial decisions are modern concepts which were non-existent in the fourth century B.C., when the theory of the Rule of Law, as we now understand that term, did not exist even in England.

The next argument in Professor Mookerjee's theory relating to the king's wielding the *daṇḍa* in order to enforce the *dharma* may now be examined. It is true that the king wielded the *daṇḍa,* and to that extent was the supreme executive. But he was also the supreme judiciary and as such was the upholder of the Sacred law. This is proved by the *Śatapatha Brāhmaṇa* in which it is stated that "the king is indeed the upholder of the Sacred law".[67] It would be incorrect on the basis of this statement to style him as a spiritual sovereign.

Thirdly, the idea of democracy descending into the villages from the top is not intelligible, since the concept of the *dharma* and of the king did not connote democracy either in the ancient or modern sense. Professor Mookerjee's idea of self-government extending from the sovereign to the villages is hardly borne out by the facts of ancient Indian history.

And, finally, the statement that Hindu monarchy was limited "under the very constitution of the State" is too confused to be intelligible. The limitations on the monarch were not imposed by the constitution but by the *dharmaśāstras* which cannot be equated with the term constitution. Neither can the word *dharmaśāstra* (or *dharma*) be considered as the spiritual sovereign, since the *dharmaśāstras* connoted not only the laws transmitted by the sages but immemorial custom and usage which certainly had no spiritual touch about them.[68]

(c) *The Third Version*

It was the one which the late Dr. Jayaswal maintained. According to this eminent scholar, the Vedic theory upheld that kingship originated under the stress of war ; that the idea of kingship was borrowed by the Aryans from the Dravidians ; that it was a contractual theory which, while being monarchical, adopted the republican theory of contract ; that the theory as given in the *Manusaṁhita* (*Manusmṛiti,* obviously)—which was the nearest Hindu approach to the divine right theory of kingship—had no direct support in earlier literature ; that it upheld the rule of the Brahman ; that it was never approved of or adopted by a single subsequent lawbook ; and that the king was a servant of the State, virtually a constitutional slave, who held his office on trust. Later on in the same work on *Hindu Polity,* Dr. Jayaswal repeats the same theory, and writes that "Hindu kingship was a trust, the trust being the tending of the country to prosperity and growth".[69]

The late Dr. Jayaswal had a genius for discovering modern theories and ideas in the ancient mind. The above is one of the many examples of constitutional juxtapositions which he invented while studying ancient Indian Polity in terms of modern political thought. Professor Ghoshal has rightly rejected the above theory on the following grounds: that, while it is true there is a theory of kingship—but not of election—in the Vedic literature, the assumption that the Aryans borrowed the institution of kingship from the Dravidians "may be treated as too original to deserve any serious notice" ; that Dr. Jayaswal's ingenious theory of the *arājaka* as being a no-ruler State which was made by that distinguished historian to be the basis of his social contract theory, must be dismissed as unproven ; that the theories of kingship in the *Manusaṁhita, Mahābhārata,* and *Arthaśāstra,* if interpreted in the sense of being the contractual origin of kingship, would give us an "altogether one-sided, and, therefore, imperfect view" of its true nature ; and that the theory of kingship as given in the *Mānavadharmaśāstra* had no direct support in earlier literature, is disproved by the reference to the story of the creation of Indra's sovereignty by Prajāpati as given in the *Taittirīya Brāhmaṇa.* The final part of Dr. Jayaswal's theory that the king held his office on trust, therefore, has to be abandoned as being untenable.[70] Dr. Jayaswal seems to have invented his contractual theory of kingship by inverting the divine right theory which he has not attempted to explain but which he merely refers to as the nearest approach to his own version in the *Manusmṛiti.*

(d) *Another Version of the Theory*

While thus refuting Dr. Jayaswal's theory, Professor Ghoshal expounds his own theory which may be summarized thus: the origin of kingship was due to the will of the Supreme Deity, as is substantiated by a passage "from an unknown *āmnāya* by Viśvarūpa, the author of the earliest extant commentary on the *Yājñavalkaya Smṛiti*". The gods and men failed to bring the people under their control through benevolence. Then the gods disappeared. When Prajāpati inquired as to who should protect the people, the gods replied: "We shall arrange for a king in human form by taking from the Moon, the Sun, Indra, Viṣṇu, Vaiśravaṇa (Kubera), and Yama respectively, majesty, brilliance, valour, victoriousness, liberality, and control." The king thus formed asked the gods to give him *dharma* as his friend, and then he would protect the people. The gods then made *dharma* his friend.[71]

While the commentator on the *Yājñavalkya Smṛiti* certainly enables us to understand the divine touch that may be given to the origin of kingship, Viśvarūpa's explanation of the same does not attribute the creation of kingship to the will of the Supreme Deity. The gods were certainly not the same as the Supreme Being! Moreover, Viśvarūpa's explanation is incompatible with that given in the *Manusmṛiti* which relates, as noted elsewhere in this work, the following: "For, when these creatures, being without a king, through fear dispersed in all directions, the Lord created a king for the protection of this whole (creation)."[72] Finally, Professor Ghoshal's theory does not help us to understand the problem, as the following criticism will make it clear. Dr. Kane, while rejecting Professor Ghoshal's theory, also refers to the same passage attributed to Viśvarūpa, and affirms that "the passages in the *Brāhmaṇas* should not be relied upon in support of the theory of the divine right of kings (as done by U. Ghoshal in 'Hindu Political Theories', pp. 28-29), since every participator (whether a brāhmaṇa or a Kṣatriya) in such solemn sacrifices as the Agniṣṭoma and Vājapēya was supposed to possess a celestial body after dīkṣā and Pravargya and was often spoken of as identified with Indra and other gods". Dr. Kane then cites the same passage from Viśvarūpa's commentary, and in this connection identifies *dharma* with *daṇḍa.*[73] Dr. Kane's criticism of the so-called divine right of kings will be cited in a later context. Here it may be obsérved that the theory, as propounded by Professor Ghoshal, fails to establish the central point in the problem, "the divine creation of the ruler so as to invest him with divine attributes or even with divinity itself".[74]

(e) *Evaluation of the Divine Right Theory*

In order to understand how far the versions of the divine right theory as advocated by Indian scholars are valid, especially as that theory has been formulated by modern Western authors, it may be described as being composed of four parts which are given by Professor J. N. Figgis. These are the following: (*a*) monarchy is a divinely ordained institution ; (*b*) the hereditary right of kings cannot be forfeited through any act of usurpation, or by any incapacity of the heirs or by an act of depositon ; (*c*) kings are accountable to God alone, there being nothing like a limited monarchy ; (*d*) and resistance to the authority of the king is a sin, obedience to be rendered to him even when he issues laws contrary to God's laws.[75]

The above theory cannot be maintained in terms of ancient Indian political thought. It appears as if there is some truth in the statement that the State in ancient India was also the result of divine creation, especially, as seen above, when in the *Manusmṛiti* it is stated that the Lord created a king for the protection of the whole world. The same work further informs us that "He (Svayambhū, i.e. the Self-Existent) having composed these Institutes (of the Sacred Law), himself taught them, according to the rule, to me (Manu) alone in the beginning . . ." ; and that Manu taught them to Marīci and other sages.[76] The evidence of the *Manusmṛiti* does not agree with that of the *Mahābhārata*, where in one context it is Manu who became the first king, and in another it was Vainya. The latter was called upon by the gods and sages to take an oath that he would protect the world.[77] Granting that this divergence in the mythological accounts is of no material significance to us, let us try to understand the theory as given in the *Manusmṛiti*. Admitting that the king was the result of divine creation, as well as the laws and even the social divisions with their respective duties as given in the same work,[78] there is nothing to prove that Svayambhū Brahmā took an active part in the direction of public affairs in the ancient Indian State in the manner of Jehovah's taking part in the affairs of the ancient Hebrew State. That the Indians were guided by the *dharmaśāstras* is no argument to prove the existence of any divine agency in their public life.

Further, even supposing that there existed a divine element in the composition of the *dharmaśāstras*, as taught to Manu, the lawgiver, it cannot be affirmed that the ancient State and its laws were theocratic in nature. Manu himself discarded the divine origin of the laws—if at all it ever existed —when he stated that "the primeval laws of the countries, of castes (*jāti*), of families, and the rules concerning the heretics and companies (of traders and the like)—all that Manu has declared in these Institutes".[79] Of these we could credit only the laws of the castes with some divine origin ; while those of the countries, of families, of heretics, and of companies of traders, etc., could not by any stretch of imagination be said to have ever been formulated by any divine agency. Their inclusion in the *Code* is a clear indication that Manu, the lawgiver, had admitted the non-divine origin of the greater part of the laws which had been associated with his celebrated name.

The unambiguous importance which Manu himself attached to the usage prevalent amongst the four castes and the mixed castes—the *anuloma* and the *pratiloma* sections, which did not come within the sphere of the orthodox society in those days—is another proof of the secular nature of the origin of the ancient Indian laws. While describing the Brahmāvarta, or the country between the Sarasvatī and the Dṛṣadvatī, Manu stated thus: "The custom handed down in regular succession (since time immemorial) among the four chief castes (*varṇa*) and the mixed races of that country, is called the conduct of virtuous men."[80] The great lawgiver was obviously referring here to the approved usage, or what might be called the unwritten or Common law of the land. Since it formed an essential part of the *dharmaśāstras,* it is clear that even Manu himself did not consider all the laws to be of divine origin and outside the scope of secular influence. Whatever tinge of divinity the laws might have possessed in the remotest periods of antiquity, it was completely wiped out in the age of Kauṭilya (fourth century B.C.), when he stated that the edicts of the king (*rājaśāsana*) were superior to the other three legs of law which we shall describe below in Part Five dealing with the Political Institutions. These considerations should suffice to show that the halo of divinity, which might have surrounded the earliest concept of the State and of its laws, had gradually disappeared in the course of time, until it was practically effaced in the age of Kauṭilya.

Turning to the next proposition of Professor Figgis relating to the hereditary right of rulers, which could not be forfeited through an act of usurpation or deposition, we shall see below, while discussing the *arājaka* (or the *arājatā*) theory, that the *Manusmṛiti* itself advocated the deposition and removal of unworthy kings, thereby proving that the second criterion on which the divine right theory rests, cannot be made applicable to ancient India. We shall also see that this concession to depose rulers had been given to the people ever since the times of the *Śatapatha Brāhmaṇa.* The "right" of the people to dethrone and kill a king conversely meant the duty of the latter towards his people which was expressed in the term protection, and which also included the duty of maintaining the laws and customs of all sections of the people. Resistance to the ruler was permissible in certain circumstances in ancient India. Since resistance to the king implied disobedience to laws as well, it meant that the third and fourth propositions as given by Professor Figgis, in the enunciation of the theory of divine right of kings, likewise cannot be applied to ancient India. The theory of divine right of kings, therefore, as understood by some Indian scholars to be a part of the ancient Indian political thought, fails to stand a critical examination.[81]

4. THE FOURTH FALLACIOUS THEORY IS THE PATERNALISTIC THEORY

(a) The Theory Stated

It is based on the assumption that, since the king is compared to a father (*piteva*), especially in the sphere of protection, it necessarily follows that he was nothing more than a patriarch who, like a benevolent head of a family, merely dictated and guided his subjects, the latter like children carrying out his behests. This theory is supposed to be based on the *Manusmṛiti* in which, as already seen above, it is declared that the king should behave like a father towards all men.[82] Even Kauṭilya follows this ideal as is clear from the following statement: "He (the king) shall regard with fatherly kindness those who have passed the period of remission of taxes" (*nivṛttaparihārān pitevānugrihṇiyāt*).[83] The paternalistic theory will appear in later Jaina works in connection with the Kulakaras and Kuladharas whom we shall describe below.

(b) Evaluation of the Theory

Professor Rangaswami Aiyangar has rejected the theory on the following grounds: firstly, since individual responsibility—"as signified in Karma—was the keynote of ancient Indian religion", the theory is inapplicable to India. Secondly, "the recognition of custom and usage of a local, family, professional or a corporate kind" does not warrant the assumption that the State treated the subjects like children. And, thirdly, the many regulations concerning the standards of life, restrictions on the liberty of the individual, etc., which are found in Kauṭilya's *Arthaśāstra* "are equally explicable on other grounds".[84]

While Professor Aiyangar has undoubtedly given cogent arguments against the paternalistic theory, it may be added that they require a further clarification in order to understand the untenable nature of the theory. In the first place, what the learned Professor says about "the individual responsibility as signified in Karma" being the keynote of the ancient Indian religion, may be interpreted in the sense that too much stress is laid on the religious side of the problem. This is not so: it is admitted that the law of *karma* was certainly the keynote of social action. But it may as well be remembered in this connection that Manu himself laid sufficient stress on human endeavour, as is proved by the following statement in the *Manusmṛiti*: "All undertakings in this (world) depend both on the ordering of fate and on human exertion ; but among these two (the ways of) fate are unfathomable ; in the case of man's work action is possible."[85] No further evidence is needed to show that the ancient Indian political theorists were fully aware of both fate and human exertion ; and that they relied more on the latter than on the former for furthering State action. The linking up of individual responsibility with the divine will, as maintained by Professor Aiyangar, hence needs some qualification.

Moreover, Kauṭilya's use of the word *piteva* was in a more restricted sense than it was used by Manu. The context clearly shows that the fatherly kindness, which the king was to show to his subjects, was in regard only to the extension of the time limit of the remission of taxes. In the *Manusmṛiti* the injunction concerning the fatherly behaviour of the king towards all men is when the annual revenue of the kingdom was collected by trusted officials, and when the ruler was to obey the Sacred law in his transactions with the people. In both the cases, therefore, there is no indication that the ruler was to behave like a father towards his subjects in all spheres of life.

Further, the paternalistic theory presupposes that the subjects were unfit either to perform their duties or urge the ruler to stand by his duties to his subjects. This assumption ignores the fact that, as related earlier, the subjects were not unaccustomed to drive out their monarchs, when the latter had consistently violated the injunctions of the *dharmaśāstras.* It also implies that the people were unfit or unmindful of their duties. This assumption is not borne out either by the ancient texts or by the available historical evidence which we do not wish to cite here.

Finally, the selective nature of the office of the king, and the important part played by the council of the ministers as well as by the assembly of the people, in their respective capacities, made it well-nigh impossible for the king to be a paternal head of his people in perpetuity. It was not the king who was in the last resort powerful but the people in whom lay his strength, as is described in the *Śatapatha Brāhmaṇa* which aptly says that he (the king) was "mighty through the people".[86] Hence it follows that outside the will of the monarch was the larger and more determined will of his subjects, who acquiesced in the actions of the ruler only to the extent he gave expression to them within the frame-work of the *dharmaśāstras.* It is here we see how the modern concept of the general will is reflected in the determined will of the bulk of the people in the ancient times. We have, therefore, to reject the paternalistic theory as being incompatible with the principles of ancient Indian Policy.[87]

B. THE ORGANISMIC THEORY OF THE STATE

The nature of the ancient Indian State is best understood when we see the organic or the organismic theory.

1. THE THEORY

According to it the State is a living organism, like animals and plants, possessing organs each of which performs a specialized function, and is subject to development and decay. The organs are dependent on each other and on the whole for their continued existence.[88] The theory can be studied from two points view—that of the component parts of the society, and that of the constituent elements of the State.

2. THE THEORY EXPLAINED

(a) *The Component Parts of the Society*

The ancient Indian society had definite organs or institutions which performed specialized functions, which became more definite and distinct in the course of ages, but which were all directed to the furtherance of the ends of the State. To a large extent the individual was merged in the society of which he was a part. The separate sections of the people like the Brahmans or priests, the Kṣatriyas or warriors, the Vaiśyas or trading class, and the Śūdras or the servile sections, were each allotted certain specific duties which they had to perform. But these different sections of the society were interdependent, all working for the common good of the community. The mutual dependence of the first two classes comprising the Brahmans and the Kṣatriyas is thus clearly stated in the *Manusmṛiti*: "Kṣatriays prosper not without Brahmans ; Brahmans prosper not without Kṣatriyas ; Brahmans and Kṣatriyas, being closely united, prosper in this (world) and in the next."[89] Then, again, Manu states that "the Brāhmaṇa is declared (to be) the root of the Sacred law and the Kṣatriya its top . . . ."[90] The importance of the third class comprising the Vaiśyas is given in the following injunction of Manu: "For when the Lord of creatures (Prajāpati) created cattle, he made them over to the Vaiśyas ; to the Brāhmaṇa, and to the king he entrusted all the created beings."[91] The fourth class of the Śūdras was unfortunately relegated to a life of servility to the three higher classes, particularly to the priestly class ; but the proviso that the priestly class should allot to the Śūdras out of its own family property a suitable maintenance, after considering the ability of the Śūdras, their industry, and the number of those whom the latter had to support, plainly indicated that Manu did not condemn the Śūdras to a life of unqualified despondency.[92]

The earlier injunctions of Manu of placing the Śūdras, we may incidentally observe, in an inferior position of workers in comparison with the first two classes, namely the Brāhmaṇs and the Kṣatriyas, were considerably modified by Kauṭilya, who said that the duty of a Śūdra is the serving of the twice-born, agriculture, cattle-breeding, and trade, the profession of artisans, and court bards (*Śūdrasya dvijātiśuśrūṣā vārtā kārukuśīlavakarma ca*).[93] While Kauṭilya followed the ancient injunction of making the Śūdras perform the duties of the Brahmans, the Kṣatriyas, and the Vaiśyas (*dvijāti*, i.e. the twice-born), he emancipated them by permitting them to take to the professions of agriculture, cattle-breeding, and trade, which had been the monopoly of the Vaiśyas, and even to adopt the duties of the artisans and of court bards which must have considerably raised their social and economic status. He thus brought the Śūdras on a level with the Vaiśyas whose duties he had enumerated in the preceding statement thus: the performance of sacrifice, giving gifts, agriculture, cattle-breeding, and trade.[94] Two of the above duties, it may be added here, were common to all the first three classes—that of performing sacrifices and of giving gifts.[95] Kauṭilya had not only raised the social status and economic position of the Śūdras but bound the first three classes in the matter of two duties, and the third (Vaiśyas) and the fourth (Śūdras) classes in three professions (cattle-breeding, agriculture, and trade), thereby combining all the four classes in an interdependent chain of duties and obligations which are not met with in the *Manusmṛiti.* And when we realize that he considered *vārtā* (agriculture, cattle-breeding, and trade) to be one of the four important sciences (the other three being *ānvikṣakī,* the triple *Vedas,* and the *daṇḍanīti,* (*ānvikṣakī trayī vārta daṇḍanītiḥ-ca iti vidyāḥ*),[96] we may maintain that he had given to the Śūdras their Charter of Liberty, and had enabled them to contribute their share to the well-being of society to which all the four castes had thus to direct their sole attention.

The interdependence of all the classes in society was made further possible by the injunction in the *Manusmṛiti* that all of them had to observe the following: "Abstention from injuring (creatures), veracity, abstention from unlawfully appropriating (the goods of others), purity, and control of the organs." Manu declared these to be the law of the four castes.[97] These six rules of conduct were meant for the common good of the community, and not for the sake of advancing the interests of any one class composing it. We have in the above ordinances, therefore, of both Manu and Kauṭilya the clearest proof of not only the specialized functions of the various classes but of their interdependence as indispensable units of a composite society, in a manner to suggest that no class could hope to live by itself without the co-operation of the other.

(*b*) *The Constituent Elements of the State*

Turning to the other aspect of the organismic theory, we may observe that the State had seven elements each of which was dependent on the other. All the seven elements that comprised the State constituted its living and growing organism. This theory has been advocated by Professors Benoy Kumar Sarkar, Rangaswami Aiyangar and D. R. Bhandarkar, Dr. Jayaswal, and Dr. Kane.[98] It will be seen in Part Five below, while describing the Political Institutions, that there is sufficient justification for upholding it, since the State was made up of interdependent parts each of which performed a specialized function all contributing to its common well-being.

While viewing the ancient State from the two aspects of the organismic theory, we find that it satisfies fully the conditions of that theory as understood by modern Western authors. There is another method of appreciating the organismic theory of the State. This is by comparing the two aspects of the ancient Indian State as given above with the description of the organismic theory as given by Aristotle (fourth century B.C.). We shall have to mention in greater detail Aristotle's concept of the State below in Part Four, when we shall compare his ideas with those of Kauṭilya. Here we may merely observe that Aristotle described the organismic theory of the State thus: governments, he said, were composed, not of one, but of many elements. One element was the food producing class, made up of husbandmen ; a second class, of mechanics, who practised arts without which a city could not exist ; the third class was made up of traders, who were engaged in buying and selling either in commerce or in retail trade ; the fourth class was made up of serfs or labourers ; the fifth class, of warriors, who were necessary in case of invasions ; the sixth class, of those who dispensed with justice ; the seventh class, of wealthy people, who ministered to the needs of the State with their property ; the eighth class, of magistrates, and officers ; and, finally, the last class, of statesmen.[99] Aristotle had only enlarged and increased the number of classes which, according to the ancient Indian concept, were only four in number. Indeed, all the nine classes he has mentioned in his *Politics* could be easily reduced to the four classes as given in the *Manusmṛiti.* His delineation of the organismic theory is in striking agreement with the view which we have proposed above relating to the specialized functions and interdependence of the different parts of the composite Indian society. Whether we examine the organismic theory of the ancient Indian State from the ancient Greek standpoint or from that of the modern times, we find that it fits in admirably with the organic nature of the elements of the State as they have been understood in the ancient and modern times.

CHAPTER V

THE FUNCTIONS OF THE STATE

A. CATEGORIES OF FUNCTIONS

1. PROTECTION

THE PROBLEM of the functions of the State is intimately bound up with that of the need of the State which we have discussed above. While explaining the justification of the State, it was stated that one of the most important grounds on which it rested was protection, which was also its foremost function. We shall have to further elucidate this function, which is considered even in modern times to be of the greatest importance,[100] and which the ancient Indian State fulfilled by enabling all classes of people to have the minimum standards of living, without destroying the initiative or responsibility of its members. In this respect the ancient State anticipated in some measure an aspect of the modern State which acts "as a great ministry of social assurance", assures the whole society of the maximum good, and maintains the individuality and privileges of the subjects who comprise it.[101]

Protection in the ancient times as well as in our own also meant, as it does today, guarding the country both against internal troubles as well as foreign aggression. Of all the ancient writers it is Kauṭilya alone who was alive to these twin dangers facing the State, as is evident from the elaborate rules which he formulated concerning the calamities that might overtake a sovereign country.[102]

2. MAINTAINING THE COMMON LAW

The next function of the State was the maintenance of the Common law as embodied in the ancient customs and usage of the land. The evidence of the *Manusmṛiti* has already been cited in this respect. Kauṭilya affirmed not only that all the righteous customs practised in a conquered country were to be maintained by the conqueror, but that the latter should adopt the same mode of life, the same dress, language, and customs as those of the conquered people.[103]

3. UPHOLDING THE SOCIAL ORDER

The third function of the State was the protection of the *dharma* of the land, within the sphere of which both the State and society moved.[104] Perhaps no writer on Politics has described the importance of social order and protection so well as Kauṭilya, who writes thus:

> As the duty of a king consists in protecting his subjects with justice, its observance leads him to heaven. He who does not protect his people or upsets the social order wields his royal sceptre (*daṇḍa*) in vain (*rājñaḥ svadharmaḥ-svargāya prajā dharmeṇa rakṣituḥ arakṣituḥ-vā kṣeptuḥ-vā mithyādaṇḍamato' anyathā*).[105]

According to Kauṭilya, therefore, the duty of maintaining *dharma* and the social order was of fundamental importance.

4. LEVYING OF TAXES

The fourth function of the State was the levying of taxes. Thus ordained Manu:

> A king who (duly) protects (his subjects) receives from each and all the sixth part of their spiritual merit; if he does not protect them, the sixth part of their demerit also (will fall on him). Whatever (merit a man gains by) reading the Veda, by sacrifice, by charitable gifts, (or by) worshipping gurus and gods, the king obtains a sixth part of that in consequence of his duty of protecting (his kingdom).[106]

What would happen to a king who, without protecting his people, extorted taxes, is given in the next verse: "A king who does not afford protection, (yet) takes his share in kind, his taxes, his tolls and duties, daily presents and fines, will (after death) soon sink into hell."[107] That the State was authorized to levy taxes only to the extent of one-sixth of the produce, after it had afforded the subjects protection, is proved by the statement of Somadeva Sūri, who wrote centuries afterwards to the following effect: *paripālako hi rājā sarveṣām dharmāṇām ṣaṣṭāṁśam-āpnoti*.[108]

5. PROMULGATING LAWS AND MAINTAINING THE JUDICIARY

Neither the protection of the social order nor the levying of taxes was possible without the fifth important function—that of promulgating laws and of maintaining the machinery of the judiciary. In the modern State, the creation of law has become an essential function of the State.[109] Law as one of the constituent elements of the State will be discussed below in

Part Five. Although in the *Manusmṛiti* there is no explicit reference to the promulgation of laws which, as must have been evident to the reader from the earlier pages of this book, had a divine tinge about them, yet when we come to the age of Kauṭilya, the promulgation of laws was definitely a function of the State. This will be further clarified in the same Part.[109a]

6. PROMOTION OF PEOPLE'S WELFARE

To the above essential functions was added another one relating to the promotion of the welfare of the people. We came across occasionally in the *Manusmṛiti* the idea that the king could think of declaring war on his enemy only when "he thinks all his subjects to be exceedingly contented".[110] Neither this assertion of Manu nor that of the *Mahābhārata*, wherein it is stated that a ruler entrenched behind the impregnable fortress of his people's love is unconquerable,[111] gives us such a clear concept of this function of the State as the following passage in the *Arthaśāstra* of Kauṭilya:

> In the happiness of his subjects lies his (the king's) happiness ; in their welfare his welfare ; whatever pleases him he shall not consider as good, but whatever pleases his subjects he shall consider as good (*prajāsukhe sukhaṁ rajñaḥ prajānām ca hite hitaṁ na-ātmapriyaṁ hitaṁ rājñaḥ prajānāṁ tu priyaṁ hitaṁ*).[112]

As to how the king was to achieve this end relating to the happiness of his people, Kauṭilya explains in the previous paragraph, thus: "Of a king, the religious vow is his readiness to action ; satisfactory discharge of duties is his performance of sacrifice ; equal attention to all is the offer of fees and ablution towards consecration."[113] Here the great Mauryan Prime Minister has likened promptitude of action on the part of the king to the latter's religious vow, satisfactory discharge of duties towards the people to the ruler's religious sacrifice, and impartial and prompt attention to all, irrespective of distinction, to the king's offering of fees and to his performing ablution during his coronation.[114] Never was the function of promoting the welfare of the people raised to such dignity as when Kauṭilya compared it to the performance of a great religious sacrifice!

In a later context in the *Arthaśāstra*, he lays further stress on the supreme importance of this function, when he writes thus: "Strength is power, and happiness is the end" (*balaṁ śaktiḥ sukhaṁ siddhiḥ*).[115] While the State was to possess power, its sole object was to promote the happiness of its subjects. Kauṭilya thus brought into relief the function of promoting the welfare of the State in the above poignant sentence, as perhaps no ancient Indian writer on Politics has done.

B. AN ANALYSIS OF THE FUNCTIONS

1. IN RELATION OF THE STATE WITH OTHER STATES

The essential functions of the State described above may be analysed in terms of the relations of the State with other States, of the State with the individual, and of the individual with individuals. While describing the sovereign power of the State, Manu and Kauṭilya enlighten us on two aspects of this important question, namely, the relation of the State with other States, and of the individual with individuals. But the ancient theorists have practically nothing to say on the second aspect, namely, the relation of the State with the individual.[116]

In regard to the first aspect of the relations of the State with the other States, Kauṭilya has more detailed information to give than Manu. While the latter dwells on the measures which a king has to undertake against his foes, and enunciates the theory of the *rājamaṇḍala* or the Circle of States in broad outline,[117] Kauṭilya elaborates it in a manner which makes his treatise both complete and illuminating. It is doubtful whether any other ancient Indian political thinker has given such a comprehensive account of the relations of the State with the other States as Kauṭilya has done.[118]

2. RELATIONS OF THE INDIVIDUAL WITH OTHER INDIVIDUALS

These are mentioned in sufficient detail in the *Manusmṛiti* while describing the relations between the various castes or *varṇas*, of the mixed classes, of the Aryans in general, of father with son and daughter, of husband with wife, and of the individual with individuals.[119] Kauṭilya's elaboration of these details concerning the relations of the individual with individuals would form a subject of discussion by itself.[120]

Since both these two aspects which aimed at securing order, justice, and security, could be regulated only on the strength of the armour of might, the ancient Indian State brought into existence the army, the police, and and a large number of executive officials, exercised powerful control, and spent large sums of money for efficiently maintaining them. In these fields, again, Kauṭilya is more helpful than Manu, whose *Code* refers more to the duties of the warrior class than to those of a large army and a larger executive staff.[121] Indeed, there is no reference to a large army in the *Manusmṛiti* ; on the other hand, there is every reason to believe that the size as well as the needs of the kingdom in the days of that work, did not necessitate the maintenance of a large army. This point may be borne in mind while discussing the Elements of the State in Part Five below.

In the age of Kauṭilya the political situation in the country had fundamentally changed. The Mauryan conqueror, under whom he served as Prime Minister, maintained an army which could overthrow not only the mighty Nandas but also compel the most powerful of the Western contemporary rulers, who had acquired the Punjab from Alexander the Great, to withdraw from that province, leaving Candragupta Maurya the undisputed master of practically the whole country stretching from the confines of Gāndhāra to those of Bihar. When it is realized that of the two enemies whom Candragupta Maurya had to face, the Nandas had frightened the invincible forces of the greatest conqueror of antiquity, Alexander the Great,[122] it will be appreciated that the army of the Mauryan monarch was precisely of that magnitude which Kauṭilya has so indirectly suggested in his great work. Indeed, the entire administrative and military machinery described in the *Arthaśāstra* bespeaks a mighty military organization as well as immense financial resources upon which alone the strength and continuity of the Mauryan monarchy could have rested.[123] These were essential for preserving the social order against internal troubles and external dangers concerning both of which Kauṭilya recommended remedial measures.[124]

C. THE ANCIENT STATE AND THE MODERN STATE

1. COMPARISON

The above clearly proves that the ancient State exercised the most essential functions which were vitally concerned with its sovereignty. In this regard it affords comparison with the modern State which also has to exercise similar essential functions in connection with its relations with other States, and with the dealings of the individual with other individuals. The modern State also maintains huge armies, raises colossal funds, has a large array of executive officials, and exercises vast powers.[125]

2. CONTRAST

But there are some essential points of difference between the ancient Indian State and the modern State in regard to their functions. The modern State has not only vast power but is continually extending its sphere of governmental control in all aspects of the individual's existence. In doing so, it may not necessarily justify its action on any moral grounds, or any code of ethics, but may be guided solely by the exigencies of the occasion, or by the programme of the party to which it belongs and which wields political power. The ancient Indian State, even as described by Kauṭilya, did not dare to transgress the limits imposed upon it by the *dharmaśāstras* and the *nītiśāstras*. Moreover, State action in ancient India was circumscribed by the ancient usage of the land ; while the modern State, although recognizing the validity of the Common law, is usually eager to narrow down the sphere of ancient usage and custom, and impose its will on both.[126] Further, the modern State, in the exercise of its functions, determines its relations with its citizens so as to decide their share in the wielding of political power. There is nothing to indicate that in the ancient State there was any attempt either on the part of the State or of the individuals to define the relations of the latter with a view to making them share in political power. The occasional privilege which the lawgivers tacitly acknowledged, and which the citizens exercised by way of deposing a king, or of otherwise expressing their disapprobation of his actions, does not suggest that they had a share in political power, as that term is understood in the modern world. Furthermore, the ancient State, particularly in the age of Candragupta Maurya, raised funds to some extent but it cannot be compared with a modern State which raises and spends huge sums of money by way of internal loans floated in the country and external financial aid secured from foreign powers. Finally, according to modern writers on Politics, the function relating to the promotion of the general welfare of the people is only an optional one on the part of the State ;[127] while, with the ancient Indian State, that function was an essential attribute of its exsitence.

CHAPTER VI

FORMS OF THE STATE

A. CAUTION IN CLASSIFICATION

ANY ATTEMPT to determine the forms of the ancient State in India is naturally influenced by the modern classifications only a few of which are useful for our purpose. The various attempts to classify modern States are not satisfactory in the sense that they do not rest upon any scientific principle by which the fundamental characteristics of the States could be distinguished. The confusion in the use of the two terms, State and government, is primarily responsible for the classification of States only on the basis of government. Further, the classification of States based on the descriptive differences of population, territory, relation of geographical and ethnical unity to State existence, and the relative degree of external independence, which has resulted in States being termed tribal, city, feudal, national, world, insular, continental, military, naval, civilized and uncivilized, has only served to add to the confusion of the subject rather than to elucidate and solve it.[128] This is of no use for our purpose, since these classifications are directed to objects other than those of a political inquiry into the State forms.

B. CLASSIFICATIONS WHICH ARE USEFUL

Modern political scientists have suggested three other classifications which are the following: the first comprises monarchies, aristocracies, and democracies, the governments of which rest upon the principle of the number of persons who share in the exercise of the sovereign power of the State. The second consists of the legislature, the judiciary, and the executive, according to the distinction between those who create law, those who apply it, and those who execute it. Under the second category is also sometimes included the distinction between the cabinet and the presidential governments, according to the nature of the relation between the legislature and the administration. These two types coming under the second category rest upon the principle of the separation of powers, that is, the distinction between organs of government on the basis of the functions performed by them. The third classification is made up of the national and the unitary or federal governments, whose distinction rests upon the principle of the division of powers between the organs of government depending upon the territorial extension over which they exercise jurisdiction.[129]

Of the above classifications that which suits best the ancient Indian State is the one relating to the number of persons who share in the exercise of the sovereign power of the State. It is the same classification which rests on the principle of how the will of the State is governed and expressed ; in other words, of the location of sovereignty within a State.[130] We may accept this classification which has been said to be the best by political thinkers like Professors G. Jellinek and J. W. Burgess ;[131] and which Aristotle adopted as the basis of his famous classification of States into monarchies, aristocracies, and democracies.[132]

C. THE CLASS THEORY EXAMINED

1. CONTENTS OF THE THEORY

Here we may examine the validity of a theory which seems to suggest that the form of the ancient Indian State may be traced to the prevalence of the four *varṇas* or castes. This is the so-called class theory advocated by Professor MacIver, which may be stated in the following terms. The Class State imposed an order based on two divisions of society—the one made up of the king, the priests, and the nobility ; and the other, of the tribute-paying and service-rendering commonalty. The conditions under which it came into being and flourished were those of primitive life, "where the herd instinct was confirmed by rigorous custom, where ignorance bred the spirit of superstitious subjection to unknown powers and to their human interpreters, and where the weakness and uncertainty of life required a rallying point in undisputed powers".[133]

In support of the above theory it may be argued (*a*) that conditions in the remote antiquity of Indian history, even during the Vedic period, were of a primitive type ; (*b*) that rigorous custom dictated the herd instinct ; (*c*) that the general ignorance of the people was responsible for their superstitious subjection to unknown powers, like those of the gods, and to their human interpreters, like the priests ; and (*d*) that the uncertainty and precarious condition of life (in ancient India, if the theory is made applicable to this country) compelled the people to acknowledge the undisputed power of the State as typified by the king.

2. EVALUATION OF THE THEORY

Whatever may be the justification for applying the class theory to the ancient States of Persia, Egypt, and Babylonia, it certainly cannot be made to apply to India during any period of her ancient history. To begin with, we may dispense with a few generalizations which cannot be seriously applied only to the ancient times. For instance, then, as now, the bulk of the citizens were, as they are, guided by the herd instinct which is only another term for the continued unthinking obedience which the many give to the will of the few, and which makes the former live, on the whole, a life of political and social inertia.[134] The crowd mentality was as much visible in the Oriental monarchies as in the Greek republican States like Athens, where its assemblies were swayed by the persuasive force of a few strenuous spirits, who imposed their will on the masses.[135]

But it is not only the existence of the herd instinct throughout human history that demolishes one of the foundations of the class theory. The nature and sanctity of custom also go against it. If, on the basis of custom, that theory were to be applied to ancient India, it would mean that its advocates have not grasped the importance of usage and custom in the history of this land. We have had many occasions of mentioning above the vital rôle which custom and usage have played in the ancient State. Here in this country, both custom and usage formed component parts of law, and along with the latter evoked obedience on the part of the citizens, who realized that both were essential, if all classes of people were to add to the general well-being of society. We might as well affirm that in the past custom as much dictated the herd instinct as law manipulates the springs of mob psychology today.

The third defect in the class theory centres round the two divisions of society which cannot be applied to India. Here in India society was divided into the four well-known classes, the king being only a member of one of them, the Kṣatriyas. There is nothing to suggest that he was superior to any one of his compatriots in the same order. In the *Manusmṛiti* it is explicitly stated that he was only a Kṣatriya, who received, according to the rule, the sacraments prescribed by the *Vedas,* and whose obligatory function was to protect the world.[136] Manu evidently had in mind the earlier use of the word Kṣatriya as given in the *Rig Veda,* where it was connected with royal authority.[137] This evidence should be sufficient to prove that the king was not apart from the Kṣatriyas but only one amongst them.[138] It would be incorrect, therefore, to single out the king as a division of society, as is done by the advocates of the class theory.

As regards the second part of the same statement, which refers to the tribute-paying and servile sections of the people, it may be observed that, while the existence of the servile class is not denied, the assumption that there was only one section of the community that paid taxes is incorrect. Even among the priestly class, it should be noted that only the Śrotriyas or those learned in the scriptures, were exempted from taxes, while the others who formed that class were not exempted from the payment of taxes.[139] Neither were the Kṣatriyas free from the same obligation.[140] Indeed, Manu's injunction that the king "after due consideration shall always fix in his realm the duties and taxes in such a manner that both himself and the man who does the work receive their due reward",[141] when read in conjunction with his other statements relating to the freedom given to the members of the priestly class to live by agriculture and money lending,[142] suggests that we have to construe the exemptions from taxation as being applicable not to all the Brahmans, but to only such of them who were learned in the Sacred law. This would mean that a large section of the priestly class, who were permitted to follow vocations other than those associated with learning, could not escape the duty of paying taxes. A division of society into those who paid taxes and those who did not, as implied in the above theory, would not be applicable to ancient India.

D. ARISTOTLE'S CLASSIFICATION OF THE FORMS OF STATE

1. THE THREE FORMS EXPLAINED

The class theory being thus of no avail in understanding the form of the State in ancient India, we may revert to the criterion of the forms of the States as given by Aristotle, and as accepted by some modern political thinkers, as being the best one. Its appropriateness for our purpose lies in the fact that it suits better the States of antiquity which were not based either on the principles of the separation of powers nor on that of the division of functions but on that of the will of the State and on how it was formed and expressed. According to this classification, there were three forms of government. The first was monarchy in which the head of the State derived his office through hereditary succession. In such a government the final and supreme authority lay in the hands of a single person, whether he secured his office through hereditary succession, election, or usurpation. The second form was the aristocratic government in which political power was vested in a comparatively small section of the people, which based its right to rule either on birth, age, wealth, priestly power, military strength, education, or a combination of some or all of these factors. Both in this form of government as well as in a monarchy, the bulk of the people was excluded from the exercise of political power. In marked contrast to these two forms was that called democracy in which the mass of the people, either directly or through their elected representatives, possessed the right to share in the exercise of sovereign power.[143]

With this as the basis, we may analyse the forms of the ancient Indian State. There is reason to believe that the three forms of government as described above, namely, the monarchical, the aristocratic, and the democratic, existed in ancient India, although in the case of aristocracies and democracies, they do not seem to have possessed all the attributes which marked their Western counterparts.

2. THE MONARCHICAL FORM OF THE STATE

(a) *Hereditary*

The ancient Indian monarchical States were divided into two broad classes—hereditary and elective. Of these the more universal type was the hereditary monarchy, while occasionally we also come across the elective type. The existence of the hereditary type is proved by the examples of kings whose descent was traced to a progenitor, as in the case of Divodāsa, Atithigva, Sudās, Pijavana, Kuruśravaṇa, Trasadasyu, Mitrātithi, Upamaśravas, etc.[144] Hereditary kings were also found among the Triṣṭus and the Purus.[145] The occurrence of the words *adhirāja* (overlord) and *ekarāja* (sole ruler) in the ancient texts,[146] seems to suggest that there was a tendency on the part of a few monarchs of antiquity to assume control over other kings. The hereditary nature of kingship is further proved by the statement in the *Śatapatha Brāhmaṇa* relating to the king, who is performing the *rājasūya* sacrifice, thus: "And to him who is his (the king's) dearest son, he hands that vessel, thinking, 'May this son of mine perpetuate this vigour of mine'."[147] A clearer and a more definite reference to hereditary monarchy is afforded in a later passage in the same *Brāhmaṇa* which refers to king Duṣṭarītu Paumsāyana, who will figure below in connection with the interesting problem of no-rule and misrule of kings. His kingdom is described in that work as having come down to him through ten generations (*daśapurusām-rājya*).[148]

(b) *Elective Monarchy*

While the evidence about the hereditary monarchy is definite, that referring to elective monarchy is inconclusive. The story of Devāpi Ārṣṭiṣeṇa and of his brother Śantanu is usually cited by scholars as an example of a monarch who was elected by the people. Both were princes of the Kurus. Devāpi was the elder brother, and Śantanu, the younger. The latter got himself anointed king, whereupon there was drought in the land for twelve years. Since this calamity was attributed by priests to Śantanu's having superseded his elder brother, Śantanu offered the kingdom to Devāpi. The latter, however, refused to become king, but acting as his younger brother's *purohita* or domestic priest, caused rain to fall. This story is met with in the *Rig Veda,* in the *Mahābhārata,* in Yāska's *Nirukta,* and later on repeated in the *Agni, Bhāgavata, Brahma, Matsya, Vāyu,* and *Viṣṇu Purāṇas.* Whatever may be the diversity in the narratives of the story in the above works—the longest and the most elaborate being in the *Mahābhārata*—there is no reason to doubt about the elective principle mentioned in it.[149]

(c) *Limited Monarchy*

Whether monarchy was hereditary or elective, the monarch inside his own State was not absolute. His powers were limited by three factors—first, by the will of the people expressed in their assembly (*samiti*) ; second, by the ancient usage of the land and by the *dharmaśāstras* ; and, third, by the "right" (tacitly admitted by the lawgivers) of the people to expel their ruler. The will of the people assembled in the *samiti* corresponded in a large measure to the general will of the modern Western authors, mentioned in the previous pages of this book. Professor Macdonell expressed the position of the king correctly when he wrote that "his (the king's) power was by no means absolute, being limited by the will of the people expressed in the tribal assembly (*samiti*)".[149a] But any restriction on the prerogatives of the king by written constitutional measures, such as those which prevail in some of the modern limited monarchies, is not met with in ancient Indian history.

3. CONFEDERACIES

Outside his kingdom the power of the king was limited by the possibility of his enemies combining against him. The history of the Vedic king Sudās, who has already figured above, will illustrate how there could be a confederacy of kings even in those ancient times. Sudās, the Triṣṭu king, is described in the *Rig Veda* as having scored a famous victory over a confederacy of twelve kings. The battle is called Dāśarājña, meaning the "Battle with Ten Kings". Although the identity of the ten kings is uncertain, yet it appears that they had formed themselves into a confederacy of ten kings.[150] That Sudās won in this war does not militate against our contention that a confederacy of kings in the ancient times was possible. Centuries afterwards western India witnessed, in the last quarter of the eighth century A.D., a confederacy of twelve kings fighting against the powerful Rāṣṭrakūṭa monarch, Govinda III, in the first year of his accession (A.D. 794).[151] This proves that confederacies were not unknown in the ancient times.

E. WERE THERE CONFEDERATE STATES IN ANCIENT INDIA?

(a) *Professor Altekar's Theory*

In this connection we may examine the view held by some distinguished Indian scholars about the existence of the so-called confederate, composite, and unitary States in ancient India. According to the late Professor Altekar, "composite and Confederate States were not unknown to ancient India". He then remarks that the Kuru Pāñcālas in the later Vedic period "seem to have formed one composite state, ruled over by a common king" ; that the Kṣudrakas and the Mālavas were separate States in the days of Pāṇini, "but are very frequently mentioned in the *Mahābharata*" ; that they formed an alliance against Alexander the Great which "seems to have lasted for about a century" ; that their alliances were cemented by 10,000 mass intermarriages ; that the Yaudheyas were republican States which comprised three sub-States ; that the Lichchhavīs formed twice an alliance, once with the Mallas, and afterwards with the Videhas ; that the Lichchhavī "federal council consisted of 18 members, nine being elected by each of the confederating State" ; but that "normally, however, States in ancient India were unitary in character", by which term is meant that the "king was the fountain source from which the ministers and provincial governors derived their power".[152]

But the learned Professor invalidated his own elaborate theory when he asserted that "we do not, however, possess sufficient information to indicate how these composite or confederate States were functioning—what powers were retained by the federating units and what authority was delegated to the federal centre". He continues to assert that the "central government of the confederating States was confined only to foreign policy and the declaration and prosecution of war" ; that otherwise each State retained its sovereignty ; and that in the campaign against Alexander the Great, the Kṣudrakas and the Mālavas elected a Kṣudraka generalissimo, "who was famous for his skill and bravery".[153]

(b) *Professor Altekar's Theory Evaluated*

(i) *Evidence of Military Alliances*

The above are a bundle of statements that cannot be tied together either by the known facts of ancient history or by the principles of Political Science. It is true that, as Diodorus remarked, the Kṣudrakas, styled by him Oxydrakai, and the Mālavas, called by him the Malloi, are said to have cemented the alliance between the two tribes by wholesale marriages, each tribe giving and taking ten thousand young women for wives.[154] This, no doubt, suggests mass intermarriages between the two tribes. But to maintain on that score that they were permanently allied to each other for about a century is rather doubtful, although Pāṇini styles them as being allied in arms (*Kṣudraka-Mālavī-Senā*),[155] which might have meant merely that they were very often allies in warfare.

(ii) *Military Alliances not Confederacies : Defect in the Kṣudraka-Mālava Alliance*

But military alliances can hardly be called confederate States. They were evidently confederacies in a loose sense, like the one met with in the Vedic age mentioned above, that is, a temporary union for a particular purpose after the realization of which the clans that had joined together dissolved. It is very uncertain whether the Kṣudraka-Mālava alliance can be called a confederacy of the type of the Achaean League in Greek history, or the Hanseatic League in the history of mediaeval Europe, or the old German Confederation of 1815-66, or the Swiss Confederacy from 1815 till 1840, or the American Confederacy from 1781 till 1789. There have been alliances of a number of States by treaty on the basis of equality and mutual benefit. But a confederation differs from an alliance in possessing common organs of government for purposes of union, in the greater variety and extent of purposes for which the union is created, and in the desire of the contracting parties for perpetuity.[156] This cannot be said of the Kṣudrakas and the Mālavas, who were more often at war with each other.[157] Indeed, although we may concede to the view that the united army of the Kṣudrakas and the Mālavas (the *Kṣudraka-Mālavi-Senā* of Pāṇini) had existed long before the days of Alexander the Great, yet the description of the two clans by the Greek writers, who had accompanied that great Macedonian Conqueror, definitely precludes any idea of a permanent constitutional union which is connoted by the term confederate State. Curtius relates that they selected, in accordance with their custom, a brave warrior of the class of the Kṣudrakas as their head, that that warrior was an experienced general, but that just when the two clans were going to give battle, the Kṣudrakas and the Mālavas fell out as regards the choice of a leader, and that they "ceased in consequence to keep the field together".[158] This fact of the disagreement between the two erstwhile allies is by itself enough to demolish the theory that the Kṣudrakas and the Mālavas were knit together into a permanent confederate State lasting for about a century.[159] If the two clans could not agree on a simple question like the choice of a military commander in times of a grave crisis, it is impossible that they could have agreed on the more complicated problems of an administrative nature extending over a long period.

(*iii*) *Difference between a Confederacy and a Federation*

Concerning the other statement which Professor Altekar has made in regard to the retaining of powers by the federal units and the delegation of authority to the federal centre, it is clear that the learned author has altogether confounded the principle of a confederacy with that of a federal State. The difference between the two types of States is fundamental. It may be summarized thus: a confederation of States is created by an agreement which is legally an international treaty, and which rests upon the consent of the governments of the member States; while a federation is created by a constitutoin which is legally a law, and which rests upon the consent of the peoples of the State. Secondly, in a confederation there are as many sovereignties as there are members; in a federation there is a single sovereign State. Thirdly, it is constitutionally legal for the members of a confederation to withdraw; while in a federation, the secession of member States is an illegal and revolutionary act. Fourthly, the member States of a confederation create the government of the confederation, which may either destroy the confederation or extend its jurisdiction; but in a federation, it is the constitution which creates the central government of the federation, the members of which are not entitled either to destroy or modify it except by constitutional amendments. Therefore, the fundamental point of difference between a confederation and a federation lies in the location of sovereignty. In the former, the individual members can withdraw from the union, if their opinions relating to their obligations under the articles of the union are not acceptable to the confederation; while in a federation, the members cannot withdraw from the union except by a revolution which is illegal; neither can the central government destroy their political existence or interfere with their legal power.[160] The difference between a confederate State and a federal State is so vital and glaring that it is confusing the issues to talk of federal powers in a confederacy, and erroneous to apply the analogy of the confederate and federal States to the constitution of the Kṣudrakas and the Mālavas about whom so little is known either from the Indian or Greek sources.

F. ARISTOCRACIES

1. EVIDENCE FROM ANCIENT LITERATURE

We may now revert to the main topic under discussion, namely, the next form of ancient Indian State. This was the government by aristocracies. The fact that the king was one amongst the many Kṣatriyas, as must have been evident to the reader from the statements in the *Manusmṛiti* cited earlier, proves that there were others, who were equally qualified to administer, and who could evoke as much respect as the king, but who, for some specific reasons, could not exercise political authority which he alone could wield.[161] In the Vedic times the term *rājan* was applied to a man of the royal family, "probably including those who were not actually members of that family, but were nobles, though it may have been originally restricted to members of the royal family".[162] It is also surmised that that term might originally have been applied to all nobles irrespective of kingly power.[163] The distinction made in the *Śatapatha Brāhmaṇa* between the *rājaputra,* one who was the son of the king, and the *rājānya,*[164] shows that the latter term was confined to definite members of the social order. They were also known by the other name of Kṣatriyas, which is mentioned so early as in the days of the *Rig Veda.*[165] That the Kṣatriyas occasionally had their own chief is evident from the *Samhitas* and the *Brāhmaṇas* which mention a *kṣatrapati* as being the equivalent of a king.[166]

The above evidence, therefore, undoubtedly points to the existence of aristocracies composed of the Kṣatriyas. But that is not equal to saying that there was government by aristocracies or that there were aristocratic republics in the ancient times. The Vedic literature does not seem to know such governments.[167] We have to come to the comparatively later times of Pāṇini, Alexander the Great, Kauṭilya, and the Buddhist *Jātakas* in order to get some idea of self-governing aristocracies in ancient India.

2. SOME MISCONCEPTIONS

(a) About Titles and Nature

Before we proceed further with the subject, it is necessary to dispense with a few untenable propositions relating to the alleged republican nature of some tribes. One of them relates to the royal titles of a whole tribe or clan. Professor Altekar maintains that the people called the Uttaramadras and the Uttarakurus were *virāṭs* ; that the whole tribes "were consecrated to the rulership" ; and that the term *vairājya* was another term for a king-less State.[168] But to say that a whole people were consecrated to the rulership of their community is not to understand the significance of either the ceremony of consecration or the impossibility of a whole people's governing themselves, especially when their States contained a large percentage of people who had no share in the exercise of political power. The latter point will be further clarified when we shall discuss below whether there were any City States of the Greek type in ancient India.

What militates against the view that all the Uttaramadras and the Uttarakurus were "consecrated to the rulership" of their clans is the fact that when the Uttarakurus are first mentioned in the *Aitareya Brāhmaṇa*, they are described as a people living beyond the Himalayas (*pareṇa Himavantaṁ*). Their mythical character is confirmed by the story of Atyarāti Jānamtapi who, although not of the royal blood, was taught *rājasūya* by Vasiṣṭha Satyahavya, and who conquered the earth. When Vasiṣṭha claimed his reward, Jānamtapi angrily replied to him that he (Vasiṣṭha) would be made king of the Earth when Jānamptapi would conquer the Uttarakurus. Vasiṣṭha retorted by saying that their land being that of the gods (*devakṣetra*), no mortal could conquer it. At last Vasiṣṭha procured the death of Jānamtapi at the hands of Amitrapaṇa Śuṣmiṇa Śaibyā.[169]

The Uttarakurus, therefore, in the days of the *Aitareya Brāhmaṇa*, lived in a semi-mythical land, where no men seem to have lived. Any interpretation leading to their alleged republican or democratic government in those distant ages would be far-fetched and doubtful.[170] What government the Uttarakurus, and their contiguous, and perhaps kindred, brethren, the Uttaramadras, later on adopted when their descendants settled down in the Punjab, is beside the point, since in the *Aitareya Brāhmaṇa* there is nothing to suggest that all the people forming these two clans were "consecrated to the rulership".

(*b*) *Aristocracies Confounded with Republican Clans and Corporations*

The second misconception which needs an explanation is that which confounds the republican clans with the so-called free aristocracies, on the one hand, and with the corporations, on the other. Professor Rangaswami Aiyangar writes of free aristocracies in the days of Kauṭilya.[171] It cannot be made out on what grounds this nomenclature of free aristocracies rests. We shall see below that Kauṭilya certainly speaks of sovereign clans. On the basis of the statements made in connection with the Kṣatriyas above, it could be interpeted to mean that they were a "free Kṣatriya aristocracy". But if it is maintained that there was a class of free Kṣatriya aristocracy as against a Kṣatriya aristocracy in bondage or under restrictions, then, adequate proof will have to be adduced from ancient literature in support of two such kinds of aristocracies. Since it cannot be done, it means that the classification of aristocracies into free and non-free is gratuitious. There is likewise no justification for confounding, as the learned historian does, the free aristocracies with the corporations which latter he cites on the authority of Kauṭilya.[172]

(*c*) *Only Aristocracies were Republican in Character*

A third misconception which might be disposed of associates the republican government only with aristocracies. We may be permitted to repeat here what was said about the Kṣatriyas above. No doubt, they formed in the Vedic age an exclusive body of aristocracies. But it has yet to be proved that they retained throughout the ancient period the exclusive monopoly of warfare with which they were credited in the Vedic age, or even in that of the *Manusmṛiti*. If the term *Kṣatriya* came to include in the days of the *Mahābhārata* not only the Aryan nobility but the aboriginal princely families as well, and all the royal military vassal and feudal chiefs, as has been assumed by Professors Hopkins and Fick,[173] then, it is futile to speak of any aristocracy based only on birth, as was originally the case with the Kṣatriyas of the Vedic times. The inclusion of non-Aryan princely families, feudal chieftains, and military vassals in the category of aristocracies in the course of ages, must have caused various problems both of a social and political nature, which preclude any idea of republican governments being associated only with aristocracies of the Kṣatriyas, as the latter term had been originally understood in the early ages. It is more reasonable to assume that republican governments were associated either with clans that had maintained their political individuality or with the rest of the warlike people, some of whom had been infused with the fresh blood of new and energetic immigrants, and who exercised administrative control over their own communities. In the former case they would be oligarchical republics ; in the latter, community corporations.

G. EXAMPLES OF OLIGARCHICAL REPUBLICS

Of the two the former approaches nearest the term conciliar oligarchy of Professor MacIver, in which a council of elders or of tribal chiefs held sway.[174] Evidence about them is available in the accounts of Greek writers, who had accompanied Alexander the Great in the course of his conquest of the Punjab, in the *Grammar* of Pāṇini, and in the *Arthaśāstra* of Kauṭilya. For instance, there was a free city of Nysa or Nicea (Skt. Nagarahara, Nangenhor, about four or five miles west of Jalalabad), which had an aristocratic council of 300 and a president over it.[175] Then, there was the republic of Peucelaotis (Skt. Puṣkalāvatī, the capital of ancient Gāndhāra, modern Hastinagar, about seventeen miles north-west of Peshawar).[176] Nothing can be gathered from the Greek accounts beyond the fact that it was a republic. Pāṇini mentions it under the name of Hastināyanasangha.[177]

He enlightens us on the nature of a *sangha* government. He uses that term for a *gaṇa* as well. It was a generic designation meant to cover the following three categories—first, a multitude, as in the expression *grāmasya-paśu-sangha,* a herd of domestic cattle. In the same sense it was used for a multitude of men. Second, it connoted a *nikāya* which is defined by Pāṇini as a corporate body where the distinction between "upper" and "lower" does not exist (*sanghe cānauttarādharye*). This was applicable to a religious *sangha* which was a fraternity in which there was no distinction between the high (*uttara*) and the low (*adhara*). And, third, there was the political *sangha* (*sangha-odghau gaṇapraśaṁsayoḥ*).[178]

These two terms, *sangha* and *gaṇa,* as Dr. Agrawala asserts, were used as synonyms for a republic. The Yaudheyas, for instance, are mentioned by Pāṇini as a *sangha* but refer to themselves as a *gaṇa* in their coins of the post-Pāṇini period. Dr. Agrawala has some pertinent remarks to make in this connection which may be read along with what has been said above concerning the so-called mass consecration of the Uttaramadras and the Uttarakurus. He writes thus:

> . . . in the Kshatriya tribes organised as *Saṅghas,* the political power vested in the hands of those families which were eligible for regular coronation (*abhiṣeka mangala*) and consecrated to rulership by that ceremony (*abhiṣikta-vaṁśyas*). Other castes in the *Gaṇa* did not share the political power, although they owed allegiance to the *Janapada* and the *Janapadins.*[179]

The distinction between classes as signified by *rājānya* used by Pāṇini only for the descendants of a *rāja*, and *rājana* for all others, in a *sangha* or a *gaṇa*,[180] makes it impossible for us to imagine of wholesale clans being consecrated to rulership, as was supposed by Professor Altekar.

H. REPUBLICAN STATES

1. SOME EXAMPLES

Our contention that there were self-governing clans which were made up of non-Aryans is proved by the fact that the Greek writers mention that Alexander the Great conquered, while sailing down the Indus, the Ossadians, the Ambastanes, and the Xathrians. They were impure tribes of mixed origin.[181] The Ambastanes are described by Arrian as being a democratic clan without a king.[182] This evidence conflicts with that of the *Mahābhārata*, Pāṇini, and Patañjali, the first two of whom would describe them as a *janapada* under a king.[183] The only way by which we can reconcile the disparity in the evidence of the Greek and Indian writers is by assuming that, as Pāṇini admits,[184] they were of mixed origin ; that in his age (the seventh century B.C.) they had not formed themselves into a republic ; that they were a republic in the days of Alexander the Great (fourth century B.C.) ; but that later on in the days of Patañjali (middle of the second century B.C.),[185] they appear to have again become a tribal monarchy.

Another self-governing clan was that of the Cathaeans mentioned by the Greek writers. They have been identified with the Kaṭṭhis of Kathiavad.[186] They do not figure in the work of Pāṇini.

One more example of a self-governing clan is that of the Yaudheyas who, as seen already, figure both as a *sangha* and a *gaṇa* in Pāṇini's work. He mentions them in the list of the *āyudhajīvin sanghas*,[187] i.e. those *sanghas* whose members lived by the profession of arms. On the obverse of their coins there is the figure of a soldier with a spear in his right hand, while his left hand is on his hip, with the legend *Yaudheyagaṇasya Jaya* (Victory to the *gaṇa* or Republic of the Yaudheyas).[188] Numismatic evidence, therefore, fully corroborates Pāṇini's statement that the Yaudheyas were *āyudhajīvins*, although centuries seem to have elapsed after that great grammarian's time, when the coins were issued in the manner indicated above. But we should be cautious in styling all the Yaudheyas as republican clans, since on some coins discovered by Major Arthur Cunningham the names *Bhāgavata Svāmina Brāhmaṇa Devasya* and *Bhānu Varma* appear, thereby suggesting that some sections of the Yaudheyas were probably monarchical in character,[189] although they might have retained their military avocations. But, on the whole, the Yaudheyas were a military clan whose form of government was republican. They evidently belonged to the category of unnamed clans described thus by Kauṭilya:

> Sovereignty may (sometimes) be the property of a clan ; for the corporation of clans is invincible in its nature, and being free from the calamities of anarchy, can have a permanent existence on earth (*kulasya vā bhavet-rājyaṁ kula-saṅgho hi durjayaḥ arājavyasanābādhaḥ śaśvadāvasati kṣitiṁ*).[190]

Kauṭilya not only pays a tribute in the above passage to the republican nature of the government of the clans but incidentally helps to substantiate the theory maintained elsewhere in these pages that *arājatā* was merely anarchy, and not a phase in constitutional development, as was erroneously maintained by Dr. Jayaswal. Kauṭilya's term for a corporation of warriors was *śreṇibalam* concerning which he has some praise to bestow, while describing the attitude of a conquered king.[191]

The exact difference between the above republics and the self-governing tribes or clans mentioned by the Greek writers, cannot be determined. We can only presume that the self-governing tribes were autonomous groups each living under a chieftain. The Greek accounts, for instance, mention a tribe called Peucelaotis (Skt. Puṣkalāvatī) which is not to be confounded with its namesake which has already figured above, and which was a republic. This other Puṣkalāvatī was under a chieftain whom the Greeks called Astes. It is mentioned by the Greeks along with the Aspasians, who were perhaps the same as the *Āśvāyanas* living as a republic, and mentioned by Pāṇini, but who, in the days of Alexander the Great, were under a governor. In the same context the Greek accounts mention the Mallians and the Oxydrakoi, who were undoubtedly the Mālavas and the Kṣudrakas of Pāṇini ;[192] the Ossadians, who were the same as the Vasāti of Pāṇini ; and the Oreitans. It is not improbable that all these are to be classed with those who followed the profession of arms, that is, with the *āyudhajīvins* of Pāṇini.[193]

2. THE GANA CONSTITUTION

Pāṇini's great work contains some features of the working of the *gaṇa* republics which may now be described. A few details about this subject have already been given above in connection with the alleged mass consecration of aristocracies. The first point that may be noted, we may repeat, is that those who were consecrated to rulership were not identical with the rest, who were merely members of an aristocracy. The next point that may be mentioned is that, according to Pāṇini, it was not all members of a class but only the heads of the *rājakulas* or royal families that constituted the governing body of a *gaṇa*. Further, the specific distinction between the *gotra*-descendant and the *yuvan*-descendant made by Pāṇini suggests that there was even in a *gaṇa* social gradations which made it impossible for all members of a *gaṇa* to be equally associated with the exercise of political power. The eldest member of a family, who was its representative, was entitled to the term *gotra*, while the junior members of a family were called *yuvan*. The eldest male member represented his *kula* (family) on all important occasions and functions.

Pāṇini also mentions a sort of a party system as connoted by the term *dvanda*. Three terms denoted party members: *vargya*, *gṛihya*, and *pakṣya*. A party was named after its leader, as in the case of *Vāsudeva-vargya*. There was an Executive Council in each *sangha* or *gaṇa*, consisting of five, ten, or twenty members. The Jaina work of the later ages, *Antagaḍadāsāo*, confirms the existence of an Executive Council in a *sangha*, when it describes the ten principal Dāśārhas among the Andhaka-Vṛiṣnis who had a *sangha* of their own. The Buddhist work *Mahāvagga* adds to the Hindu and Jaina testimony that there were Executive Councils of four, ten, twenty, or more members.[194] But beyond these details it is not possible to say to what extent exactly the *gaṇa* constitution was republican in character.

3. THE BUDDHIST SANGHAS: INTRODUCTION

It would be worthwhile to discuss here the nature of the Buddhist *sanghas* concerning which there has been a good deal of speculation. We have seen above that, according to Pāṇini, one type of *sanghas* was the religious one in which there was no distinction between the high (*uttara*) and the low (*adhara*). Were the Buddhist *sanghas* of the later ages radically different from the religious *sanghas* mentioned by Pāṇini? It is true that there was no Buddhism in the days of that great grammarian ; and, that, therefore, no connection need necessarily be maintained between the concept of Pāṇini and that of the Buddhists. Nevertheless it is profitable to discuss whether the latter deviated from the ancient practice relating to the nature of a *sangha* in such a manner as to give a radically new concept to the world.

(*a*) *Theory about the Sanghas*

The sources of information on this particular aspect of the question are the Buddhist works like the *Majjhima Nikāya*, the Buddhist *Jātaka Stories*, the *Dialogues* of Buddha, etc. On the basis of these it has been maintained by scholars that the Buddhists had assemblies ; that the members of these assemblies were known as *rājās*, and their sons, *uparājās* ; that they had a Central Assembly consisting, as in the case of the Yaudheyas, of 5,000, and as in that of the Lichchhavīs, 7,707 members ; that there were two Houses, one Upper and the other Lower, which possessed sovereignty and controlled the foreign policy of the Central Assembly ; that the latter was sometimes converted into a place of discussion on political matters, and, at other times, on socio-religious questions ; that there was a definite procedure relating to the business of the Assembly ; that there were parties and a quorum for deciding issues ; that there was an Executive Council of the Central Assembly, a President of that Council, who was also the President of the Central Assembly ; and that there was an apportioning of portfolios among the members of the Central Assembly. To give a semblance of reality to all these speculations, it is asserted that the city of Nysa (Nicea), which has figured above in connection with Alexander the Great, had an Assembly of thirty councillors ; and that, therefore, a big State like that of the Yaudheyas might have had a larger assembly of 5,000 members. And to make this picture still more appealing the evidence of Kauṭilya's *Arthaśāstra* is pressed into it ; and we are told that the president and members of the *sangha* mentioned by Kauṭilya were members of the Executive Council of the Central Assembly, that they were under the law of the land, and that if they violated it, they were liable to be dismissed and punished by the State tribunals.[195]

(*b*) *Evaluation of the Theory*

The learned advocates of the above theory (Drs. Jayaswal, Altekar, and D. R. Bhandarkar) have mixed fact with fiction in expounding it. In the elucidation of the above theory, the following points may be readily admitted: firstly, that the Buddhists had assemblies in which business was conducted according to a well laid-out plan ; secondly, that there might have been parties and a quorum for the conduct of business ; thirdly, that the larger assemblies might have been broken up into smaller committees ; and that over the larger assemblies there were presidents, who conducted the business of those bodies ; fourthly, that Kauṭilya devotes a whole chapter styled *sanghavṛittam* to this subject ; and, fifthly, that the Greek writers, who accompanied Alexander the Great, certainly mention the number of persons who comprised the assemblies of certain self-governing clans.

But all this does not entitle us to postulate the elaborate theory of a Central Assembly and the Executive Council mentioned above. The Greek accounts, while mentoining the presidents of some assemblies, do not refer to the Executive Council and the division of work among the members of the Assembly. Kauṭilya does not mention in his *Arthaśāstra* that the President or the members of the Executive Council as being specifically punishable for embezzlement of public funds or for contravening the law of the land. The elaborate rules mentioned in the *Arthaśāstra* in connection with these two grave offences, which will be referred to in a later context in this work, were meant for all, high and low, who had violated the law of the country. The entire chapter on the *sanghavṛittam* deals with the problem of bringing the corporations under the iron rule of the conqueror, the Emperor, by various means like sowing the seeds of dissension among members of the corporations by means of immoral women, spies, and mendicants. The only object of these measures was to make the conqueror "the only monarch of all the corporations". Kauṭilya's reference to the leaders of the *sanghas* (*sangha-mukhya*) in this and other contexts, cannot be interpreted to mean presidents of republics, unless there is valid ground for proving it. One fails to see how the above account of the *sanghas* or corporations, as given in the *Arthaśāstra*, can be made applicable to an imaginary picture of the republican constitution, especially when one realizes that in the description of Kauṭilya, it is not the republican leader who figures but the inexorable imperial head, the single monarch (*ekarājaḥ*), who cannot tolerate any republican spirit. Indeed, the whole chapter on the *sanghas*, as given by Kauṭilya,[196] is a negation of the republican government, as imagined by Professor Altekar and others.

(c) *Nature of the Buddhist Sanghas Analysed*

(i) *Criteria of Study*

The *Arthaśāstra* and the Greek accounts being of no avail in supporting the above theory, let us see how far the actual conditions prevailing in the Buddhist *sanghas* or congregational meetings, could be made to agree with it. Here, too, we should admit that the Buddhist Church assemblies were undoubtedly self-governing and democratic in character; and that by the very spirit of Buddhism, there could never have been any distinction between the high and the low, and the rich and the poor in such congregational assemblies. But the advocates of the above theory have not taken notice of three questions: firstly, did the political *sanghas* serve as a model for the religious *sanghas*, or *vice versa*? Secondly, is there any justification for confoundnig the republican or self-governing constitution among tribes or clans like the Lichchhavīs with that prevailing among the Buddhists? And, thirdly, did the Buddhist congregations, which were pledged to the furtherance of the *dharma*, ever transact political business sometimes, and religious business at other times, in their synods?

(ii) *On What were the Sanghas based?*

We may examine the above points in detail. There is no agreement among the three eminent propounders of the above theory on the first point relating to the relative position of the political and religious *sanghas*. Professor Altekar maintained that in regard to the details of the rules of procedure of the so-called Central Assembly, such rules served as a model for the rules of the Buddhist *sanghas*. But in the very next sentence the same authority asserted that the Buddhist practice of having twenty members for a quorum was imitated by the political *sanghas*![197] But the concept of a quorum was by no means introduced by the Buddhists. We see it in Pāṇini, who refers to *gaṇa-tīrtha* which term has rightly been interpreted to mean as a person, whose attendance completed the *gaṇa* (*gaṇasya-pūraṇaḥ*).[198] The *Mahāvagga* likewise refers to a *gaṇa-pūraka*,[199] thereby suggesting that the Buddhists merely continued the earlier concept of a quorum in regard to their assemblies. If the idea of a quorum had existed in political bodies long before the days of Buddhism, it is futile to maintain that the religious congregations of the Buddhists set an example for the political assemblies to imitate in this regard.

The uncertainty in the mind of Professor Altekar as to who imitated whom—whether the Buddhist *sanghas* imitated the political *sanghas,* or *vice versa*—is probably due to the fact that he wished to depart from the stand adopted by the two earlier exponents of the theory. According to the late Dr. Jayaswal, who was followed in this respect by the late Professor D. R. Bhandarkar, the procedure prescribed by Buddha for the deliberations of the congregations or *sanghas,* as given in the *Mahāparinirbbāṇa Sutta,* was borrowed from the procedure followed by the republics in their deliberations. Dr. Jayaswal, therefore, naturally concluded that there was no difference between the procedure conducted in the Buddhist *sanghas* and that prevailing among the republican clans.[200] There is some justification for the view that the Buddhist synods copied the procedure from the political *sanghas,* when it is realized that the latter were anterior to the former. We shall revert to this point presently. On the first detail, as regards the relative position of the *sanghas,* therefore, there is no agreement among the advocates of the above theory.

(iii) The Lichchhavī Organization

We may now take up the second detail which may be stated thus: is there any justification for confounding the republican or self-governing constitution, as it prevailed amongst some of the ancient clans like the Lichchhavīs, with that existing amongst the Buddhist clergy? Buddhist works give many details about the States of the Lichchhavīs, the Śākyas, the Moriyas, the Mallas, etc. The assemblies of all these had members of the Kṣatriya aristocracy, each called *rājan,* and who, as in the case of the Lichchhavīs, were 7707 in number, and were entitled to consecration. Clans like the Lichchhavīs, the Mallas, etc., might have had an oligarchical or republican constitution. The late Professor D. R. Bhandarkar, while describing the constitution of the Lichchhavīs and the Mallas, as given in the Buddhist canonical works like the *Majjhima Nikāya,* wrote that those two clans were organized in *sanghas* and *gaṇas* ; that they had the right to banish, burn, or kill a man in their own *vijita* or State ; that the preambles to the *Jātakas* tell us in two places that there were 7707 Lichchhavī kings staying at Vaiśāli, the capital of their State ; that these latter administered the affairs of the State ; that their sons were called Lichchhavīkumāras or Lichchhavī princes, and as kings, were entitled to coronations ; that there was a special tank in Vaiśāli (called *puṣkariṇī*) the water of which was used for sprinkling on their heads, when they were crowned ; and that that tank was especially guarded in order to prevent any one from taking water from it.[201] But the learned historian writes: "It is not, however, clear whether these Lichchhavī kings were crowned all at one time, and if so, on what occasions." In a later context, the same eminent authority further informs us that in another *Jātaka*, it is related that all the 7707 Lichchhavī kings staying at Vaiśāli (modern Basaṛh in the Muzaffarpur district of Bihar) had as many *uparājās* or viceroys, *senāpatis* or generals, and *bhaṇḍāgarikas* or treasurers, all staying with them.[202] Professor Bhandarkar supplements the above with the evidence of the *Aṭṭakathā* and the *Sumangalavilāsinī*, which were two Buddhist commentaries on the Buddhist Pali works, written in about the fifth century A.D. The evidence of these two commentaries is then cited in order to show that the final decision in a legal dispute lay with the *rājan* or king.[203]

But the learned Professor is not prepared to accept all the evidence about the republican nature of the Vaiśāli constitution. He rightly doubts "whether there were as many as 7707 Lichchhavī kings ever staying at Vaiśāli", as the *Jātakas* inform us. According to him, the number of kings constituting the Lichchhavī *gaṇa* was pretty large. "It again seems that the Lichchhavī kings had each his separate principality where he exercised supreme power in certain respects." It is only on this supposition that the statement that each king had his own *uparāja, senāpati*, etc., becomes intelligible. If the kings had separate States, it cannot be understood why all of them stayed in the capital, leaving their subordinate staff like the *vinascaya, mahāmātra, vyavahārika*, etc., in their native States. Finally, "in what matters individually in the several States, and in what matters conjointly in the whole kingdom, the Lichchhavī kings exercised autonomy, is not clear".[204]

The above doubts raised by Professor Bhandarkar come in the way of our accepting as valid all that has been said regarding the republican nature of the Lichchhavī constitutoin. His conclusion in this regard is interesting. "This, however, is certain that their *saṁgha* was a federation of the heads of some of the clans constituting the tribe."[205] To this sober judgment we might add another consideration which prevents us from giving all credence to the evidence of the *Jātakas* relating to the political nature of the Buddhist congregations. It relates to the meaning attached to the terms *kṣatriya* and *rājan* in Buddhist literature. Professor Bhandarkar, while discussing the origin of kingship as given in the *Aggañña-suttanta* of the *Dīgha-Nikāya*,[206] affirms that the person selected as king by the men who had assembled together, received three different appellations to suit his three different stages—that of being selected, that of being called the punisher of the wicked, and that of receiving a portion of their rice—*mahāsammata*, because he was selected by all men (*mahājanasammata*) ; *kṣatriya* or the lord of all the fields (*khettanampatīti*) ; and *rājan*, because he delighted others through righteousness (*dhammena pare rañjetīti*).[207]

We shall describe below in Part Five, while discussing the Elements of the State, the position of the king in Buddhist political philosophy. But for the present, we may observe that there is nothing in the above to suggest that the Buddhists had either advanced upon the earlier concepts or had discarded them in order to formulate new ideas either of kingship or of a republican government. The etymology of the word *rājan* as given in the Buddhist works is the same as that given in the Śāntiparvan of the *Mahābhārata*.[208] This points to the fact that Buddhists followed the earlier Hindu concept of a *rājan* which meant a member of the royal family. The other word *kṣatriya,* according to the ancient Hindus, covered the whole class of nobles, a social order distinct from the other three orders of priests, traders, and serving classes. The slight twist which the Buddhists gave to the word *kṣatriya* was to make it applicable to lords of all the fields, presumably as owners of land. The Buddhist connotation of the word *kṣatriya,* in the sense of protecting the people, was in accordance with the *Manusmṛiti* in which the Kṣatriya is described as carrying arms, evidently in the discharge of his duties as the protector of the people.[209] One cannot help feeling that the Buddhists used the two terms *kṣatriya* and *rājan* in a looser sense than they had been used in the earlier times ; and that the connotation of those two words, as given in the Buddhist canonical works, cannot be interpreted to mean that the 7707 *rājas,* who were concentrated in the Lichchhavī capital of Vaiśāli, formed a republican government. The utmost that might be conceded in regard to the nature of the constitution of the Lichchhavīs is that it was a sort of a confederacy of independent tribal units, whose powers and jurisdiction cannot be distinguished from each other with the help of the available sources.

(iv) The Buddhist Sanghas and the Lichchhavīs

There seems to be hardly any difference of opinion among scholars about the oligarchical nature of the Lichchhavīs and the republican or democratic nature of the Yaudheyas, the Mālavas, and other tribal bodies. The major point which the advocates of the republican nature of the Buddhist *sanghas* have not clarified is whether there is any justification for maintaining that what prevailed among the Lichchhavīs, the Yaudheyas, and the other self-governing clans was necessarily identical with what existed in the Buddhist congregational meetings ; or for asserting that the Buddhist Church organization could be made applicable to the clans mentioned above. One flaw in the above analogy of the Buddhist clannish organizations is admitted by the advocates of the above theory when they say that some of the clans like the Yaudheyas, the Mālavas, etc., showed definite signs of a monarchical government in the third century A.D.[210] This fact is by itself enough to prove that there was nothing like an age-long republican or democratic constitution of those tribes ; and that even if they had earlier a democratic constitution, they had eschewed it for a monarchical one in the early centuries of the Christian era.

Coming to the Buddhist *sanghas* themselves, we have now to see whether the constitution of those synods, could be applied to the political organization of the clans. We get a good glimpse of the Buddhist congregational meetings in the Buddhist literature. In the *Mahāparinirbbāṇa Sutta,* Buddha is said to have told the prime-minister of king Ajātaśatru of the Madras, who contemplated attacking the confederacy of the Vajjians, that the latter would not decline but prosper as long as they observed seven conditions. These seven conditions were prescribed by Buddha for the welfare of the *sanghas.* The rules of procedure which the *sanghas* had to follow in their deliberations are given in detail in the Buddhist works called *Mahāvagga* and the *Cūlavagga* ; while the seven conditions for the welfare of the Vajjians and the *sanghas* are set forth in the *Mahāparinirbbāṇa Sutta.* The seven conditions are the following: holding full and frequent public assemblies ; meeting together in concord and carrying out undertakings in concord ; enacting nothing not already established and abrogating nothing that had already been enacted ; acting in accordance with the ancient institutions established in the former days ; honouring and respecting and supporting elders, and hearkening to their advice ; not detaining women or girls of their classes by force or abduction ; honouring and supporting Vajjian shrines in town and country, and not allowing proper offering and rites to fall into a state of disuse ; and protecting and supporting the Arhats (or Buddhist sages) amongst them.[211]

The above general directions of policy, which aimed at the moral well-being of society, do not help us to postulate any theory. They could be as well applied to the Vajjians as to any other people. They were rules of moral conduct ; and excepting the reference to the preservation of ancient enactments, there is nothing in them to suggest that they were of a political nature that could be adopted by political bodies like the Vajjians, who were a confederation of eight classes of which the Lichchhavīs and the Videhas were the most prominent.[212]

That the set-up of the Buddhist democratic clans was different to the one which existed in the Buddhist synods will be evident when we note how the Śākyas, for instance, carried out their administrative and judicial business in their halls called *santhāgāra* at Kapilavastu. Professor Rhys Davids, who gives these and other details of the eleven Buddhist republics, as he calls them, and particularly of the Śākyas, states that the latter chose a single chief, although it cannot be made out how and for what period he was selected. The chief presided over the session of the congregation, but when there was no session of the congregation, he presided over the State. He bore the title of *rāja* which, we may note by the way, was borne by Buddha's cousin as well as by Buddha's father.[213] Even this bare outline of the working of one of the Buddhist clans is enough to show that their constitution was not identical with that of the Buddhist synods.

(*v*) *Business Transacted by the Sanghas*

The working of the Śākya constitution enables us to dispose of the third point raised above, viz., whether the Buddhist congregations transacted sometimes political business and at other times Church business. The very nature of the Buddhist synods precluded any association of politics with their working. What the Śākyas as a clan did the Buddhist synods would never have contemplated of doing, namely conducting political and judicial business in addition to their own Church affairs. We may, therefore, conclude that the Buddhist synods had their rules of procedure which were devoted more to the furtherance of the cause of the Buddhist *dharma* than to that of the temporal side of their life, although they must have formulated rules for the proper management and continuance of their properties on which their subsistence depended. It is also clear that they had their rules of procedure in their congregational assemblies without which fruitful discussions on theological matters could never have come to a successful issue.

(*vi*) *Conclusion*

But to institute any large scale comparison between the Buddhist synods and the assemblies of the Vajjians, the Lichchhavīs, the Videhas, etc., and to confound the former with the latter, would be as erroneous as, for instance, to compare the administration of the various Indian States, particularly in western India, in the eighth century A.D., and onwards, with that of the great Pontificate of Śringeri, or of the self-governing cities in Italy and Germany, in the early mediaeval ages, with that of the Holy Roman Empire.[214] No one would question the soundness of basing one's remarks on the Buddhist canonical works for constructing the history of the administration of the Buddhist Church ; but what is unsound is the applicability of Buddhist ecclesiastical regulations to the political conditions of the republican clans, especially when so little is known about the latter, and when, as Dr. Kane rightly states, the Buddhist literature itself does not enlighten us on the vital questions of voting in and membership of assemblies.[215] And when we realize that the Buddhist sources, particularly the *Jātakas*, do not know anything about the *samiti*, which seems to have disappeared as an effective political institution in the epics, in the law books,[216] and in the Buddhist texts, we may conclude this part of our survey of the Buddhist republican institutions by saying that, in the present stage of our historical knowledge, there is no justification for constructing an elaborate superstructure of the so-called republican States of the Buddhists.

4. THE COMMUNITY CORPORATIONS

The discussion we have entered into regarding the republican constitution of the Buddhist States, and particularly the conclusion we have arrived at above, do not mean that ancient India was unaware of democratic organizations. One such type of organizations was that of the *śreṇis* or community corporations, which are met with in Pāṇini in connection with the *āyudhajīvins,* or those clans that lived by the profession of arms.[217] The exact connotation of the term *śreṇi,* however, in the days of Pāṇini cannot be determined.[218] We have to come to the times of Kauṭilya, who explicitly states that the corporations of warriors (*kṣatriya-śreṇi*) of Kāmbhoja, Surāṣṭra, and others lived by agriculture, trade, and wielding of weapons; while those of the Lichchhavīs, Vrijikā, Mallaka, Madraka, Kukkuru, Kuru, Pāñcāla, and others lived by the title of rāja (*Kāmbhoja-Surāṣṭra-kṣatriya-śreṇyādayo vārtāśastropajīvinaḥ Lichchhavika-Vrijika-Mallaka-Madraka-Kukkura-Kuru-Pāñcālādayo rāja-śabda-upajīvinaḥ*).[219]

It is not improbable that the *kṣatriyaśreṇis* of the Kāmbhoja, Surāṣṭra, and other regions, were made up of mercenary soldiers who, although given to the traditional use of arms, nevertheless took to the pursuits of agriculture and trade in times of peace. Since in the chapter of the Conduct of Corporations (*Sanghavṛittam*) in which he mentions them, he classes them under the *sanghas,* and clearly distinguishes them from the corporations which were invincible to the enemy, and from those whose services were to be secured by the king through gifts and conciliation, and from other corporations which were opposed to the ruler, and which were to be put down by sowing seeds of dissension among them and by secretely punishing them, it is clear that we have to understand by the term *śreṇi* used in connection with the corporations of warriors those who were not sovereign but subject to the ordinary law of the land. Otherwise the whole tenor of the chapter is unintelligible. Indeed, the concluding part of the chapter indicates beyond doubt that such corporations were within the jurisdiction of the king. For it says the following: "Thus he (the monarch) should live as the only monarch of all the corporations; the corporations also, under the protection of such a single monarch, should guard themselves against all kinds of treachery."[220]

Our presumption that the corporations connoted by the term *śreṇi* were directly under the State is borne out by two previous references to them in the *Arthaśāstra.* In one context it is stated that a confederacy of persons, which has hurt another person, shall be punished with the usual fine.[220a] The next reference to the *śreṇis* is in the chapter entitled Protection against Artisans, wherein Kauṭilya states that the guilds (*śreṇi*) shall receive their deposits back in times of distress; and that they will be under the jurisdiction of three commissioners or three ministers of the State.[221] Such corporations, therefore, may not be considered on a footing of equality with the sovereign clans which Kauṭilya, as already remarked above, has described as being invincible in nature, and as having a permanent existence on earth because of their freedom from anarchy.

5. OTHER AUTONOMOUS COMMUNITIES

Before we pass on to the next important subject in the comparative study of the Indian and Greek republics, it may be observed that Pāṇini mentions two terms under the generic designation of *sangha*, the exact meaning of which cannot be determined. These are *pūga* and *vrāta*, the former of which was organized under the *grāmaṇi*, and the latter which lived by violence and depradation.[222] Professor Agarwala's conjecture that "pūga was less developed than a regular *āyudhajivīn* sangha but better organized than a vrāta",[223] is not helpful in ascertaining the exact significance of those two terms. It appears that *pūga* was a term that was in vogue long after the *Vedas*, since it is not met with in the Vedic literature.[224] But the terms *vrāta* and *gaṇa* occur in the *Rig Veda* denoting the troops of the Maruts.[225] Vrātapati, in the sense of "Lord of the Troops", is one of the epithets given along with that of "Ganapati, Lord of Gaṇas", to Rudra in the *Yajur Veda Samhita*.[226] We have to conclude from the above that, although the two terms *vrāta* and *gaṇa* are met with in the Vedic times, they did not acquire the specialized meaning of republican corporations which seems to have been associated with them probably in the age of Pāṇini. But the mercenary nature of *vrāta* is evident from the fact that that term, used in the sense of *Vrātapati*, connoted the "Lord of Troops".

6. THE INDIAN REPUBLICS AND THE GREEK CITY STATES

(a) *Theories*

At this stage we may examine the validity of the arguments brought forward by modern Indian scholars in regard to the alleged similarity between the Indian democratic governments and the Greek City States. The analogy centres round two ideas—one which likens the Indian self-governing communities mentioned above to the Greek City States ; and the other, the *janapada* States to the Greek City States. The former view is advocated by Professor Altekar ; the latter, by Professor Agrawala. Professor Altekar writes thus:

> We can, therefore, legitimately describe the ancient *gaṇa* states as republics in the same sense in which the standard works on the political science describe the States of Athence (sic), Sparta, or Venice, as republics, remembering at the same time that they were not democracies of the modern types, where the franchise is vested in as large a number of citizens as possible.[227]

Professor Agrawala, in a well drawn-out parallel, asserts: "A comparative study of human societies affords innumerable analogies, and we find unmistakable parallels between the Janapada State in India and the City State in Greece."[228]

(b) *Evaluation of the Theories*

The two propositions given above are wide apart—one would limit the comparison of the *gaṇa* republics with the Greek City States; while the other would compare the larger units called the *janapadas* mentioned by Pāṇini with the Greek City States. Before we see how far these two analogies are historically tenable, it is necessary that we should mention here the methods of approach to this part of the subject, the existence of democratic characteristics in the organizations of the ancient communities in general, the main features of the ancient Greek City States, and the possible points of analogy and contrast between them and the ancient Indian city republics.

(i) *Criteria of Judgement*

When we wish to ascertain a few facts about organizations or persons or events of the past, relating to two different countries, we could utilize either the comparative method or the method of survivals for our purpose. According to the former method, the institutions of various tribes or clans which are reputed to have developed similar political organizations in India may first be compared, so as to gain some general idea of the manner in which such tribes or clans lived, and of the conditions out of which their States grew. The next step in this method would be to compare the results thus arrived at with what we actually know about similar foreign communities, preferably of the same age. And, finally, the third step would be to verify the results by seeing whether the conditions out of which the Indian tribal organizations are supposed to have originated, continued to survive in any shape after their States had been formed.[229] The comparative method, which has been so profitably used in the case of the Greek and the Roman City States, appears to be unsuited for our purpose, because we know so little about the actual conditions prevailing in the ancient Indian republics that it is almost impossible to form a general idea of their political organization excepting on the basis of imagination. Any idea of comparing, therefore, the organization of one republic with that of another is plainly impossible.

The method adopted by some historians which has been described above, namely, of forming a general picture of the Indian republics based mostly on the Buddhist canonical texts, supplemented by stray references in the *Mahābhārata*, and in Kauṭilya's *Arthaśāstra*, is not fruitful in the sense that, not only are the principles of Buddhist Church organization not applicable to the non-Buddhist Hindu communities of the early times, but, what is more important, the difference in the age in which the various republics flourished makes it almost impossible for us to know the conditions out of which such republics might have grown. The evidence of Pāṇini supplemented by the comments of Patañjali in some cases, and of the author of the *Kāśikāvritti* in many others, is certainly valuable but not so conclusive as to make us dogmatically maintain that the republican communities of ancient India possessed features which were identical with those of their Western counterparts. If the first step in the comparative method is thus so very unsatisfactory, we have hardly any justification for comparing our republics with those of the foreign countries of the same age. The second step is likewise extremely difficult in view of the fact that in comparatively later times, excepting a few names and still fewer technical terms mentioned in some inscriptions, there is nothing even to indicate that the republican communities of ancient India functioned in the manner of the Greek City States. A comparison between the Indian republican States with the Greek City States thus becomes extremely difficult.

The second method of studying with the aid of the survivals is essentially connected with the third step in the comparative method described above. According to the second method we argue backwards from the nature of the institutions of the later times, of which we know something, to their probable origins or early history, of which we know nothing.[230] In this case, too, we in India are unfortunately faced with a great difficulty. It relates to the complete wiping out of the traces of even the names of the republics after the fourth century A.D., due to a number of causes into which we shall not enter.

Since neither of the two historical methods is possible in regard to a comparative study of the ancient Indian republics and the Greek City States, we can only fall back on such of the generalizations as are permissible because of a similarity in some of the features of the ancient political institutions not only of India and of Greece but of the other parts of the ancient world as well. It is generally agreed that the early tribes and other ancient communities were in a certain sense democratic in their character. But, as Professor MacIver rightly affirms, it was as communities, and not as States, that they were democratic.[231] It was a stage in the growth of the tribal and community life in which the sense of responsibility and of effort was that of the community as a whole, and not that of the individuals, as in Greece. And, further, the democratic nature of the ancient communities revealed itself in a formless equality of tribal life ; while, in some of the advanced Greek City States, their democratic nature was reflected in the organized and progressive control of government by a large section of the citizens.[232]

(ii) History of the Greek City States : Definition of a City State

In order to see how far the Indian self-governing communities were similar to the Greek City States, we have to understand what was meant by a Greek City State. While it is admitted that there was no uniformity in the manner in which the different City States of Greece grew,[233] yet the fact remains that, on the whole, they were formed on certain general lines. A City State in Greece grew around a hill called the *acropolis*. On its top was a fort, and around the latter the temples of the gods. Close by was a market place, where the people met to transact business and to conduct meetings. In fact, it was the centre of their public and private life. The entire area within the walls of the fort and the neighbouring district, where also the people lived, was called a City State (*polis*). The total size of the City State hardly extended beyond a few dozens of square miles around the city.

Causes of the Origin of the City State. There were two causes which were responsible for the origin of a Greek City State—firstly, the fear of a common danger, and the consequent necessity of self-defence ; and, secondly, its common gods, whose protection against enemies was as much needed for the safety of the citizens as for the preservation of their ancient forms of worship.[234]

Main Features of the City States. The main features of the citizens of the Greek City States were the following: their intense patriotism, and their great desire to participate in the many public duties like serving on the jury, in the army and navy, in public worship, in constructing works of public utility like ships and beautiful edifices in the city, and in bestowing patronage on artists, musicians, men of letters, etc. But the duty of policing the city, which was shunned by the citizens, particularly, the Athenians, was left to the Scythians. Another important feature of their public life was that they held land in common. In a Greek City State, city and land were one whole, which did not admit of any division of natural interest.[235] A further feature of their public and private life was that they believed in the institution of slaves and aliens, who did not possess rights. The size of the population of a City State varied from about 50,000 to about a quarter of a million ; but those who were over thirty years of age and who were entitled to vote in the popular assembly could, at any time, be brought together within the hearing of a single voice.[236]

Nature of their Government. The nature of their government is best exemplified by that which prevailed in Athens. The whole Athenian body of citizens was not only identified with the State but was the State itself, all sharing equally in government, education, and pleasures. This equality of right and opportunity was responsible for the development of the Athenian genius in a manner unknown in any other Greek City State. The entire assembly of the privileged citizens constituted the sovereign body of the State. Two of their most important classes of officials were the following: those who comprised the Council of 500, and those who filled the long series of administrative posts from the Archons and Generals at the top to the overseers, who supervised the markets, the police, and the victims of the public sacrifices.[237]

(iii) The Janapadas and the Greek City States: Professor Agrawala's Theory Evaluated

We may stop here in order to examine the analogy of the Indian republics or self-governing communities and the *janapadas* on the one hand, and the Greek City States on the other. Of the two Indian types, the republics made up the smaller units ; while the *janapadas* comprised the larger units. We shall first deal with the question of the *janapadas* and the Greek City States. It is not possible to agree with Professor Agrawala that the *janapadas* bear an analogy with the Greek City States. He has compared the *janapadas* with the Greek City States on the basis of the following: the wide extent over which the *janapadas* and the City States were spread ; the *acropolis* of the Greek City States which is compared to the sixteen *mahājanapadas* and the twenty-five *janapadas* mentioned in the Buddhist and Jaina texts respectively ; and the evolution of the City States and the *janapadas* on the parallel lines of the clans (*genos*), which Professor Agrawala interprets to mean *jana,* of the families (*phratries*) which he interprets as *kula,* and of the city (*polis*) which he interprets as *janapada.* Professor Agrawala further strengthens his theory by maintaining that the *janapada,* like a City State, was a cultural unit, that its people were as much actuated by loyalty to the *janapada* as the citizens were to a Greek City State ; that there was citizenship in the *janapada* as connoted by the term *sa-janapada* ; and that, as in Greece, where a citizen became a member of an assembly on his attaining the age of eighteen or twenty, when he had to undergo military training for two years, so in the *janapadas* of Pāṇini, a young Kṣatriya, when eighteen years of age, acquired the privilege of being declared fit for military duty (*vayasi-ca*), and when twenty-one, the privilege of exercising all political rights and duties (*Kavacaharah-Kṣatriya-kumārah*).[238]

Evaluation of the Theory. Much as one would have liked to have agreed to the analogy of the Indian *janapadas* with the Greek City States, as propounded by Professor Agrawala, one cannot help feeling that it is more ingenious than convincing. The learned Professor has read much more into the terms mentioned by Pāṇini than perhaps what that great grammarian himself intended, and has misunderstood the essential features of the Greek City States, while attempting to formulate an analogy of the Indian *janapadas* with the Greek City States. In the first place, whatever may be the importance of Pāṇini for other purposes, the evidence of that great grammarian is not of much avail unless otherwise corroborated by the available historical evidence, both Indian and foreign, to establish the working of the political institutions of the age in which he lived. A purely grammatical construction of words and phrases interpreted to mean, as in the case of *vayasa-ca* or *kavacaharah-kṣatriya-kumārah*, while being of much importance in understanding them from the purely literary point of view, does not help us to understand whether such terms were actually in vogue in those times, and whether they definitely had the connotation, especially in the political sense, which Professor Agrawala would attach to them. It may be remembered in this connection that many interpretations were given to Pāṇini's terms and phrases by the author of the *Kāśikāvṛitti* long after that great grammarian's own times, as is clear from Professor Agrawala's excellent work itself. Literary interpretations may be given to words and phrases long after their actual use has been forgotten, or without reference to the prevailing conditions amidst which they had originated, which may not by themselves, without the help of other evidence, be taken seriously to decide issues of a political nature.[239]

The next objection to Professor Agrawala's theory centres round some considerations relating to the *janapadas* as given by Pāṇini. The latter mentions thirty *janapadas* bounded by the Kambhojas in the north, Sauvīra in the west, Aśmaka in the south, Kalinga in the south-east, and Sūramasa in the east. They comprised kingdoms like those of the Kurus, the Śālvas, the Madras, the Ambaṣṭhas, the Kālakūṭas, Magadha, Avanti, etc., self-governing communities like the Brāhmaṇakas, mere countries like those of the Bharadvājas, confederacies like those of the Śālvāyanas, and undesignated *janapadas* or country parts like Kachchha.[240] It cannot be understood how these political organizations of different types could be called by the general designation of republics. No point is made by comparing these kingdoms of diverse nature, size, resources, and potentialities, with the Greek City States. A better case could be made by comparing the above *janapadas*, as mentioned by Pāṇini, with the monarchies like those of Thebes, democracies like those of Athens, and oligarchies like those of Sparta, etc., as obtaining in Greece. But it is not such a general and broad-based comparison that would help us in our study. Neither is it so much a comparison between the monarchical organization in India and in Greece that would elucidate the problem before us. We shall have something to say about the latter below. But the main problem confronting us here is whether a comparison between the different types of *janapadas* as given by Pāṇini and the Greek City States is possible. Professor Agrawala clouds the issue when he writes that "the Janapada States in India had different systems of government just as the city states in Greece", and then proceeds to mention the terms given by Pāṇini, namely, *gaṇa, sangha, avayavas*, or members of a union, *trigarta-ṣaṣṭha* or members of a confederacy, *dvanda* or party system, etc. And not content with this, he affirms that "just as bands of mercenary armed soldiers existed in many *Āyudhajīvī Sanghas*, similarly they existed in Greece and many were enlisted in Alexander's army recruited from the Greek cities and the highlands in Thrace. The code of honour with these fighters also offers scope for comparative study."[241]

7. COMPARISON BETWEEN THE INDIAN REPUBLICS AND THE GREEK CITY STATES

Instead of pursuing further this method of confused reasoning, it would be better if we confined ourselves to some definite points like the following: firstly, whether and to what extent the self-governing communities of ancient India—and not all and sundry types of political organizations under the general designation of *janapada*, as maintained by Professor Agrawala—could be compared with some of the well-known City States of Greece ; secondly, where exactly the Indian and Greek types differ ; and, finally, what conclusions could be drawn from this comparative study of the Eastern and Western types of political organizations.

There appears to be no doubt that the Indian self-governing communities afford comparison with the Greek City States in certain respects. We do not refer here to the analogy between the Indian *janapadas* and the Greek City States in the matters of the evolution of the classes, families, tribes, and cities, as propounded by Professor Agrawala, since this development was common to most ancient peoples all the world over. The specific points of comparison may be stated thus: the need of defence ; the tie of the worship of common gods ; the fact that most of them were political units that were governed either by the majority of their citizens, or by aristocracies, or by an elected king or a president ; and the smallness and compactness of the areas comprising the republics.

Need of Defence. We can only assume that the ancient Indian republics were brought into existence by the need of self-defence, since there is no evidence to support this assumption of ours. The Greek City States, as already seen above, were likewise brought into existence by the need of self-defence.

Tie of Worship. As regards the tie of worship, that, too, may be conceded in view of the fact that in India, as elsewhere, it was one of the strongest links that bound the different sections of a people into a political unit. Whatever religious beliefs they followed, whether they were of the Hindus, the Jainas, or the Buddhists, or even the atheists, it is clear that they all had their own duties, which came within the framework of the *dharma* they followed, and which they wished to protect against their enemies. They were evidently animated by the same desire to maintain their respective *dharma* as the Greeks were prompted to foster their religious and moral codes. In this particular regard the ancient Indians were similar to the Greeks, who preserved their gods, whom they considered as their guardians, and whose benedictions were necessary for their continual welfare. Indeed, "wherever we turn in Greek or Italian history, we find that all unions of communities, small and great, are invariably held together by the bond of common worship, a special devotion to some protective deity, or combination of deities".[242] To what extent the ancient Indian self-governing communities, like all the later Indian cities and States, were given to the worship of special protective deities, will be evident from the history of many kingdoms and of cities which we shall not describe here. It could form a study by itself. But a word of caution is needed here. While broadly speaking both the ancient Indian self-governing communities and the Greek City States may be said to have been held together by the bond of religion, there was a marked difference between the two types of organizations, as will be pointed out below.

Share in Government. There is another point of comparison between the Indian self-governing communities and the Greek City States. In both there was an appreciable proportion of people who had no share in the administration of their States. Although no definite details are available in regard to the precise sections of the people that were excluded from the right of participating in government, yet we may imagine that in the purely Kṣatriya self-governing communities like the *āyudhajīvīns* mentioned by Pāṇini, it is not unlikely that the majority of the Brahmans and the Vaiśyas, and all the Śūdras were excluded from this privilege. They may be likened to the aliens and the slaves in the Greek City States, who did not possess any rights and privileges. But this comparison cannot be stretched too far in the case of the Brahmans and the Vaiśyas, who were never denied their social status and privileges, even in the most republican of the Indian self-governing communities, since they were guaranteed to them by the *dharmaśāstras*.

Size of the States. As regards the size of the States, we have no definite data concerning the Indian self-governing communities. All that we may say is that they were small and compact when compared with the larger kingdoms over which the monarchs exercised their sway. In Greece the area covered by a City State seldom exceeded a few dozens of square miles around the city or the *acropolis.* Whether this could also be said of the ancient Indian self-governing communities is doubtful. The examples of the Auḍumbaras or Oḍumbaras and the Trigartas, whose coins have been found in the Pathankot district itself ;[243] of the Kuṇindas, whose coins have been discovered between Ambālā and Shahrānpur ;[244] and of the Yaudheyas, whose coins have been unearthed over a large area stretching between the Sutlej and the Jamunā rivers,[245] suggest that we have to assume that the above States comprised compact areas, the largest of which seems to have been that of the Yaudheyas. The find-spots of the above self-governing communities reveal that their States, excepting that of the Yaudheyas, were not bigger in extent than one or two districts of the modern times.

Forms of the States. About the next point of comparison, there is more definite evidence. This refers to the nature of the ancient Indian self-governing communities. The Greek writers, who accompanied Alexander the Great in his Indian campaigns, as we have aldeady seen, are definite about the republican nature of their States. The one indisputable fact that is evident from their accounts is that the Indian self-governing communities were not ruled by kings. Some of them, like the republic of Nisaea, were governed by presidents ; others, like Peucelaotis (Puṣkalāvatī, not the one mentioned already), seem to have had two governors suggesting dual kings.[246] It is not improbable that in some of these republican communities there were Councils of Elders corresponding to the Council of 500 in Athens. But no further details about the republican States in ancient India are available. The utmost we might say is that, in so far as these were States ruled by the people themselves, they offer comparison with some of the City States like Athens, where the people themselves comprised the sovereign body.

8. CONTRAST BETWEEN THEM

(a) *The Acropolis*

But with the above the comparison between the Indian republican States and the Greek City States ends. The points of contrast may now be enumerated. The first significant point of difference between them centres round the *acropolis*. A mere comparison between the fortified towns of ancient India and the Greek City States, as is done by Professor Agrawala, is misleading.[247] The *acropolis* was not a fortified town, as he imagines ; it was the hill on which stood the fort around which were the temples of gods. The idea of a hill with a fort on it was, of course, not peculiar to the Greeks alone. Almost all the hill forts of India were of this type. But they cannot be compared with the *acropolis* of Greece for three reasons. Firstly, the forts in India, especially in the ancient, and, to some extent, in the mediaeval times, contained towns in them. This is proved by the detailed description of the construction of forts as given in Kauṭilya's *Arthaśāstra*.[248] If in the age of Kauṭilya towns were inside the fortresses, it cannot be understood how they could be compared with the *acropolis* around which the towns grew in Greece. Secondly, as is also evident from the same chapter on the construction of forts in the *Arthaśāstra*, there were other types of forts besides those which were on hills. These were the water, mountain, desert, and forest forts—none of which could be compared with the *acropolis*. Finally, in one essential detail the fortified cities of India fall short of the *acropolis*. Granting that in India, as elsewhere, the cities inside the forts were centres of human activity, which, to a certain extent, reflected the strength of the rulers and the people who occupied them, it is very doubtful whether the Indian fort-cities ever came to the level of the *acropolis* which, as in the case of Athens, was the visible embodiment of the united life and strength of the Athenians and the personification of their indomitable will.[249] This is not to belittle the importance of the Indian forts but to merely indicate that the peculiar feature of Greek life which was visible in the City States like Athens was missing in the Indian republican States, which were nurtured in an altogether different socio-political atmosphere.

(b) Tie of Kinship

As regards the tie of kinship, too, the analogy between the Indian republican States and the Greek City States does not hold good. Kinship in ancient Greece was a strong bond that knit the Greeks into a powerful socio-political fabric upon which the City States were built.[250] This cannot be said of the ancient Indian republics. Indeed, Professor Agrawala admits that the *janapadas* were formed of small communities of men, who traced their descent from a fictitious founder ; and that this false claim was perpetuated throughout generations.[251] It is not so much the disparity in the matter of tracing the ancestry of the people which contrasts the Indian republics with the Greek City States, as the diversity in the racial origin of the different sections of the Indian people, which makes it impossible for them to be compared with their Greek counterparts in regard to the structural base of their political organization.

(c) Position of Priests

We now come to the next point of difference between the Indian republics and the Greek City States. The former had, as seen earlier, presidents. But in no case were the heads of the Indian republics also the chief priests of those self-governing communities. The functions of the priests were different from those of the rulers in ancient India. While in ancient Athens, at least in its earliest stages, the head of the *gens* was also its chief priest.[252]

(d) Religious and Ethical Sanctions

Allied to the above is another point of difference between the Indian republics and the Greek City States. We have seen in the earlier pages of this book that, in the case of a conflict between the *dharmaśāstras* and the *arthaśāstras,* the former prevailed. This was because, in terms of government, the moral code and behaviour of the States were determined by the *dharma* of the land. From this it may not be inferred, as has been erroneously done by some, that the Eastern people, at least of India, were essentially a superstition dominated people, who lived under the "fearful sanction of the prescriptions of a not-to-be-questioned morality".[253] We shall have to revert to this topic later on in these pages. The rulers of the Indian republics, like those of kingdoms, were to some extent under the influence of religion in the sense that, as stated above, they could not transgress the limits of the *dharmaśāstras.* But it would be entirely a travesty of fact to infer from this that they lived a life of perpetual fear of the religious sanctions. The whole concept of *dharma* which was evolved by the genius of the Indian people was absent in Greek thought. By keeping within bounds of the *dharma,* the rulers of the republics like those of kingdoms, not only championed its cause but also perpetuated their own self-governing communities, some of which continued to exist till the days of Samudragupta the Great. Further, their deference to *dharma*, which never amounted to a slavish following of the injunctions of all priests, was also responsible for preserving the healthy and noble ideals of government which continued to exist till our own days.

This was not the case with the Greeks. In the earlier and healthier days religion played an important part in the evolution of the City States. Professor Duncker related long ago that, the forming of the agricultural communities around the *cecropia* (i.e. the later *acropolis*) under the protection of Athena, around Eleusis under the protection of Demeter, and the community of shepherds in the south under the protection of Pallas, is the oldest known fact in Attic history.[254] Gradually the religious bond which took the shape of common worship of a protecting deity or a combination of deities, gave place to reason ; and as the City States developed, "their religion was rather the adaptable personified expression, set in aesthetic rather than dogmatic forms, of their concept of nature".[255] It was undoubtedly a sign of their independent thought, and to some extent, of their political progress. It led to the Age of Illumination (530-400 B.C.) which produced some of the greatest names in history like those of Xenophon, Plato, Socrates, Thucydides, Euripides, and Aristotle.[256] But it also witnessed the growing spirit of rivalry and the monopoly of political power that brought about the disease called *stasis* by the Greeks which ultimately drowned the City States in internicine war, and, finally, led to their decay and disappearance.[257] Here we have, therefore, an essential point of difference between the ancient Indian political organizations, republican and monarchical, and the Greek City States: the former lived within the framework of the *dharmaśāstras* and survived the shocks of Time ; the latter brushed aside religious considerations, enthroned reason on the pedastal of political power, rose to unrivalled brilliance, and finally disappeared from the ken of mankind.

(*e*) *Land and Property*

We now come to the next point of difference between the Indian republican States and the Greek City States. It centres round the question of land and the institution of property. We must confess that no details about these questions are available in the annals of the Indian republics. But a careful study of Pāṇini's great work and of Kauṭilya's *Arthaśāstra* will reveal that an analogy between the *janapadas* and the Greek types of republics is untenable, so far as the vital questions of land and property are concerned. The concept of a *janapada* in Pāṇini takes us to a large country-side ; whereas in the Greek City States, as related earlier, the city and the land were one whole.[258] This fact alone should suffice to disprove the analogy. Further proof is afforded in the fact that in ancient India land belonged to the State. It was never the monopoly of a ruling class. Although Pāṇini does not explicitly maintain that all land belonged to the State, yet the reference to the measurement of land by royal officers (*kṣetrakara*), the division of land by the officers into *kṣetras* or holdings, the distribution of plots among individuals, the fixing of their size, the granting of loans to farmers for raising crops, particularly barley, and the guarding of barley fields by royal officials,[259] these undoubtedly bespeak control over land by the State. The same is true of land in the age of Kauṭilya.[260]

In ancient Greece the conditions were quite different. The aristocrats, as in Sparta, formed the bulk of the landowners.[261] Aristotle informs us that in Sparta, land was in the hands of the few, that is, the oligarchs.[262] Much more than land, the concept of property in ancient India precludes an analogy of the self-governing communities in this country with those in Greece. The detailed regulations concerning property from the days of the *Manusmṛiti* till those of the *Arthaśāstra* prove that the whole concept of property in ancient India was as broad as it was complicated.[263] But in ancient Greece, the concept of property was narrow, limited as it was to the disputes arising out of it.[264] Aristotle, who criticizes Plato's idealistic concept of community property, relates that the Lacedaemonians used others' property as if it were their own, appropriating for themselves even the produce of the fields belonging to others![265] They were so unlike the citizens of Tarentum, who shared their own property with the poor![266] It is true that we have no evidence relating to the concept of property in the republican States of ancient India; but it is permissible to presume that the republics in this matter could not have had a concept different to the well developed one prevailing in the monarchies. One has only to read the references to the corporations of warriors (*kṣatriyaśreṇi*) described in Kauṭilya's *Arthaśāstra*, and to the numerous measures suggested by him to bring them under the control of the State,[267] in order to convince oneself that the above presumption is correct. For our purpose, it may be noted that in ancient Greece a well developed concept of property did not exist; and that, hence, from the standpoint of land and property, the Indian republican communities cannot be compared with the Greek City States.

(f) *The Individual and the State*

Nowhere do we see so clearly the contrast between the Greek City States and the Indian republican communities as in the identification of the individual with the State. In a previous context it was stated that the democratic nature of the Greek City States was seen in the organized and progressive control of government by a large section of the people. In addition to that feature there was the other one relating to the idea of political order, "not of order only in the sense of traditional and trustful obedience to a hereditary monarchy, but order in the sense of conscious organisation by an intelligent body of privileged individuals".[268] Further, the Greek City States, as in the case of Athens, made a conscious endeavour to bring about a profound change in their political order, without seriously dislocating their existing social system. For instance, the great constitutional changes brought about by Solon gave the ordinary Athenian citizen "exactly that share of power for which he was naturally fitted". This was done by two simple and effective methods—first, by reclassifying the body of Athenians, not according to descent, but according to a specified annual income from land. On the basis of this economic criterion, the old social order comprising the Eupatridae, the Georgi, and the Demiurgi was replaced by the lowest class which was not elevated to the executive itself but to a position in the constitution from where it could, as it were, survey and control the executive. Their control over the executive was done in the following manner: all citizens above thirty years of age were entitled to become members of the Athenian Assembly; they shared in the election of the magistrates; they judged the conduct of the magistrates when the year of the office of the latter was over; and perhaps they had the right of deciding questions of war and peace. These changes did not constitute democracy, "a form of government then unknown, and for which there was as yet no word in the Greek language". But they initiated the democratic spirit.[269] The reins of government came to be kept in the hands of men who were qualified to wield them. The democratic spirit thus introduced into Greek life was fully realized in the days of Pericles (middle of the fifth century B.C.), when every Athenian not only became a citizen in the fullest sense of the word but identified himself to the full with the State.[270]

Admitting that the other points of contrast mentioned above are of not much consequence, the preceding one dealing with the identification of the individual with the State is enough to disprove any analogy between the Greek City States and the Indian republican communities. By no stretch of imagination can it be maintained that there was at any time any self-governing State in ancient India of the type of Athens; that there was any conscious endeavour made by the legislators in ancient India to uplift the lower social orders with a view to pitching them against the privileged ones; and that the former were given constitutional powers with which they could curtail or annul the privileges of the latter. Neither can it be affirmed that, in any age of ancient Indian history, the individuals ever identified themselves with the State, as the Athenians did with their own State.

9. CONCLUSION

The above does not mean that we have to deny the existence of oligarchical and republican States in ancient India. Not only do the accounts of the Greek historians, who accompanied Alexander the Great, confirm their existence, but the works of Pāṇini and Kauṭilya testify to their widespread and continued existence. Even in the Buddhist work called

Avadānaśataka, which was not earlier than A.D. 100, there is a reference to a *gaṇa* or republican government. A ruler of the Deccan asked a company of merchants from the Madhyadeśa as to who were the kings in their own land. They replied thus: "Sire, some countries are under the *gaṇas,* and some others are under the *rājās*" (*deva kecid-deśa gaṇādhīnaḥ kecid-rājādhīnaḥ iti*).[270a] The existence of the *gaṇas* in the early centuries of the Christian era is further proved by a legend on one of the coins of the Yaudheyas which we have cited earlier, and which reads thus: *Yaudheya gaṇasya jaya* (Victory to the *Gaṇa* of the Yaudheyas).[270b] Since the Yaudheyas were one of the clans subjugated by Samudra Gupta in the fourth century A.D., it may safely be concluded that the *gaṇas* as self-governing communities continued to exist from the seventh century B.C. till the fourth century A.D.

While we are thus sure about their prolonged existence, at the present stage of our historical knowledge, we have no information about their internal organization excepting some vague references to some kind of a council among oligarchical governments, and positive references to presidents among the republican States. When it is denied that there were republican States in ancient India identical to the Greek City States in Athens, it is not intended either to belittle or disparage the ancient system of republican government in India. The criterion of appreciating it should not be in terms of Greek history, although, as will be evident from Part Four below, a comparative study of socio-political institutions in India and in the contemporary Western world would be most fruitful from the historical point of view. The proper standard of judging the ancient Indian republican States, like all other Indian political institutions, should be to study them in the context of the ancient Indian political theories and of the environment amidst which they originated and into which after centuries of existence the republican States finally disappeared.

Whether we take the republican or the monarchical or the oligarchical forms of government in ancient India, we find in all of them the perfection of a co-ordinated partnership of all classes of people which is not met with in the history of the Greek City States. Here in India was a community fellowship of the various sections of the people in the truest sense of the term, which were held together as much by the deliberate provisions made for their material prosperity in the *dharmaśāstras* and the *nītiśāstras* as by their willing acquiescence in the need of maintaining the ideals of their respective orders. When all has been said about the citizens of the Greek City States, their unique political sense, their conscious effort at raising the lowest classes to almost the highest constitutional status, and their identification of themselves with the State, the undisputed fact remains, as Professor MacIver admits, that the Greek City State was the best example of an inclusive partnership which aimed at the ideal of a universal partnership but which, in reality, became "a bitterly exclusive" partnership that was confined to the small circle of the privileged classes beyond whom lay the masses of serfs, aliens, and slaves. This cannot be said of the ancient Indian States which were nurtured in the spirit of the *dharmaśāstras*, guided by the dictates of the *nītiśāstras*, and which worked for the welfare of all the sections of the people, on whose co-ordinated endeavour the welfare and progress of the Indian State depended.

10. CAUSES OF THE DISAPPEARANCE OF THE INDIAN AND GREEK CITY STATES

(*a*) *Decay of the Greek City States*

The difference in the outlook and nature of the Indian republican States and of the Greek City States was due to various factors amongst which their environment, their traditional legacy, and their leadership played an important part. But in the causes which brought about their decay and ultimate disappearance, we may perhaps find some similarity. Two categories of causes were primarily responsible for the disappearance of the Greek City States—internal and external. Among the former were the following: their perpetual feuds and State rivalries, their decadence in politics, and their imperfect sense of political justice ; while among the external causes mention may be made of their tendency to form leagues amongst themselves ; the desire of some to perpetually dominate over the rest ; the baneful influence of their tyrants ; the attempts of the Persians to subjugate them ; and, finally, their complete disappearance at the hands of Alexander the Great.[271]

(*b*) *Decay of the Indian Republics*

Of the above causes which brought about the decay and death of the Greek City States, a few are common to the Indian republican States as well. The first cause relating to feuds and jealousies may be said to be a fell disease which enveloped the Greeks as well as the Indians.[271a] It is this which explains the successful manner in which Alexander the Great managed to set one Indian republic against another, and conquer all of them. We may presume that the mutual jealousies and feuds among the Indian monarchical and republican States of Taxila, Peucelaotis (Puṣkalāvati), Nysa—the first of which was under a king, while the second and third were under their presidents—gave that Macedonian Conqueror the necessary handle to subvert them and the other Indian States. There is definite proof in the accounts of Greek historians, who had accompanied Alexander the Great, of the bitter rivalry between the Indian republican and monarchical States. In addition to the three examples, we have mentioned above, we may add that of the unnamed Indian communities that divulged to Alexander the secrets of the impregnable rock fortress of Aornos, and enabled him to conquer it. The king of Taxila, whom the

Greeks called Taxiles, and who had sided with Alexander from the beginning, was responsible for divulging news about the great Porus. There was another, and a less significant Indian ruler called also Porus, who also betrayed to Alexander the news of the great Porus, and who was likewise an enemy of the latter. Indeed, the whole story of Alexander's conquest of the Punjab seems to suggest that there was no unity of purpose at all amongst the Indian republican and monarchical States, that they were guided by decadent politics, and that, like the Greeks, they had an imperfect sense of political justice.[272] Alexander the Great was the common enemy of both the Greek City States and the Indian republics, with this difference that, whereas the Greek City States were practically wiped out never to raise their heads again, here in India notwithstanding their having been subjugated, and in some instances, completely annihilated, republican States continued to exist till the fourth century A.D., when they seem to have finally succumbed to the great Samudra Gupta and to the complex surroundings that followed in the wake of the invasions of the Huns in the reign of his son and successor Candra Gupta II Vikramaditya, and particularly in that of the next ruler, Kumāra Gupta.

One interesting cause of the disappearance of corporations (*śreṇi*) is given by Kauṭilya, who discusses the major question of the calamities that were to be overcome by the State. He cites his own teacher's view that the troubles due to a corporation of people cannot be put down, since a corporation consists of a number of men and causes oppression by theft and violence. Kauṭilya, on the other hand, said that it was very easy to get rid of the troubles from a corporation, since it rose or fell with a king, and since the king could put down a corporation either by arresting its leader (*śreṇimukhya*) or by a pact with the corporation itself (*Śreṇimukya-ekadeśopagraheṇa va*).[272a] To what extent he himself recommended this measure to his royal master in the matter of wiping out the republican communities of his own days cannot be determined for want of evidence. But here was a cause fraught with the greatest danger to the Indian republican States.

Finally, there is another reason which explains the disappearance of the republican States of ancient India, and which is not met with in the history of the Greek City States. This refers to the tendency of the republican or self-governing communities to change over to the monarchical form of government. The coins of the Yaudheyas, who have figured above as a self-governing community of the *gaṇa* type, illustrate this point. Some of the coins of the Yaudheyas, like the one cited earlier, contain the legend of the *Yaudheya gaṇa* ; but others unmistakably contain the names of rulers like Bhānuvarma, or merely the name *Mahārājasa,* or the legend *Bhagavato Svāmina Brāhmaṇa Yaudheya,*[272b] thereby suggesting that, although the Yaudheyas reckoned themselves, on the whole, as a *gaṇa* or a republican clan, yet they had sections amongst them which had kings or chieftains. In other words, it appears as if we are to understand from the history of the Yaudheyas themselves that the republican form of government gradually gave place to the monarchical form of government amongst them. If this presumption is correct, their disappearance as a self-governing community is easily understood: they were simply absorbed by the larger monarchical States like those of the Mauryas, or the Imperial Guptas or of the Huns under Toramāṇa and and Mihirakula. The history of the republican communities has completely disproved the statement of Kauṭilya that "the corporation of clans being invincible in its nature, and being free from the unrestrained calamities of anarchy can have a permanent existence on earth".[272a] Kauṭilya has used a phrase in this context—*arāja vyasanābādhaḥ*—(unrestrained destruction during a period of *arāja*) which now requires a more detailed explanation.

CHAPTER VII

ANARCHY AND INTERREGNUM

A. THE INDIANS NOT IDEALISTS

THE INFERENCE need not be drawn from the foregoing estimate of the republican and other forms of governments that the ancients either believed in or created visionary conditions for the people to live in. There was no Plato in ancient India. The Hindu theorists and statesmen were far too realistic to think of an age of idyllic felicity. They were aware of periods of misrule, confusion, and anarchy, which sometimes haunted them. After all in a vast sub-continent like India, whose ancient boundaries had far transcended the north-western regions, and whose population was composed of diverse races, it was impossible that there could have been everywhere and in all ages a perfect type of government that created ideal conditions of life. We find, therefore, in ancient literature repeated references to anarchy and its evil effects on society.

B. THE TERMS CONNOTING ANARCHY: APARUDDHA AND ARĀJATĀ

A brief survey of this side of the ancient Indian political thought will reveal that throughout ancient history, the people were confronted with the dread of political confusion. The two technical terms which denoted political turmoil were *aparuddha* and *arājatā* or merely *arājatam*, or, as in some instances, *arājaka*. The first two terms are met with in the *Atharva Veda*, the *Samhitas*, and the *Brāhmaṇas* thereby suggesting that anarchy was a feature of periodic occurrence in the life of the ancient Indian State. *Aparuddha* referred to the expulsion of kings from their realms, and to their efforts to regain their lost kingdoms ;[273] while *arājatā* connoted the period of no-rule. The difference between the two terms lay obviously in the relative degree of political and social confusion that marked them.

C. ANTIQUITY OF APARUDDHA

The story of Duṣṭarītu Paumsāyana, who has figured above in connection with the problem of hereditary monarchy, illustrates the term *aparuddha*. It is given in the *Śatapatha Brāhmaṇa* thus: a people called Sriñjayas expelled king Duṣṭarītu from his kingdom, which had come down to him through ten generations. They had also expelled Revottaras Pāṭava Cakra Sthāpati, who was, as his name implies, a sage.[274] He said to Duṣṭarītu Paumsāyana: "I will perform the Sautrāmaṇi (sacrifice) for thee, and will confer upon thee the dominion over the Sriñjayas." The latter seem to have been helped by the Kaurava king, Bālhika Prātipīya, who stoutly opposed the restoration of king Duṣṭarītu to his kingdom. This is apparent from what follows in the *Śatapatha Brāhmaṇa*:

> Now Bālhika Prātipīya, the Kaurava king, heard people say this—'There is that Duṣṭarītu Paumsāyana who has been expelled from the kingdom which has come down to him through ten generations: for him Cakra Sthāpati wants to perform the Sautrāmaṇi and to confer upon him the dominion over the Sriñjayas'. He said—'I will just tell him that if he wants to confer dominion upon him, he will indeed exclude him from dominion'. But Cakra Sthāpati performed the sacrifice, and re-instated Duṣṭarītu on the throne of the Sriñjayas.

It is then related that "he (Bālhika Prātipīya) then went home and said, 'It is not so (as we had thought): that kingdom of the Sriñjayas now belongs to Duṣṭarītu ; in such and such a manner has that Cakra Sthāpati this day performed the sacrifice' ".[275]

The above story refers to the expulsion of both king Duṣṭarītu and of his priest Cakra Sthāpati by the people, obviously with the aid of a friendly neighbouring king. The story also relates that Duṣṭarītu was re-instated by the priest with the aid of a supernatural agency. But it is evident from it that monarchs were driven out by their people in the ancient times ; and that the former made every attempt, including that of invoking heaven, to regain their lost thrones.[276]

From the time the Sriñjayas drove out king Duṣṭarītu till his re-instatement by Cakra Sthāpati, the Sriñjayas appear to have been under the form of *arājatā*, that is, the condition of being without a king. It is not clear from the *Śatapatha Brāhmaṇa*, which relates the above story, whether the Sriñjayas during that period were subject to all the horrors of anarchy which are described in the later epic literature. Perhaps there was some confusion in their kingdom which gave Duṣṭarītu a chance of regaining his lost throne. But that there were spells of anarchy in the history of the ancient Indian States is apparent from the occurrence of the word *arājatā* in the *Taittirīya* and *Aitareya Brāhmaṇas*.[277]

D. HISTORY OF ANARCHY

The possibility of the people's expelling their kings and the justification for such action are both apparent from the *Manusmṛiti* which states the following:

> A king who properly inflicts (punishment) prospers with respect to (those)

three (means of happiness) ; but he who is voluptuous, partial, and deceitful will be destroyed, even through the (unjust) punishment (which he inflicts). Punishment (possesses) a very bright lustre, and is hard to be administered by men with unimproved minds ; it strikes down the king who swerves from his duty, together with his relatives.[278]

We have in these statements the clearest indication that the people could not only depose a king but even kill him together with his relatives, if he swerved from his duty as laid down in the *dharmaśāstras*. The reference to the death also of the relatives of the king suggests the extremination of the royal family. It seems as if Manu in the above verses tacitly sanctioned the outbreak of a sort of a violent revolution which ended with the wiping out of the royal family, although there is no explicit reference to a revolution anywhere in the *Manusmṛiti*. But in a later context, Manu undoubtedly refers to the deposition and death of a king at the hands of the people. "That king who through folly rashly oppresses his kingdom, (will), together with his relatives, ere long be deprived of his life and of his kingdom."[279] No clearer proof than this is needed that, even according to the authors of the *dharmaśāstras*, the people could, in certain grave contingencies, depose and kill a bad ruler together with his relatives. This has been considered by some scholars as a political right although, in our opinion, it is not specifically called a right granted to the people in the sense of the rights which will be discussed below.

That this rare privilege was, indeed, an acknowledged one is apparent from the *Mahābhārata*, wherein it is stated that the people should gird themselves up and kill a cruel king, who does not protect his subjects, who extracts taxes and simply robs them of their wealth, and who gives no lead to his subjects. Such a king is an incarnation of Evil and Strife (Kali). If a king after declaring "I shall protect you" does not protect his subjects, he should be killed (by the people) after forming themselves into a confederacy, like a dog that is afflicted with madness.[280] The deposition of a ruler and tyrannicide are again justified in the same epic in another context.[281] The failure of a king in his primary duty of protecting his subjects, his greed, and his tyrannical rule—these were sufficient causes, therefore, which entitled the subjects to form themselves into a confederacy and depose and kill their king. We may presume that the people in such circumstances were powerful enough to take the drastic action of killing their ruler ; but the explicit reference to the wiping out of even his relatives, as given in the *Manusmṛiti*, and to the forming of a confederacy by the people, as mentioned in the *Mahābhārata*, suggests that they could perhaps invoke the aid of a neighbouring ruler, who was inimical to the king but friendly to the people themselves. This, however, is only a supposition.

E. ANARCHY DESCRIBED

That the ancient Indians were fully aware of the horrible consequences of a State's being without a ruler is clear from the detailed picture of a kingless State as given in the *Rāmāyaṇa,* in the *Ayodhyā Kāṇḍa* of which we have the following:

> On the departure of Rāma to the forest, the aged Emperor Daśaratha out of sorrow died. There was lamenting and weeping in the capital, and on the next day the Brahman advisers to the State, together with the ministers and other illustrious wise men, met together in the royal assembly; and, in the presence of the illustrious sage Vasiṣṭha, after briefly relating the sad events, declared their mind thus: 'A member of the House of Ikṣvāku must be appointed king lest the country fall into ruin. On a kingdom destitute of a ruler, clouds charged with lightning and thunder pour down rains and hail (*arājakam hi no rāṣṭram na vināśam avāpnuyāt*). In a rulerless land (*na-rājaka*), the peasants sow no grain; fathers and sons oppose each other, and wives no longer remain subject to their husbands! In a rulerless land, there is no peace, thieves and brigands exercise their power; women, unfaithful to their consorts, leave their homes. Where women lose their virtue, truth is also lost. In a rulerless land, there are no assemblies, nor do the people visit pleasant parks and gardens or build temples and homes of rest. In such a land, the self-controlled Brahmans offer no sacrifice, nor do those of pious vows, assist them in the sacred rites. In a rulerless land, the Brahmans do not receive their due share of the sacrificial fees; neither do actors nor leaders of song or dance find joy in such a land. The holy festivals promoting the land's prosperity are no longer held, nor do those reciting the holy tradition give satisfaction to their hearers. In a rulerless land, virgins adorned with golden ornaments, do not frequent the flower gardens at the close of day, nor do the devotees of pleasure, riding swift chariots in company with charming damsels, repair to the forest. In such a land, the wealthy are not protected, nor does the husbandman, the cowherd, and the shepherd sleep at ease with open doors. In a rulerless land, great elephants of sixty years of age do not wander on the king's highways adorned with tinkling of bells. The twanging of the archer's bow is no longer heard, nor do the merchants travelling on the roads in security bring their goods to sell them from distant lands. In a rulerless land, the self-controlled sage, fixing his mind, in contemplation, on his identity with the all-pervading spirit (*ātman*), receives no hospitality when night falls. Wealth is not unassailable, nor are man's needs supplied, the armies have no leaders, nor can they match the enemy in war. In a rulerless country, no man, gorgeously apparelled, riding in an excellent chariot, drawn by swift steeds, can go forth without

fear; nor can the learned disputant propound his doctrines in the city or forest. In such a land, garlands and sweatmeats, alms and other gifts, are not offered by worshippers at a sacrifice, nor in the springtime, do the princes, like blossoming trees, adorned with sandalwood and aloe paste (*candana-āgarūḥ-rūṣitāḥ*), walk abroad. A kingdom without a sovereign is like a river without water, a forest without vegetation, or a cow without a cowherd. As a chariot is known by its standard, as a fire is indicated by smoke. so the king, a light representing the kingdom, has been extinguished. No man loves his own kind in a rulerless land, but each slays and devours the other daily like fish (*narājake janapade svakaṁ bhavati kasyacit matsyā ivaṁ narā nityaṁ bhakṣayanti parasparaṁ*). Atheists and materialists, exceeding the limits of their caste, assume dominion over others, there being no king to exercise control over them. As the eyes continuously point out what is dangerous to the body, promoting its welfare, so the king regards the advantage of his people, promoting truth and *dharma*. The king leads his people on the path of righteousness and guides them in integrity; he is the parent of his subjects and their benefactor (*yathā dṛṣthiḥ śarīrasya nityaṁ-eva pravartate tathā narendro rāṣṭrasya prabhāvaḥ satya-dharmayoḥ rājā satyaṁ ca dharmas-ca kulavatāṁ-kulaṁ rājā mātā pitā ca-eva rājā hitakaro nṛiṇām*). In the path of duty, he excels even Yama, Kubera, Indra, and Varuṇa. The king, discerning good and evil, protects his kingdom; bereft of him, the country is enveloped in darkness. Oh holy Vasiṣtha, while the king lived, we obeyed thy mandates like the ocean kept within its boundaries. Oh great Brahman, consider our words and the danger threatening this, our kingdom, and appoint some one king if he be of the House of Ikṣvāku.'[282]

F. INTERREGNUM

The above long passage is important from the following points of view: firstly, it fully justifies the need of State concerning which we have already discussed above.

Secondly, it refers to one of the theories also discussed in the earlier pages of this work, namely, the Paternalistic theory, in the sense that it compares the king to a father. But the explicit statement that it is the duty of the king to protect the subjects is a qualification which does not permit a ruler to be an irresponsible father.

Thirdly, it clearly points to what might be called an *interregnum*, and to the action taken by the *mantripariṣad* or council of ministers, to solve the problem of electing the next ruler. Although Emperor Daśaratha had already bequeathed the kingdom to Bharata, as Daśaratha's spiritual adviser, Vasiṣtha, himself admits in the next chapter, yet from the implorations of the *mantripariṣad* to the same sage, it may be concluded that, during the interval after the death of the Emperor and before the accession of the next ruler, Bharata, some time elapsed when the *mantripariṣad* led by the sage Vasiṣṭha was the controlling factor in the State. We are thus led to presume that, during an *interregnum*, which was legally unavoidable, the power of deciding as to who was to be the next ruler, rested with the *mantripariṣad* led by the chief spiritual adviser or, in his absence, by the prime minister.

Fourthly, the continued use of the word *janapada* meaning the country in general, or the land, confirms the meaning given to it in this book, namely, the realm, or the kingdom, or the country, rather than the fantastic one attributed to it by some historians.

And, finally, the admirable picture of a kingless State given above definitely points to a stage in the history of the State when there was *arājatā*, that is, when the stronger daily devoured the weaker like fish (*matsyā ivaṁ narā nityaṁ bhakṣayanti parasparam*).[283] This unmistakably refers to a condition when there was absolutely no safety in the kingless State.

The whole picture of such a State as described in the *Rāmāyaṇa* unequivocally points to a state of continued confusion and chaos in the land which made it impossible for either law to continue or society to prosper. That such a pitiable state of affairs should ever have been described in that great epic is a point which seems to have escaped the notice of scholars till now. Why should such a picture of anarchy ever have been described at such length only in that epic, and not in any earlier work? To this question we have only a hypothetical answer to give, since there is nothing to substantiate it. It appears that in some age immediately preceding that depicted in the epic, there was a period of confusion which had witnessed a complete collapse of both the social and political order unleashing the forces of turmoil. It was precisely to warn the people against a repetition of such a chaotic condition of life, when men behaved like fishes, that the author of the *Rāmāyaṇa* seems to have inserted it in his great poem.

The evils of anarchy thus pictured in the *Rāmāyaṇa* are repeated in the *Mahābhārata*, and by the later writers like Kāmandaka, who was a close follower of Kauṭilya, and by the author of the *Mastya Purāṇa*.[284]

G. ANARCHY IN JAINA AND BUDDHIST WORKS

Lest it might be said that the concept of a kingless State was the invention of the fertile brain of the Hindu writers on Politics, we may turn to Buddhist and Jaina literature in order to see whether the Buddhists and the Jainas also had any concept of anarchy in a kingless State. The *Jātaka Stories* contain the statement that a country without government cannot ever exist (*arājakam nāma raṭṭhum paletuṁ na sakakā*).[284a] In the famous words attributed to Buddha, as given in the *Mahāparinirbbāṇa Sutta*, cited elsewhere in this work, in regard to the Vṛijjian (Vajjian) confederacy, there is the clearest evidence of the lack of unity in the republican communities,[284b] although there is no specific reference to anarchy in this passage. We have to read the Jaina works in order to get a clearer concept of anarchy. In the Jaina canonical work called *Ācārango Sūtra* (*Āyaranga Suttam*), the following is said:

> A (Jaina) monk or nun on a pilgrimage, whose road lies through a country where there is no king, or which is ruled by a *gaṇa* form of government, or by a *yuvarāja* or crown prince, or by two kings, or which is *vairājya* State, or which is a *viruddharājya*, should, if there be some other places for walking about or friendly districts, not choose the former road for their voyage. The Kevalin says, 'This is the reason: the ignorant populace might bully or beat, etc. the mendicants': (*gāmāṇugāmam dūjjamāṇe aṁtara se arāyāṇi va gaṇarāyāṇi va juvarāyāṇi va dorajjāṇi va verajjāṇi va viruddharājjāṇi va sati lāḍhe vihārāe saṁtharamāṇehim janavaehiṁ no vihara-vattiyāe pavajjejjā gamaṇāe Kevali būya āyāṇaṁ eyaṁ te naṁ bālā ayaṁ teṇe taṁ cevajava gamaṇāe tato saṁjayāṁ eva gāmaṇugāmaṁ dūjjejjā*).[285]

As to which age the above account of the different forms of government under which anarchy prevailed refers, is a difficult matter, since the date of the *Jaina Sūtras* is itself not decided. But since the first edition of the *Sūtras* took place under the Venerable Devarddhigaṇi in A.D. 453, they may be assigned to the early centuries A.D., as has been opined by Professor Hermann Jacobi.[286] We have seen above that the republican communities finally disappeared from history only in the age of the Imperial Guptas (fourth century A.D.). We may, therefore, presume that the above Jaina account refers to the first three centuries of the Christian era. It cannot be made to apply either to western or southern India, where there were no *gaṇa* republics, and where, as is evident from the available historical records, there was stable monarchical government from the early centuries A.D. onwards. On the strength of the *Avadānaśataka* cited earlier, which has also to be assigned to the early centuries of the Christian era, it may be said that the *gaṇa* form of government, where, according to the *Ācārango Sūtra*, anarchy prevailed, has to be assigned to the Madhyadeśa.

H. KAUṬILYA ON ANARCHY

The point to be noted is not so much the locale of anarchy as the nature of the kingless State itself, and the justification for assuming that there were in any period of ancient Indian history spasms of misrule. Here it would be worth while to remember the passage from Kauṭilya cited above, relating to the invincibility of clans and to their being free from unrestrained calamities. The fact that Kauṭilya refers to the *arāja vyasanābādhaḥ* proves that he was aware of chaotic conditions in a State.[286a] We cannot think of the Mauryan Government of which he was the great Prime Minister tolerating misrule or anarchy of any type whatsoever. Indeed, the whole tenor of Kauṭilya's *Arthaśāstra* bespeaks a stern attitude to miscreants both of the political and the social types. And, as remarked elsewhere in this book, Kauṭilya stood for the unequivocal sway of the central government which would tolerate no maladministration on the part of guilds and corporations. We have, therefore, to imagine that Kauṭilya had in mind the condition of some parts of the country outside the Mauryan dominion or of an earlier age when there were republican governments in north-western India, as is proved by the accounts of Greek historians and by the famous work of Pāṇini.

Kauṭilya refers to anarchy not only in the passage cited above but elsewhere in his great book, where we have unmistakable allusions to the migrations by the people, anarchy, and national disturbances. Sometimes he hints at one or all of them indirectly; at other times, he plainly mentions them. In Book I, Chapter X on Ascertaining by Temptations the Purity or Impurity in the Character of Ministers, Kauṭilya makes a dismissed priest, who plays the rôle of a tempter, instigate a minister, with a view to finding out the integrity of the latter, thus:

> This king is unrighteous, well, let us set up in his place another who is righteous, or who is born of the same family as of this king, or who is kept imprisoned, or a neighbouring king of his family and of self-sufficiency (*ekapragriham*), or a wild chief (*āṭavikam*), or an upstart (*aupapādikam*); this attempt is to the liking of all of us; what does thou think?[287]

Since we cannot conceive of a lawful ruler's being displaced by an unlawful ruler like a forest chieftain, and an upstart, we have to assume that Kauṭilya had in his mind, while writing this passage, a state of affairs which amounted to anarchy.

In another context Kauṭilya clearly refers to a stage in the life of a State when there was confusion in the land resulting in the migration of people. This is in connection with the question of ownership and resumption of gifts. The passage is the following:

> When the owners others than minors, the aged, those that are afflicted with disease, or calamities, those that are sojourning abroad, or those that have deserted their country during a civil war, neglect for ten years their property which is kept under the enjoyment of others, they shall forfeit their title to it (*yat svaṁ dravyaṁ-anyaiḥibhujyamānaṁ daśavarṣāṇi-upekṣeta hīyetāsya anyatra bālavṛiddha-vyādhita-vyasaniproṣita-deśatyāgarājyavibhramebhyaḥ*).

The term *rājyavibhrama* could have referred only to the unsettled conditions resulting from a civil war like the one which the country witnessed when his own royal patron had overthrown the Nandas.[288]

Kauṭilya recommended that a king may be deserted by his people in certain contingencies. In the course of a long discussion of the views of his political predecessors on time-serving, he affirmed that "when wealth and honour are discontinued, such a king may be abandoned" (*artha-mānā-pakṣepe ca parityāgaḥ*).[289]

I. DR. JAYASWAL'S THEORY OF ANARCHY

1. THE THEORY STATED

With the above discussion of the antiquity and nature of *arājatā* or anarchy before us, we are in a position to evaluate the theory of anarchy as propounded by the late Dr. Jayaswal. Basing his remarks on the same passages from the Hindu, Jaina, and Buddhist works which have been cited above, that eminent historian evolved an elaborate theory of anarchy which may be briefly stated thus: the *arājaka* was an idealistic non-ruler State "which came to be the object of derision of political writers of Hindu India. The ideal of this constitution was that Law was to be taken as the ruler and there should be no man-ruler. The basis of the State was considered to be mutual agreement or social contract between the citizens. This was the extreme democracy almost Tolstoïan in ideal." The *Jaina Sūtras* (cited earlier in this work) take it "as a constitutional experiment which had been tried more than once in this country. The *Sūtra* mentions the form as a living institution. The group where this constitution occurs is composed of all real and historical forms of government." Then, referring to the passage in the Jaina work *Ācārango Sūtra* cited above, the author states that it mentions the following forms of government—the non-ruler States, the *gaṇa*-ruled States, the *yuvarāja*-ruled States, the two-ruled States, the *vairājya* States, and the *viruddharājjāṇi* or States ruled by parties. Of these the *yuvarāja* States were evidently of the type referred to in Khāravela's famous Hāthigumpha inscription as one which that great monarch is said to have presided over before his coronation (*Yuvarājam pasāsitam*). "Legally such a period of rule was considered as interregnum. Government was probably in the hands of some council of regency, the sovereign being too young." The *viruddharājjāṇi* States were typified by the Andhaka Vṛṣni State. The discussion of the *arājaka* State in the *Mahābhārata* also "shows familiarity with a written theory of the State of the Arājaka constitution". The monarchists really adopted the social contract theory "originally formulated by the Arājakas".[290]

2. EVALUATION OF THE ABOVE THEORY

The above theory has been altogether discounted by Dr. Kane, and Professors Rangaswamy Aiyangar and U. N. Ghoshal, as being the result of the over-patriotic desire of its learned exponent to find the latest European thought in our ancient books, and as being both novel and unproven.[291]

But more valid reasons are necessary before we could reject Dr. Jayaswal's theory. At the outset it is better if we recollect the Hindu, Jaina, and Buddhist authorities cited above, which have dwelt on the nature of *arājatā*. If the evidence of all these sources is accepted, then, Dr. Jayaswal's theory has no basis in ancient Indian political thought. Firstly, as remarked earlier, there is no proof of there having been in ancient India at any time an Indian Plato, who visualized an ideal condition of socio-political existence which was permeated by an atmosphere of extreme individualism. Secondly, whatever may be the reflex of the concept of individualism in the ancient Aryan philosophical speculation, it is not visible in the writings of the Indian political thinkers. Thirdly, extreme individualism, which Dr. Jayaswal would make the essence of an *arājaka* or *arājatā* State, was altogether incompatible with the age-long concept of co-ordinated partnership which was preached by the *dharmaśāstras* and the *nītiśāstras,* and concerning which we have given ample evidence in the previous pages of this book. Fourthly, the concept of "a no-ruler constitution" is as much misleading as it is incorrect. The term *arājaka* denoted a simple phenomenon of a country's being without a ruler with the possible attendant consequences of confusion, in case such a condition was allowed to continue. The state of being *without a ruler,* which is certainly intelligible, was not the same as the condition of a *no-ruler-constitution,* that is, of an idyllic people enjoying an extreme form of democracy, having realized that government was an evil. This involves the social contract theory which will be discussed below. As an attempt to explain a phase in the history of ancient Indian political thought, the *arājaka* theory, as expounded by Dr. Jayaswal, fails to explain the origin of the State, because it does not account for this phenomenon, viz., how a people disbelieving in government, came to bind themselves with a constitution which presupposes a government! And as an essay in grafting the comparatively modern Western theory of individualism, as expounded by Herbert Spencer, on the ancient Indian soil, it fails to meet the biological aspect of the theory of individualism. And, finally, Dr. Jayaswal's theory is self-contradictory in the sense that we cannot conceive of a people's enjoying unrestricted felicity, and as considering government an evil, basing their socio-political organization on a legal and communal foundation which is in itself the result of the legislative action of the State. The *arājaka* theory of Dr. Jayaswal has to be discarded as being fallacious and self-contradictory.

CHAPTER VIII

THE SOCIAL CONTRACT THEORY

A. THE BASIS OF THE THEORY

THE *arājatā* theory which, according to some, is supposed to involve the social contract theory, thus leads us to a study of the latter. We may first describe the basis of the theory as it appears in the ancient Indian political works, and how it has been interpreted by modern Indian historians ; then, explain the social contract theory as it has been understood in Western political thought ; and, finally, see how far the ancient Indian thought is in accordance with its modern counterpart.

1. IN THE MANUSMRITI AND IN THE MAHABHARATA

The social contract theory in the Indian political thought is supposed to rest on the statements in the *Manusmṛiti,* in the *Mahābhārata,* and in the *Arthaśāstra* of Kauṭilya. After stating that the duty of the Kṣatriya (the king)—who has received, according to the rules, the sacrament prescribed in the *Veda*—was to protect the whole world, the *Manusmṛiti* says thus: "For, when these creatures, being without a king, through fear dispersed in all directions, the Lord created a king for the protection of the whole (creation)."[292] The basis of the social contract theory, as given in the *Śānti-parvan* of the *Mahābhārata,* is related to the divine right of kings, which has been cited in an earlier context in this book. In this version the first king was Vainya, and not Manu, as already stated above. Vainya is called upon by the gods and the sages to take an oath that he would protect the world, and that he would carry out his duties, not according to his own fancy, but according to the science of government.[293]

2. IN KAUTILYA

Kauṭilya's version of the theory is interesting. He refers to it in two contexts —in an earlier and in a later context. In the earlier one he merely states that when the law of punishment is kept in abeyance, it gives rise to such disorder as is implied in the law of the fishes ; for in the absence of a magistrate, the strong will swallow the weak, but under his protection, the weak will resist the strong *(apraṇīto hi mātsyanyāyam-udbhāvayati balīyān-abalaṁ-hi-grasate daṇḍadharābhāve tena guptaḥ prabhavat-iti*).[294] There is no reference to any contract in this passage which merely introduces us to the first stage in the chaotic condition of society, when the law of the jungle prevailed. Instead of a contract, we have the positive assertion that such an anarchical condition could be prevented only by the appointment of a magistrate, under whose protection the weak would resist the strong.

In a later context, however, Kauṭilya writes:

> People suffering from anarchy, as illustrated by the proverbial tendency of a large fish swallowing a small one (*mātsyanyāyābhibhūtaḥ prajāḥ*) first elected Manu, the Vaivasvata, to be their king; and allotted one-sixth of the grains grown and one-tenth of the merchandise as sovereign dues. Fed by this payment, kings took upon themselves the responsibility of maintaining the safety and security of their subjects (*yoga-kṣemāvahāḥ*), and of being answerable for the sins of their subjects, when the principle of levying just punishments and taxes has been violated. Hence, hermits, too, provide the king with one-sixth of the grains gleaned by them, thinking that 'it is a tax payable to him who protects us'.[295]

B. THE SOCIAL CONTRACT THEORY AS INTERPRETED BY PROFESSOR BHANDARKAR

1. HIS THEORY

Historians have taken the above to be the Indian version of the social contract theory as given by Kauṭilya.[296] Superficially it appears as if we have in the above the counterpart of the social contract theory as it was known in the West. Professor D. R. Bhandarkar, while describing the theory of kingship, and while commenting on the same passage in *Arthaśāstra* of Kauṭilya, affirms that it is "the same story which is repeated but at greater length in Chapter 67 of the Śānti Parvan"; that it is similar to the account of the origin of monarchy as described in the Buddhist canonical works like *Aggañña-suttanta of the Dīgha Nikāya,* and the *Mahāvāstu*; that these accounts make it clear that sovereignty in ancient India "originated in a social contract"; that the state of nature as described in the above theory was one of war, "which came to an end only when men agreed to give their liberty into the hands of a sovereign"; that this theory bears a remarkably close resemblance to the one propounded by Hobbes; but that while Hobbes "expounded this notion of Agreement by saying that absolute power was irrevocably transferred to the ruler", the social contract theory, as advocated by the Hindu *Arthaśāstras,* maintained that "the king was still the servant of the people", the sixth part of the grains and the tenth part of the merchandise (obviously as recommended by Kauṭilya) being the wages which he received for the services rendered to the pople. Professor Bhandarkar goes to the extreme length of maintaining that the Hindu theory was superior to that propounded by Hobbes, since it limited the king's power making the king appear "as merely a public servant though of the highest order".[297]

2. EVALUATION OF PROFESSOR BHANDARKAR'S THEORY

We cannot help remarking that the distinguished historian in his exposition of the contract theory has done scant justice to both Kauṭilya and Hobbes. In the first place, Professor Bhandarkar failed to notice the two contexts in which the *mātyasanyāya* or the law of the fishes occurs in the *Arthaśāstra*. In the earlier context, as stated above, Kauṭilya explicitly mentions the presence of a magistrate, whom he would liken to a king, because he wielded the *daṇḍa* but without reference to any contract. This precludes the association of any agreement between the king and the people, although it certainly refers, as remarked earlier, to a state of anarchy. Secondly, in the later passage, Kauṭilya puts the whole passage in the mouth of a spy. Indeed, the passage referring to the so-called social contract is in the chapter entitled Protection of Parties For or Against One's Own Cause in One's Own State. Kauṭilya begins this chapter by stating that the king should set up spies over his own prime ministers, and then proceed to espy both the citizens and the country people. He then pitches one spy against another, and makes the latter utter the words relating to the alleged social contract theory. This makes the whole case, which scholars have made out for a social contract theory, supposed to have been enunciated by Kauṭilya, rather weak in the sense that it is not an equivocal statement relating to any contract but an indirect reference to it which is supposed to rest on some foundation. If we have to accept as valid this part of the passage in the *Arthaśāstra,* which a spy is made to utter, then we have to accept as valid also the opinion of the earlier spy, who maintained that the king, being endowed with all desirable qualities, was a stranger to such tendencies as would lead him to oppress citizens and country people by levying heavy fines and taxes. We should likewise accept as valid the latter part of the passage in which the alleged social contract theory is supposed to be couched, wherein Kauṭilya makes the spy say that in the king the duties of Indra (the rewarder) and Yama (the punisher) are blended, that he is the visible dispenser of punishments and rewards, and that if any one disregarded kings, that person would be visited with divine punishments.[298] The contexts in which the so-called social contract theory occurs in the *Arthaśāstra* seem to suggest that the great Mauryan Prime Minister was more for rejecting its validity and less for accepting it as a political axiom. Indeed, the whole trend of Kauṭilya's great book is a negation of any contract between the king and the people, being entirely in the direction of extreme centralization and of the supreme will of the ruler. It is this which explains why Kauṭilya, while explaining the law of the fishes in an earlier context, does not refer to any contract between the ruler and the people but merely to the existence of a magistrate under whose protection the weak will even resist the strong. One fails to see, therefore, how on the strength of the statements made by Kauṭilya, one could maintain with another eminent historian, Professor Rangaswami Aiyangar, that "a theory like this, sanctifying not merely the state and the institution of kingship, but also the reciprocal duties of the sovereign and subject", was "accepted by the leading political writer and renowned statesman of the fourth century B.C."[299]

C. THE SOCIAL CONTRACT THEORY AS EXPOUNDED IN THE WEST

A detailed examination of the social contract theory, as described by the ancient Indian writers, and of the modern version of the same by the Western theorists, reveals that the resemblance between the two is superficial, while the contrast between them is marked. Both the theories are of great antiquity. Mention has already been made of the *arājatā* concept which may be said to have had within it the germs of a contract. In Western political thought the social contract theory goes back to the fourth century B.C., when the Greek City States were faced with the question of annihilation, first, at the hands of the Macedonian Conqueror, and, then, at those of the Romans. When the Greek philosophers were confronted with the loss of their independence, they turned to the question of replacing civic life by mere happiness which the individual might need. The Sophists took the lead by stating that the State was the result of a voluntary agreement among men, but that it was a hindrance to self-realization, and, therefore, opposed to nature. The Epicurians maintained that the State rested upon individual self-interest. Accordinng to them law was an agreement of utility entered into by the individuals in order to secure protection against violence. Here was the beginning of the later idea of a deliberate agreement amongst men to which the later system of Roman law gave a further impetus, when it developed the concept of obligation by contract. Gradually the Roman jurists incorporated in it the idea of government by contract, when they said that the power of the Roman Emperor was based upon the consent of the Roman people. That this idea was, indeed, common to the ancient peoples is proved by the fact that in the Old Testament there is a covenant made before God by king David and the Elders of Israel.[300]

When Hobbes took up the idea of contract, it had already passed the stages of agreements in the feudal system and of the Conciliar movement in the Church which had revived the concepts of natural rights, social contract, and popular consent. But these ideas were lost in the struggles that followed in the seventeenth and eighteenth centuries, when the theory of the divine right of kings unsuccessfully fought against the growing strength of popular sovereignty based on the freedom of the individual and his right to rebel. It was at this stage that Hobbes (*The Leviathan*, 1651). Locke (*Two Treatises on Government*, 1690), and Rousseau (*Du Contrat Social*, 1762) took up the thread of contract shaping it in three different ways which are familiar to students of Politics.[301]

D. CONCLUSION: THE APPLICABILITY OF THE THEORY TO INDIAN CONDITIONS

(*a*) *Comparison*

With the above sketch of the origin and development of the social contract theory in the West, let us see how far it existed in ancient Indian thought. The first point of analogy is the one relating to the antiquity of the theory both in India and in the West. In both the Indian and Western theories, there is an inconvenient stage of society preceding the rule of either a leader or a king. And in both protection follows the establishment of government. Here the resemblance between the Indian and the Western versions of the theory ends.

(*b*) *Contrast*

The contrast between the two versions is marked. The Indian version would make the condition of society as one of evil. In this it partially approaches the state of society as envisaged by Hobbes but it is dissimilar to the one described by Locke and Rousseau. To Hobbes the state of nature was one of war and aggression because men were brutal and selfish ; to Locke it was one of equity and freedom, because men were peaceable and sociable ; while to Rousseau, it was one of idyllic happiness, because men were perfect. The Hindu theory, if at all it could be construed as one of contract, approached in this particular detail only the concept of Hobbes but not that of Locke and Rousseau ; while the Buddhist and, particularly, the Jaina, anticipated some of the ideas of Hobbes.

The next point of contrast refers to the question—Who abandoned the anarchical state of nature? It is not clear from the Indian version as to who abandoned the state of nature—whether the people of their own accord abandoned the anarchical state of nature, or whether they were made to abandon it. In one of the passages in the *Arthaśāstra* of Kauṭilya cited above, we are merely told that, in the absence of a magistrate, the strong will devour the weak. Neither in this passage nor in the later one in which a spy describes the creation of Manu Vaivasvata, is it clear whether the people themselves abandoned the anarchical state of nature, or whether they were compelled to abandon it. In all likelihood it was the latter, as will be evident from the emphasis laid on the supernatural element relating to the election of Manu Vaivasvata. The reader may recall here the remarks that have been made elsewhere in these pages in connection with the need of protection and with *arājatā,* according to the Hindu, Buddhist, and Jaina sources. In this respect the Indian version affords a contract to the Western theory in which men themselves abandon the state of nature. Hobbes, Locke, and Rousseau are all unanimous in this vital detail, viz., that it was men themselves who agreed to surrender their rights to a common authority. There is no trace of men's surrendering their rights to a ruler in any version of the Indian theory.

Thirdly, the State, according to the Indian version, was originally the result of divine action. But the State, according to the Western version, was the result of deliberate human action. It follows from this that in the Indian version governmental authority in its origin could be ultimately traced to the influence of God ; while in the Western version, it could be traced only to the people.

Fourthly, in the Indian version the first ruler, who was not a party to the contract, appears to have been ordained by God. This is probably what the spy in the *Arthaśāstra* means when he talks of Manu Vaivasvata. But in the Western version, it was either the people, who bestowed the right to govern upon the ruler, or they themselves who remained sovereign. In the theory of Hobbes, too, the ruler was not a party to the contract, and he was not appointed by God. Since the ruler was not bound by the contract which the people had made amongst themselves, he was above it. According to Locke, the ruler was a party to the contract ; while, according to Rousseau, the government was not a party but merely an agent to carry out the general will. It is clear from the different interpretations, given by the three great thinkers, that the essential idea of the ruler's being or not being a party to the contract, as described in the Western version, is absent in the Indian version in which there is an element of divinity in the appointment of the first monarch. Indeed, Manu, on being appointed as the first ruler, makes no promise at all, the promise of obeying being entirely on the side of the people. This defect robs the Indian theory of the essence of a contract between the ruler and the people.

Fifthly, according to the Indian version, the people agreed to obey the king, there being no indication whether such submission on their part was the result of their decision to abjure their inherent rights. But in the Western theory, it is the people who agreed among themselves to surrender their rights either to the absolute ruler, as described by Hobbes, or to the ruler with limited powers, as maintained by Locke, or to the representative government, as advocated by Rousseau. The main idea in the interpretations of the three great exponents of the Western theory centres round the importance of the individual which is entirely missing in the Indian version.

And, finally, the Indian version does not mention at any stage the political rights of the people. There is a reference only to the protection that was to be given by the king to the people ; while in the Western theory, the main emphasis is laid on the political rights and obligations without which the State cannot exist. We thus come to the conclusion that the Indian theory bears a pale resemblance to only some of the points in the theory of social contract as expounded in the West.[302]

Part Four

A COMPARATIVE STUDY

CHAPTER I

NEED OF A COMPARATIVE STUDY

A. INTRODUCTION

FROM THE previous pages the reader will have realized that we have on many occasions indulged in comparisons with a view to arriving at some reasonable conclusions in Indian political theory. In this Part we shall elaborate this method of evaluation. While studying the problem of the Indian republics and the Greek City States, it was stated above that there was no justification for assessing the Indian institutions and theories in terms of later Western thought ; and that they should be studied in the context of the indigenous conditions and environment which had produced them. We thereby arrive at the springs of their growth and the causes that helped their development and enabled them to survive the shocks of ages till our own days. This by itself is a most valuable part of our study. But it would not be complete in the sense that it would not enable us to find out in what manner they contributed to the world-picture of the contemporary times. That is, a true and final appraisal of the contribution of the Indian thinkers and of the political institutions which they helped to evolve would be complete only when we study the thought of our ancestors in relation to that of their contemporaries. Of the many illuminaries of the ancient times, the greatest names that invite comparison are Manu, Hammurabi, Aristotle, and Kauṭilya.

B. MANU AND HAMMURABI—A STUDY IN THE CONCEPT OF LAW

1. MANU'S IMPORTANCE

Manu is one of the most fascinating figures in the history of the lawgivers of antiquity. His importance in Indian history lies in the fact that it was he who gave the stamp of sanctity and permanence to the socio-political institutions of the land, and left to the Indian world the first code of civil and criminal law. His greatness in the history of the contemporary world can be gauged by the analogy and contrast which he offers to the other great lawgiver of antiquity, Hammurabi, and by perennial interest which he evokes in the mind of the students of the modern times.

2. MANU AND HAMMURABI

(a) A Comparison

(i) The Age in Which They lived

The two greatest lawgivers of antiquity afford points of comparison and contrast. The ages in which both lived are still a matter of speculation. While discussing the historicity of the pre-Kauṭilyan schools of political thought in an earlier context, it was stated that Manu could be hypothetically assigned to *circa* 1800 B.C. It is the same age to which Hammurabi has been assigned by Professor Gordon Childe.[1]

(ii) Both represented the Height of their Culture

But whereas in regard to Hammurabi, sufficient sources of information relating to the laws promulgated by him are available in the archaeological finds discovered in the ancient cities of Babylonia,[2] no such firm data are available for Manu, whose *Code* was orally transmitted for centuries before it was finally reduced to writing. Both Manu and Hammurabi were the greatest kings in their respective countries, and the *Codes* of both marked the apex of the socio-political advancement in their respective lands. While Manu represented the height of the Indo-Aryan culture, Hammurabi stood for the perfection of the Semitic traditions.

(iii) Both codified Laws after achieving Political Unity

As lawgivers both Manu and Hammurabi bear some resemblance. It has been assumed that the codification of laws ascribed to Hammurabi took place when the City State was absorbed in the territorial State, and when the realities of the economic needs necessitated their codification.[3] In this regard, too, there is some resemblance between the two *Codes,* although, it cannot be maintained with certainty that the *Code* ascribed to Manu was composed at a particular point in the history of the transformation of the City State in India into a territorial kingdom. There is abundant evidence, as is well-known, of the existence of cities in the Mohenjo Daro and Harappa epoch (*circa* 2500 B.C.). But beyond their general lay-out, the articles in which they traded, and some general observations in respect of their buildings, civic life, etc.,[4] no complete details are available in the archaeological finds discovered in those cities. Their bearing on the culture and cvilization in Manu's *Code* is still an unexplored study.

In that *Code* there is definite proof of the existence of towns which were built by the king with walls and ditches, and with pasture grounds around them.[5] The references to the king's castles[6] prove that in the art of constructing buildings, the people in the age of that *Code* had reached a high state of efficiency. The towns described in the *Code* were evidently the capitals and chief cities of the territorial State over which ruled the sovereign. About the latter there is ample proof, as, for instance, in the invocation by the divine sages to Manu, in which the latter is called "a sovereign ruler".[7] That Manu was, indeed, no small ruler but a sovereign lord is proved by a later context in the same work in which he is not only compared to Pṛithu but said to have gained sovereignty by humility like that ruler.[8]

More substantial evidence that the State was a vast one is afforded in the later contexts of the *Manusmṛiti* in which the country between the two mountains (the Himālayas and the Vindhyas) as far as the eastern and the western oceans called Āryāvarta, and the different regions comprising it, viz., Brahmāvarta (or the land between the Sarasvatī and the Dṛṣadvatī), Brahmarṣi (or the land comprising Kurukṣetra, Mastya, Pāñcāla, or Kānyakubja, and Sūrasena or Mathurā), and the Madhyadésa (or the land between the Himālayas and the Vindhyas to the west of Vināśanā and the east of Prayāga), was declared to be the land where the *Code of Manu* and the immemorial customs relating to the four *varṇas* and the mixed castes were in force.[9] Thus, in both cases, a codification of laws was made only after political unity had been achieved.[10]

(*iv*) *Both the Codes mirror a Developed Socio-Economic Organization*

The *Codes* of both the great lawgivers of antiquity give the first clear picture of the social and economic organization of their respective peoples. But the *Code of Manu* is more comprehensive in the sense that it deals with moral problems like penance and expatiation, and even purely religious topics like the transmigration of souls and final beatitude,[11] which are missing in the great Babylonian lawgiver's *Code*.

(*v*) *Identity of Views on Property, Wages, etc.*

On Property, both the *Codes* cover almost all the important aspects of an urban civilization like property, wages, fees, slavery, domestic relations, and crime with this difference that, whereas the *Code of Manu* dwelt at minute length on even such questions like lawful and forbidden food, which affected the progress of society, Hammurabi's *Code* knew only two kinds of landed property—land given by the king in return for military service which could not be disposed of by its possessor, and land held with the full rights of sale, lease, mortgage, and bequest.[12] But in the *Code of Manu* we have a more advanced and a more comprehensive concept of property which covered seven lawful modes of acquiring it, viz., inheritance, finding or friendly donation, purchase, conquest, lending at interest, performance of work, and the acceptance of gifts from virtuous men.[12] Further, the concept of property in Manu's *Code* included in it the law of limitations,[14] which would justify the assumption that it was of a high order which is not met with in the Babylonian *Code*.[15]

On Wages. In regard to the question of wages and fees, we see, again, that Manu's *Code* compares favourably with the Babylonian lawgiver's *Code*. In the latter, if a cultivator failed to produce any grain, he was to account for it by the person from whom he had leased the field ; and he had to make good the loss to the owner of the field by giving grain on the basis of the adjoining fields. When a gardener received an orchard for management, he was to give to the owner of the garden two-thirds of the produce of the orchard, retaining for himself one-third.[16] Manu's regulations were more precise and advanced. While dealing with women employed in the royal service, he says that for them and the menial servants, the king (i.e. the State) should fix a daily allowance in proportion to their position and to their work. One *paṇa* was to be given daily as wages to the lowest, six to the highest, likewise clothing every six months, and one *droṇa* of grain every month.[17] Non-payment of wages was one of the eighteen topics covered by the Civil Law in the *Code of Manu*.[18] The law of non-payment of wages clearly establishes the superiority of the Indian *Code* over the Babylonian. In the *Manusmṛiti* it is stated that a hired servant or workman, who, without being ill, fails out of pride to perform his work according to the agreement, shall be fined eight *kṛṣṇalas*, and that no wages shall be paid to him. But if he is really ill, and after recovery performs his work according to the original agreement, he shall receive his wages even after the lapse of a very long time. But if he, whether sick or well, does not perform or will cause to be performed by others, his work, according to the agreement, the wages for that work shall not be given to him, even if it be only slightly incomplete.[19] The concept of the non-payment of wages as promulgated by Manu is not only superior to anything similar in Hammurabi's *Code* but approaches modern labour legislation in this particular respect.

On Slavery. Turning to slavery, we find in Hammurabi's *Code* that slaves were branded, and that they were required to wear a special dress. If they ran away or if they attacked a freeman, they were subject to severe punishment. They were entitled to three days' rest in a month. They could acquire town property and could buy their liberty. Special protection was given to slave concubines. Owners of slaves did not possess the right of life and death over their slaves.[20]

Slavery was also known to Manu, who was more conservative than Hammurabi in this regard. In the *Manusmṛiti*, seven kinds of slaves are mentioned—he who is made captive under a standard, he who serves for his daily food, he who is born in the house, he who is bought, and he who is given, he who is inherited from ancestors, and he who is enslaved by way of punishment.[21] But a slave could not own property. He shared this short-coming with a wife and a son, all three of whom could own no property. The priest (*Brāhmaṇa*) could confidently seize the goods of his slave![22] Evidently Manu was less liberal than Hammurabi in regard to the right to property which the Babylonian lawgiver conceded to the slave. Manu classed a slave with a number of persons, among whom figured the king, a student of the *Veda*, and others, who were debarred from being witnesses in lawsuits.[23] But if qualified witnesses failed to give evidence, then a slave could do so.[24] Householders were forbidden to quarrel with slaves.[25] The *Code of Manu* does not specifically mention anywhere whether the owners of slaves had the right of life and death over their slaves. In all likelihood, the masters of slaves did not possess the right which was vested only in the king as the head of the State. A study of the social institution of slavery as depicted in the two *Codes* reveals that the Babylonian *Code* was undoubtedly more liberal than its Indian counterpart in this particular respect.

On the Judiciary. Some resemblance between the ancient Indian and Babylonian judicial procedure may be noted. Prior to the days of Hammurabi, the priest-rulers themselves were the dispensers of justice. Hammurabi substituted them by magistrates and judges selected from those landowners who held fields under the king, and who performed military service to the State. Both civil and criminal cases were heard in temples. The priests administered the oaths to the witnesses but the decisions were given by the secular judges. Verbal evidence was taken but greater stress was laid on written evidence, particularly where landed property was concerned. Appeals were permitted from the lower to the higher courts.[25a]

The judicial procedure as laid down in the *Code of Manu* is so elaborate and detailed that it could well merit a treatment by itself. The two points of superficial comparison between the Babylonian and Indian judicial procedure centre round the priests and evidence. In both the countries the priests, in the sense of learned men, formed an integral part of the legal machinery although, there were others, too, "experienced councillors", who could constitute a court of law. It may be noted that in India, a member of the fourth caste of the Sūdras could not become a judge, which ban does not appear to have been laid on the other two castes, the Kṣatriyas and the Vaiśyas.[25b] From the statement in the *Manusmṛiti* that "a king, desirous of investigating law cases, must enter his court of justice, preserving a dignified demeanour" together with Brahmans and experienced councillors,[25c] it is clear that there was a separate court of justice which was, unlike the Babylonian one, not situated in a temple.

On another point there is a similarity between the Babylonian and Indian judicial procedure. Evidence in both was most often verbal but, unlike in India, greater stress was laid on written evidence in Babylonia.

Excepting the above two points of comparison, the Babylonian court cannot be compared with the Indian court of justice. Here in this country a court consisted of three Brahmans learned in the *Vedas* and a judge appointed by the king, it being understood that the latter was to investigate all cases arising out of the eighteen titles of law. These were the following: the non-payment of debts, deposits and pledges, sale without ownership, concerns among parties, restitution of goods, non-payment of wages, non-performance of agreements, rescission of sale and purchase, disputes between the owner of cattle and his servants, disputes regarding boundaries, assault, defamation, theft, robbery, violence, adultery, duties of man and wife, partition of inheritance, gambling and betting, and miscellaneous cases all of which have been most minutely described by Manu.[25d] The careful manner in which justice was to be administered, the penalties imposed on judges, who were unjust, the rule in regard to the behaviour of the judges in a court, and the entire method of judicial investigation—all these prove that the Indian court of justice was superior to the more primitive and less dignified Babylonian court as described either in Hammurabi's *Code* or in the Babylonian texts.

On Criminal Law. In the sphere of criminal law, there are again points of similarity and contrast between the two *Codes.* The law of relation (*lex talionis*) governed, on the whole, the *Code of Hammurabi*: "If a man has caused the loss of a gentleman's eye, his eye one shall cause to be lost. If a man has made the tooth of a man, that is his equal, to fall, one shall make his tooth to fall out."[26] This may be compared with what Manu says about cases of theft and assault. "With whatever limb a thief in any way commits (an offence) against men, even of that (the king) shall deprive him in order to prevent (a repetition of the crime)."[27] As regards an assault, Manu says: "He who raises his hand or a stick, shall have his hand cut off; he who in anger kicks with his foot, shall have his foot cut off."[28]

Incidentally it may be observed that the *lex telionis* governed not only the Indian and the Babylonian *Codes* but also that of the Hebrews. In the *Bible* in the *Leviticus* we have the following: "Breach for breach, eye for eye, tooth for tooth: as he hath caused a blemish in a man, so shall it be done to him again."[29] It is repeated in the *Deuteronomy* later on in identical terms.[30] The *lex talionis* continued to persist in the Roman times, when one of the provisions of the Roman law, as given in the Twelve Tables (Table 8th, Provision 2nd) (*circa* 449 B.C.),[31] enacted "retaliation against him who breaks the limb of another and does not offer compensation".[32]

Social Differences and Punishments. In Hammurabi's *Code* the social differences were reflected in the various modes of punishment for crimes against freemen, priests, and princes. If, for instance, a man stole an ox or a sheep, a pig, or an ass, or a boat, if the owner was a priest or a prince, the thief had to restore it thirty-fold; if the owner was a freeman, the thief restored only ten-fold.[33] A similar class distinction to a certain extent is visible in the *Code of Manu,* in which it is said that "with whatever limb a man of a low caste does hurt to (a man of the three) highest (castes), even that, limb shall be cut off; that is the teaching of Manu."[34]

On Drastic Punishments. Before we see the redeeming features in the Criminal Code of Manu, which are not noticeable in that of Hammurabi, we may continue with the nature of the drastic punishments noticeable in the *Codes* of both the great lawgivers. Hammurabi enjoined that in crimes like rape, kidnapping, incest, brigandage, burglary, cowardice in battle, and adultery, the punishment was either impaling or death by drowning. Trial by ordeal, in cases of witchcraft and false accusations, took the shape of drowning persons in rivers—if they swam, they were set free, if they sank, it marked their guilt. If thieves or burglars caused loss to the citizens, the governors of their cities, where the thefts and burglaries had occurred, had to make good the loss. Divine acts were outside the ambit of the Babylonian criminal law.[35]

On Crimes in Detail : Adultery. We may take crime by crime, and see what Manu has to say on the various types of crimes. On almost all the crimes we shall cite, the great Indian lawgiver has detailed injunctions to give. On the whole, he was very severe with those who committed sins against society. He ordained thus: "Men who commit adultery with the wives of others, the king shall cause to be marked by punishments which cause terror, and afterwards banish." The reason for this severity is given in the next passage. "For by adultery is caused a mixture of the castes (*varṇa*) among men; thence (follows) sin, which cuts up even the roots and causes the destruction of every thing."[36] On the question of rape, he enjoined as follows: "He who violates an unwilling maiden shall instantly suffer corporal punishment; but a man who enjoys a willing maiden, shall not suffer corporal punishment, if (his caste be) the same as hers."[37] Even priests were not free from punishment if they committed such crimes. "A Brāhmaṇa who carnally knows a guarded Brāhmaṇī against her will, shall be fined one thousand (*paṇas*); but he shall be made to pay five hundred, if he had connexion with a willing one."[38] Then, again, "Tonsure of the head is ordained for a Brāhmaṇa (instead of) capital punishment; but (men of) other castes shall suffer punishment".[39] Here in this case Manu has obviously made a distinction in punishments based on class lines.

Brigandage and Thefts. Manu's exposition of the question of brigandage and theft was far more detailed and equitable than the summary dictates of Hammurabi. It is not possible to go into the many aspects of these questions described in Manu's *Code,* but it is evident that the great Indian lawgiver considered theft as a social evil that had to be dealt with in the different contexts in which it had been performed. Brigandage on a vast scale is not seen in the Indian *Code.* It would not be an exaggeration to maintain that lawless robbery of great magnitude was practically unknown in ancient India. Kidnapping was a most serious crime. For kidnapping men of noble family, and, especially women, and for stealing the most precious gems, the offender was given corporal punishment. And for stealing large animals, weapons, or medicines, the king could fix a punishment after considering the time and the purpose for which they were destined.[40]

Common Crimes. In regard to the more common crimes of stealing and theft, Manu laid down minute rules which are too numerous to be mentioned here. No doubt, the class bias is certainly visible in Manu who, as is only natural with a lawgiver of antiquity of his type, could only be partial to the Brahmans, who were considered as the custodians of knowledge and ritual in those ages. If a man stole cows belonging to the Brahmans, or pierced the nostrils of a barren cow, he was punished with the loss of half of his feet![41] But in very many other cases ranging from the stealing of thread to abetting stolen property, Manu ordained fines ranging from five *kṛṣṇalas* to depriving of the limbs of the thief, as mentioned above.[42]

Restitution of Stolen Property. But that there was equity in the ordinances of Manu is seen not only in the differences in the fines imposed for committing various kinds of thefts but also in the provision made by him for the restitution of stolen property. If in Hammurabi's *Code* it was the governors of the cities, who were required to make good the loss by thefts incurred by the citizens, in Manu's *Code* it was the king who was to restore stolen property to men of all castes (*varṇa*). If the king used such property for himself, he incurred the guilt of a thief.[43]

Cowardice in Battle. Cowardice in battle was not a crime in ancient India. It was social ignomy which could not be condoned. Heaven itself was denied to a coward on the battlefield. Manu maintains that "not to turn back in battle" is one of the best means for a king to secure happiness.[44] If a king did not turn his back in war, he would go to heaven.[45] In a later context, he further states that if a Kṣatriya "turns back in fear", he takes upon himself all the sin of his master, whatever it might be.[46] How far this standard of considering bravery in battle as one of the most valued of moral prizes remained throughout ancient India, and what lasting effect it had on the longevity or otherwise of political structures are subjects well worth separate treatment by themselves. All that may be said in regard to this detail, with reference to its counterpart in Babylonian law, is that there was no need for the State in ancient India to list cowardice in battle as a crime, since ancient Indian society did not consider a soldier, who turned his back in battle, as worthy of any respect. Social reprobration was a more potent deterrent than the punishment by drowning which was awarded to a coward in battle in the Babylonian *Code*.

Adulteration of Goods. On adulteration of merchandise, Manu in an earlier context stated thus: "One commodity mixed with another must not be sold (as pure), nor a bad one (as good), nor less (than the proper quantity or weight), nor anything that is not at hand or that is concealed."[47] Obviously the social crime of adulteration had already gone so deep in the life of the people by Manu's time that that injunction by itself was not enough to wean them from this nefarious practice. Hence in a later context he states: "For adulterating unadulterated commodities, and for breaking gems, or for improperly boring (them), the fine is the first (or lowest) amercement."[48] Looking back through the vista of centuries one cannot help regretting that the great lawgiver was not more drastic in his punishment of adulterators ; and that he allowed the socially despicable criminals of this type to get off with a bare fine. If he had ordained severer and more deterrent punishments for the crime of adulteration, perhaps, as in the case of rape and similar gross examples of social degradation, the crime of adulterating goods, including food grains, would have been held within bounds, and would not have been allowed to assume the alarming proportions of a national evil which it has unfortunately attained in our own days.

Witchcraft. Witchcraft and black-art seem to have been known in the days of Manu, who ordained: "For all incantations intended to destroy life, for magic rites with roots (practised by persons) not related (to him against whom they are directed), and for various kinds of sorcery, a fine of two hundred (paṇas) shall be inflicted."[49] As regards ordeals, Manu is silent. He describes only the administration of oath, mentioning the ordeals of water and fire in a cursory manner.[50] We are to infer from this that the penalty of drowning, which was meted out to those who were accused of witchcraft and false accusation in the Babylonian *Code*, was not recommended by the great Indian lawgiver.

(*vi*) *A Criticism of Manu's Criminal Law : Urbanity of His Laws*

We have not exhausted either the criminal *Code of Manu* or the different modes of punishments which he advocated for various crimes. Such a study would deserve a treatment by itself. Neither do we wish to justify the criminal law of Manu on all counts. There was undoubtedly a vein of severity, almost amounting to savagery, in some of his measures. But while judging his criminal law, two points may be borne in mind—firstly, to what extent his criminal law could be compared with that of his great Babylonian contemporary ; and, secondly, whether severity was the special feature only of the Babylonian and the Indian criminal *Codes.* On the first point, the reader must have realized from the few examples cited above that, while Manu certainly could be compared with Hammurabi in regard to certain aspects of the *lex talionis,* and also in regard to the class bias which is visible in the differential punishments advocated by Manu for the various castes, yet, on the whole, Manu cannot be accused either of barbarism or a want of equity in regard to the dispensation of justice. A lawgiver, who had the boldness to declare that "where another common man would be fined one *kārṣāpaṇa,* the king shall be fined one thousand", and to state that that was the settled rule, while describing the punishments that were to be given to all,—father, mother, teacher, friend, wife, son, and domestic priest, who did not conform to their duties[51]—may be considered to have maintained, as we might say in modern parlance, the rule of the law even where the king was concerned. Indeed, any impression that might have been created in our mind from the slight leaning on class distinctions, which Manu has shown in some of his injunctions cited above, is wiped out when we note that the same lawgiver adjudged the relative guilt of the various classes, in an inverse proportion, thus: "In (a case of) theft the guilt of a Śūdra be eight-fold, that of a Vaiśya sixteen-fold, that of a Kṣatriya two and thirty-fold. That of a Brahman sixty-fold, or quite a hundred-fold, or even twice four-and-sixty-fold, (each of them knowing) the nature of the offence."[52]

Manu's Positive Theory of Punishment: It is not merely this urbanity mixed with equity which we notice in the *Code of Manu*, and which is missing in that of Hammurabi ; we see also a positive theory of punishment in Manu which is not met with in the *Code* of the great Babylonian lawgiver. Punishment by the State, according to Manu, was of four kinds—the king was to punish first by gentle admonition, afterwards by a harsh reproof, thirdly, by a fine, and, finally, by corporal punishment. If, however, culprits could not be restrained even by corporal punishment, the king could apply all the four modes conjointly.[53] Further, punishment was to depend upon the nature and motive of the crime committed. "Having fully considered the time and place (of offence), the strength and knowledge (of the offender), let him (the king) justly inflict that (punishment) on men who act unjustly."[54] In a later context, Manu is almost modern in his concept of punishment. "Let the king, having fully ascertained the motive, the time and place (of the offence), and having considered the ability (of the criminal to suffer), and the (nature of the) crime, cause punishment to fall on those who deserve it."[55] After all punishment is not an end in itself: it is the means to redemption. Hence Manu states that "men who have committed crimes and have been punished by the King, go to heaven, being pure like those who performed meritorious deeds".[56]

This theory of punishment which had ultimately the object of helping the criminal to regain his moral purity is not met with in the Babylonian *Code* which, in spite of its urbanity in a few cases, made no such provision for the moral uplift of the criminal. The case for justice was nowhere better stated in antiquity than when Manu declared thus: "Where justice is destroyed by injustice, or truth by falsehood, while the judges look on, there they shall also be destroyed." In the admonition which follows, and which Manu would make the assessors address a judge, who had acted against the law, we have the enthronement of Justice on the seat of Power. "Justice, being violated, destroys ; justice being preserved, preserves: therefore, Justice must not be violated, lest violated Justice destroy us."[57] The emphasis on equity and on the fundamental duty of not violating justice, which is noticeable in the *Code of Manu*, is not visible in that of his great Babylonian contemporary. We have to come to the modern times in order to see the vindication of the eternal principle of Justice as enunciated by Manu.

(*vii*) *Severity in all Codes—Past and Present*

We have now to explain whether severity was the marked feature only of the ancient Indian and Babylonian *Codes* of law. Western jurists like Professors Stephens, Hart, and Brew have admitted that even in a country like England, "there can be no doubt that the legislation of the eighteenth century in criminal matters was severe to the highest degree and destitute of any sort of principle or system".[58] At the beginning of the nineteenth century A.D., in England more than a hundred offences were punished with death.[59] The barbarous nature of the British Criminal Law is seen so late as 1832 when a child was convicted at Ludgate Hill for stealing a box of paints worth two pence, tried at the Old Bailey, and hanged![60] Making due allowance for all other factors, we might justifiably maintain that Manu's *Code*, in spite of its defects, never reached the level of either its contemporary Babylonian *Code* or of the comparatively later British Criminal Code, particularly in the matter of meting out punishment.

(*viii*) *Domestic Relations in Manu and Hammurabi*

We may now turn to the question of domestic relations as given in the two *Codes*.

In Hammurabi. In Hammurabi's *Code,* the husband and father possessed paramount rights in the family. Marriages were made by contracts. The system of dowries to be given by the fathers of the brides prevailed, the prospective bridegrooms being required to make suitable gifts to the fathers of the brides. Divorce was possible in case the wife was barren, or the husband could take a second wife or even a concubine with the consent of his first wife. Drowning was the punishment for adultery. The wife who roamed about was punished with drowning ; while if she conspired to kill her husband in order to marry another husband, she was impaled. The utter helplessness of the wife and children could be seen in the law which permitted the husband to pledge them for the debts he had contracted! If the debt was not redeemed, the creditor could claim the wife and children of the debtor for three years. But in case a husband had an invalid wife, he could not throw her out of his house but he could replace her by a concubine.[61]

Inferior Position of Women in Manu. Abundant materials are available in the *Code of Manu* on almost all the details mentioned above. We shall confine ourselves only to such of them as will give us a fairly accurate idea of the domestic relations in the *Code* of that great lawgiver. Manu ordained: "In childhood a female must be subject to her father, in youth to her husband, when her lord is dead, to her son ; a woman must never be independent."[62] In this famous dictum which he reiterates in a later context,[63] it appears as if Manu had condemned woman to a position of eternal dependence. We shall see at once that, notwithstanding this rigorous interdict,

Manu had made ample provision for the husband's liberal treatment of the wife. Thus he stated: "Reprehensible is the father who gives not (his daughter in marriage) at the proper time ; reprehensible is the husband who approaches not (his wife in due season), and reprehensible is the son who does not protect his mother after her husband has died."[64] The husband, according to Manu, was to employ his wife in the collection and expenditure of wealth, in keeping everything clean, in the fulfilment of religious duties, in the preparation of his food, and in looking after the household utensils.[65]

Were Women perpetually condemned in Manu? It need not be inferred from the above that women were prepetually condemned to a life of inferior status. Manu, no doubt, explicitly states that "Women (who are) destitute of strength and destitute of (the knowledge of) Vedic texts are as impure as falsehood itself, that is a fixed rule".[66] But the equal importance of the wife and the husband is evident from the following: "To be mothers were women created ; and to be fathers men ; religious rites, therefore, are ordained in the *Veda* to be performed (by the husband) together with the wife."[67] The interdependence of husband and wife is nowhere better illustrated than in the two following verses in Manu: "Let mutual fidelity continue until death—this may be considered as the summary of the highest law for husband and wife. Let man and woman, united in marriage, constantly exert themselves that (they may not be) disunited and may not violate their mutual fidelity."[68] The immunity which the wife enjoyed is clear from the injunction of Manu that, if she was defamed by her husband, the latter had to pay to the king 100 *paṇas*.[69] If the husband forsook his wife, he was fined 600 *paṇas* by the king.[70] Indeed, according to the law made by the Lord of Creatures (Prajāpati), a wife could not be released from her husband either by sale or by repudiation. This was an old law.[71]

Relation between Husband and Wife. Manu has given in detail "the pure popular usage" which regulates the relations between husband and wife, which may not be repeated here.[72] He made detailed provisions for securing offspring on various occasions like misfortune, departure of husband for more than a special period, and such other contingencies[73] which bespeak a well advanced social code prevalent in his age. In case the wife bore no children, Manu permitted the raising of offspring on her by a *sapiṇḍa* (a brother-in-law or some other relative) of her husband.[74] In a later context Manu has the following interesting ordinance in regard to a barren wife: "A barren wife may be superseded in the eighth year, she whose children (all) die, in the tenth, she who bears only daughters, in the eleventh, but she who is quarrelsome without delay."[75] As regards a sick wife, he enjoined the following: "But a sick wife, who is kind to her husband and virtuous in her conduct, may be superseded (only) with her own consent and must never be disgraced."[76] Concerning marriage outside one's own circle, Manu laid down the severest penalties which point to a rigidly maintained social structure that is not seen in the Babylonian *Code*.[77]

Dowry. The question of dowry was carefully considered by Manu under two aspects—as nuptial fee and as *strīdhana*. The former which amounted to selling one's daughter was prohibited. "Even a Śūdra ought not to take a nuptial fee, when he gives away his daughter ; for he who takes a fee sells his daughter, covering the transaction by another name."[78] Soon after this he says the following: "Nor, indeed, have we heard even in former creations, of such (a thing) as the covert sale of daughter for a fixed price, called a nuptial fee."[78a] But a woman could certainly claim as her own six kinds of property, one of which was *strīdhana* or the ornaments and jewellery and the means of subsistence, as the following ordinance clearly proves: "Whatever (was given) before the (nuptial) fire, what (was given) on the bridal procession, what was given in token of love, and what was received from her brother, mother, or father, that is called the six-fold property of a woman."[79]

C. CONCLUSION IN REGARD TO THE TWO CODES OF LAW

1. CONTRAST BETWEEN THE TWO CODES

The meagre sketch of the regulations bearing on domestic relations and on some other aspects of life as given in the *Codes* of both Manu and Hammurabi will have. convinced the reader that in the celebrated lawgiver of ancient India, we have a figure of a higher stature with a more catholic, practical, and lasting outlook than that of the Babylonian contemporary. Manu's *Code* marked the zenith in the development of the Aryan culture in the long period of antiquity, so far as India is concerned. The Babylonian *Code* was urban, while that of Manu was more universal. The former satisfied the needs of the commercial instincts of society ;[80] while the latter, the needs and aspirations of an everlasting social fabric.

While the law *Codes* of both the ancient lawgivers of antiquity guided the destiny of their respective countries during their life-time, that of the Indian lawgiver continued to regulate the conduct and nature of Indian society for three millenniums after his age. It is here that Manu scored a decisive victory over Hammurabi: the archaeologist's spade in the Middle East had to save Hammurabi from falling completely into oblivion. But in India it is society itself that refused to allow Manu to fade from the memory of man.

2. MERITS OF MANU'S CODE

The inherent merits in the *Code of Manu* are themselves responsible for this eternal tribute which posterity has paid to the cosmopolitan, realistic, and comprehensive ordinances of Manu,[81] which are the richest heritage of an urban civilization. It was because Manu's *Code* had a utility for all sections of the people and for all ages that it continued to maintain its high position in the socio-political life of the people. In spite of its bias on social rigidity, its tendency to explain the origin of kingship in terms of the divinity, and its drastic methods of punishment which were perhaps inevitable in those ancient times when such ideas were common to the peoples of antiquity, Manu's *Code* stood for the free development of all those social forces which came within the purview of the Hindu *dharma,* and which were necessary for the stabilization of religion and the State. No other Code in the long range of ancient Indian history was so clearly responsible for augmenting and enriching the Hindu civilization from generation to generation. Manu's *Code,* so unlike that of the great Babylonian lawgiver, or, indeed, any other Code of antiquity, laid down stress on the co-ordinated partnership of all classes of people,—the orthodox and the non-orthodox, the pure and the mixed, the citizens living within the urban areas, and those inhabiting the border and forest areas—which was so essential for the realization of the objectives as laid in the *dharmaśāstras.*

Finally, Manu's *Code,* and all the Indian *Codes* written after him, embodied an ideal and certain standards which were always kept in view by the States and society that came long after that celebrated lawgiver. It is true that the States differed in many respects from each other ; and that society likewise underwent vital changes due to the influx of new peoples, the preaching of great reformers, the growth of materialism, and other causes of socio-economic and political nature. But the ideal of maintaining the *dharma* of the ancients was never lost sight of ; and centuries afterwards it became the ambition of the Hindu rulers to "follow in the path of Manu", as is proved by inscriptional evidence of the comparatively later times. The high standards, goal, and ideal which Manu had first promulgated served to preserve Hindu society, and prevent it from disintegrating, even when the most ruthless foreign invaders threatened to wipe it out. The celebrated Babylonian lawgiver's *Code* obviously did not possess any ideal, goal, or standards which the States and society that came after him could follow. If it had possessed them, the world of antiquity would not have witnessed the sad spectacle of the disappearance of the ancient Babylonian States, and particularly the Babylonian society millenniums ago.

CHAPTER II

THE INDIAN AND THE BABYLONIAN CONCEPT OF THE STATE

A. INTRODUCTION

THE COMPARATIVE study of the ancient Indian and Babylonian concept of law made above refers to only one side of the major question of the State. We may now turn to the other aspects of the same problem which may be grouped under the following heads—the divine nature of the foundation of the State, kingship, administrative hierarchy, taxation, and the nature of the police force.

B. THE DIVINE NATURE OF THE FOUNDATION OF THE STATE

The Babylonian idea of government was different to the one which obtained in India in the age of Manu. It has been assumed by some scholars that originally to the Babylonians government was only a form of magic, that later on they came to look upon rulers as gods, and that afterwards they considered political institutions as having been divinely established.[82] The theory of the foundation of the State, as described in the *Code of Manu,* does not make provision for the inclusion of magic at all, although undoubtedly there is a touch of the divinity in the institution of the first king Manu, as explained in an earlier context in this work.

C. THEORY OF KINGSHIP IN HAMMURABI

The Babylonian concept of kingship centred round the idea of *ishakku's* being the Vice-Regent of the city-god. He was essentially the tenant-farmer of the city-god. He stood at the head of the State as an uncontrolled despot, who ruled by divine right. While his person was sacred, his judgments formed law. He was responsible only to his god, and he possessed the power of life and death over his subjects. His absolute power swayed between that of an unbridled autocrat and an uncontrolled executioner. The only people, who could oppose him inside his territory, were either the powerful officials, who formed an hierarchy, or the priests, who were the repositories of magic and the messages of the gods. The *ishakku,* as the Akkadian called the king, and the *patesi,* as the Sumerians styled him, conducted the administration of the land, which was marked by continual intrigue between the members of the royal court. He maintained himself on the voluntary offerings of the peasants and herdsmen. The king supervised the estates and workshops of the temples, legalized all business, agreements, fixed weights and measures, and defended the city which was considered as the god's property. He supervised also the commercial life of the city, and maintained a close watch on the canals and dykes of the country. The principle of heredity governed the selection of the king, who held theoretically the city under a lease from the city-god.[83]

2. IN MANU

(a) *King Not an Unbridled Despot*

Excepting the fact that the first ruler, as stated above, had been ordained, according to the ancient texts, by Brahmā ; and that, on the whole, he was the head of the State in all vital matters, there was little in common between the king as conceived of among the Babylonians, and the ruler, as described in the *Manusmṛiti*. From the elucidation of the powers of and the limitations on the king, as given elsewhere in this work, it will have been evident to the reader that the ancient Indian king, whether in the age of Manu or afterwards, cannot be considered as an unbridled despot. No doubt, his person was to some extent sacred, and his judgment was considered final. But the latter could be given only in accordance with the ancient usage of the land and in the context of the *dharmaśāstra*. Like his Babylolian counterpart, the Indian ruler undoubtedly possessed the power of life and death over his subjects. But these privileges were hedged in by limitations which made him less of an executioner and more of a constitutional monarch. Like the Babylonian ruler, who was afraid only of the powerful officials and the priests, the Indian king was perhaps, we may presume, afraid of the Kṣatriyas, between whom and himself there was no difference so far as valour and social status were concerned. But the Kṣatriyas did not make up the official hierarchy, and, therefore, could not offer to the king the stoutest opposition which, as mentioned elsewhere in these pages, came from all sections of the people. The priests never formed an opposition to the king, as they did in Babylonia. The king was afraid not so much of the Kṣatiryas and of even the people as of infringing the injunctions of the *dharmaśāstras* which governed him as much as the rest of the people. In short, the Indian king offers a marked contrast to the Babylonian king, who knew no such body of regulations like the *dharmaśāstras*.

(*b*) *King Not the Vice-Regent of God*

Further, the Indian monarch did not conduct the government of the country as the Vice-Regent of the city-god, or of God, as was done by his Babylonian counterpart, or by the Hebrew rulers of the later times. In India, no doubt, the principle of heredity governed monarchy; but we have seen that Manu certainly made provision for the overthrow, and even killing, of the monarch by the people, in case the latter proved to be a tyrant or had violated the precepts of the *dharmaśāstras*. Since in ancient Babylonia each city-god chose his tenant-farmer as a king, different cities had different lines of kings, or dynasties, which were contemporaneous with one another.[84] In India, too, there were different dynasties contemporaneous with one another; but it was not each city-god that chose a tenant-farmer as his king. On the other hand, each dynasty had its own capital city and its own deity.

(*c*) *Regal Funeral Custom missing in Manu*

Finally, the peculiar custom of Babylonian regal ritual, according to which, on the death of a monarch, soldiers fully armed, women attired in finery, jewels, vehicles, oxen, gaming boards, and embellished harps were all buried along with him,[85] is altogether missing in the concept of kingship as described by Hindu writers beginning with Manu, although, as pointed out by us elsewhere, that peculiar regal custom was noticeable in some parts of western India and in Assam in comparatively later times.[86]

D. ADMINISTRATIVE HIERARCHY

1. IN HAMMURABI

In the administrative hierarchy of ancient Babylonia, the temple priests played a decisive part, although there were others, too, the powerful officials of the monarch, the officials of the court, those of the provincial governors, those of the districts, the judges, the clerks, and the accountants. The royal court through its army, fiscal officials, priests, and favourites controlled the whole realm. The provincial rulers were generally independent of the royal authority. The judges were concerned with cases involving breaches of law and with complaints against officials. In the districts the local officials dealt with the questions of raising military levies, collection of taxes, imposition of forced labour (*corvée*), etc. The tax collectors earned notoriety for their rapacity. The clerks and accountants were trained for managing and recording governmental proceedings. Self-interest appears to have been the guiding principle of the Babylonian official hierarchy.[87]

The above is by no means an exhaustive account of the Babylonian administrative machinery. But it will have convinced the reader that there was some system in the administration of the Babylonians. A few points of interest in it may be particularly noted. Firstly, the absence of the hold of the central government over the provincial governors, who were practically independent in their respective regions. Secondly, the judges dealt with simple cases involving the officials and the violation of law. Thirdly, the officials, particularly the tax-collectors, were noted for their rapacity. And, finally, the want of provision in the Babylonian *Code* for counteracting the evil of corruption or negligence of duty on the part of the officials.

2. IN MANU

(a) *Similarity between the Babylonian and the Indian Machinery*

Let us turn to the picture of the administrative machinery as given in the *Manusmṛiti*. As in Babylonia, the monarch in India appointed all officials. It was laid down in that work that, so far as deliberating on "the most important affairs which relate to the six measures of royal policy" was concerned, the king was to entrust that work to the most distinguished of his ministers. He was to be a learned Brahman with whom the king was to deliberate but the final responsibility of taking a decision rested with the king alone.[88] To the extent of entrusting the work of deliberation on the most important matters to a priest, the ancient Indian and the Babylonian administrative conventions agreed.

(b) *Contrast between the Two : All Appointments by the King*

But beyond it there was no similarity between the Indian and Babylonian governmental practice. The Indian king decided himself all fundamental questions. He appointed other officials of integrity, who were wise, firm, able to collect money, and well tried. They were to be free from sloth. As many persons as were needed for the due performance of the State business were appointed. And, in particular, the king was to appoint "the brave, the skilful, the high born, and the honest in (offices for the collection of) revenue", e.g., in mines and in manufactories, and the timid in the interior of his palace.[89] In the last part of the preceding sentence we have a judicious provision for restricting the influence of court intrigue which is not seen in the Babylonian *Code*. As regards the appointment of ambassadors, special care was to be taken to get the best men which system we have described elsewhere,[90] and to which we shall revert in the next Part.

Official Hierarchy covers the Country. The official hierarchy in the *Code of Manu* covered even the villages. A battalion of soldiers commanded by a trusted officer was placed over a group of two, three, or five hundred villages for protection. Over each village a lord or governor was appointed, and likewise over ten, a hundred, and a thousand villages. The lord of one village had to inform the lord of ten villages of the crimes committed in his village, and the lord of ten villages to the governor of twenty, the lord of twenty villages was to report all such matters to the lord of a hundred, and the latter, to that of a thousand villages. Food, drink, and fuel were to be daily supplied by the villagers to the lord of one village ;[91] and, we may presume, the same obligation was imposed on the villagers in regard to the governors of a hundred and a thousand villages. Obviously this was a compulsory levy from which the villagers could not escape. It cannot be made out whether any payment or compensation was made to the villagers for supplying thus daily food, drink, and fuel to the king's officers. Neither can we make out whether any provision was made for the maintenance of the lord of one village, as in the case of higher officials. For instance, the ruler of ten villages was entitled to levy one *kula* (i.e. as much revenue as land for one family yielded) ; the governor of twenty villages, five *kulas* ; the governor of a hundred villages, of one village ; and the lord of a thousand villages, the revenues of a town.[92] We have in the above administrative machinery pertaining to the villages an admirable system of royal supervision which is not met with in the Babylonian *Code*.

Supervision the Keynote of Manu's Machinery. Manu did not leave anything to chance in the matter of administrative efficiency ; nor did he consign himself to the care of priests. For the governmental departments, the king was to appoint intelligent supervisors, who were to inspect all the acts of those men who transacted State business.[93] In other words, supervision was one of the chief features of the administrative machinery in the *Code of Manu*. All officials, including those appointed by the king over the villages, were supervised by a minister specially selected for that purpose, who was to be loyal, and who could "never remiss". The minister in question had under him a superintendent of all affairs in each town, who was to personally visit by turns all other officials, and to "properly explore their behaviour in their districts through spies (appointed to) each".[94] That the State was well aware of the rapacity of officials is proved by the following passage in the *Manusmriti*: "For the servants of the king, who are appointed to protect (the people), generally become knaves who seize the property of others ; let him protect his subjects against such (men)."[95]

Measures against Corruption. Greed and corruption are the twin evils which, if left unchecked, eat into the life of governments. Corruption must certainly have existed as much in ancient India as elsewhere, but it was severely dealt with by the State. It was ordained by Manu that "the whole property of those (officials) who, evil minded, may take money from suitors", was to be confiscated, and that they were then to be banished.[96] Those officials, who were convicted of stealing property lost and found, were ordered to be killed by elephants.[97]

Neglect of Duty. Neglect of duty was equally reprehensible but the penalty was not so heavy as in the case of misappropriation of property lost and found. If a man "who subsists by (the fulfilment of) the law, departs from the established rule of the law, the king shall severely punish him by a fine, (because he) violated his duty".[98]

Protection against Official Rapacity. The above ordinances show that, unlike the Babylonian regulations, those enacted by Manu made ample provision for the protection of the common people against the rapacity and dishonesty of officials. They prove, no doubt, that self-interest did mark the activities of the officials in the days of Manu ; but they also show that the State was not only alive to that danger but made safeguards to combat it. Another point of difference between the Babylonian and Indian administrative hierarchy is the selection of officials after great care, particularly in regard to their qualifications and their fitness to do the work entrusted to them. And the third point of difference relates to the supervision of one set of officials by a higher one, and of all by a minister, who was specially appointed for the purpose. It will be seen from above that, unlike the Babylonian official hierarchy, its Indian counterpart could not become a destructive element in the State because of the system of checks devised by it. The direst punishment awaited those who were charged either with embezzlement of public funds or with disobedience of royal authority. "On those who rob the king's treasury and those who persevere in opposing (his commands), he shall inflict various kinds of capital punishment . . . ."[99]

E. TAXATION

1. IN ANCIENT BABYLONIA: SOURCES OF REVENUE

In the history of the ancient Middle East, taxation was meant not so much for the furtherance of the welfare of the State as for that of the monarch. There were five important sources of revenue in ancient Babylonia—the annual produce of the land, the income derived from *corvée* or forced labour, the tribute from the conquered people, the income derived from customs, port duties, and markets, and finally, the profits from the exploitation of mines and industries. The last two sources became more important with the expansion of river and maritime trade. The land revenue was paid to the king, who was the agent of the city-god. Theoretically all land belonged to the city-god, that is, to the king. The income from forced labour was more in the shape of human labour rather than in that of actual receipts. Every year cultivators had to do forced labour by way of repairing embankments, constructing bridges, and digging irrigational canals. The temple craftsmen laboured for the welfare of the priestly class ; and the profits of trade also went to the same section of the people, obviously because they were the lieutenants of the king, who was the Vice-Regent of the city-god.[100]

2. IN ANCIENT INDIA

(a) *Limitations on the King*

The conditions in ancient India were, on the whole, different to those prevailing in Babylonia. Taxation was not a matter of either chance or caprice on the part of the monarch. Even in regard to this vital problem of taxation, the action of the king was circumscribed by the regulations laid down in the *dharmaśāstras*. The *Manusmṛiti* clearly enjoined thus: "Let him (the king) cause the annual revenue in his kingdom to be collected by trusty (officials), let him obey the Sacred law in his transactions with the people, and behave like a father towards all men."[101]

(b) *Based on Justice*

Manu's injunctions in regard to customs duties were based on considerations of justice. "Having well considered (the rates of) purchase and (of) sale, (the length of) the road, (the expenses for) food and condiments, the charges for securing goods, let the king make the traders pay duty. After (due) consideration, the king shall always fix in his realm the duties and taxes in such a manner that both he himself and the man who does the work receive their due reward."[102]

Then, again, in a later context Manu says the king should fix "one-twentieth of that (amount) which men, well acquainted with the settlement of tolls and duties (and) skilful (in estimating the value of) all kinds of merchandise, may fix as the value for each saleable commodity". The rates of purchase and sale of "all marketable goods" were fixed after the king had "duly considered whence they come, whither they go, how long they have been kept, the (probable) profit and the (probable) outlay".[103] It is incredible that such minute considerations relating to the marketable goods should have weighed on the mind of the great Indian lawgiver, whose injunctions in this respect are undoubtedly more liberal and equitable than anything similar in the ancient Babylonian *Code*.

(c) *General Principle of Taxation*

As regards the general principle on which taxation was based, it was summed in the following statement of the *Manusmṛiti*: "As the leech, the calf, and the bee take their food little by little, even so must the king draw from the realm moderate annual taxes."[104] In a later context, Manu says the following: "Let him (the king) not cut up his own root (by levying no taxes), nor the root of other (men) by excessive greed; for by cutting up his own root (or theirs), he makes himself or them wretched."[105] The ancient Indian ruler could not, therefore, imitate his Babylonian counterpart, and become a thorough-going imperial exploiter, who could levy either an annual indemnity or special taxes at will.

(d) *Rate of Taxation*

Indeed, the rate of taxation itself was so carefully and minutely laid down as not to permit the ruler from deviating from it. "A fiftieth part of (the increments on) cattle and gold may be taken by the king, and the eighth, sixth, or twelfth part of the crops. He may also take the sixth part of the trees, meat, honey, clarified butter, perfumes, (medical) herbs, substances used for flavouring food, flowers, roots, and fruit; of leaves, pot-herbs, grass (objects) made of cane, skins of earthen vessels, and all (articles) made of stone."[106] The differential rate of taxation on crops (one-eighth, one-sixth, and one-twelfth), obviously depended on the nature of the soil, the monsoons, and the availability of water from artificial sources. It compares favourably with the Babylonian rate under Hammurabi, which ranged from one-third to one-half of the crop.[107] The general rate of taxation on crops in ancient India was not insisted upon in the case of Vaiśyas or traders, who were required to pay one-eighth as tax on grain, and one-twentieth on the profits on gold and cattle, which amounted to at least one *kārṣāpaṇa,* while the Śūdras, artisans, and mechanics were to benefit the king by doing merely work for him which, as will be seen below, was only for one day in a month.[108]

Concerning tolls, the *Manusmṛiti* said: "Let the king make the common inhabitants of his realm who live by traffic, pay annually some trifle, which is called a tax."[109] The weightage given to river traffic in the Babylonian *Code* is not met with in the *Manusmṛiti,* probably because here in India the State depended more on income accruing from agricultural produce than on that derived from river and oceanic traffic.

(e) *Forced Labour: Similarity between the Babylonian and Indian Types*

On one detail there is a superficial resemblance between an item among the sources of taxation as described in the *Manusmṛiti* and those described in Hammurabi's *Code.* It refers to forced labour. We have seen above that it formed the second major source of revenue in the Babylonian State. Forced labour certainly existed in the age of Manu and long after. But it never formed a major source of revenue in any age of Indian history. Manu undoubtedly made provision for forced labour when, for instance, as we have already seen above, he ordained that the villagers should bring the daily food, drink, and fuel necessary for the governor of each village. But it may also be realized that that official had no other income on which he could maintain himself ; and unlike the officials placed over ten, twenty, a hundred, and a thousand villages, no land or revenue from land was set apart for his maintenance. There appears, therefore, some justification for the billeting of the governor of a village on the villagers in the age of Manu.

The above is no extenuation of the legalization of forced labour by Manu, who ordained that "mechanics and artisans, as well as Śūdras who subsist by manual labour, he (the king) may cause to work (for himself) one (day) in each month".[110] In the above regulation we have a wider class of people compelled to do forced labour than those mentioned in the *Code of Hammurabi*. It is not only the cultivators but the mechanics and artisans, too, who were compelled to do physical work for the State. Ancient India, particularly in the north, did not possess the huge temples, the mighty embankments, the irrigational canals, and the bridges which were a prominent feature of the public life in ancient Babylonia. But there were the roads, the market places, the temples of ordinary size, and the public buildings of a smaller nature on the repairs, and perhaps on the construction of which, forced labour might have been requisitioned by the State in ancient India.

Contrast between the Two as regards the Duration of Forced Labour. But there was an essential point of difference between the duration of forced labour in India and in Babylonia. Here in this country, according to the *Manusmriti,* it was only for one day in a month that the State could conscript forced labour ; while in ancient Babylonia, it was for the duration of the construction of such huge walls like those of Uruk and of great embankments that it was demanded. The working classes, as represented in the famous *Epic of Gilgamesh,* complained of the excessive labour demanded of them in the construction of the mighty walls of Uruk.[111]

As regards Exemptions. There was another point of difference between the forced labour in India and that in Babylonia. While the other classes of people were taxed, those who were compelled to do forced labour like the Śūdras, the mechanics, and the artisans, were exempted from the payment of taxes. This is evident from the rules regarding the rate of taxation described above. Such exemption from taxation, relating to the sections of the people conscripted for forced labour, is not seen in the case of the cultivators, who were compelled to do forced labour for the greater part of the year, and, perhaps, of their lives in ancient Babylonia.

An essential point of difference between the system of taxation in ancient Babylonia and that in ancient India refers to the exemptions from taxation. Nothing like exemption from taxation seems to have been known to the Babylonians: it was one endless mechanical process of merciless extraction of taxes from the people for the maintenance of the magnificence of the great monarch. But in ancient India the rigour of taxation, if at all it ever existed, was tempered with exemptions. It is true that the particular section of the people that benefited most from exemptions was made up of the Śrotriyas or those who were proficient in the sacred lore. These were not to be taxed even though a king was dying from want of finances![112] But it would be wrong to infer from this that the entire priestly community composed of Brahmans enjoyed this immunity. In the first place, all Brahmans were not necessarily Śrotriyas, as will be evident from what we shall state below. It was only such of the few among them, who were proficent in the Sacred lore (that is, in the knowledge of the *dharmaśāstras*, and, in particular, of the *Vedas* and the *Vedāṅgas*) that were considered as Śrotriyas. Hence, the exemption referred to above concerned only a section of a community which had the onerous duty of studying the Scriptures. The entire priestly community in ancient India did not enjoy the privileges and immunities which its counterpart in Babylonia possessed. For in a later context Manu ordained that if the members of the priestly class did not invite their neighbours, especially those worthy of honour, for a festival at which twenty Brahmans were entertained, or did not invite virtuous Śrotriyas at auspicious festival rites, the ordinary Brahmans were made to pay a fine of one *māṣa* each, while the Śrotriya was subjected to a fine that was twice the cost of the meal and a *māṣa* of gold which latter was to be paid to the State.[113] This passage is important not only because it proves the statement we have made above relating to the non-immunity of the priestly class from State action but also because it supports our contention that Śrotriyas were distinct from the ordinary Brahmans, and that even they were subject to fines levied by the State.

Continuing the topic of exemptions from taxation, we may observe that sons were exempted from paying unpaid fines, taxes, duties, and money due by a surety, or lost at play.[114] In addition to the above two categories of Śrotriyas and sons, who were exempted from certain taxes, there were blind men, idiots, cripples who moved with the help of boards, men seventy years old, and those who conferred benefits on the Śrotriyas, who were all exempted from the payment of a tax. The pregnant women carrying two months and more, ascetics, hermits in the forests, and Brahmans, who were students of the *Vedas*, were not required to pay tolls at any ferry.[115] And when we add to these the Śūdras, the artisans, and the mechanics, who were not taxed at all but made to work for the State for one day in the month, we have a fairly large percentage of the population which was exempted from taxes of all kinds. It is true that we have no stsatistical data relating to the total number of people who were thus exempted from taxation ; but it appears certain that, making allowance for the special favour shown to a small section of the priestly class, which was made up of the Śrotriyas or those learned in the *Ved*as and the law, there were many sections of the people who enjoyed the benefit of the exemption. In this regard ancient India was undoubtedly more progressive than ancient Babylonia.

F. POLICE FORCE

1. BABYLONIA

We are concerned here with the actual methods used by the two ancient governments to coerce and intimidate the population. In this connection we may recall the theory of *daṇḍa* or punishment pervading the entire history of ancient Indian political thought, and the careful manner in which force or coercion was to be used by the monarchs. No such theory is seen in the history of ancient Babylonia, where force was used in all its pristine rigour without any limitations imposed on it. A full picture, it is true, of the police force as it existed in ancient Babylonia is not available. But it is surmised that originally the police force was attached to the temples in Sumer. To what extent it formed the nucleus of the later Babylonian police force is problematical. The fact that Hammurabi charged the feudal lords, who acted on behalf of the monarch, both in the military and civil capacity, with the maintenance of the law and order,[116] suggests that there was nothing in the *Code* of that great Babylonian law-giver that could be compared with the theory of a *daṇḍa* so carefully elaborated in the *Code of Manu,* and so scrupulously followed by all the later Indian writers on political and legal thought.

2. IN ANCIENT INDIA

The convention that existed in Babylonia of holding down conquered peoples by either regular or mercenary soldiers, the methods of sending punitive raids into the territories of the enemies, of demanding hostages, and of forced migrations,[117] are not met with in the *Code of Manu* in which specific and humane regulations are laid down in regard to the method of warfare and conquest.[118]

The king in India was to behave in a generous and gracious manner towards the conquered people. On conquering an enemy, he was to grant exemptions and to cause promises of safety to be proclaimed. Having fully ascertained the wishes of all the conquered people, the king was to place in the conquered territory a relative of the vanquished ruler, and to impose his conditions on the latter. What is more important was that the conqueror was to "make authoritative the lawful customs of the inhabitants, just as they are stated to be, and let him honour the new king, and his chief servants with precious gifts".[119] From whatever angle of vision we may view the ancient State as described in the *Code of Manu,* we find it impossible to equate it with the Babylonian State which was merely a stupendous machinery of might that was shorn of all ethical standards, and which existed only for enhancing the magnificence of the monarch.

CHAPTER III

MANU AND THE MODERN WORLD

A. SHORTCOMINGS IN MANU

1. THE SIZE OF THE STATE

BEFORE WE describe in what manner Manu's concept of the State is of interest to a modern student of Politics, it would be necessary to mention a few shortcomings in that concept which might come in the way of our appreciating that great lawgiver's idea of the State. It may be argued, for instance, that, since the territorial extent of the State as given in the *Manusmṛiti* did not go beyond the limits of Āryāvarta, that is, the land between the Himalayas and the Vindhyas, extending as far as the eastern and western oceans;[120] since in the preceding verses of the same chapter in which the definition of Āryāvarta is found, Manu describes the land between the two sacred rivers, the Sarasvatī and the Dṛṣadvatī, as Brahmāvarta, the plains of the Kurus, the Pāñcālas, and the Śaurasenas as forming the land of the Brahmarṣis, and the land between the Himavat and the Vindhyas to the east of Prayāga and to the west of Vinaṣanā, as Madhyadesa,[121] there was nothing like a single unified political structure that could be called an empire; and that, at the utmost, Manu's concept of a kingdom was nothing more than the emergence of a tribal organization into some faint beginnings of a territorial State. In other words, an imperial power had not yet emerged, and, therefore, we cannot credit Manu with the many attributes of a well developed and multipurposed political structure of the modern times.

The above appears to be a valid argument which comes in our way of maintaining that Manu's concept of the State is in all respects one that has an appeal to the student of the modern times. But on a closer examination it will be found that, notwithstanding any explicit statement relating to a single mighty State in the *Code of Manu,* there is enough justification for us for asserting that in his concept of the State provision was made for a fully grown imperial power that extended its authority over a wide and unified area. We have referred in an earlier context to the concept of a sovereign in the *Manusmṛiti,* who was more powerful than a tribal king. The entire picture of the elaborate legal and judicial machinery in that work presupposes a large and complicated social order which can be associated only with an extensive kingdom. The system of taxation, which likewise has been alluded to above, strongly suggests that we have to consider Manu's State as an empire rather than as a small kingdom. What definitely proves that the political structure in the *Manusmṛiti* was of an imperial type is the idea of conquests, diplomacy, and six-fold policy which cannot be made to agree with a small-sized kingdom of the tribal type. Indeed, when Manu describes the six-fold policy and the ambition of a king,[122] he explicitly refers to a *vijigīṣu* or would-be conqueror, whose ambitious designs we have described elsewhere.[123] On the strength of these considerations it is justifiable to conclude that Manu has described an imperial State ; and that, therefore, we could take into account some of the attributes of his State as being valid for an understanding of the problem from the standpoint of the modern times.

2. EMPHASIS ON THE PRIESTLY CLASS

The second objection that may be levelled against Manu is that he has laid undue emphasis on the priestly class ; and that consequently his concept of the State is not of any interest in the modern age in which the priests have ceased to exist as an integral part of the socio-political life of the people. It is not denied that Manu has assigned a high place to the learned section of the priestly class. But we have to recollect here the many limitations imposed upon the priests by the State mentioned in an earlier context in this work, and especially their prescriptive rights which did not empower them to play the dangerous part in Indian politics which their counterparts had so disastrously played in the history of ancient Babylonia. There is no evidence in Indian history of the priests dominating the entire political atmosphere of the ancient Indian State.

3. NATURE OF THE RULER

Thirdly, it might be objected that sovereignty, according to the concept of Manu, is only intelligible in terms of the master-servant relationship, more in accordance with the idealistic concepts of Hobbes, Bentham, Austin, and others, and not in accordance with the modern concept of the State. In this case, too, it is necessary to recollect that, even when the king was absolute, he was as much required to be subservient to the *dharmaśāstras* as any section of the people ; and that an unbridled despot had no place in the socio-political life of the people. Indeed, there is no room for such an unqualified tyrant in the concept of Manu.

4. BASED ON POVERTY AND SUPERSTITION

And, finally, an objection allied to the previous one may be raised by saying that the mighty all-embracing sway of the king in the *Manusmṛiti* exercised its control over the masses sunk in poverty and superstition ; and that the deep ignorance of the people permitted the personal prerogative of the ruler. Manu's was nothing but a primitive State over which ruled an irresponsible will. Nothing can be farther from the truth than the above estimate of the king in the *Manusmṛiti.* In addition to the obligation of the king to maintain and foster the usages of the older times, and of all sections of the people, which really formed the Common Law of the realm, and his duty to observe the dictates of the *dharmaśāstras,* Manu, as we have stated elsewhere in these pages, permitted the driving out, and in certain cases, the destruction of a wicked king along with his relatives at the hands of the people. To a certain extent, the masses were sunk in poverty and superstition. But these evils have not yet disappeared from many countries ; and even in the most progressive countries of the world, the eradication of poverty has not been finally and completely achieved. While a belief in the potency of the unknown forces of nature has to a great extent been removed from many lands, its place has been taken by a tenacious credulity in the superhuman powers of individuals in the modern world. The primitive cult of the mysterious unknown has given room to the progressive cult of personality in our times. But the practical result in both the cases is much the same: the originality of the individual is lost in the artificial halo of splendour created around the leader. This is, of course, not defending the condition of society in the distant days of Manu. A State might exercise its mighty and all-embracing sway over a population steeped in ignorance, as in the days of Manu, or over a progressive people, as in our own days, the *rationale* of its commands being as much in the needs of the times as in the nature of the people themselves.

B. MANU AND THE MODERN WORLD

The above objections being thus found to be untenable, let us proceed to the next question—Whether and to what extent Manu is of interest to the modern world? This aspect of the question may be studied by analysing some of the characteristics of the ancient and modern State in terms of the following: (1) The State as the Embodiment of Force ; (2) Force in relation to Protection ; (3) Protection and Social Order ; and (4) Social Order, Solidarity, and Develoment.

1. THE STATE AS THE EMBODIMENT OF FORCE

Modern authors on Politics are agreed that the modern State cannot be divested of its armour of might ; that it uses its vast coercive power which cannot be wielded by the citizens but by itself ; and that it displays its untrammelled authority in conquest and expansion, in the war of steel and gold, and in alliances and in diplomacy. Indeed, each State, in the ultimate analysis, is nothing but the personification of Force.[124]

Manu's State is intelligible in the context of the nature of the modern State. Enough has been said above to prove that the theory of *daṇḍa* really converted the State into crystallized force. As in the modern State, so in that of Manu, the coercive power inherent in the State was not meant so much for the citizen as for the State itself. But Manu made it clear: "If (punishment) is properly inflicted after (due) consideration, it makes all people happy ; but inflicted without consideration, it destroys everything."[125] It was justified only to the extent that it prevented the stronger from devouring the weaker. But, it may be argued that the coercive power in a modern State is sanctioned by the judgment of society ; while in the ancient times it was permitted by the judgement of the ruler himself, since ancient society cannot be said to have possessed a judgment of its own.[126] Whatever may be the validity of this assessment of ancient society in other parts of the world, it is inapplicable to the society of ancient India. Viewed from the modern standpoint, it was perhaps defective in the sense that it could not intelligently formulate its will on any given question, particularly that relating to the use of force. This shortcoming in Indian society, on the whole, may be said to have possessed throughout centuries down to our own days. But it was more than compensated for, especially in the ancient times, by the weighty sanction of the "sacred tradiion" of the *smṛitis,* of the customs of virtuous men, and of the conduct of those who knew the *Vedas,*[127] which no ruler could dare to challenge. And since no tradition, customs, and conduct would have been preserved unless sanctioned by society, it is evident that coercion, which was resorted to by the king in the *Manusmṛiti,* could have been in the long run only conditioned by the will of the society.

Allied to the above is another feature of the use of force which is visible in a modern State. The latter denies to the citizens as individuals the use of force "which it restores to them as members of the Leviathan".[128] This idea in its entirety is the result of the growth of modern political consciousness, and is, therefore, hardly visible in the State of Manu, who denied to the individuals the use of force excepting in certain grave contingencies which we have mentioned in an earlier context, viz., in the case of the failure of the king to rule according to the dictates of the *dharmaśāstras,* wilful perversity, etc., and such other cases.

In the unrestrained sweep of the might of the modern State, the aspirations of the individual run the risk of being suppressed, his free expression of thought curtailed, and his daily wants like food, dress, etc., either diminished or diverted even in times of peace, precisely by those "members of the Leviathan" who, once enthroned on the seat of Power, might arrogate to themselves the power of an omnipotent Censor. In this respect, particularly in suppressing the aspirations, opportunities, and needs of the people, the modern State only takes a leaf from the book of Manu which. as remarked earlier, imposes certain restrictions and disabilities on some sections of the people.[129]

2. FORCE IN RELATION TO PROTECTION

We have now to see the *raison d'être* of the use of force in the ancient as well as in the modern State. With the power sanctioned to him by the *dharmaśāstras,* the king in Manu's State appeared *par excellence* as a Censor. That was inevitable when there was no concerted expression of popular voice called public opinion which, in a modern progressive society, is the greater Censor. Manu was concerned with the suppression of the anti-social impulses within society, and, in particular, with the problem of preventing a recurrence of lawlessness which had marked the ages preceding the establishment of the State, when the weaker had been devoured by the stronger. In other words, Manu was faced with the great question of maintaining social order, and of giving to the Stāte its first primary need of protection. Now modern Western writers admit: "To protect the weak against the strong is on the whole a modern reinterpretation of the State's function."[130]

But there is a difference between the concept of protection as it is visible in the *Manusmṛiti* and as envisaged by modern writers. In the age of Manu, protection was needed to guard the weak against the strong, and to provide them with the means of realizing their best within the terms of the *dharmaśāstras.* But in the modern world, although protection continues to mean what it connoted in the ancient days, yet it has taken the shape of the establishment of the minimum standards of living, the provisions of requisite health and decency, and in short, of the State itself becoming what Professor MacIver aptly calls "a great ministry of social assurance",[131] so that the members of the State could compensate for their natural or accidental loss from the generosity of the State. As to how far this could be actually realized is for the present problematical ; but the general principle of the State's providing the necessary means of making up for the deficiencies in its members without destroying either their responsibility or their initiative, appears to be accepted.[132] It is thus clear that the use of force in the ancient Indian State is intelligible, even though its objectives were different to those facing a modern State.

3. PROTECTION AND SOCIAL ORDER

Manu realized that order was the next most essential business of the State. But the order in his mind was that which covered all the four orders of the people—the students, the householders, the hermits, and the ascetics, and all the four *varṇas* or castes. The relation between force or punishment and social order is given in the statement in the *Manusmṛiti* that "the whole world is kept in order by punishment", and that "All castes (*varṇas*) would be corrupted (by intermixture), all barriers would be broken through, and all men would rage (against each other) in consequence of mistakes with respect to punishment".[133] Manu's concept of a social order was a peculiar feature of those distant days, when one of the greatest social questions was the maintenance of the purity of the race. The State was created with an environment in the midst of which the four orders, the four castes, and even the mixed castes together with the people of the forest regions, could all lead their lives in a co-ordinated relationship with one another, and within the limits imposed by the *dharmaśāstras*. It was likewise concerned with the question of directing the degrees of social intercourse so that the framework of the social order was maintained,[134] and the chances of communal friction and chaos, and with it the exercise of coercion, gradually lessened. In doing so it was necessary to maintain and foster the ancient customs of the various sections of the people.[135]

We have to see how far the above general outline of the concept of order is similar to that of the modern State. To begin with, it may be observed that modern writers are agreed that order is the first business of the State.[136] But instead of there being the interests of the four orders and the four castes, that is, instead of the considerations of either racial or religio-occupational significance, as in the days of Manu, there are now-a-days vast spheres of social order like those of custom, morality, business usage, and special associations, the interests of all of which, in addition to its own, the modern State has to uphold and foster. Indeed, it is no more a limited social order as in the days of Manu: it has assumed the magnitude of a universal social order of various forms and potentialities, which are the results of the many complex socio-economic and political tendencies of the modern world. Nevertheless, it is interesting to observe that, as in the case of the State of Manu, so in that of the modern State, the primary function of the State is:

> To provide such conditions that people can lead their lives in decent relation to one another, to prevent confusion and chaos, to regulate the forms of intercourse and communication so that life shall run more smoothly for all concerned, to see that every thing has and holds its appointed place,—including itself, and finally to take in its sole keeping and to so to minimize the exercise of coercion necessary for the fulfilment of these tasks. . . .[137]

4. SOCIAL ORDER, SOLIDARITY, AND DEVELOPMENT

The regulations of Manu pertaining to the purity of the race and to the duties of the various castes unmistakably point to the great objective which he seems to have kept before him, viz., the maintenance of the solidarity of the whole social fabric. It is perhaps this laudable object which made him, after delineating in detail the duties, of all the main four castes in various contexts,[138] issue a general order to the following effect: "Abstention from injuring (creatures), veracity, abstention from unlawfully appropriating (the goods of others), purity, and control of the organs, Manu has declared to be the summary of the law of the four castes."[139] How permanently this all-round directive came to stay in the country will be evident when we observe that centuries after the days of Manu, the very same order became the basis of the noble injunctions of Aśoka the Great. For our purpose we may note that the above general order occurs in the middle of the description of the mixed castes. The only way by which it could be explained is not to consider it as an interpolation, which would hardly solve the problem, but to suppose that the particular ordinance relating to all the four castes was obviously meant to promote the well-being of the whole society. It is this which explains why, in an earlier context, we are informed in the *Manusmṛiti* that the good and bad qualities of human action, and the immemorial rule of conduct are meant to be followed by all the four castes.[140] We may reasonably conclude from the above regulations as well as from those relating to the interdependence of the castes and the careful adjustment of duties amongst them that Manu's ordinance had in view, not the interest of any particular caste, but the furtherance of the social solidarity of all the sections of the people.

If it is true that order is to be maintained not for itself but for the sake of protection, conservation, and development, as suggested above, then, it may be asked to what extent were these objectives furthered in the State of Manu? We have to remove from our minds the modern concept of development and conservation as implying an extensive utilization by the State of the resources, the execution of enterprises on a vast scale, the preservation of the beauties of the natural regions, the establishment of industries, the lessening of the hardships arising out of industrialization, and the like, which only modern governments with huge finances and the advantages of scientific and technical skill can successfully perform.[141] We have, on the other hand, to visualize conditions of an altogether different nature where the twin problems of conservation and development implied more the preservation of the ancient law, the Sacred teachings, the standards of virtuous conduct, and the building up of character than the expansion of the materialistic aspect of life. Manu's age had not outgrown the stage of the sanctity of the sacred fire, the sacraments, and the sacrifices.[142] It still believed in the imperative need of conserving and transmitting the Sacred knowledge to posterity. It stood for the development of character upon which depended the continuance of the *dharma* of the various *āśramas* and the *varṇas*.

The conservation and development with which Manu was concerned were of an altogether different type from those which confront a modern State. But it does not mean that the State in the days of Manu had a less onerous task to perform than that which faces the modern State. On the other hand, its performance has to be judged from the legacy which it has left behind it. The fact that, inspite of its all-round limitations and its perennial source of anxiety in the form of alien ideas and forces, the ancient Indian State survived for centuries and succeeded in conserving all that was abiding and virtuous in ancient Indian life and thought is by itself, the best tribute which posterity can pay to the nature, strength, and outlook of the State of Manu. No student of modern Politics can fail to observe that, when all things have been said, the *Code of Manu* created a universal frame of social order within which, according to the prevailing notions of freedom, the lives of the members of all the orders and castes were so regulated as to move voluntarily towards the fulfilment of the one great objective for which the ancient State and society stood—the realization of the ends as prescribed in the *dharmaśāstras*. It is in the nature of freedom, more than in its contents, which it allowed the members of the society that we see how the State of Manu is of some interest to us in the modern times.

CHAPTER IV

MANU AND KAUṬILYA

A. THE ARTHAŚĀSTRA A DEPARTURE FROM THE MANUSMṚITI

1. BEGINNING AND ENDING

CENTURIES AFTER the times of Manu, there appeared in the fourth century B.C. one of the most original thinkers in the field of politics, Kauṭilya, the great Prime Minister of Candragupta Maurya. A comparative study of the *Arthaśāstra* which he wrote, with the *Manusmṛiti* reveals that the former was a bold departure from the latter. According to the historical data available till now, the first and the greatest reaction against the concept of the State of Manu was at the hands of Kauṭilya. To what extent the intervening authors on Politics between Manu and Kauṭilya were responsible for preparing the ground for the latter is unfortunately a point that cannot now be determined, since the works of those teachers have been lost, the only reference to most of them being in the *Mahābhārata*, and particularly in the *Arthaśāstra* itself. We may, however, with the meagre sources available on the subject, surmise that the earliest signs of a breaking away from the school of Manu in certain respects was probably the School of Uśanas, which is mentioned by Kauṭilya immediately after the School of Manu. We may, likewise, presume that the reaction against the earliest orthodox School, thus established, must have had a sufficiently good response necessitating, as centuries passed by, the compilation of all such liberal views at the hands of Kauṭilya himself. This is clear from the opening sentence of the *Arthaśāstra*, immediately following the salutation to Śukra and Brihaspati, thus: "This Arthaśāstra is made as a compendium of almost all the Arthaśāstras, which, in view of acquisition and maintenance of the earth, have been composed by ancient teachers."[143] Towards the end of his book Kauṭilya repeats this in a slightly different way, thus: "This Arthaśāstra, or Science of Polity, has been made as a compendium of all those Arthaśāstras which, as a guidance to kings in acquiring and maintaining the earth, have been written by ancient teachers."[144]

In the above two almost identical statements Kauṭilya seems to suggest that his work is different from the one of Manu. In the *Code*, of the latter, as we have already seen above, there is no reference to its being a guide to kings, who desired to acquire and maintain the earth. On the other hand, Manu explicitly refers to the sacred character of the laws of the four castes and the four orders, to the ancient customs and usage, to the regulations relating to intermediate castes, and to the duties of the king, etc.[145] Kauṭilya would not break away altogether from the moorings of the ancient *dharmaśāstras* but was not prepared to grant them their sacredotal hold over political institutions. This is proved, firstly, by the manner in which he defines the *Vedas* ; secondly, by the place of importance which he assigns to the *Vedas* in the list of the four sciences ; thirdly, by the stress which he laid on wealth ; and, fourthly, by the manner in which he mentions the relative importance of the Sacred law and the State law.

(*a*) *Definition of the Vedas*

According to Kauṭilya, "the three *Vedas, Sāma, Ṛik,* and *Yajus,* constitute the triple *Vedas.* These together with the *Atharva Veda* and the *Itihāsaveda* are (known as) the *Vedas.*"[146] As to what was meant by *Itihāsaveda,* he relates in a later context, thus: "*Purāṇa, Itivritta* (history), *Ākhyāyika* (tale), *Udhāraṇa* (illustrations), *Dharmaśāstra* and *Arthaśāstra* are (known by the name) *Itihāsa.*"[147] Although he has mentioned apart the three *Vedas,* yet the inclusion of the *Itihāsaveda* among the Vedas unmistakenably points to a more radical interpretation of the term "Sacred lore" than which Manu was prepared to concede.

(*b*) *Place of Importance given to the Vedas*

That Kauṭilya was not prepared to give the first preference to the *Vedas* in the field of knowledge is proved by the place of importance which he assigns to them in the list of the four sciences which he enumerates thus: *Ānvikṣakī,* the triple *Vedas* (*Trayī*), *vārtā* (agriculture and trade), and *daṇḍanīti* (science of government) are what are called the four sciences (*vidyāḥ*).[148] As to what he meant by *ānvīkṣakī,* he defines it as comprising the philosophy of Sānkhya, Yoga, and Lokāyata. The supreme importance of *ānvīkṣakī* is given thus by him:

> When seen in the light of these sciences, the science of *ānvīkṣakī* is most beneficial to the world, keeps the mind steady and firm in weal and woe alike, and bestows excellence of foresight, speech, and action. Light to all kinds of knowledge, easy means to accomplish all kinds of acts and receptacle of all kinds of virtues, is the science of *ānvīkṣakī* ever held to be.[149]

Kauṭilya's insistence on the *ānvīkṣakī* and on the logic of the Lokāyatas amongst the sciences is by itself enough to prove that he was vitally different from Manu in whose political philosophy logic had no place whatsoever. Unlike Manu, who was concerned solely with righteous behaviour flowing from a study of the ancient scriptures, Kauṭilya was faced with the problem of righteous and unrighteous conduct, and with that of wealth on which alone the State could be firmly planted. It is this which perhaps made him affirm that "it is from these sciences (mentioned above) that all that concerns righteousness and wealth is learnt".[150]

We may not deduce from this discussion that Kauṭilya altogether ignored the importance of the *Vedas*. On the other hand, he agreed with Manu, whose injunctions we have already seen, that the triple *Vedas*, which definitely determined the general conduct of social behaviour of all the sections of the people, were most useful. This is inferred from his statement that the world maintained in accordance with the triple *Vedas* would surely progress but never perish (*Trayyā hi rakṣito lokaḥ prasīdati na sīdati*).[151]

(c) *Importance of Wealth*

Kauṭilya also differed from Manu in regard to the importance of *daṇḍanīti*, and the stress which was to be laid on wealth. He maintained that the first three sciences (*ānvīkṣakī*, the triple *Vedas*, and *vārtā*) are dependent for their well-being on the science of government.[152] Unlike Manu, Kauṭilya made wealth, as connoted by *vārtā*, and *daṇḍanīti* interdependent. This was because the strength of the king, who was to wield his sceptre, depended on wealth which came through agriculture, cattle-breeding, and trade.[153] Wealth, according to Kauṭilya, was productive of dangerous, provocative, and doubtful consequences. The detailed manner in which he describes these three kinds of wealth,[153a] and the emphasis which he placed on wealth in general, suggest that in his concept of the State, wealth played a most important part which is missing in Manu's concept of the State.

(d) *Sacred Law and State Law*

Kauṭilya's independent and rational outlook is proved further by the way he discriminates between Sacred law and State law. He admits, no doubt, the importance of the Sacred law (*dharma*) in the following statement: "The king who administers justice in accordance with Sacred law (*dharma*), evidence (*vyavahāra*), *saṁsthā* (precedents? history?), and *nyāya* (equity) which is the fourth, will be able to conquer the whole world bounded by the four quarters (*caturantāṁ mahīṁ*)."[154] The subordinate position of the Sacred law is visible, not when it conflicts with history—in which case the Sacred law prevails—but when it is at variance with rational or State law (*dharma-nyāya*), in which case "reason shall be held authoritative". The reason for this is given by Kauṭilya in the next part of the same sentence—"for there the original text (on which the Sacred law has been based) is not available".[155] It is astonishing that

Kauṭilya should have upheld reason against authority, especially when we realize that he himself was a member of the priestly class which believed in classical domination ; and when around him the atmosphere was still saturated with sacredotal sanctity. Moreover, in his great work the main idea was the stabilization of monarchical authority. Viewed from this standpoint, he appears to have supplanted the theocratic concept of law by the secular idea of law.

2. MANTRIPARISAD AND OTHER ITEMS

Kauṭilya differed from Manu also on the composition of the council of ministers (*mantripariṣad*). Manu had laid down that it was to consist of twelve members, as Kauṭilya himself relates. But in the same context Kauṭilya states that the *mantripariṣad* shall consist of as many members as the needs of his dominion require (*yathāsāmarthyaṁ*).[156] Likewise on the question of punishing a government official, who was negligent in his duties, Manu, according to Kauṭilya, held that a fine equal to the loss of revenue and multiplied by the serial number of the circumstances of the guilt (narrated by Kauṭilya in the preceding paragraph) should be imposed upon him. But Kauṭilya objected to this by saying that the fine should be proportional to the guilt.[157]

Manu enjoined, according to Kauṭilya, that false witnesses should be fined ten times the amount which, no matter whether it was true or false, they caused to be lost. But Kauṭilya asserted that it was truth which the witnesses had to hear (when they were called to attest to any transaction) ; if they did not mind it, they were to be fined twenty-four *paṇas* ; if they attested to a false case (without scrutiny), they were to be fined half of the above amount.[158] Concerning robbery, too, Kauṭilya differed from Manu. The latter, again as given in the *Arthaśāstra,* held that the fine for the direct seizure of precious stones and superior and inferior raw materials shall be equal to their value. But Kauṭilya was of the view that it should be proportional to the gravity of the crime.[159]

3. THE SIZE OF THE STATE

From a description of Āryāvarta as given in the *Manusmṛiti* cited above, it must have been apparent to the reader that the State in the age of Manu was sufficiently large enough to justify the title of sovereign given to the ruler in that work. We may be permitted to repeat that Manu's regulations referring to the ambassadors, and in particular to the *rāja-maṇḍala* theory,[160] point to a powerful monarch who had passed from the stage of a tribal chieftain to that of a territorial ruler.

But Kauṭilya's sovereign was of a larger, more powerful, and more aggressive type than the one described in the *Manusmṛiti*. In the latter work the king had an exalted position because of the divine sanction behind him. There is nothing of that halo around the sovereign in the *Arthaśāstra*. In this work the king starts as a small ruler, and then assumes the status of a great sovereign by conquering the whole world. Kauṭilya gave a new idea of kingship when he wrote: "A wise king, trained in Politics, will, though he possesses a small territory, conquer the whole earth with the help of the best fitted elements of his sovereignty, and will never be defeated."[161] In this statement Kauṭilya had discarded, once for all, the Kṣatriya claims of the ruler. Unlike the monarch in Manu, the one in Kauṭilya received no inspiration from any divine source. At best he could claim only the *daṇḍanīti* and wealth as his support. Kauṭilya's monarch was not content with a large kindom: it was the conquest of the whole earth (as signified by the geographical boundaries of northern India) that satisfied his ambition. Such a conqueror was essentially the royal patron on whose behalf Kauṭilya, as the latter informs us towards the end of his great book, wrote the *Arthaśāstra* after rescuing "the scriptures and the science of weapons and the earth which had passed to the Nanda king".[162] The conqueror described by Kauṭilya was, as already stated earlier, no other than the Narendra on whose behalf he had composed his work.[163] Since this Narendra is known from other sources to have been the same as Candragupta Maurya, it follows that Kauṭilya had in his mind no other ruler but the Mauryan leader, whom he has rightly pictured as an aggresive sovereign. The State which Kauṭilya's Narendra brought into existence was much larger than the one which Manu had ever contemplated for his sovereign. We see, therefore, that it was not merely a monarchical State but a huge imperial machinery which Kauṭilya describes in his *Arthaśāstra*.[164]

B. THE PROBLEMS FACING THE STATE: NATURE AND NUMBER OF PROBLEMS

Kauṭilya's State was confronted, no doubt, with most of the problems which had faced Manu's State. But some of them had assumed such large dimensions as to change the nature of the State itself. Without going into the details of the numerous problems which the State of Manu attempted to solve, and which, considering the period of antiquity in which he lived, were of a varied and complicated nature, we may merely observe that, on the whole, Manu's State seemed to lean more on the ethical than on the material side of life. This explains why we find elaborate regulations on the observance of the *dharmaśāstras*, on the duties of the four castes and the four orders, on the dangers of an admixture of castes, on the purity of family life, on the duties of children, wives, etc.,—in a word, on the need of maintaining a high moral life which could never transgress the limits imposed upon it by the *dharmaśāstras*. Sanctity of the institutions, sacredness of the orders, inviolability of married life, maintenance of the glory of the ancient learning—these were some of the great questions which, along with others like those of trade, inheritance, civil and criminal law, faced the State of Manu.[165]

But with Kauṭilya the weightage had shifted to graver and more vital problems. There were the army, battles, strategy, war, peace, policy, intrigue, espionage, conduct of governmental departments, national calamities, internal and external dangers to the State—that is, complicated problems which are not met with in the *Manusmṛiti*. Even if we examme the fines imposed in connection with numerous crimes, we see that the State in the *Arthaśāstra* had far transcended the limits mentioned by Manu.[166] The magnitude of the problems confronting the State of Kauṭilya proves that it was no more the comparatively simple State it had been centuries earlier in the days of Manu, but that it had grown into a costly, complicated, and colossal machinery resting on the pillars of wealth and power.

C. OTHER QUESTIONS: SOVEREIGNTY AND POLITICAL STRENGTH

1. SOVEREIGNTY

The wide gulf between the State of Manu and that of Kauṭilya will be further evident when we examine the concept of sovereignty in their words. The concept of sovereignty as discussed in the *Arthaśāstra* is missing in the *Manusmṛiti*. A plausible explanation of this is that in the concept of Manu, the king had a supernatural touch about him, although, as we have already remarked, that great lawgiver had made definite safeguards on behalf of the people, including the overthrow of the king in certain circumstances. But the statements that the king was a great deity in human form, and that no man was to transgress the law made by him,[167] clearly indicate that Manu's concept of sovereignty was couched more in terms of moral sanctity than in those of political power.

That this was not the case with Kauṭilya is evident when we note that he used the terms *rājatva* and *prakṛitiḥ* for sovereignty and its attributes, and described the elements and calamities of the same in a manner to suggest that there was practically no trace of the divinity around his sovereign.[168]

2. POLITICAL STRENGTH

The new concept of political strength which Kauṭilya introduced in the history of political thought is expressed in the analysis of strength. Strength, according to him, was of three kinds—the power of deliberation which is intellectual strength ; the possession of a prosperous treasury and a strong army is the strength of sovereignty ; and martial power is physical strength (*śaktiḥ—trividhā jñānabalaṁ mantriṣaktiḥ kośa daṇḍa balaṁ prabhuśaktiḥ vikrama-balaṁ utsāhaśaktiḥ*). In the preceding statement that Strength is Power and Happiness is the End (*balaṁ śaktiḥ sukhaṁ siddhiḥ*),[169] Kauṭilya had epitomized the new concept of political strength. We seek for it in vain in the *Manusmṛiti*.

CHAPTER V

KAUṬILYA AND ARISTOTLE

A. INTRODUCTION

THE HIGH place which Kauṭilya gave in his concept of the State to power and happiness tempts us to seek for similar ideals in the same age but outside the confines of India. We find them in the writings of a celebrated political thinker, who also dwelt on them but in a way suited to the conditions of his own country. It was Aristotle between whose concepts and those of Kauṭilya we may now institute a comparison in order to see, in general, how far the two great thinkers were similar in their ideas, where exactly they differed in their views, and in what respects one falls short of the other. This side of our comparative study may be grouped under the following heads: the environment in which the two great thinkers lived ; their views on the origin of the State, on its evolution, its requisites, elements, forms, machinery, functions, and its ends, including their views on citizens ; and, finally, a study in their method. Viewed from these standpoints, Aristotle and Kauṭilya afford more scope for a comparative study than Kauṭilya and Machiavelli, as some scholars have done.[170]

Aristotle and Kauṭilya were chronologically near each other but were not exactly contemporaries. Aristotle died in 322 B.C. ;[171] while Kauṭilya was the Prime Minister of Candragupta Maurya (320-296 B.C.).[172] Nothing is known either of the ancestry or antecedents of Kauṭilya. But since he is generally believed to have been responsible for overthrowing the Nandas through the instrumentality of Candragupta Maurya, and since this event may be placed in 323 B.C.,[173] we may justifiably assume that Kauṭilya, who three years later assumed the onerous duties of a prime minister, might have been born about twenty-five years earlier. That is, he might have been born in *circa* 346 B.C. which was about the time Aristotle had left Athens for seeking service under foreign rulers. Only in this way could we look upon them as contemporaries, that is, Aristotle as belonging to the greater part of the fourth century B.C., and Kauṭilya, to the latter part of the same century B.C. and to the early part of the third century B.C.

B. THE ENVIRONMENT IN WHICH THEY LIVED

1. HISTORY OF ARISTOTLE

There was little in common in their environment, antecedents, and experience. All these three factors were to a great extent responsible for shaping their respective concepts of the State. Aristotle was a native of the City State of Stageria which stood on the border of the Greek world. While a youth at Athens, he had studied philosophy under Plato, the profoundest thinker Greece had till that time produced. After Plato's death (347 B.C.), Aristotle left Athens, and took service under new monarchs who, not being Greeks, had taken upon themselves the duty of diffusing Greek culture among the barbarians of the East, as all non-Greeks were then called. Aristotle first served under the insignificant tyrant Hermias of the city of Atarneus ; but in 342 B.C., he went to the court of Philip of Macedon, where he became the tutor of the future Aleaxnder the Great. He gained much experience while in Macedonia, particularly about the despotic rule of both Philip and Alexander. When in 335 B.C. Alexander started on his unrivalled career of conquests, Aristotle left Macedonia, returned to Athens, where he incurred the wrath of the Athenians, who charged him with impiety, and compelled him to take shelter in Chalcis, a Macedonian centre, where he died in 322 B.C. What the civilized Greeks had failed to give him, he received at the hands of the barbarians—a generous treatment![174]

Aristotle's youth and early manhood had been spent in Athens, his mature life in Macedonia, and his last years in a stronghold that was imperial in spirit. While at Athens he had ample opportunities of studying the history and constitutions of the many Greek City States ; and while at Macedonia, of the new and powerful imperial structure built by Philip and Alexander. He was, therefore, admirably qualified to be a student of the then existing constitutions, which were both varied and complex in their nature. His study of philosophy under Plato, while at Athens, his mastery of all the political theories prevailing till his time, and his wide experience of administration, while at the Macedonian court, made him look at the problem of the State both from the abstract and the practical points of view. He never desisted from criticizing his illustrious teacher, sometimes not justly, but he could not escape the influence of Plato. He lived in an age that was surcharged with conflicting ideals ; and he appears to us in the rôle of a mediator in the controversies ranging in his own and previous times. We find him, therefore, tackling both beliefs and practices with a view to laying the bare truth before us.[175] This point may be borne in mind when we shall evaluate his method below.

2. SIMILARITY BETWEEN THE TWO

(a) *Little Knowledge about Their Lives*

There are some points of similarity between Aristotle and Kauṭilya. As in the case of the great Greek political philosopher, so in that of the Indian thinker, we know very little about their early life. Like Aristotle, Kauṭilya was fearless in his criticism of his own teacher, but unlike the great Greek, Kauṭilya was never unjust to his own teacher,[176] whom unfortunately he never mentions by name. Like Aristotle, who had studied under previous teachers like Plato, Phalaes, and Hippodamus,[177] Kauṭilya had studied all the theorists who had preceded him. Like Aristotle, Kauṭilya was constrained to take up service under an imperial ruler. Like the great Greek thinker, Kauṭilya also tackled both beliefs and practices with a fundamental point of difference in his method which will be discussed later on in these pages. But unlike Aristotle, who turned his back on Macedonia, Kauṭilya did not forsake Magadha, because his royal master wished to embark upon a career of conquest. And unlike the Greek political thinker, the Indian politician did not appear as a mediator in the controversies of the age. On the other hand, because of the dangerous times in which he lived, he was an uncompromising advocate of only one form of government. The internal danger of the followers of the intolerant, irreligious, and tyrannical Nandas, and the external danger of the admirers and hirelings of one of the most intrepid of Alexander the Great's generals, were responsible for transforming Kauṭilya into the staunchest champion of imperialism India had ever seen.

(b) *Both did not originate Political Science*

Both Aristotle and Kauṭilya were not originators of Political Science: they were merely heirs to a rich heritage which they enlarged with their wide experience and penetrating skill.[178]

(c) *Both wrote with Prejudiced Minds*

Both were great thinkers whose minds were prejudiced. Aristotle had an inborn contempt for all Asiatics, whom he considered as barbarians, and amongst whom he might have counted the Indians. This is proved by the following passages in his *Politics.* While describing one kind of monarchy, he writes: "There is another sort of monarchy not uncommon among the barbarians, which nearly resembles tyranny. But even this is legal and hereditary. For barbarians, being more servile in character than Hellenes (that is, the Greeks), and Asiatics, than Europeans, do not rebel against a despotic government."[179] Then, again, he writes that a second kind of royalty "is that of the barbarians, which is an hereditary despotic

25

government in accordance with law".[180] In a later context Aristotle, while contrasting the people of Europe, who live in a cold climate, and who preserve their freedom, with those who live in warmer regions, says: "Whereas the natives of Asia are intelligent and inventive, but they are wanting in spirit, and therefore they are always in a state of subjection and slavery."[181] In a still later context, he seems to point to the Indians when he writes that "kings have no marked superiority over their subjects, such as Skylax affirms to be found among the Indians, it is obviously necessary on many grounds that all citizens should take their turn of governing and being governed".[182] Whatever may be the correctness of the view which Aristotle held in regard to the other Asiatic governments, it cannot be made to apply to the ancient Indian governments for reasons already stated in this book. But Aristotle's obliquity of judgment became an article of faith with all later European scholars, many of whom like Sir Henry Maine, Professor T. H. Green, and others have not failed to dwell on the alleged subservient nature of the Indian people.[183]

The antipathy which Aristotle had to all Asiatics was much the same as the hatred which Kauṭilya, and the Indian political thinkers after him, bore for the Mlechchhas. While describing rules regarding slaves, he writes thus: "It is no crime for Mlechchhas to sell or mortgage the life of their own offspring."[184] In this single sentence there is more of the denunciation of the Mlechchhas than in the passages from Aristotle concerning the Asiatics cited above. Kauṭilya's contempt for the Mlechchhas is also seen in the manner in which he classifies them along with thieves and wild tribes. He relates that if a king is destitute of an army, he should as far as possible attract to himself the brave men of corporations, of thieves, of wild tribes, of Mlechchhas, and of spies who are capable of inflicting injuries upon enemies.[185]

(d) *Their Works as a Whole*

Their works taken as a whole may now be compared. Professor Davis states that Aristotle's book is unfinished, full of repetitions, with some subjects which are promised but never discussed, and with the connecting links between subjects not understood.[186] None of these defects is visible in the *Arthaśāstra* of Kauṭilya. Both in design and execution, it is a work in which the topics are not only well arranged and in their proper sequence, but treated in such an admirable manner as to leave little room for improvement. There is hardly any repetition in any chapter. Indeed, as a manual on statecraft, the *Arthaśāstra* is a masterpiece of workmanship superior not only to the work of Aristotle but to that of the comparatively later great Italian thinker Machiavelli, who has been compared so often with Kauṭilya, as related in the notes of this book.

(e) *The Objectives before Them*

We may now come to the next point—the objectives which Aristotle and Kauṭilya had in view. Aristotle conceived of a City State limited in territory and in population, although he was certainly aware of an empire like that of Philip and Alexander under whom he had served. But he had an instinctive hatred for empires, the possible services of which to civilization he, no doubt, granted.[187] Kauṭilya was, on the other hand, an unequivocal champion of a large kingdom ever growing into a mighty empire. Indeed, as stated elsewhere in these pages, he wrote his work for a monarch—and for all those like him who came after his time—who, starting as the ruler of a small kingdom, rose to the position of an emperor and aspired to universal dominion.

(f) *Both justified Authority and Force*

It is interesting to see how far both the Greek and the Indian political thinkers justified authority and the use of force. Aristotle's justification of authority may be traced to his ideas of the eternal and unbridgeable difference between the male and the female. He writes that the relation between the male to the female is apparent because the inequality between them is permanent. The rule of the husband over the wife is a constitutional one, while that of the former over the children is royal rule but rule it is all the same in both the cases.[188] In an earlier context he stated that the male is by nature superior, the female, inferior ; and the one rules, and the other is ruled ; this principle, of necessity, extends to all mankind.[189] Then, again, he says that the courage of a man is shown in commanding, while that of a woman, in obeying.[190]

The great Greek political philosopher expressed precisely the same opinion about man and woman which Indian thinkers since Manu had maintained. We have already seen in this Part, while discussing the problem of the domestic relations as given in the *Code of Manu* and in that of Hammurabi, that Manu had consigned woman to the care of her father in childhood, to that of her husband in her youth, to that of her sons on the death of her husband, and that independence was altogether denied to her.[191] This subjection of woman ordained by Manu seems to have been maintained by all later Indian political thinkers, including Kauṭilya, although the latter does not explicitly repeat the famous statement of Manu regarding the inferior position of woman cited above. But it is clear from the rule laid down by Kauṭilya that, even when girls attained majority at the age of twelve, if they proved disobedient to lawful authority (which is not stated but which was obviously that of their parents or husbands), (*ata ūrddhvam-aśuśrūṣāyaṁ*), then they were to be fined fifteen *paṇas*.[192] We have here the same justification of authority which we notice in Aristotle.

Much more than the difference between the male and the female, it was in the nature of man himself that both Aristotle and Kauṭilya ultimately justified the use of force by the State. According to Aristotle, man's inherent nature was one addicted to war and wickedness which necessitated the exercise of power and the infliction of punishment. While explaining the theory that the State was by nature prior to the family and the individual, he writes that man, when perfected, is the best of animals, "but, when separated from law and justice, he is the worst of all". If man is without virtue, "he is the most unholy and the most savage of animals, and the most full of lust and gluttony".[193] Aristotle amplifies this point, while explaining the evils arising out of the possession of private property. "These evils, however," he writes, "are due to a very differtnt cause—the wickedness of human nature."[194] Although Aristotle does not explicitly mention the relationship between the wickedness of man and the need of maintaining force, yet it appears that, when he affirmed that the king must have force in order to maintain law,[195] he had in mind practically the same idea relating to *daṇḍa* which, as already seen in these pages, Kauṭilya had when the latter justified the use of *daṇḍa* in order to maintain the State. Indeed, Aristotle had forestalled the Kauṭilyan principle when he wrote that, as a general principle common to all governments, the portion of the State which desires permanence ought to be stronger than that which desires the reverse.[196]

Emphasis laid on Military Strength. The emphasis laid on military strength, which is precisely the keynote of the internal and external policy of the *vijigīṣu* of Kauṭilya, is quite evident when we note what Aristotle has to say on the art of war and its relationship to government. In one context, while discussing the concept of property, Aristotle says that the art of war is a natural art of acquisition, "for it includes hunting, an art which we ought to practise against wild beasts, and against men who, though intended by men to be governed, will not submit ; for want of such a kind is naturally just".[197]

Importance of Force. While criticizing the view of Phaleas of Chalcedon, one of the theorists who had written on constitutions, Aristotle came nearest to Kauṭilya in the following statement: "The government must be organized with a view to military strength ; and of this he (Phaleas) has not said a word."[198] A further point of comparison between Aristotle and Kauṭilya in regard to the importance of force as the mainstay of the State refers to the significance of the army. While rejecting Plato's view that the legislator should have his eye on two points—the people and the country—Aristotle writes that the legislator should not forget the neighbouring countries, and that "a state must have such a military force as will be serviceable against her neighbours, and not merely useful at home".[199] It would be tedious to give parallel passages to the above in Kauṭilya's *Arthaśāstra* ; but a glance through Books VI, VII and VIII of the latter will suffice to prove that Kauṭilya had done more than justice to the above view of Aristotle relating to the maintenance of a strong military force.[200]

C. ORIGIN OF THE STATE

1. INTRODUCTION

The many points of comparison between the views of Aristotle and Kauṭilya discussed above, would make us naturally hope for a further identity of interests between the two great thinkers. But these hopes are belied when, for example, we examine the various aspects of the State beginning with the question of its origin, as revealed in their writings. To Aristotle the State was a creation of nature. He came to this conclusion after stating: "When several villages are united in a single large community, perfect and large enough to be nearly or quite self-sufficing, the state comes into existence, originating in the bare needs of life, and continuing in existence for the sake of a good life."[201] In the latter part of the same sentence, Aristotle enunciated a famous principle which all progressive governments ever since his time have placed before themselves. His statement that the State is a creation of nature followed by the observation that man is a political animal,[202] is to be read in conjunction not only with what he writes in connection with the union of villages forming a State given above, but also together with the later statement that "the state is by nature clearly prior to the family and to the individual, since the whole is of necessity prior to the part ; for example, if the whole body be destroyed, there will be no foot or hand, except in an equivocal sense, as we might speak of a stone hand ; for when destroyed the hand will be no better".[203]

2. ARISTOTLE ON THE ORIGIN OF THE STATE

Aristotle is not quite intelligible in his discussion of the origin of the State as given above.[204] If the State originated as a union of villages, it is clear that it could not have been prior to the family, for we cannot think of villages existing without families and individuals. Further, if the State were prior to the family and the individual, all the attributes of the State, including those of law, should also be prior to the individual and the family which, however, is as much irrational as it is unhistorical. We cannot likewise think of law existing for abstract purposes unrelated to the needs and motives of individuals, and prior to them. Laws in that case would have already been made by the time the family had came into existence. Even when applied to the Greek City States and Macedonia, Aristotle's theory is historically untenable. The origin of the State is to be ultimately traced to the existence of man and to his first subjection to some sort of authority exercised over him by other individuals.[205]

3. KAUTILYA ON THE ORIGIN OF THE STATE

Neither the inconsistency about the existence of the State and of the individual nor the unhistoricity of the origin of the former prior to that of the latter is seen in Kauṭilya. He could have, like Aristotle, indulged in speculation about the origin of the State but like a true practical statesman, he took the existence of the State as a *fait accompli*. The reason for this was obvious. He was concerned with the State that had existed before his royal patron, Candragupta Maurya, had wrested it from the Nandas. He was not interested with the question as to how the State, which had come into the possession of Candragupta Maurya, had been brought into existence but with the more urgent problem of how to make it a mighty and vigorous State that could withstand both internal and external dangers. These two dangers we have already mentioned above. Kauṭilya dwells at length on the internal danger which sometimes becomes the main theme of some of his chapters. For instance, Book V, Chapter I, entitled the Awards of Punishments begins thus: "Measures necessary to remove the thorns of public peace, both in fortified cities and country parts, have been dealt with. We shall now proceed to treat of measures to suppress treason against the king and his kingdom."[206] At the end of the next chapter dealing with the replenishment of the treasury, he reiterates the same paramount problem, viz., that measures such as above (narrated by him) shall be taken only against the seditious and the wicked, and never against others (*evaṁ duṣyeṣu-adhārmikeṣu-ca varteta na-etareṣu*).[207] These considerations should enable us to appreciate the altogether different viewpoint of Kauṭilya, whose failure to discuss the problem of the origin of the State thus becomes intelligible. Unlike him Aristotle, who had left the patronage of the Macedonian court, had to find a new haven and to justify the same. Filled as Aristotle was with the experience of many Greek City States, he could naturally think of the origin of the State in a manner which was impossible in the case of Kauṭilya. At best the Mauryan Prime Minister could trace the origin of the Mauryan State to the misdeeds of the Nandas. And there he left it without further comment.

D. EVOLUTION OF THE STATE

With the above vital difference between the antecedents and environment of Kauṭilya and Aristotle, and between their views on the origin of the State, it is easy for us to examine now their views on the evolution of the State. The Indian thinker has nothing to say about this problem, although he dwells in detail on some of the matters on which Aristotle has written in connection with the origin of the State, viz., the ultimate relationship between the husband and wife, father and child, master and slave, and the ruler and the ruled, as being responsible for the source of authority which came to be exercised by the State,[208] and about the States's being formed out of a union of several villages, which we have mentioned above.[209] Kauṭilya also describes in detail the formation of villages; indeed, his description of this topic is almost perfect in its exposition, dealing as it does with almost all the aspects of village and town life.[210] But there is no reference to the origin or evolution of the State; all that Kauṭilya does is to impose upon the villages and the towns the authority of the monarch.[211] Once again we see that, as between Aristotle and Kauṭilya, it was a difference between an idealist, who was seeking the realization of a perfect State, and a realist, whose sole concern was to preserve what had been realized.

E. REQUISITES OF AN IDEAL STATE

This problem has a double aspect—one which refers to the requisites of an ideal State as pictured by Aristotle but not by Kauṭilya; and the other referring to the elements of the State about which both the great thinkers have left some account behind them. An ideal State, according to Aristotle, would require a defensible position, a small-sized naval force, and an intelligent and courageous body of citizens, which did not include mechanics and artisans. It was also to include slaves and the Perioeci, who were to till the soil, and to have common meals; land divided into State and private land; its capital situated near but not upon the Sea; a good water supply; a healthy environment with proper walls and fortifications; houses and streets well laid-out in a manner to combine beauty with security; an *acropolis* where the temples were to be situated; and government buildings, freemen's *agora,* and tradesmen's *agora.*[212]

1. IN KAUTILYA

The whole concept of Aristotle as given in the above passage was that of a City State. It only affords a sharp contrast to that of Kauṭilya, who was concerned with an imperial State. But all the same, Kauṭilya gives us valuable and full details about the lay-out of a city, particularly the capital city inside the fortress. In other words, he describes the imperial capital of a growing Empire. Inside the fort the land was to be demarcated by opening three royal roads from the west to the east, and three from the south to the north. The fortress was to have twelve gates provided with land, water, and secret passages. Chariot roads, royal roads, and those leading to the *droṇamukha, sthānīya,* country parts, and pasture grounds were to be each four *daṇḍas* (or twenty-four feet) in width; while roads leading to *sayonīya* (?), military outposts, *(vyūha),* burial or cremation grounds, and villages were to be eight *daṇḍas* in width. Those leading to gardens, groves, and forests shall be four *daṇḍas* in width; those leading to elephant forests, two *daṇḍas* in width. Roads for chariots shall be five *aratnis* (or seven-and-a-half feet); those for cattle, four *aratnis*; and those for quadrupeds and for men, two *aratnis.* Royal buildings were to be constructed on strong grounds. The king's palace was to be constructed in the midst of the houses of the people of all the four castes, and to the north from the centre of the ground inside the fort, facing either the north or the east. The residences of royal teachers, ministers, and priests, sacrificial places, and water reservoirs were all to be located east by north of the palace ; while east by south were to be located the royal kitchen, the elephant stables, and the store house. Kauṭilya explicitly mentions that there shall be a water well for every ten houses ; that hospitals were to be constructed to the north by west ; and that the city should be endowed with quite a number of buildings, offices, and manufacturies which are too detailed to be narrated here.[213] It is evident from the minute care bestowed by Kauṭilya on the construction of the capital city that he was as careful as Aristotle in providing it not only with all the amenities and advantages which were necessary to make it both self-sufficient and progressive but also with the benefits of security and protection without which its existence would have proved futile. The duties of the Superintendent of the Capital City (*nāgaraka*), which he describes in detail in a later context,[214] are by themselves enough to demonstrate the magnitude of the capital as well as of the problems connected with its administration.

2. IN ARISTOTLE

Aristotle's description of the elements of the State is less exhaustive than that of Kauṭilya but it contains significant principles which are missing in the *Arthaśāstra.* It has been seen above that, while picturing the condition of an ideal City State, Aristotle had laid down certain conditions relating to the territory, position, and population of the State.[215] In this connection, his observation on the citizens is important. Since we shall discuss this particular aspect of the State presently, we may merely observe that in this regard he lays stress on an aspect of the State which is not dealt with by Kauṭilya. Apart from the elements of a perfect State which he had in mind, Aristotle also describes the many parts of the State, obviously as the result of his close study of the different forms of governments in Greece. It is in this connection that he writes that the different parts of the State are like the different organs of an animal ; and he enumerates the many elements of the State thus: the food producing class called the husbandmen ; the class of mechanics who practise arts and without whom a city cannot exist, since some of these arts are absolute necessaries, while others merely contribute to the luxury or grace of life ; the class of traders who are engaged in buying and selling ; the fourth class made up of serfs and labourers ; and the fifth class, of warriors who are "as necessary as any of the others, if a country is not to be the slave of another".[216]

3. CRITICISM OF ARISTOTLE

Before we see what was Kauṭilya's concept of the elements of the State, it is worth while noting one or two observations of Aristotle in regard to the elements of the State. While analysing the causes of revolutions, he says that as a body is made up of many members, every member ought to grow in proportion in order to preserve the symmetry of the body, as otherwise it would lose it. He illustrates this by giving the example of an abnormal growth of a foot of four cubits in a body the other parts of which are only two spans.[217] Leaving aside the bearing of this point on the cause of revolution, it is clear that Aristotle had enunciated here an important principle relating to the proportional and symmetrical growth of all the elements of the State which we do not come across with in Kauṭilya. The importance of the many parts or elements of the State is also indicated by Aristotle in another context where he says that if a constitution is to be permanent, all the parts of the State must wish that it should exist and be maintained.[218]

F. ELEMENTS OF THE STATE

1. IN KAUTILYA

Kauṭilya analysed the elements of the State from an altogether different standpoint. Although we shall have to revert to this topic at greater length below under Part Five, yet for the sake of the completeness of this part of the subject, we may briefly allude to Kauṭilya's description of the elements of the State. We have seen above that he was concerned primarily with the monarchical State which was to reach the magnitude of a great empire. According to him, there were eight elements of the State—the king, the minister, the country, the fort, the treasury, the army, the friend, and the enemy.[219] He does not analyse the interdependence of the various elements of the State in the manner of Aristotle. But he was, as we shall see later on, fully aware of the principles of interdependence which he expressed thus: "Sovereignty (*rājatva*) (which to him was the equivalent of the State) is possible only with assistance. A single wheel can never move."[220] It is true that Kauṭilya refers here to the necessity of the king's consulting ministers on important matters.[221] Since he lived in an entirely different political environment, Kauṭilya was more concerned with the calamities confronting the elements of the State than with the question of their interdependence. It is this which explains why he devotes one whole chapter on the Aggregate of Calamities facing the Elements of Sovereignty. How important was the necessity of protecting all the elements of the State in the same efficient manner lest one should destroy the other is evident from the concluding sentences of the same chapter, which run as follows:

When any two elements of sovereignty are equally under troubles, they should be distinguished in respect of their progressive or declining tendency, provided that the good condition of the rest of the elements needs no description. When the calamities of a single element tend to destroy the rest of the elements, those calamities, whether they be of the fundamental or any other element, are verily serious.[222]

2. CRITICISM OF KAUTILYA

Kauṭilya's seven elements, which we shall have to discuss again in the following pages, were reduced by him to two major ones—the king and the territory, since the minister and the army formed only a part of the king; the country, the fort, and even the treasury constituting essentially the various aspects of the territory without which none of them could be evolved; while the friend and the enemy were really extraneous elements with which the State was only indirectly concerned. It is this which perhaps makes Kauṭilya dwell at some length on the king and the territory in his chapter on the Elements of Sovereignty, in which he admits at the end: "Excepting the enemy, these seven elements, possessed of their excellent characteristics are said to be the limb-like elements of sovereignty" (*arivarjāḥ prakritayaḥ sapaitāḥ svaguṇodayāḥ uktāḥ, pratyanga-bhūtāḥ tāḥprakritā rājasampadaḥ*).[223] In the last part of the above statement, Kauṭilya would compare the State to an organism in the manner of Aristotle. But he is not in favour of reducing the elements of the State to three which modern writers are inclined to fix as the elements of the State.[224] Neither was Kauṭilya inclined to dwell on the importance of one of the elements—the citizens—as making up an essential part of the population, on whose character, as Aristotle unequivocally maintained, depended the nature and the form of government. Since we shall have to discuss this question of the citizens in a later context, we may leave it at this stage.

G. FORMS OF THE STATE

1. SIMILARITY BETWEEN ARISTOTLE AND KAUTILYA

Keeping in mind the fundamental difference in the antecedents, environment, and outlook of the two great political thinkers of Greece and India, let us now try to see how far their ideals of the forms of government were similar. Aristotle, as is well-known, has many observations to make on the forms of government which were those in which one, or the few, or the many governed with an eye to the common interest. But when the one, or the few, or the many governed with a view to private interests, they became perversions of the governments by the one, the few, or the many. In other words, governments were either monarchies, aristocracies, or constitution or polity which when perverted became tyrannies, oligarchies, and democracies respectively.[225] We do not find these normal and abnormal forms of government in the *Arthaśāstra*. On the ancient Indian political horizon, as has been shown in these pages, we certainly come across monarchies, tyrannies, aristocracies, and republics. Kauṭilya does mention the corporations of the Lichchhavikas, Vṛijika, Mallaka, Madraka, Kukura, Kuru, Pāñcāla, and others that lived by the title of rāja.[226] But beyond these names and others mentioned by the Greek writers, who had accompanied Alexander the Great in the latter's compaigns, we have no details either in Kauṭilya's *Arthaśāstra* or in any other work which could enlighten us on the nature of the republics or on their classifications or on their perverted forms.[227]

2. ARISTOTLE ON MONARCHIES

Here in India that form of government which Aristotle did not favour but under which he had served for some time, and which nevertheless he mentions in some detail, was the normal form of government. This was the monarchical form of government. Aristotle mentions five kinds of kingship giving, wherever possible, examples. These were the monarchy according to law, as in Lacedaemonia; the monarchy "not uncommon among the barbarians, which nearly resembles tyranny", and which was legal and hereditary; the third form of monarchy which existed in ancient Hellas, which was called Aesymnetia or dictatorship, which Aristotle styled "elective tyranny", and "which, like the barbarian monarchy, is legal", but which differed from it in being not hereditary; the fourth form of monarchy which was limited to a term of years; and the last one which was limited until certain duties were performed.[228] Aristotle's contempt for the Asiatics, amongst whom he must have included the Indians, is seen when he describes the second type of monarchy which he calls legal and hereditary. His explanation for its existence is, we may be permitted to repeat, that the "barbarians, being more servile in character than the Hellenes, and Asiatics, than Europeans, do not rebel against a despotic government".[229]

3. ARISTOTLE'S JUSTIFICATION OF KINGSHIP

Before we comment on Aristotle's observations on the different types of monarchies, particularly those which obtained in the land of the so-called barbarians, that is, the Asiatics, as he calls them, we may note how he justifies kingship. With all his admiration for the rule of the many, and his inborn hatred of the Asiatics, Aristotle gave expression to views on royalty which one would expect of an Asiatic political theorist. Commenting on royalty, he writes that "we admit (it) to be one of the true forms of government".[230] While describing the rule of the father over his children which he calls royal, he writes that "a king is the natural superior of his subjects, but he should be of the same kin or kind with them".[231] Obviously when Aristotle wrote these lines, he remembered with some gratitude his erstwhile royal patrons, the Macedonian monarchs, father and son, who, as is well-known, certainly considered themselves as superior to their own subjects.

4. ARISTOTLE COMES VERY NEAR THE ASIATIC CONCEPT OF KINGSHIP

It is not so much in the above as in the following estimate of kingship that Aristotle, inspite of his aversion to the Asiatic concept of kingship, came very near it. Virtues, according to him, were not the same in or for all. "Hence the ruler ought to have moral virtue in perfection, for his duty is entirely that of a master artificer, and the master artificer is reason ; the subjects, oṅ the other hand, require only that measure of virtue which is proper to each of them."[232]

Brushing aside the temptation to compare the estimate of the king as given by Aristotle in the above citation with that given by Manu on the same point,[233] we may restrict ourselves to Kauṭilya's view on the same. According to Kauṭilya, the king when very young was to undergo severe discipline ; then, observe celibacy till he was sixteen ; then, observe the ceremony of tonsure (*godāna*), and marry ; and, then, "iṅ view of maintaining efficient discipline, he shall ever and invariably keep company with aged professors of sciences, in whom alone discipline has firm root" (*asya nityas-ca vidyāvriddha-saṁyugo vinaya-vṛiddhyarthaṁ tat-mūlātvāt-vinayasya.*)[234] Kauṭilya devotes an entire chapter styled Restraint of the Organs of the Senses (*indriya-jayaḥ*) on the manner in which the young king was to be virtuous ; and after giving the examples of eleven rulers who were vicious, and of two, who were virtuous, drives home the significant lesson that the young king should be virtuous in conduct.[235] In the next chapter on the Life of a Saintly King, Kauṭilya further dwells on the necessity of the king's leading a virtuous life.[236] Kauṭilya does not explicitly say in the above contexts, after the fashion of Aristotle, that the master artificer in the king is reason ; but it is evident from the many qualifications, restraints, and duties which he imposed on the king that the latter could not possess, observe, or fulfil them without possessing the first requisite of an administrator—Reason.

5. CRITICISM OF ARISTOTLE'S DESCRIPTION OF MONARCHIES

When Aristotle enumerated the five kinds of monarchies described above, and when he condemned the Asiatics, he was probably aware of only those types of monarchy which had prevailed in Persia, Egypt, and the neighbouring countries, but not those which had existed in India, where the *dharmaśāstras* and the *nītiśāstras* guided the actions and thought of the monarchs. His elucidation of the different kinds of monarchies, and, in particular, of the other forms of government, refers to one major aspect of the problem ; while the restricted view of Kauṭilya may be said to refer to an aspect which is missing in Aristotle. That is, if we take the world of the fourth and third centuries B.C. as a whole, while Aristotle's classification helps us to understand all about the different forms of the State as they prevailed in Greece and Macedonia, Kauṭilya's account enables us to know about the form of the State concerning which Aristotle is silent. That is the imperial State about which we find no trace in Aristotle beyond the statement that empires, which he equated with despotic governments, were unnecessary to the happiness of men.[237] This is rather strange, especially when we realize that, as stated above, Aristotle had lived at the court of Philip of Macedon, and, then, for some time at that of Alexander the Great, which were undoubtedly the greatest imperial centres of the Western world. If we consider the totality of ancient political thought, Eastern and Western, in the fourth and third centuries B.C., we may say that Kauṭilya began where Aristotle ended, and completed the history of ancient governments by adding the description of the imperial State to that of the many forms which Aristotle has so admirably described.

H. MACHINERY OF THE STATE: JUDICIAL AND EXECUTIVE

1. LAW AS A PART OF THE STATE

A State of small size, limited in population, and with restricted problems like the one which Aristotle had in mind, cannot be expected to have an elaborate machinery which can be associated only with an imperial State described by Kauṭilya. It is not surprising, therefore, that the machinery of the State is more perfectly described by Kauṭilya than by Aristotle. Of the main subjects falling under the category of the organization or machinery of the State, as that term is understood in the modern world, mention has already been made of the form of government in the previous section. It is idle to expect of the ancients, Eastern or Western, a knowledge of some of the other topics falling under this head like, for instance, the theory of Separation or Division of Powers, Electorate, Political Parties, and Public Opinion which in the modern times are an integral part of the organization of the State. We shall, however, have an occasion of discussing some aspects of the Electorate and Public Opinion while dealing with citizens and their relationship to the State in a later context in this work. Here we may be content with two important parts of the governmental machinery—the law-executing and the law-interpreting bodies. That is, we shall restrict ourselves to the executive and judicial sides of the State as described in the works of Aristotle and Kauṭilya. As regards the law-making body, or the legislature, while we have many details in Aristotle, we have little information about it in Kauṭilya since law flowed from the *dharmaśāstras* except when it was made by the monarch.

2. ARISTOTLE ON LAW

(a) *Nature of Law*

To Aristotle law was the rule of God.[238] In the same context he states that law is reason unaffected by desire.[239] Law derives its force from habit.[240] It must be supported by force in the ruler.[241] Aristotle enthroned law on the seat of power when he stated: "The law ought to be supreme over all, and the magistracies and the government should judge only of particulars."[242] The ethical side of law is given by him when he writes that virtue must be the serious care of a State that truly deserves the name; and that law is only a convention, a surety to one another of justice.[243] The duty of the legislator is to make good men, and to see how this could be accomplished, and what is the end of a perfect life.[244]

(b) *Characteristics of Law*

A few more characteristics of the law as delineated by Aristotle may be given, before we pass on to the question of the executive and the judiciary, and to the concept of the three powers of government as given by Kauṭilya. A peculiarity in the concept of law of Aristotle is that he considers law as a mean.[245] Another important idea in the legal system of Aristotle is: "Even when laws have been written down, they ought not always to remain unaltered."[246] Further, Aristotle maintains that the rule of the law is preferable to that of any individual, and that kings are only guardians and ministers of law.[247] Moreover, he affirms that laws exist only for equals. "Hence we see that legislation is necessarily concerned only with those who are equal in birth and in power; and that for men of pre-eminent virtue there is no law—they are themselves as a law."[248]

3. ARISTOTLE AND KAUTILYA ON LAW

(a) *Limitation of Comparison*

Excepting the view that the rule of law is preferable to that of any individual which, in terms of Indian thought, may be equated to some extent with the idea of *dharma's* being superior to the rule of a king, it is difficult to find exact parallels to the above characteristics of law as given by Aristotle in the work of Kauṭilya. In the latter's opinion, as narrated elsewhere in these pages, Sacred law or *dharma* was one of four legs of law. *Dharma* is eternal truth holding sway over the world. The second leg of law was *vyavahāra* which may be interpreted to mean usage, rather than evidence, as was done by Dr. Shama Shastry.[249]

(*b*) *Both Compared*

(*i*) *Habit and Usage*

If to Aristotle law derived its force from habit, to Kauṭilya usage, or habitual practice, was so important that it was obligatory on the part of the State to maintain it. In fact, the partition of inheritance, for instance, was to be made in accordance with the customs prevalent in the country, caste, guild, or the village of the inheritors (*deśasya jātyā saṅghasya dharmo grāmasya vā'pi yaḥ ucitaḥ—tasya tenaiva dāyadharmaṁ prakalpayet*).[250]

(*ii*) *Emphasis on Custom*

To both Aristotle and Kauṭilya custom was an integral part of law. The Greek thinker affirmed: ". . . customary laws have more weight, and relate to more important matters, than written laws, and a man may be a safer ruler than the written law, but not safer than the customary law."[251] About the inherent permanence of customary laws, he wrote that, even after the establishment of a revolution, "The laws which existed previously continue in force".[252] Aristotle in the above statements laid more emphasis on custom than on written law. In this respect he slightly differed from Kauṭilya in the sense that the latter, while admitting, as we have seen above, that *vyavahāra* or usage was one of the four legs of law, also maintained that in case of disagreement between Sacred law (*dharma*) and *vyavahāra* or usage, the former prevailed.[253] But this difference between the two thinkers may be reconciled when we note that, according to the Indian concept of law as enunciated by Manu, and as remarked elsewhere, usage formed a part of *dharma* itself; and that, therefore, it played a vital part in the assertion of law. Kauṭilya fully recognized the importance of usage even in minor matters like disputes of village boundaries. While dealing with the question of the settlement of boundaries of villages, he enjoined that neighbours or elders of five or ten villages should investigate the case of evidence, and decide the issue,[254] evidently according to the custom of the localities.

(*iii*) *Stress on Reason*

In another respect Kauṭilya's idea comes very near the concept of Aristotle, when the former says that whenever Sacred law is in conflict with rational law (i.e. *dharmanyāya* or edicts of kings), "then reason shall be held authoritative".[255] The importance which Kauṭilya gives to reason in this context may be studied along with the emphasis which be laid on *ānvikṣakī* which we have already cited in the earlier pages of this work. While both Aristotle and Kauṭilya, therefore, are comparable in regard to the stress which they laid on reason, the Indian thinker apparently deviated from the Greek theorist when he stated that the king was the fountain of justice.[256] This, however, is to be understood not in the sense of the king's being superior to *dharma*, which neither Kauṭilya nor any other ancient Indian theorist was prepared to admit, but in the sense of the king's fulfilling his fundamental duty of upholding the *dharma* of the land. We infer this from the whole passage which runs thus:

> In virtue of his power to uphold the observance of the respective duties of the four castes and of the four divisions of religious life, and in virtue of his power to guard against the violation of the *dharmas*, the king is the fountain of justice (*caturvarṇāśramasyāyaṁ lokasya-ācāra-rakṣaṇāt naśyatāṁ sarvadharmāṇām rājā dharmapravartakaḥ*).[257]

The Aristotlean idea that the end of law was to produce a good man is missing in Kauṭilya, who was concerned, as will be pointed out later on, with happiness and not with a perfect life.

4. THE JUDICIARY

(a) *Aristotle on Theories of Justice*

The next power in the State is justice concerning which we have valuable details both in Aristotle and Kauṭilya. The Greek political thinker's inherently analytical mind is seen in the manner in which he discusses the theories of justice. In an illuminating passage dealing with virtue, power, and justice, he writes thus:

> Virtue, when furnished with means, may be deemed to have the greatest power of doing violence: and as superior power is only found where there is superior excellence of some kind, power is thought to imply virtue. But does it likewise imply justice—that is the question.

And in answer to this question, he states that some assert that justice is benevolence; that others say that it is nothing more than the rule of a superior; that if these two views are considered as antagonistic and exclusive (i.e. if the notion that justice is benevolence excludes the idea of the just rule of a superior), the alternative (viz., that no one should rule over others) has no force or plausibility, because it implies that not even the superior in virtue ought to rule, or be master. Some others, Aristotle continues, consider law and custom as some sort of justice, and justify slavery in war. This is an untenable position because it cannot be maintained that a man can be a slave when he is unworthy to be a slave. Aristotle would not grant this in the case of the barbarians for he believed that, as in the case of nobility, slavery was absolute and relative.[258]

Before we proceed to examine further Aristotle's views on justice, it may be observed that the Westerners, whose ideas of justice he had summarized in the passage, did not possess any concept of justice which approached the Indian concept of *dharma*. This fact may be borne in mind throughout our study of ancient Indian political thought and institutions, since the Indian concept of *dharma* played a vital rôle in the shaping of both the political thought and institutions of the ancient Indians.

(*b*) *Aristotle's Idea of Justice*

To continue with Aristotle's views on justice as given in the above passage, we may note that, while he discussed the different theories, he did not define justice in that context. We have to search elsewhere in the *Politics* for his theory of justice. In one place he writes that justice was peculiar to man inasmuch as "it is characteristic of man that he alone has any sense of good and evil, of just and unjust".[259] Aristotle then affirms that justice is the bond of union between men in a State.[260] This, too, being inadequate, we have to seek elsewhere in the work of Aristotle for a clearer concept of justice. Once again he discusses the conflicting views of justice; and with that penetrating acumen so characteristic of him, he rejects illogical or unsatisfactory notions, and arrives at an admirable solution thus:

> All men cling to justice of some kind, but their conceptions are imperfect and they do not express the whole idea. Some consider justice to be equality, not for all, but only for equals; others, look upon it as inequality; but the more sensible view is that justice implies a relation to persons as well as to things, and a just distribution embraces alike persons and things.[261]

A definition of justice, which is of especial interest to us in our comparative study, is given by Aristotle in a still later context where he states the relation between all sciences and justice thus: "In all sciences and arts the end is good, and especially and above all in the highest of all—that is, the political science of which the good is justice, in other words, the common interest."[262]

(c) *Aristotle and Kauṭilya : Identity of Views in regard to Justice*

(i) *Justice is the End of Political Science*

In the above passage we have an admirable identity of views in Aristotle and Kauṭilya. The latter, it must be admitted, does not discuss the views on justice, because, as must have been evident to the reader from the previous pages of this work, the concept of justice (*dharma*), like the other fundamental concepts, had already been formulated centuries before the times of Kauṭilya. A change in the concept of justice in ancient India was unthinkable, although an enlargement in the scope of law was permissible. This explains why we have no conflicting views on justice like those mentioned by Aristotle. But in regard to the end of all sciences, the importance of Political Science, the end of Political Science, and the ultimate ends of the State, there was complete agreement between Aristotle and Kauṭilya. As regards the end of all sciences, the Indian thinker first enumerates the essential sciences. As mentioned earlier, they were only four—Ānvīṣakī, the triple *Vedas* (*Trayī*), *vārtā* (agriculture, cattle-breeding, and trade), and *daṇḍanīti*. This view of Kauṭilya ran counter to that of Manu, who maintained that they were only three —the triple *Vedas, vārtā* and *daṇḍanīti* ; to that of Bṛihaspati, who affirmed that they were only two—*vārtā* and *daṇḍanīti* ; and to that of the School of Uśanas which declared that there was only one science—the science of governmment, all other sciences having their origin and end in it. While affirming his own view that "four and only four are the sciences", Kauṭilya stated that "it is from these sciences that all that concerns righteousness and wealth is learnt" (*tābhiḥ dharmārthau yat-vidyāt-vidyānām vidyātvaṁ.*)[263] In the last sentence, Kauṭilya not only gives the identical end of all sciences which Aristotle expressed by the term "the good", as connoted by the term *dharma* or righteousness, but gives an additional end, *artha* or wealth, which is missing in Aristotle.

As regards the importance of the science of government, it must have been evident to the reader from the elucidation of this point earlier in these pages, while describing the theory of Punishment, that Kauṭilya explicitly states that "that sceptre on which the well-being and progress of the sciences of Ānvikṣakī, the triple Vedas, and Vārtā depend is known as Daṇḍa (punishment). That which treats of Daṇḍa is the law of punishment or the science of government" (*Daṇḍanīti*). On the importance of the science of government, he continues thus: "It is a means to make acquisitions, to keep them secure, to improve them, and to distribute among the deserved the profits of improvement. It is on this science of government that the course of the progress of the world depends."[264] Kauṭilya thus confirms the opinion of Aristotle in regard to the supreme importance of the Science of Politics. He likewise endorses the view of Aristotle about the aim which Political Science should place before itself. It was the common good of all the people. We shall revert to this detail below when we shall describe the comparative views of the Greek and the Indian political thinkers on the functions and ends of the State.

(ii) *Importance of Justice and Punishments*

On another detail, too, there is an identity of views between those of Aristotle and Kauṭilya. The former writes that "judicial decisions are useless if they have no effect ; and if society cannot exist without them, neither can it exist without the execution of them".[265] The same principle is expressed in a later context, while illustrating his statement that the realization of happiness by the perfect exercise of virtue is not conditional but absolute, thus: "Take the case of just actions ; just punishments and chastisements do indeed spring from a good principle, but they are good only because we cannot do without them."[266] Aristotle, therefore, subscribed to the view that society cannot exist without judicial decisions and punishments. In other words, he admitted that for the ultimate realization of the ends of the State and the progress of the world, punishment was perfectly necessary.

Kauṭilya's view on the same problem, viz., that punishment was indispensable for the proper realization of the ends of the State, is given in connection with the discussion of the view of his unnamed teacher that "whoever is desirous of the progress of the world shall ever hold the sceptre raised (*udyata daṇḍa*). Never can there be a better instrument than the sceptre to bring people under control." The teacher of Kauṭilya obviously held the view that severe punishment was the panacea for all human ills, suggesting thereby that it should be used on all occasions. Kauṭilya rejects this extreme view of his teacher, and says:

> No, for whoever imposes severe punishment becomes repulsive to the people ; while he who awards mild punishment becomes contemptible. But whoever imposes punishment as deserved becomes respectable. For punishment (*daṇḍa*), when awarded with due consideration makes the people devoted to righteousness, i.e. *dharma*, or, as Aristotle would term it, *the good*) and to works productive of wealth and enjoyment ; while punishment, when ill-awarded under the influence of greed and anger, or owing to ignorance, excites fury even among hermits and ascetics dwelling in forests, not to speak of householders.

It is then that Kauṭilya concludes by referring to the famous law of the fishes (*mātsyanyāya*) and to the general need of protecting the weak against the strong with the help of punishment, which we have described in an earlier context in this work, while dealing with the justification of the State.[267] When Kauṭilya writes that neither severe nor mild but deserving punishment is to be given, he perhaps approaches nearest the dictum of

Aristotle, which we have cited already, viz., that "in seeking justice men seek for the mean or neutral, and the law is the mean".[268]

(d) *Composition and Appointment of the Judiciary*

(i) *In Aristotle*

The composition of and appointment to the judiciary in the writings of both the great thinkers may now be examined. Aristotle analyses the problem of the judiciary under three heads: firstly, the persons from whom the judges were to be recruited ; secondly, the matters with which they were concerned ; and, thirdly, the manner of appointment. He starts the discussion by enumerating eight kinds of law courts—the court of audit or scrutiny ; that of cognizance of ordinary offences against the State ; that which was concerned with treason against government ; that which determined disputes respecting penalties, whether raised by magistrates or by private persons ; that which decided the more important civil cases ; and that which tried homicide of four types—pre-meditated, unpremeditated, cases in which the guilt was confessed by justice disputed, and murderers who had fled from justice but who were tried on return to their native land. The seventh court was meant for strangers of two kinds—those foreigners who disputed with one another, and those who disputed with the citizens. And the eighth court was meant for small suits from about the sum of a *drachma* up to five *drachmae* or a little more, which had to be decided but without many judges.[269]

Turning to the first question as to the persons from whom the judges were to be appointed, Aristotle maintained that all the citizens could be judges in which case they were to be appointed to the various courts by vote or by lot, or sometimes by lot and sometimes by vote, or when a certain class of cases were tried, the judges who decided them, could be appointed, some by lot and some by vote. These were the five methods of appointing judges from the whole people. Even when they were elected from a part only, there were likewise four methods: they might be appointed from some by vote and judge in all causes ; or they may be appointed from some by lot and judge in all cases ; or they may be elected in some cases by vote, and in some by lot ; or sometimes, even when judging the same cases, some courts may be composed of members, some appointed by vote and some by lot.[270] In reality, Aristotle's methods of appointment of judges could be reduced to two—appointments by lot and by vote, all the other methods being their modifications.

Aristotle's provisions for safeguarding impartiality among the judges, and for preventing the judiciary from being turned into a monopoly may now be noted. According to him, the judges were not to communicate with one another in a court of law.[271] He rightly maintained that judges should not hold office for life, "for the mind grows old as well as the body".[272] He would make provision for an equal distribution of opinion among them.[273] And he would distinguish the judges who inflicted punishment from those who carried out executions.[274]

(ii) The Judiciary in Aristotle and in Kauṭilya Compared and Contrasted

Since we shall have to describe the Indian judiciary in some detail below under the head Elements of the State, it will suffice if we give here only some of the few points of comparison and the many points of contrast between the judiciary of Aristotle and that of Kauṭilya. We do not come across in the huge governmental machinery described by Kauṭilya any such method of the appointment of judges by lot or by vote as advocated by Aristotle. In the Kauṭilyan concept appointment by the State was the only method that was permissible. Likewise we do not come across in the Kauṭilyan State the eight types of courts described by Aristotle. Kauṭilya would classify courts under four categoris, as will be narrated below, all of them being State courts. Both the judicial machinery and procedure as described by Kauṭilya were very elaborate. The judges in Kauṭilya were never mere ordinary citizens: they could have belonged to the ordinary ranks of life but they were experts in the *dharmaśāstras* and the *nītiśāstras*. They could, of course, take the advice of ordinary citizens in certain circumstances. Kauṭilya like Aristotle was very careful about equity being maintained by the judiciary; but unlike the Greek thinker imposed such a number of restrictions on the judges that must have made them extremely cautious in the discharge of their duties. That they were to be strictly impartial is proved by the following injunction of Kauṭilya: "Judges shall thus settle disputes free from all kinds of circumvention, with mind unchanged in all moods or circumstances, pleasing and affable to all."[275] Even Aristotle could not have described the rôle of the judges in a clearer manner than that given in the above statement.

5. THE EXECUTIVE

(a) In Aristotle

(i) Executive in General

The Executive in Aristotle and Kauṭilya may now be studied. The Greek political philosopher describes the executive in some detail. The distribution of offices was, according to him, a part of Politics. Their number, their nature, and their duties are described first followed by a discussion of the right distribution of offices. Aristotle guards against the common belief that in a democracy all hold office. In a political community, no doubt, many officers are needed ; but not every one who is chosen by vote or by lot can be regarded as a ruler. That is, "they are to be called offices to which the duties are assigned of deliberating about certain measures and of judging and commanding, especially the last ; for to command is the especial duty of a magistrate".[276]

(ii) Their Number

Concerning their number, Aristotle admits that "in great States, it is possible, and indeed, necessary, that every officer should have a special function ; where the citizens are numerous, many may hold office".[277] Although he repeats the question relating to the number of magistrates, yet he does not come to any final decision in regard to this point. All that he says is that they vary between small and great States, and between the different types of constitutions.[278] This, of course, does not help us in ascertaining his views on the exact number of magistrates in a given State.

(iii) Tenure of Office

About their duration or tenure of office, Aristotle says that the magistrates may last for six months, sometimes for a lesser period, sometimes they may be annual, while in other cases, they may hold office for still longer periods.[279] The same indecision is seen in regard to the question as to who appoints them. Sometimes all the citizens, or only some, appoint magistrates. These latter are chosen out of all or out of some who are distinguished either by property qualification, or by birth, or merit, or for some special reason, or when they had returned from exile and fought together with their countrymen against a common enemy. As in the case of judges, the executive officials were to be chosen either by lot or by vote or by a combination of these two methods which amounted to twelve in all.[280] Incidentally it may be observed that most of the methods of selecting magistrates which Aristotle describes were prevalent in oligarchical constitutions, while one or two (by vote or by lot by all people) were common in democratic States.[281]

(iv) Kinds of Executive

The kinds of executive offices which Aristotle mentions are interesting. In oligarchical States there were magistrates who formed the *Bule* or council ; others whose duty was to prepare measures for the people so that the latter might not be diverted from their business ; then, there was the magistracy that controlled the boys and women but not the wives of the oligarchs, for "the wives of the oligarchs are too fine to be controlled".[282] Later on he elucidates the problem of the kinds of executive when he writes that "first among the necessary offices is that which has the care of the market" over which a magistrate was to be appointed in order to maintain order. The second office was that of the magistrate who undertook the supervision and embellishment of public and private buildings, the maintenance and repairs of houses and roads, the prevention of disputes about boundaries and other similar matters. This magistrate called the City Warden had various departments under him like those of walls, fountains, and harbours. The third category of magistrates was made up of Wardens of the Country or Inspectors of the Woods. They were concerned with similar questions like those mentioned above but outside the walls of the city and in the country. The fourth kind of magistrates was called Receivers or Treasurers, whose function was to receive taxes, and who had under them the revenue which they distributed among the various departments. Then came the magistrates called the Recorders or the Sacred Recorders, or Presidents, who looked after all private contracts, decisions of courts, all public indictments, and all preliminary proceedings. They had under them, as in the case of the City Wardens, minor officers. Next came an office which had the most necessary and the most difficult duties to perform, viz., executing the punishments, exacting fines from those whose names were listed in public registers, and looking after prisoners. To this office much odium was attached with the result that "no one will undertake it unless great profits are to be made, and any one who does it is loth to execute the law". But this office was necessary for, as related earlier, without it the judicial decisions could never be executed. It was not entrusted to one person but distributed among several officials taken from different courts. Next to them came the Guards of the City and those to whom military duties were allotted. These were subdivided according to the size of the State and its civil and military needs. Then came the magistrates entrusted with the work of examining and auditing accounts, called Scrutineers, Auditors, Accountants, and Controllers. Next came the magistrates who, especially in democratic States, were entrusted with the duty of presiding over the assembly, and of introducing and rectifying measures. Because of the three powers which they possessed, that of presiding over assemblies, that of introducing measures, and that of rectifying them, they were considered as magistrates of very great importance. In some States they were called the Probuli but in a democracy merely Councillors. Then came the magistrates whose duties were to maintain religion, preserve and repair temples, and look after religious matters. In small States only one magistrate did all this work but in larger States, there were Superintendents of Sacrifices, Guardians of Shrines, and Treasurers of Sacred Revenues. Connected with them were the magistrates whose duty was to look after the performance of public sacrifices, excepting where by law the priests were to perform such sacrifices. Those magistrates were called sometimes *Archons* or kings, or *Prytanes*.[283] To this long list Aristotle adds in a following paragraph magistrates who were called the Guardians of Women, Guardians of Laws, Guardians of Children, Directors of Gymnastics, and Superintendents of Contests and other similar spectacles.[284].

(b) *In Kauṭilya*

(i) *Nature of the Government in Kauṭilya*

Since the conditions existing in India were quite different from those obtaining in Greece, it would be futile to expect in this country the exact nomenclature of the magistrates mentioned by Aristotle. Nevertheless we may venture to see how far the duties of the different magistrates of Aristotle could be made to agree with their counterparts as described in the *Arthaśāstra* of Kauṭilya. In that work we have a bewildering description of the many executive officials who were needed for the government of the large empire of Candragupta Maurya. Here in India there was no question of selecting the magistrates either by lot or by vote. All authority, of course, flowed from the monarch, who delegated powers to a number of larger officials under whom worked smaller officials. The whole governmental machinery appears to have been of a well-knit and graded bureaucratic type which owed its existence to the monarch. The magistrates were answerable not to the privileged body of citizens but to the monarch. If the rules laid down in the *Arthaśāstra* regarding the appointment and character of ministers and royal priests were rigorous and comprehensive,[285] we may well assume that all other lower executive officials, who will be described below, must likewise have been subjected to a severe scrutiny as regards their character, antecedents, and ability before being selected for their respective appointments. This assumption is supported by the opening sentence of the chapter entitled Examination of the Conduct of Government Servants (*upayukta parīkṣā*), which runs thus: "Those who are possessed of ministerial qualifications (which Kauṭilya has already described in detail in Book I, Chapter IX) shall, in accordance with their individual capacity, be appointed as superintendents of government departments. While engaged in work, they shall be daily examined . . . ."[286] When we realize the intricate technical nature of the duties many of them had to perform, we cannot help imagining that, unlike the executive heads described by Aristotle, who were selected from amongst the general body of citizens, those in India must have been restricted to the experts in the various professions and trades which were essential for the progressive working of the machinery of government. In other words, in ancient India it was not the whole body of citizens from whom the executive officials were selected but a limited number who fulfilled the requisite conditions of character, ability, training, and experience in their respective subjects.

(ii) *General Observations on Executive Departments by Kauṭilya*

Before we undertake a rapid survey of the chief executive offices in the *Arthaśāstra*, and compare them with those described in the *Politics*, it may be desirable to note certain general observations made by Kauṭilya in regard to the various departments of government. He states that "the superintendents of all the departments shall carry on their respective works in company with accountants, writers, coin examiners, treasurers, and military officers". Then again he writes: "Each department shall be officered by several temporary heads."[287] In these two regulations we have, firstly, the principle of co-ordinated work amongst all departments; and secondly, the principle of not overburdening the governmental machinery with permanent heads unrelated to the relative needs of the various departments.

The whole bureaucratic machinery, as stated earlier, had at its apex the monarch under whom were councillors of the rank of *amātyas* and ministers of the status of *mantris*. The prime minister was, of course, the *pradhāna mantri*. It would be both long and tedious to go into all the details of the administrative machinery of Kauṭilya.[288] We may, therefore, briefly describe the executive organization as given by him.

(iii) *The Executive in Kauṭilya Described*

While describing the departments of the State Records Keeper (*akṣa-paṭalaḥ*),[289] and of Accounts, Kauṭilya states that "all departmental heads (*mahāmātrāḥ*) shall together narrate the whole of the actual accounts pertaining to each department" (*pracārasamaṁ mahāmātrāḥ—samagrāḥ śrāvayeyuḥ*).[290] This makes it clear that each department was under a *mahāmātra*, who may not be confounded with an *amātya* or a *mantri*,[291] although, in Book IV, Chapter I, entitled Removal of Thorns, he would assign the work of maintaining peace in the land to the *amātyas*, if commissioners were not available.[292] The *amātyas* here were evidently in the over-all charge of the work of maintaining the peace of the country parts.

Under the *mahāmātras*, whom we may provisionally call Executive Heads of Departments, was the Collector-General (*samāhartṛi*), who had various duties of a most important nature.[293] The supreme importance of the office of the Collector-General may be seen in the general order given by Kauṭilya, thus: "Commissioners appointed by the Collector-General, shall first check (the proceedings of) superintendents and their subordinates" (*samahārtṛi-pradeṣṭāraḥ pūrvaṁ adhyakṣāṇāmadhyakṣa-puruṣāṇām ca niyamanaṃ kuryuḥ*).[294] In an earlier context, he says that the "Collector-General shall thus energetically attend to the affairs of the kingdom".[295] The Commissioners (*pradeṣtarāḥ*), therefore, were subordinate to the Collector-General.[296] Next to the Commissioner came the Chief Superintendent (*sarvādhikaraṇam*).[297] Below him came the Superintendent who was usually called *adhyakṣa*, or sometimes *adhikāraḥ* or *adhikaraṇam*.[298] Below him came the Chief Officer (*yukta*) under whom came the officer (*karaṇika*) followed by the clerks (*lekhaka* or *kārmika*).[299] The ministerial servants of officers were called *mantri-vaiyāvrityakaraḥ*.[300]

To this list are to be added the informants (*sūcakaḥ*), who spied on the public and private work of officials.[301]

(c) *The Executive in Aristotle and Kauṭilya Compared*

(i) *Appointment*

With this bare sketch of the executive structure as given in the *Artha-śāstra,* let us try to see how many of the officials mentioned by Aristotle had their counterparts in Kauṭilya's work, and how many altogether indigenous to the country. The reader must have already noticed that, unlike the executives in Aristotle, who were appointed either by vote or by lot, or by a combination of the two methods, those in India were appointed by the ruler. Here in India, therefore, all appointments were made by the supreme executive head, the ruler. This is proved by the statement of Kauṭilya who, while describing the daily duties of the monarch, relates that during the fourth-eighth part of the day, the latter was not only to receive the revenue in gold but also to attend to the appointment of the superintendents, who are styled here *adhyakṣaḥ*.[302] From the many punishments described by Kauṭilya, it is clear that all executives were responsible only to the monarch.[303]

(ii) *Council of Magistrates*

Aristotle begins with a reference to some of the oligarchical States in which there were magistrates who constituted the *bule* or *probuli* or council. These were perhaps identical with the *mantripariṣad* described by Kauṭilya in Book I, Chapter XV under the heading *Mantrādhikāraḥ* or Business of the Council Meeting rather than with the *Amātyas* described in Chapter VIII of the same work. The reason is that in the former Chapter, Kauṭilya specifically refers to all kinds of administrative measures which were preceded by deliberations, and which were discussed in that Council.[304]

There was no question of the members of the *mantripariṣad* presiding over their assembly or introducing or ratifying measures, like their counterparts in Aristotle, since here in India it was only a question of expounding the *dharmaśāstras* and the *nītiśāstras* with which the ministers were concerned. The deliberations of the Council of Aristotle were marked by a spirit of independence and initiative both of which are lacking in the *mantripariṣad* of Kauṭilya. The king presided over the *mantripariṣad,* and he asked the advice of the ministers, either individually or collectively. In other words, the Council in Kauṭilya was only a consultative body without powers of either initiating measures or ratifying them. At best the king could depute ministers to do important work, especially when he could not himself attend to it. Thus says Kauṭilya: "As works do not happen to be simultaneous, are various in form, and pertain to distant and different localities, the king shall, in view of being abreast of time and place, depute his ministers to carry them out. Such is the work of ministers."[304a]

Magistrates to enforce the Duties of the People. Aristotle mentions magistrates, also in aristocracies, whose duty was to prepare measures for the people so that the latter might not be diverted from their business. It is not clear from Aristotle's work as to what exactly was this function of the magistrates, and what was meant by the business of the people—whether it refers to their daily vocations, or professions, or religious duties. In the *Arthaśāstra* this all-embracing function of seeing that the people were confined to their respective duties belonged only to the king. Kauṭilya states thus in regard to this function: "This people (*loka*), consisting of the four castes and the four orders of religious life, when governed by the king with his sceptre, will keep to their respective paths, ever devotedly adhering to their respective duties and occupations" (*catur-varṇāśramo loko rājñā daṇḍena pālitaḥ svadharma-karmābhirato vartate sveṣu vartmasu*).[305]

(iii) Magistrates controlling Boys and Women

Then there were the magistrates who controlled boys and women but not the wives of oligarchs. This office was suited to aristocracy. These magistrates may have been similar to another category of magistrates whom Aristotle describes later as Guardians of Women and Children. Here again it cannot be made out whether the magistrates were in general charge of all women or only of the disabled, the forsaken, and the destitute. Kauṭilya is more explicit in this case. The duty of maintaining orphans, youths, and women was an exclusive function of the monarch himself. While delineating the various duties of the king, Kauṭilya writes thus:

> He (the king) shall, therefore, personally attend to the business of the gods, of heretics, of Brahmans learned in the *Vedas*, of cattle, of sacred places, of minors, the aged, the afflicted, and the helpless, and of women ; —all this in order (of enumeration), or according to the urgency of pressure of those works. . . .[306]

In an earlier context he had stated that the orphans (*asamandhinaḥ*) were to be necessarily fed by the State, and were to be put to the study of science, palmistry, sorcery, the duties of the various orders of religious life, legerdemain, or conjuring tricks, and the reading of omens and augury. Some of them were also to be trained as spies.[307]

(iv) Magistrates in charge of Markets

Among the necessary magistracies first in the list of Aristotle came the magistrates of the market, whose duty was to inspect contracts and maintain order. From the Indian point of view this magistracy was performing two incongruous duties—one, looking after the market itself, and the other, after what might be called civil contracts and the maintenance of order. But a market in the Greek sense was quite different to its counterpart in India, where only transactions in the purchase and sale of articles of food consumption, like grains, vegetables, etc., took place. Amongst the Greeks a market was the centre of public life ; and no place was liable to disorder so much as a market. Hence it is obvious that a magistrate had to maintain order in a market. In the *Arthaśāstra* market towns (*panyapaṭṭaṇa*) were directly under the king's supervision.[308] The designation of the official placed over the markets cannot be made out.

(v) Magistrates in charge of Public Buildings

Next in importance came the magistracy that looked after the supervision, maintenance and embellishment of private and public buildings, roads, boundary disputes, and similar questions. They also looked after the (city) walls, fountains, and harbours. In the above category were miscellaneous duties which, being possible in small States like those dealt with by Aristotle, were impracticable in the imperial State of Kauṭilya. For instance, the maintenance of roads was the direct responsibility of the king. Kauṭilya states: "He (the king) shall not only clear roads of traffic from the molestations of courtiers (*vallabha*), of workmen (*kārmika*, clerks?), of robbers, and of boundary guards, but also keep them from being destroyed by herds of cattle."[309] Boundary disputes in India assumed larger proportions than those in Greece, and consequently are treated in a separate section entitled Sale of Buildings, Boundary Disputes, Determination of Boundaries, and Miscellaneous Hindrances by Kauṭilya in Book III, Chapter IX. It does not appear as if there was a special official to look after boundary disputes, since Kauṭilya says: "In all disputes regarding the boundaries between any two villages, neighbours or elders of five or ten (*pañcagrāmi daśagrāmi vā*) shall investigate the case on the evidence to be furnished from natural or artificial boundary marks." In the next sentence he affirms: "Elders among cultivators and herdsmen, or outsiders who have had the experience of former possession in the place, or one, or many persons (not) personally acquainted with the boundary marks under dispute, shall first describe the boundary marks, and, then, wearing the unusual dress (*viparītaveṣaḥ*), shall lead the people (to the place)." Guilty persons, or those misleading judges, were to be fined 1,000 *paṇas*.[310]

(vi) Fountains, Harbours, and Naval Force

Although Kauṭilya, as we shall see later on, mentions fountains in the imperial capital, yet the Greek idea of beautifying cities with fountains and with artistic works may be said to have been non-existent as a part of governmental policy. We have to come to comparatively later ages in order to see this side of the city life in India. Aristotle mentions the duty of looking after harbours as coming within the sphere of the City Warden. But in Kauṭilya it did not form a part of the function of the Superintendent of the City whose duties we shall describe presently. The care of harbours in the state manual of Kauṭilya was the duty of the Superintendent of Ships, whose onerous and multifarious duties given in detail by him form a marked contrast to the regulations relating to the naval and maritime side of the city administration as described by Aristotle. In the concept of the latter, the State was to possess a naval force. This is evident from his statement that "there can be no doubt that the possession of a moderate naval force is advantageous to a city". It was required for the needs of the citizens and also as a precaution against their neighbours "in certain cases". The number and magnitude of the naval force depended upon the character of the State, and particularly upon the part it played in contemporary politics.[311] After saying so much Aristotle is silent about the interesting point whether any special magistracy was placed in charge of the naval affairs of the State. This is rather surprising when we note that the Greek City States, excepting in some cases, always devoted their most serious attention to this side of their public life. Aristotle's silence on this vital point is inexplicable.

Kauṭilya had, on the other hand, in his mind a land empire that was governed from a capital in the country. It had, no doubt, a seaboard and large navigable rivers. He describes the duties of the Superintendent of Ships in such detail that it is really surprising that he should have devoted such minute care to this side of State activity. The Superintendent of Ships (*nāv-adhyakṣa*) had to examine the accounts relating to navigation not only in oceans (*samudra samyāna*) and mouths of rivers, but also on lakes, natural and artificial, and rivers in the vicinity of *sthānīya* and other fortified cities. Villagers on seashore, or on the banks of rivers and on lakes, fishermen, merchants, passengers, arriving on board either the king's ships or on private vessels, those who went a-fishing in State boats in search of conch shells and pearls, ships that touched the harbours, pirate ships (*hiṁsrikā*), large and small boats, those who forded rivers (a great number of whom are mentioned), foreign merchants, persons who abducted women and girls, and suspects of all kinds—these miscellaneous persons came within the purview of the Superintendent of Ships.[312] We have in the above account an infinitely greater number of problems concerning naval and maritime matters than those mentioned in the *Politics*.

(*vii*) *Wardens of the Country or Inspectors of Woods*

We may now come to the next magistracy in Aristotle called by him Wardens of the Country or Inspectors of Woods. Their duties are not described by Aristotle, who merely says that they were similar to those of the City Wardens. But this is not intelligible since the country sides can hardly be said to have had the problems of maintaining public buildings, boundary disputes, walls, fountains, and harbours associated with the City Wardens. At any rate we may find the counterparts of the Wardens of the Country of Aristotle in two types of officials mentioned in the *Arthaśāstra*. The first was made up of the Superintendent who looked after the villages. Kauṭilya does not give any designation to this official but from the fact that the vital problem of the formation of villages was included among the duties of the government Superintendents (*adhyakṣaḥ*),[313] we are justified in assuming that the entire question of looking to the country sides was entrusted to the Superintendents. The second type was made up of the Superintendents of the Country (*rāṣṭrapāla*), who approached nearest the Wardens of the Country of Aristotle. Kauṭilya mentions them in connection with the measures which he recommended for putting down wild tribes or recalcitrant villages. He writes that if the king failed in certain measures, which he mentions in the preceding paragraphs, he "may send a seditious minister with an army of inefficient soldiers and fiery spies to put down a rebellious wild tribe or a village, or to set up a new superintendent of countries . . . or to bring under control a highly rebellious city. . . ."[313a]

What great importance was attached to the country sides in the concept of Kauṭilya is clear from the fact that he assigns to the king the duty of looking after the affairs of both citizens and country people during the second one-eighth part of the day (*dvitīye paurajānapadānām kāryāṇi paśyet*).[314] Unlike the State in the *Politics*, that in the *Arthaśāstra* made special provision for a Superintendent of Forests (*kuppyādhyakṣa*), whose duty in general was to collect forest produce by employing those who were appointed to guard forests. The numerous specimens of trees, grass, animals, and metals mentioned in this connection, presuppose that this high official must have had an uncommon knowledge of Botany, Zoology, and Minerology. One of his main duties was the manufacture of all kinds of articles which were necessary for life or for the defence of forts.[315] From this it is clear that not only were there in India the counterparts of the Wardens of the Country and Inspectors of the Woods mentioned by Aristotle, but that the Indian political thinker bestowed more careful attention on the country sides than the illustrious Greek philosopher.

(viii) *The Receivers or Treasurers*

Next in importance in the list of Aristotle came the Receivers or Treasurers, who had under them the charge of revenue, and who received the taxes. Kauṭilya considered this function as one of the greatest importance. He was of the opinion that "wealth, and wealth alone, is important, inasmuch as charity and desire depend upon wealth for their realization" (*artha eva pradhānaḥ iti Kauṭilyaḥ arthamūlau-hi dharmakāmāviti.*)[316] The onerous duty of looking after the collection of revenues and of allotting it to the various departments was entrusted to the Collector-General (*Samahartṛi*). He was to collect the revenue from forts, country parts (*raṣṭra*), mines (*khaṇi*), buildings and gardens (*setu*), forests (*vana*), herds of cattle (*vraja*), and roads of traffic (*vaṇikpatha*). In this capacity the following came under his jurisdiction: tolls, fines, weights, measures, the Superintendent of the Capital City (*nāgaraka*), the Superintendent of Coinage, the Superintendent of Seals and Passports, the Superintendent of Liquor, the Superintendent of Slaughter Houses, the Superintendent of Threads, Oils, Ghee, and Sugar, the State Goldsmith, the Superintendent of Ware Houses of Merchandise, the Superintendent of Prostitutes, the Superintendent of Gambling, the Superintendent of Building Sites (*vāstuka*), the Superintendent of the Corporations of Artisans and Handicrafts, the Superintendent of Gods, and the Superintendent of Taxes collected at the gates and from people called Bāhirikas. All the produce from the Crown lands (*sītā*), portion of produce payable to the State (*bhāga*), religious taxes (*bali*), taxes paid in money (*kara*), merchants, the Superintendent of Rivers, Ferries, Boats and Ships, the Superintendent of Towns, pasture grounds, road cess (*vartaṇi*), ropes (for land measurement?), ropes to bind thieves (*corarajju*), all precious minerals like gold, silver, and diamonds, pearls, conch shells, corals, metals, salt, and other minerals extracted from plains and mountain slopes, all kinds of vegetables, fruits, flowers, wild game as well as domesticated amimals, and land and water ways—these were the multifarious subjects which this high dignitary had to deal with.[317] The duties of the Receivers or Treasurers of Aristotle pale into insignificance when contrasted with the innumerable fields of activity of the Collector-General of Kauṭilya.

The minute care with which the Indian political thinker viewed the vital question of State revenue is also seen in the manner in which he made provision for dividing the whole country into four provinces, then subdividing them into villages of first, middle, and lower ranks, appointing village accountants called *Gopas*, who were to look after the revenue from the villages, district officers called *Sthānikas*, who were each entrusted with the duty of collecting the revenue of one-fourth of the kingdom, and laying down details in regard to the fixing and realization of revenue.[318] These injunctions in the *Arthaśāstra* will have proved to the reader that the Indian political thinker bestowed more attention on the problem of the revenue of the State than Aristotle.

(ix) Sacred Recorders or Recorders

Aristotle next mentions the Sacred Recorders or Recorders, whose duty was to register all private contracts, court decisions, public indictments, and all preliminary proceedings. These appear to be restricted mostly to the judicial proceedings, although Aristotle is not explicit on this point. The Recorders of Aristotle may be compared with the Superintendent of

Records (*akṣapaṭalaḥ*), who has figured above in connection with the maintenance of revenue accounts. Since he was concerned with the accounts of all departments and of all types, including loans and contracts,[319] he performed some of the functions of the Recorder of Aristotle. Kauṭilya describes in great detail debts, contracts, deposits, and pledges in a later context ;[320] and we may presume that there must have been another official of the status of a Superintendent to look after these matters which were essentially of a judicial nature.

(x) Executors of Punishments

We may now come to the magistrates who according to Aristotle, executed orders of punishments, or held the prisoners in custody, or exacted fines according to the official records. In this category three different duties are classed together which in a small State, as envisaged by Aristotle, could have been perhaps performed by a single magistrate but not in a large State like that of Kauṭilya. Aristotle admits the impracticability of a single magistrate's fulfilling all these duties when he says that one magistrate has the custody of prisoners, while another executes the sentence, as, for example, was done by the Eleven at Athens. He even suggested that the jailorship should be separated.[321] Taking the first of the duties of the above magistrate, viz., carrying out of punishments, we may compare it with the duty of the Superintendent of Jails, who is mentioned in connection with offences which he might commit against prisoners of all kinds. The Superintendent of Jail was called *bandhanāgāra-adhyakṣa,* the jail being called *bandhanāgāra,* the lock-up being called *cāraka.*[322] The detailed punishments given to offenders who had violated justice, as described in Book IV. Chapter XIII entitled Punishment for Violating Justice (*aticāra-daṇḍah*),[323] prove not only that there were various offences against justice but that there must have been a hierarchy of officials to execute the judicial decisions. We have to assume also that there must have been a separate minor official, like the executioner, who carried out the odious duty of executing death penalties. The death penalty occurs so frequently in the *Arthaśāstra,*[324] that we cannot help concluding that there was a State Executioner in the civil list of Kauṭilya. This official, who had to perform unwholesome duties, may not be confounded with other minor officials, whose duties were to meet out corporal punishment, which was common in those days, and to realize fines, which abound at almost every step in the state manual of Kauṭilya.

(xi) Guards of the City

Aristotle mentions Guards of the City whose duty was to guard the city in peace and war times, to defend the gates of the city, and to muster and marshal out the citizens.[325] The Guard of the City of Aristotle may be compared with the Superintendent of the City of Kauṭilya. But the duties of the two were slightly different. In Indian life the citizens have never been accustomed to the rigorous discipline of some of the Greek City States, and, therefore, we would not be justified in finding out whether the Superintendent of the City (*nāgaraka*) in the *Arthaśāstra*[326] had the duty of mustering and marshalling out the citizens in a daily drill. But the many functions the Superintendent of the City had to perform in Kauṭilya —like those of having accountants called *Gopas* under them to look after the accounts of ten, twenty, or forty householders, to know the caste, names, *gotras*, and occupations of both men and women in all those households, and their income and expenditure as well, and likewise of having under him officials called *Sthānikas*, who were to attend to the needs of the four quarters of the kingdom, and to various other functions, point to the complicated aspects of the city life in the days of Kauṭilya which perhaps did not exist in the smaller cities of Aristotle.

(xii) Auditors of Accounts

In the City State of Aristotle, there was a magistracy to look after the auditing of accounts, which did not do any other duty.[327] In Kauṭilya the final responsibility of looking after the auditing of accounts was that of the Collector-General. This is evident from the following injunction: "The business of upkeeping the government (*saṁsthānaṁ*), the routine work (*pracāraḥ*), the collection of the necessaries of life, the collection and auditing of all kinds of revenue—these constitute the work in hand" (*saṁsthānaṁ pracāras—sarīrāvasthāpanaṁ—ādānaṁ sarvasamudayapiṇḍa-sañjātaṁ—etat—karaṇiyam.*)[328] We have already referred to the State Records Keeper. In that dignitary's office, with its face constructed with four doors facing either the north or the east, were seats for clerks kept apart and shelves for accounts books well arranged (*vibhaktopasthānaṁ nibandha-pust.ıkasthānaṁ kārayet*). Here again Kauṭilya lays down minute details of how the revenues from various sources were to be received, entered, and checked.[329] This extremely detailed working of a part of the revenue department cannot be expected of small City States like those of Athens, where the revenue as well as the staff dealing with it were both limited.

(xiii) Superintendents of Shrines and Sacrifices

Aristotle would have in some City States a magistrate to look after the maintenance of religion, preservation and repair of temples; but in large States, Superintendents of Sacrifices, Guardians of Shrines, and Treasurers of Sacred Revenues.[330] It should be realized that religion played a considerable part in the life of the Greeks. The duties enumerated above may be compared with those of the king and of the Superintendent of Religious Institutions in ancient India. It was the personal duty of the monarch to look after the religion of the country. We have seen this while describing another duty of the king, viz., looking after the minors, the aged, the afflicted, the helpless, and the women.[331] That it was obligatory on the part of the king to look after, in general, the religion and the religious observances is further proved by the passage in the *Arthaśāstra* which we have cited earlier, and which, we may be permitted to repeat, relates: "In virtue of his power to uphold the observances of the respective duties of the four castes and of the four divisions of religious life, and in virtue of his power to guard against the violation of the *dharmas*, the king is the fountain of justice" (*dharma pravartaka*).[332]

The existence of the office of the Superintendent of Religious Institutions (*devatādhyakṣa*) is proved by the following injunction of Kauṭilya, who deals with the main question of the Replenishment of the Treasury. "The Superintendent of Religious Institutions may collect in one place the various kinds of property of the gods of fortified cities and country parts, and carry away the property (to the king's treasury)."[333]

(d) *Aristotle and Kauṭilya Contrasted in regard to the Executives*

(i) *Gymnastics and Contests*

We thus see that almost all the executive offices mentioned by Aristotle have their counterparts in Kauṭilya, the only exception being the magistracy to control gymnastics and contests. This did not obtain in India since the Indians do not seem to have attached much importance to the care of the physical development of the youth of the country.

(ii) *Other Numerous Executives*

It is not so much this which marks the difference between the executives mentioned in Aristotle and those in Kauṭilya as the host of other executives which the latter has mentioned but which are not found in Aristotle. Thus, for instance, there were the Superintendents of *vārtā* (wealth?), Conches and Pearls, Metals, Coins, Mint, Ocean, Mines and Salt, Gold, Store House, Royal Writs, Commerce, Armoury, Chariots, Cows, Horses, Elephants, Liquor, Passports, Pastures, Prostitutes, Slaughter Houses, Weights, and Measures, and Weaving.[334] We have to assume that quite a number of important subjects like slaves and labourers, resumption of gifts, etc., artisans and weavers, physicians, musicians, moral offences, and the like were likewise under the charge of their respective Superintendents. Kauṭilya's meticulous care in describing every one of these various subjects, and the way in which he guards the interests of the king, the State, and the people in general are in striking contrast to the perfunctory manner in which Aristotle describes the magistracies and their respective duties,

(iii) Corruption amongst Magistrates

On another important detail, too, we see how the Indian thinker excelled his Greek counterpart. This refers to the corruption among magistrates. Aristotle relates that magistrates should not be allowed to make money. He dwells on this point on many occasions. The general rule which he framed in this connection was to the following effect: "But above all every State should be administered and so regulated by law that its magistrates cannot possibly make money."[335] Although Aristotle says in the next sentence that special precautions should be taken against this evil in oligharchies, yet it is not clear from what follows what exactly were the measures which the Greek philosopher had in mind to remedy this evil. The emphasis laid on this side of the problem clearly proves that it existed in ancient Greece. There is no doubt that it was also rampant in ancient India. Kauṭilya was fully alive to this great danger as is proved by the detailed provisions which he made to suppress it. After stating that "all undertakings depend upon finance. Hence foremost attention shall be paid to the treasury", he lays down minute rules for punishing either with fines or with corporal punishment various categories of executive officials who were found guilty of forty different types of embezzlement.[336] We see, therefore, that unlike Aristotle, who merely alluded to the evil of corruption amongst the executives, Kauṭilya not only mentions various types of corruption but prescribes the severest remedies for eradicating them.

I. FUNCTIONS AND END OF THE STATE

1. ARISTOTLE ON THE FUNCTIONS OF THE STATE

(a) On the Conditions necessary for a State

Having seen in some detail the parallelism in the Aristotlean and Kauṭilyan machinery of the State, we may now proceed to the question of how the two great thinkers tried to solve the problem of the functions and end of the State. Aristotle discusses the question of the problem of the State in the context of the necessary conditions of a State, thus: "We must see also how many things are indispensable to the existence of a State . . . . Let us then enumerate the functions of a State." He then gives the necessary conditions of the State, thus:

> First, there must be food ; secondly, arts, for life requires many instruments ; thirdly, there must be arms, for the members of a community have need of them in order to maintain authority both against disobedient subjects and against external assailants ; fourthly, there must be a certain amount of revenue ; both for internal needs and for the

> purpose of war; fifthly, or rather first, there must be a care of religion, which is commonly called worship; and sixthly, and most necessary of all, there must be a power of deciding what is for the public interest, and what is just in man's dealings with one another. These are the things which every state may be said to need.[337]

The aim of the State is to attain self-sufficiency. Therefore, a State should have husbandmen, artisans, a warlike class, a wealthy class, priests, and judges. Since the best form of government is that which makes the State most happy, and since happiness cannot exist without virtue, it clearly follows that "in the state which is best governed the citizens who are absolutely and not merely relatively just men must not lead the life of mechanics or tradesmen for such a life is ignoble and inimical to virtue. Neither must they be husbandmen, since leisure is necessary both for the development of virtue and the performance of political duties."[338]

(b) *Criticism of Aristotle*

From the foregoing sketch of the needs of the State as given in Aristotle, it is clear that the problem of protection which is the foremost function in Kauṭilya, appears to be third in the list of Aristotle. This is rather not intelligible in the sense that neither the first need of food nor the second one of arts can be secured and fostered without protection which forms the basis of the life of a State. But it should be remembered in this connection that Aristotle was not confronted with the grave problem which faced Kauṭilya, viz., that of uprooting an internal danger (as represented by the Nandas and their innumerable sympathizers and supporters), and that of driving out an external enemy (as represented by Seleukos Nikator and the latter's henchmen in north-western India). Aristotle wrote at a time when the Greek City States had succumbed to the Macedonian conquerors, father and son, and when the last vestiges of their greatness were gradually becoming merely ideas to be dreamt of by the decadent Greeks and by the rising Macedonians. Protection in the days of Aristotle was more the concern of the Macedonians than that of the Athenians or the Spartans. No wonder Aristotle was constrained to view the problem of food and arts as being more important than that of protection.

2. ARISTOTLE AND KAUTILYA

(a) *The State to be Self-Sufficient*

But in the passages cited above, the great Greek philosopher has given three ideas which we may now analyse in order to see how far they existed in Kauṭilya. These three ideas refer to (*a*) the self-sufficiency which each State was to aim at; (*b*) the relative "ignoble" position of the mechanics and artisans in society ; and (*c*) the importance of leisure. Aristotle's idea of self-sufficiency is amply borne out by the plentiful provision made by Kauṭilya in every sphere of State activity for adequate finances, food, and stores. The Superintendent of the Store House (*koṣṭāgārādhyakṣa*) was to supervise the accounts of agricultural produce, taxes coming from the *rāṣṭra* or country, commerce, barter, begging for grains, grains borrowed with promise to repay, manufacture of rice, oil, etc., accidental revenue, statements to check expenditure, and recovery of past arrears. The numerous duties of the Superintendent of the Store House[339] made it incumbent upon him to see that the essential need of self-sufficiency was fulfilled.

(*b*) *Attitude towards the Mechanics and the Artisans*

Kauṭilya's superiority over Aristotle as an impartial observer of human nature is seen in the manner in which he considers the artisans as a class. While he agrees with Aristotle that they were prone to dishonesty, he does not condemn them as a community, as the great Greek thinker does. And he gives them special privileges which Aristotle does not give. The artisans and other handicraftsmen were permitted by him, on their own responsibility, to allow others of their profession to reside wherever they wanted so long as they carried on their own work. The same privilege was given to the merchants.[340] The City Superintendent controlled both the artisans and the merchants. Later on Kauṭilya gives detailed regulations to counteract the oppression which the artisans, weavers, washermen, scavengers, medical practitioners, musicians, and beggars might inflict on the rest of the people.[341] The Superintendent of Commerce took every care to see that the trading communities did not have recourse to deception in weights and measures, and to look after exports and imports.[342] These two regulations indicate that Kauṭilya, while giving the artisans some privileges, was aware of their innate propensity to defraud which he expressed in the following stricture: "Artisans are naturally of an impure character (*aśucatho hi kāravaḥ*). It is not an approved custom with them to deposit for some reliable reason" (*na eṣām kāraṇapūrvo nikṣepa dharmaḥ*).[342a] There was something in the artisan class which, so it appeared, could not be easily be rectified. That alone explains why in a later context, he writes thus:

> Artisans shall, in accordance with their engagement as to time, place, and form of work, fulfil their engagements. Those who postpone their engagements under the excuse that no agreement as to time, place, and form of work has been entered into shall, except in troubles and calamities, not only forfeit one-fourth of their wages, but also be punished with a fine equal to twice the amount of their wages. They shall also make good whatever is thus lost or damaged. Those who carry on their work contrary to orders shall not only forfeit their wages, but also pay a fine equal to twice the amount of their wages.[342b]

The above undoubtedly points to the defective nature of the artisans. But it is also evident from the same passage that Kauṭilya did not consider the artisans as wholly being incorrigible and outside any kind of compassion, as is done by Aristotle, who writes that the artisan attains excellence only in proportion as he becomes a slave (i.e. is under the direction of his master). But the artisan, unlike the slave, does not exist by nature.[342c] Aristotle's contempt for labour is seen in his statement that no man can practise virtue who lives the life of a mechanic or labourer.[342d] Further, according to the same great thinker, there is no room for moral excellence in any of their employments, whether they be mechanics or traders or labourers.[342e] The artisans had no place in the democratic concept of Aristotle. For he writes that in the best form of government in which citizens are absolutely and not merely relatively just, "men must not lead the life of mechanics or tradesmen, for such a life is ignoble and inimical to nature".[342f] It is here that we see the difference between the Greek and the Indian political philosophers: the former adopted an uncompromising and, in a sense, unjustifiable attitude towards a class of people, and condemned them and their profession for ever as being ignoble and unfit for any recognition at the hands of the State; while the latter, while admitting the inherently defective nature of the same class, gave them some privileges and a place in the State. To Aristotle social prosperity could never be achieved through labour; while to Kauṭilya it was possible to secure it through properly guided labour.

(c) *Importance of Leisure*

Aristotle's third idea refers to leisure. He maintained that, since the ends of the best men and of the best State are the same, there ought to exist in both of them the virtue of leisure without which there could not be progress in any direction.[343] This was a unique idea inasmuch as Aristotle attributed to leisure the development of virtue and the performance of political duties. He also believed that a State could lead a life of virtuous activity isolated from others.[344] We shall have to revert to these ideas but here we may note that both these concepts are not found in the *Arthaśāstra*. To Aristotle and to the Greeks they were the natural corollaries of the position of political subservience to which the Greek City States were reduced in the age of the Macedonian conquerors. They were to some extent the index of the character of the Greeks who had collapsed before their aggressive northern neighbours. That is, the Greeks could conveniently think of leisure and a life of isolated virtuous activity when they had, politically, nothing to strive for, and when their whole concern was how to preserve what they had so magnificently achieved in the hey-day of their political greatness.

It was otherwise with Kauṭilya. During his age it was not leisure but vigilance that was the keynote of the life of the State and of the citizen—vigilance against both the internal danger and the external enemies we have mentioned above. While Aristotle, therefore, contemplated on leisure, Kauṭilya concentrated on security. And since leisure was unthinkable in the political context of the times, a life of isolated virtuous activity was likewise unimaginable. It was not a single virtuous individual or State that mattered but a well-knit, co-ordinated, and impregnable State that was the most urgent need—a State which permitted no leisure to itself nor prescribed it to its citizens, in view of the dangers which perennially faced it. Aristotle could contemplate only on leisure because the sun had set on his political horizon ; Kauṭilya, on the other hand, could dwell only on vigilance because his age ushered in the dawn of the political greatness of his land. What was only natural to Aristotle was alien to Kauṭilya in terms of the different political situations in which they lived.

(d) *On Conquest*

We may at this stage examine two more ideas of Aristotle, and see to what extent they were visible in Kauṭilya, before we pass on to the identity of views of the two great thinkers. These two ideas related to conquest and education. Aristotle unequivocally maintained that a State was not happy by conquests.[345] To Kauṭilya conquest was the *sine qua non* of existence. His concept of a *vijigīṣu* or a would-be-conqueror, and of the elaborate preparation for war, as described in detail in the *Arthaśāstra*, cannot be appreciated except in terms of conquest. Kauṭilya was essentially an imperialist to whom peace only prepared the State for war.

(e) *On Education*

(i) *Aristotle on Education*

Aristotle's other idea relating to education is likewise not visible in Kauṭilya. Aristotle laid very great emphasis on education. Children were to be trained by education "with an eye to the state".[346] The legislator was not to aim at the equalization of properties but a moderation in their amount, since it is "not possessions but the desires of mankind which require to be equalized".[347] Aristotle promulgated an eternal principle when he stated that "the best laws, though sanctioned by every citizen of the State, will be of no avail unless the young are trained by habit and education in the spirit of the constitution, if the laws are democratic, democratically, or oligarchically, if the laws are oligarchical". It is this adaptation of education to government that made for the permanence of constitutions.[348] After repeating what he had said earlier, viz., that the legislator "should direct his attention above all to the education of youth", since the neglect of education did harm to the State, Aristotle put forward the case for the education of the youth, thus:

The citizen should be moulded to suit the form of government under which he lives. For each government has a peculiar character which originally formed and which continues to preserve it. The character of democracy creates democracy, and the character of oligarchy creates oligarchy; and always the better the character, the better the government.[349]

(ii) Kauṭilya on Education

Never was the relationship between education, character, and government so clearly and so magnificently stated as in the above passage in Aristotle, whose delineation of this vital problem had such a profound effect on the concept of citizenship and on the nature of government of the later Western world. In the elucidation of this question Aristotle scores a victory over Kauṭilya in whose work the relationship between education and government is unfortunately not visible. We need not infer from this that Kauṭilya was unaware either of the importance of education or of its relationship to government. The importance of education, if we take the bulk of the citizens, and, in particular, its bearing on the nature of government, is missing in the *Arthaśāstra*; but it is certainly noticeable if we take the head of the State. While describing the life of the king from the time he underwent the ceremony of tonsure onwards, Kauṭilya states that the king, as a student, shall learn the alphabet and arithmetic, study the triple *Vedas*, the science of *ānvikṣakī*, the science of *vārtā* and of *daṇḍaniti* both in theory and practice, "ever and invariably keep company with aged professors of sciences, in whom alone discipline has its firm root", receive military lessons in the forenoon, hear *itihāsa* (history) in the afternoon, and "during the rest of the day and night, he shall not only receive new lessons and revise old lessons, but shall hear over and over again what has not been clearly understood". Kauṭilya then gives in the next sentence the importance of knowledge thus: "For from hearing (*śruta*) ensues knowledge; from knowledge steady application (*yoga*) is possible; and from application self-possession (*ātmavattā*) is possible. That is what is meant by efficiency of learning" (*vidyā sāmarthyam*). Kauṭilya finally explains the fruits of such perfect education. "The king who is well educated and disciplined in sciences, devoted to the good government of his subjects, and bent on doing good to the people, will enjoy the earth unopposed" (*vidyāvinīto rājā hi prājānāṁ vinaye ratah ananyāṁ pṛithvīṁ bhuṅkte sarvabhūtahite ratah*).[350]

(iii) Criticism of Education in Kauṭilya

In the above we have an ideal system of education so far as the head of the State is concerned, which had before it two objectives—the spirit of the constitution as the ancient Indians understood it, and the ultimate good of the people. These two objectives came very near those of Aristotle. But while they help us to understand the rigorous training which the monarch in ancient India underwent, they do not enlighten us on the specific point in the above account of Aristotle, viz., in what manner the generality of the citizens were trained with an eye to the State. Education in the Aristotelean sense was absent in India, where the orthodox method of study, while it undoubtedly developed character, remained rooted in the traditions of the past. When Kauṭilya wrote that the duty of a youth (*Brahmacārin*) consisted in learning the *Vedas*, fire worship, ablutions, living by begging, and devotion to his teacher, even at the cost of his own life, or in the absence of his teacher, to the teacher's son, or to an elder classmate,[351] he had virtually slammed the door of enterprise and free thinking on the face of the Youth of the country. Perhaps he could not help being the transmitter of the traditional type of education: the legacy to which he was an heir, particularly in the wide field of learning, was of the conservative mould which he did not dare alter. Even while describing the education of the king, as seen above, he was compelled to step along with his ancestors on the path of the *śrutis*, the *yoga* (steady application), and the *ātmavatta* (self-possession), although like a wise person he left the third term vaguely undefined. It is a matter of misfortune that Kauṭilya, who had introduced many radical ideas in statecraft, and had the courage to reject the views of not only Manu and other great ancient sages but also of his own unnamed teacher, did not think it desirable to change the concept of education both for the ruler and for the youth of the country. Evidently this was not in his mind, pre-occupied as he was with the supreme need of rescuing the scriptures and the land from the wicked Nandas.[352] We may only suppose that if the great Mauryan Prime Minister had advocated new ideas in the ancient system of education, he would not have failed to have received an all-round denunciation which he got for his statecraft at the hands of the champions of orthodoxy who came long after him, like the illustrious Bāṇabhaṭṭa (seventh century A.D.)[353] So far as our study is concerned, Kauṭilya's adherence, without any modification whatsoever, to the ancient system of education, precludes any comparison between it and that which Aristotle had so boldly advocated not only for the youth of the latter's State but for those of all Time.

3. WHERE ARISTOTLE AND KAUTILYA MEET

(*a*) *Comparison in General*

Notwithstanding the wide divergence between the two great thinkers in the matter of education, it is worthwhile seeing how far they approached each other in regard to the functions of the State in general. On the whole, there was nothing fundamentally different between the views of Aristotle and those of Kauṭilya concerning the functions which the State had to perform by way of having self-sufficiency in food, encouraging arts, maintaining an adequate army, looking after religion, and having enough revenue for internal and external purposes. These basic functions of the State appear to have been common to the Greek and Indian political thinkers.

(b) *Justice and the State*

If we study a little deeper we find that there are still other points of comparison between the two great writers. These are, firstly, in regard to the relationship between justice and the State. According to Aristotle, the State rests upon justice. He amplifies this by saying that "no government can stand which is not founded upon justice".[354] Kauṭilya echoes the same idea but in a different way, thus:

> As the duty of the king consists in protecting his subjects with justice, its observance leads him to heaven. He who does not protect his people or upsets the social order wields his royal sceptre (*daṇḍa*) in vein. It is power and power alone which, exercised by the king impartially and in proportion to guilt, either over his son or his enemy, maintains both this world and the next.[355]

(c) *Care of Virtue*

The second common idea between the two great thinkers is that the State must have a care of virtue.[356] Since Kauṭilya maintained that the king, as the head of the State, was to overthrow the aggregate of six enemies (lust, anger, greed, vanity, haughtiness, and overjoy), to restrain the organs of the senses, and to keep away from unrighteous transactions,[357] it follows that the State in Kauṭilya was not only brought into existence in an atmosphere of virtue but that it took care of virtue throughout its career.

(d) *Happiness*

The third concept which is common to Aristotle and Kauṭilya relates to happiness. Aristotle's idea of happiness in relation to the State requires some clarification. In an earlier context while criticizing Socrates' theory (as given in Plato's *Republic*) that the legislator must make the whole State happy, Aristotle writes that "the whole cannot be happy unless most, or all, or some of its parts enjoy happiness". He qualifies this in the next sentence thus: "In this respect happiness is not like the even principle in numbers, which may exist only in the whole, but in none of the parts; not so happiness."[358] But in a later context, the great philosopher, while dealing with the governing classes, writes the following: ". . . for happiness cannot exist without virtue, and a city is not to be termed happy in regard to a portion of the citizens, but in regard to them all".[359] Evidently the all in the last sentence is to be equated with the whole in the earlier passage. But Aristotle does not press this point further. What appears clear from his discussion is that the State should aim at the happiness of the largest number of people.

Kauṭilya likewise lays stress on happiness but in clear terms thus: "In the happiness of his subjects lies his (the king's) happiness; in their welfare his welfare; whatever pleases him he shall not consider good but whatever pleases his subjects he shall consider good" (*prajāsukhe sukhaṁ rājñaḥ prajānāṁ ca hite hitaṁ na-ātmapriyaṁ hitaṁ rājñaḥ prajānāṁ tu priyaṁ hitaṁ.*)[360] We shall see below, while narrating the qualities of a good country, which formed one of the seven Elements of the State, that Kauṭilya had some specific ideas in his mind, when he wrote about the happiness of the people. It might be observed here that he was vigorously opposed to the impoverishment of the people; and that he recommended remedial measures against such a danger, since impoverishment and discontent were potent causes of trouble within a country; while it was only in their loyalty that all other good qualities had their strength.[361] Kauṭilya's idea of happiness, therefore, obviously referred more to the material existence of the people rather than to their aesthetic plane which perhaps was also included in the concept of Aristotle.

(*e*) *Good Life*

The fourth idea in Aristotle relating to the end of the State refers to good life. Aristotle's arguments in this regard are interesting. Since men are by nature political animals, even when they do not require one another's help, they desire to live together all the same, and "are brought together by their common interests in proportion as they severally attain to any measure of well-being. This is certainly the chief end, both of individuals and of States." His elucidation of this point in the following lines reflects the temperament of the Greeks of that age. "And also for the sake of mere life (in which there is possibly some noble element) mankind meet together and maintain the political community, so long as the evils of existence do not greatly over-balance the good. And we all see that men cling to life even in the midst of misfortune, seeming to find in it a natural sweetness and happiness."[362] But in an earlier context Aristotle maintained that the "State comes into existence, originating in the bare needs of life, and continuing in existence for the sake of a good life".[363] And later on he comes almost to accept the view which he appears to have once rejected, in the following statement: A State "is a community of well-being in families and aggregation of families, for the sake of a perfect and self-sufficing life".[364]

Leaving aside the point that a perfect life is not necessarily a good life, it is clear that in the statement that "men cling to life even in the midst of misfortune, seeming to find in it a natural sweetness and happiness",

Aristotle had echoed the plaintive cry of the later Greeks, who reconciled their unfortunate lot with the exigencies of the times, and who were so unlike their earlier robust countrymen, who had made no compromise with the desperate situations which had faced them. What else but this compromising attitude was left to Aristotle when his two great erstwhile royal masters, the Macedonian Conquerors, Philip and Alexander, had destroyed the last traces of the independence of the Greeks, and compelled them to lead only good but not valiant and independent lives?

There is nothing of the Aristotelean spirit of reconciliation with despair in the *Arthaśāstra* of Kauṭilya who, if he stood for anything, was against compromise on fundamentals. It was stated above that he gave no latitude to the king in regard to the latter's duty to his people: the king was to consider that good which his subjects considered good. We have also seen in the earlier pages of this work that the king, who was well educated and disciplined in sciences, devoted to the good government of his subjects, and bent on doing good to all the people, was sure to enjoy the earth unopposed.[365] These statements make it perfectly clear that the good of all the people was the most important end in view of the State in ancient India. But Kauṭilya was not concerned with the perfect life which Aristotle had in view, since, according to the ancient Indian concept, such perfect life was commensurate with the fulfilment of the respective duties which had been ordained since time immemorial to each of the four castes and the four religious orders, and which could not be transgressed without the fear of incurring the gravest of punishments. We may recount here the injunction of Kauṭilya: "This people (*loka*), consisting of four castes and four orders of religious life, when governed by the king with his sceptre, will keep to their respective paths, devotedly adhering to their respective duties and occupations.[366] With the firm setting of the classical tradition around him, it is futile to expect of Kauṭilya that he should have had any other concept than the one given above of the perfect life that was expected of the various classes of the people in the Indian society.

J. THE CITIZENS AND THE STATE

1. ARISTOTLE ON CITIZENSHIP

On two important topics there was wide divergence between Aristotle and Kauṭilya. These are the concept of citizenship and the method of treatment of their subjects. The former will lead us to an elucidation of the idea of citizenship and its corollary, the concept of rights; and the latter, to a comparative study of the method they adopted in writing their great books.

We shall first deal with Aristotle, whose one aspect of the important question of citizenship has already been dealt with above in connection with the education that was to be imparted by the State. Aristotle dwells on the importance of citizenship on many occasions thereby suggesting that, according to him, it was a question of fundamental importance. He states that a good man is not necessarily a good citizen. The latter should know how to govern like a freeman, and how to obey like a freeman. These are the two virtues of a citizen which are not the same which a good man might possess, although in an ideal State they may coincide.[367] Who, then, was a citizen? In defining a citizen, he warns that what he says is true of democracies, and not necessarily of other States.[368] Speaking in general, he says that "he who has the power to take part in the deliberative or judicial administration of any State is said by us to be a citizen of that State"; while a State "is a body of citizens sufficing for the purposes of life".[369] Therefore, the main criterion is that if men shared in the government of the State, they were citizens.[370]

2. CRITICISM OF ARISTOTLE'S CONCEPT OF CITIZENSHIP

(a) *His Partisan Spirit*

Aristotle's avowed partisan spirit is apparent when he describes the character of the citizens. He says that the character of the citizens "can be easily understood by any one who casts his eye on the more celebrated States of Hellas, and generally on the distribution of races in the habitable world".[370a] About the former, that is, the "celebrated States of Hellas" (Greece), he was certainly in a position to write with authority, although during his days the greatest of them, Athens, Sparta, Thebes, and Corinth, had already fallen low and were on their decline. But on what grounds he could pass any judgment on "the distribution of races in the habitable world" passes one's comprehension, since he has not given any evidence of his ever having personally visited any other part of the world, leaving aside the Greek States and Macedonia. Even when he writes of the Indian kings, it was only what he had gathered from Skylax. This was Skylax of Karyanda, the commander of the Persian Emperor Darius (521-485 B.C), whom the latter had dispatched soon after his accession to find out the feasibility of a sea voyage from the mouth of the Indus to Persia. Skylax's fleet was assembled on the upper waters of the Punjab in the Gāndhāra region. Sailing down the Indus to the west, he reached the Red Sea within thirteen months.[371]

(b) *The Source of His Information*

Here we have the source of information which refers to a province of India, and on the basis of which Aristotle, we think, has generalized in regard to the Asiatics. But it is worthwhile noting what he says after stating that one should see the celebrated States of Greece and the races in the habitable world:

> Those who live in a cold climate and in (northern) Europe are full of spirit, but wanting in intelligence and skill; and, therefore, they keep their freedom, but have no political organization, and are incapable of ruling over others. Whereas the natives of Asia are intelligent and inventive, but they are wanting in spirit, and, therefore, are always in a State of subjection and slavery. But the Hellenistic race, which is situated between them, is likewise intermediate in character, being high spirited and also intelligent. Hence it continues free, and is the best governed of any nation, and if it could be formed into one State, would be able to rule the world.[372]

(c) *His Estimate of the Hellenes*

Aristotle erred not only in his estimate of the Asiatics but also in that of the Hellenes; and in his admiration of the latter suggested a solution which he had elsewhere condemned. We may first dispense with the second point. It has been seen above that he was averse to conquest and to empire-building. He maintained that an empire was unnecessary for the happiness of States.[373] And yet he seems to imply in the above passage that if only the Greeks could form themselves into one State, they would be able to rule the world! That is, he would give to the Greeks what he denied to the tyrants and the Asiatics, viz., the right of ruling over others. But unfortunately in his days the Greeks had fallen so low that there was no chance whatsoever of their ever realizing his dream!

This brings us to the first part of the above passage relating to the character of the Greeks and the nature of their rule. Here, too, the great Greek political philosopher is unhistorical. He affirms, we may be permitted to repeat, that the Hellenes continued to be free, and that they were the best governed of any nation. In a later context he repeats the encomium which he had bestowed on the government of the Greeks thus: "Whereas even the Hellenes of the present day, who are reputed to be best governed"; although in the next part of the same sentence he admitted that their legislators, who gave them their constitutions, did not frame their governments with regard to their best end, or gave them laws and education with a view to all the virtues, having fallen back "in a vulgar spirit" which promised to be more useful and profitable.[374]

(d) *Criticism of His Estimate of Greek Character and Political Institutions*

Was Aristotle correct in the estimate of either the character of the Greeks or of the nature of their government? We have to follow the course of events in the history of Greece during this age, and in particular listen to what one of the greatest historians of the early times, Thucydides, had to say on the nature of the government of the Greeks. Before the days of Aristotle the Greek City States were moving fast to their great crisis which came in the shape of the Peloponnesian War. But already in the fifth century B.C., almost every State in Greece was either a decided oligarchy or a decided democracy or a confirmed tyranny, and practised a novel method of imposing the rule of those who were in power, viz., getting rid altogether of the most dangerous section of their opponents. The result of this most uncompromising and fatal spirit of revenge was internal dissension and its accompanying evils of revival of old jealousies and calling in a common non-Hellenistic enemy to solve local feuds. The history of the City States of the island of Naxos, Miletus, and Epidamnus only proves that this disease had already set in amongst the Greeks. Thucydides, while describing the opening phase of the great Peloponnesian War which was fought between Athens, on the one side, and Sparta, on the other, with almost all the Greek States joining one or the other party, gives a vivid picture of the disease which the Greeks themselves called *stasis,* i.e. taking up a definite stand in a State with the malicious intention of ruining the opposite party.[375]

How virulently this epidemic of *stasis* was spreading, and what havoc it was causing among the Greeks is also related by the same great historian thus: What in ordinary times would be defects of character, laid claim now to be considered as excellences of character. "Reckless daring was held to be loyal courage ; prudent delay was the excuse of a coward ; moderation was the disguise of unmanly weakness ; to know everything was to do nothing. The lover of violence was always trusted, and his opponent suspected. . . . The tie of party was stronger than that of blood, because a partisan was more ready to dare without asking why."[376]

The effect of all this on the public and private life of the Greeks was both lasting and profound. Family life and affection were replaced by clubs and coteries ; simplicity and straightforwardness were laughed at ; and, so far as government was concerned, as Thucydides relates, party principles became corrupt, and the "life-giving middle class" was destroyed. Love of power originating in avarice and ambition, according to the same great historian, and party spirit were mainly responsible for ushering in evils which completely undermined the political life of the Greeks.[377]

Now Aristotle wrote some sixty or seventy years after Thucydides.[378] If by the time of Thucydides, as that great historian candidly admits, Greece had already fallen on evil days ; if the life-blood of the city States was already poisoned and had become feverish ; if the true end of the State, as he imagined it, was no longer pursued ; and if every organ of the State had lost its healthy and natural action,[379] one cannot understand on what justifiable grounds Aristotle could have maintained that during his own age the Hellenes were the best governed people in the world! We have to discount this particular part of Aristotle's study as being altogether unhistorical and prejudiced. Indeed, viewed in the light of the impartial observations of Thucydides, Aristotle's work, particularly Book V in some editions, and Book VIII in others, has been condemned as a treatise on the pathology of Greek society.[380] If this judgment has already been passed by historians on Aristotle's famous work, we may wonder whether we have to pursue further the concept of citizenship which that great Greek political thinker has given in the particular part of the book mentioned above, or be content with noting a few observations which would be germane to our study.

(*e*) *Lasting Effect of His Concept of Citizenship*

There is no denying the fact that Aristotle gave expression to a new concept of citizenship to the world. This is particularly true of one aspect of citizenship which, in the long run, was to have the most lasting effect on the history of all later progressive governments. It relates to rights. According to Aristotle, residence in a place did not make a person a citizen of that locality; nor did the enjoyment of legal rights of suing and of being sued make a man a citizen.[381] Nor was it enough if a man's parents were citizens;[382] nor was usage a criterion of citizenship;[383] nor was it citizenship in which a citizen shared in the administration of justice and in offices.[384] An approved citizen is one who knows how to obey.[385] Aristotle laid down in the last definition an eternal principle of citizenship for posterity to follow.

(*f*) *Aristotle's Concept of Citizenship in terms of the End of the State*

In order to find out how far the above view relating to citizenship was obtainable in India in the age of Kauṭilya, we have, firstly, to study it together with Aristotle's view on the end of the State; secondly, to see whether Kauṭilya provided for citizens participating in the administration of the State; and, thirdly, to ascertain whether any theory of rights is discernible in the *Arthaśāstra*. And in so doing we shall have to traverse some part of the ground already covered.

On the first point we have to remember here what was said above in regard to the good life for all that was to be aimed at by the State. Although Aristotle maintained in one context, as remarked earlier, that a good man was not necessarily a good citizen, yet in another connection he affirmed that the virtue of a citizen was identical with that of a good man in a perfect State.[386] Since Aristotle lapses into the mood of a visionary in search of an ideal State, more after the pattern of his great teacher Plato than after the model of a practical statesman, we may take his description of a citizen in a perfect State as being suitable for our purpose. In other words, whatever rights a citizen possessed, so it appears, were meant only for the furtherance of common good. It is only in this sense that one can interpret his statement that "all must have the virtue of the good citizen—thus, and thus only, can the State be perfect ; but they will not have the virtue of a good man, unless we assume that in the good State all the citizens must be good".[387]

If goodness is the ultimate end of the State, the question arises: is it necessarily attained only by having rights or could it be secured by any scheme of social order which taught the people to live within bounds, to perform their allotted duties, and thereby to add to social good and yet to possess certain rights? When we discuss the State in Aristotle, we should remember that it did not comprise classes of people whose duties had been fixed for them by immemorial usage. It is no wonder, therefore, that Aristotle is constrained to talk in terms of rights which, when properly exercised, were to enable them to lead a happy and good life. The same objective was reached in the *Arthaśāstra* of Kauṭilya, and in ancient India, where the respective duties of the different classes of people compelled them to work in a vast social order of co-ordinated partnership, in which there was no possibility of one order's or class' encroaching on the duties of another without coming under the influence of law and the opprobrium of time-honoured custom. Moreover, if rights, in the Aristotelean sense, in the long run, were merely privileges that enabled one to participate in government and to share in the honours of the State, that freedom was conceded by Kauṭilya to the citizens of his State, whose active assistance was perennially needed for the efficient working of the vast and complicated governmental machinery described by the great Indian political thinker.

3. DID THE ANCIENT INDIANS POSSESS A THEORY OF RIGHTS?

(a) *Divergent Theories among Modern Indian Scholars*

At this stage we might ask the question: Did the ancient Indians ever possess a theory of rights? Opinion seems to be divided on this question among Indian scholars. On the one hand, we have the late Professor Altekar and Professor V. P. Varma maintaining that the Indian political thinkers did not dwell on any theory of rights, since the concept of *dharma* covered the basic principles involved in the theory of rights, duties, and freedom. On the other hand, Professor U. N. Ghoshal mentions the civil rights not only of individuals but even of classes and communities.

(b) *Professor Altekar's Theory*

(i) *The Theory Stated*

We may first take up the view of Professor Altekar. "While discussing the relations between the State and the citizen the political science (*sic!*)

seeks mainly to define the mutual rights of the two parties. Hindu constitutional writers have approached the problem from quite a different point of view." They usually describe not the rights of the citizens, but the duties of the State ; the former are to be inferred from the latter. Similarly they discuss the duties of the citizens, from which we are to indirectly infer the extent of the control the State could exercise over its subjects. In our ancient works, therefore, there is no systematic discussion of the problem from the point of view of the rights of either party. European writers, whether of the ancient or modern times, further look at the question from a purely secular and constitutional point of view. They separate the civic and political life of the citizen from his religious and moral life ; and define rights as against the State, which is often assumed to be hostile to them. Ancient Hindu writers, on the other hand, considered the political duties of the citizen as part of his general duties (*dharma*), and assumed that normally there should be no conflict between the State and citizen, necessitating a clear-cut definition of the rights and obligations of both. The very aim of the State was to promote the all-sided progress of the citizens both in this life and the life to come.[388]

(ii) *Evaluation of Professor Altekar's Theory*

The above is neither an appreciation of the Indian concept of rights nor an understanding of the Western theory of rights. It abounds more in half truths than in principles. The above passage from the learned Professor's work starts with the dictum that Political Science, while discussing the relations between the States and the individual, seeks mainly to define the mutual rights of the two parties. This is a confused way of expressing the functions and end of the State in the elucidation of which the political scientist attempts to solve the problem whether the State is an end in itself or whether it is merely a means to enable the individuals to realize their ends. In doing so, the political scientist has not only to give the theories relating to the State but also those relating to the individual, to analyse the functions of the State, and to discuss the functions in regard to the sovereignty of the State, on the one hand, and the liberty of the individual, on the other, so as to bring out their mutual interdependence.[389] Therefore, any postualtion of the theory that Political Science is mainly concerned with the "mutual rights of both the parties" would be stating the principle in an incomplete and unsatisfactory manner.

European Authors have not ignored the Moral Side of Man. Professor Altekar further maintains that European writers, "whether of the ancient or the modern times", looked at the question of rights "from a purely secular and constitutional point of view", separated the civic and political life of the citizen from his religious and moral life, and defined his rights as against the State "which is often assumed to be hostile to them". The statement that Western authors of the ancient or modern times examined the question of rights purely from the secular and constitutional points of view is incorrect. The reader has only to remember what has been said about the Aristotelean concept of citizenship as summarized above. Aristotle's insistence on virtue and moral good was not with a view to divorcing the civic and political life of the citizens from their religious and moral life but to unifying the political and moral sides of man. To some extent it is true that Western authors did not, as they do not, project their religious and moral ideas into the political sphere, while dealing with the vital problem of the State and the individual. But this is not equal to saying that they have either ignored or minimized the importance of the moral basis of both State and individual action.

Examples of European Authors to prove the Above. A cursory study of the writings of some modern Western writers on Politics will convince the reader that it is futile to generalize in the manner of Professor Altekar. Three examples may suffice to prove our point. Professor Harold Laski wrote thus: "Every government is thus built upon a contingent moral obligation."[390] As to how this statement has been elaborated by the eminent Western political thinker is well known to all those who have studied his works. Professor H. T. Green had expressed earlier the moral basis of the State thus: The only acts which it (the State) ought to enjoin or forbid are those of which the doing or not doing, from whatever motive, is necessary to the moral end of society.[391] This is because, as Professor McIver rightly says, the law of the State, notwithstanding its universality, its coercive sanction, and its imperative will, can regulate "only the exterior order of society", touching the outer aspects of man's conduct.[392] and not the moral domain over which no State has any control. Those who would arbitrarily accuse modern Western political thinkers of divorcing morality from State action would do well to study Professor MacIver's admirable exposition of this side of the vital question, when he discusses the larger issue of the limits of political control.[393]

Deposing and Killing a Wicked King Not a Right in the Modern Sense. Professor Altekar's statements would seem to suggest that, unlike the Western political thinkers, the Indian theorists considered political duties as part of the general duties of the citizens, and assumed that normally "there should be no conflict between the State and the citizen, necessitating a clear-cut definition of the rights and obligations". This is far too speculative an assertion which could be accepted on the basis of either the *dharmaśāstras* or the *nītiśāstras*. As remarked in an earlier context, the only political right—if we might call it so!—which the *smṛitis* and the *Mahābhārata* conceded to the people was that of deposing and even killing their king, in case the latter failed to rule justly, proved to be voluptuous, mean, and deceitful, and misused the right of wielding the *daṇḍa* or punishment. Kauṭilya echoed the view of the *smṛitis* when he wrote thus: "But an erring king, who is bent upon doing what is against the science (i.e. of *daṇḍanīti*) brings about destruction to himself and his kingdom by maladministration."[394] Even in this case, it is not stated as a right in the modern sense, that is, a privilege granted by the State to the people for being used against itself, but only as a measure which might be used by the people in a contingency when the king ruled unjustly and misused his powers. We have only to realize here that such a contingency could not arise always, and that the people could not exercise the drastic privilege of deposing and killing their monarch on all occasions, in view of the sacred halo which Manu had created around the person of the king, whom he eulogized in the highest terms as "a great divinity in human form".[395] The above measure has to be studied along with another one which Kauṭilya has laid down, and which we have discussed above in connection with the *arājatā* theory. It is this that "when wealth and honour are discontinued, such a king may be abandoned".[396] It must be admitted that this injunction as well as the previous one smacks of a political privilege in the sense that both were laid down as a possibility on the part of the people. But they were to be used under the greatest provocation. Perhaps the second privilege of deserting a wicked ruler may be considered as a right of the people, since perhaps Kauṭilya had actually put it into practice against the Nandas.

Beyond this we fail to see where exactly, either in the *smṛitis* or elsewhere, the State gave to the citizens any political rights or defined the latter in relation to its own rights. Professor Altekar has merely assumed that there were political rights without either naming or defining them. As regards any conflict between the State and the citizens, the *smṛitis* are very clear on the subordinate position of the latter. Whatever may be the possibility of a conflict between the State and the citizens, according to any other work, in the *Arthaśāstra* of Kauṭilya it certainly does not exist. In this connection it is worthwhile noting that on two occasions he fully describes the calamities that overtook kings. These he divided into providential and human. Among the former he classed eight kinds of calamities—fire, floods, pestilential diseases, famine, rats, tigers, serpents, and demons. Among the internal calamities he mentions the troubles arising from a minister, divided rule between father and son, or between two brothers, a blind king, or a king who erred against the science of Politics, a diseased king, a new king, a weak but high born king, a strong but low born king, and the destruction of crops and grains. In the above list of internal calamities, the contingency of people's having recourse to the drastic measure of deposing or even killing the king is obviously in connection with the ruler who had erred against the *daṇḍanīti* or the science of Politics discussed above. Among the external calamities, Kauṭilya mentions foreign rule.[397] This is by itself enough to demonstrate that during his age, any trouble arising out of the people's vindicating their so-called right of deposing their king was practically non-existent, although, strange enough, he himself was instrumental in overthrowing the lawful rulers, the Nandas, as he admits towards the end of his book![398]

Guiding Citizens to the Next World was not the Function of the State. Finally, in regard to the end of the State, Professor Altekar rightly affirms that it was directed to promote the all-sided progress of the citizens in this life. But when he adds to that sentence the words "and the life to come", one feels that the learned Professor went beyond the injunctions laid down in the classical texts in this behalf. It is not unlikely that the alleged duty of the State to lead the citizen to the life to come might have been based on statements like these occurring in the *Manusmṛiti*. In this work, for instance, one whole chapter is devoted to the question of the transmigration of souls; and while recounting the various penalties in the next life for sins committed in this world, it is related in it that a Brahman, a Kṣatriya, a Vaiśya, and a Śūdra, if they fell off from their respective duties, would become a particular *preta* (or spirit named), or servants of the Dasyus, after migrating into despicable bodies.[399] Passages like these cannot be interpreted to mean maxims for the guidance of the State in regard to the life of the citizens in the next world. We could take them only as warnings to those who might think of transgressing the duties imposed on them by usage and by the *smṛitis*. The duty of looking after the material and moral interests of all sections of the people was undoubtedly that of the State, but not that of leading them to the next world which was a matter that was left entirely to the invididuals themselves. It does not appear from any ancient text that the State usurped to itself this heavenly duty in the purely mundane surroundings in which it moved.

Conclusion in regard to the Alleged Political Rights. In regard to the so-called political rights, therefore, it may be concluded that, excepting the tacit sanction of deposing and even killing a wilfully and persistently wicked monarch, and the right of deserting a tyrannical ruler, there were no other privileges which amounted to rights that were conceded to the people in the ancient times.

(c) *Professor Ghoshal's Theory*

(i) *The Theory Stated*

One of the reasons why some modern Indian scholars are inclined to think that there were political rights in the ancient days is due to the fact that they seem to have confounded immunities with political rights, particularly the civil, economic, and legal rights, which thinkers like Kauṭilya have elaborately given. An instance of immunities being confounded with rights is afforded in the theory propounded by Professor U. N. Ghoshal. According to this eminent historian, individuals, classes, and the community had all civil rights. These referred to the upper classes of people:

> The rights accorded to the individuals of the upper classes in the last and most complete sense of the foregoing passage (Viṣṇu, III 45-46 ; Vasiṣṭha, III 24 ; Baudhāyana, II 2, 4 ; 16-18) comprise those of self-defence and defence of the social order (based upon the strict rules of inter-marriage between the castes) as well as that of protection of the nearest and most honoured persons and the most cherished dumb animals.

Elaborating this view towards the end of his illuminating book, Professor Ghosal recounts again the civil rights as he understands them, and as given in the "two early *Smṛtis* of Vasiṣṭha and Baudhāyana" and by the later work *Viṣṇusmrti*. If we are to conclude from the next author he mentions, Manu also seems to have followed them. Professor Ghoshal's arguments may be cited in order to understand his view point:

> The above view of the popular rights is set forth by the *Smṛtis* side by side with their idea of the Kṣatriya's exclusive occupation of bearing arms in accordance with the law of the social order. This illustrates once more the characteristic *Smṛti* principle of adjustment of the law to the needs of the people. Supplementing these private rights of the individuals, Bhīshma in the *Mahabharata* advocates not only the passive resistance of the subjects against a bad or an incompetent ruler, but he also condones or even approves of their armed rising for slaying a tyrant.

Professor Ghoshal concludes by saying: "The Brahmanical authors in general asserted the claim of their class to private rights of persons and property and to public rights on special occasions, while their Buddhist and Jaina rivals failed to make any systematic or serious attack upon those claims."[400]

(ii) *Evaluation of Professor Ghoshal's Theory : Immunities Explained*

There seems to be no doubt that, if not in the age of the *smṛtis,* certainly in (that) of Kauṭilya, the State acknowledged the rights of the people. But it is doubtful whether we have to agree with the learned Professor when he states that individuals, classes, and communities, and in particular, the upper classes, possessed civil rights. Leaving aside the point whether one would be justified in studying the sources, as Professor Ghosal does—Vasiṣṭha and Baudhāyana preceding Manu—without assigning valid reasons for such a procedure, one cannot help stating that Professor Ghoshal has confounded rights with immunities in his enumeration of civil rights. We admit that, according to the modern concept, civil rights are considered as legal immunities enjoyed by the citizens. But it is essential that such immunities are protected by the State against interference, and that, at the same time, they are guaranteed against other persons and against the State itself.[401] There may be no objection to consider the rights mentioned by Professor Ghoshal as immunities guaranteed by the State to certain sections of the people.

It was not Upper Classes but all Classes Who enjoyed Immunities. Incidentally we may mention that it was not only the upper sections, that is, the Brahmans, who were privileged to have recourse to professions outside their normal and prescribed spheres. That concession was given by Manu to all the other classes—the Kṣatriyas, the Vaiśyas, and even the Śūdras. The Kṣatriyas and the Vaiśyas could be employed by wealthy Brahmans, if they were distressed for a livelihood.[402] Just as a Brahman, unable to subsist by his special profession, could live according to the law applicable to the Kṣatriyas, so also the latter could live, in distressed circumstances, according to the Vaiśya mode of life but could not have recourse to agriculture. Both the Brahmans and the Kṣatriyas could sell the commodities usually sold by the Vaiśyas but with some restrictions.[403] A Vaiśya, unable to subsist by his own duties, could maintain himself by a Śūdra's mode of life, provided he avoided certain forbidden acts.[404] Learning, mechanical arts, work for wages, service, rearing cattle, traffic, agriculture, contentment (with little) alms, and receiving interest on money were the ten modes of subsistence permitted by Manu to all classes in times of distress.[405] Likewise Manu enjoined seven lawful modes of acquiring property to all communities—inheritance, finding or friendly donations, purchase, conquest, lending at interest, performance of work, and acceptance of gifts from virtuous men.[406]

Upper Classes were not Privileged Classes. From the above it is clear that it was not only the upper classes, the Brahmans, who enjoyed the privilege of living by professions other than their legitimate and prescribed ones but all classes of people. Manu gave the freedom to live by trades other than those which he himself had sanctioned to all communities. We cannot, therefore, single out any upper class like the Brahmans from amongst the rest of the communities, as being entitled, for instance, to take up arms (which was essentially the duty of the Kṣatriyas) in the defence of either their own community or of the country. We have to interpret the freedom given to the Brahmans in the context of the general freedom given to all castes, in order to realize that such concessions were not necessarily rights in the sense that that term was understood even in the later days of Kauṭilya. If we are to accept the interpretation of Professor Ghoshal that such latitude necessarily connoted a right given to the superior classes, then, we should take the following one, too, in the same sense with the resultant absurdity that might follow. In the *Manusmṛiti* it is said: "The taking of roots and of fruit from trees, wood for sacrificial fire, and of grass for feeding cows, Manu has declared to be no theft."[407] If it is true that adopting the profession of arms in times of distress was a special right given to the Brahmans, then, according to the above injunction, they were also given the right to steal roots, fruits from trees, wood for sacrificial fire, and grass for cattle even in normal times! Nothing could be more absurd to imagine than that the great lawgiver should have ever thought of perpetuating an iniquity of this type!

Immunities were more Indulgences than Rights. We have, therefore, to reject the theory that the special concessions given to the upper classes necessarily meant rights or privileges which they could claim. We could perhaps better appreciate the theory of immunities mentioned above in the sense that they were certain indulgences granted to the various classes to tide over times of difficulty. The explicit ban put on them by way of not allowing the communities to do certain specified duties, points to the fact that such latitude as was given to them could not have been used by them in normal times. This removes from the theory any semblance of rights which, as stated above, are privileges granted by the State to an individual or individuals against others and against itself. Viewed from the modern standpoint, they were not even legal immunities, since the State that granted them did not protect any one of the four castes against interference by the remaining castes. The essential idea behind a right, viz., that it could be used either against the State itself or against other members of the society, is absent in the immunities mentioned above. They cannot be compared with the so-called natural rights in the sense of being inalienable under the law of nature.[408] We have, therefore, to seek elsewhere for a concept of rights that would satisfy two conditions: (*a*) their relationship to the contemporary standards ; and (*b*) their relationship to the concept of freedom as it then prevailed.

4. CONCEPT OF RIGHTS IN KAUTILYA

(*a*) *Introduction*

Both these considerations lead us to the times of Kauṭilya, when we see for the first time the formulation of what may be termed rights even in the modern sense, that is, privileges given by the State which the State itself was not in a position to subvert, and which could be claimed by the individuals even against the State. A careful analysis of the *Artha-śāstra* of Kauṭilya reveals that that thinker made provision for three different kinds of rights—civil rights, economic rights, and legal rights. As already narrated, the times in which he lived precluded any idea of political rights being granted to the citizens. But there is hardly any doubt that Kauṭilya was both sincere and definite about these three types of rights which he conceded to the citizens.

(*b*) *Rights in Kauṭilya Enumerated : Civil Rights*

(*i*) *Rights of Women*

We shall first deal with civil rights as mentioned by Kauṭilya. By the term civil rights we may understand the rights and privileges which the State creates and protects for its subjects.[409] The first of the civil rights refers to women. Kauṭilya has a great deal to say about women. But the rights which he has given to them make interesting reading. He gave them the right to certain types of property, thus: "Means of subsistence (*vritti*), jewellery (*abadhya-aniyamaḥ*) constitute what is called the property of a woman. Means of subsistence valued at above two thousand (*paṇas*) shall be endowed (in her name). There is no limit to jewellery." It was no guilt on her part to make use of this property in maintaining her son, daughter-in-law, and herself, particularly when her absentee husband had made no provision for her maintenance. This property could be used by the husband only in calamities, diseases, famines, warding off dangers, and charitable gifts. The minute rules made in this connection as well as in the case of widows, who remarried, are truly enlightening in the sense that the State made definite provision to safeguard the interests of the wife even against her husband, and to protect her property in certain circumstances.

It is interesting to note that Kauṭilya prohibited a widow after remarriage from using her own property. "No woman with a son or sons shall (after remarriage) be at liberty to make free use of her own property (*śrīdhana*) ; for that property of hers, her sons shall receive." Further, on the death of the wife, the law prevented the husband from acquiring her property. Her sons and daughters were to divide her property amongst themselves ; in the absence of the sons, it went to the daughters ; and it was only in their absence that the husband could claim only the *śulka* (or amount of money which had been given to her), while her relatives were entitled to retake whatever in the shape of dowry or gifts had been given by them to her.[410] In the above regulations we see that the State protected the interests of the sons against their own father!

Woman's Right to Property in Manu. Kauṭilya had evidently the following ordinance of Manu in mind when he stated that the sons and daughters were to divide the property of their mother on her death. "But when the mother has died, all the uterine brothers and the uterine sisters shall equally divide the mother's estate."[411] But in regard to the definition of property, Kauṭilya was more comprehensive than Manu, who had laid down the following six-fold property of a woman—what was given before the nuptial fire, what was given on the bridal procession, what was given in token of love, and what was received from her brother, mother and father.[412] While the resemblance between Kauṭilya and Manu in regard to the above two points is clear, that concerning the inviolability of the woman's property in the shape of jewellery is not visible in Kauṭilya. Manu had enjoined thus: "The ornaments which may have been worn by women during their husbands' lifetime, his heirs shall not divide; those who divide them become outcastes."[413] Here was, indeed, the State protecting the woman against her own children, although no other penalty excepting that of excommunication from society—which in those distant days was perhaps more poignant than punishment at the hands of the Superintendent of Jails!—was imposed on the erring children.

Kauṭilya More Progressive than Manu: Widow Remarriage Permitted. But Kauṭilya was undoubtedly more advanced than Manu in regard to the question of women. Manu had expressly forbidden the marriage of widows, although he had permitted the marriage of virgin widows.[414] Kauṭilya not only gave a woman the right to remarriage on the death of her husband but laid down rules as regards her right to certain kinds of property. Further, it appears that she could marry as many times as she wanted on the death of each husband. This is inferred from the statement: "If a woman has as many male children by many husbands, then, she shall conserve her property in the same condition as she had received from her husbands."[415]

Right for Maintenance Conceded. The woman was also given the right of maintenance (*bharman*). A woman who has the right to claim maintenance for an unlimited period of time shall be given as much food and clothing as is necessary for her, or more than is necessary in proportion to the income of the maintainer. But she could not sue her husband for maintenance if she placed herself under the protection of any one belonging to her father-in-law's family, or if she began to live independently.[416]

Right of Divorce Granted. Kauṭilya's injunctions in regard to divorce are of special interest to the modern world. He granted divorce to women in certain circumstances but denied to them the same in certain others. He writes:

> A woman hating her husband, cannot dissolve her marriage with him against his will. Nor can a man dissolve his marriage with his wife against her will. But from mutual enmity divorce may be obtained (*parasparaṁ dveṣān mokṣaḥ*). If a man, apprehending danger from his wife, desires divorce (*mokṣam ichchhet*), he shall return to her whatever was given (on the occasoin of her marriage). If a woman, under the apprehension from her husband, desires divorce, she shall forfeit her claim to property.

While Kauṭilya explicitly permitted divorce in the above cases, he prohibited it in marriages which had taken place according to certain specified rules, which he had given earlier. These were the following: the *ārṣa* type of marriage in which a maiden was married for a couple of cows; the *daiva* type, in which a maiden was married to an officiating priest;

the *gāndharva* type, in which there was a voluntary union of a maiden with her lover ; and the *āsura* type, in which a maiden was married after receiving plenty of wealth (*śulka*). He enjoined that marriages contracted in accordance with the customs of these four types of marriage could not be dissolved.[417]

Ordinance on Divorce Relaxed. But this ordinance on divorce he later on relaxed, while dwelling at length on the question of the remarriage of wives, who belonged to the Śūdra, Vaiśya, Kṣatriya, and Brahman castes, and who had not given birth to children. They had to wait for the return of their husbands, who might have gone abroad, for a short time ; but if they were such as had given birth to children, they were to wait for their absentee husbands for more than a year. If they were provided with maintenance, they were to wait for two years. If they were not so provided, then, well-to-do *jñātis* (or communities) were to provide them for either four or eight years. Then, the *jñātis* should permit them to remarry, after receiving from them what had been presented to them on the occasion of their marriage. If the wife of an absentee husband lacked maintenance, and was deserted by the well-to-do *jñātis,* she could marry any one she liked, who was in a position to maintain her and relieve her of her misery. The right of remarriage, however, was denied to the wife of the king's servant, who was abroad. But if she bore children to a *savarṇa* husband (i.e. a second husband belonging to the same *gotra* as her former husband), she was not liable to contempt. If the husband was a Brahman, who was studying abroad, and his wife had no issue, she had to wait for ten years ; but if she had given birth to children, she had to wait for twelve years before remarriage. A young wife (*kumārī*), who was wedded according to the customs of the first four kinds of marriage described above, whose husband had gone abroad, and was heard of, was to wait for him for a period of seven menses, provided he had not announced his departure ; but if he had announced his departure, for a year. Kauṭilya then gives further details in regard to the right of remarriage in various other contingencies.[418]

Importance of the Above Rules regarding Foreign Travel. Parenthetically we may observe here, before continuing with the main topic of the rights given to women by Kauṭilya, that the above passages have an important bearing on an aspect of Indian life which has been so often condemned by Western authors, and whose criticism has been taken for granted to be correct. This refers to the interesting question: did the ancient Indians ever go abroad for study or for other purposes? We need not cite here the oft-repeated charge against the ancient and later Indians that they confined themselves to within the boundaries of their country, and that they were averse to foreign travel. Whatever may be the truth of this charge in the later ages—when, too, it does not hold good!—it certainly cannot be maintained, so far as the history of the ancient times is concerned. We have shown elsewhere that this charge is entirely unfounded.[419] In the regulations cited just above, Kauṭilya makes provision twice for the remarriage of women, whose husbands had gone abroad either for study or for a short time, obviously for commercial purposes. General rules like those given above would not have been formulated if there had not been a sufficiently large number of persons, who had gone abroad for specific purposes. We have, therefore, to take it as an established fact that in the Mauryan age, people did go abroad for study or for other purposes.

Summary of the Five Rights hitherto granted to Women. We may now continue with the subject of the right of divorce given to women by Kauṭilya. In all the cases mentioned above, the rights of the husbands were duly protected against those of their wives. From what has been narrated only about women, it is clear that they possessed the following rights, according to the *Arthaśāstra* of Kauṭilya: the right to property, the right to remarriage, the right to maintenance, the right to earn an independent livelihood, and the right to divorce. But the number and variety of fines imposed on women in the same chapter under the section Transgression and Forbidden Transactions are a clear indication that, while he was prepared to go a long way in the matter of granting freedom to them, he was loath to give them every kind of liberty that might come in their way of either their conjugal devotion to their husbands, or their duties in their households, and their general demeanour as members of society.[420]

Further Rights of Women: Right of Freedom from Torture. In addition to the five rights mentioned above, which Kauṭilya granted to women, he gave them an additional one. This refers to trial and the use of torture to elicit confession. It was more of a legal type than of a civil nature. We may mention it for the completeness of the subject dealing with women. Kauṭilya ordained that, while those whose guilt was proved, should be subjected to torture, "women who are carrying or who have not passed a month after delivery", shall not be subjected to torture. As regards other women, he stated that "Torture of women shall be half of the prescribed standard. Or women with no exception may be subjected to the trial of cross examination (*vākyanuyogo vā*).[421]

Right to State Relief. Women possessed a seventh right. This related to State relief which will be mentioned below.

Kauṭilya and Manu in regard to the Rights of Women. Before we proceed to cite the next right in the category of civil rights, we may mention here that Kauṭilya had gone far beyond the limits of Manu in regard to the rights which the latter had granted to women. That great lawgiver of antiquity had merely stated that the right of women to property was not lost by limitations.[422] The careful distinction which Kauṭilya made in regard to the position of the wife, the provision he made to safeguard her interests against those of her husband and sons, and the rules he formulated to protect the claims of the husband, are naturally missing in the earlier and comparatively more orthodox surroundings in which Manu wrote his celebrated work.

(ii) Right to Property Ownership and Possession

The right to property which was thus guaranteed to women, was extended even to the slaves. A slave was entitled to enjoy not only whatever he earned without prejudice to his master's work but also the inheritance he had received from his father. On his death his property passed into the hands of his kinsmen, and, in their absence, it went to his master.[423]

Since property and ownership are cognate concepts, we may consider Kauṭilya's injunctions on ownership. "As to the title of an owner to his property: the owners who have quitted their country where their property lies shall continue to have their title to it." The question as to when a person lost his title to his property is explained in the next sentence thus:

> When the owners other than minors, the aged, those who are afflicted with disease or calamities, those that are sojourning abroad, or those that have deserted their country during national disturbances, neglect for ten years their property which is under the enjoyment of others, they shall forfeit their title to it.

The right to possession is explained, in the next paragraph thus: Buildings left for twenty years in the enjoyment of others shall not be reclaimed. But the mere occupation of the buildings of others during the absence of the king by kinsmen, priests, or heretics shall not give them the right of possession. The same rule holds good in regard to open deposits, pledges, treasure troves (*nidhi*), boundary, or any property belonging to the king or priests (*Śrotriyas*). Even ascetics and *Brahmacārins* had their own proprietary rights. The property of hermits (*vānaprastha*), ascetics (*yatis*), or bachelors learning the *Vedas* (*Brahmacārins*), shall on their death be taken by their preceptors, disciples, their brethern (*dharma-bhṛitri*), or classmates, in succession.[424]

That the above were, indeed, rights in the modern sense, that is, privileges granted to the citizens by the State against itself, is proved by the provision which Kauṭilya made for the recovery of property. In the same chapter entitled Resumption of Gifts, etc., he ordained:

> Whatever of the property of his own subjects the king brings back from the forests and countries of the enemies, shall be handed over to its owner. Whatever the property of citizens robbed by thieves the king cannot recover, shall be made good from his own pocket. If the king is unable to recover such things, he shall either allow any self-elected person (*svayamgrāha*) to fetch them, or pay an equivalent ransom to the sufferer.[425]

In this last detail, viz., of paying compensation from the king's personal funds for the non-recovery of stolen property, the Kauṭilyan State appears to have been more advanced than the modern State which, after real or feigned attempts at recovery stolen property, merely writes it off as being "untraceable".

(iii) Right to possess Rent Free Lands

The right to possess rent free lands was shared by two classes of people—those learned in the ancient lore, and those who were in State service. The former comprised those who performed sacrifices (*ṛitvik*), those who were spiritual guides and priests, and those who were proficient in the *Vedas.* The State had to give them lands yielding sufficient produce and exempted from taxes and fines. The second category of the recipients was made up of superintendents, accountants, *gopas, sthānikas,* veterinary surgeons, (*anīkastha*), physicians, horse-trainers, and messengers. The State endowed them with lands which, however, they could not sell or mortgage.[426]

(iv) Right to State Relief

The next civil right was that of State relief. Kauṭilya laid down that the king should provide the orphans (*bāla*), the aged, the infirm, the afflicted, and the helpless with maintenance. The king was also to provide subsistence to helpless women when they were carrying, and also to the children they gave birth.[427] State aid was also provided when Brahmans, ascetics (*pravrajita*), children, the aged, the afflicted, royal messengers, and pregnant women were to cross rivers. The State Superintendent was authorized to cross them free of charge.[428] In the enumeration of these rights which could be claimed by men and women, Kauṭilya had definitely advanced on the views of Manu, who had earlier merely said that the king shall protect the inherited and other property of a minor, until the latter returned from his teacher's house, or until he had passed his minority. In like manner, according to Manu, the king was to take care of barren women, those who had no sons, those whose family was extinct, wives and widows faithful to their lords, and women afflicted with diseases.[429]

(v) Right to Medical Relief

The great care which Kauṭilya bestowed on State relief is also seen in the provision he made for proper medical attendance. Physicians undertaking medical treatment without intimating to the State the dangerous nature of the disease, shall, if the patient dies, so enjoins Kauṭilya, be punished with the first amercement (i.e. a fine ranging from forty-eight *paṇas* to ninety-six *paṇas*). If the death of a patient under treatment is due to carelessness in treatment, the physician shall be punished with the middlemost amercement (i.e. a fine ranging from 200 to 500 *paṇas*). Growth of disease due to negligence or indifference (*karmavadha*) of a physician shall be regarded as an assault or violence.[430] That such a right to receive adequate medical treatment should have been provided for by Kauṭilya shows the highly progressive views which that great statesman held about one of the most important functions of government. We seek in vain for such solicitude for the physical welfare of the people on the part of the State in the *Politics* of Aristotle. Neither does it exist in India today.

(*vi*) *Right to Adequate Personal Attention*

Kauṭilya mentions a unique right which is not met with in Manu. He affirms that those who do not heed to the claims of their slaves (*dāsa*), hirelings (*āhitaka*), and relatives shall be taught their duty.[431] This ordinance affords another proof to demolish the view that only the upper classes enjoyed certain privileges. It is an indication that the State was not only concerned with the material well-being of even slaves and hirelings, but that it was prepared to grant them the right of proper personal attention at the hands of their masters.

(*vii*) *Right to Graze and Fodder*

Agriculture being the only major industry of the land, it was only natural that adequate attention should have been paid to it by the State. While cowherds and herdsmen, who came under the authority of the Superintendent of Cows, had to fulfil certain regulations regarding the care and maintenance of cows, horses, asses, camels, and hogs, they had the right of taking their cattle, according to their protective strength and the capacity of the cattle, to graze either far or near. This rule applied to all the animals mentioned above. The State provided draught oxen and cows supplying milk (*payaḥ*) with subsistence in proportion to the duration of time the oxen were kept at work, and the quantity of milk the cows supplied. "All the cattle shall be supplied with abundance of fodder and water." When we realize that the Superintendent of Cows had the charge of eight varieties of cattle mentioned at the beginning of the chapter relating to his duties, we may imagine the huge expenditure involved by the State on the single item of fodder.[432]

(*viii*) *Right to Free Movement*

During certain hours of the night movements of people were restricted. But the following categories of people could always move about without being arrested: those who went about at night to attend to the work of midwifery or medical treatment, or those who attended a funeral procession ; or those who went about with a lamp in their hands, or those who visited the officer in charge of the city, or those who went about to find out the cause of a trumpet sound, or to extinguish the outbreak of fire, or under the authority of a pass.[433]

The right to free movement, however, was denied to two classes of people—strangers and labourers. It will be seen below under the section on City Administration that masters of houses had to report about strangers arriving at or departing from their houses. We shall likewise see, in connection with Community Projects and Coercion in Labour, that there was nothing like free movement of labour, the labourers being compelled to work in their respective companies. There seems to be some incongruity in Kauṭilya in regard to the right of free movement which he thus denied to labourers, while otherwise giving them the right to wages. We are unable to explain as to why he was so severe with the labouring class in this particular sphere. The regulations we have mentioned here will have to be read in conjunction with what will be mentioned below under Civic Life in order to realize that the right of free movement was circumscribed by limitations.

In this connection we may observe that there was free movement into or from the country, provided certain conditions were fulfilled. These came within the sphere of the Superintendent of Passports (*mudrā-adhyakṣa*). He was authorized to issue passports at the rate of one *māṣa* per pass. Whoever was provided with a pass was at liberty to enter into or go out of the country. Foreigners were entitled to enter the country with a pass.[434]

(ix) *The Right to manufacture and drink Liquor*

The whole problem of prohibition, as we now understand the term, makes interesting reading in the *Arthaśāstra*. The manufacture of liquor was a State monopoly. Subject to the over-all control and supervision of the Superintendent of Liquor (*surā-adhyakṣa*), the trade in liquor was open to the public. The right of drinking was regulated thus—those who were well known and of pure character could take liquor out of the licensed shops ; or all could be compelled to drink it in the shops. Liquor was sold to persons of well known character. The citizens could not only drink on all days of the week but claim compensation for loss incurred when they were intoxicated! "When customers under intoxication lose any of their things, the merchants of the shop shall not only make good the loss, but pay an equivalent fine." The merchants of the shops appear to have been servants of the State. This is inferred from the opening sentence of the chapter, dealing with the duties of the Superintendent of Liquor, which runs thus: "By employing such men as are acquainted with the manufacture of liquor and ferments", he shall carry on liquor traffic not only in forts and country parts but also in camps. Moreover, in the next sentence it is stated that the Superintendent alone could either centralize or decentralize the sale of liquor, in accordance with the requirements of demand and supply. We are justified, therefore, in assuming that the men under intoxication, who lost their goods, could claim damages for their full loss against State officials.

We may observe by the way that the people could claim the right of manufacturing liquor under a licence, on some special occasions. For instance, on special occasions (*kṛityeṣu*), wholesale families (*kuṭumbinaḥ*) were entitled to manufacture white liquor (*śvetasurā*), *ariṣṭas*, or medicated liquors, and other kinds of liquor. And on festive occasions like fairs (*samāja*) and pilgrimages, the right of manufacturing liquor for four days was to be allowed.[435]

Without commenting on some of the aspects of prohibition in the days of Kauṭilya, we may observe that he went beyond any modern government in giving a drunkard the right of claiming damages from the State for the loss of the latter's goods when he was in a state of intoxication!

(x) *Right of Prisoners to regain Freedom*

Kauṭilya mentions another civil right of the people. This refers to the prisoners regaining freedom. "On the date to which the birth star of the king is assigned, as well as on full moon days, such prisoners as are young, old, diseased, or helpless (*anātha*) shall be let out from the jail (*bandhanāgāra*)." Prisoners could also obtain their ransom if people of a charitable disposition sought for their liberation by paying an adequate ransom. Moreover, "Once in a day, or once in five months, jails may be emptied of prisoners in consideration of the work they have done, or of whipping inflicted upon them, or of an adequate ransom paid by them in gold". On the conquest of a new country, or on the installation of an heir-apparent on the throne, or when a prince was born to the king, prisoners were usually set free.[436] We cannot make out whether this last was a privilege the prisoners could claim or was an act of generosity and goodwill on the part of the State. But the provision by which a prisoner could obtain his freedom by paying a handsome ransom was clearly a right which he could exercise in order to win his freedom.

That such a right was a real one can be seen when we examine the condition in which even slaves could regain their freedom:

> On paying the value (for which one was enslaved), a slave shall regain his Āryhood. The same rule shall apply either to born or pledged slaves. The ransom necessary for a slave to regain his freedom was equal to what he had been sold for. Any person who had been enslaved for fines or court decrees (*daṇḍapraṇītaḥ*) shall earn the amount of work. Any Ārya made captive in war shall for his freedom pay a certain amount proportional to the dangerous work done at the time of his capture, or half the amount.

The right of a slave to regain liberty could not be withheld from him. "Failure to set a slave at liberty on the receipt of a required amount of ransom was punishable with a fine of twelve *paṇas*. And selling or mortgaging the life of a male or female slave, who was once liberated, was punishable with a fine of twelve *paṇas*, with the exception of those who enslaved themselves."[437] These regulations covered not only the Āryas but all slaves born or pledged, who could exercise this right.

(*c*) *Economic Rights in Kauṭilya*

(*xi*) *Right of Sale and Purchase*

Subject to the control of the Superintendent of Commerce (*paṇyādhyakṣa*), who was authorized to ascertain the existence of demand or absence of demand for, or the rise or fall in, the price of all commodities, and the time suitable for their distribution, centralization, purchase, and sale, merchants could import goods and sell them without hindrance. Only those goods of State manufacture of a local nature were centralized; imported merchandise could be freely distributed. There was no restriction as to the time of the sale of those commodities for which there was frequent demand; nor were they subjected "to the evils of centralization" (*saṅkuladoṣa*). Pedlars could sell goods of State manufacture at a fixed price in many markets. Merchants were shown favour by the Superintendent of Commerce, when they imported foreign merchandise. This applied especially to mariners and merchants, who imported foreign goods. They were exempted from the payment of trade taxes. Foreign merchants were exempted from being sued for debts except when they were members of local trade associations. Such of them who often visited the country as well as those who were well known to the local merchants were allowed to land in port towns.[438]

(*xii*) *Right of Wages: Labour Legislation*

In spite of the severity which marked the State of Kauṭilya, there was equity in its dealings with labour. The right to adequate wages, which in the modern world is so constantly engaging the attention of the State, was an established right in Kauṭilya. We shall take labourers one by one in order to illustrate this point. The weavers came under the direct control of the Superintendent of Weaving (*sūtra-adhyakṣa*). The wages of the weavers were to be fixed according as the threads spun were fine, coarse (or big, *sthūla*), or of a middle quality, and in proportion to a greater or less quantity manufactured, and in consideration of the quantity of thread spun, those who turned out a greater quantity being presented with oil and dried cakes of myrobalan fruits (to keep their heads and eyes cool, and as an inducement to others to work). If the weavers were made to work on holidays (*tithiṣu*), they had to be paid special rewards (*pratvā-padānamānaiḥ*).

While wages were thus guaranteed, work on the part of the labourers was demanded. "Wages shall be cut if, making allowances for the quality of raw material, the quality of the threads spun out is found to fall short."

We may incidentally note that labourers in fibrous cloths, raiments, silk cloths, woollen cloths, and cotton fabrics were specially rewarded for good work by presentations like scents, garlands of flowers, or higher wages.

Women Labourers. Those who finished their quota of work were to exchange their spinnings for wages. The moral code prevalent in the labour world of those ages is reflected in the regulation which said that if the Superintendent of Weaving cast any looks at such women or even talked with them about any other work, he was to be punished with the middlemost amercement (i.e. a fine ranging from 200 to 500 *paṇas*). The same punishment was to be inflicted on him for paying wages for incomplete work. If a woman labourer after receiving wages did not turn out the work, her thumb was cut off. Labourers, when guilty, were fined out of their wages in proportion to their offences.[439]

From the above it is evident that, while the labourers could claim wages according to their output, also special rewards for working on holidays, even hope for prizes by way of encouragement, and insist on the prompt payment of their wages, they were entitled to receive wages only for good and complete work done, the women labourers being fully protected against the State official's indecorous behaviour.

Labourers and Workers of Other Categories. They were also entitled to wages, according to law. "Artisans, musicians, physicians, buffoons, cooks, and other workmen, serving of their own accord, shall obtain as much wages as similar persons employed elsewhere usually get or as much as experts (*kuśalāḥ*) shall fix."[440]

The State guaranteed redress in the disputes of the labourers. Disputes regarding wages were decided on the strength of evidence furnished by witnesses. In the absence of witnesses, the master who had provided the servants with work was examined. If he failed to pay wages, he was punished with a fine ten times the amount of the wages or six *paṇas*; if he misappropriated the wages, he was fined with a fine of twelve *paṇas*, or four times the amount of the wages.[441]

Labour Regulations. Kauṭilya's regulations about labourers are far too detailed to be enumerated here. His major dictum is of interest to us nowadays. He writes that "wages are to be paid for work done but not for work that is not done". His sense of justice is evident from the next sentence: "If an employer, having caused his labourer to do a part of work, will not cause him to do the rest for which the latter may certainly be ready, then, the unfinished portion of the work has to be regarded as finished." These rules were applied to guilds of workmen (*sanghabṛitāḥ*), which were evidently associations or unions of workers in the modern sense.[442]

What if the labourers worked half but gave substitutes in their place? After repeating his earlier injunction that cultivators and merchants, at the end or in the middle of their cultivation or manufacture, shall pay to their labourers as much as the latter's share in proportion to the work done, Kauṭilya says that if the labourers gave up their work in the middle but supplied substitutes, they were to be paid in full.[443]

Of particular interest is the classification of sacrificial priests among labourers, and the division of their wages when they co-operated in performing sacrifices like *Agniṣṭoma, Madhyandina, Sutya, Ahargaṇa,* etc.[444]

Not only were the labourers guaranteed their wages, but all government servants from the highest to the lowest entitled to money payments in proportion to the services they rendered. Equally interesting is the statement in the same connection: "The sons and wives of those who die while on duty shall get subsistence wages." Moreover, "infants, aged persons, or deceased persons related to the deceased servants, shall also be shown favour" by the State.[445]

Thus did Kauṭilya guarantee State aid to the relatives of the deceased servants of the State, and introduce important aspects of labour legislation anticipating in both the spheres by centuries the action of modern governments.

(*xiii*) *Right to receive Deposits*

Individuals as well as guilds enjoyed the right to receive deposits. Kauṭilya's regulations concerning deposits are so minute that it may be tedious to enumerate them. We shall, therefore, mention a few points relating to this particular right, and explain how it was guaranteed by the State on behalf of citizens against citizens.

A man who deposited either goods or money with a depository had certain rights against the latter. If the depository made use of the deposit for his own comfort, he had to pay a compensation which was to be fixed according to the place and the circumstances, and, in addition, a fine of twelve *paṇas*. If there was any loss in the value of the deposit, it was to be made good along with a fine of twenty-four *paṇas*. Deposits damaged or lost in any way were to be made good. But if the depository was involved in calamities or died, the man who had deposited could not sue him. If, however, the depository either mortgaged or sold the deposit, he had not only to pay as compensation four times its value but pay a fine five times the stipulated value. But if the depository exchanged the deposit for a similar deposit, only its value was to be paid. These rules held good also in regard to pledges, order (*ādeśa*), property entrusted for delivery to a third person (*anvādhi*), and sealed deposits (*upanidhi*).

Kauṭilya made identical rules relating to pledges and deposits applicable to trade guilds (*samvyavahārika*). But the trade guilds were shown some preference because of their corporate nature. Where individuals had to make good the merchandise lost while in their custody, merchants who belonged to trade guilds, and those who were trustworthy, or those who had not been condemned by the king, were not required to restore even the value of the merchandise which was lost or destroyed owing to its inherent defects or due to some unforeseen accidents. "But of such merchandise as is distanced by time or place, they shall restore as much value and profit as remains after making allowance for the wear and tear of the merchandise ; and also proportional part of every commodity."[446] The guilds, (obviously of the artisans, called in the text merely *śreṇi*) had the right of receiving the deposits they might have given to certain types of persons in times of distress.[447]

(*xiv*) *Right of being exempted from paying Revenue*

While the king could legally demand as revenue one-fourth of the grain from the people in general, he could not demand such revenue from the following categories of people: those living in middle or low quality ground ; those whose help was needed to construct fortifications, gardens, buildings, roads for traffic ; those who colonized waste lands, exploited mines, and formed forest reserves for timber and elephants ; those who lived on the borders of the kingdom ; and those who had not enough subsistence. This meant that agriculturists living in low lands, labourers whose help was needed for State purposes, including construction of timber and forest reserves, those who were on the frontiers of the kingdom, and those who were indigent—all those could claim exemption from the payment of revenue. Those who colonized waste lands had a right against the State in the sense that the king had to supply them with grain and cattle.[448]

Kauṭilya, while continuing the ancient precepts, had considerably advanced on the views of Manu, although in one respect he fell short of that great lawgiver of antiquity. Manu had enjoined thus: that no taxes were to be paid by blind men, idiots, cripples, old men who were seventy, and those who conferred benefits on the Śrotriyas.[448a] The Śrotriyas were fully exempted from paying taxes. Even if the king was dying for want of funds, he could not levy a tax on the Śrotriyas. The Mauryan Prime Minister continued the earlier injunctions in the sense that he gave the right of being exempted from taxation to the indigent like the four classes of people mentioned in the *Manusmṛiti*. He was below the standard of the classical ordinance in regard to those who conferred benefits on the Śrotriyas, and in regard to the latter themselves. But he had considerably advanced on Manu in the wide range of remissions given to those who had helped the material prosperity of the land. In the last sense Kauṭilya had anticipated some of the modern revenue concessions in regard to the colonization and development of uncultivated lands.

(*d*) *Legal Rights*

(*xv*) *Right to have recourse to Justice*

In the State of Kauṭilya the right of having recourse to justice was given to both individuals as well as to associations. This is inferred from, firstly, the number of places where the judicial courts were set up ; secondly, the transactions that were held valid, and the details of the procedure of trial ; and, thirdly, the punishments given to judges for withholding or otherwise delaying justice.

The Location of Courts. The courts were set up in the cities of the *sangrahaṇa* (a city in the midst of a collection of ten villages), *droṇamukha* (a city in the centre of four hundred villages), and *sthānīya* (a city in the centre of eight hundred villages), and at places where districts met (*janapada sandhi sangraha*). Those who comprised these courts were three members acquainted with the Sacred law (*dharmasthas*) and three ministers of the king (*amātyas*). They were to administer justice.[449] Since there could not have been as many courts as there were cities, we are to presume that these were Courts of Circuit, which were meant to satisfy the needs of the country parts, as distinct from the court in the capital which we shall mention later on in connection with the Elements of the State. It was because every citizen had a right to seek justice that such Circuit Courts were established in the most distant parts of the country.

The Transactions that were held as Valid. The jurisdiction of the Courts of Circuit comprised cases which were valid and invalid. From the detailed description of the valid and invalid transactions as given in the *Arthaśāstra,* it is clear that the jurisdiction of the Circuit Courts covered practically all categories of citizens. The details of filing suits, the provision for irrelevant issues, the payment of witnesses, the right of instituting counter-suits, and the adjournments on behalf of the plaintiffs and defendants suggest that every citizen could have recourse to law. We shall see below, while discussing the Elements of the State, more about justice in Kauṭilya.

Punishment of Judges. What definitely proves that justice was not the monopoly of either the few or the rich or the powerful but the right of all is the long list of punishments which were meted out to the judges, who had abused their powers, or postponed their cases, or otherwise interfered with the course of law. These details will likewise be described later on in connection with the Elements of the State. Since it was only one of the contending parties to a suit that could have been responsible for drawing the attention of the State to the misdemeanour of a judge, it follows that an individual had the right granted to him by the State against the judiciary.[450]

(*xvi*) *Right to a Fair Trial*

The preceding right to have justice involved in it the right to have a fair trial. Kauṭilya dwells on this important aspect of the life of the citizens in many places in his work. He conceded this right even to government servants charged with embezzlement of public funds. Government officials of various categories (mentioned in detail) were to be examined separately. A public proclamation (*pracāra*) was to be made to the effect that "Whoever has suffered at the hands of this offender may make their grievances known to the king". Those who responded to this call were awarded compensation equal to the loss they had sustained.[451] This proves that the State protected the rights of the individual against the servants of the State itself! The public servants thus charged with an offence were given every opportunity of clearing themselves in any manner open to law.[452] The right given to those charged with the crime of possessing stolen property, of bringing forward evidence, and of witnesses to prove his charge, shows that they could always hope for a fair trial.[453] The careful manner in which all kinds of circumstantial evidence was to be examined,[454] suggests that trials were as fair as could be possible in those distant days. The explicit provision made in the *Arthaśāstra,* while describing trial and torture to elicit confession, that an accused shall be acquitted if he answered questions which were attested to by reliable witness,[455] is a further proof of the chances given to the accused to have a fair trial. The proviso that "when a person accused of theft proves in his defence the complainant's enmity or hatred towards himself", he shall be acquitted,[456] only confirms our contention that every citizen had the right to fair judicial proceedings.

The guarantee to individual liberty, if we may be permitted to use that modern term, is again proved by the proviso which said: "Three days after the commission of a crime, no suspected person (*śaṅkitakaḥ*) shall be arrested, inasmuch as there is no room for questions unless there is strong evidence to bring home the charge."[457] We may interpret this claim to mean that the executive could not arrest and imprison a man on suspicion for any length of time. Indeed, citizens could not be arrested and imprisoned without showing cause of their guilt. If this was done, the Superintendent of Jails was punished. Thus ordained Kauṭilya: "When the Superintendent of Jails puts any person in lock-up (*cāraka*) without declaring the grounds of provocation (*saṁkruddhakamanākyāya*), he shall be fined twenty-four *paṇas.*"[458]

(*xvii*) *Right to produce Witnesses*

Each party in a contending suit had the right of producing three witnesses, who were to be honest, reliable, and respectable. At least two witnesses on each side, who were acceptable to either party, were necessary. But in the case of debts, it was laid down that one witness was not permitted.[459] The right of citing witnesses conceded to the contending parties is apparent from the following injunction: "Parties shall themselves produce witnesses who are not far removed either by time or place." But witnesses who were very far removed either by time or place, and those who were very far, or those who would not stir out of their place, "shall be made to present themselves by the order of the judges" (*dūrasthānaprasārānvā svāmivākyena sādhayet*).[460]

Persons exempted from being Witnesses. In this connection it is interesting to observe that, among the persons who were exempted from being called as witnesses, were the following—the king, persons learned in the Vedas (i.e. the Śrotriyas), persons depending for their maintenance on villages (*grāmabhṛitaka*), persons of mean avocations, egoistic persons, women, and government servants (*rājapuruṣāḥ*). The clause at the end of this injunction that those persons "shall not be taken as witnesses excepting in case of transactions in one's own community"[461] is not clear, since it cannot be made out whether that proviso was also applicable to the servants of the State. Neither is the statement of Kauṭilya that women were exempted from being witnesses intelligible in the light of one of his previous statements cited above, viz., that "women with no exception may be subjected to the trial of cross-examination".

(*xviii*) *Right of Inheritance*

This was an ancient right which has been delineated in detail by Manu.[462] Without going into the many aspects of this right, we may merely observe that the right to inheritance could not be claimed by sons when their parents were alive. It was only after the death of their parents that the sons could claim a division of ancestral property but calculating it according to fathers (*per sterpes*).[463] The right to inheritance could be claimed by the inheritors only after they had attained majority. Any one of the claimants could claim a redivision of the inheritance, if he suspected a bad, unequal, or deceptive division.[464] Even the children of the mixed classes were entitled to equal divisions of inheritance.[465]

(*xix*) *Right of Claiming Remission of Taxes*

Certain categories of people, who worked for public good, could claim remission of taxes. Thus, for instance, those who constructed new works such as tanks, lakes, etc., could claim remission of taxes for five years. This refers to the lands below such tanks. For repairing neglected or ruined works of such a nature, remission could be claimed for four years. For improving or extending or restoring water works overgrown with weeds, it could be claimed for three years. But in the case of new lands acquired by mortgage of purchase, it could be claimed only for two years. But it need not be understood from the above that such a right of enjoying rent free land could be secured without a corresponding duty on the part of the person who received it. Kauṭilya says that "persons who are permitted to enjoy such lands free of rent of any kind, shall keep the tanks, etc, in good repair ; otherwise they shall be punished with a fine of double the loss".[466]

(xx) Right to settle Boundary Disputes

In all disputes regarding the boundary between any two villages, neighbourers or elders of five or ten villages (*pañcāgrāmī daśa grāmī vā*) were entitled to investigate the cases on the evidence which was to be furnished from natural or artificial boundary marks.[467]

(xxi) Right to receive Interest

Citizens were entitled to receive interest at the rate of a *paṇa* and a quarter a month. This was the non-commercial rate of interest ; while the commercial rate of interest (*vyavahārika*) was five *paṇas* a month. Among those working in forests, ten *paṇas* could be levied ; while among the sea traders, twenty *paṇas* could be levied. Those who levied a higher rate of interest or caused to be levied a higher interest, were punished with the first amercement (i.e. a fine ranging from forty-eight *paṇas* to ninety-six *paṇas*) ; while the hearers of such transactions were to pay half of the above fine.[468]

(xxii) Right of Exemption from being Sued

Cultivators and government servants were given the right of being exempted from being sued in their professional capacity. Kauṭilya writes that they shall not be caught hold of while engaged in their duties (or at work). In the same context earlier the great Prime Minister stated: "Excepting the case of a debtor going abroad, no debtor shall simultaneously be sued for more than one debt by one or two creditors." As regards the debts contracted by husbands and wives, the *Arthaśāstra* says the following:

> A wife, who has (not) heard of the debt (*pratiśrāvaṇi*), shall not be caught hold of for the debt contracted by her husband, excepting in the case of herdsmen and joint cultivators (*gopālakāraddhasītikebhyaḥ*). But a husband may be caught for the debt contracted by his wife. If it is ad-

mitted that a man fled the country without providing for the debt contracted by his wife, the highest amercement shall be meted out; if not admitted, witnesses shall be depended upon.[469]

From the above passage the following may be deduced—firstly, that people did go abroad. This fact has been proved by more than one reference in the same work cited earlier in these pages. And, secondly, there were four categories of citizens who were exempted from being sued under certain circumstances: wives and husbands, debtors of all kinds, cultivators, and government servants. The right of exemption from being sued given to the last two, viz., cultivators and government servants, while engaged in their duties, is of special interest to us in the modern world. They were given this right obviously because they were considered, to use a term from modern phraseology, to have belonged to the essential services. The wide range of people who were given this right suggests that it was extended to the majority of the people. It cannot be made out why the wives of herdsmen and joint cultivators were denied this right excepting on the supposition that they worked in conjunction with their husbands in the performance of their duties.

The right of exemption from being sued which Kauṭilya had given to certain categories of people, including women, is really to be traced to the right of exemption which Manu gave to some sections of the people. In the *Manusmṛiti* it is stated that the king could not take action against the infants, the aged, the sick, and the litigants, even when they inveighed against him.[470] One could understand why State action could not have been taken against the first three classes of people—the infants, the aged, and the sick, but one wonders as to why the litigants were given this exemption. It is not unlikely that, then as now, the litigants must have became bankrupt by the time the judicial action in which they were already involved was complete. The king, therefore, would have gained nothing by instituting proceedings against such harmless people.

(*xxiii*) *Right to summon Help while in Danger*

If a person was in danger and called a neighbour to help him, the neighbour was compelled to go to the help of the former. "When a person does not run to render help to another in danger", he was to be fined 100 *paṇas*.[471]

(*e*) *Nature of Rights in Kauṭilya*

Before we pass on to the last detail in the comparative study of Aristotle and Kauṭilya, it is necessary to make a few observations on the nature of rights mentioned in the *Arthaśāstra*.

(i) *Rights not the same as Immunities*

The above rights enjoyed by the people may not be confounded with immunities which a section of the people could claim in certain circumstances. Thus, a Brahman could claim exemption from torture but not from being convicted and branded "so as to leave a mark indicating his crime" which Kauṭilya has described in detail.[472] Indeed, the impartiality of the law in the Kauṭilyan State is evident when we observe that the punishment of drowning was awarded to a Brahman convicted of treason.[473]

(ii) *Rights were of Universal Application*

The above helps us to formulate the next proposition that rights in Kauṭilya were of universal application without distinction of classes. The fact that the Brahmans were exempted from one type of punishment does not prove that they were not punished at all or that they were exempted from all punishments. The alternate punishments recommended by Kauṭilya, which we have not mentioned here, were of a more humiliating nature to the members of the learned professions than any physical torture that might have been inflicted on them. When they were thus compelled to come within the orbit of law, it meant that they were on a level with the rest of the citizens, so far as rights and punishment were concerned.

(iii) *Were Rights in the Kauṭilyan State Rights in the Modern Sense?*

We have next to consider whether the rights mentioned above were rights in the modern sense. It has been seen above that, according to the modern concept, rights are privileges created by the State and protected by it. This was essentially the case with rights in Kauṭilya, since in every instance he left no discretion to the State to deviate from the rights enjoyed by the citizens. They were created by the State and guaranteed to the citizens. Every right mentioned above permitted the citizens to do what they choose but within the limits set down by law. The righs in Kauṭilya were rights in the modern sense also because they involved protection from interference not only at the hand of other members of the community but protection from interference even at the hands of the State itself. The example of weavers, persons convicted of thefts, persons under trial, and drunkards suffering from intoxication, which have been given above, conclusively prove that the citizens could claim their rights against the State. The rights of being cited as witnesses and of exemption from being sued which were given to government servants were unique in the sense that they point to two vital principles so essential to the proper and efficient working of government, viz., that government servants should not be burdened with the duty of attending at the courts as witnesses, and that there should be no interference in the discharge of their official duties. The right to have recourse to justice suggests that it anticipated by centuries the modern right of access to law, and along with it, to some extent, the right of equality before law, which are some of the most essential features of modern progressive governments. In certain matters like the right to receive adequate wages, and the right to receive special wages for work done on holidays, Kauṭilya was, indeed, far ahead of his times. We seek in vain for these rights in the *Politics* of Aristotle.

(*iv*) *Conclusion about Rights*

We may conclude our brief survey of the rights in ancient India by saying that it is incorrect to maintain that, in the general context of the Hindu *dharma*, there were no rights but only immunities, but that there were political rights emanating from that *dharma*. On the other hand, our study of the rights enables us to postulate the view that the civil and legal rights, which were first formulated by Manu, were confirmed and elaborated by Kauṭilya, who added in minute detail a number of economic rights which were necessary in the Mauryan days, obviously because of the growth of the country. As regards the emphasis laid on overthrowing and killing a wicked ruler, who had misused his powers and violated *dharma*, which we see both in Manu and Kauṭilya, it was more of an extreme contingency than a political right, since neither of the two great thinkers was prepared to raise it to the sanctity of a right, although, as narrated above, Kauṭilya had himself had recourse to it before ushering in a new era in Indian history.

K. GENERAL CHARACTERISTICS OF THE STATE—A COMPARATIVE ESTIMATE

1. INTRODUCTORY REMARKS: DIFFERENCE IN OUTLOOK

It is necessary to pause here in order to assess the identity and difference in the views of Aristotle and Kauṭilya in regard to the general characteristics of the State, since such a study will enable us better to appreciate the next and the last important point in our comparative study, viz., an evaluation of the method of the two great thinkers. Here it would be necessary to recapitulate a few facts mentioned earlier. When Aristotle mentions the characteristics of the State, it should be remembered that, unlike Kauṭilya, he had visualized an ideal State to which he would add a few of the features of the existing States whose constitution and working he had studied. But there was no idealism in Kauṭilya. On the other hand, there is a sense of grim reality and dreadful earnestness which make his work a state manual of practical statesmanship. In the last Part of this book it will be shown to what extent Kauṭilya continued to cast his influence on the succeeding generations. And, secondly, Aristotle dwells on democracies and oligarchies in comparatively small sized City States, with passing reference to monarchies; while Kauṭilya concentrates on a single, centralized, and ever-growing imperial State with fleeting reference to oligarchical and republican communities. The *Arthaśāstra* of Kauṭilya is complimentary to the *Politics* of Aristotle, as a study in World Politics, in the sense that it gives a full, vivid, and detailed picture of a form of government which is not found in Aristotle.

2. POINTS OF SIMILARITY BETWEEN ARISTOTLE AND KAUTILYA

(a) *Defence of the State*

On many points there is a resemblance in the characteristic features of the State as described in the *Politics* and as given in the *Arthaśāstra*. The first refers to the vital question of defence. Aristotle maintained that the State must be able to defend itself. Even while framing an ideal, Aristotle admitted that we may wish but should avoid impossibilities. Rejecting the view of Plato that only the people and the country are important, Aristotle maintained that a State should have such a military force as would be serviceable against neighbours, and not merely useful at home.[474] Then, again, he says that the government must be organized with a view to military strength.[475] Commenting on the need to have wealth, freedom, justice, and valour, he says that without military strength (i.e. valour), a State cannot exist well.[476]

There was complete agreement between Aristotle and Kauṭilya on the above point. The emphasis which Kauṭilya places on the army, and the minute and considered attention which he bestowed on raising, supervising, maintaining, training, equipping the army, and keeping it in a perfect condition of efficiency prove that he was more alive to the importance of the army than Aristotle.[477] With Kautilya it was not a mere question of the State's existing well: it was one of existing so efficiently and so powerfully as to subvert oppositoin at home and prevent threats from abroad. The army described in the *Arthaśāstra* was essentially that of a *vijigīṣu* or would-be conqueror, who could brook no insubordination within his territory nor insolence from across his frontiers.[478]

(b) *The State is built upon Justice*

When Aristotle said, as remarked earlier in connection with law and justice, that, in addition to wealth and freedom, justice and valour were equally important,[479] he had acknowledged the fact that the basis of the State was not only the army but justice. Here he was in agreement with the view of Kauṭilya, cited earlier, that on the science of government depended the progress of the world; that the king should maintain the world in accordance with the triple *Vedas* and the three other sciences, which we have already mentioned ; and that righteous and unrighteous actions depended upon the triple *Vedas*.[480]

(c) *The State should be Self-Sufficient*

Aristotle repeatedly affirms that the State should be large enough to be entirely self-sufficient.[481] That was exactly the view of Kauṭilya whose provisions for administering the country sides, for inducing local people to take up productive work, for attracting foreign immigrants, for sending out the excessive population from the thickly populated centres to thinly occupied areas in the kingdom, for proposing remedies against national calamities that caused damage to food and goods, and for looking after the welfare of the agricultural, labouring, and manufacturing sections of the people—all these and many others which only reveal his grave concern at maintaining the productive capacity and wealth of the country that could make it completely self-sufficient and independent of foreign aid.[482] The concept of a self-sufficient country which Kauṭilya had in mind will be further explained below under the Elements of the State.

(d) *The State must have a Care of Virtue*

Aristotle maintained that those who care for good government take into consideration (the greatest question of) virtue and vice in States ; and that "virtue must be the serious care of a State which truly deserves the name".[483] Later on he says that "virtue and goodness are not a matter of chance but the result of knowledge and purpose".[484] No one who has carefully studied the *Arthaśāstra* of Kauṭilya can fail to have noticed that, in spite of his bias to the use of coercive power—which was so necessary in the age in which he lived—he was undoubtedly an advocate of good and efficient government in which the questions of virtue and vice ever presented themselves, the former ultimately prevailing over the latter. Kauṭilya had no illusion either about human nature, or about the type of men who had sold their country to Alexander the Great,[485] or about the irreligious and unprincipled Nandas and their hirelings still rampant in the country.[486] It is this which made him regard the State (that is, the king) not as a repository of all good but as an instrument that could remove hindrances and enable society to lead a good life. That explains why, among other things, he gave rewards for good conduct (*caritānugrahaḥ*), as one of the factors conducive to financial prosperity.[487] Nothing could be more erroneous than to imagine that Kauṭilya discarded religion in order to achieve his objective: he only minimized its importance to enlarge the sphere of State action. The continual stress which he laid on "harmlessness, truthfulness, purity, freedom from spite, abstinence from cruelty, and forgiveness are duties common to all",[488] and the various measures which he promulgated for the continued maintenance of equity and virtue in all departments of the State, are the strongest evidence in support of the view that in his concept of the State, virtue had the foremost place of honour. A political thinker like him who, as we have pointed out earlier, affirmed that in the happiness of the subjects lay the happiness of the king, that in their welfare was the king's own welfare, and that what pleased them—and not what pleased the ruler—was to be considered good,[489] cannot by any stretch of imagination be accused of having perverted virtue in order to gain the end of the State. Indeed, as will be seen from the remarks to follow on the Elements of the State, his idea of population was one of loyal and good citizens. From whatever angle of vision we view Kauṭilya's concept of the State, we cannot escape the fact that it fostered virtue in order to realize its end.

(*e*) *The State must make all Citizens Happy*

Aristotle was of the opinion that all the parts of the State should be happy, that "a city is not to be termed happy in regard to a portion of the citizens, but in regard to them all".[490] Here, again, there was complete identity of interest between him and Kauṭilya. The ideal set before the State as given in the above passage should be read along with Kauṭilya's statement relating to the king's governing with his sceptre the people (*loka*) consisting of the four castes and the four orders, and especially his injunction that the king who is bent on doing good to all the people will enjoy the earth unopposed,[491] in order to understand that he was not advocating the good of any particular section but of the entire people.

(*f*) *The State and Education*

Although Aristotle and Kauṭilya had different objectives in regard to education, yet in the long run their views on education might be reconciled. According to Aristotle women and children were to be trained with an eye to the State.[492] Leaving aside his inconsistency in regard to education which he says in one place was not to be the same for all, and in another that it should be one and the same for all,[493] we may observe that the main object of his education was to mould the citizen in order "to suit the form of government under which he lives".[494] But he was definite about the rôle which the State had to play in regard to this subject. He opens the chapter on Education by saying: "No one will doubt that the legislator should direct his attention to the education of the youth, or that the neglect of education does harm to states."[495]

Kauṭilya's idea about education was different from that of Aristotle but there was agreement between him and Aristotle in regard to the control of education by the State. Kauṭilya could not extricate himself from the clutches of ancient custom in regard to the general content of education, although he seems to have thrown it open to all sections of the people. He does not define education nor does he specifically say that it was meant for all. But there is reason to believe that he did not restrict it to any particular section of the people. He defined efficiency in learning (*vidyāsāmarthyaṁ*), as remarked earlier, thus: From hearing (*śruta*) ensues knowledge; from knowledge comes steady application (*yoga*); and from application self-possession (*ātmavatta*) is possible (*Śrutāddhi prajñopajāyate prajñayā yogo yogāt-ātmavatteti vidyāsāmarthyaṁ*).[496]

That the study of the alphabet (*lipi*) and arithmetic, along with a more advanced course included in the compulsory syllabus of the king was meant also for the bulk of the citizens will be evident from the following consideration. We have seen above that the State, according to Kauṭilya's concept, comprised many departments among which were those of Records Keeping and Accounts. We cannot conceive of a very huge and complicated governmental machinery like the one described in the *Arthaśāstra* functioning with an army of clerks for whom ample provision was made for sitting and keeping account books necessary for the various departments,[497] without adequate and wide provision having been made for their efficient training in the many branches of governmental service. In other words, a general scheme of education meant for all sections of the people from whom the numerous clerks and officials of the bureaucratic government of Kauṭilya were recruited, was a prerequisite of the continuous and efficient working of the huge administrative machinery of State as described in the *Arthaśāstra*. It is impossible that the large body of clerks could have been recruited only from the priestly class. In the first place, we cannot conceive of the priestly class having outgrown in size the other classes in a manner to swamp the administrative services. And, secondly, it cannot be that the priestly class was the only section gifted with the intelligence needed for manning the administration. We have to assume that the huge body of clerks and officials came from the priestly as well as the other classes, particularly the trading sections, since the general bulk of the warrior classes were, on the whole, averse to the avocation of the pen. This would mean that education must have been open to all; and that, since the clerks were employed in the most onerous and responsible duties some of which we have narrated earlier in this work, education was controlled by the State both for the sake of the uniformity and efficiency of the administration.

Our assumption in regard to the general proposition that education was open to all is proved by the following facts. Thus, for instance, the profession of the writers (*lekhaka*) was open to all. Any "one who is possessed of ministerial qualifications, acquainted with all kinds of customs, smart in composition, good in legible writing, and sharp in reading will be apointed as a clerk" (*tasmāt amātyasaṁpadopetaḥ sarvasamayavidāśu granthascārvakṣaro lekhavācanasamartho lekhakaḥ syāt*).[498]

There is nothing either in this general order or in any other regulation in the *Arthaśāstra* to suggest that the clerical profession, which was to possess the ministrial qualifications, was restricted to any particular community. What was meant by ministerial qualifications has been described in detail earlier in the *Arthaśāstra*, thus:

> Native (i.e. domicile in the modern parlance), born of a high family, influential, well trained in arts, possessed of foresight, wise, strong of memory, bold, eloquent, skilful, intelligent, possessed of enthusiasm, dignity, endurance, pure in character, affable, firm in loyal devotion, endowed with excellent conduct, strength, health, and bravery, free from procrastination and fickle mindedness, affectionate, and free from such qualities as excite hatred and enmity—these are the qualifications of a ministerial officer (*amātyasampat*).[499]

The opening words of the above passage, *jānapado' abhijātaḥ*, "one born in the country", conclusively proves that Kauṭilya had in his mind, while dealing with the vital problem of recruiting ministerial officials and clerks, all the people in the land.

As regards the other assumption made above, viz., that the State controlled education, it is proved by fact that in the scales of pay meant for all government servants, teachers and learned men were paid at a rate ranging from 500 to 1,000 *paṇas* according to their merit.[500] Since we cannot conceive of the State's paying high salaries to those who were merely learned, without receiving any work in return from them, we would be justified in assuming that the teachers (*ācārya*) and learned men (*vidyāvanta*) mentioned in the preceding context, could have referred only to the teachers and learned men in the service of the State. If they had not been in government service, they would not have been mentioned in what might be called the Civil List of the king. And when we add to this consideration the one relating to the verification of the educational qualifications required of a candidate for ministerial employment, namely, that those qualifications would be tested by teachers of equal learning (*samānavidyebhyaḥ śilpaṁ śāstracakṣuṣmattāṁ ca*),[501] we cannot but conclude that education was not only open to all but was under the control of the State.

(g) *The State must not be left to Fortune*

While criticizing the oligarchical government of the Carthegenians, Aristotle writes that "the legislator should be able to provide against revolution without trusting to accidents".[502] No elaborate proof is needed to show how this characteristic of the State was understood and provided for by Kauṭilya, whose minute precautions against internal and external troubles, human and natural, and against all kinds of calamities facing sovereignty, and the remedial measures thereof comprise a large part of the *Arthaśāstra*.[503] Indeed, if Kauṭilya did anything, it was to prevent fortune from playing havoc with the State which he had wrested from the Nandas and which he lived to consolidate.

(*h*) *The State is not the Growth of a Day*

In the course of describing the causes of revolution, Aristotle writes that "a State is not the growth of a day, neither is it a multitude brought together by accident".[504] To Kauṭilya, the State which he had wrested from the Nandas, was not the work of a day but the fruit of long exertion. As regards multitudes, Kauṭilya did not believe in them. His faith was pinned on efficient and well trained personnel, who would help him to maintain his State and further its aims. His disbelief in dumb multitudes will be further evident when we shall see below the good qualities of the country under the Elements of the State. He will lay stress on good and active agriculturists and a population noted for their loyalty and good character.

(*i*) *The State may sometimes be under the Control of the Army*

Aristotle relates that in some oligarchical States, from mutual distrust the rival parties would hand over the defence of the State to the army which would often become the master of both.[505] In other words, it seems as if we were to infer from this that the army which looked after the defence of the State also ultimately looked after the civil administration of the State. With Kauṭilya there is no question of there being two parties in the State inviting the army to become the decisive factor in it in the long run. In the State of Kauṭilya the only party is that of the monarch, who entrusts the army with the work of looking after the defence of the country as well as the calamities inside the realm. We may recount here the references to the army and its efficient working given elsewhere in these pages.

(*j*) *The State secures Permanence only by the Toleration of All Elements*

What Aristotle meant by the permanence of the State is expressed in the statement that "if a constitution is to be permanent, all the parts of the State must wish that it should exist and be maintained".[506] In another context he has a more comprehensive explanation of the term "permanence of the State". In a well tempered polity (which contains the system of filling in the offices both by lot and by selection), "the government should rely on itself, and not on foreign aid, not on the goodwill of a majority of foreign States but . . . on the general willingness of all classes in the State to maintain the constitution".[507] Here was a principle of stability which Aristotle had laid down for the Greek States but which was meant for all time and all governments. We have already cited earlier his statement that "as a general principle common to all governments, that the portion of the state which desires permanence ought to be stronger than that which desires the reverse".[508]

The last principle was perhaps nowhere better illustrated than in Kauṭilya whose State was the embodiment of strength. In his cryptic statement "strength is power" (*balaṁ śaktiḥ*),[509] he had given an eternal ideal for India to follow. As regards foreign aid or the goodwill of the foreign States, neither idea had any room in the concept of Kauṭilya, who was as much an enemy of the foreigner in India as he was of the unrighteous Nandas of Magadha. No politician kept before him the ideal of self-reliance so consistently as Kauṭilya. And as regards the support of all the sections of the people, upon whom alone the ultimate prosperity of the State depended, enough has been said to show that Kauṭilya believed in the bulk of the loyal and good people for the maintenance of the State.

3. POINTS OF CONTRAST BETWEEN ARISTOTLE AND KAUTILYA

(a) *The State can lead an Isolated Virtuous Life*

Aristotle's ideal State was supposed to be happy in isolation, well administered, with good laws, but without any eye to conquest.[510] A life of inaction, he maintained, did not necessarily mean having relations with others. Virtuous inactivity was an end in itself which could be attained by a State.[511] Aristotle could visualize a life of inaction because, as we have pointed out earlier in these pages, he lived in an age of decadence when virtuous activity, which the Greeks of the earlier days had kept as an ideal before them, had become a thing of the past. It mattered little if a State lived in isolation: there was the mighty State of Macedonia to look after the isolated lives of all Greek City States. Amidst such a decadent situation, conquest was an impossibility. It simply meant annihilation at the hands of the northern conquerors. Hence, Aristotle's State could dispense with conquest, and, somewhat in the manner of the French Vichy Government of our own days, could think of leading a virtuous life if only the conqueror permitted it to live in happy isolation.

Isolation was unthinkable to Kauṭilya, who believed in being surrounded by numerous States every one of which was to fall a victim to his master. Kauṭilya's theory of *rājamaṇḍala* or Circle of States[512] referred to the neighbouring as well to the distant States. His State lived a life of constant friction with the other States. In the very opening sentence of the section on the Elements of sovereignty, which will be discussed in detail below, Kauṭilya made full provision for the inclusion of the friend (or the ally) and the enemy which would mean that he never contemplated living in a condition of happy isolation.

(*b*) *The State is not made Happy by Conquest*

From the above it follows, so far as Aristotle is concerned, that conquest was not a necessary condition of the existence of a State. The Lacedaemonian doctrine of war was unacceptable to Aristotle, who considered peace and leisure better than the strain and stress of war. He writes that most men desire an empire in the hope of accumulating the goods of fortune. But such people like the Lacedaemonians, when their empire passed away, were not happy.[513]

Kauṭilya's outlook was different. He had ushered in a new era in his country's history by helping his young royal patron to uproot an ancient royal family, and, thereby, making military strength the *terra-firma* of his State. The scriptures had to be saved, the science of weapons rescued, and the earth won ; and in order to do this, he had to spur on the young Candragupta Maurya to become a conqueror. Further, a large part of the country had to be recovered from the foreigner, who had entrenched himself in the north-western parts of India. We do not, of course, find any explicit reference in the *Arthaśāstra* to this side of the question. But it is implied in those sections which deal with the foreigners and conquest. Conquest was to Kauṭilya what peace was to Aristotle—the prerequisite of a progressive and good life.

(*c*) *The State should not exceed a Certain Size*

From the above followed a further point of contrast between Kauṭilya and Aristotle. Since to the latter conquest was not an adjunct to greatness and wealth, he could be content with a State limited in size. It was no use having a large population: even a population of 5,000 was enough to fill in a large city like Babylonia. A large population would mean a multitude of idlers. A city like Babylonia would be more like a nation. To Aristotle it was a small city that was in view.[514] What counted was not numbers but power.[515] The two great thinkers agreed on the importance of quality.

Kauṭilya's capital city, whose Superintendent has figured above, was, evidently according to the standard of Aristotle, more a nation than a city. There was, indeed, a complete contrast between the concept of the State in Aristotle and that in Kauṭilya in this regard: the former could not outgrow the size of a City State ; the latter could think only in terms of a mighty imperial State.

(d) *The State must have Leisure*

Since Aristotle's State could never think of embarking upon war, because it had no aggressive designs, it could always think of peace and leisure. Peace is the end of war, and leisure, of toil.[516] Amidst which surroundings such a concept could originate and nourish has already been explained above, while discussing the virtuous life of a State.

But to Kauṭilya leisure meant disaster. The prime necessity of maintaining order in the conquered country of Magadha, the continued vigilance that was needed to guard against the innumerable supporters of the dispossessed royal family, and the sustained watchfulness that was required against the foreigners in the north-western parts of the country—all these precluded any idea of leisure which was impossible in the context of the political events that had brought Candragupta Maurya into power. Any relaxation of the efforts which Kauṭilya has so carefully described in his book, especialy in the direction of maintaining the might and efficiency of the government, would have spelled disaster to the new Mauryan State. We do not find, therefore, any reference in the *Arthaśāstra* to leisure which Aristotle could think amidst the serene surroundings of the decadent Greek States.

L. ARISTOTLE AND KAUṬILYA—A STUDY IN THEIR METHOD

1. SIGNIFICANCE OF THIS PART OF OUR STUDY

We have now come to the last stage in our comparative estimate of the two great political thinkers. It refers to the method which they adopted in their works. When we shall have analysed their method and explained it, we shall be in a position to understand which of the two master-minds had a more lasting effect upon human thought, and give reasons for the same. In other words, we shall then have explained their importance in the history of Political Science.

2. METHOD IN ARISTOTLE

This could be studied under two heads: the general aim which Aristotle set before himself, and the method he adopted to achieve it.

(a) *The General Aim of Aristotle*

Aristotle wished to "lay bare the grain of truth which exists at the core of every political practice and belief".[517] His aim is expressed in the following statement: "Let no one suppose that in seeking for something beyond them (the practical and theoretical forms which he wished to study), we at all want to philosophize at the expense of truth; we can only undertake the enquiry because all the constitutions with which we are acquainted are faulty."[518]

(*b*) *The Method adopted by Him*

The method which was adopted by him to achieve his aim leads us to the manner in which he studied the subject, and the way he arrived at the general laws. The manner adopted by him was inductive which was supplemented by a study of examples of the various constitutions then prevailing, or which had existed in Greece in the past. Aristotle explains as a part of his manner of study when he writes:

> As in other departments of science, so in politics, the compound should always be resolved into the simple elements or least parts of the whole. We must, therefore, look at the elements of which the State is composed, in order that we may see in what they differ from one another, and whether any scientific distinction can be drawn between the different kinds of rule.[519]

What is meant by the study of the whole in relation to its parts is given by him, while criticizing Socrates' theory of government, thus: "...he (Socrates) deprives the guardians of happiness, and says that the legislator ought to make the whole State happy. But the whole cannot be happy unless most, or all, or some of its parts, enjoy happiness."[520]

We have now to see how he applies the principle of the whole in relation to its parts. This is best done by selecting a few subjects like (*i*) the origin of the State, (*ii*) nature of property, (*iii*) members of the State, (*iv*) equality and inequality, (*v*) causes of civil strife, and (*vi*) government.

(*i*) *The Origin of the State*

As regards the origin of the State, he writes: "Thus the State is by nature clearly prior to the family and to the individual, since the whole is of necessity prior to the part; for example, if the whole body be destroyed, there will be no foot or hand, except in an equivocal sense, as we might speak of a stone hand; for when destroyed the hand will be no better."[521]

(*ii*) *Nature of Property*

This problem, too, he analyses in the same manner on the analogy of the whole and its parts. In answer to the vital question whether the citizens of a perfect State should have their possessions in common—which was allied to the other equally important question of women and children—

he says that three cases are possible: first, whether the soil may be appropriated but the produce may be thrown for consumption into the common stock, as was done among some nations; second, whether the soil was common, and may be cultivated in common, but the produce divided among individuals for their private use, which was said to exist among the barbarians; and, third, the soil and the produce may be alike common.[522] After discussing the respective merits and demerits of the three forms of property, from the point of the whole in relation to its parts, he concludes: "It is clearly better that property should be private, but the use of it common."[523]

(iii) Members of the State

While discussing this he utilizes the example of the rulers and the ruled, the slave, and the freemen, and women and children, in regard to the major question of the State. In all these cases, as in that of property, he proposes one of the three courses—either all things or nothing in common, or some thing in common and some not.[524] He had earlier referred to the same problem but from the standpoint of each possessing virtue.[525] His conclusion in regard to the latter was that "all may be supposed to partake of them (virtues), but only in such a manner and degree as is required by each for the fiulfilment of his duty".[526] Although this conclusion is difficult to be reconciled with the one he had earlier arrived at, while referring to the ruler and the subject, viz., that the difference between the two is one of kind and not of degree,[527] yet it appears as if he had in mind, especially while describing the filial relations, how "we may pursue the good and escape the evil", while discussing later on the different forms of government.[528]

(iv) Equality and Inequality

Aristotle affirms that common interest, or justice, or good is the end of Political Science, but where lies equality and inequality? He discusses this question thoroughly, and illustrates it from the other arts like those of flute players, and from other subjects like the height of men, the ability of men in some games, like gymnastics, etc.[529] The whole discussion is then directed to the State—how, if the existence of the State is concerned, the different grades of equality and inequality may be considered; but if the good life of the State is taken into account, then, only education and virtue have superior claims.[530]

(v) Causes of Civil Strife

In the elucidation of this problem, too, Aristotle would adopt the same method of studying the whole in relation to its parts. His analysis of civil strife is the following: civil strife may arise out of inequality of property among common men, inequality of honour among higher classes, or because of crimes. All these he finally relates to the welfare of the State.[531]

(*vi*) *Government*

While discussing the whole of any subject, we should consider all that appertains to a single subject, and not to any part only. Illustrating this from the examples of gymnastics, medicine, shipbuilding, and the making of cloths, he says that "government too is the subject of a single science" in which the legislator should be aquainted not only with that which is best in the abstract but that which is best relatively to circumstances.[532]

Now to the general laws which he deduced from a study of particular events. Aristotle's thorough acquaintance with the different constitutions, prevailing earlier or during his lifetime in Greece, gave him an uncommon advantage in the use of his inductive reasoning. A comparative study of the most important, and in some instances, even of comparatively insignificant States, enabled him to postulate laws which were of universal application. A most typical example is that of law. His conclusions about law were based on the study of the constitutions of Sparta (Lacedaemon), Crete, Carthage, and of the lawgivers like Solon of Athens, Zaleucus of Epizephyria, Phaleas of Chalcedon, Charondas of Catana, Philolaus of Thebes, Androdamus of Rhegium, and others.[533] Indeed, at every stage Aristotle refers to one State or the other before formulating his conclusions.[534]

(*c*) *The Technique of his Method*

We may first ascertain the method Aristotle used in his Politics, and, then, assess its importance before proceeding further to see to what extent it is discernible in the *Arthaśāstra* of Kauṭilya. Aristotle used essentially what has been called the historical or the critical or the comparative method of investigation. Its technique consisted of the following: (*i*) collection of all data on a given subject; (*ii*) their classification; (*iii*) their critical appraisal; (*iv*) their application to a given set of events, ages, or persons; and (*v*) their presentation without embellishments.[535] Lord Acton centuries afterwards described it as the sublime art of investigating material, and of discerning truth from falsehood, and certainty from doubt.[536] Aristotle applied this technique to Political Science in the same manner as Thucydides (*circa* 470-396 B.C.) had done in the case of History, when that great historian wrote that he would not give credence to accounts sung by poets, or to chronicles composed by writers with a view to please the ear, or to chance information, but would give credence only to truth after investigating with the greatest possible accuracy each detail.[537] The essence of the historical method—as, indeed, of method in general—is the reduplication of common sense.[538] Aristotle's mastery of the historical method would have been perfect but for his presentation of principles which is sometimes wanting in clarity and cogency,[539] and his tendency to lapse into the mood of a visionary. His method, however, was destined to live; and about two thousand years afterwards was perfected at the hands of Leopold von Ranke. In other words, the method first shown by Thucydides and then adopted by Aristotle came to stay in Europe.

3. METHOD IN KAUTILYA

To what extent could we compare Kauṭilya with Aristotle in regard to the adoption of the historical method? In order to answer this question, we have (*a*) to see what modern Indian scholars have to say about Kauṭilya's method; (*b*) to examine how far that estimate is valid; (*c*) to understand the *rationale* of Kauṭilya's work; and (*d*) to see the difference between his method and that of Aristotle.

(*a*) *Modern Indian Scholars on Kauṭilya's Method*

(*i*) *Their Views*

Modern Indian scholars are of the opinion that Kauṭilya followed the historical method. Describing the mental stagnancy that was witnessed in India after Kauṭilya, Professor Rangaswami Aiyangar wrote thus:

> After the days of Kauṭilya, the conditions were, in a sense, unfavourable to the advance of political speculation. The extraordinary thoroughness of Kauṭilya's work, its eminent inductiveness and practical character, its unflinching logic and heedlessness of adventitious moral or religious standards, and its wide range of subjects and interests—which gave it a unique combination of features that, in European literature, we find only separately in an Aristotle, a Machiavelli, and a Bacon—must have co-operated with the rise of a well-knit empire of unprecedented dimensions, under the Mauryan and succeeding dynasties, to depress creative political thought in the centuries after Kauṭilya.[540]

Professor U. N. Ghoshal comments thus on the method followed by Kauṭilya:

> The method of the science, in other words, is primarily an empirical (if not a scientific) one. In Kauṭilya's work this is supplemented by some interesting applications of what may be called the historical method as the author occasionally draws upon traditional history to justify his arguments. This is however made, in the words applied by a modern historian of political theory to the thought of Machiavelli, to point a moral which has already been told.[541]

(ii) The Above Views Examined

Neither historian has explained what exactly is meant by the historical method. It is not enough if we merely assert with Professor Aiyangar that Kauṭilya's work had the characteristics of "eminent inductiveness"; nor with Professor Ghoshal that Kauṭilya's method was an empirical one because the latter supplemented his statements with references to historical examples. Both the above estimates are confusing and indefinite. In Professor Aiyangar's opinion, Kauṭilya was eminently inductive and practical in character, and heedless of casual moral and religious standards; while in that of Professor Ghoshal, Kauṭilya could be compared to Machiavelli in driving home a moral which had already been set forth. The issue is not whether the Mauryan Prime Minister was inductive in his method, and, at the same time, whether he gave no heed to religious standards; nor whether he was merely adorning a tale which had already been told with a moral. The main questions are, firstly, did Kauṭilya ever have any method at all? And, secondly, to what extent was that method scientific or historical?

(b) Did Kauṭilya ever have a Method at all?

On this question there can be no difference of opinion. Kauṭilya not only followed a method but pursued it so well as to give to the world a concise and condensed work divided into fifteen books, 150 chapters, 180 sections, and 6,000 *ślokas.*[542] No author could have written such a compact, well-knit, and comprehensive work if he had not followed a method. We shall analyse his method presently. In the meanwhile, we may see to what extent it was scientific or historical.

(c) The Rationale of His Method

An appreciation of the method followed by Kauṭilya leads us to the question of the *rationale* of his work. He based his work not only on religion to the extent it came within the *dharmaśāstras*, but, what is more important, on reason. From this it may not be inferred that he was either irreligious or unmindful of the obligations of the State to moral and religious principles. Such an inference would violate all the evidence in the *Arthaśāstra* which unmistakably points to Kauṭilya's having fully realized the part which religion had to play in the general life of the State and of the citizens. We may be permitted to recall here some of the observations made above, while explaining to what extent Kauṭilya had deviated from Manu. Kauṭilya's insistence on the study of the triple *Vedas* as being important for determining the respective duties of the four castes and the four orders of religious life; his statement that righteous and unrighteous acts are learnt from the triple *Vedas*; his warning that "the observance of one's own duty leads to *svarga* (heaven) and infinite bliss (*ananta*)" ; his conviction that "the world, when maintained in accordance with the injunctions of the triple *Vedas*, will surely progress, but never perish" ; and his explicit assertion that he wrote the book after he had rescued the scriptures, the science of weapons, and the earth which had passed on to the Nanda king[543]—these unmistakably prove that Kauṭilya recognized that religion was a vital force in the maintenance of the public life in the State. But a grim realist that he was, he minimized the part of religion in order to enlarge the scope of State action.

In so doing he had necessarily to rely not on dogma and belief but on reason and experience. It is in this connection that we see the basis of his work. His logical process was expressed in the term *ānvīkṣakī* (*ānvīkṣikī*). But here there seems to be a division of opinion among scholars as to what was meant by the term *ānvīkṣakī*. Professor Ghoshal consistently interprets it as "the whole of scholiastic philosophy".[544] This view is really to be traced to Kāmandaka, who had identified it with philosophy.[545] But Professor Aiyangar interprets Kauṭilya's use of the term *ānvikṣakī* as referring, not in the sense used by Kāmandaka, but in the sense of including only Sānkya, Yoga, and Lokāyata.[546] The third view is that of Dr. N. N. Law, who interprets it as a branch of *vārtā*, but meaning logic and philosophy.[547] The fourth view is that of Dr. Kane who, after studying the interpretation given by different writers, came to the conclusion that Kauṭilya "uses it not only in the sense of logic based on premises derived from ordinary experience (loka), though in later literature Lokāyata came to mean *nāstika* (atheist, materialist). Among those authors who understood by *ānvikṣakī* only logic were Amarasimha, the commentators Viśvarūpa on Yājñavalkya, Haradatta on Gautama, Aparārka, and others. In this sense, *ānvikṣakī* means the science of ratiocination."[548]

Confining ourselves only to Kauṭilya, it seems that the last interpretation as given by Dr. Kane is the happiest one. Ānvikṣakī cannot be linked merely with *vārtā*, since Kauṭilya clearly differentiates between *ānvikṣakī*, the triple *Vedas*, *vārtā*, and *daṇḍaniti*,[549] thereby proving that *vārtā* (agriculture, cattle-breeding, and trade) was not the same as *ānvīkṣakī*. But in a later context he defines *ānvīkṣakī* as comprising Sānkhya, Yoga, and Lokāyata[550]—an elucidation which seems to have prompted Kāmaṇdaka in later ages, and others in our own, to identify that branch of knowledge with philosophy. On the strength of Kauṭilya's own arguments the identification of *ānvīkṣakī* with mere philosophy is not possible. Firstly, there is nothing to suggest anywhere in the *Arthaśāstra* that Kauṭilya indulged in mere philosophical speculation. We might have said that Kauṭilya was more of a philosopher than a practical statesman if, like Aristotle,[551] he had dealt with an abstract State, and if he had given in the *Arthaśāstra* the least hint that he loved to think of an ideal government. On the other hand, he is concerned with a practical government, as will be seen below when we shall see to what extent his principles guided the course of State action after him. There is nothing of an idealist in him which, for instance, we see in Plato. The monarch whom he describes is not the philosopher king pictured by that great teacher of Aristotle,[552] but a relentless conqueror who was the head of a well-organized and centralized bureaucratic machinery of government.

Secondly, Kauṭilya lays repeated stress on *vārtā* which increases the wealth within the country, and which enables the king to control both his and his enemy's party.[553] He maintained that "wealth and wealth alone is important, inasmuch as charity and desire depend upon wealth for their realization".[554] It is impossible to think of an author, who would have made philosophy the basis of his observations, giving wealth a place of such importance in his work. If by *ānvikṣakī* he had meant philosophy, even as one of the aspects of Political Science, he would not have either described or analysed the various problems of the State in the matter-of-fact manner he has done. Neither would he have advocated various measures of State activity which cannot in any manner be connected with philosophy, and which cannot be solved by an appeal to philosophy. Perhaps it may be argued that he was a follower of the Sānkhya philosophy, and that his preference to the State laws as against the *dharmaśāstras* is the best proof of his materialistic outlook and of his being the follower of the atheistic side of the *ānvikṣakī* philosophy. But we should remember here that his preference to the king's law in any conflict between it and the Sacred law is due to the fact that, like a realist, and unlike a philosopher, he explains fully when such preference could be given to the king's law. It was only when the original text on which the Sacred law was based was not available.[555] The entire scheme of diplomatic action in his work would be unintelligible if we were to assume that he wrote it with philosophy of any type as his background. He would not have recommended the secret means of destroying the enemy,[556] if his intention had been merely to expound the principles of a particular kind of philosophy. When, as we have seen above, he lays down as the motto of the State that Strength is Power, he did not mean the strength of the soul, which a philosopher would certainly have emphasized, but only the physical and intellectual strength of an active, ever watchful, and well-meant monarch.

Finally, if we are to construe *ānvīkṣakī* in the sense of scholiastic philosophy, the whole purpose of Kauṭilya's work would be meaningless. The entire work stands for timely, calculated, and ruthless State action which can be associated not with any idealistic thinking but only with deep and profound reason driven by political necessity.

While Kauṭilya thus gave the most predominant place to reason in his work, he was not prepared to cut himself away from past experience, and be merely a visionary. This is proved by the many references he makes to past historical events and personages. While warning monarchs not to lead vicious lives, he refers to twelve examples of rulers and corporations which came to grief because they had failed to restrain their organs. They were Bhoja, also called Dāṇḍakya, Karāla of Videha, Janamejaya, Tālajañgha, Aila, Ajabindu the Sauvīra, Rāvaṇa, Duryodhana, Dambodbhava, Arjuna the Haihaya, Vātāpi, and the corporation of the Vṛiṣnis; while Ambarīṣa of the family of Jāmadagni, and Nābhāga ruled over the earth for a long time because they had restrained their organs.[557] Commenting on the evidence of the earlier author Vātavyādhi, Kauṭilya, while discussing the problem of the protection of the princes, refers to the former's having cited the examples of Aditi and Kauṣika, whose maternal relations went a-begging.[558]

His intimate knowledge of history is further proved by the many examples of kings who had lost their lives because they were careless about the strict rules to be observed inside the royal harem. These were king Bhadrasena, who was killed by his own brother hiding in the queen's chamber; king Kārūśa, who fell at the hands of his son hiding himself under the bed of the latter's mother; king Kāśirāja, who was killed by his queen with rice served with poison; king Vairantya, who lost his life at the hands of his queen, who killed him with an anklet filled with poison; king Sauvīra, whose queen killed him with a gem of her zone bedaubed with poison; king Jālūtha, who was killed by his queen with a looking glass painted with poison; and king Vidūratha, who was killed by his queen with a weapon hidden in her tuft of hair.[559] Then, again, Kauṭilya refers to Piśuna's examples of kings Jayatsena and Duryodhana as rulers who were expert gamblers; while he himself cites the examples of Naḷa and Yadhiṣṭira, who suffered from defeat in gambling.[560] While discussing the major problem of doubts about wealth, Kauṭilya illustrates his statements relating to a contingency when no help from any quarter is possible. In such a case one should run away, leaving all that belongs to him; for if one does it, one may return and be sure of regaining one's power, like kings Suyātra and Udayana.[561] By way of a general rule, he enjoins: "Even if the king is held by the chiefs under their influence, the minister may, through the medium of the king's favourites, teach him the principles of polity with illustrations taken from *itivṛitta* (*itihāsa*) and *purāṇa*."[562].

That he was conversant not only with the working of monarchies but also with that of republican communities and oligarchical corporations is proved by his reference to them in many contexts, in some of which he names them. Thus, as remarked elsewhere in this book, while contrasting the nature of sovereignty in a monarchy with that in a corporation of clans, he states that the former is subject to dangers, excepting when it falls to the lot of the eldest son of a king, when it is always respected. But the sovereignty of a corporation of clans is invincible, "and being free from the calamities of anarchy, can have a permanent existence on earth".[563] He has much to say about combinations of corporations which were to be won over by certain specified measures.[564] The corporations of warriors (*kṣatriyaśreṇi*), which were obviously oligarchies, are named by him as those of Kamboja and Surāṣṭra and of other countries, who lived by agriculture, trade, and wielding of weapons. The other corporations were those of the Lichchhavika, Vṛijikas, Mallakas, Madrakas, Kukura, Kuru, Pāñcāla, and others who lived by the title of *rāja*.[565] The whole chapter entitled the Conduct of Corporations in which these corporations are mentioned, is a tribute to Kauṭilya's profound knowledge of the working and behaviour of the governments of oligarchies and of the republican communities of his age.

(d) *Kauṭilya's Technique Analysed*

His method, therefore, revolved round two important factors—reason as connoted by *ānvikṣakī*, and past experience as gathered from history. With the help of the former, he analysed the principles of Politics ; with the help of the latter, he drew general conclusions. But unlike Aristotle, he never ventured to go beyond the boundaries of India in order to find examples of constitutions which were to receive an unfavourable treatment at his hands ; and, further, even though he was a firm believer in centralized monarchy, he did not underrate the importance of non-monarchical forms of government, as Aristotle did with monarchies and oligarchies while championing the course of democracies. In his method there was an admirable combination of two of the essentials of the critical or historical method to which he added the third one relating to a comparative study. Kauṭilya's skill in this direction is seen in the manner in which he cites the evidence of his predecessors, including his unnamed teacher, and in most instances differs from them. Leaving aside the other occasions, when he disagreed with his predecessors, we may confine ourselves to the following instances in which he makes a comparative estimate of every one of the problems. These are the comparative importance of the king and the minister ; the comparative seriousness of the troubles due to the want of finance and forts, and of the army and the ally ; the comparative evils of language and of money, of hunting and gambling, of drinking and addiciton to women, of fire and floods, of quarrels among peoples and kings, of the king's being sportive and of the country's being sportive, of a favourite wife and prince, of the oppression caused by the chamberlain and the collection of revenue ; and the comparative merits of enthusiasm and power.[566]

So far as Kauṭilya's technique of the historical method is concerned, it appears as if we have to agree with the opinion of distinguished Indian historian cited above, that Kauṭilya adopted the empirical and the scientific method almost to perfection, as is revealed in his desire to arrive at truth, in his collection of all the data required for his subject, in his critical estimate of the principles of his predecessors, in the manner he arrived at general conclusions from many facts, and in his admirable presentation of his work without vague statements, without repetitions, without any reference to idealistic conditions, without embellishments, and strictly adhering to reason.

4. DIFFERENCE BETWEEN ARISTOTLE AND KAUTILYA IN THEIR METHOD

There is no doubt that both the great thinkers were prompted by a desire to arrive at Truth, that both used reason as the main key to unlock the treasures of Political Science, that both looked upon their predecessors with respect,[567] that both declared Political Science to be the best of all sciences,[568] and that both used the historical method involving induction, comparative study, and analysis in arriving at conclusions. While Aristotle, according to some, epitomized the best thoughts of a nation and of a stage in human history,[569] Kauṭilya compressed within 6000 *ślokas* (that is, within 1,92,000 syllables),[570] the wisdom and experience of almost a millennium of one of the most civilized peoples.

We have now to see wherein lay the fundamental difference between the two great thinkers. That Kauṭilya adopted the comparative method in the study of the composition and behaviour of the Indian State there cannot be any doubt. But, in our opinion, he seems to have suffered from some shortcomings. In the first place, he restricted himself to the study of only one form of government, that is, the monarchical in the sense that, as related above, while he was certainly aware of the working of the constitutions of the republican and oligarchical communities, he concentrated his attention only on the imperial State. When he paid a compliment to the ever lasting nature of sovereignty among the corporation of clans, on comparing it with that existing in a monarchy, one would have wished that he would have given a few more details about the working of the constitution among the republican clans. This he failed to do with the result that the student of Political Science is at a loss to know what precisely was the merit of the constitution of those republican clans, some of which claimed considerable antiquity. We come, therefore, to the second shortcoming in Kauṭilya, viz., that he either ignored or failed to take note of an important aspect of the comparative study which, if only he had undertaken, would have made his work invulnerable from all points of view.

Professor Ghoshal's Theory Examined. Here it is necessary to examine Professor Ghoshal's theory that "the most complete analysis is of *sanghas* (comprising under this head both the political type and the military-cum-agricultural and trading types)" in Chapter XI of the *Arthaśāstra* from which one of the two citations mentioned above was taken. The eminent historian affirms that Kauṭilya in this particular context "deals with a king's policy towards the *sanghas* and their reciprocal policy towards himself".[571] Professor Ghoshal is certainly correct in so far as he states that Kauṭilya deals with the interaction of the policy of the king and that of the *sanghas*. But it is possible to disagree with the view that this necessarily is the same as analysing the constitution of the *sanghas*, as Professor Ghoshal would maintain. A study of their constitution would have led Kauṭilya to the delineation of the elements of their constitution or that of the oligarchies, of the relative powers of their executives and of the others in their constitutions, of the end of such States, and similar subjects which are mentioned by Kauṭilya in such minute detail concerning the imperial State but not in regard to the constitution of the corporations. On the other hand, in the chapter entitled the Conduct of Corporations, the main theme is that of winning over such corporations. The opening sentences of the chapter clearly enunciate this policy in the following terms:

> The acquisition of the help of corporations is better than the acquisition of an army, a friend, or profits. By means of conciliation and gifts, the conqueror should secure and enjoy the services of such corporations as are invincible to the enemy and are favourably disposed towards himself. But those who are opposed to him, he should put down by sowing the seeds of dissension among them and by secretely punishing them.[572]

We have, in this passage and in the succeeding ones, the major policy of the king towards the corporations described, viz., of winning over them, if they were well disposed towards the monarch, or of putting them down, if they were too powerful.

In the whole of the above chapter in the *Arthaśāstra*, Kauṭilya definitely refers to the powerful nature of the corporations to whose sovereignty, as remarked above, he paid a tribute when he stated that they were invincible and free from anarchy which was a feature of the monarchies. But it was precisely here that Kauṭilya failed: while he devoted minute attention to the means by which the recalcitrant republics could be reduced to subjection, he did not think it worthwhile to dwell on their other good points, nor explain how, for instance, the Lichchhavikas, the Vṛijikas, the Mallakas, etc., had survived through centuries, and what precisely were their features which were worth imitation by the monarchical forms of government. In other words, Kauṭilya unfortunately did not pay attention to that aspect of comparative study to which Aristotle had devoted his most serious attention, viz., where exactly the redeeming features of the constitutions of the different States lay, and to what extent he could recommend them for adoption by his own ideal State. In this detail Aristotle scored a complete victory over Kauṭilya, whose zeal in perfecting all the aspects of one type of State, the imperial, was perhaps responsible for clouding his imagination in regard to the merits of the republican and oligarchical constitutions whose nature of sovereignty alone came in for a favourable comment at his hands. This solitary reference to the invincibility of the constitutions of the corporations of clans and their freedom from anarchy does not compensate for the indifference which he, on the whole, showed to the working of their constitutions. It was not enough if a comparative study was made, as pointed out earlier in these pages, between the various organs of the same type of the monarchical government. Kauṭilya would have earned the gratitude of posterity in a greater measure than he did by his extraordinary and incomparable study of only one type of the State, if he had included in it the comparative aspects of the organs of government, their functions, and their end as prevailing in the different types of States of his own and the previous ages.

The above was an inherent defect in Kauṭilya which perhaps because of the exigencies of the critical times in which he lived he could not rectify. There is another reason for which he was, however, not responsible but which explains why he did not secure that universal approbation which Aristotle, in spite of the latter's shortcomings mentioned earlier, has won for himself. This refers to the unfortunate fact that Kauṭilya's admirable method of study was not followed, excepting in one instance, by the later Indian political thinkers. The only example of a later writer who scrupulously kept Kauṭilya as his model was Kāmandaka, who opens his work by confessing that he was a follower of Kauṭilya.[573] Kāmandaka "merely versified the passages of the *Arthaśāstra*, sometimes without even understanding them or verifying their references".[574] Another example of a still later author, who followed to a lesser extent Kauṭilya, was the Jaina writer Somadeva Sūri (tenth century A.D.), who has figured in Part Two of this book. Somadeva Sūri may be compared to Kāmandaka in the sense that he did not care even to acknowledge all that he borrowed from Kauṭilya, and unlike Kāmandaka, modified the opinions of Kauṭilya when they came into conflict with those of the Jaina religion.[575]

But what was needed was not an imitation—and that a faulty one!—of Kauṭilya's cryptic statements but a continuation and perfection of the method which he had so boldly and so successfully adopted in his work. It was thus lost to his country not because of any inherent defect in that great writer but because his successors took shelter behind the antiquated method of treading on the path of the traditional writers and of duplicating versions of theories which had already been made known, without allowing their reason either to enlarge or analyse them, and without having the rational and independent outlook of Kauṭilya.

To sum up. A comparative estimate of the two great political thinkers which has been made above, reveals that they were not antagonistic but complimentary to each other. We may repeat that, while Aristotle dealt with all forms of the State other than the imperial one, prevailing in Greece, Kauṭilya concentrated on the imperial State to the exclusion of others, as obtaining in India. The two political thinkers complete the picture of political organization in a unique manner. What Aristotle does not give, Kauṭilya supplies in detail. They were the two outstanding representatives of Aryan thought in their respective ages, discussing the logical basis of political existence and the nature and end of the many fundamental problems confronting the State. In the totality of human intellectual endeavour which aimed at finding out the Truth, the *Politics* of Aristotle and the *Arthaśāstra* of Kauṭilya may be considered as two components of one whole of the Book of Political Thought which Greece and India gave to the world.[576]

Part Five

POLITICAL INSTITUTIONS

(ELEMENTS OF THE STATE)

CHAPTER I

THE THEORY OF THE CONSTITUENT ELEMENTS

A. INTRODUCTION

By the term elements of the State is meant the essential factors that make up a State, that is, those integral parts without which it cannot exist.[1] The elements of the State are to be distinguished from the institutional organizations like those of the ambassadors, etc., which, though necessary for the proper fulfilment of the objectives of the State, do not constitute its essential factors. The institutional organizations came to be set up with the gradual growth of the State, and did not at any time encroach on the province of the elements of the State.[2] During our discussion of the elements of the State, we should recollect one of the theories of the origin of the State which was given earlier, viz., the organismic theory which is intimately connected with the elements of the State ; and likewise the statements made above, while comparing Aristotle's ideas of the elements of the State with those of Kauṭilya. An elucidation of the constituent elements will reveal that they form the basis of the organic growth of the State.

B. ANTIQUITY OF THE THEORY OF THE CONSTITUENT ELEMENTS

The ancient Indians had a definite concept of the elements of the State. They called them the seven *prakṛitis* of the State. The antiquity of the concept of the elements or *prakṛits* cannot be determined. From the Vedic literature, it is apparent that the number seven had a fascination for the ancients. Thus, the number seven figures in the *Rig Veda* ; there is the seven-tongued Agni, the Sapta-Sindhu or the seven rivers, the *sapta-sūryāḥ* or the seven suns, the *sapta-mānuṣa* (an epithet of Agni), the *sapta-vadhri* (a protege of the Aśvins), and *sapta-gu* (a reputed author of a verse in the *Rig Veda*)—these are met with in the Vedic literature.[3] In the age of *Śatapatha Brāhmaṇa*, we come across the term *sapta-hotri* or seven sacrificing priests.[4] In the same work a hymn of seven verses is eulogized ; and we are told that the fire altar consists of seven layers ; that there are seven seas, seven regions, seven worlds of the gods, seven *stomas*, seven *priṣṭhas* (*sāmas*), seven metres, seven domestic animals, seven wild ones, seven vital airs in the head, and whatever else there is of seven kinds.[5] These examples prove that some specific significance was attached to the number seven; but they do not enable us to find out exactly when the concept of the seven constituents of the State originated. It may have been in the ages after that of the *Śatapatha Brāhmaṇa,* or perhaps in that which immediately preceded the composition of the *Manusmṛiti.* At any rate it is only in the latter work that we see the earliest enumeration of the theory of the constituent elements or of the seven *prakṛitis.*[6]

C. THE THEORY OF THE ELEMENTS OR PRAKṚITIS: IN RELATION TO THE STATE

This theory has two aspects—one which concerns the State as an independent unit; and the other, the State as a unit in a circle of States. The former is elucidated here while the latter will be discussed in connection with foreign policy below.

1. MANU ON THE THEORY

It is in connection with the latter that Manu first uses the term *prakṛiti,*[7] and, then, later on in connection with the seven limbs of the State, enumerates them thus: the king, his minister, his capital, his realm, his treasury, his army, and his ally which are the seven constituent parts of a kingdom; "hence a kingdom is said to have seven limbs (*aṅga*)". The relative importance of every one of the seven parts, and the importance of all the seven so far as the State is concerned, is given by Manu in the next two verses, thus:

> But let him know (that) among those seven constituent parts of a kingdom(which have been enumerated) in due order, each earlier (named) is more important and (its destruction) the greater calamity. Yet in a kingdom containing seven constituent parts, what is upheld like the triple staff (of an ascetic), there is no (single part) more important (than the others), by reason of the importance of the qualities of each for the others.[8]

Manu's Theory Examined. There appears to be some apparent contradiction in the above statements—that each preceding part is more important than the following one, since the destruction of the former would be a greater calamity; and that no single part is more important than the other, because of the qualities of each for the others. This contradiction is probably resolved by Manu in the next verse in which he explains the second part of the above statement, and thereby justifies the enunciation of the organismic theory that was made in Part Three above. Manu states the following: "For each part is particularly qualified for (the accomplishment of) certain objects, (and thus) each is declared to be the most important for that particular purpose which is effected by its means."[9] This does not explain his earlier statement as to how the destruction of the preceding element is a greater calamity than the destruction of the following one. But it certainly enables us to substantiate the organismic theory by stating that, accroding to Manu, each element of the State had a definite duty to perform.

2. MANU FOLLOWED BY LATER WRITERS

These views are almost identical with those in the *Śāntiparvan,* wherein it is stated that it is not possible to say definitely whether any one of the seven elements excels the others in merit, but that at different times a different element assumes importance over the others, since that particular element is in the particular circumstances capable of accomplishing the purpose in hand.[10] In order that the organismic theory may be complete to some extent, we may cite the view of the seven constituent elements as given in the later work, *Śukranītisāra,* which compares them to the organs of the body, thus: the king is the head ; the ministers are the eyes ; the ally is the ear ; the treasury, the mouth ; the army, the mind ; the capital, the hand ; and the *rāṣṭra* or kingdom, the feet.[11]

3. KAUTILYA IMPROVES UPON MANU

(a) *Defect in Manu*

Manu in the passages cited above not only enunciated the theory of the elements but described their relative importance. The order of preference which he gave, viz., the king, the minister, the capital, the realm, the treasury, the army, and the ally, remained the model for almost all later works like *Yājñavalkyasmṛiti, Gautama, Viṣṇudharmasūtra,* the *Śantiparvan,* and others.[12] No attempt was made by Manu, and those following him, to reduce the number of the constituents. That was the work of Kauṭilya, who restated their relative importance, and then reduced their number. The relative importance of the constituents was stated by him thus: the king, the minister, the country, the fort, the treasury, the army, the friend, and the enemy. These are the elements of the State (*svāmi-amātya-jana-pada-durga-kośa-daṇḍa-mitrāṇi prakritayaḥ*).[13] The change in the relative importance as well as the increase in the number of elements from seven to eight are significant. Kauṭilya adds the eighth element, the enemy but retains the others as given by Manu. In the final analysis, however, he agreed with Manu when he stated: "Excepting the enemy, these seven elements, possessed of their excellent characteristics, are said to be the limb-like elements of the State."[14]

(b) *Kauṭilya on the Relative Importance of the Elements*

The indefiniteness which is visible in Manu in regard to the relative importance of the elements of the State is not seen in Kauṭilya who, in a well-thought-out passage, clearly sets forth their relative importance in a manner which is suggestive of the analytical approach to the problem. He starts with his teacher's statement, and citing the evidence of Bharadvāja, Viśālākṣa, Parāśara, Piśuna, Kauṇapadanta, and Vātavyādhi, finally gives his own opinion on this important question. His teacher maintained, evidently following Manu, that of the calamities, viz., the king in distress, the minister in distress, the people in distress, the distress due to bad fortifications, financial distress, the army in distress, and an ally in distress, that which is first mentioned is more serious than the one following in the order of enumeration. Before we proceed further, we may observe that the enumeration of the elements as given by the teacher of Kauṭilya is the same as that found in Kauṭilya but for the inclusion of the friend by the latter, and for the element of the country in Kauṭilya which the teacher would call the people.

Kauṭilya next cites the opinion of Bharadvāja, according to whom the distress of the minister is more serious than the distress of the king, because of the reasons stated by Bharadvāja. To this Kauṭilya objects by saying that, since the ministers are the creatures of the king, it is only the latter who is more important. Indeed, "the king is as it were the aggregate of the people".

He next refers to the opinion of Viśālākṣa, who maintained that as between the troubles of the minister and those of the people, the troubles of the people were more serious. Viśālākṣa also gave reasons for his opinion. But Kauṭilya rejects it by saying that, as all activities proceed from the minister, it is the latter who is superior to the people.

Parāśara is the third thinker cited by Kauṭilya. According to Parāśara, the distress caused by bad fortifications was more serious than that caused by the people, for reasons stated by him. But Kauṭilya objects to this by saying that, since forts, finance, and the army depend upon the people, the latter are more important than the fortifications.

Piśuna was of the opinion that of the troubles due to the absence of forts and those due to the absence of finance, the latter was more serious ; and he likewise gives reasons to substantiate his conclusions. But Kauṭilya rejects it by saying that, since it is in the fort that the treasury and the army are safely kept, the fort is more important than finance.

Kauṇapadanta's view was that distress due to an inefficient army was more serious than that due to want of finance, for reasons stated by him. But, according to Kauṭilya, since the army is dependent on finance, the troubles from the latter are more serious than those from the army.

Vātavyādhi maintained that of the distress of the army and that of an ally, the latter was more serious also for reasons given by him. But Kauṭilya rejected this too, and in doing so, although his reasoning is not very clear, he seems to place more reliance on the army as well as on finance. From this discussion it appears as if Kauṭilya was, on the whole, in agreement with the views of his unnamed teacher, who followed Manu.

(c) *Kauṭilya adds a New Idea*

But in the succeeding statements Kauṭilya is more cautious than either his teacher or Manu in assessing the relative importance of the component parts of the State. He writes thus:

> When a part of one of the elements of sovereignty is under troubles, the extent, affection, and strength of the serviceable part can be the means of accomplishing a work. When any two elements are equally under troubles, they should be distinguished in respect of their progressive or declining tendency, provided that the good condition of the rest of the elements needs no description.[15]

While Kauṭilya had thus extended the theory of Manu and of his own teacher on the relative importance of the component parts of the State, he had, at the same time, introduced the new idea that the relative importance of each .part would depend on the good conditions of the rest of the elements. By so doing, he had neutralized the superiority of the first over the second element in the order of enumeration, and thereby added to the growth of political thought. Kāmandaka, it may be added by the way, merely echoed Kauṭilya's opinion when he stated that each of the seven elements is complimentary to the other; and that if the State is defective even in one out of the seven elements, it would not work well.[16]

(d) *Eight Elements reduced to Two*

Kauṭilya went further than his predecessors when, as if anticipating the modern classification of the elements, he reduced the eight elements to two. While discussing the troubles of the king, he writes: "The king and his kingdom are the two primary elements of the State" (*rāja rājyaṁ-iti prakṛiti-saṁkṣepaḥ*).[17] There was some justification for this drastic reduction in the number of the elements to two when we realize that, in truth, out of the seven recognized elements, it was only the king and the country that were of ultimate significance in the sense that the former appointed the ministers and the army, and selected his ally, while it was in the country that a fort could be constructed and through its resources, a treasury filled. In this connection it is interesting to observe that, according to modern thinkers, the elements of the State are reducible to four—population, territory, government, and sovereignty.[18] Although Kauṭilya was aware of the concept of sovereignty, yet he did not distinguish between government and sovereignty; neither did he distinguish between people and territory, since the one without the other would have been meaningless. He, therefore, thought of the king as symbolizing sovereignty, and of the *rājya* or kingdom as connoting territory, both of them forming the two most important elements.[19]

CHAPTER II

THE ELEMENTS DISCUSSED IN DETAIL

A. THE KING

1. STRESS ON SECULAR ORIGIN

IN EVERY classification of the elements of the State, the king leads thereby showing that to the ancients the concept of kingship was indissolubly bound up with that of sovereignty. While describing the place of the king among the elements, it would be necessary for us to recall the theory of the divine origin of kingship which was discussed in some detail earlier in these pages. Without covering the same ground, it may be observed that, whatever may have been the sanctity around the king in the days of Manu, it had disappeared with Kauṭilya to whom the king was by no means endowed with any divine sanction or attributes. There is nothing in the *Arthaśāstra* to suggest that Kauṭilya ever considered the king as a god on earth. On the other hand, all the regulations which he has mentioned in connection with the education, duties, work, etc., of the king point to a member of the Hindu society, who was only one amongst the many that could hope to become a king.[20] When Kauṭilya makes provision for a stupid and a wise king (*bāliśāt-prājñād-vā*),[21] he had exploded the myth of the divinity that had surrounded the kings.

This aspect of the question seems to have escaped the notice of historians. What was the significance of the complete rejection of the earlier concept of either the sanctity or the divinity of the king by Kauṭilya? Before we give an answer to this question, it is better that we realize that Kauṭilya was not against the omniscient power of the king. Indeed, he refers to the omniscient power (*sarvajñatva, rājñaḥ prabhāvaḥ*) of the king in two places in one and the same context, while describing the duties of the Superintendent of the Tolls (*Śulkādhyakṣa*).[22] The omniscient power of the king mentioned here is obviously to be taken in the sense of vast and detailed knowledge of the many aspects of statesmanship. But it has nothing to do with either the divinity or the sanctity of the king as suggested in the *Manusmṛiti*. The reasons for the secular, and, to some extent, perhaps the non-Kṣatriya, origin of the king pictured in the *Arthaśāstra* are not far to seek. The rulers whom Kauṭilya helped his royal master Candragupta Maurya to dethrone were not of any divine origin. Neither was Candragupta himself of divine sanctity, nor were the foreigners, who had squatted in the north-western regions of divine extraction. The entire theory of the divine origin of kings seemed to Kauṭilya to be utterly false and unreasonable. It is not surprising, therefore, that it should have found no place in his work. From the orthodox point of view, Kauṭilya had, of course, committed a sacrilege, so far as the sanctity and the halo of divinity around the king were concerned. But the young person whom Kauṭilya had helped to become king, and who was in some way connected with the Nandas,[23] had not even the faintest claims to Kṣatriyahood! In these circumstances it is not surprising that Kauṭilya should not even hint at the sanctity that had once been attached to the person of the king, although he was scrupulously careful in guarding the person of the monarch,[24] and warned those who disregarded the king with the infliction of divine punishments (*tānavamanyamānān daivo'pi daṇḍaḥ spraśati*).[25]

2. THE KING AND CORONATION

(a) *Importance of Coronation*

One of the most important attributes of kingship in ancient India was the coronation which from the Vedic times had been endowed with great significance. The performance of the coronation (*mahābhiṣeka*) and of allied ceremonies alone entitled a prince to claim the rank of a king or even of a great king. The *mahābhiṣeka* ceremony was one of great antiquity going back to the Vedic days, and especially described in the *Brāhmaṇa* works like the *Taittirīya Brāhmaṇa,* the *Aitareya Brāhmaṇa,* the *Pañcaviṁsa Brāhmaṇa,* and the *Śatapatha Brāhmaṇa.*[26] It was equivalent to the performance of the *rājasūya* sacrifice, and was associated with celebrated rulers like Janamejaya Parīkṣit and others. The *abhiṣeka* was an essential part of the *rājasūya* or sacrifice of royal inauguration, being the second of its component parts.[27]

(b) *Description of the Abhiṣeka or Coronation Ceremony*

(i) *The Simple Ritual of the Early Times*

The ceremony of coronation may now be briefly described. It began with the chanting of seven *mantras* by the officiating priest (*purohita*), who performed a *homa* or sacrifice before the ritual of sprinkling took place. The first *mantra* referred to the prince's rebirth as the son of the *ṛitviks* or sacrificial priests, with his vigour increased by his symbolic entry into the *homa* fire, and his exit therefrom, and wished him ability to keep his subjects away from sinful ways. The second *mantra* blessed him with an extended kingdom, a stout physique for its efficient administration, and an abundant supply of cattle for performing sacrifices. The third *mantra* desired of him a solemn promise that he would protect the good and punish the wicked, and be the guide of men. The fourth and the fifth invoked blessings on him for his prosperity ; and the sixth and the seventh prayed for the glorification of the castes by his power, the continued prosperity of his people, and the extension of Prajāpati's protection to him.

After the performance of the *homa,* the prince was made to sit on a tiger skin, and was blessed by the priest with an unconquerable life, with loyal subjects, and with a firm kingdom. The priest then sprinkled over the prince water in which barley and the *dūrvā* grass were steeped, blessing him all the while. The prince then ascended a chariot which stood before the *āhavanīya* fire of the sacrificial ground. This evidently symbolized the prince's prospective conquests and firm rule. The prince then prayed to the priest to help him in the maintenance of his duties, in keeping the kingdom free from danger, and in contributing to its well-being. The priest as well as the king's relatives and friends then embraced him, after which his body was smeared with unguents. The prince then looked to the sun, when the priests blessed him with a reign as lustrous as the rays of the sun, and with peace and plenty in his realm. Then the prince was made to sit on a throne of *uḍumbara* wood, when the *purohita* or priest asked him for his fees. The priest then shaved the king's head with a *mantra* in imitation of what Prajāpati had done for Soma and Varuṇa, collected the king's hair on a tuft of *kuśa* grass with the object of preserving the king's strength ; and, then, anointed the king with a mixture of *ghī* and milk with the same object, and with a formula which said that the Aśvins might see that the king's beauty was devoted only to his queens.

(ii) *The Elaborate Ritual of the Later Days*

The simple ritual of the coronation, as given in the earlier texts, was elaborated in great detail in the later ages. In the two epics, the collection of the waters from the seas and the rivers in golden pitchers, the sprinkling of the same on the prince, who was made to sit on a throne, the offering of presents by the subjects to the prince, and many other details were added to the earlier simple ritual. In the *Agni Purāna* it became still more elaborate with these and other details. In addition to the *homa,* there was the symbolic bathing with earth brought from various places (*mṛittikāsnāna*) ; the sprinkling of water over the prince by the ministers ; the sprinkling of liquids by the Rig Vedic and Sāma Vedic Brahmans and by the royal priest ; the sprinkling of water by the priest through a pitcher perforated with a hundred holes ; the seeing of auspicious things by the prince ; his crowning, presentation of officials to the prince, payment of fees to the priests, a coronation feast, and a royal procession through the metropolis and its return to the royal palace where gifts were made to the people.[28]

(c) *The Significance of the Ceremony*

A few points deserve notice in the short description of the coronation given above. In the coronation ceremony the *mantras* uttered were seven, thereby adding to the evidence already adduced that that number had a peculiar significance attached to it in the ancient times. In the days of the *Brāhmaṇas,* the *mantra* relating to the rebirth of the prince as the son of the sacrificial priest obviously meant, as Dr. Law rightly maintained, the prince's becoming a totally different person with his faculties developed and his vigour increased for the onerous duties which he would be called upon to discharge. The third *mantra* was equivalent to the coronation oath of the kings of the West, its chief import lying in the fulfilment of the paramount duty of protecting the life and property of the subjects.[29] The next point to be noted is that in the epic times, the inclusion of the waters of the oceans signified the expansion of the territory to the seas; while the collection of the waters of the rivers in golden pitchers showed the growing economic prosperity of the country. In the still later days, the coronation ceremony became the symbol of the unity of the country in the sense that the bath with earth from the various regions and the association of the officials and the people with the ceremony made the ruler think more in terms of the whole kingdom rather than in terms of himself and of the priests, as was the case in the days of the simple ancient ritual.

(d) *Coronation in Kauṭilya*

What is of importance for our purpose is that in the detailed description of the education and duties of the prince, the ceremony of abhiseka does not figure at all in the *Arthaśāstra* of Kauṭilya. This is surprising because Kauṭilya describes what the young prince is to do from the time he was to undergo the ceremony of tonsure till late at night when the ruler was to "hear over and again what has not been clearly understood".[30] Kauṭilya's silence in regard to this celebrated ritual is inexplicable. Perhaps, as in the case of Manu, it was not felt necessary to mention a ritual in a treatise on statecraft, although it was most vitally connected with the legality of the actions of the king.

3. EDUCATION AND TRAINING OF THE PRINCE IN MANU AND KAUTILYA

Both Manu and Kauṭilya dwell at some length on the education and training which was to be given to a prince, who was to become king.

(a) *According to Manu*

The first part of a Kṣatriya's name was to be connected with power, and the second, with protection.[31] A Kṣatriya's initiation was to take place in his sixth year ;[32] and as a student his girdle was to be of a bowstring made of *mūrvā* fibres.[33] His sacrificial string was to be of hempen threads,[34] while his staff was to reach his forehead.[35] An initiated Kṣatriya was to beg for food beginning his request with the word "Lady!" in the middle of the sentence.[36] The ceremony of clipping hair (*keśanta*) was to be performed in his twenty second year.[37] Since Manu explicitly states that the king was "a Kṣatriya, who had received, according to the rule, the sacrament prescribed by the Veda",[38] we are to presume that all the above regulations, which were meant to be applied to the rest of the Kṣatriyas, held good also in his case.

The next stage in the life of the ruler was reached when we are told that, after rising early in the morning, he worshipped the Brahmans, who were well versed in the three-fold Sacred science, and who were learned in polity, and followed their advice.[39] Later on in the same chapter, Manu explains what was meant by the three-fold science thus: the primeval science of government, the science of dialectics, and the knowledge of the supreme soul which he was to learn from those versed in the three *Vedas* ; while the theory of the various trades and professions he was to learn from the people.[40] He was to exert day and night in conquering the senses, and to scrupulously avoid the ten vices which are enumerated in detail in the *Manusmṛiti*.[41] He was to daily consult with the seven or eight ministers of approved character and qualifications, the latter of which are given in the same work. The subjects on which he was to take the advice of his ministers were the following: the ordinary business referring to war and peace, revenue, protection of the kingdom, and the sanctification of his gains by pious gifts. Having first ascertained the opinion of each minister separately, he was then to consider the views of all together, and finally to do what was most beneficial to him in his affairs. With the most distinguished of his councillors, he was to deliberate on the six measures of State policy.[42] His daily programme was as follows: rising in the last watch of the night, performing the rites of personal purification, offering with a collected mind the oblations in the fire, worshipping Brahmans, and, finally, entering the hall of audience where he was to tarry gratifying his subjects by a kind reception, dismissing them, and consulting with ministers in a lonely place on the important questions before him.[43]

(b) *Education of the King in Kauṭilya*

A similar account of the daily routine and education of the king is given by Kauṭilya. He mentions of course the injunctions of the earlier legists that the duty of a Kṣatriya is to study, perform sacrifices, give gifts, take to military occupations, and protect life. He then recounts the duties of the other classes of people, and says: "Harmlessness, truthfulness, purity, freedom from spite, abstinence from cruelty, and forgiveness are duties common to all." The king was not to allow people to swerve from their duties.[44] If the duties common to all were also meant for the king, it cannot be understood how the uncompromising and unprincipled life of a conqueror, which Kauṭilya has described in his work, could be made to agree with the life of forgiveness and abstinence from cruelty which he had prescribed as duties to all including the Kṣatriyas. This inconsistency was, we suppose, inescapable in a practical statesman like the author of the *Arthaśāstra*.

Kauṭilya advocated a very severe life of discipline to the prince. He does not mention the age on reaching which the prince was to perform the various duties, but merely observes that after having undergone the ceremony of tonsure, the student-prince should learn the *lipi* (alphabet) and arithmetic. We have to infer from what will be stated below that the tonsure ceremony was undergone when the prince was about sixteen years of age. After the investiture with the sacred thread (for which Kauṭilya, unlike Manu, has not assigned any age), the prince was to study the triple *Vedas* and the science of *ānvīkṣakī* under teachers of acknowledged authority (*śiṣṭebhyaḥ*), the science of *vārtā* under State Superintendents (*adhyakṣas*), and the science of *daṇḍanīti* under theoretical and practical politicians (*daṇḍanītim vaktṛiprayoktṛibhyaḥ*). Kauṭilya seems to have advanced on the theory of Manu in this respect since he lays stress, not on those who were merely learned in the three *Vedas*, as Manu had enjoined, who were to instruct the prince, but on teachers of acknowledged authority, that is, on experts, and on State Superintendents, thereby suggesting that mere knowledge in the sciences was not enough qualification for teaching a prince but acknowledged proficiency which alone was the criterion of a teacher who taught the prince. In addition to them were the State Superintendents, who were to teach the prince the science of *vārtā*, and practical statesmen, the science of *daṇḍanīti*. Since we know that learned men were paid by the State regular salaries, it means that the greater part of the education of the young prince was completed under the direction of teachers and officials, who were servants of the State. The curricula which the prince had to follow laid equal stress on theory and practice, a feature of the study which is not met with in the *Manusmṛiti*.

Kauṭilya next proceeds to narrate that the prince shall observe celibacy till he was sixteen years of age after which he had to observe the ceremony of tonsure (*godāna*) and marry. The next sentence is as much a comment on the learned professions of the age as on Kauṭilya's own sense of justice. He writes thus: "In view of maintaining efficient discipline, he shall ever and invariably keep company with aged professors of sciences in whom alone discipline has its firm root" (*asya nityas-ca vidyāṛiddha samyogo vinaya-vṛiddhyarthaṁ tat mūlatvāt-vinayasya*).[45]

Routine Time-Table in General. The king's routine time-table is next described in general in the *Arthaśāstra* thus:

> He should spend the forenoon in receiving lessons in military arts concerning elephants, horses, chariots, and weapons ; and the afternoon in hearing *itihāsa* (which is mentioned in detail). During the rest of the day and the night, the king shall not only receive new lessons and revise old ones, but shall hear over and over again what has not been clearly understood.[46]

Routine Time-Table in Detail. The daily routine duties of the king are given in detail. The whole day and night was to be divided into eight *nāḷikas* (of one-and-a-half hours each), or, according to the length of the shadow (given in detail). During the first one-eighth part of the day, the king was to post watchmen and attend to the accounts of receipts and expenditure ; during the second part, to look into the affairs of both citizens and country people ; during the third, to bathe, study, and dine ; during the fourth, to receive the revenue in gold (*hiraṇya*) and look to the appointment of superintendents ; during the fifth, to correspond in writs (*patra-saṁpreṣaṇena*) with the council of ministers, and to receive secret information from spies ; during the sixth, to engage himself in his favourite amusements or in self-deliberation ; during the seventh, to supervise the training of elephants, horses, chariots, and infantry ; and during the eight, to consider various plans of military operations with his commander-in-chief. At the close of the day, he was to observe the evening prayer (*sandhyā*).[47]

The night was likewise divided into eight parts. The first one-eighth part was spent in receiving secret emissaries ; the second, in attending to bathing and supper ; the third, in entering the bed chamber amidst the sound of trumpets ; the fourth and the fifth, in sleeping ; the sixth, in being awakened by the sound of trumpets, when he was to recall to his mind the injunctions of the sciences as well as his daily duties ; the seventh, in considering administrative measures and sending out spies ; and the eighth in receiving benedictions from the sacrificial priests, teachers, and the high priest, in seeing his physicians, chief cook, and astrologer, and in saluting a cow with its calf and a bull and in circumambulating round them, after which he was to proceed to his court. Kauṭilya's realism is seen in the last sentence of the above passage that, as an alternative to the above severe and heavy programme, the king "in conformity to his capacity, he may alter the time-table and attend to his duties".[48]

(c) *Criticism of the Daily Time-Table of the King as given in Kauṭilya*

It appears incredible that a ruler should have had such a rigorous and heavy time-table like the one mentioned above! One wonders whether one could give credence to the divisions of the day and night into sixteen parts in the manner done by Kauṭilya, especially when one realizes that the period of rest enjoyed by the king was only two parts comprising in all three hours! We could have entertained the above doubt but for the fact that very many of the injunctions laid down in the *Arthaśāstra* were actually observed by the greatest of the Mauryan Emperors, as will be shown in Part Six below. Whatever may be the scepticism with which we have to view the period of rest assigned to the king, there is hardly any doubt that Kauṭilya had in mind a ruler who was, indeed, the most heavily worked servant of the State.[49]

Another point of interest in the above account is its divergence in many details from the daily programme as laid down by Manu. The severe restriction of time, and the allotment of the several duties to the various parts of the day and night, clearly point to the enormous growth in the nature and volume of State work since Manu's time, and particularly in the days of Kauṭilya, which can be associated only with the large and complicated bureaucratic machinery of an Empire like that of the Mauryans.

4. DUTIES OF THE KING

(a) *In the Manusmṛiti*

The uncommonly strenuous life of the king as depicted in the *Arthaśāstra* has to be appreciated in the context not only of the duties of the king as given in that work but also in that of those described in the *Manusmṛiti*. If the latter is to be relied upon, the duties of the ruler were, indeed, abnormally heavy even in those comparatively early times. The duties of the king as enumerated in the *Manusmṛiti*, for the sake of convenience, may be analysed under the following eight heads—Executive, Judicial, Legislative, Administrative, Ecclesiastical, Revenue, Military, and Enlightened.

(i) *Executive Duties*

This was the most important duty, since without it most of the other duties could not be fulfilled. It had two aspects—protection and punishment. The first referred to the protection of all castes and creeds with special reference to the minors and women.[50] Oppression through folly entailed the loss of life and kingdom.[51] The duty of protection was to be carried out zealously and carefully. It involved three ideas—prevention of the confusion of castes, and protecting the weak against the strong. And protection alone entitled the king to receive one-sixth part of the spiritual merit of the people. But protecting the weak against the strong could be done only by punishing those worthy of corporal punishment. The wicked were to be restrained by three methods—by imprisonment, by putting them in fetters, and by various kinds of corporal punishments.[52] Punishment was sanctified in the sense that it was declared to be the son of the Creator, and an incarnation of law, formed out of Brahmā's glory.[53] In the previous pages of this book, it was seen what an important part *daṇda* or punishment played in the political thought of the ancients. It formed the essence of the executive power of the State.

A third significant aspect of protection referred to the king's duty to the young and the infirm. He was to protect the inherited and other property of the minors, until they had returned from their teachers' houses, or until they had attained majority. In like manner care was to be taken of barren women, those who had no children, those whose family was extinct, of wives and widows who were faithful to their lords, and of women afflicted with diseases. A righteous king was entitled to punish like thieves those relatives, who had appropriated the property of such women (like those mentioned above) during their lifetime.[54]

(ii) Judicial Duties

These have been set forth in the *Manusmṛiti* in such a thorough manner that we cannot but conclude that the judicial procedure was as perfect as those distant times could permit. The king was the supreme judge. He was to enter the court "preserving a dignified demeanour", together with the Brahmans learned in the *Vedas,* and experienced councillors. He was to examine the cases either seated or standing, but without ostentation in his dress and ornaments. This was to be done daily, the judicial cases falling under the eighteen titles of law being enumerated in detail. The decisions were to be just, since justice when violated was destroyed, but when preserved, preserved. The laws of castes (*jāti*), of districts, of guilds, and of families were to be studied by the king, who was to settle the peculiar law of every one of them. Neither the king nor any of his servants was entitled to cause a law suit to be begun, neither could they hush up a case brought before them by some one else.[55] As to how the actual judicial procedure was to be conducted is mentioned in detail, special attention being paid to witnesses, oaths, and ordeals.[56] If his minister or ministers settled cases improperly, the king himself was to re-try the cases, and fine them 1,000 *paṇas* each.[57] A thief could not be put to death unless taken along with the stolen goods in his possession. But if found in possession of stolen goods and implements of burglary (*in flagranti*), he could, without hesitation, be put to death.[58] The king could not take action against the infants, the aged, the sick, and the litigants, even when they inveighed against him.[59]

(iii) *Legislative Duties*

In the age of Manu there was no question of taking into account the king's *śāsana* or written law which was going to be a special feature of Kauṭilya's legal system. The eighteen titles mentioned earlier were already laid down, according to the principles drawn from local usage and from the *Institutes of the Sacred Law* (*dharmaśāstras*).[60] This reduced one of the major duties of the king to the mere application of the regulations already laid down before him, and meant that, so far as the duty of promulgating laws was concerned, he was to restrict himself to the sphere allotted to him by the Common Law, that is, the local usage.

A genuine difficulty arose when, in respect of specific points of law, no provision had been made in the *Institutes of the Sacred Law*. This was solved in this manner: the opinion of Brahmans, who were *Śiṣṭas*, was to have the force of law. These Brahmans were not the ordinary ones, who had not fulfilled their sacred duties, who were unacquainted with the *Vedas*, and who subsisted only by the name of their caste. They were *Śiṣṭas*, who alone in accordance with the Sacred law, had studied the *Veda*, together with its appendages, and who were able to adduce proof perceptible by the senses from the revealed texts. Either a maximum number of ten, or a minimum number of three, of such persons constituted an assembly, and their decision was to have the force of law which none could dispute. The composition of a judicial board was as follows: three persons, each of whom knew one of the three principal *Vedas*, a logician, a Mimāmsaka, an expert in Nirukta, one who recited the *Institutes of the Sacred Law*, and three men, who belonged to the first three orders (the Brahmans, the Kṣatriyas, and the Vaiśyas). If the board was made up of three members, then, the distribution was as follows: one who knew the *Rig Veda* ; the second, who knew the *Yajur Veda* ; and the third, who knew the *Sama Veda*. The specific injunction that "even that which one Brāhmaṇa versed in the *Veda* declared to be law must be considered (to have) supreme legal (force but) not that which is proclaimed by myriads of ignorant men" clearly shows that the interpretation of law was not left to any charlatan but was the work of an expert in law.[61]

(iv) *Administrative Duties*

Apart from the three kinds of duties mentioned above, there were the administrative duties which related to two categories—appointments and administrative problems. The former referred to the appointment of seven or eight ministers, and of other officials. The number of the latter depended on the nature of the State business.[62] As regards the administrative problems, the king decided questions of property, treasure troves, and weights and measures. Property, the owner of which had disappeared, was kept as a deposit with the State for three years within which period the owner could claim it, and after that term, the king could take it.[63]

(v) *Ecclesiastical Duties*

The king was to appoint the chief priest (*purohita*), and choose other officiating priests (*ṛitviks*). They were to perform his domestic rites and sacrifices for which three fires were required. He was to offer various *Śrauta* sacrifices at which liberal fees were to be distributed, and he was to give to the Brahmans legal enjoyment and wealth for their services.[64] The king was to offer oblations to the fire before entering the hall of audience.[65]

(vi) *Revenue Duties*

The revenue duties comprised fixation of the rates of taxes and duties. The principle of taxation was the following: after due consideration the king was always to fix in his realm the duties and taxes "in such a manner that both he himself and the man who does the work receive (their due) reward". It was expressly laid down that like the bee, the calf, and the leech taking their food little by little, the king was to levy moderate annual taxes.[66] The annual revenue was to be collected by trusted officials. In his transactions with the people, the king was to obey the Sacred law, and "behave like a father towards all men".[67] But no taxes were to be paid by blind men, idiots, cripples, old men who were seventy years, and those who conferred benefits on the Śrotriyas.[68]

(vii) *Military Duties*

It was the king who selected his royal residence and the fortress.[69] It was his duty as a Kṣatriya to fight bravely and honourably, and not turn back in fear. It was likewise his duty to see that asylum was granted to all who had surrendered to him.[70] The right of distributing the booty belonged to him ; but, where it was not taken by one but many, it was to be distributed among all soldiers.[71] He had also the right of inspecting the army,[72] and we may suppose, naturally that of appointing it.

(viii) *Enlightened Duties*

The enlightened duties referred to the king's being the promoter of learning and culture. He was to worship every morning the learned men, well versed in the three-fold sacred sciences and learned in polity.[73] He could not tax a Śrotriya, or a learned priest, even though he might be dying for want of finances.[74] Presents, including costly jewels, of all sorts were to be given to the Brahmans, who performed sacrifices.[75] We have already seen that it was one of his duties to study the three-fold sciences of government, dialectics, and the soul from those who were well versed in the three *Vedas*, and the theory of the various trades and professions from the people.[76]

(b) *Duties of the King in the Arthaśāstra of Kauṭilya*

Let us now see to what extent the duties of the king, as given above, remained the same, or were altered, in the days of Kauṭilya. Since the whole administration was centralized, according to the latter, it was evident that all power was vested in the king himself, who delegated it to the various heads of the departments under whom worked their numerous subordinates. The eight categories of duties mentioned in the *Manusmṛiti* remained unchanged in the *Arthaśāstra*, but the items under every head had grown to an appreciable extent necessitating certain new ideas.

(i) *Executive Duties*

Protection continued to be the foremost of all the duties of the king in the age of Kauṭilya. Along with it was the good government of the subjects, and the duty of doing good to all the people.[77] It has been seen above that it was the duty of the king to provide the orphans (*bāla*), the aged, the infirm, the afflicted, and the helpless with maintenance. He was also to provide subsistence to helpless women, when they were carrying, and also to the children they gave birth.[78] That is, in modern phraseology, the State conducted a State Orphanage, a Widows' Home, and a State Relief Centre for the infirm, etc. Kauṭilya wisely continued the policy of Manu in this respect.

But a departure from the earlier policy was made in regard to protection against national calamities. It was the duty of the king to protect the kingdom against the eight types of national calamities described elsewhere in these pages, viz., fire, floods, pestilential diseases, famines, rats, tigers, serpents, and demons.[79] These do not figure in the *Manusmṛiti*. Likewise Kauṭilya laid stress on a new subject of protection—the need to remove the disturbing elements of peace. This was entrusted to the Collector-General, whose duty was to protect the country against thirteen kinds of criminals mentioned in detail by Kauṭilya.[80] Robbers figure prominently in the *Arthaśāstra* thereby suggesting that they had become a serious menace either in Kauṭilya's time or were legacy of the misrule of the previous monarchs, the Nandas. The growth in population and in the extent of territory, we may imagine, since the days of Manu perhaps explains the emergence of these new internal dangers to the State in the *Arthaśāstra*.

(ii) *Judicial Duties*

The king was the head of the judiciary but not the fountain of law. We shall see below that Kauṭilya had a definite concept of law-making bodies in which the laws passed by the king formed only one group of laws. We shall see likewise how the judges were punished for contravening law or delaying justice. The picture of the law courts and of the judges as given in the *Arthaśāstra* only proves that the ultimate power of controlling the judges lay entirely in the hands of the king.[81]

(iii) *Legislative Duties*

In regard to these duties, it is doubtful whether, on the whole, Kauṭilya had made much progress since the days of Manu. He had, no doubt, added to the organs which interpreted the existing law, as will be narrated below in connection with the four legs of law, one of which may, with some certainty, be said to have formulated new law.[82] In this particular sense alone it may be said that there was some legislative activity in the Kauṭilyan State. But it may not be confounded with the punishments imposed on the judges referred to above, as has been done by some modern Indian historians.[83]

(iv) *Administrative Duties*

In this sphere there was a marked difference between the State of Manu and that of Kauṭilya. As in the earlier times, the appointment of ministers and the control to be exercised over them was the duty of the king.[84] It was remarked above that in the daily routine time-table of the ruler, the fifth one-eighth part of the day was reserved for the king's correspondence in writs with the assembly of ministers. In two respects Kauṭilya definitely had advanced on Manu—that in regard to the conduct of the government servants, and that in regard to the protection of all government departments.[85] From the daily programme of the ruler, it is clear that his administrative duties, in all spheres of governmental activities, were unusually heavy.

(v) *Ecclesiastical Duties*

The king appointed the high priest, whose qualifications are given in detail in the *Arthaśāstra*. Only such a person was to be appointed as a *purohita* or high priest, whose family and character were highly spoken of, who was well educated in the *Vedas* and the six *Angas*, who was skilful in reading providential or accidental portents, who was well versed in the science of government, who was obedient, who could prevent providential as well as human calamities, and one who could perform soul expatiatory rites as were prescribed in the *Atharva Veda*. Such a person, when once appointed, apparently had great control over the king, for the next sentence runs thus: "As a student his teacher, a son his father, and a servant his master, the king shall follow him."[86]

The qualifications of the high priest (*purohita*) require some comment. He was evidently not of the ancient orthodox type as described in the *Manusmṛiti*, viz., one who could perform the *Agnyādheya Pākajñāsa*, and the *Śrauta* sacrifices.[87] The domestic priest and the officiating priests, as we have already seen above, appointed by the king, as given in the *Manusmṛiti*, performed his domestic rites and the sacrifices for which the three fires were required.[88] But the times had, indeed, changed: it was no more a question of merely performing sacrifices; it was also necessary to perform the rites as prescribed in the *Atharva Veda*, to read providential or accidental omens, to prevent providential or human calamities, and to be well versed in the science of government. In other words, the high priest of Kauṭilya was more secular than spiritual. As to how he could perform some of the functions mentioned above relating to portents and calamities, it is impossible to know. But he was the right type of a high priest who could fit into the scheme of things evolved by Kauṭilya which included strange devices for conquering an enemy.[89]

(*vi*) *Revenue Duties*

The elaborate bureaucratic machinery evolved by Kauṭilya rested upon the solid foundation of finance. In this sphere, too, the financial powers of the ruler were both final and extensive. It was his duty to see that the treasury was not depleted, since an empty treasury ate into the very vitality of both the citizens and the country people (*alpa-kośo hi rājā paurajānapadān—eva grasate*).[90] In the programme of the king, the first item during the day, as already seen above, was looking into the accounts of receipts and expenditure; and the fourth item, receiving the revenue in gold. What this must have meant to the king can well be imagined, since it was he who appointed and supervised the Controller-General, whose duties were as onerous as they were multifarious.[91] The revenue thus collected by the Collector-General was received by the Chamberlain (*sannidhātā*), who attended to it assisted by trustworthy officials.[92] In assigning one-fourth of the total revenue of the State for meeting the salaries of the officials and servants of the State,[93] Kauṭilya showed how vast the administrative machinery and the needs of the State had grown since the times of Manu.

(*vii*) *Military Duties*

As supreme commander of the army, the king in the *Arthaśāstra* had the duty of inspecting the elephants, the horses, the chariots, and the infantry during the seventh one-eighth part of the day.[94] We have no means of ascertaining the exact strength of the army described in the *Arthaśāstra.* But it is evident that Candragupta Maurya's army which had the double task of uprooting the Nandas and of driving the Macedonians out of the Punjab, could only have been of a very large size. The daily supervision of such an army was, inded, a heavy item in the already over-burdened programme of the monarch.

In the *Manusmṛiti* the king was to select the site of his palace as well as that of the fortress. Kauṭilya is more explicit in this detail. The residential palace of the ruler was to be after the model of the treasury house, although three other alternate constructions were also permissible.[95] In this detail Kauṭilya is different from Manu.

Earliest Reference to Red Cross. It is not possible to give in this work a detailed account of the care that was bestowed on the army by Kauṭilya. We may only mention an innovation which might appeal to the modern times. The army of Kauṭilya was accompanied by physicians with surgical instruments (*śastra*), machines, remedial aids, and cloth in their hands. And there were also women who stood behind the fighting forces, with prepared food, and beverages, "uttering encouraging words to fighting men" (*cikitsakāḥ śastra-yantra-agadasneha-vastra-hastāḥ striyaḥ-ca-anna-pāna-rakṣiṇyaḥ puruṣāṇām-uddharṣaṇīyāḥ prasṭhataḥ-tiṣṭheyuḥ*).[96] Kauṭilya had considerably progressed since the days of Manu, who has nothing to say about the physicians and women accompanying the army.[97] Kauṭilya's explicit mention of physicians with surgical instruments, medicinal oils, and cloth, and of women with food and beverages is the earliest reference we have in Indian history, and perhaps in that of any part of the world, of a Red Cross Organization during military action.

The super-size to which the State of Kauṭilya had attained necessitated a re-orientation of its foreign policy in regard to the other States. We may not enter into this interesting side of the question, which would require a dissertation by itself. It may be stated here that Kauṭilya had in the clearest manner indicated the new concept of the imperial State when he dwelt at length on the *rājamaṇḍala* theory and its complicated working.[98]

(*viii*) *Enlightened Duties*

Patronage of learned men, of those who were experts in *yoga,* and even of those who were experts in witchcraft,[99] and providing them with rent-free villages (*Brahmadeya* lands),[100] continued to be the policy of the king in the days of Kauṭilya. In the construction of hospitals (*bhaiṣajyagṛihaṁ*) in the capital city,[101] Kauṭilya once again showed that the State had progressed considerably since the age of Manu.

5. WAS THE KAUTILYAN KING A TYRANT OF THE GREEK TYPE?

A question that naturally arises, in view of the extreme centralization advocated by Kauṭilya, is whether the king as depicted by him was a tyrant in the Greek sense. To answer this question we have to understand the significance of the term tyrant as used by Aristotle rather than to judge the Kauṭilyan king by the standards of our own days.

(a) The Tyrant in Greece described by Aristotle

While discussing the question of the preservation of monarchies, Aristotle refers to the traditional method in which most tyrants administered their governments. He then cites the examples of Periander of Corinth and the Persians, and gives the following "ancient prescriptions for the preservation of a tyranny":

> . . . the tyrant should lop off those who are too high ; he must put to death men of spirit ; he must not allow common meals, clubs, education, and the like ; he must be upon his guard against anything which is likely to inspire courage or confidence among his subjects ; he must prohibit literary assemblies or other meetings for discussions, and he must take away every means to prevent people from knowing one another (for acquaintance begets mutual confidence). Further, he must compel the inhabitants to appear in public and live at his gates ; then he will know what they are doing ; if they are always kept humble, they will learn to be humble. In short, he should practise these and the like Persian and barbaric arts which all have the same object. A tyrant should also endeavour to know what each of his subject says or does, and should employ spies, like the 'female detectives' at Syracuse and the eves-droppers whom Hiero was in the habit of sending to any place of resort or meeting ; for the fear of informers prevents people from speaking their minds, and if they do, they are more easily found out. Another art of the tyrant is to sow quarrels among the citizens ; friends should be embroiled with friends, the people with the nobles, and the rich with one another. Also he should impoverish his subjects ; he thus provides money for the support of his guards, and the people, having to keep hard at work, are prevented from conspiring.

Aristotle then gives the examples of the public buildings like the Pyramids of Egypt, the offerings of the family of Cypselus at Corinth, the temple of Olympian Zeus built by the Pesistratidae, and the great Polycratean monuments at Samos, all of which "were alike intended to occupy the people and keep them poor". Another practice of the tyrants was to multiply the taxes, after the manner of Dionysius of Syracuse, "who had contrived that within five years his subjects should bring into the treasury their whole property". The tyrant also made war "in order that his subjects may have something to do and be always in want of a leader". "And whereas the power of a king is preserved by his friends, the character of a tyrant is to distrust his friends, because he knows that all men want to overthrow him, and they above all have the power."[102]

(b) *Tyrant's Method Analysed*

The methods used by the Greek and the Persian tyrants may be reduced to the following: (*i*) weed out all opposition in the shape of highly spirited men or leaders ; (*ii*) disallow all measures that would unite the people like common meals, clubs, common education, literary or public meetings ; (*iii*) guard against anything that might inspire courage and confidence among the people ; (*iv*) compel people to appear in public with a view to humiliating them ; (*v*) know every thing which the people do or think by a rigorous system of espionage ; (*vi*) sow dissensions among the people ; (*vii*) impoverish them by unbearable and excessive taxation ; (*viii*) construct public buildings or make war in order to divert their attention and keep them engaged ; and (*ix*) distrust friends.

(c) *The Greek Tyrant and the King in Kauṭilya Compared*

(*i*) *Points of Comparison*

Removal of All Opposition. There are some points of striking resemblance between the Aristotlean tyrant and the Kauṭilyan king. Thus, for instance, in regard to the removal of all those who were men of spirit, or too high, and, in particular, in regard to the institution of a strict system of espionage, there is no doubt that the Kauṭilyan king was a faithful reproduction of the Greek model. When Kauṭilya states that "disaffection or disloyalty (*virāga*) can be got rid of by putting down the leaders",[103] he approaches almost the characteristic of the Greek tyrant, who did away with all leaders and men of spirit. We may presume that, as in the case of the Greek tyrant, the Kauṭilyan king was extremely careful to see that there was no movement which united the people, since such a course of action would have meant perhaps the consolidation of the pro-Nanda forces in the country which Kauṭilya himself had been instrumental in destroying.

Espionage. What makes us suspect that the Kauṭilyan king had such an idea in his mind is the extremely powerful and all-embracing system of espionage that shadowed the people practically in all the walks of life. It is true that the spies played a most important part in detecting treason and in sowing seeds of dissension among the enemy ; but it is also a fact that they pried into the revenue collection, detected criminals, found out disloyal ministers, covered the activities of even the *mahāmātras*, and espied the doings of the citizens in towns and the people in the country. Spies ascertained the total number of men and beast (*jaṅghāra*) as well as the amount of income and expenditure of each family. Even the quantity and price of the royal merchandise, like minerals, products of gardens, etc., forests, fields, and manufactured articles came within their purview. Indeed, they formed an efficient weapon in the hands of the Collector-General.[104] With such a huge octopus-like network of spies, the Kauṭilyan autocrat could feel the pulse of the people better than his counterpart in Greece or Macedonia. Judged from the manner in which he held the people within his iron grip, it seems that there was no difference between him and the tyrant described in Aristotle. The similarity between the Indian and Greek tyrant is heightened by the fact that, as in the case of the latter, so here in India the king was ever engaged in war, which could only have diverted the attention of the people from the pressing problem of uniting against the king in regard to his schemes of glorious aggrandizement.

(*ii*) *Points of Contrast*

On a closer examination, however, we find that the Kauṭilyan king had some redeeming features which distinguish him from his Greek counterpart, and which justify the assumption that he was not an uncontrolled despot of the Western type.

Conciliation of Conquered People. War in the age of Kauṭilya was inevitable for reasons stated elsewhere in these pages. The two dangers, one within the country and the other on the north-western regions of India, compelled the Kauṭilyan king to look upon war more as a necessary step in the stabilization of the country than in that of his own autocratic position. Although Kauṭilya was for completely wiping out all opposition, yet he made provision for conciliation. Thus, for instance, he advocated: "Honours and rewards should be conferred upon those that are contented, while those that are disaffected shall be brought round by conciliation, by gifts, or by sowing dissension, or by punishment." This course of action was particularly directed against those people who were likely to fall a prey to foreign intrigue.[105]

Public Meetings Not Prohibited. The Greek institution of common meals, clubs, and education did not exist in India, where the places and the methods by which people were brought together were quite different. Here it was in the temples, religious fairs, market places, etc., where the people assembled together and exchanged views. There is nothing in the *Arthaśāstra* to suggest that such meetings of the people were prohibited. Perhaps no special measures were needed in this direction because the army of spies made it practically impossible for the people to think of conspiring against the State. Likewise it cannot be made out from Kauṭilya's injunctions that he imitated the Greek tyrant in compelling the people to appear in public with a view to humiliating them. While the Kauṭilyan autocrat certainly sowed seeds of dissension, especially among the enemy, it does not appear that he followed this policy in regard to his own people. If he had followed such a disastrous policy, the entire economy of the State as typified in the many excellent rules relating to the pasture lands, fields, etc.,[106] and in those concerning the commercial life of the people,[107] would have been ruined.

Judicious Taxation. Much more than the continual humiliation of the people and the measures to prevent them from communicating with each other was their impoverishment that was brought about by a heavy taxation. Its only object, so far as the State of the Greek tyrant was concerned, was the enrichment of the latter at the expense of the people. But with Kauṭilya it was altogether different: it was both the king and the people who were to be wealthy. Indeed, when Kauṭilya had raised *vārtā* to the status of a science, and included it among the four sciences which the king had to study,[108] he had proclaimed the supreme importance of wealth not only for the king but for the people as well. He explicitly states, while describing the duties of the Superintendent of Commerce, that the latter "shall avoid such large profits as will harm the people".[109] The whole commerical policy of the State, as revealed in the same connection, was one of judicious taxation. Kauṭilya warns the king: "An impoverished people are ever apprehensive of oppression and destruction (by over taxation, etc.), and are desirous of getting rid of their impoverishment, or of waging war, or of migrating elsewhere."[110]

Before we proceed with our main topic we may observe that in the above passage we have a striking proof of what was stated above in regard to the alleged right of the people of rebellion and of killing a tyrannical ruler. Although the expression "of waging war" seems to mean that Kauṭilya might have had in mind a contingency when all impoverished people might have thought of waging war against their own ruler, that is, of waging a civil war, yet the explicit omission of any reference to the right of killing a bad ruler in the above passage suggests that Kauṭilya was not prepared to grant any such right to the people. On the other hand, the last alternative of permitting them to migrate elsewhere seems to negative such an assumption on the part of the people.

Restrictions on Taxation. We may now continue with the main subject of the comparison between the Kauṭilyan king and the Greek tyrant. It is true that "in a great financial trouble", when the king was in need of money, he could collect revenue in various ways which have been given in detail by Kauṭilya. But even in this contingency, the king could not lay his hands on certain categories of lands and of people, who were exempted from these unusual levies. The only exception was the community of goldsmiths, whose entire property could be confiscated by the king. No offence of theirs could be forgiven, "for they carry on their fraudulent trade while pretending at the same time to be honest and innocent". Kauṭilya, as was noted earlier, shared the views of Aristotle on the artisan class, who were devoid of honesty. But even when the king levied money from all quarter in financial crises, Kauṭilya ordained that "such demands shall be made only once and never twice".[111] This injunction clearly proves that the king was not entitled to extort money on the pretence of financial stringency at will. The restriction thus imposed on the king, and the judicious maner in which he levied taxation, prove that he stood in sharp contrast to his Greek counterpart who prospered on unjust levies and unbridled extortion.

Character of the King. What establishes beyond doubt the claims of the Kauṭilyan king to be considered as apart from, and in a sense, superior to the Greek tyrant, is the stress Kauṭilya laid on the character of the king. We may be permitted to repeat this side of the question, some aspects of which we have already noted above. Kauṭilya laid down at the very outset the severest restrictions on the king. He opens the chapter on the Aggregate of the Six Enemies of the King thus:

> Restraint of the organs of the sense, on which success in study and discipline depends, can be enforced by abandoning lust, anger, greed, vanity (*māna*), haughtiness (*mada*) and overjoy (*harṣa*) . . . . Strict observance of the precepts of sciences also means the same ; for the sole aim of all the sciences is nothing but restraint of the organs of sense.

Kauṭilya's warning that follows is very clear: "Whosoever is of reverse character, whoever has not got his organs of the senses under control, will soon perish, though possessed of the whole earth bounded by the four quarters." The twelve examples of tyrants who had violated the ancient precepts of the control of the senses, are given next ; and these are followed by two noble examples of great rulers like Ambarīṣa of the Jāmadagnya family, and Nābhāga, who had driven out the aggregate of six enemies relating to the senses.

This wise counsel is followed in the next chapter by further advice which runs thus:

> Hence by overthrowing the aggregate of the six enemies, he (the king) shall restrain the organs of the senses ; acquire wisdom by keeping company with the aged ; see through his spies ; establish safety and security by being ever active ; maintain his subjects in the observance of their respective duties by exercising authority ; keep up his personal discipline by receiving lessons in the sciences ; and endear himself to the people by bringing them in contact with wealth and doing good to them.

In the next paragraph, Kauṭilya cautions further that the king should not be a tyrant:

> Thus with his organs of the senses under his control, he shall keep away from hurting the women and property of others; avoid not only lustfulness, even in dream, but also falsehood, haughtiness, and evil proclivities, and keep away from unrighteous and uneconomical transactions. Not violating righteousness and economy, he shall enjoy his desires. He shall never be devoid of happiness.[112]

In the above detailed injunctions Kauṭilya sapped the strength of the Greek tyrant which had grown fat on pride, avarice, lust, and unrighteousness, and thus made it impossible for an Indian king to imitate his Greek counterpart. If the warning given above was not sufficient, Kauṭilya supplemented it in the folowing words: "If the king is energetic his subjects will be equally energetic. If he is reckless, they will not only be reckless likewise, but also eat into his works. Besides, a reckless king will easily fall into the hands of his enemies. Hence the king shall ever be wakeful."[113]

The King worked for the People's Welfare. Unlike his Greek prototype, the Kauṭilyan king worked hard for the welfare of his subjects. Indeed, as related elsewhere in these pages, his greatest concern was the good of his subjects. "In the happiness of his subjects lies his happiness; in their welfare his welfare; whatever pleases himself he shall not consider as good, but whatever pleases his subjects he shall consider as good."[114] Herein we have the ideal which the king had to set before him from which there could be no deviation without incurring the penalty of the loss of the crown at the hands of the people.

Not an Autocrat. There was another sphere where the Indian king could definitely maintain that he was not like the Greek tyrant. This was the meting out of justice which was unknown to the latter. In ancient India *dharma* or righteous conduct was the keynote of the socio-political structure. In addition to the remarks we have made in the earlier pages of this book, relating to the interdependence of *dharma* and *daṇḍa*, which must have made it clear to the reader that *daṇḍa* could never transgress the boundaries of *dharma*, we may note the following specific regulations in Kauṭilya, which made it impossible for the king to continuously play the part of a tyrant. We do not mean to say that he was not an autocrat. Indeed, his supreme position in the State made it incumbent upon him to play the rôle of an autocrat. In this context it is worthwhile examining the view of Professor Rangaswami Aiyangar, who writes thus:

> The king is practically an autocrat, who is generally inaccessible, showing himself to the people only once in a month or two months, in order to prevent disturbances caused by the rumours of his death. He is so removed from common folk that he is to converse with envoys and subjects only through his ministers.[115]

There is no justification for the above estimate of the Kauṭilyan king which, if true, would have reduced him forthwith to the position of his Greek counterpart. It is not correct to say that the king showed himself to the people only once in a month or two. The daily programme of the king, as given elsewhere in these pages, made definite provision for the king's daily personal investigation of important administrative questions relating to the people. During the second one-eighth part of the day, he was to look to the affairs of both the citizens and the country people ; and during the eighth division of the night, he was to receive the benedictions of the sacrificial priests, the high priest, and the teachers, and, finally, go to the court. When in the court, he was never to cause his petitioners to wait at the door. Kauṭilya warns that "when a king makes himself inaccessible to his people, and entrusts his work to his immediate officers, he may be sure to endanger confusion in business, and to cause thereby public disaffection, and himself a prey to his enemies."[116]

We may next examine the other part of the statement relating to the king's showing himself to the people once in one or two months. It appears that the learned Professor has confounded the directions given to spies, who were to verify the character of ministers, with what he would like to describe as a normal practice. In the various directions given to the spies is one which required of them the following: that they should investigate the character of each minister, one after another, saying on oath—"this king is unrighteous, well, let us set up in his place another king who is righteous, etc".[117] The various measures adopted by the ministers to avert calamities in which the king was involved, and which are too numerous to be cited here, likewise seem to have given an occasion for the above erroneous view that the king made himself inaccessible to the people. Indeed, in Book V, Chapter VI of the *Arthaśāstra,* which deals wtih the major topic of the consolidation of the kingdom and of absolute monarchy, and in which the measures taken by the ministers are described in detail, we have also the statement that the minister was to be the medium of communication between the various officials of the palace and the people.[118] All these measures refer to abnormal occasions, when the king was faced wtih great difficulties, and not to normal times which are mentioned in the daily programme of the ruler.

Justice to All. While it may be conceded that the Kauṭilyan king was an autocrat, it cannot be maintained that he was an unprincipled despot of the Greek or Persian type. Nothing proves this so much as the stress which Kauṭilya laid on the subservience of *daṇḍa* to *dharma* concerning which enough has been said in the earlier pages of this book.[119] Much more than that is the importance given to righteous conduct (*dharma*) in the state manual of Kauṭilya. No tyrant of the Greek model, if at all he ever lived in India in the days of Kauṭilya, would have organized his law courts in the manner we shall describe below. They were located in the cities of the *sangrahaṇa, droṇamukha,* and *sthānīya* types, and at all places where the district boundaries met.[120] The Kauṭilyan king, as we have already seen, was compelled to portion out justice according to the four sources of law, one of which was the Sacred law (*dharmaśāstra*) which he could not transgress. In this connection it was specially laid down by Kauṭilya: "As the duty of a king consists in protecting his subjects with justice, its observance leads him to heaven. He who does not protect his people or upsets the social order wields his royal sceptre (*daṇḍa*) in vain."[121] Even the commissioners of the districts, when discharging their duties, were ordered to take "into consideration (the socail position of) persons, the nature of the offence, the cause, whether grave or light (that led to the perpetration of the offence), the antecedents and the present circumstances, the time, and the place, and without failing to notice the equitable distinctions among the offenders, whether belonging to royal family or to the commercial people", were to determine the propriety of imposing the first amercement (i.e. a fine ranging from fortyeight *paṇas* to ninety-six (*paṇas*), or the middlemost amercement (i.e. a fine ranging from 200 to 500 *paṇas*), or the highest amercement (i.e. a fine ranging from 500 *paṇas* to 1,000 *paṇas*).[122] If the king himself punished an innocent person, he was to throw into water dedicating to god Varuṇa a fine equal to thirty times the unjust imposition, which was afterwards to be distributed among the Brahmans.[123]

Conclusion. When to the above considerations we add the cumulative evidence of the *Arthaśāstra* relating to the king's maintenance of peace and happiness among his people, to his patronage of industry and commerce, and to his efforts to protect the kingdom against the national calamities, we cannot help concluding that, however autocratic the king was in some matters, he could not, by the established precepts in the *dharmaśāstras* and the *nītiśāstras,* afford to play the part of the Greek tyrant without losing his kingdom and his life at the hands of the people.[124] Although the king was exalted, he was neither apart from or alien to the people, who were never mere objects of his will. On the other hand, he was only the aggregate of the people (*tat-kūṭasthāniyo hi svāmi-iti*) in the sense: "When the king is well off, by his welfare and prosperity he pleases the people ; of what kind the king's character is, of the same kind will be the character of his people ; for their progress or downfall, the people depend upon the king."[125] Herein we have the essential point of difference between the Kauṭilyan king and the Aristotelean tyrant.

CHAPTER III

THE KING ACCORDING TO THE BUDDHIST AND JAINA CONCEPTS

A. THE BUDDHIST CONCEPT OF KINGSHIP

1. SOURCES OF INFORMATION

(*a*) *Enumeration*

THE BUDDHIST concept of kingship is based mostly on the Buddhist works like the *Tripīṭaka* or *Three Baskets* (*Sutta, Vinaya*, and *Abhidhama*), and the *Jātaka Stories.* Of the *Nikāyas* or Collections comprising the *Sutta Basket,* the *Dīgha or Love,* the *Majjhima* or *Middle,* and *Samyutta* or *Miscellaneous* have some bearing on our subject. Amongst these the most important is the *Dīgha Nikaya* for our purpose. In addition to these works written in Pāli and in mixed Sanskrit, there are the Sanskrit works like Ārya Śūra's *Jātakamālā,* Aśvaghoṣa's *Saundara Nandam Kāvyam,* another work of his called *Buddhacarita,* and later works. Finally, there is a Tibetan work on the *Life of Buddha* which is a Vinaya compilation, and which is of some importance for our study.[126]

(*b*) *Chronology of the Sources*

Here it would be better if we noted the chronological periods to which these works could be assigned. There is no agreement among the Buddhist scholars as regards the exact date of the *Tripīṭaka work.* That famous work has been assigned to a period ranging from fourth century B.C. to fourth century A.D.[127] As regards the *Jātaka Stories,* Buddhist tradition relates that they were taken by the royal missionary Mahinda (Mahendra) to Ceylon during the reign of Aśoka in the middle of the third century B.C. But the *Jātakas* were known to the modern world only through the translations from Pāli into Singhalese in the fifth century A.D. On the value of these stories, Dr. Keith wrote thus: " . . . as folklore its (the *Jataka* book's) contents are often of undeniable age, but as Buddhist fables their antiquity is uncertain."[128] Aśvaghoṣa composed his works in the first century A.D. ; while Ārya Śūra's *Jātakamālā* has been assigned to the fourth century A.D.[129] The Tibetan version of the *Life of Buddha* in thirteen volumes (the *Dulva*) is a work of uncertain date which may be assigned to the later times.[130]

Before we pass on to the question of the Buddhist contribution to political thought, it may be necessary to point out here that, as is well-known, the Buddhists and the Jainas had led two vigorous protestant movements against Hinduism from the fifth century B.C. onwards. Both the Buddhists and the Jainas were essentially concerned with ridiculing the earlier Hindu political concepts, although that did not prevent them from either adopting or modifying to some extent the concepts of their predecessors.[130a] Neither of them could escape the influence of the ancient Hindu political thought, as will be shown below.

2. BUDDHIST CONTRIBUTION TO THEORY

The Buddhist contribution to the totality of Indian political thought may be studied from the following two points of view: firstly, what was their contribution to the purely theoretical aspect of government? And, secondly, whether and to what extent the greatest Buddhist Emperor, and one of the greatest in Indian history, followed the Buddhist principles as enunciated in some of the Buddhist texts cited above.

The Dīgha Nikāya. Of the earlier Buddhist works the *Dīgha Nikāya* is of particular interest in the sense that it gives us an insight into the fanciful picture which the Buddhists conjured up in connection with the primeval condition of human society. The occasion was the following: the Brahman Vaseṭṭha (Vasiṣṭha) inquires of Buddha if the claims of the Brahmans to supremoacy were just. "The Buddha, or rather the author, replied in the negative, and called a fanciful history to support his view." There was a long period of perfect happiness when men had nothing corporeal about them, and when the ethereal beings shone in splendour, enjoyed peace and effulgence. At last this age of pristine purity declined, the differences in sex and colour manifested themselves, mankind descended from the ethereal to the physical plane, and the age of rottenness began. The questions of food, drink, and shelter cropped up ; there was the need of some order ; and people entered into agreements among themselves and formed the family and private property, two of the greatest human institutions. With these there appeared greed, selfishness, and theft ; and in order to maintain the social order, once more the people assembled and agreed to choose a chief who was to maintain the social order and judicially inflict punishment. In return they would give him a part of their paddy. Thus arose the institution of kingship, and the rise to power of the Great Elect or the *mahāsammata.* He was the *rājan,* one who delighted the people, the leader and guide of the people. In the *Kuṭadanta Sutta,* the king supplies food, seeds, capital, and wages to the followers of the various occupations, according to their needs ; and thus frees them from want and disorder, increasing thereby his revenue and bringing peace and plenty to all.[131]

The Dulva. The Buddhist version of the origin of society and government is given in greater detail in the fifth volume of Tibetan version of the

Life of Buddha, the *Dulva,* in which the story of the restoration of the world after its destruction is given. In the region of the Ābhāsvara, the *devas* with ethereal bodies, free from all impurity, moved in perfect delight for ages. Gradually the solid earth was formed, the sun, the moon, and the stars appeared ; distinctions of time became perceptible ; differences in sex manifested themselves followed by feelings of love and conjugal relationship ; and differences in the quantity and quality of food appeared followed by the habit of sinful beings of constructing houses, of hoarding, and of quarrelling among men. At this stage the people assembled together, and chose the finest looking, the strongest, and the largest among them as a chief whom they made their lord over their fields, endowing him with the right of punishing those who deserved punishment and of recompensing those who deserved recompense. For this work of the king they gave him a portion of the produce of their fields and of the fruits they gathered. Because he received the homage of the many, he was called "honoured by the many, the *mahāsammata*" ; because he was the lord of the fields and protected them from harm, he was called "*kṣatriya,* or the protector of the fields" ; and because he brought happiness to mankind according to law, he was called "king or rāja". After this appeared caste distinctions based on occupations. The king was called "lord of the law", since on his decision depended the lawfulness or otherwise of the divisions of houses among the people. The third volume of the *Dulva,* in which divine inter-position is absent, narrates that the formation of the State was determined by reason and expediency, government deriving its validity from the consent of the governed. And it fulfilled certain definite needs.[132]

Criticism of the Dulva. The *Dulva* had improved upon the *Dīgha Nikāya* only in one or two respects. For instance, it relates that the king whom the people selected was the finest looking, the largest, the handsomest, and the strongest amongst them, who was known as their *mahāsammata.* This is in confirmity with the earlier injunction of Manu which we have cited already, viz., that the king was one amongst the many Kṣatriyas. Secondly, the *Dulva,* the king is called Kṣatriya because of his two functions—he protected the people, and was lord of their fields. In these two details, too, the Buddhist had not advanced on the earlier Hindu concept except in rejecting the Kṣatriya nature of the ruler and in relegating the claims of the Kṣatriyas to some recognition as a class from whom the king was chosen. And, thirdly, the *Dulva* gives the origin of the caste distinctions after the election of the king ; while the *Dīgha Nikāya* would place it before the election of the *mahāsammata.* But neither it nor the *Dulva* had materially added to the ancient Hindu concept of kingship except by way of indirectly ridiculing the claims of the Kṣatriyas to kingship. As to what extent the Buddhists were indebted to the ancient Hindus in regard to certain vital concepts is proved by the statements relating to the State in the third volume of the *Dulva* cited above. There is no divine disposition in the matter of the creation of the State ; on the other hand, reason and expediency alone determind the formation of the State.[133] The *Dulva* was merely echoing the ideas in Kauṭilya's *Arthaśāstra*, consciously or unconsciously, wherein, as we have already mentioned, *ānvikṣaki* was given the place of honour by placing it first in the list of four sciences (*ānvīkṣakī trayī-vārtā daṇḍanīti-ca-iti vidyāḥ*).[134]

Aśvaghoṣa. We may examine the remaining Buddhist works before finally assessing their importance in the history of Indian political thought. These are the works of Aśvaghoṣa and Ārya Śūra. The former relates in his *Saundara Nandam Kāvyam* that some princes, who had founded a city, discovered that they could not prosper without a king. The earth without a supreme lord was like the firmament without the moon. So the princes elected one amongst themselves, who was senior to them in age, discipline, and accomplishments, to be their sovereign. The king thus chosen had nothing of the divine ruler about him. He was to use the sceptre for the sake of virtue, and not for his own selfish gratification. He was to be the guide and teacher of his subjects.[135] Aśvaghoṣa's other work, the *Buddha Carita*, depicts the king as a mighty and glorious teacher of the people, who showed them the path to follow, who had numberless councillors, who admonished guilty persons with gentle words, and who took only one-sixth of the produce as the price of the protection he afforded to the people.[136]

Criticism of Aśvaghoṣa. Aśvaghoṣa had nothing new to say in regard to the theory of kingship. When he affirms that the ruler was to use his sceptre for the sake of virtue, and not for his own selfishness, he merely falls back upon the ancient Hindu concept. Likewise the rate of taxation was the accepted ancient rate. Even when he affirms that there was no divine element in the king, he does not improve upon Kauṭilya, who had made it clear centuries before the age of Aśvaghoṣa.

Ārya Śūra. Now there remains chronologically Ārya Śūra, whose work *Jātakamālā* ("Garland of Birth Stories") belongs to the northern Buddhist canon. It has been assigned to the fourth century A.D. It contains thirty-four stories. The king (who in that work was Bodhisattva) was distinguished by energy, discretion, majesty, and power. He was the embodiment of all the virtues pertaining to *dharma*, *artha*, and *kāma*. The Bodhisattva ruled the subjects like his own children. He gave succour to the needy and poor. None in his kingdom suffered from want of food, drink, dwellings, gold, etc. People declared by proclamation what they needed. He handled the sword and dispensed law, while discharging his duty of protection. He dealt with punishments without infringing righteousness. The Bodhisattva became a universal monarch in the tenth story. When his realm was afflicted by famine, his Brahman councillors advised him to propitiate the disaster by performing a Vedic sacrifice. To this he would not agree, since he would not sacrifice animals. Instead he sacrificed a thousand blackguards, and set an example to all to lead virtuous lives. He gave enough succour to those who were in want.[137]

Criticism of Ārya Śūra. As in the case of the other Buddhist authors, so in that of Ārya Śūra, there is nothing new or original in the Buddhist version of kingship. On the other hand, Ārya Śūra was more under the influence of the ancient Hindu than under that of the Buddhist ideas. This is proved by the following: he says that the king was the embodiment of the ideas of *dharma, artha,* and *kāma,* which, as Professor Beni Prasad rightly said, is "a reminiscence of Brahmanic thought".[138] In the second story he describes the king as pouring out gifts "not unlike a cloud of the Kṛita Yuga".[139] This was also a Hindu idea. Ārya Śūra then describes in the eighth story the king wielding his sword and meting out justice, while protecting the people. Here, again, he harks back on the Hindu idea of protection which has been fully described above. Ārya Śūra states in the same story that the king inflicted punishment without infringing righteousness.[140] This was nothing more than an unconscious repetition of the ideas of Manu and Kauṭilya. The king in the tenth story declined to sacrifice animals, according to the Vedic rites, but preferred to slay 1,000 human beings[141]—an act which was non-Hindu and anti-Buddhist. The fact that he performed a sacrifice is enough to show that he was inclined to follow his Brahman councillors who had, of course, never recommended human sacrifice. Finally, in the eleventh story he refers to the king's mastering the contents of the *trayī* (the triple *Vedas*) and metaphysics.[142] This stamps him more as a follower of Kauṭilya than as an original Buddhist writer.

Conclusion. The brief analysis of the Buddhist political thought made above enables us to dispose of the first point with which we started this part of our study, viz., to what extent it contributed to the totality of Indian political thought. It may be safely maintained that, so far as the ancient Indian political thought relating to kingship is concerned, the positive contribution of the Buddhists to it was practically nil, excepting the picture of an idyllic condition of society in the primeval ages before the formation of the State. On the negative side, the Buddhists denied that one of the duties of the king was to maintain the social order, and to see that the four *varṇas* and the four *āśramas* were confined to their respective spheres of duties. This was because the Buddhists disbelieved in caste which they said was useless for attaining *nirvaṇa.*[143] They further denied the restriction of kingship to the Kṣatriyas in the social order, for to them the Kṣatriyas were to be called so primarily because they looked after the fields. Thirdly, they disbelieved in the sanctity that surrounded the person of the king, whom they would describe only as one who was elected by common consent—*mahāsammata.* This would seem to rule out the possibility of heredity among the kings of the Buddhist mould. And, finally, the Buddhists denied that the sword could be used for punishment: it was merely an ornament so that other kings might wait on the king respectfully for orders.[144] While the Policy described in the *Jātakas* and other Buddhist books may perhaps serve to illustrate better the conditions prevailing in some of the Buddhist republican States, it is very doubtful if they help us to understand the concept of kingship, so far as the latter is concerned.

Our doubt is heightened by the elucidation of the other point, viz., to what extent the greatest of the Buddhist monarchies, Aśoka, put into practice the Buddhist theory of kingship. We shall see below in Part Six, that a careful comparison made between the *Arthaśāstra* of Kauṭilya and the Edicts of Aśoka, will reveal that there is little or no ground for maintaining that that great Emperor had given expression to the Buddhist principles in his royal proclamations. On the other hand, the available evidence will tend to prove that he followed closely the precepts of Kauṭilya.

B. THE JAINA CONTRIBUTION TO THE THEORY OF KINGSHIP

Jainism became prominent in the same century and in the same region as Buddhism, although in its origin was perhaps older than the latter. While the latter had to disappear from the land, Jainism continued to live in the country, its influence being restricted to certain regions.[145]

1. SOURCES OF INFORMATION

In Part Two above we had an occasion of referring to some of the post-Kauṭilyan Schools in which figure some Jaina authors. The remarks that were made in that context may be recalled in the present connection. The sources of information on our subject may be grouped thus: the first category is made up of the Jaina canonical works. Of these the most important for our purpose are the *Jaina Sūtras,* the dates of which are uncertain. Professor Hermann Jacobi wrote in 1894 that the exact date of the composition of the *Sūtras* cannot be satisfactorily solved. He said that most parts of the *Sūtras* were old ; that the redaction of the *Angas* took place at an early period (tradition placing it under Bhadrabāhu) ; and that, as related earlier in these pages, the first edition of the Jaina canonical works took place under the Venerable Devarddhigaṇi in A.D. 453.[146] Of the *Jaina Sūtras* the most important for our purpose are the *Uttarādhyāna Sūtra,* and, to some extent, the *Ācārāṅga Sūtra.* It will be seen below that Professor Beni Prasad's verdict on the *Jaina Sūtras* in general, that "to the student of governmental theory, the *Sūtras* as a whole are rather disappointing",[147] cannot be entirely endorsed.

The next category of Jaina works centres round the famous Jaina teachers Jinasenācārya and his pupil Guṇabhadra. The teacher began the work called *Ādipurāṇa,* and the pupil continued it under the name of *Uttarapurāṇa.* Jinasena was the preceptor of the Rāṣṭrakūṭa monarch Amoghavarṣa (A.D. 815-77), and the author of another work called *Pārśvābhyudaya.*[148] Guṇabhadra completed his work in A.D. 897 in the reign of the next Rāṣṭrakūṭa monarch Kṛṣṇa II.[149]

The third category of Jaina works centres round the figures of Somadeva Sūri and Hemacandrācārya. The former has already figured in Part Two above as one of the teachers of the Post-Kauṭilyan Schools. The latter was a celebrated author and teacher, who really falls outside the scope of our study which ends with A.D. 1000, but whom we cannot leave out of account in our appraisal of the Jaina contribution to the volume of ancient Indian thought. We shall have to briefly describe his life and mention his contribution to poltiical thought below.[150]

2. THE JAINA SUTRAS AND POLITICAL THEORY

The *Jaina Sūtras* may be said to be the earliest Jaina works throwing some light on the ancient Indian political thought. Of all the *Sūtras* the most important for our purpose are the *Uttarādhyāyana Sūtra* and the *Ācāranga Sūtra* (*Āyārangasuttam*). The former enlightens us on the concept of monarchy; and the latter, on one of the forms of State-lessness.

Uttarādhyāyana Sūtra. In this *Sūtra* there is an interesting description of the ideals of Kṣatriyahood and of the concept of monarchy. Concerning the former, we have the following in the conversation between Nami, who had descended from the world of gods, and was born as a man, and Indra, disguised as a Brahman. The occasion is one which refers to the complete retirement of Nami to the life of meditation, when he reached the excellent stage of *pravrjya* at which Indra drew his attention to the uproar in his erstwhile capital of Mithila, thus: "Erect a wall, gates, and battlements; dig a moat; construct *śataghnis,* then, you will be a Kṣatriya." Nami answered that his faith was his fortress; self-control, the bolt of its gate; patience, its strong wall; zeal, his bow; carefulness, its string; contentment, the top of the string; truth, the strength with which he pierced the arrow; penance, the foe's mail; and *karman* with which he could be a victor in the battle with *saṁsāra* or life. Indra then said: "Build palaces, excellent houses (*vardhamānagraha*), and turrets, thus will you be a Kṣatriya." Nami answered that he who built houses on the roads would certainly get into trouble; he may take up his lodgings wherever he wanted to go. Then Indra said: "Punishing thieves and robbers, cut-purses and burglars, you should establish public safety; thus will you be a Kṣatriya." Nami replied: "Men frequently apply punishments wrongly: the innocent are put in prison, and the perpetrator of the crime is at liberty." Indra answered: "O king, bring into subjection all princes who do not acknowledge you: thus will you be a true Kṣatriya." At this Nami replied that, although a man might conquer thousands and thousands of valiant foes, yet his greater victory would be when he would conquer himself. Indra then said: "Offer great sacrifices, feed Śramaṇas and Brāhmaṇas, give alms, enjoy yourself, and offer sacrifices: thus you will be a true Kṣatriya." To this Nami replied that he who controlled himself was better than he who gave every month thousands of cows. Then Indra said: "Multiply your gold and silver, your jewels and pearls, your copper, fine robes, and carriages, and your treasury; then you will be a true

Kṣatriya." Nami replied by saying that, since there was no end to man's greed, it was best to practise austerities. In the end Indra failed to entice the enlightened Nami with the pleasures, power, and privileges of the Kṣatriyas.[151]

In the above we have, among other things, the following concepts common among the Jainas, although not relished by the Jaina teachers: (*i*) that relating to the duty of a Kṣatriya (i.e. of a king), who was to fortify his capital ; (*ii*) that concerning his duty of punishing the wicked and of establishing public safety ; (*iii*) that relating to his subjugation of all recalcitrant chieftains, that is, his ambition as a conqueror ; (*iv*) that relating to his patronage of *dharma* in the shape of performing sacrifices and feeding Śramaṇas and Brahmans ; and (*v*) that relating to his increasing material wealth in the shape of gold, silver, jewels, etc. In all these details the *Jaina Sūtras* are in perfect agreement with what has been stated in the *Manusmṛiti*.[151a] Here we have, therefore, unanimity of opinion between the ancient Hindus and the Jainas on certain important aspects of kingship.

Even in regard to their concept of a universal monarch, the Jainas merely followed the earlier Hindu tradition. The ideal universal monarch was, of course, Bharata, the son of Vṛiṣabha. About Bharata it is said that after learning the pure creed, "which is adorned by truth and righteousness, he gave up Bharatavarṣa and all pleasures and entered the Order". The pure creed is defined thus: "A wise man believes in the existence of the soul ; he avoids the heresy of the non-existence of the soul ; possessing true faith one should practise the very difficult law according to the faith." Next to Bharata was Sāgara, who likewise gave up the ocean-girt Bharatavarṣa, and his unrivalled kingly power, and reached perfection through compassion. Then came Maghavan, a universal monarch of great power, who also gave up the sovereignty of Bharatavarṣa before taking to the life of the pure faith. Next came Sanat Kumāra, another *cakravartin,* who abdicated in favour of his son before practising austerities. Śānti, the next monarch, followed suit. He was succeeded by king Kunthu, the bull of the Aikṣvāku race, who likewise became a member of the Order. Then came Ara, who likewise gave up the sovereignty of the sea-girt Bharatvarṣa, before becoming perfect. Mahāpadma forsook his large kingdom, arms, war chariots, and exquisite pleasures before becoming likewise perfect. He was followed by Hariṣeṇa, Jaya, Daśārṇabhadra, the king of Daśārna, Karakaṇḍu of Kalinga, Dvimukha of Pāñcāla, Nami of Videha, Naggati or Nagnajñit of Gāndhāra, Udyāna of Sauvīra, Nandana of Kāśi, Vijaya, the son of Brahmaraja of Dvārakāvatī and Mahābala of Hastināpura.[151b]

The above long list of universal monarchs as given in the *Jaina Sūtras* proves, firstly, that the concept of a universal monarch was the same as that among the ancient Hindus ; and, secondly, that, as amongst the latter, there were many illustrious names in Jaina history of rulers who, after enjoying sovereignty for a long time, abandoned it for attaining salvation.

About one kind of political States, we have evidence in the *Ācāranga Sūtra* cited earlier while describing the forms of government. This is the *arājatā* form of State as exemplified by the States ruled over by the *gaṇas*, those ruled over by *yuvarājas*, those ruled over by two kings, those ruled over by *vairrājya*, and, finally, those ruled over by *vairuddha-rājya*.[151c] Here, indeed, we have a unique feature which, for want of a better title, may be called the negation of kingship. These names of the different types of anarchical States are not met with, excepting the States ruled over by the *gaṇas*, in ancient Hindu literature. Perhaps in this detail the Jainas added to ancient Indian political thought in the sense that they at least gave some idea of anarchical States, thereby completing the picture of the forms of government in ancient India.

3. THE THEORIES OF THE JAINA TEACHERS JINASENA, SOMADEVA SURI, AND HEMACANDRA

(a) *Jinasenācārya*

This learned Jaina *guru* may be said to have been the clearest exponent of Jaina idealism, in particular of the Jaina theory of cycles. We may study him under the following heads: (*i*) his concept of the origin of society or the theory of cycles; (*ii*) his idea of the origin of lordship or the theory of patriarchs or Kulakaras; (*iii*) his view of castes; and (*iv*) his theory of *daṇḍa* and of government.

(*i*) *The Jaina Theory of the Origin of Society or the Cycles of Ages*

The Jaina lore which was reduced to writing in the fifth century A.D. in the Council of Valabhi, presided over by the venerable Devarddhigaṇi, stretched back to centuries, and was anterior to the Buddhist literature which it rivals both in variety and vastness. We have to assume that the Jaina versions of the origin of society and of kingship were of some antiquity; and, that, therefore, they have some claim to recognition at our hands, although it cannot be determined as to when exactly they originated. One of the clearest presentations of the Jaina theory of the origin of society is that given by Jinasena in his *Ādipurāṇa*, and continued by his eminent pupil Guṇabhadra in the latter's *Uttarapurāṇa*.[152]

Jinasena visualized the origin of society amidst surroundings which were of pristine purity. The times fell from a state of virtue and happiness, the decline being gradual and extending over millions of centuries. Up to this point Jinasena is like the Buddhists and the ancient Hindus, but from now onwards he evolves his own theory. He advocated a two-fold cycle of progressive evolution (*utsarpiṇī*) and regressive evolution (*avasarpiṇī*) which rotate one after another like the two successive fort-nights. Each of these cycles consists of six ages or time-divisions which are the following: bliss-bliss (*suṣamā-suṣamā*) ; bliss (*suṣamā*), bliss-sorrow (*suṣamā-duhṣamā*), sorrow-bliss (*duhṣamā-suṣamā*), sorrow (*duhṣamā*), and sorrow-sorrow (*duhṣamā-duhṣamā*). We have in these six ages the gradual linking up of the preceding age with the following one in such a manner as to indicate the evolution of society from an age of idyllic felicity to one of misery and pain. The cycles vary in duration so as to permit longer spans of happiness. The exact computation of the ages is a feat of mathematical skill. As to what exactly Jinasena had in mind when he pictured the first stage will be clear when we note the descriptoin of the men and women in that age. They enjoyed a span of existence which cannot be adequately computed. Hence, so far as their age is concerned, it was aeons. They had a golden complexion, their countenance being as beautiful as their virtue was perfect. There was no question of their earning bread, since they spent their lives in idyllic surroundings which yielded Kalpadrumas or radiant trees which, at the merest prompting of the heart, yielded every thing they desired—from houses to clothes, from flowers to food.

The above age of indescribable happiness gradually declined in the second cycle ; and in the third cycle to a still lower level when there took place some profound changes in the world. Among these was the appearance of the sun and the moon in the heavens, and the consequent alarm and surprise which they caused among men. These latter then went to Pratiśruti, the one person who was pre-eminent in that society of perfect equality and happiness. Here we are introduced to the theory of the Kulakaras or patriarchs described below. Jinasena, when describing the *avasarpiṇī* or regressive evolution, would refer them to the Āryakṣetra of the Bharatavarṣa, that is, probably to the Āryāvarta of the Hindus, or the region lying between the Himalayas and the Vindyas, perhaps excluding the eastern parts of India and the south-western parts of Sind and Surāṣṭra.[153] It was here in the Āryakṣetra that Jinasena placed the life history of the Kulakaras to whom we may now turn.

(*ii*) *The Concept of the Origin of Lordship or the Theory of Patriarchs or Kulakaras*

Pratiśruti was the first Kulakara or patriarch in a line of fourteen patriarchs. These were called by four different names, according to the functions performed by them: Manus, because they knew and taught the people the means of their livelihood ; Kulakaras, because they taught the Āryas how to live together ; Kuladharas, because they established many families ; and Yugādhipuruṣas, because they were the embodiments of the age-cycles.

The first Kulakara explained that the light of the Kalpa trees was fading away, and the plants had, therefore, become visible. There was no cause of fright among the people. At this the latter felt reassured, and profusely thanking and praising him, in obedience to his wishes, returned to their homes. But the countless aeons rolled on, and other more alarming and profound changes came into view. The stars appeared in the heavens, and the mountains and rivers became visible on earth. Animals which till now had remained docile became more ferocious. The innocent people were seized with alarm at the growing sense of insecurity around them. At this stage there appeared the other patriarchs, who taught men how to adapt themselves to the changing environment. These new teachers told men how to protect themselves from ferocious brutes, how to tame and break elephants, horses, and other animals, how to climb mountains, and how to cross rivers by means of canoes. In the meanwhile the Kalpa trees were steadily declining in number. Over the remaining Kalpa trees the people, who had now become selfish, began to quarrel with ever increasing ferocity.

From the fifth patriarch order comes out of chaos. He was Sīmantaka, who marked the trees and fixed their bounds. His successor Sīmandhara demarcated them still more clearly. During the age of the eleventh patriarch, Nābhi, the Kalpa trees altogether disappeared. Clouds and rain came for the first time ; and the earth began to shoot forth ordinary trees, herbs, flowers, and fruits. The people approached Nābhi and inquired of him as to what they were like—whether beneficial or injurious. He gave them a long discourse along with a demonstration of their value ; and taught them the art of cooking the products of the earth but warned them against poisonous plants. This brought about a complete transformation in the life of man.

(*iii*) *The Concept of Castes*

It was left to the last of the patriarchs, Vṛiṣabhadeva, to establish the six occupations relating to the martial, agricultural, literary, artistic, commercial, and industrial aspects of man's life. He instituted the three castes of the Kṣatriyas, the Vaiśyas, and the Śūdras. In each group were men who were best fitted to fulfil the object of the caste. The Śūdras were further subdivided into two sections—the washermen, barbers, etc., and the rest. The latter were again subdivided into the touchables and the untouchables. Vṛiṣabhadeva planned towns, built villages, grouping them into circles of eight hundred, four hundred, and two hundred. He apportioned the earth among four great kings, each of whom being the lord of a thousand smaller monarchs under him.

(*iv*) *The Theory of Daṇḍa*

It was now when the political institution of government was established that Vṛiṣabhadeva founded the institution of punishment and imprisonment. The justification for creating punishment was that hitherto men had obeyed when they were rebuked mildly; but now they ceased to listen to mild rebuke: chastisement of a severer type was needed, and that was in the shape of punishment. As to how punishment came gradually to assume its full shape, we are informed in the *Ādipurāṇa* that, with the increased wickedness of man, the patriarchs progressively increased their penalties for offences. Thus, the first five patriarchs and their successors had merely prescribed for offenders the punishment of crying alas (*hā!*) to which the next five added that of warning (*mā!*) against the repetition of the offence; the last four prescribed for offenders the punishment of crying shame (*dhik!*); while it was only Bharata who, on realizing that men could not be weaned from crimes. instituted corporal punishment, imprisonment, and even death.[154]

Thus was the transformation of the earlier *bhogabhūmi* or the land of enjoyment into *karmabhūmi* or the land of action made complete, and coercive punishment, so essential in preserving social order, introduced in the history of man. It was only in this way that the strong could be prevented from swallowing the weak, as is indicated by the proverbial law of the fishes.[155]

(*v*) *The Concept of Government*

So that we might complete the picture of Jinasena s idea of government, we may summarize his views on this subject as given in the *Ādipurāṇa*. In that work he enumerates the king's obligations to the subjects thus: the obligation to preserve the *kula* (family), meaning perhaps, as Professor Ghoshal rightly interprets, that the king had to preserve the family customs (*kulanyāya*) of his own and other families. Then, there was the obligation to divide society into two classes—those who should be protected, and those who were to be made to devote themselves to their professions. The next obligation of the king was to follow the law (*dharma*) and lead others on the same path. The fourth obligation was to inflict punishment. Then came the king's obligation to preserve his subjects like a cowherd preserving his herd of cattle. In this connection Jinasena elaborates his theory of *daṇḍa,* and says, among other things, that punishment should not be severe but appropriate to the crime committed. The comparison between the cowherd and the king is worked out in a detailed manner by Jinasena. He mentions in this context the king's cherishing his hereditary troops (*maulam tantram*), and the ruler's strengthening himself within the sphere of the Circle of States (*maṇḍala*). The last function of the king was the preservation of prosperity (*samjña-sattva*). Jinasena states in this connection that the king should cherish the good (*śiṣṭa*), who lived according to their occupations, and punish the wicked (*duṣṭa*), who committed crimes.[156]

(*vi*) *Criticism of Jinasena*

Excepting for the picture of pristine purity which Jinasena has drawn in his *Ādipurāṇa,* there is hardly any detail in his theory that could be said to be at variance with the ancient Hindu concept of kingship. Indeed, it might not be erroneous to state that Jinasena, inspite of his strong Jaina bias which allotted certain duties to the Kulakaras in an age of idyllic happiness, only helps to confirm the view that he merely restated the ancient Hindu theories in a Jaina garb. Even his Kulakaras were probably no other than the Hindu *devas* under a new denomination. What stamps Jinasena as a firm believer in the ancient Hindu ideals is the following: he appears to have upheld the caste system, although it was so repugnant to the Jainas. In his caste system, the Brahmans, of course, found no place of importance. This is evident when we see what Bharata, the son of the last of the Kulakaras and the first of the Tirthakaras, did in reorganizing society. Bharata assumed the status and powers of a world-ruler (*cakravartin*), and of the founder of families (*Kuladhara*). He selected a number of persons from the three castes, grouped them together into a fourth caste and called it Brahman. The avowed policy of the Jainas of putting the classes of society in contra-position to that prevailing amongst the Hindus, is seen in the manner Jinasena would create the four castes. Vṛiṣabhadeva, as is related in the *Ādipurāṇa,* instituted the order of the Kṣatriyas with the weapons in his hands, brought the Vaiśyas into existence with his thighs, indicating the ways of travel, and created the Śūdras with his feet. It was left to Bharata to bring into existence the Brahmans by teaching the *Śāstras* with his mouth, and in the manner indicated above. All the four castes, we may note by the way, had professed originally Jainism but later on when they fell into "falsehood", abjured Jainism and embraced Hinduism. This was foretold to Bharata in an ominous dream.[156a] There was nothing evolutionary in the creation of society by Bharata or by his father, Vṛiṣabhadeva ; on the other hand, Jinasena endeavoured in a clumsy manner to indicate the origin of society which millenniums before his time had already been well established and adequately described.

Jinasena likewise believed in touchability and untouchability, as these two terms are known now-a-days. That is, he made provision in his concept for social distinctions of the extreme type, like those prevailing among the Hindus.

His idea of having circles of 800, 400, and 200 villages was nothing but an adaptation of what is given in the *Manusmṛiti,* thus: "Let him (the king) place a company of soldiers, commanded (by a trusty officer), in the midst of two, three, five, or hundreds of villages, (to be) a protection of the kingdom. Let him appoint a lord over (each) village, as well as lords of ten villages, lords of twenty, lords of a hundred, and lords of a thousand."[157]

Jinasena's theory of punishments was likewise a repetition of the ancient Hindu concept of *daṇḍa* reinterpreted in terms of Jainism, but almost in the manner of the ancients. His idea of the king's cherishing the good (*śiṣṭa*), who lived according to their respective professions, and of punishing the wicked (*duṣṭa*), who committed crimes, was borrowed entirely from the *Manusmṛiti* where, as we have already seen, this concept is described in full.[158] When Jinasena says that punishment should not be severe but in proportion to the crime committed, he was not enunciating a new principle but merely repeating an old one as given in the *Manusmṛiti*.[159] In the same manner, Jinasena's statement that the king's obligation was to divide society into two classes—those who should be protected, and those who were to be made to devote themselves to their profession, was an awkward rendering of the same idea as given in the *Manusmṛiti*, thus: "The king has been created (to be) the protector of the castes (*varṇa*) and orders, who, all according to their rank, discharge their several duties."[160]

When Jinasena writes about the rapacity of men and the wickedness of human nature by giving the example of the fishes, he is certainly not adding to political theory but repeating a well known illustration concerning which enough has been said in these pages.

Then, again, when Jinasena states that the king should follow *dharma*, and lead others on the same path, he merely repeats the ancient Hindu ideals about which, too, we have mentioned above.

Jinasena's comparison of a king with a cowherd is not a new idea but is the old one which the ancients have so clearly expressed. Indeed, it is involved in the whole theory of protection which has been discussed in detail in these pages.

When Jinasena states that the king should cherish his hereditary troops, he was unconsciously repeating one of the injunctions of Kauṭilya relating to the army which is described in detail in connection with the Elements of the State in this book.

Finally, Jinasena's statement that the king should strengthen himself in the sphere of the Circle of States was a mere repetition of the *rājamaṇḍala* or *maṇḍala* theory of Manu and, in particular, of Kauṭilya.[161]

An Estimate of Jinasena. If Jinasena's theory of kingship, therefore, was modelled on that of the ancient Hindus, where exactly is the claim of that learned Jaina teacher for recognition at our hands? We began the criticism of his theory by saying that, excepting for the picture of a period of pristine glory, he had practically nothing new to say. It is here in drawing that picture that Jinasena's uniqueness is seen. Firstly, like all other Jainas, and to some extent like the Buddhists, he divested the socio-political institutions he had conjured up of all divinity, and attributed their growth to changes in environment,[162] although in doing so he could not help giving his Kulakaras a touch of the divinity in the manner of the Hindus. But it must be admitted that, in his ideal picture, the influence of the environment was much more than that of inspiration. Secondly, Jinasena did not consider the economic and political institutions connoted by the term *vārtā* and *daṇḍa,* as being essential to the advancement of happiness. Here he differed from the ancient Hindus to whom there could be no material progress and no happiness without the development of *vārtā* and *daṇḍa.* And, thirdly, according to the ancient Hindus, the king was to create an environment in which the people were to bestir themselves in order to attain progress. That is, the initiative for development was to come from the people themselves, the king being merely the repository of all might which was to be used against the wicked. But in the ideal picture of Jinasena, the patriarchs or Kulakaras led men from the aeons of perfect happiness into progress in the economic and political fields. That is, the primary function of the king was to guide and educate men in all spheres of human activity. That was precisely what Vṛisabhadeva did, as is related in the *Ādipurāṇa.*[163] In Jinasena's idealistic picture, therefore, the men are shorn of their initiative, being merely led like sheep in a flock by their shepherd, the king. The best comment of Jinasena's idealism was made by scholars of his own faith like Somadeva Sūri who, only a century after Jinasena, discarded the latter's idealism for the realism of Kauṭilya.[164]

What demolishes the theory of Jinasena, particularly in regard to one fundamental idea which lay at the root of kingship as conceived of by him, is the behaviour of his royal patron Amoghavarṣa. The ruler was to be the embodiment of all virtues, and was to direct his untiring energy to the protection of his people. *Ahiṁsā* or non-violence was to be the essence of State action ; and the universal conquest of the world by *ahiṁsā* was the aim of Jinasena's political philosophy. His royal patron, Amoghavarṣa, may be said to have directed his full attention to the protection of his subjects, like any other Hindu monarch. But it is questionable whether he observed the fundamental principle of his preceptor that *ahiṁsā* should be the keynote of his royal policy. Two facts are enough to disprove Jinasena's view on this matter. King Amoghavarṣa, at the very commencement of his reign, destroyed his enemies and reconquered his kingdom which had fallen off or tottered.[165] There is nothing objectionable in this: it was his foremost duty to have put down his enemies and to have regained his lost dominions. But it was certainly not in the spirit of Jinasena's teaching. Further, king Amoghavarṣa's method of conquering his enemies violated the Jaina principle of *ahiṁsā,* particularly when he sent a chieftain, named Bankeśa, to uproot the ancient province of Gangavāḍi.[166] Whether our conclusion is correct or not, it is clear that Jinasena's picture of a ruler's conquering the land around him by *ahiṁsā* was disproved even in his own days.

(*b*) *Somadeva Sūri*

(*i*) *His Life*

This Jaina writer stands in contrast to Jinasenācārya. The first point of difference between them has been mentioned just above. He was as much a realist as Jinasena was an idealist. Like the latter, Somadeva Sūri, too, served under a Deccan ruler; but Somadeva Sūri's patron, unlike Jinasena's, was a minor feudatory called Yaśodhara, under the powerful Rāṣṭrakūṭa monarch Kṛṣṇa III. Somadeva wrote two works—one called *Nītivākyāmṛita* ("The Nectar of Political Maxims"), and the other *Yaśastilaka*. In the latter work he states towards its end that it was finished on the 13th Caitra when 881 years of the Śaka king had elapsed, the cyclic year being Siddhārtin, during the rule of Yaśodhara in the reign of the latter's suzerain Kṛṣṇarājadeva.[167] Somadeva Sūri, therefore, lived in A.D. 959, just about a century after Jinasenācārya. He was a great dialectician, a poet of considerable merit, and a master of Jaina theory and tradition.[168] The *Nītivākyāmrita* is in the *sūtra* form, and the *Yaśastilaka*, in the *campū* style. The former work contains a more comprehensive treatment of government and allied subjects than the latter which is referred to in the former work. It is only in the third *āśvāsa* of the *Yaśastilaka* that he describes king Yaśodhara, and mentions a number of political topics. His third work *Trivargamahendramātalisañjalpa*, being a dialogue between Indra and his charioteer Mātali on *dharma, artha,* and *kāma,* refers to Politics.[169]

(*ii*) *Somadeva's Contribution to Political Thought: He deifies the State*

Unlike any previous writer, Somadeva Sūri deified the State in the first *sūtra* of the *Nītivākyāmrita,* thus: *atha dharmārtha phalāya rājyāḥ namaḥ* (now, to the State, the source of *dharma* and *artha,* Salutation!). Somadeva thus anticipated by almost a millennium the Hegelian concept of the State's being the chief good of human existence.[170] The fact that, instead of saluting the Tīrthakaras, as any orthodox Jaina author would have done, Somadeva opened his work with a salutation to the State, suggests that he was more inclined to lay stress on logic and reasoning than on mere sentiment and loyalty, while dealing with the material side of man's existence. In this Somadeva Sūri followed more Kauṭilya, who had, as we have demonstrated enough in these pages, laid all emphasis on *ānvīkṣakī,* than Jinasena, who had soared high in the sphere of idealism.

Knowledge is the Prime Requisite. Both according to Kauṭilya and Somadeva, knowledge was essential for an intelligent study of the State. Indeed, according to the latter, it was the prime requisite in worldly affairs. He even went to the extent of maintaining that anarchy was preferable to a rule by a king, who was uninstructed in the art of government. A perverse king was worse than a calamity; while a worthy king, who was the repository of all goodness and merits, was extolled by all wise men.[171] Somadeva had thereby merely reinterpreted Kauṭilya's verdict on an erring king, "who is bent upon doing what is against science", and who "brings about destruction to himself and his kingdom by maladministration".[172]

Theory of Protection and Punishment. What was the end of the State? To this question Somadeva would answer in the Kauṭilyan manner that prosperity was the end of the State. But prosperity was impossible without protection which, in its turn, could not be maintained without punishment. It is here we see how Somadeva completely repudiates Jinasena's idealistic theory of guidance. In order to understand Somadeva's concept of punishment, we shall follow him in his description of the king and of the latter's functions. The king was a god on earth, who bowed only to his ancestors and *gurus.* His prime duty was protection. Somadeva asks a pertinent question—How can he be a king who does not protect his subjetcs (*sa kiṁ rājā yo na rakṣati prajāḥ*)?[173] Protection surpasess all royal duties in importance and religious merit. The protection of the subjects is the king's sacrifice (*prajā pālanaṁ hi rājño yajñaḥ*).[174] And when the king protects his people justly, the skies pour forth all desires (*nyāyataḥ paripālaka rājñī prajānāṁ kāma dughā diśaḥ*).[175]

But protection was impossible without being strict in regard to sinners and criminals. They were obstacles in the way of the happiness of the people. No mercy was to be shown to them; they were just to be weeded out. The king was not to condone crime; he had to repress it. If the king did not put down the wicked, he was on the road to perdition. This could be done only by wielding *daṇḍa* or punishment which was to maintain the social order. Indeed, the king was to set before himself, like the God of Death, the task of inflicting punishment, so that people did not transgress their prescribed limits, and so that they could attain the three ends of life. Punishment was to be used by the king for the protection of his subjects, and not for amassing money. In this Somadeva merely followed the *smṛiti* tradition and the views of Kauṭilya which we have described at length in these pages.[176]

Ministers. On ministers and on the need of the king to consult them and to listen to their advice, Somadeva again followed closely Kauṭilya. The ministers were to be men of character, free from sensual pleasures, reliable and courageous, but they were never to be foreigners. As regards deliberation, secrecy was to be maintained. The king was not to be satisfied with a single minister but with many.[177] Somadeva dwells on the problem of the ministers also in his *Yaśastilaka.*[178] The details about the ministers given in his two works, *Nītivākyāmṛita* and *Yaśastilaka* are far too many to be narrated here; but they are, on the whole, in agreement with those given in Kauṭilya's *Arthaśāstra.*[179]

Army. On the next important element of the State, the army, Somadeva has something to say. Army officers were not to be consulted on questions of policy as they would be only too ready to cling to war to solve them. Further, if they were to be placed in control of civil policy, they might grow proud and powerful.[180] The army was the main support of sovereignty. Of the many branches of the army, the elephants were the most important. Unlike Kauṭilya, who relied on mercenary troops, Somadeva declared that hired troops were not of much value. Those soldiers were the best who were tied to the sovereign by bonds of sentiment. Everywhere the soldiers put forth their best, not because of prospective monetary gain (by way of a share in the booty), but because of the honour expected from their royal master. That is, Somadeva gave expression to the concept of patriotism which in those days centered round the personality of the ruler. But he was careful in warning the king that the latter should be punctual in paying his forces. What was the use of a cloud if it did not bring forth rain in time?[181] While Somadeva, on the whole, followed the precepts of Kauṭilya in regard to the army, his predilic-tion to troops attached to the ruler by bonds of sentiment, and his insistence on prompt payment of the forces by the king, marked him to some extent from the Mauryan Prime Minister.

Diplomacy and Foreign Policy. But in the delineation of the foreign policy he followed implicitly Kauṭilya.[182] The army was certainly useful but diplomacy was not less important. Allies were to be secured in as many ways as possible.[183]

The King is the State. Somadeva identified the State with the king to such an extent that he maintained that the safety of the monarch was the safety of the State. He said that a people may prosper, but if they had no government, they would come to no good. He firmly believed in protecting the king from all kinds of temptations, including those from women whom he unduly condemned as being a source of evil and a bundle of craft and hypocrisy. The young princes were to be respectful to their parents even in thought, otherwise they would fall into misery.[184] Somadeva's attitude to women was illiberal when compared with the saner views of Kauṭilya on the same subject. As regards his precautions to guard the king against temptations, and his precepts concerning the young princes, they were less perfect than those of Kauṭilya.[185]

Taxation. Somadeva's views on taxation were after the ancient Hindu model. He warns the State against over-taxation, since taxation was to be in proportion to the resources of the people. Expenditure was never to exceed income. The rate of taxation was one-sixth of the produce which was to be levied only in return for the protection given by the king to the people. The king was to receive not only one-sixth of the produce of land but a corresponding portion of the increase in the spiritual merit of the people, as a result of protection, which he expressed thus: *paripālako hi rājā sarveśām dharmāṇām ṣaṣṭam-āpnoti.*[186] The reader will recollect all that has been stated in the previous pages of this work from the *Manusmṛiti* and the *Arthaśāstra* of Kauṭilya in order to see how closely Somadeva followed the ancient Hindu precepts in regard to taxation.

(iii) Criticism of Somadeva Sūri

Notwithstanding the fact that he borrowed profusely from Kauṭilya, sometimes even without acknowledging his indebtedness to the latter,[187] yet it is possible to assign to him a place in the history of ancient political thought. Firstly, he re-enforced the principles of Kauṭilya as no other writer, excepting Kāmandaka, had done, thereby proving that Kauṭilya's theories had definitely come to stay not only in the Hindu but in the Jaina world as well. That is, Somadeva's testimony establishes beyond dispute the oneness and continuity in ancient Indian political thought. Secondly, Somadeva showed that the idealistic stand taken by Jinasena was too impracticable to be followed. Indeed, he seems to have cast to the winds Jinasena's theories. He took his stand on the realistic grounds of Kauṭilya. Thirdly, Somadeva like a true Jaina eliminated all privileges, although he recognized caste and upheld adherence to hereditary professions, and was even prepared to regard the Brahmans with some consideration. But he was unequivocal in maintaining the equality of all before the law.[188] In this regard he again followed Kauṭilya, who had unmistakably enunciated the policy of treating all citizens alike by the State, as has been amply shown in these pages. And, finally, Somadeva went a step further than Kauṭilya in idealizing the State. By anticipating Hegel's idea of the State to some extent, Somadeva had vindicated the position of the Indian political thought in the international field. Somadeva's deification of the State, and the practically negligent part which the individual played in his concept of the State, forestalled in a measure the celebrated nineteenth-century political thinker G. W. F. Hegel who, in his *Philosophy of Right,* taught that the State was the real person, its will being the manifestation of perfect rationality. In his own way Somadeva, too, had stated, after the model of Kauṭilya, that knowledge was the prime requisite in worldly affairs, thereby emphasizing the importance of rationality. When Hegel maintained that the "State is the divine idea as it exists on earth", he seemed to express Somadeva's dictum that the king is a great god to whom all excepting ancestors and teachers had to bow. And in the statement of Hegel that "all the worth which the living being possesses—all spiritual reality—he possesses only through the State", he had admirably conveyed the idea of Somadeva expressed in the salutatoin to the State cited above, viz., *atha dharmārtha phalāya rājyāḥ namaḥ*! But Somadeva stopped with this, while Hegel developed his philosophical theory of the State transcending the limits of Somadeva.[189] Nevertheless the tenth century Indian political thinker, inspite of his shortcomings, has earned his place in the history of Indian political thought by adhering to the principles of Kauṭilya, and in the history of international political thought by deifying the State.

(c) *Hemacandrācārya's Contribution to Political Thought: a Parenthetical Study*

(i) *His History*

Notwithstanding the fact that Hemacandrācārya falls outside the scope of our study, yet it is essential that we should briefly allude to his life and theories in order to understand how Jinasena, who was discarded by Somadeva Sūri, was vindicated by Hemacandrācārya. There is hardly a greater, and in some sense, a nobler name in the entire range of Jainology than that of Hemacandrācārya, more popularly called Hemācārya. He lived from A.D. 1089 till A.D. 1173. His royal patrons were, firstly, the famous Siddharāja Jayasingha of Gujarat (A.D. 1094-1143); and then, the latter's successor, the celebrated Kumārapāla (A.D. 1143-74). Hemacandra was an encyclopaedist in addition to being a great philosopher and a profound scholar both in Sanskrit and Prakrit. We shall not be concerned with his numerous works on grammar, prosody, genders, local and provincial words, rhetoric, and history; but shall confine ourselves to the first book of his *Triṣaṣṭhisālākapuruṣacaritra* or *Lives of Sixty-three Jaina Saints*, called *Ādīśvaracaritra*, and to his *Laghu Arhannīti* which "draws freely upon its Brahmanical predecessors".[190]

(ii) *Hemacandra follows Jinasena*

In the *Ādīśvaracaritra* he harked back to Jinasena to some extent but could not help following the earlier Hindu writers on Polity in certain other respects. In his account of the origin of the social and political order, Hemacandra treads in the footsteps of Jinasena. The above work is more after the pattern of the *Ādipurāṇa* inasmuch as it introduces the reader to the twelve-spoked Wheel of Time with its two great divisions or cycles of *avasarpiṇī* and *utsarpiṇī*. The *avasarpiṇī* cycle had six ages in a descending order, namely, Pure-Bliss (*ekānta-suhṣamā*), Bliss (*suhṣamā*), Bliss-Sorrow (*suhṣamā-duhṣamā*). Sorrow-Bliss (*duhṣamā-suhṣamā*), Sorrow (*duhṣamā*), and Pure-Sorrow (*ekānta-duhṣamā*). *The utsarpiṇī* cycle had the same spokes but in the reverse order. The succession of the six ages in the *avasarpiṇī* cycle was attended by a gradual decline in the longevity and health of man, in his food, and even in the *Kalpavṛikṣa* (or the Wish-giving Tree). It was in the third age of the *avasarpiṇī* cycle that the hero Vimalavāhana and his wife were born as twins in the southern part of of the Bharatavarṣa in the Jambudvīpa, in the region between the Ganges and the Sindhū.

Vimalavāhana and his wife were the progenitors of a line of chiefs.

When in the course of time, the Wish-giving Tree diminished in potency, one of the twins (born in the manner of the progenitors) wished to acquire a *Kalpavṛikṣa* at which the other afflicted twins made Vimalavāhana their chief with ruling authority. Then Vimalavāhana divided the Wish-giving Tree among his followers, thereby originating the institution of property. He instituted the penalty of *hākāra* for punishing any one who crossed the boundary from desire for another's Wish-giving Tree. Gradually with the still declining morality, the fourth descendant from Vimalavāhana instituted the penalty of *mākāra,* and the sixth descendant, the penalty of *dhikkāra.* In the days of the seventh patriarch called Nābhi, they made, at his desire Ṛiṣabha their king, who introduced the institution of punishment in its civil and criminal aspects.[191]

Notwithstanding the above approach to the problem of society and punishment by Hemacandra in the manner of Jinasena, we may observe that that great author was far too practical a teacher to be carried away by mere idealism. It was not that he had discarded Jinasena's theory. But he was, as will be seen presently, a realist who could not live in a world of theory unrelated to facts. Indeed, it is doubtful whether any Jaina teacher exercised such a powerful sway over his royal patron for the good of the people as Hemacandra did in the twelfth century.

(iii) Hemacandra follows Hindu Authors

He drew freely from the earlier Hindu works on Polity. He pays greater attention than any of his predecessors of the Jaina faith to civil and criminal law; recommends the use *sāma, dāna, bheda,* and *daṇḍa* much in the manner of the earlier Hindu political thinkers; and fearlessly enjoins that war should be conducted at all cost, declaring boldly that the Jaina scruple of regarding the destruction of life caused in war, would not debar him from advocating such a view.[192] That Hemacandra followed Kauṭilya in some respects is clear when we observe what he states about a conquered country. After the king has won a victory, he should grant amnesty to the followers of the conquered king, and taking into consideration their wishes, install a scion of the subjugated family, who was devoted to himself. The new ruler as well as the conquered subjects should be gratified with rewards.[193] This may be compared with what Kauṭilya says in Book XIII, Chapter V entitled the Restoration of Peace in a Conquered Country, in which he gives in detail the measures which the king had to take in order to restore peace in a conquered country.[194]

(iv) Hemacandra's Personal Influence

Jinasena had merely written about the conquest of the world by *ahiṁsā.* But Hemacandra made it the foundation of his royal master

Kumārapāla's policy. It is impossible to describe in detail the incalculable good this great Jaina *guru* did for Gujarat and India. We can at best only give a few of his many activities. He prevailed upon the king, Kumārapāla, to forego the claim of the State to the property of those who died issueless. Under his advice, the same monarch gave up the use of flesh and wine, ceased to take pleasure in the chase, and by beat of drum forbade throughout his vast kingdom the taking of life. King Kumārapāla withdrew from hunters, fowlers, and even fishermen, their licenses, and compelled them to adopt other avocations. He ordered that only filtered water was to be given to the animals employed in the royal army. When a Bania of Sāmbhār, which distant part of Rajputana had been conquered by king Kumārapāla, had been caught killing a louse, he was brought to Aṇahilavāḍa (modern Pāṭan, the capital, in North Gujarat) in chains, his property was confiscated, and it was used for constructing a building for a louse temple or *yūkā-vihāra* in the captial. On another occasion, when a woman of Nador in Marwar had offered flesh to a field-god (*kṣetrapāla*), her husband was put to death by Khelna, the chief of Nador, in order to escape the wrath of king Kumārapāla.[195] Truly had *ahimsā* become the pivot of State policy under the guidance of Hemacandrācārya, who thus raised Gujarat to the premier position in the land ; and made it possible for that province to give to India eight centuries later a moral guide, who was to make *ahimsā* the basis of his great movement that was to end the career of the most powerful Colonial Empire in the twentieth century.

CHAPTER IV

THE ELEMENTS OF THE STATE (*Contd.*)

B. MINISTERS: INTRODUCTION

THE MINISTERS formed the next important element in the State. We may study this element under the following heads: (1) the need of ministers; (2) their qualifications; (3) their composition; (4) their responsibility; (5) their salary; (6) their relationship with the judiciary; (7) their relationship with the administration; (8) public service conduct rules; and (9) welfare schemes.

Before we explain the necessity for having ministers, we might observe that the minister, who was the second important element in the State, was connoted by the technical terms *amātya, saciva,* and *mantri,* although sometimes a distinction seems to have been made between them. Of these the last two were more or less synonyms, while, according to Kauṭilya, the *amātyas* were, on the whole, inferior to the *mantris*. This is inferred from his statement that the king "Having divided the spheres of their powers and having definitely taken into consideration the place and time where and when they have to work, such persons shall be employed, not as councillors (*mantriṇaḥ*), but as ministerial officers (*amātyāḥ*).[196] It is also proved by the provision which Kauṭilya made to test the character of the ministerial officers which will be cited below in the sub-section on Public Service Conduct Rules. For our purpose we may consider all the three categories of officers as being of the same executive importance.

1. THE NEED OF MINISTERS

The *Manusmṛiti* gives the need of ministers thus: "Even an undertaking easy (in itself) is (sometimes) hard to be accomplished by a single man; how much (harder is it for a king), especially (if he has) no assistant (to govern) a kingdom which yields great revenues?"[197] Kauṭilya expressed the same idea in the progressive surroundings in which he lived in the following manner: "Sovereignty (*rājatva*) is possible only with assistance. A single wheel can never move. Hence he shall employ ministers and hear their opinion" (*sahāyasādhyaṁ rājatvaṁ cakraṁ-ekaṁ na vartate kurvīta sacivān-tasmāt-teṣāṁ ca śriṇūyān-mataṁ*).[198] Herein we have the principle that government should be conducted, not by the will of a solitary person, as in the case of a Greek or Persian tyrant, but with the aid of councillors whose advice was to be respected by the sovereign.

2. THEIR QUALIFICATIONS

The *Manusmṛiti* had laid down the qualifications of the ministers ; but between them and those mentioned in the *Arthaśāstra,* there was much difference, showing in this, as in other cases, a progressive evolution of political thought in ancient India. Manu had enjoined that the king was "to appoint seven or eight ministers whose ancestors have been loyal servants, who are versed in the sciences, heroes skilled in the use of weapons, and descended (from) noble families, and who have been tried". Then, again, he states that with "the most distinguished among them, a learned Brāhmaṇa, let the king deliberate on the most important affairs which relate to the six measures of royal policy".[199]

Kauṭilya is more explicit on their qualifications. He writes thus:

> Native, born of high family, influential, well trained in arts, possessed of foresight, wise, of strong memory, bold, eloquent, skilful, intelligent, possessed of enthusiasm, dignity, and endurance, pure in character, affable, firm in loyal devotion, endowed with excellent conduct, strength, health, and bravery, free from procrastination and ficklemindedness, affectionate, and free from such qualities as excite hatred and enmity—these are the qualifications of a ministerial officer (*amātyasampat*).[200]

The additional qualifications to those given by Manu, as laid down by Kauṭilya, were the following—that they should be natives (*jānapado abhijātaḥ*), possessed of enthusiasm, dignity, and endurance (*pratipattit māna-utsāha-prabhāva-yuktaḥ*), and firm in loyal devotion (*dhṛiḍhabhaktiḥ-śīla*), all of which reflect the changed times in which Kauṭilya lived. In the same chapter he gives further details as to how these qualifications were to be ascertained. It speaks volumes for the Mauryan Prime Minister that he could with such acumen lay down the hardest qualifications which any progressive modern government could have prescribed for recruiting the highest officials of the State ; and that he could, at the same time, make ample provision for finding out whether the prospective ministers really possessed them.

3. THE COMPOSITION OF THEIR COUNCIL

Kauṭilya's radical manner of thinking is seen in the rules he laid down concerning the council of ministers (*mantripariṣad*). While Manu, according to Kauṭilya, had advocated a council of twelve ministers (in the *Manusmṛiti* to which Kauṭilya always refers but which has been lost to us). Bṛihaspati, sixteen, and the School of Uśanas, twenty, Kauṭilya maintained that it should consist of as many members as the needs of the ruler's dominion required (*yathāsāmarthyaṁ iti Kauṭilyaḥ*).[201] There is some latitude in this injunction, since the number of ministers comprising their council increased or decreased in number, with the increase or decrease in the number of problems facing the State.

4. MINISTERIAL RESPONSIBILITY

Manu had laid down a general principle that the ministers were to be jointly and severally consulted by the king in the following statement: "Having (first) ascertained the opinion of each (minister) separately and (then the views) of all together, let him do what is (most) beneficial in his affairs."[202] In the last sentence Manu, no doubt, admitted that the sovereign alone was ultimately responsible for his policy. This was but natural because in a monarchy, the final voice in all matters lay with the king.

As to when the king was to take the advice of his ministers is related thus in the *Manusmṛiti*: the king was to entrust all official business relating, for instance, to the six measures of royal policy to the ministers chosen by him, and after "having his final resolution with him, let him (the king) afterwards begin to act".[203] In a later context, in the same work it is stated that, after certain specified ceremonies, the king was to enter the hall of audience. "Tarrying there, he shall gratify all subjects (who come to see him by a kind reception) and afterwards dismiss them ; having dismissed his subjects, he shall take counsel with the ministers. Ascending the back of a hill, or a terrace, (and) retiring (there) in a lonely place, or in a solitary forest, let him consult with them unobserved."[204] It cannot be made out why Manu advocated the retirement of the king to a hill or a terrace or a lonely place or a solitary forest for consulting with his ministers, when he certainly had a well guarded privy chamber and an audience hall, where he could as well have conducted the State business.

There is no such incongruity in Kauṭilya, whose description of the Business of the Council of Ministers (*mantrādhikāraḥ*) appears to be almost modern in its contents and nature:

> Having gained a firm hold on the affection of both local and foreign parties, both in own and enemy's State, the king shall proceed to think of administrative measures (*kṛitaḥ-svapakṣa-parapakṣopagṛihaḥ-kārya-ārambhān-cintayet*). All kinds of administrative measures are preceded by deliberations in a well formed council (*mantra-pūrvāḥ-sarvārambhāḥ*). The subject matter of a council shall be entirely secret, and deliberations in it shall be so conducted that even birds cannot see them ; for it is said that the secrecy of counsels was divulged by parrots, mainas, dogs, and other low creatures of mean birth. Hence without providing him-

self with sufficient safeguard against disclosure, he (the king) shall never enter into deliberations in a council. Whoever discloses counsels shall be torn to pieces.

Kauṭilya then explains what is meant by the disclosure of counsels and change in attitude and countenance that would help in the detection of the leakage of news. The maintenance of the secrecy of council matters and keeping guard over officers, who had taken part in the deliberations over it, was to be strictly observed till the time of starting the work so considered approached.

After enumerating the causes of the betrayal of counsels, Kauṭilya makes a comparative estimate of the views of his predecessors in regard to the importance of taking counsel jointly or severally by the king with his ministers. The earlier thinkers whom he cites in this context are Bharadvāja, Viśālākṣa, Parāśara, and Piśuna. The divergent views which they maintained, help us to form an idea of the intense agitation in their minds in regard to this vital problem, and the practical ways they suggested to solve it.

According to Bharadvāja, the king was to singly deliberate over secret matters, "for ministers have their own ministers, and these latter have some of their own; this kind of successive line of ministers tends to the disclosure of counsels". Hence only those who were employed to carry out the works, which the king had in view, shall know it, "either when it is begun or when accomplished". But Viśālākṣa rejected this theory, and upheld the view that "no deliberation made by a single person will be successful". Since the nature of the work which a sovereign had to do was to be inferred from the considerations of both the visible and invisible causes, it was only the ministers who could make the decisions. Hence the sovereign should deliberate along with ministers. "He shall dispise none, but hear the opinions of all. A wise man shall make use of even a child's sensible utterance." Parāśara called this "ascertaining the opinion of others" but not keeping counsels. He was for the king's asking for the opinion of the ministers on a given project, and for doing as they recommended. Piśuna would not rely on all the ministers; he recommended that the sovereign should consult only such of the ministers who were "capable of giving decisive opinion regarding those works about which he seeks for advice".

Kauṭilya rejected all this argumentation regarding seeking advice as being "infinite and endless". According to him, the sovereign was to consult only three or four ministers, since "consultations with a single (minister) may not lead to any definite conclusion in cases of complicated issue"; while deliberating with two ministers, the sovereign may be "overpowered by their combined action, or imperilled by their mutual dissension". Hence Kauṭilya advocated that the king should consult three or four ministers in order to arrive at satisfactory results. Consultations with ministers more than three or four meant a good deal of trouble, and the possibility of secrets leaking out. After stating that the king shall consult three or four ministers, Kauṭilya recommended below in the same passage that the sovereign "in accordance with the requirements of place, time, and nature of work in view", if he thought it proper, should "deliberate with one or two ministers, or by himself", thereby finally agreeing with the earlier precept of Manu.

Joint Responsibility. Before we proceed further with the question of the council of ministers as given by Kauṭilya, we may observe that, while discussing the views of his predecessors, the great Prime Minister, in the above passage, appears to have rejected the earlier theory of the ministers being responsible jointly and severally, as maintained by Manu, Viśālākṣa, and Parāśara, and to have endorsed the view of Piśuna of having a smaller number of ministers with whom the king was to consult. But in a later passage in the same chapter, Kauṭilya advocated the theory of the king's consulting jointly or individually with the ministers. "The king may ask his ministers for their opinion, either individually or collectively, and ascertain their ability by judging over the reasons they assign for their opinions." That Kauṭilya clearly distinguished between the council of ministers and the ministers themselves is further proved from the concluding passages in the same chapter in which he writes: "In works of emergency, he (the king) shall call both his ministers and the assembly ministers (*mantriṇo-mantripariṣadaṁ ca*), and tell them of the same."[205] In other words, while Kauṭilya was for the ruler's consulting with the ministers either in their individual or collective capacity, he would hold none but the king himself responsible for all final decisions. In this he followed evidently the injunctions of Manu cited above.

But in a later context Kauṭilya seems to have advocated what may be construed as the joint responsibility of the ministers. This was when the ministers in charge of finance had to submit their accounts at the end of every financial year. All the ministers (who are now called *mahāmātras*) shall, he writes, together narrate the whole of the actual accounts pertaining to each department. If any one of them (or their clerks) was of undivided counsel, or kept himself aloof, or uttered falsehood, he was to be punished with the highest amercement (i.e. a fine ranging from 500 to 1,000 *paṇas*).[206] If the finance ministers were thus jointly held responsible for submitting their accounts, it cannot be understood why Kauṭilya should have denied the same privilege to the other ministers. One cannot help feeling that the great Prime Minister is not very clear on this important question of ministerial responsibility. Indeed, if we were to take into account the severe restrictions imposed on the *amātyas* described below under the sub-title of the Examination of the Daily Work of the Ministerial Officials, it appears as if we have to doubt any such thing like even independent initiative on the part of the ministerial officials!

As to how the sovereign was to be guided by the deliberations of the council of ministers, is given by Kauṭilya thus: "He (the ruler) shall do whatever the majority (*bhūyishṭāḥ*) of the members suggest, or whatever course of action leading to success (*kāryasiddhikaraṁ vā*) they point out".[206a]

The sphere of their works is given thus in the *Arthaśāstra*: "Those ministers shall have to consider all that concerns the parties of both the king and his enemy. They shall also set themselves to start the work that is not yet begun, to complete what has been begun, to improve what has been accomplished, and to enforce strict obedience to orders" (*niyoga-sampadaṁ*).[206b]

5. SALARY OF MINISTERS

Before we pass on to the question of the relation between the ministers, the executive, and the judiciary, the salary paid to the ministers may be noted. Kauṭilya made provision for the payment of salaries to all the State servants. One-fourth of the total revenue of the State was set apart for this purpose. The reason why liberal salaries were given to the State servants is given in the statement that the sovereign "should look to the bodily comforts of his servants by providing such emoluments as can infuse in them the spirit of enthusiasm to work". But this did not mean that the ruler could "violate the course of righteousness and wealth". The highest salary of 48,000 (*aṣṭacatvārivimśatsahasrāḥ*) *paṇas* was paid to the minister (*mantri*).[207] Opinion is divided among scholars as to whether this high salary was per annum or per mensem. Dr. N. N. Law and Professor Rangaswami Aiyangar maintained that it was per month ; while Dr. R. Shama Sastry stated it was per annum.[208] In view of what we shall say below regarding the financial year as instituted by Kauṭilya, it appears that the view that the salaries were per annum seems to be correct. Whether it was per mensem or per annum, it is clear that the highest salary was paid to the ministers in Kauṭilya's State.[209]

6. MINISTERS AND THE JUDICIARY

Since the ministers formed an essential part of the executive, we may in this section see the relation of the executive with the judiciary. Kauṭilya differentiated the judges from the ministers not only in his description of their respective duties but even in the matter of providing separate chambers for them, when he wrote that the court and the offices of the *mahāmātras* shall be built in a separate locality in the capital city (*pṛithak-dharmasthīyam mahāmātrīyaṁ*).[210] Notwithstanding this he included the ministers (*amātyas*) amongst the judiciary when he stated that what may be called the itinerant justices should be made up of the following— three members acquainted with the Sacred law (*dharmasthas*), and three ministers (*amātyas*), who were to carry on the administration of justice, as related earlier, in the cities of *sangrahaṇa*, *droṇamukha* and *sthānīya*, and at places where districts met (*dharmasthāḥ-trayaḥ-trayo' amātyā janapada - sandhi - sangraha - droṇamukha - sthānīyeṣu - vyāvahārikānarthān kuryuḥ*).[211]

As to what was meant by the cities of the *sangrahaṇa, droṇamukha,* and *sthānīya* types, is related in an earlier context where is stated the following: that a *sthānīya* (a fortress of that name) was to be set up in the centre of eight hundred villages, a *droṇamukha* in the centre of four hundred villages, a *khārvāṭika* in the centre of two hundred villages and a *sangrahaṇa* in the midst of a collection of ten villages.[212] From the gradation given above, it is evident that the smallest city was the *sangrahaṇa* above which was the *khārvāṭika* above which was the *droṇamukha* at the top of which was the *sthānīya* which was the biggest unit of civic life. Kauṭilya's injunctions seem to imply that the itinerant justices were to hold their sessions in only three out of the four categories of cities—the *sangrahaṇa,* the *droṇamukha,* and the *sthānīya.* As to why the *khārvāṭika* centre was not included in the list of cities where the administration of justice was to be carried out by the itinerant justices, cannot be understood.

The association of the ministers with the judiciary in the *Arthaśāstra* of Kauṭilya is to be traced to the *Manusmṛiti,* wherein it is stated: "Whatever matter his ministers or the judge may settle improperly, that the king himself shall (re-) settle and fine (them) each one thousand (*paṇas*)."[213] Manu herein recommended the punishment of judges for negligence. In other cases he imposed the severest punishment on corrupt officials including the judges. If the royal officials took money from suitors, their whole property was to be confiscated, and then they were to be banished.[214] Those who were entrusted with the safe custody of lost property, if found guilty of stealing it, were caused to be slain by an elephant.[215]

Kauṭilya was even more stringent in his attitude to unworthy judges. When a judge threatened, browbeat, sent out, or unjustly silenced any one of the disputants in his court, he was first of all to be punished with the first amercement (i.e. a fine ranging from forty-eight *paṇas* to ninety-six *paṇas*). If he defrauded or abused any one of them, the punishment was to be doubled. If he did not ask what ought to have been asked, or asked what ought not to have been asked, or left out what he himself had asked, or taught, or reminded, or provided any one with previous statements, he was to be punished with the middlemost amercement (i.e. a fine ranging from 200 to 500 *paṇas*).

Kauṭilya's next paragraph regarding the behaviour and attitude of judges, contains some admirable injunctions which one wishes were made applicable to the modern times:

> When a judge does not inquire into necessary circumstances, inquires into unnecessary circumstances (*deśa*), makes unnecessary delay in discharging his duty, postpones work with spite, causes parties to leave the court by tiring them with delay, evades or causes to evade statements

that lead to the settlement of a case, helps witnesses by giving them false clues, or resumes cases already settled or disposed of, he shall be punished with the highest amercement (i.e. a fine ranging from 500 to 1,000 *paṇas*). If he repeats the offence, he shall both be punished with double the fine and dismissed.[216]

The above passages proves that, among other things, the judges were as much under the State as the ministers. The concept of justice in the *Arthaśāstra* is given thus: "Judges shall thus settle disputes free from all kinds of circumvention, with mind unchanged in all moods of circumstances, pleasing and affable to all."[217]

7. MINISTERS AND ADMINISTRATION

(*a*) *Administration in General: the Theory of Co-ordinated Administration*

We have to revert to the *Manusmṛiti* in order to get some idea of the theory of administration. "In governing his kingdom let him (the king) always observe the following rules: for a king who governs his kingdom well, easily prospers." Manu then enjoins, as seen earlier, that the king was to place a company of soldiers commanded by a trusted officer, in the midst of two, three, five, or hundreds of villages, for the protection of the kingdom. A lord (or governor) was to be appointed over each village, other lords over groups of ten, twenty, a hundred, and a thousand villages. "The lord of one village himself shall inform the lord of ten villages of the crimes committed in his village, and the ruler of ten shall make his report to the ruler of twenty." The ruler of twenty was to report all such matters to the lord of a hundred villages, and the lord of a hundred villages shall himself give information to the lord of a thousand. Adequate provision was made for the maintenance of these governors; and they were all placed under the jurisdiction of a minister, who was to inspect their work. In each town the king was to appoint one Superintendent of All Affairs, "elevated in rank, formidable, resembling a planet among the stars". That high dignitary was "to personally visit by turns all those (other officials)" and to "properly explore their behaviour in their districts through spies appointed to each".[218]

In the above we have the clearest exposition of the theory of co-ordinated administration in which the lowest unit of administration is connected with the highest in such a manner that every unit, while working within its sphere, is connected with every other unit, and the whole chain of units connected with the highest executive, viz., the king, through the superintendent. It has to be studied along with the theory of the elements or *prakṛitis* in relation to the State discussed in the previous pages of this book. The keynote of the theory was the close co-operation of the different executive units in a manner to secure the protection of the kingdom.

(b) *Financial Year and Annual Auditing*

Kauṭilya perfected the above theory by knitting together all the departments of the State into a centralized administrative machinery. The minute care which he bestowed on this side of the question is seen in the provision he made for the exact working days in a year, and for the commencement of the financial year. Three hundred and fifty-four days and nights, he ordained, formed an official year. Work done by government servants, especially of a profitable nature, was to be "paid for more or less in proportion to its quantity at the end of the month of Āṣāḍha (about the middle of July)". But the work done during the intercalary month was to be separately calculated.[219] That the financial year ended with the close of the month of Āṣāḍha is further proved by the regulation that "accounts shall be submitted at the close of Āṣāḍha", that is, at the end of the financial year;[220] while the examination and verification of accounts began on *vyuṣṭa* or the New Year's day.[221] The financial year was called the royal year (*rājavarṣaṁ*).[222]

(c) *Departments under Government*

The administration, according to Kauṭilya, was divided into departments which have already been mentioned above. It appears that there were in all twenty-eight departments in the Mauryan Government.[223]

A picture of the departmental organization is given in the chapter on the Business of Keeping Accounts in the Office of the Records Keeper (*akṣapaṭale gāṇanikyādhikāraḥ*), some aspects of which have already figured earlier in these pages. The office was really that of the Superintendent of Records, or, in modern language, of the Director of Archives, or Keeper of Records. It was to be so constructed as to face either the north or the east. It contained seats kept apart for clerks, with shelves of accounts books well arranged.[223a] The importance of writers is given in a later context, thus: only those were to be appointed as writers or clerks (*lekhaka*), who possessed ministerial qualifications, who were acquainted with all kinds of customs, smart in composition, good in legible writing, and sharp in reading.[224] The accountants and writers were paid each 500 *paṇas*.[225]

They were to enter the various topics relating to the several departments in a detailed manner given by Kauṭilya. Over them were the chief superintendents, who were authorized to look into all details relating particularly to the revenue and expenditure of the State. The accountants were to present their accounts in time, that is, as related above, on the New Year's day. If they failed to do so, and if they did not bring their account books along with the net revenue, they were fined ten times the amount due from them! If a superintendent of accounts (*kāraṇika*) did not at once proceed to receive and check the accounts, when the clerks (*kārmika*) were ready, he was punished with the first amercement. If, on the other hand, the clerks were not ready, they were fined double the first amercement. But if an accountant was not ready with the table of daily accounts, he was to be given one month's time to prepare it. After the lapse of that time, he was to be fined at the rate of 200 *paṇas* for each month during which he delayed submitting the accounts. If any clerk violated or deviated from the prescribed form of writing accounts, entered what was unknown to him, or made double or treble entries, he was to be fined twelve *paṇas*.[226] In addition to these permanent members of the staff, there were several temporary heads in each department.[227]

(*d*) *The Civil List*

The following salaries were paid, perhaps annually, to the officials: the highest salary of 48,000 *paṇas* was paid, as seen earlier, to the minister, and likewise to the sacrificial priest (*ṛitvik*), the teacher (*ācāryāḥ*), the high priest (*purohita*), the commander of the army (*senāpati*), the heir-apparent, the mother of the king, and the queen. Next came the door-keeper, the superintendent of the harem (*antarvaṁśika*), the commander (*praśaṣṭṛ*), the collector-general, and the chamberlain, each of whom received 24,000 *paṇas*. The third category was made up of the prince (*kumāra*), the nurse of the prince, the chief constable (*nāyaka*), the officer in charge of the town (*paura*), the superintendent of law or commerce (*vyavahārika*), the superintendent of manufactories (*karmāntika*), the members of the council of ministers, and the superintendents of the country parts and of boundaries, each one of whom received 12,000 *paṇas*.. The fourth category comprised chiefs of military corporations, chiefs of elephants, horses, chariots, and cavalry, and commissioners (*pradeṣṭārah*), who received each 8,000 *paṇas*. Below them came the superintendents of infantry, cavalry, chariots, and elephants, and guards of timber and elephant forests, who received each 4,00 *paṇas*. The sixth category was made up of the chariot driver, the physician of the army, the trainer of horses, the carpenter (*vardhaki*), and those who reared animals (*yoniposaka*), who were paid each 2,000 *paṇas*. The seventh category included the fortune-teller, the reader of omens, the astrologer, the reader of the *Purāṇas*, the story-teller, the bard (*māgadha*), the retinue of the priest, and all superintendents of departments, all of whom received each 1,000 *paṇas*. The eighth category was made up of trained soldiers, and the staff of accountants and writers, who received each 500 *paṇas*. The ninth category comprised musicians (*kuśīlava*), who received each 250 *paṇas*. Of these the trumpet blowers (*tūryakara*) received twice as much wages as others. The tenth category was made up of artisans and carpenters, who received each 120 *paṇas*. The eleventh category including servants in charge of quadrupeds and bipeds, workmen doing miscellaneous work, attendants upon the royal person, bodyguards, and the procurer of free labourers, received each sixty *paṇas*. The twelfth category comprising the honourable playmate of the king, (*āryayukta*), the elephant-driver, the sorcerer (*māṇavaka*), the miners of mountains (*śailakhaṇaka*), all kinds of attendants, the teachers and learned men received each an honorarium ranging from 500 to 1,000 *paṇas*, according to their merit. The thirteenth category was made up of ambassadors (*dūta*). Of these those of middle quality received each 10 *paṇas* for every four *yojanas* they travelled ; and twice as much when they travelled from ten to 100 *yojanas*. The fourteenth category included the person who represented the king in the *rājasūya* and other sacrifices. He got three times the salary that was paid to others who were equal to him in learning ; while the charioteer of the king (in the sacrifices) received 1,000 *paṇas*. The fifteenth category was made up of spies of the types of the fraudulent, the indifferent, the householder, the merchant, and the ascetic. The spies were paid (each) 1,000 *paṇas*. Servants leading the spies were paid 250 *paṇas*, or in proportion to the work done by them. Finally, the last category comprised the village servants (*grāmabhṛitaka*), fiery spies (who were different to the preceding five kinds of spies), poisoners, and mendicant women, who received each 500 *paṇas*.[228]

(*e*) *City Administration*

(*i*) *The Gopas and the Sthānikas*

We get a glimpse of the administrative set-up of a city in the chapter on the Duty of a City Superintendent. The Superintendent of the City (*nāgaraka*) was of the status of the Collector-General. He looked after the capital. Under him worked the Gopa, who was to look after ten, twenty, or forty households. The Gopa was to know not only the caste, *gotra*, name, and occupation of both men and women in their households, but also ascertain their income and expenditure. In other words, the Gopa was to collect the census of the men, women, and children in the city, and to prepare the statistics of the income and expenditure of the families.

The same duties were entrusted to the Sthānikas but with reference to the accounts of the four quarters of the capital.

(*ii*) *Their Powers*

The powers of both the Gopas and the Sthānikas were wide and great. They were authorized to receive information from the managers of charitable institutions (*dharmāvasthinaḥ*) about any heretics (*pāśaṇḍa*) and travellers arriving to reside in their institutions. The managers of charitable institutions were to allow ascetics and men learned in the *Vedas* to reside in such places only when those persons were known to be of reliable character. Artisans, merchants, vinters, sellers of cooked flesh and cooked rice, prostitutes, and physicians—all came within the jurisdiction of the Gopas and the Sthānikas.[229]

State Control over the Physicians. The State control over the physicians might be of some interest to the modern world. Any physician who undertook to treat in secret a patient suffering from ulcer or excess of unwholesome food or drink, as well as the master of the house, where such treatment was attempted, were declared innocent only when the physician and the master of the house reported about the same to the Gopa or the Sthānika; otherwise both of them were equally guilty with the sufferer. Kauṭilya appears to have gone beyond even modern regulations relating to the medical profession in the matter of controlling the physicians.

State Control over the Masters of Houses. Not only were the masters of houses responsible thus to the State in the above matter; they were to report about strangers arriving at or departing from their houses. If they failed to do so, they were guilty of the offence of theft, etc., committed during the night. Even during safe nights (i.e. nights when no thefts, etc., seem to have been committed), they were liable to a fine of three *paṇas* for not making such a report. The masters of the houses, therefore, performed a part of the duties which managers of hotels are required to perform in the modern times.

Loiterers at nights, persons suffering from wounds, or ulcers, or possessing destructive instruments, or tired of carrying head loads, timid persons, or those indulging in too much sleep, or those fatigued, or strangers who were found inside or outside the capital, temples of gods, places of pilgrimage or burial grounds—any one of these or all of them—could be caught hold of by wayfarers on the high road or those who walked on footpaths, and evidently brought to the presence of the Gopa. Spies were also empowered to perform the same duty. Indeed, they were even authorized to search for suspicious persons in the interior of deserted houses, in the workshops, in the houses of vinters and sellers of cooked rice and flesh, in the gambling houses, and in the abode of heretics.

In addition to the Superintendent of the City and the Gopa under him, we have to assume that there were other officials like the officer in charge of the town (*paura*), the chief constable (*nāyaka*), the superintendent of gambling (*dyūtādhyakṣa*), and the accountants and writers, who are mentioned in different contexts.[230]

(*f*) *Civic Life*

(*i*) *Dangers of Fires: Precautions against Them*

The civic life of the people was to a certain extent regulated by the State. These ordinances are to be read along with those referring to the masters of houses mentioned just above, and to the right of free movement commented upon in the previous pages of this book. Owners of houses could carry on cooking operations outside their houses. This meant that permission from the Gopa had to be previously obtained for this purpose. It was incumbent upon them to have the following ready with them—five water pots (*pañca ghaṭīnām*), a *kumbha* (a vessel of that name), a *droṇa* (a water tub made of wood and kept at the door of each house), a ladder, an axe (to cut off beams), a winnowing basket (to blow off smoke), a hook (such as was used for driving an elephant (to pull down burning door panels), pincers (*kacagrāhiṇī*) (to remove hay stack), and a leather bag (*dṛiti*). If a houseowner failed to keep the above articles ready with him, he was to be fined one-fourth of a *paṇa*. It was also required of them to remove thatched roofs. Those who worked by fire (like the blacksmiths) were to live together in a single locality. Indeed, the duties of the householders did not end with these: each houseowner was to be ever present at night at the door of his house. It cannot be made out to what length of time he was subjected to this restriction.

The State had recourse to the above precautions evidently to prevent the danger of fires which seems to have been rather common in the days of Kauṭilya. We infer this not only from the above regulations, particularly those referring to the maintenance of the nine articles mentioned above, but from what follows in the *Arthaśāstra*. Vessels filled with water were to be kept in thousands in a row without confusion not only in big streets and at places where four roads met but also in front of the royal buildings (*svagṛihapradvāreṣu gṛihasvāmino vaseyuḥ asaṁpātino rātrau rathyāsu kaṭavrajāḥ-sahasraṁ tiṣṭheyuḥ catuṣ-pathadvāra-rāja parigriheṣu ca*). Any houseowner, who did not run to give help in extinguishing the fire of whatever was burning, was to be fined twelve *paṇas* ; and a renter (*avakrayi*, i.e. a tenant) not running to extinguish a fire was to be fined six *paṇas*. And, furuther, whoever carelessly set fire to a house was to be fined fifty-four *paṇas* ; but he who intentionally set fire to a house was to be thrown into the fire!

One wonders what necessitated the above detailed regulations regarding the outbreak of fires in houses. We cannot make out whether most of the people lived in thatched houses ; or whether it was common to set fire to one's neighbour's house ; or whether houses were built of inflammable materials ; or whether it was an age when setting fire to houses, like theft and gambling, was indulged in as a profitable pastime until caught by law. At any rate their fire brigade was composed essentially of citizens, one of whose duties was to prevent the spread of fire in their own localities.

(*ii*) *Sanitation*

Equally stringent were the regulations regarding sanitation and cleanliness. Whoever threw dirt in a street was punishable with a fine of one-eighth of a *paṇa* ; whoever caused mire or water to collect in a street was fined the same amount; but whoever committed the above offences in the king's highway (*rājamārga*) was punishable with double the above fines. Kauṭilya's regulations were more modern in this respect than those which govern our civic life today.

That the State took scrupulous care of the sanitation of the cities and towns is further proved by the regulations that whoever excreted faeces in places of pilgrimages, reservoirs of waters, and in royal buildings were to be punished with fines ranging from one *paṇa* in the order of the offences; but when such excretions were due to the use of medicine or to disease, no such punishment was to be imposed.

Moreover, the defilement of a city with the carcass of animals such as a cat, a dog, a mongoose, and a snake was punishable with a fine of three *paṇas*; of animals such as an ass, a camel, a mule, and cattle, with a fine of six *paṇas,* and a human corpse, with a fine of fifty *paṇas.* If a dead body was taken out of a city through a gate other than the usual or prescribed one, or along a path other than a prescribed one, those who carried it were punishable with the first amercement; while the guards of the gate, who permitted them, were fined 200 *paṇas.* A fine of twelve *paṇas* was imposed on those who interred or cremated a dead body in places other than the prescribed ones.

(iii) Movements of Citizens Restricted

Regulations governing the movements of citizens mentioned in this connection are to be read along with those narrated under Civil Rights in Part Four above. Several restrictions were placed on citizens moving between six *nāḷikas* ($2\frac{2}{5}$ hours) after the fall of night and six *nāḷikas* before dawn, when a trumpet was sounded prohibiting the movements of people. No movement of people was permitted in the vicinity of royal buildings and the defensive fortifications of the capital. Here Kauṭilya seems to have forestalled modern regulations of the same nature. We have mentioned above under Civil Rights the categories of people who were exempted from restrictions for moving at night time in certain specified circumstances. If severe penalties were imposed on citizens for violating these regulations, equally severe punishment, including death, was inflicted on watchmen at night time, who contravened law.

(iv) The City Superintendent Not Free from Punishment

The Superintendent in charge of the City (*nāgaraka*) could not claim any immunity in regard to his duties. If he did not report to the king any nocturnal nuisance of an animate or inanimate nature (*cetanācetana*) which had occurred in the city, or showed carelessness in discharging his duty, he was to be punished in proportion to the gravity of his crime. What this punishment exactly was is not related by Kauṭilya. Among the other duties of the City Superintendent were the following: a daily inspection of the reservoirs of water, of roads, of hidden passages for going out of the city, of forts, of fort walls, and of other defensive walls. He was also to keep in his safe custody whatever things he came across as lost, forgotten, or kept behind by others. We are to presume that he had likewise the duty of freeing the prisoners on certain days and occasions mentioned elsewhere in this work. The categories of such prisoners have also been described in the same connection. Since this duty of releasing the prisoners was included among the other duties of the City Superintendent, we are justified in assuming that they formed a part of his work.[231]

8. PUBLIC SERVICE CONDUCT RULES

(a) Character Test

We have already seen that Kauṭilya laid down severe regulations relating to the qualifications of ministers.[232] To these he added the measures through which the purity or impurity in the character of ministers could be tested. These ministers are explicitly stated to have been in charge of government departments of an ordinary nature. In ascertaining their purity or impurity, the king was to be assisted by the prime minister (*mantri*), the high priest (*purohita*), and the spies (*satri*). It is here that we see clearly that the *mantris* were superior to the ministerial officers of the status of *amātyas,* since the character and work of these latter were examined by the king along with the *mantri.*

The four methods by which the character of the ministers was tested were the following: the religious allurement, the monetary allurement, the amôurous allurement, and the allurement under fear, all of which are explained in detail by Kauṭilya. Those ministers whose character was tested under the religious allurement, and who were found fit, were employed in civil and criminal courts (*dharma sthānīya kaṇṭhaka śodhaneṣu*) ; those whose purity was tested under the monetary allurement, were employed in the work of revenue collectors and chamberlains ; those who were tried under the allurement of love were appointed as superintendents of pleasure grounds (*vihāra*), both internal and external ; those who were tested by the allurement of fear were appointed for "immediate service" ; those whose character was tested under all kinds of allurements were appointed as prime ministers (*mantriṇaḥ*) ; and those who proved to be impure under one or all of the allurements were appointed in mines, timber and elephant forests, and manufactories.[233]

(b) Daily Examination of Work

With such severe tests like those mentioned above, it is not surprising that Kauṭilya should have recommended the daily examination of the work of those who possessed the ministerial qualifications (i.e. the *amātyas*). Not only were the agency and the tools made use of by them in the fulfilment of their duties, but the place and the time of their work they were engaged in, the precise form of the work, their outlay, and the results they obtained—all these came in for a close scrutiny by the king. They were to carry on their normal work without dissension and without any concert among themselves. Without bringing to the knowledge of their master (*bhartṛ*, king), they could undertake nothing but remedial measures against imminent dangers. This clearly proves that the final decision in all important matters rested with the king.

(c) *Increase or Decrease in Revenue*

Inadvertance on their part was punishable with a fine of twice the amount of their daily pay and of the expenditure incurred by them ; but if they made as much, or more than, the prescribed revenue, they were honoured with promotion and rewards. If a minister was responsible for the lessening of revenue, he had to make good the loss ; and if he doubled the revenue, he was warned in the first instance ; and if he committed the same offence, he was proportionately punished. If an officer merely spent the revenue without bringing any profit, he was punished in proportion to the value of the work done, the number of days taken, the amount of capital spent, and the amount of daily wages paid.

Inconsistency apparently marks the ordinances relating to the increase in revenue. In one place we are told that if the ministerial officials made as much, or more than, the prescribed revenue, they were honoured with promotion and reward. But in the next sentence it is stated that if the *amātya* doubled the revenue, he was warned in the first instance ; and if he committed the same offence, he was proportionately punished. It cannot be understood how an increase of revenue in one instance won its reward, and in another case secured its condemnation, excepting on the assumption that the increase in the former case was according to justifiable methods, while that in the second instance was by the wrong means.

(d) *Embezzlement*

That Kauṭilya was perfectly aware of the inherently weak side of human nature, and that he made provision to set it right is proved by what he says of embezzlements in detail, as seen in an earlier context above, and when he writes the following:

> Just as it is impossible not to taste the honey or the poison that finds itself at the tip of the tongue, so it is impossible for a government servant not to eat up, at least, a bit of the king's revenue. Just as fish moving under water cannot possibly be found out either as drinking or not

drinking water, so government servants (*yuktāḥ*) employed in the government work cannot be found out (while) taking money (for themselves). It is possible to mark the movements of birds flying high up in the sky; but not so is it possible to ascertain the movement of government servants of hidden purpose.

After having thus pointed to an inherent defect in the character of the servants of the State, Kauṭilya devised the severest measures to eradicate this ancient evil of embezzlement. He recommended the confiscation of the ill-earned wealth of the government servants, and their transfer from one walk to another, "so that they cannot either misappropriate government money or vomit what they have eaten up".[234]

(*e*) *Criticism*

The above will have made it clear to the reader that, while Kauṭilya laid down the severest tests for the recruitment of the ministerial officials, he also made ample provision for meeting the danger of corruption amongst them. Whatever else it might serve to show, the whole chapter entitled the Examination of the Conduct of Government Servants is a realistic picture of the government service conditions and of the actual practice in the days of Kauṭilya. Here, again, as in many other matters discussed above, that great Prime Minister dealt with a problem which was anything but idealistic in its nature. The final impression that is left in our mind is that, as stated just above, he admitted the existence of corruption in the highest government circles, but that, at the same time, strenuously endeavoured to improve the tone of the whole administration. There is a vein of outspokenness in his regulations, particularly in the dangers of public service which he describes, when he writes thus:

> Self-protection shall be the first and constant thought of a wise man; for the life of a man under the service of a king is compared to life in fire; whereas fire burns a part of the whole of the body, if at all, the king has the power either to destroy or to advance the whole family, consisting of sons and wives of his servants.[235]

Kauṭilya wrote thus about the conduct of a courtier; but in doing so, he had given expression to the severest judgment on State service in general which any author on Politics could ever have passed! He had made ample provision for the efficiency of government and for the continued good behaviour of its servants, including the highest officials of the ministerial cadre, but he had evidently no guarantee to offer to any one in regard to the safety of the life of the officials serving under the king. From the above it appears as if we are to assume that public service under the Mauryan State was rather precarious.

9. MINISTERS AND WELFARE SCHEMES

(a) *Uncertainty was not the Feature of the Mauryan State*

But it would be erroneous to conclude that uncertainty of life was the daily feature of the Mauryan public service. We have to recall here the many checks which were imposed on officials, including those of the highest category, and even on the king himself, mentioned in the previous pages of this book, in order to realize that neither royal vagaries nor individual caprice was allowed to come in the way of the smooth working of the administration. If uncertainty was the keynote of the Mauryan State service, the huge bureaucratic machinery described in the *Arthaśāstra* would have become an impossible achievement. Moreover, what goes against the view that the officials in the ancient Indian State lived a life of perpetual peril is the fact that stability was guaranteed to them in the shape of annual salaries mentioned earlier which would have been superfluous if the State service was hedged in by continual insecurity.

The Mauryan State was the opposite of the ancient Persian type and of that of the Greek tyrant of the contemporary times. To what extent it kept before itself the welfare of the people, and implemented such an ideal will be evident when we examine the following seven problems facing the Mauryan Government. These were house building, public morality, public health, food, labour, public transport, and national calamities. A cursory examination of every one of these problems will reveal that the Mauryan sovereign could not have held the lives of his officials in continued suspense, if he wished to bring into existence what may be called in modern terms a Welfare State.

(b) *Welfare Schemes of the Mauryan State*

(i) *Rules in regard to House Building*

Nothing is discernible in the *Manusmṛiti* in regard to this problem. The only detail about houses refers to the boundary marks of houses concerning which Manu has laid down a few regulations.[236] But this is not the case with Kauṭilya, who not only gives the earlier injunctions of Manu, regarding the disputes concerning buildings, including houses (*vāstu*), but elaborates them in great detail, thereby suggesting that the problem of buildings had assumed large proportions in the days of the Mauryan Prime Minister. A few of them may be given in order to show what care the State took concerning the important problem of house building. The roof of a house had to be fastened to the traverse beam by iron bolts. According to this (which was called *setu*) the houses were to be constructed. The roof of adjoining houses could be either four *anguḷas* apart, or one of them may cover the other. The front door (*āṇidvāra*) was to measure a *kikṣu* ; there was to be no impediment inside the house for opening one or the other of the folds of the door. Here the author in regard to this particular injunction is not clear. The upper storey, however, was to be provided with a small but high window. If the neighbouring house was obstructed by it, the window was to be closed. With a view to warding off the evil consequences of rain, the top of the roof (*vānalaṭyāscordhvaṁ*) shall be covered with a broad mat, not blowable by the wind. Neither was the roof to be such as would easily bend or break. Violation of this rule was punishable with the first amercement. The same punishment was awarded to those who caused annoyance by constructing doors or windows facing the houses of others, except when those houses were separated by the king's road or the high road.

Without encroaching on what belonged to others, the foundation of a house (*pade bandhaḥ*) was to be laid at a distance of two *aratnis* or three *padas* from the wall of the neighbouring house.[237] Between any two houses or between the extended portions of any two houses, the intervening space was to be four *padas* or three *padas*. The only temporary structures permitted by law were those meant for the confinement of women for ten days ; all others had to be permanent structures which were to be provided with a dunghill (*avaskara*), water course (*bhrama*), and a well (*udapānam*). Violation of this rule was punishable with the first amercement. From each house a watercourse of sufficient scope at a distance of three *padas* or one-and-a-half *aratnis* from the neighbouring site was to be so constructed that water was to flow from it in a continuous line or fall from it into a drain. If this rule was violated, a fine of fifty-four *paṇas* was to be imposed.

At a distance of a *pada* or an *aratni* from the wall of the neighbouring house, an apartment for bipeds and quadrupeds, a fire place (*agniṣṭhaṁ*), a water butt (*udañjaram*), a corn mill (*rocanīṁ*), and a mortar (*kuṭṭinīṁ*) were to be constructed. Violation of this rule was punishable with a fine of twenty-four *paṇas*.

(ii) *Nuisance Forbidden*

Householders were punishable with fines if they caused nuisance to their neighbours. For instance, if they constructed a pit, a water course, a ladder, a dunghill, or any other part of the house, or caused annoyance to outsiders, or in any way obstructed the enjoyment of others (*bhoghanigrahe ca*), or caused water to collect and thereby injured the wall of the neighbouring houses, they were punishable with a fine of twelve *paṇas*. If the annoyance was caused by faeces and urine, the fine was doubled. If the water course or gutter did not offer free passage for water, the fine was twelve *paṇas*.

(*iii*) *Tenancy Laws*

Tenancy rights were regulated in the following manner: if a tenant refused to vacate a house when asked to do so, and continued to remain in it, he was fined twelve *paṇas*. The same penalty was imposed on the owner of a house who forced a tenant, who had paid rent, to vacate the house, unless the renter was involved in acts of defamation, theft, robbery, abduction, or enjoyment with a false title. But if the renter voluntarily vacated the house in which he lived, he had to pay the balance of the annual rent.

(*iv*) *Community Living*

Although the ancient Indians did not know the community life of the Greek type, yet to a certain extent there was a sort of a community life in those days. If any one of a party did not take part in the construction of a building which was intended for the common use of all the members of a family, or if any one obstructed another member of a party in making use of any part of such a building, he was fined twelve *paṇas*. Similarly if any one marred another's enjoyment of such a building, he was fined double that amount. With the exception of private rooms and parlours (*aṅgaṇa*), all other open parts of a house as well as apartments where fire was kindled for worship or a mortar was situated, were to be thrown open for common use.[238]

(*v*) *Sanctity of a Citizen's House*

With what sanctity a citizen's house was looked after is evident from the regulation that he who forced his entrance into another's house during the day was punished with the first amercement; and during the night, with the middle amercement. And, further, if any person, with a weapon in hand, entered another's house, either during the day or night, he was to be punished with the highest amercement. Incidentally we may note that if a man mounted the roof of his own house after midnight, he was punished with the first amercement; and if he mounted the roof of another's house, he was punished with the middlemost amercement.[239] The significance of these crimes cannot be made out. Perhaps they refer to the possibility of stealing. At any rate, the severity of the fine of the middlemost amercement appears to have deterred persons from infringing the sanctity of others' houses.

(*vi*) *Conclusion*

From the above the following may be deduced: firstly, the construction of houses was acording to certain definite rules laid down by the State.

Secondly, violation of those rules was punishable with heavy fines. Thirdly, the State was keen not only on formulating rules regarding the construction of houses but also on the attitude of the citizens towards one another. In other words, the State insisted on certain standards of civic behaviour. Fourthly, the State guarded as much the rights of the houseowners as those of the tenants. And, finally, the State laid sufficient stress on the advantages of community life even in private houses. A State that looked so carefully after these aspects of the civil existence of the people could never have made life uncertain or unbearable either for its citizens or for its officials.

(c) *Public Morality*

There were four major aspects of this grave problem which the State tackled—that referring to gambling ; that concerning prostitutes ; that dealing with a number of immoral crimes ; and finally, that pertaining to orphans. A brief elucidation of these four aspects of public morality will show that Kauṭilya had definitely advanced on Manu. Of the four aspects of public morality two had received some attention at the hands of Manu. These were gambling and prostitution.

(i) *Controlling Gambling*

The former was a vice of great antiquity. The *Rig Veda*, the *Atharva Veda*, the later *Samhitas*, and the *Brāhmaṇas* mention many details of the game of dice (*akṣa*).[240] Manu had unequivocally condemned gambling (*dyūta*) and betting (*samāhvaya*). He prescribed corporal punishment by the king for all those who indulged in gambling and betting.[241] Gambling was forbidden to kings.[242] Likewise the Snātakas or priests were forbidden to gamble.[243] Since in a former *kalpa* the vice of gambling had caused great enmity, wise men were not to have to recourse to it even in amusement.[244] This injunction of the *Manusmṛiti* is echoed in the *Udyogaparvan* of the *Mahābhārata*.[245]

Gambling in Kauṭilya. Opinion was divided among ancient writers whether gambling was to be controlled by the State or whether the king was to receive only a share of the stakes. Practical in his views, Kauṭilya permitted gambling under the strict control of the State, since it brought revenue to the king, and since it led to the detection of thieves. There was a Superintendent of Gambling (*dyūtādhyakṣa*), who granted licenses for gambling, charged fees for supplying water and accommodation, supplied dice and other accessories of the game, levied five per cent of the stakes from every winner, and, in general, controlled the playing of the game in all its aspects.[246]

(ii) Controlling Prostitution

In the same manner the State controlled the other social vice—that of prostitution which Kauṭilya considered to be more dangerous than gambling.[247] Prostitution, too, was a vice of antiquity which Manu had likewise condemned.[248] In the Kauṭilyan State there was a Superintendent of Prostitutes (*gaṇikādhyakṣa*), whose duties are enumerated in great detail.[249] In the matter of controlling prostitution by the State, Kauṭilya had advanced on the views of Manu, who merely enjoined that prostitutes should be watched by spies.[250]

(iii) Controlling Immoral Crimes

In the array of fines which Kauṭilya advocated to suppress vices of all kinds, especially those which were of the worst moral turpitude,[251] we have further evidence of the endeavours of the State in controlling vice, and thereby in trying to improve the morals of the people. The many social crimes mentioned in the *Arthaśāstra* do not figure in the *Manusmṛiti*, thereby adding one more proof to the indisputable fact that society since the days of Manu had grown in size, and that the social problems likewise had become more complicated and more difficult than in the earlier days of the author of the *Manusmṛiti*. What effect this growing degeneracy had, in the long run, in heralding a period of a moral change-over in the reign of Emperor Aśoka, and how ultimately it led to the collapse of the mighty fabric of the Mauryan Empire are problems which suggest themselves to us but which are outside our present purview.

(iv) Care of Orphans

The attempts of the State to usher in a Welfare State covered the orphans (*asambandhinaḥ*) as well. It was the duty of the State to feed them, and to teach them science, palmistry (*aṅgavidyā*), sorcery (*māyāgata*), the duties of the various orders of religious life, legerdemain (*jambhakavidyā*), and the reading of omens and augury (*antara-cakra*). Their classmates were spies, amongst whom were those who learnt by social intercourse (*saṁsargavidyā satrinaḥ*).[252] That it was the duty of the State to look after the orphans is proved by a later statement in the *Arthaśāstra* in which it is stated that the king shall provide the orphans (called in this context *bāla*) with maintenance along with the aged, the afflicted, the helpless, and the helpless women who were carrying, and also the children the latter gave birth to.[253]

(d) *Public Health*

Manu had laid down that physicians, officials of high rank who acted improperly, and prostitutes were to be watched by spies, and were to be considered as thorns on the side of the people; and that unskilful physicians, who wrongly treated both human beings and animals, were to be punished with the first (or lowest) and the middlemost amercements.[254]

(i) *State Control of Physicians*

The above injunctions were elaborated by Kauṭilya, who brought the important question of public health completely under the control of the State. It has been already seen above in connection with the duties of the City Superintendent that they included a strict control of the physicians, who treated in secret patients suffering from ulcers or excess of unwholesome food or drink.[255] Physicians with surgical instruments (*śastra*), machines, remedial oils, and cloth in their hands, as we have likewise seen above, were to stand behind the army, while in action, ready to render first aid to the armed forces.[256] They formed a regular part of the army, as is evident from an earlier context in the *Arthaśāstra* which speaks of the physicians of the army being paid 2,000 *paṇas*.[257] That the State maintained hospitals is proved by a still earlier context in the same work which, while describing the buildings within the fort, relates that to the north by west there should be shops and hospitals (*uttara-paścimaṁ bhāgam paṇya bhaiśajya gṛihaṁ*).[258]

Private Medical Practitioners also under State Control. The reader will have to recollect here all what was stated above under the sub-section of the topic on City Administration dealing with the State Control of the Physicians. Physicians who were not in State service, or, as they would be now-a-days called, private medical practitioners, were also controlled by the State. If they undertook medical treatment without intimation to the Government the dangerous nature of the disease, and if the patient died, they were punished with the first amercement. If the death of a patient under treatment was due to carelessness in the treatment, the physician was punished with the middlemost amercement. Growth of disease due to negligence or indifference (*karmavadha*) on the part of the physician, was considered as asault or violence.[259] Abortion was punished in the severest manner. The woman who committed it was torn off by bulls, "no matter whether or not she is big with a child or has not passed a month after giving birth to a child".[260] Kauṭilya's anxiety in preserving a high moral code is intelligible but the punishment recommended by him for this particular crime, which no one would extenuate, was perhaps more of a barbarous and less of a cultured type. While imposing the above terrible punishment on the guilty woman, Kauṭilya does not mention the retribution that was to overtake the man who was a party to it, nor the physician who abetted it.

(ii) Control of Food

The Welfare State of Kauṭilya also controlled the vital question of food. The regulation of food implied in its turn the control over agriculture and the ancillaries on which the material prosperity of the country depended. Food was controlled by means of regulations relating to adulteration. The Superintendent of Store House (*koṣṭāgārādhyakṣa*) had multifarious duties among which were the following: he was personally to supervise the increase or decrease in grains when they were pounded (*kṣuṇṇa*), or frayed (*ghṛiṣṭa*), or reduced to flour (*piṣṭa*), or fried (*bhṛiṣṭa*), or dried after soaking in water. In the same chapter we are informed that the State even standardized the meals which were to be taken by the Aryans, the women, the children, and the low-castes. One *prastha* of rice, pure and unsplit, one-fourth *prastha* of *sūpa,* and clarified butter or oil equal to one-fourth part (of *sūpa*) were declared to be sufficient for one meal for an Aryan ; one-sixth *prastha* of *sūpa* for a man (who was evidently not an Aryan) ; and half the above quantity of oil was said to be the ration for low-castes (*avara*). The same rations less by one-fourth the above quantities formed one meal for a woman ; while half the above rations (of an Ārya and of the low castes) was meant for children. The detailed regulations in regard to the dressing of flesh and the cooking of *śākas* (dried vegetables) and fish given in this connection, clearly point to the desire of the State to regulate the minutest details regarding food in the days of Kauṭilya.[261]

Adulteration of Food Punished. Adulteration of articles of food was severely punished. Adulteration of salt was punished with the highest amercement.[262] Selling rotten flesh was forbidden. If it was sold, the punishment was twelve *paṇas.* This fell within the jurisdiction of the Superintendent of the Slaughter House (*sūnādhyakṣa*).[263] Adulteration of grains, oils, alkalis, salts, scents, and medicinal articles with similar articles of no quality was punished with a fine of twelve *paṇas.* We are to infer that the imposition of this fine was one of the duties of the Superintendent of Commerce (*saṁsthādhyakṣa*), since this regulation is mentioned in the chapter on that high dignitary.[264]

The State paid the greatest attention to agriculture which was under a Superintendent (*sītādhyakṣa*). He had multifarious and onerous duties which need not be enumerated here. It is enough to say that every care was bestowed by the State on questions like the protection of agriculture, cultivation of State lands, guarding the fields and pasture lands, and preventing them from being destroyed.[265] The minutest regulations relating to cowherds milking cows many times a day, to persons in charge of water courses neglecting their duties, to people setting fire to fields and pasture lands, and the fines imposed on those who violated rules regarding the above,[266] show the great solicitude which the State bestowed on these matters on which the prosperity of agriculture ultimately depended. The Kauṭilyan State devoted much attention to the great question of agriculture. particularly to that of cultivating pasture lands on uncultivable tracts, to the importance of raising crops, and to the measures which had to be taken to protect agriculture from all kinds of vexations including oppressive fines and forced labour.[267]

(iii) Irrigational Works

Water reservoirs and irrigational works, without which it was impossible to improve agriculture, came under the close notice of the State. The king was to construct reservoirs (*setu*) filled with water either perennial or drawn from some other source ; or he was to provide with sites, roads, timber, and other necessary things to those who were willing to construct reservoirs of their own accord.[268] As in some other matters detailed above, Kauṭilya seems to have anticipated long ago the methods adopted by the modern State in augmenting agricultural production. The City Superintendent was to make a daily inspection of the reservoirs of water, evidently those which were near the city.[269] Irrigational works (*setubandha*) were rightly considered as the source of crops, although good showers were also held responsible for plentiful crops, especially below the irrigational works.[270]

(iv) State Control of Labour

The Welfare State of Kauṭilya was built upon the joint endeavours of all the sections of the people but under the supervision of the State. Indeed, it would not be erroneous to maintain that it was one of the earliest experiments in history of a Co-operative State built by the people. We have to realize how Kauṭilya, who helped Candragupta Maurya to overthrow the Nandas and to found the Mauryan dynasty, would not have been able to effect a revolution all by himself or even with the help of the Mauryan ruler, if both of them had not the whole-hearted co-operation of the army and of the bulk of the people. Indeed, the emphasis which Kauṭilya laid on the co-operative side of their public life is intelligible only from this point of view. Co-operation was the keynote of all their activities. We saw just above that the State paid great attention to agriculture. Co-operative effort was the essence of agricultural advancement. Whoever stayed away from any kind of co-operative construction (*sambhūya-setubandhāt*) was to send his servants and bullocks to carry on his work, and was to have a share in the expenditure but not any share in the profit of that undertaking.[271]

(v) Community Projects

The co-operative nature of their public life is seen in the regulations relating to labourers and co-operative undertakings. If a cultivator arrived at a village for work but did not perform it, the fine levied on him was to be taken by the village itself. He was to refund not only double the amount of the wages he received when he had promised to work, but also double the value of food and drink with which he had been provided. If the work was a sacrificial performance (*prahavaṇeṣu*), then also he was to pay double the amount of the wages. Any person who did not co-operate in the work of preparing for a public show was, together with his family, to forfeit his right to enjoy the show (*prekṣā*). If a man, who had not co-operated in preparing for a public play or spectacle, was found hearing or listening to it under hiding, or if any one refused to give his aid in a work beneficial to all, he was compelled to pay double the value of the aid due from him.[271a]

Coercion in Co-operative Undertakings. It is interesting to observe how such large scale co-operative undertakings were performed, that is, whether they were all voluntarily done, or whether there was an element of force in them. Coercion was inevitable in the fulfilment of such co-operative enterprise. We see it clearly in the next injunction of Kauṭilya, who enjoins that the order of any person, who attempted to do a work beneficial to all, should be obeyed. Disobedience in such cases was punishable with a fine of twelve *paṇas.* If others unitedly beat or hurt such a person (obviously with a view to preventing him from doing the work), each of them had to pay double the amount of the fine usually imposed for such an offence. If among the above offenders, there was a Brahman or a person superior to a Brahman (by which we are to suppose was meant a Snātaka), he was first to be punished, the exact nature of the punishment being left vague. The favour shown to the Brahmans in this regard is seen in the regulation that if a Brahman did not take part in the co-operative performance of any sacrifice in his village, he was not to be violated but merely persuaded to pay a share. These regulations were applicable to the non-performance of agreements in the country (*deśa*), and among castes, families, and assemblies.[271b] That is, they were universally applicable.

Further proof of the use of coercion in the fulfilment of co-operative undertakings is afforded in the regulations relating to labourers and priests. If a servant neglected or unreasonably put off work for which he had received wages, he was not only fined twelve *paṇas* but was to be caught hold of till the work was done. But when a labourer thus engaged on a work was incapable to turn out (for some reason or other), or was engaged to do a mean job, or suffered from some disease, or was involved in calamities, he was to be shown some concession. His master was even permitted to get the work done by a substitute. The loss incurred by the master or employer owing to such delay was to be made good by extra work.[272] Thus, there was no escape from the work allotted to a labourer. In other words, it appears as if there was some sort of conscription in the Mauryan times.

To what length coercion could go is seen in such regulations like the following: when the headman of a village had to travel on account of any business of the whole village, the villagers by turns had to accompany him. Those who failed to do this duty were fined one and a half *paṇa* for every *yojana.*[273]

Neglect of Work Punished. That conscription was a special feature of the Mauryan age, at least in the times of Kauṭilya, is further proved by the following regulations. A healthy person, who deserted his company after work had begun, was to be fined twelve *paṇas,* for none was permitted, of his own account, to leave his company. It is interesting to note how shirkers of work were treated. Any one who was found to have neglected his share of work by stealth was to be shown mercy (*abhayaṁ*) for the first time. He was to be given a proportional quantity of work anew with a promise of proportional share of earnings as well. If he continued to be negligent in his work for the second time, or went elsewhere, he was to be thrown out of the company (*pravāsanaṁ*). If he was guilty of a grave offence (*mahāparādhe*), he was to be treated as one condemned![274]

Spiritual Co-operation. Co-operation in the spiritual field was as important as in the material spheres. Priests co-operating in a sacrifice were to divide their earnings either equally or as agreed upon, excepting what was especially due to each or any of them. In case priests died while performing specified sacrifices like Agniṣṭoma, Soma, Madhyamopasad, Pravargyodvāsana, Sutya, Maya, Prātassavana, Madhyandina, Bṛihaspatisavana, and Ahargaṇa, specified rules were laid down as to what wages were to be paid to them. Proportional presents (mentioned in detail) in every case were to be paid to the claimants of the deceased priests. The surviving priests, who carried on the remaining part of the sacrifices, or any other relatives of the dead priests, were to perform the obsequies of the dead for ten days and nights. It was obligatory on the part of the remaining priests to complete the sacrifice, and to claim the presents.[274a]

Co-operative Companies: *Guilds.* These played an important part in the fulfilment of the community projects of those days. They were given some special privileges. Thus, the guilds of workmen (*sanghabhṛitāḥ*) were given the right of having a grace of seven nights over and above the period agreed upon for fulfilling their engagement. Beyond that time they were to get substitutes and get the stipulated work completed. Guilds of a co-operative nature (*sambhūya samutthāthāraḥ*) as well as guilds of workmen were to divide their earnings (*vetanaṁ,* or wages) either equally or as agreed upon among themselves.[274b]

Concessions for Co-operative Undertakings. The State gave special concessions to those who by their co-operative effort constructed roads and buildings of any kind (*setubandha*), which were beneficial to the whole country; and who not only adorned their villages but also kept watch on them. The favourable concessions (*priyahitaṁ*) given by the king, however, are not specified.[274c]

(*e*) *Public Transport*

(*i*) *Highways in the Manusmṛiti*

A certain amount of co-operative endeavour, no doubt, had existed in the earlier days of Manu. Thus, for instance, it is related in the *Manusmṛiti* that those who did not give assistance, according to their ability, when a village was being plundered, or when a dyke was being destroyed, or when a highway robbery was committed, were to be banished with their goods and chattels.[275] The highways which are referred to in the above passage were under State control. Indeed, it was the duty of the citizens to keep them clean. If any one, except in cases of extreme necessity, dropped filth on the king's highway, he was fined two *kārṣāpaṇas*, and was required to remove it immediately.[276] A further proof that even cross-roads were under State control is afforded in the passage which relates that assembly houses, houses where water was distributed, well-known trees, festive assemblies, play houses, concert rooms, cross-roads, and many other places (given in detail) were to be guarded by companies of soldiers, both stationary and patrolling, and by spies.[277]

(*ii*) *Highways in the Arthaśāstra*

Notwithstanding the above injunctions regarding the king's highway and the cross-roads, it does not appear from the *Manusmṛiti* that in the days of Manu the problem of transport had assumed that magnitude and importance which later on it attained in the days of Kauṭilya. The Mauryan Prime Minister's transport policy was directed as much against highway robbers as against the servants of the Government itself! This explains why he enjoined that the king should not only free the roads of traffic from the molestations of robbers but also from that of courtiers (*vallabha*), workmen (*kārmika*), boundary guards, and protect the roads from being destroyed by herds of cattle.[278]

What care was bestowed on the roads by the State is seen in the regulations relating to their measurements, their obstruction, and their importance in war time. Rules were laid down regarding the width, number, and purpose of roads. There were royal roads (*rājamārga*), and roads leading to *droṇamukha, sthānīya,* and country parts. These were to be four *daṇḍas* or twenty-four feet in width. Those to *sayoniya* (?), military barracks (*vyūha*), burial or cremation grounds, and villages, which were called merely *patha,* were to be eight *daṇḍas* in width. The roads to gardens, groves, and forests were to be four *daṇḍas* in width. Those leading to elephant forests were to be two *daṇḍas* in width. Roads for chariots were of two types—the broader roads each four *daṇḍas* in width ; and the narrower, five *aratnis* or seven and a half feet in width. These two types of chariot roads were evidently meant for two different kinds of chariots.

Roads for cattle were to measure four *aratnis* ; and roads for minor quadrupeds and men, two *aratnis* (*dvau kṣudra-paśu-manuṣya-pathaḥ*).[279]

Obstruction to roads was punished with fines ranging from twelve *paṇas* to 1,000 *paṇas*, thereby showing that the State attached very great importance to the free flow of traffic on roads of all categories. If roads were blocked for inferior beasts or for men, the penalty was twelve *paṇas*. Obstruction to roads for superior beasts was punishable with a fine of twenty-four *paṇas* ; to roads for elephants or to those leading to fields, fifty-four *paṇas* ; to those leading to any building or forests (*setuvanapatham*), 600 *paṇas*(?) ; to those for burial grounds or villages, 200 *paṇas* ; to those for *droṇa-mukha*, a fortress, 500 *paṇas* ; and to those leading to a *sthāniya*, country parts, and pasture lands, 1,000 *paṇas*. Even in the matter of the upkeep of the roads, the State imposed fines. The same fines as those mentioned above were imposed in the case of ploughing the several roads too deep (*atikarṣaṇe caiṣām*) ; and one-fourth of the same fines for ploughing merely on their surface.[280]

The importance of roads of traffic (*vaṇikya patha*) for purposes of war was fully realized by Kauṭilya, who wrote that the roads of traffic were a means to over-reach the enemy. It was through them that armies and spies were led (from one country to another) ; that weapons, armours, chariots, and drought animals were purchased ; and that entrance and exit in travelling were facilitated.[281]

Security on the Roads: *Wayfarers' Privilege*. A singular privilege was given to wayfarers on the public roads and footpaths (*pathikāḥ utpathikāḥ*), which we have already noticed above. They were empowered to catch hold of any person whom they found to be suffering from wounds or ulcers, or possessed of destructive instruments, or tired of carrying heavy loads, or timidly avoiding the person of others, or indulging in too much sleep or fatigue from a long journey, or who appeared to be strangers to the place in localities like inside or outside the capital, temples of gods, places of pilgrimage, or burial grounds.[282]

The above general permission given to wayfarers looks strange from some points of view ; but its main object seems to have been to help the State in maintaining security on the highways and footpaths. There is reason to believe that there was enough security on the roads and in the country sides. This is inferred from the regulations relating to the travelling merchants. Whatever of their merchandise was stolen or lost in the intervening places between any two villages, the Superintendent of Pastures (*vivītādhyakṣa*) was to make good. If there were no pasture lands (in such places), the officer called Corarajjuka was to make good the loss. From his designation, it appears as if this officer's duty was to bind thieves with ropes. If the loss of merchandise occurred in such parts where there were no Corarajjukas, the people in the boundaries of the place should contribute to make up the loss.[283] If there were no people in the boundaries, the people of five or ten villages of the neighbourhood were to make up the loss. While this was, no doubt, forced co-operation on the part of the people in maintaining public security, it also meant punitive action on a vast scale unprecedented anywhere else in the contemporary world. These regulations of Kauṭilya and his great desire to maintain the public highways, and even the footpaths, in the best condition, and free from all possible kinds of vexations and dangers, point to the fact that he had in this respect gone far beyond the scope of the *Manusmṛiti* or of any other ancient work on Polity.[284]

(*f*) *Welfare State and National Calamities*

(*i*) *Kinds of Calamities*

Nowhere do we see the trend of the Kauṭilyan State to move in the direction of a Welfare State so clearly as in the case of national calamities, and the measures it took either to ward them off or to overcome them. Some of these have been mentioned in the earlier pages of this work. But we may be permitted to deal with them at length here. They may be subdivided into calamities which were the result of human action, and those which were caused by natural agencies. The former were represented by wars against which adequate provision was made by the Kauṭilyan State. We shall not be concerned with them so much as with the latter which are called providential visitations (*daivānyaṣṭau mahābhayāni*). They were eight in number: fires, floods, pestilential diseases, famines, rats, tigers, serpents, and demons (*agniḥ-udakaṁ vyādhiḥ-durbhikṣaṁ mūṣikā vyālāḥ-sarpā rakṣāṅsi-iti*). From these the king shall protect the kingdom (*tebhyo janapadaṁ rakṣet*).[285]

(*ii*) *Remedies against Pestilences*

Detailed regulations are given in the *Arthaśāstra* for dealing with these providential calamities. We shall restrict ourselves to three of them which have recurred in Indian history down to our own days. These are pestilences, floods, and famines. About pestilences, particularly the disease called *maraka* ("killer"), measures which are intelligible, and those which appear to us rather incomprehensible, were proposed. Among the latter were remedial measures of the magical and Tāntric types.[286] The more intelligible methods against pestilences were confined to physicians, who were to overcome them with medicines, the ascetics and the prophets aiding them with their auspicious and purificatory ceremonials. These measures were especially to be adopted against the epidemics of the type of *maraka*, the nature of which cannot be made, but which may have been the plague of antiquity. Besides the above measures, provision was also made for the oblations to gods, the performance of ceremonials called *mahākachchhavardhana*, the milking of cows on cremation or burial grounds, the burning of the trunk of a corpse, and the spending of nights in devotion to God.

(iii) *Remedies against Cattle Diseases*

Of particular interest to veterinary students of the modern times are the measures to ward off cattle diseases (*paśuvyādhimaraka*). The ceremony of waving lights in cow sheds (*nīrājanaṁ*) was to be done, and also the worship of the family gods. But it need not be imagined that credulity was the keynote of State action in regard to this problem. We have to recall here the fact that, as related earlier in these pages, there were physicians who looked after the units of the army, and others who looked after the elephants. And in addition there was the Superintendent of Cows (*go-adhyakṣa*) under whom were cowherds. Of the duties of the latter was one of applying remedies to calves or aged cows or cows suffering from diseases (*bāla-vṛiddha-vyādhitānām gopālakāḥ pratikuryuḥ*).[287] This regulation should dispel any misgiving in our mind that the ancients believed only in sorcery in combating the diseases among cattle.

(iv) *Floods*

More harmful than the diseases among cattle were the floods and famines. We shall first deal with the former. Here again we see how commonsense was balanced with superstition in providing remedies against floods. Villagers living on the banks of rivers were, during the rainy season, to remove themselves to up-countries. They were to provide themselves with wooden planks, bamboos, and boats. They were further to rescue persons, who were carried off by floods, by means of bottle gourds, canoes, trunks of trees, or boats. Persons neglecting this work of rescuing others, with the exception of those who had no boats, were fined twelve *paṇas*. The supernatural element in the system of flood relief is seen in the provision made for worshipping rivers on new and full moon days, and in persons, who were learned in the *Vedas*, and who were experts in sacred magic and mysticism (*māyāyogavidaḥ*), performing incantations against rains.[288]

But as in the case of floods, every thing was not left either to fate or to magic. Even small rivers were provided with small boats, especially when they were in floods in the rainy season. Since this detail is mentioned under the heading of the Superintendent of Ships (*nāvādhyakṣa*), we may presume that providing small rivers with boats was one of the duties of that high dignitary.[289]

As regards the relative harm caused by floods and fire, Kauṭilya did not agree with the view of his unnamed teacher, who considered the destruction caused by fire to be irremediable, while that due to floods could be passed over. On the other hand, Kauṭilya thought that, whereas fire destroyed only a village or a part of the village, floods carried off hundreds of villages.[290] From the last statement it may be inferred that floods were, inded, a major national calamity which the State had to face in those times.

(v) Famines in Early Times

Equally destructive were famines concerning which we have more details in the *Arthaśāstra* than in any other ancient text, although they are referred to in earlier literature. For instance, in the *Cāndogya Upaniṣad* there is the story of Uṣati Cakrāyana, who took *kulamāṣas* from the plate of another person (i.e. ate *ucchiṣṭa* food). This was when the land of the Kurus was struck by a shower of hail (or by locusts).[291] There is no reference to famines in the *Manusmṛiti*. In the *Rāmāyaṇa*, however, there is a reference to a famine (*anāvṛiṣṭiḥ*) in the country of Aṅga under Romapāda.[292] A famine extending over twelve years in the kingdom of Śantanu is referred to in the *Nirukta*.[293]

Famine Policy in Kauṭilya. While these instances prove that the calamity of famines is to be dated to a remote period of Indian history, there is nothing to suggest that any measures to counteract their effects were undertaken before the days of Kauṭilya. What may be called in modern phraseology a famine policy is seen for the first time only in the *Arthaśāstra*. This policy was implemented in the following manner: firstly, during a famine, the king was to show favour to his people by providing them with seeds and provisions (*bījabhaktopagrāhaṁ*). Secondly, he was to execute such works as were usually resorted to in times of calamities, obviously like repairing ruined buildings and constructing new ones, repairing tanks, etc. Thirdly, he was to show favour to the people by distributing either his own collection of provisions or the hoarded income of the rich amongst his subjects. Fourthly, he was to seek for help from his allies. Fifthly, he could adopt the policy of thinning the rich either by excessive taxation (*karśaṇam*) or by causing them to disgorge their accumulated wealth (*vamanaṁ*). Sixthly, the king along with his subjects could migrate to another kingdom which had abundant crops, evidently ruled ever by a friendly king. Next he could remove himself along with his subjects to the seashore or to the banks of rivers and lakes. Further, he could cause his subjects to grow grains, vegetables, roots, and fruits wherever water was available. And, finally, he could hunt and fish on a large scale, and provide the people with the flesh of wild beasts, birds, elephants, tigers, or fish.[294]

Of the nine methods advocated by Kauṭilya to meet the grave danger of famines, the first five deserve comment. Almost all of them have a modern touch about them. The first method of providing the people of the famine-stricken areas with seeds and provisions, is still being followed in the modern times. Constructive public works is another method by which the misery of the people was, as it is now-a-days; alleviated in such contingencies. Distribution of royal wealth and provisions has also been resorted to by later kings during famine times. But what is of particular interest is the levy on the rich: the distribution of their excessive wealth and ill-gotten gains among the suffering people is a measure which the more radical Socialist governments of the present day would not hesitate to adopt in our own times, if they, too, were faced with the calamity of a famine. The sixth and the seventh methods suggest that the consequences of the calamity must have been, indeed, so terrible as to compel the ruler to have recourse to wholesale migration to a neighbouring kingdom. The eighth method was a reasonable one which is sometimes adopted even in the modern times. The last method reveals that the bulk of the people were not necessarily vegetarians.

(vi) *Other Calamities*

We may briefly pass over the other national calamities like fire, rats, snakes, tigers, and demons. As regards the danger from fire, the villagers were to provide equipment mentioned above in these pages. Observers (who were perhaps spies) were responsible for finding out the fire.[295] The danger of rats, cats, and mongoose was met by a specified kind of food which was to be used for killing them. Similar means were to be used for meeting the dangers from locusts, birds, and insects. The reference to locusts is particularly interesting inasmuch as it proves that by the time of Kauṭilya, the danger from these pests had already become common in the country. This means that we have to assume that locusts had already visited northern India ages before Kauṭilya. Snake charmers were to tackle the problem of snakes. Those who killed tigers were to be awarded an unspecified sums of money. Negligence to rescue a man from the clutches of a tiger was punished with a fine of twelve *paṇas*. The superstitious tinge in the mind of Kauṭilya is seen in the provision he made for combating the danger from demons. They were warded off by incantations from the *Atharva Veda*. Indeed, in the case of all these five calamities, supernatural measures like incantations, prayers to Mahā-kachchha, etc., were advocated.[296] Leaving aside the supernatural aspect of it, the existence of rats, snakes, and tigers on a vast scale suggests that the country sides still formed the larger part of the Kauṭilyan State.

(vii) *Conclusion about the Welfare State*

The reader will have realized from the above that the measures advocated in the above regulations relating to the seven problems facing the State, point to the endeavours made by Kauṭilya to bring a Welfare State, as then understood, into existence, in which the supreme consideration was the material and spiritual good of the people rather than the increase in the power and prestige of the monarch. We have to add here the careful manner in which the State solved the many troubles facing it from internal and external enemies[297] in order to understand that in such a State the life of its servants could never have been one of precariousness, as one might be superficiously inclined to think in terms of some remarks made by Kauṭilya himself in a few contexts in his work.

CHAPTER V

THE ELEMENTS OF THE STATE (*Contd.*)

C. THE PEOPLE

1. DIFFERENT TERMS USED FOR THE PEOPLE

IN THE elucidation of this essential element of the State, it is necessary to remember a few ideas which we mentioned at the beginning of Part Three above. These refer to what is known in the modern world as the general will of the community, and to the assemblies which limited the powers of the king. We may also observe here that, as in the other spheres of our study, we are faced with the paucity of materials on the subject, and with the divergent theories maintained by modern scholars which have only added to its complicated nature. The technical terms around which there has been much controversy are the following: *janapada, paura-jānapada, sabhā,* and the synonyms of the last term, *vidhatha, pariṣad,* and *samiti.* These terms are of great antiquity, which seem to have varied in their connotation in the different ages, but all of which seem to have had much to do with the people or with their representatives through whom the general will was made coherent.

2. JANAPADA

(*a*) *Connotation of the Term in the Ancient Texts*

This term occurs in the *Brāhmaṇa* literature in two senses—that of people or subjects, and of land or realm. The subjects were denoted by the adjectival form *jānapada.*[298] The *jānapada* was also used to distinguish the people including the nobles as distinguished from kings, as the following passage in the *Śatapatha Brāhmaṇa* would show:

> He (the Advaryu) sąys—'Ye Guardians of the Quarters, those who go on to the end of this (horse sacrifice) become sharers of the royal power, they all become kings worthy of being consecrated ; but those who do not go to the end of this (sacrifice) will be excluded from royal power, they will not become kings, but nobles and peasants, unworthy of being consecrated.[299]

The importance of the people is given in the statement that in them lay the strength of the people. Thus in the *Śatapatha Brāhmaṇa*: "O! Brahman! thus he addresses him in the third name. The other answers—'Thou art Brahman! Thou art Indra, mighty through the people (i.e. the *viś, viśaḥ*),—he thereby lays vigour unto him, and causes Indra to be mighty through the people."[300]

An identical estimate of the importance of the people in general is given in the *Maitrāyaṇī Samhita* and the *Taittirīya Brāhmaṇa.*[301] This concept of the importance of the people is to be traced to the *Atharva Veda,* where the people are classed with *bald* or power, the *viś* being associated with the *sabhā, samiti,* and the *senā,* the two former representing the assemblies of the people, and the third, the armed host obviously composed of all the able bodied sections of the people.[302] The general term *janapada* or people seems to have comprised all—those who formed the subjects of the sovereign, those who lived in the country sides, and those who came to be classed into the four castes and the four classes, whose earliest traces are found in the *Rig Veda,* where the people are divided into *Brahma, Kṣatram, Viśaḥ,* and the servile population.[303]

(b) *Jānapada in the Manusmṛiti*

The term *jānapada* acquires a clearer meaning with Manu, who enjoined that "(a king) who knows the Sacred law, must inquire into the laws of the castes (*jāti*), of country parts (*jānapadān*), of guilds, and of families, and (thus) settle the peculiar law of each".[304]

(c) *Jānapada in the Rāmāyaṇa*

In the *Rāmāyaṇa* the terms *jānapada* and *paurajānapada* figure prominently. Both of them are used in the singular and plural but when used collectively as *paurajānapada,* evidently refer to two different bodies—the *jānapada* or the body consisting of the representatives of the country sides, and the *paura,* or the body consisting of the representatives of the cities, but acting together in one capacity as the General Assembly of both types of representatives on certain occasions. It is only in this sense that we can understand the term *paurajānapada-jana* to which Rāma addressed on one occasion.[305]

(d) *Jānapada in the Arthaśāstra*

Kauṭilya used the terms *jānapada* and *paura* in a manner which leaves no doubt in our minds as to their precise connotation. *Jānapada* meant essentially the realm, or the people of the country, while *paura* stood for the citizens of the towns and of the capital. This is proved by the following: "Having set up spies over his ministers (*mahā-amātya* or *mahā-*

mātra), the king shall proceed to espy both the citizens and the country people" (*gūḍha puruṣa-praṇidhiḥ kṛita-mahāmātya apasarpaḥ paura-jānapadān-apasarpayet*).[306] In a later context he writes that the Collector-General (*samāhartṛ*) having divided the country (*janapada*) into four divisions, and having also subdivided the villages (*grāma*) into specified grades, shall bring them under one or the other of the heads which he has mentioned in detail (*samāhartā caturthā janapadaṁ vibhajya*).[307] That the term *jānapada* was used in connection with the realm or country as a whole is further proved from the same work, where later on the qualities of a good country (*janapada sampat*) are mentioned.[308] We shall have to describe these qualities below in this Part. In the same sense is the word *janapada* used in a still later context in the *Arthaśāstra*, when Kauṭilya refers to one's own and a foreign country.[309] But when he uses the term *deśa*, it is in the sense of a larger unit—*pṛithvī*, a vast Empire.[310] We shall cite further evidence in regard to the *janapada* from the *Arthaśāstra* below.

3. PAURAJANAPADA

(a) Dr. Jayaswal's Theory

Keeping in view the above meanings of the term *jānapadān* as given in the various texts, let us now examine Dr. Jayaswal's theory. This distinguished historian interpreted in some contexts the term *paurajānapada* as Realm, Diet, and the Paura Assembly;[311] in some other contexts, the term *jānapada* as a political nation;[312] and in still other contexts, *jānapada* as "the whole area of a kingdom, minus the capital constitutionally".[313] In the same connection he would call *jānapada* as a collective institution, the plural *jānapadāḥ* as "the members of the *jānapada*—institution" as well as the people of the *jānapada*.[314] Earlier the term *jānapada* is taken by the author as a synonym of *rāṣṭra* and *deśa*.[315]

Dr. Jayaswal supported his theory by adducing the following arguments: the *jānapadas* as corporate bodies had their own laws which were recognized by the *dharmaśāstras*. The *Manusmṛiti* recognized the laws of the *jāti* and the *jānapada*. The evidence of the *Rāmāyaṇa* proves that the *jānapada* (as a corporate body) was working for the consecration of the heir apparent. The *jānapadas* in the plural had come to a unanimous agreement with the *pauras* and others on the question of the consecration. The *Rāmāyaṇa* speaks of the *paura* and the *jānapada* each having an Inner and an Outer Body, the former of which was the Executive Council consisting of the Elders, which sat permanently, while the latter Body (the Outer) is left undescribed by the learned historian. There is unquestionable evidence in the Hāthigumpha inscription of king Khāravela (*circa* 170 B.C.) that that ruler "granted privileges to the *jānapada* (or the singular *jānapadaṁ*)". Some of the seals discovered at Nāḷanda confirm the corporate nature of the *jānapadas* by their statement—*paurikā-grāma-jānapadasya*.[316] The term "Paura does not relate to all the towns in the kingdom", but it means a corporate body "mentioned in the singular like *jānapada* in the inscription of Khāravela", who granted privileges to the *paura*. The corporate sense of the *paura* is seen in the Buddhist work *Divyāvadāna* "Where Kunāla is supposed to have entered the paura (used in the singular, that is, the Paura Assembly)". Dr. Jayaswal further says that the author of the *Vīramitrodaya* definitely states that the *paura* was a body (*samūha*) of the capital (*pura*). The *paura* was a commercial association in which was vested the municipal administration of the capital. Apart from its municipal work it exercised great constitutional powers. It was presided over by a leading citizen, generally a banker or a merchant. It was not appointed by the king. It had a number of non-political functions like the administration of estates, construction of public works, etc. And the capital of the Mauryan Empire, Pāṭaliputra, was an example of *paura* administration.[317]

(*b*) *Evaluation of Dr. Jayaswal's Theory*

There can be no doubt that Pāṭaliputra was a well administered city. We shall mention below in Part Six the opinion of Megasthenes on its administration. But this does not mean that the theory of *paurajānapada* as propounded by Dr. Jayaswal is historically correct. In view of the fact that he has adduced formidable arguments in support of his theory, it is desirable to analyse it in order to see how far it is historically acceptable.

Manu referred to Common Law and Not Particularly to the Jānapadas. In the first place, the fact that the *Manusmṛiti* recognized the laws of the *jāti* (castes) and the *jānapadas* (provinces, rural areas, or districts) means nothing. We are to construe from this injunction of Manu that that great lawgiver paid adequate attention to the customs and usages of the country as a whole, that is, of the people in general, as distinct from the *varṇas* or castes and *āśramas* or orders of life. Manu referred here, as we had an occasion of mentioning earlier, to the Common Law of the land without dwelling on any aspect of the so-called constitution of the *jānapadas*.

The Singular and Plural use of the Term Inadequate to prove Anything. Secondly, the distinction between the singular and plural use of the word *jānapada* is more ingenious than convincing. The use of both the forms in the *Rāmāyaṇa* disproves that any special significance was attached to the use of the term *jānapada* in the plural.[318] To maintain with Dr. Jayaswal that "the plural *jānapadāḥ* may equally denote 'the ministers of the *Jānapada*—institution' as well as 'the people of *Jānapada*'"[319] is merely to beg the question. There is nothing to suggest that the ancients ever distinguished between the singular and the plural use of the word *jānapada* in the sense given to it by Dr. Jayaswal. Even in regard to the existence of two committees or sections in the *paurajānapada* bodies, the *bāhya* or Outer and the *abhyantara* or Inner, which two terms are certainly mentioned in the *Rāmāyaṇa*,[320] there is no adequate data on which one could build one's theory of the two bodies. The *abhayantara* and *bāhya* people mentioned in that epic, were evindently sections of the general body of the people as represented by the term *paurajānapado janaḥ*. In what manner the *bāhya* committee or section of the *paura* was connected with its counterpart in the *jānapada* proper,—if at all there were such committees,—cannot be satisfactorily explained for want of sufficient evidence.[321] At any rate to invest the *paurajānapada* assembly with an "institutional significance", as is done by Dr. Jayaswal,[322] is to stretch the significance of the term *paurajānapada* beyond its limit. Likewise all the assumptions relating to the *pauravṛiddhas* or Council of Elders, and to their being equated with the Inner or *abhyantara* committee of the *paura-jānapada* mentioned in the *Rāmāyaṇa*, as is done by Dr. Jayaswal,[323] is to postulate assumptions that have no foundation on fact.

Evidence from the Hāthigumpha Inscription of No Avail. Now we come to the considerations centering round the Hāthigumpha inscription of king Khāravela. The evidence of this inscription does not prove the contention of Dr. Jayaswal. The precise sentence on which the learned historian based his theory is the following: *rājasūyam saṁdasayaṁto sava-kara-vaṇaṁ anugha anekāni sata sahasāni visajati poraṁ jānapadaṁ*, which the same scholar had once translated as "remits all tithes and cesses, bestows many privileges amounting to hundreds of thousands on the *paura* and *jānapada*", but which he rejected later on.[324] Scholars are not agreed that this rendering of the sentence is correct;[325] neither was he himself sure of his own reading! In view of the uncertainty in regard to the precise meaning of the sentence in that inscription, any reliance on the latter to prove that the *paurajānapada* was a Parliament or a Diet is unsafe. It would be altogether misleading to affirm, therefore, that "the technical significance of the *Jānapada* as a collective institution has now been established by Khāravela's inscription of *circa* 170 B.C.".[326] A simple consideration which requires no proof may be mentioned here: throughout ancient and mediaeval Indian history during the Hindu period, the kings granted concessions of taxes and of various other matters, not necessarily to bodies with an "institutional significance" but to corporate bodies, individual citizens, or groups of citizens. These latter were not necessarily knit together into institutions of political or constitutional significance.

The Buddhist Evidence does not prove the Theory. Turning to the evidence which Dr. Jayaswal has tried to get from the Buddhist work *Divyāvadāna*, we may affirm that it is of no avail in proving his theory. The reference in the *Divyādāna* to Tiṣyarakṣita's addressing to the *pauras* need not be construed as being made to "an organised body", but may be interpreted as an address to the representatives of the city. Indeed, the protests made by the representatives of Takṣaśīla to Prince Kunāla, as given in the same work cited by Dr. Jayaswal in a later context, only proves our contention that they were merely acting in their representative capacity, and that they did not have any "institutional" character.[327]

Incongruity in Dr. Jayaswal's Statements. Dr. Jayaswal wrote in one and the same breath that the *paura* was "a communal association", and that it was "vested with the municipal administration of the capital".[328] There is something incongruous in this statement: a purely communal body does not seem to have been entrusted with the administrative, and particularly, municipal, affairs of the capital. We have to recall here the excellent picture of the City and of the City Superintendent as given in the *Arthaśāstra*, which has been cited elsewhere in these pages, in order to discountenance any such theory like the one maintained by Dr. Jayaswal relating to the communal nature of the municipal organization of the ancient Indian cities.

Evidence from Vīramitrodaya Unconvincing. We now come to the next argument that the *paurajānapada* possessed non-political and constitutional powers. Among the former are included the administration of estates, public works which contributed to the material welfare of the people, policing the capital, judicial work, "limited to the matter of municipal administration", and the charge of sacred and public places.[329] Dr. Jayaswal attempts to prove that the above powers were given to the *paurajānapada* by citing Bṛihaspati's *Digest* as cited in the *Vīramitrodaya*, and by giving the example of the organization of Pāṭaliputra as described by Megasthenes.[330] The *Vīramitrodaya* was the encyclopaedic work of Mitramiśra, the famous commentator on *Yajñavalkyasmṛiti*. There is no doubt that Mitramiśra's authority was acknowledged everywhere excepting in Bengal,[331] and that his opinions are to be respected. But Mitramiśra lived in the seventeenth century A.D.,[332] and his interpretation of the ancient texts cannot be taken as the last word on the significance of technical terms like *paurajānapada* which figure in them. Admitting that we may, for argument's sake, rely on Mitramiśra's testimony, the citation from *Vaśiṣṭhadharmaśāstra* given by Dr. Jayaswal, does not help to establish his contention. The citation is as follows: "They (i.e. the *nāgaraiḥ*, citizens) were authorized by the king to administer, along with government officers, property left by a deceased person."[333] There is nothing to suggest in this passage that the *paurajānapada* were an institution. On the other hand, the specific statement that the citizens (*nāgaraiḥ*) were to administer the property of a deceased person along with the government officers (*tato' anyathā rājā mantribhiḥ saha nāgaraiḥ-ca kāryāṇi kuryāt*, as given in *Bṛihaspati*) points essentially to the State machinery with which the citizens were to co-operate, since they were naturally in the best position to know about the financial standing of one amongst themselves.

Construction of Public Works Not the Duty of Paurajānapada. As regards the construction of public works, policing the towns, and doing some kinds of judicial work, all of which are alleged by Dr. Jayaswal to have been within the jurisdiction of the *paurajānapada*, the least that could be said about this set of arguments, is that these different duties could not always have been performed by the *paurajānapada,* especially when we remember that there were State officials to execute them along with various allied duties. Nothing prevented the *paurajānapada,* of course, from offering their co-operation to the officials of the State in the execution of these and other duties. In fact, we have to assume that there was always a close *liaison* between the State officials and the country people, in view of the fact that the ancient Indian governments, as must have been evident to the reader from the earlier pages of this work, were extremely scrupulous in respecting, and in being guided by the ancient usage of the land, and, in particular, by the experience of the elders of the localities in the country sides. No one was better qualified to offer guidance to the State than the country people, who were the repositories of the past usage of the land.

The Constitutional Significance of the Paurarajānapada Not Their Special Peculiarity. In this connection it is necessary to examine the so-called constitutional powers supposed to have been possessed by the *paurajānapadas.* Dr. Jayaswal enumerates these powers thus: appointment of a *yuvarāja* or crown-prince (whom he styles king-assistant), taking part in the consecration or coronation of the prince, interfering with succession, preventing unworthy princes from succeeding to the throne, appointing chief ministers or *mantris,* and deciding questions of taxation and of State policy.[334] It must be admitted that the representatives of the country sides as well as of the cities, indeed, all the people in the kingdom, were concerned with the question of the appointment of the crown-prince, with the celebration of the coronation, and with the vital question of preventing unworthy members of the royal house from ascending the throne. The people in general could not be indifferent to these grave questions. Even in dethroning a wicked king, who had consistently failed to do his duty, and who had violated the precepts of the *dharmaśāstras* and the *nītiśastras,* the people acted together, and their action was condoned, and, to some extent, legalized in the sense that the lawgivers from Manu onwards tacitly admitted their action. The evidence of the *Mṛichchhakaṭikā,* which Dr. Jayaswal cites in this connection,[335] does not help to legalize that privilege which was exercised by the people on the gravest of provocations ; it merely echoes the opinion of the *smṛitikāras* and the *nibandhakāras* on this important question of deposing an unworthy and wicked ruler. The equation of the passage in the *Arthaśāstra* with that given in the *Mṛichchhakaṭikā,* which Dr. Jayaswal has done,[336] can only confound an incautious student, who does not know the exact context in which that passage occurs in Kauṭilya's work. It is in connection with the protection of the parties in one's own State.[337] Even granting that that passage is of some use in proving Dr. Jayaswal's theory, the opening sentence of that chapter in Kauṭilya's work completely violates Dr. Jayaswal's theory. The sentence in question has already been cited above in connection with the definition of *janapada* in the *Arthaśāstra*. It clearly distinguishes between the citizens (*paura*) and the country people (*jānapada*).[338]

Selection of Prime Ministers Not the Function of the Paurajānapada. On the question of the appointment of the prime minister, there was no doubt that, as is related in the *Mahābhārata*, the king had to select as his minister one who had the confidence of the citizens and of the country people.[339] But this means nothing more than the fact that the king had to select as prime minister a person who was known for his integrity among the people. There is no indication in the *Mahābhārata* that the *mantri* so selected was necessarily a person who "has legally earned the confidence of the Paurajānapads", as Dr. Jayaswal asserts.[340] In the first place, there is nothing in the ancient texts to show that a person can "legally earn the confidence of the Paurajānapada", or illegally lose it, before or after being selected by the king. The custom of choosing as a minister one who was held in high respect by the people was common throughout the country; and it did not possess any legal tinge about it. And, secondly, even admitting the construction of that passage in the *Mahābhārata*, as is done by Dr. Jayaswal, it cannot be made to agree either with the view of Manu or that of Kauṭilya, both of which we have cited elsewhere in these pages, but which we may be permitted to repeat in order to understand the erroneous nature of the theory of Dr. Jayaswal. Manu enjoined that those persons were to be appointed as ministers, who were well versed in the sciences, who were skilled in the use of weapons, who were descended from noble families, and who were well tried. As regards entrusting a *mantri* with the affairs of the State, Manu merely stated that such a *mantri* alone, who was most distinguished among all the ministers, could be given the duty of looking after the six-fold royal policy.[341]

Kauṭilya, as narrated earlier, is even more pronounced than Manu in regard to the appointment of ministers. The very first two conditions in the long list of qualifications mentioned by him, for the recruitment of ministerial officers, prove that he certainly made provision, not for the right of either recommending or confirming the appointment of ministers on the part of the *paurajānapadas*, but merely for their good antecedents and their domicile—that is, for satisfying that they were sons of the soil, and not foreigners whom Kauṭilya rightly distrusted. The conditions are expressed in the two words—*jānapado abhijātaḥ* (native and high born).[342] The assumption, therefore, that the previous sanction of the *paurajānapada* was needed to appoint a person as a prime minister is without any foundation in ancient Indian political thought.

State Policy Not decided by the Paurajānapada. Equally futile is it to maintain that the questions of State policy were decided ultimately by the *paurajānapada*, after they had been discussed by the king with his ministers, as has been maintained by Dr. Jayaswal.[343] If the *paurajānapada* were the ultimate authority in deciding intricate questions of State policy, there was no need of having the *mantripariṣad,* and the many highly qualified and experienced dignitaries like the ministers for war and peace, etc., with whom the king always consulted before embarking upon any political venture relating to the neighbouring States.[344] Moreover, as we have seen, the final verdict on State or domestic policy rested with the king, who, as narrated elsewhere in these pages, had to take the final decisions himself in a lonely place, after having consulted with his ministers either individually or collectively. If decisions on State policy had to be placed before a large, unqualified, and inexperienced multitude of representatives of the citizens and the country sides, previous to their ratification by the king, nothing but chaos would have resulted in the foreign policy of the State. The entire concept of the executive as given in the ancient texts violates the assumption that the *paurajānapada* had the final voice in the determination of State policy.

The Paurajānapada Not entitled to decide Questions of Taxation. We now come to the assertion that the *paurajānapada* decided the taxes levied by the king. While affirming that the "taxes were fixed by common law", Dr. Jayaswal in the next sentence writes that "the king often had the necessity and occasion to apply for an extraordinary taxation" which assumed the form of *praṇaya* or benevolences or forced levy. He further states that "it is evident that proposals for such taxation were first submitted to the *Paura-Jānapada*". And then he cites a sentence from the *Arthaśāstra* —*etena pradeśena rājā paurajānapadān bhikṣet,* which he translates thus—that the king "had to beg of the *Paura-Jānapada*" for these levies.[345]

One cannot help feeling that the versatile historian has altogether misled his readers by citing a passage in its incomplete context. The whole chapter from which this sentence is taken is styled *kośābhisamharaṇaṁ* which the late Dr. Shama Sastry rightly translated as "Replenishment of the Royal Treasury". The opening sentence of this chapter (II in Book V) would have dispelled any uncertainty in regard to the use of the term *jānapada* and the nature of the financial demands which the State made, and which Dr. Jayaswal himself partially admitted when he wrote that they referred to the necessity of having recourse to extraordinary taxation. The chapter in question begins thus:

> The king who finds himself in a great trouble and needs money may collect (revenue by demand). In such parts of his country as depend solely upon rain for water and are rich in grain, he may demand of his subjects one-third or one-fourth of their grain, according to their capacity (*kośaṁ-akośaḥ prati-utpanna-arthakṛichchhaṁ sangraṇhīyāt janapadaṁ mahāntam-alpapramāṇaṁ vā devamātṛikaṁ prabhutadhānyaṁ dhānyasya-aṁśaṁ tṛitīyaṁ caturthāṁ vā yāceta*).[346]

In the above passage we have two important ideas—first, that relating to the bankruptcy of the royal treasury (*kośam-akośaḥ*), and the king's right of demanding (*sangraṇhīyāt*) taxes, in order to replenish it, and his levying of graded taxation from the country sides (*janapadam*) according to the fertility of the soil.[347] It is true that in thus levying extraordinary taxation, the king had to solicit (*yāceta*) the help of the people much in the manner which will be indicated below. But this need not be interpreted to mean that the king had to get the prior permission of the *paurajānapada* before having recourse to extraordinary taxation. The verb *yāceta* may as well be construed to mean *demand*, and not necessarily *beg*. That in the matter of taxation there was no question of the king's asking any one, either an individual or an association of people, to grant him prior permission is proved when we peruse the duties of the Revenue Collectors as given in Book II Chapter XXXV of the *Arthaśāstra*.[348] Indeed, the right of imposing or levying taxation was vested only in the king, and not in the *paurajānapada* or in any other body or association, as is evident from the following injunction of Kauṭilya: "Lands prepared for cultivation shall be given to tax payers (*karada*) only for life (*ekapuruṣikāṇi*)." Then again, we have the regulation:

> The king shall bestow on cultivators only such favour and remission (*anugṛihaparihārau*) as will tend to swell the treasury, and shall avoid such as deplete it. A king with depleted treasury will eat into the very vitality of both citizens and country people. Either on the occasion of opening new settlements or on any other emergent occasions, remissions of taxes will be made. He shall regard with fatherly kindness those who have passed the period of remission of taxes.[349]

The right of the king to levy and remit taxes is implied in the above passage which merely refers to the impoverishment of both the citizens and the country people in case the royal treasury was empty (*alpa kośo hi rājā paurajānapadān-eva grasate*).[349a]

Paurajānapada Never meant an Institution. That the term *paurajānapada* or *jānapada* never meant an institution is proved not only by what has been stated earlier in connection with *jānapada* in the *Arthaśāstra*, but by the many references to that term in the same work, which means merely country sides or the realm. It is in the last sense of a realm that it is used in the chapter on villages (*janapada niveṣaḥ*).[350] We have in the same chapter the importance given to the elders of the villages. They were to improve the property of the bereaved minors till the latter attained their age, and they were likewise to look after the property of the gods.[351] If in the matter of looking after the property of the gods and the minors, Kauṭilya made no provision for the prior permission of the so-called *paurajānapada* "institution",—a privilege that was granted by the king to the elders, and not claimed by them as their right—, it cannot be understood how Kauṭilya could have advocated the securing of the prior permission of the *paurajānapada* by the king in the more vital question of replenishing the royal treasury. Indeed, Dr. Jayaswal has not only missed the general tenor of the injunctions of Kauṭilya in regard to taxation, but, what is unfortunate, has, in his enthusiasm to support an untenable theory, torn a sentence from out of its general context in order to create a wrong impression. The exact context, in which the passage cited by Dr. Jayaswal referring to the "begging" by the king of his people occurs, is one where, after permitting the king to make specified demands on herdsmen (*yoniposakaḥ*), Kauṭilya enjoins the following:

> Such demands shall be made only once and never twice. When such demands are not made, the Collector-General shall seek subscriptions, (or beg for benevolences) from citizens and country people alike under false pretences of carrying this or that kind of business (*sakrid-eva na dviḥiḥ prayojyaḥ tasya-ākaraṇe vā samahārtā kāryaṁ apadiśya paura-jānapadān bhikṣeta yogapuruṣās-ca-atra pūrvaṁ atimātraṁ dadyuḥ etena pradeśena rājā paurajānapadān bhikṣeta*).[352]

The late Dr. Shama Shastry had rightly translated *bhikṣeta* as "benevolences".[353] Here we have, therefore, the fact that it was not the king, as incorrectly stated by Dr. Jayaswal, who "begged" but the Collector-General (no doubt, on behalf of the king) who sought subscription, or begged for benevolences, not of the usual kind of taxes but of the unusual type in order to meet a grave financial contingency. If we might be permitted to clarify this detail relating to the soliciting of public contributions, we might say that the Collector-General as much begged of the people to give to the State their contributions as any of the officials of a modern government would do when a State Loan is floated, and when citizens are requested, directly or indirectly, to subscribe liberally to them. In either case there cannot be any question of "begging": it is only a matter of soliciting the aid of the people in order to tide over a grave financial crisis.

That Kauṭilya never attributed any special significance to the word *paura-jānapada* will be evident when we peruse the same chapter where, in a later context, it is related that the Superintendent of Religious Institutions (*devatādhyakṣa*) was empowered to do many things, amongst which were the following: to cause a false panic by the news of an evil spirit residing in a tree or in a city, wherein a man is hidden making all sorts of devilish noises, and then to have money collected by means of spies from the country people (*manuṣyakaraṁ vā vṛikṣe rakṣobhyaṁ rūpayitvā siddhavyañjanāḥ paurajānapadānāṁ hiraṇyena pratikuryuḥ*).[354] The interpretation of *paurajānapada*, therefore, in the sense of an institution with any political or constitutional bias, based on the *Arthaśāstra*, is unwarranted.

Numismatic Evidence is of No Avail. Let us turn now to the last argument in support of Dr. Jayaswal's theory which rests on numismatic evidence. The learned historian maintained that the inscription on some of the seals discovered at Nāḷanda, viz., *purikā-grāma-jānapadasya* ("of the town, village, and *jānapada*"), refers to the "corporate body" of the *jānapada*, although he admits in the same context that, in the age of the seals (sixth or seventh century A.D.), *jānapada* as meaning "the whole country or province, i.e. the Deśa-sangha", had ceased to exist, as the term was transferred to the *grāma-sangha*. "But the corporate character of the term is still there."[355] Evidently the versatile scholar was at great pains to reconcile the conflicting data found in the seals with the corporate nature of the *pura*, the *grāma*, and the *jānapada*. The question is: if every one of them (the town, the village, and the *jānapada*) possessed a corporate character of its own, then, why should special significance be attached only to that of the *jānapada*? To this question no answer is forthcoming in Dr. Jayaswal's work. On the other hand, it might be safely maintained that, instead of proving that corporate character was the special characteristic of the *jānapada*, the Nāḷanda seals attest to the corporate life of the towns, the villages, and the country sides thereby demolishing the theory of Dr. Jayaswal that the last named (*jānapada*) alone had any special attributes.

What has to be decided is not whether the corporate life of the *paura*, the *grāma*, and the *jānapada* is indicated in the Nāḷanda seals but whether the corporate nature of the *jānapada* as given in the Nāḷanda seals was an attribute of the whole country, thereby justifying Dr. Jayaswal's contention that that term (*paurajānapada*) has to be understood in the sense of an institution with political and constitutional significance found all over the country. We could arrive at an answer to this question by a comparative study of the numismatic evidence relating to similar corporate bodies. For instance, there were the Yaudheyas, who have already figured earlier in these pages, and whose coins contain the legend—*Yaudheya gaṇasya jaya* (Victory to the corporation of the Yaudheyas!).[356] It cannot be maintained on the strength of these coins that the Yaudheya constitution was of universal application: at the most we could affirm that the Yaudheyas possessed a constitution that was republican in character. Likewise all that could be said about the *paura*, *grāma*, and *jānapada* mentioned in the Nāḷanda seals is that they had a corporate existence. But this by itself, again, disproves Dr. Jayaswal's contention that the *jānapada* alone were an institution of constitutional significance—a fact which the learned historian seems to partially admit in the statement that the "general *jānapada* of the whole country or province, i.e. the Deśa-sangha had ceased to exist, as the term is here transferred to the *grāma-sangha*". We could go to the extent of affirming that the *paura* and the *grāma* had an equal status with the *jānapada*, thereby robbing the last of any special significance which Dr. Jayaswal would like to give it as a Hindu Diet or Parliament!

Conclusion. From a detailed examination of the *paurajānapada* theory promulgated by Dr. Jayaswal, it is clear that it cannot stand a critical examination, since it is based neither on political theory nor on historical facts. Scholars like the late Professor Altekar and Dr. Kane have rejected it as being fanciful and ingenious but on different grounds.[357] We are inclined to agree with the view of the latter scholar that the term *paura* refers to the residents of the capial, and *jānapada*, of the country other than the capital.[358] We would only add that, since the capital was not the only town in the ancient Indian State, there being other towns also, we may include under the term *paura* the residents of the major towns of the kingdom including those of the capital. As to how they functioned when they assembled, whether they had a joint session of all their representatives, or whether they met separately, cannot be determined for want of sufficient data.

4. SABHA, SAMITI, PARISAD, AND VIDATHA

(a) *Their Antiquity*

These terms, especially the first three, appear to have been synonyms but seem to have been used in different contexts. As in the case of *janapada* and *paurajānapada*, speculation has been rife as regards their exact significance and their relationship to each other. All the above terms are of considerable antiquity, since they figure in the Vedic literature. Of these we shall first select the *sabhā* and, then, the *samiti* for discussion on the ground that the *samiti* is sometimes mentioned with the *sabhā*,[359] thereby suggesting that the latter term had a claim to priority. There is of course no specific mention in any ancient text of the relative position of the two bodies. The statement in the *Atharva Veda* that the *sabhā* and the *samiti* were the two daughters of Prajāpati,[360] clearly shows that we have to give the same importance to both, although it cannot be made out what exactly was their relative importance.

(b) *Theories regarding the term Sabhā*

This term occurs often in the *Rig Veda* and in the later works[361] but its exact nature cannot be determined. In the *Rig Veda* the *sabhā* appears as a hall used for gambling, "presumably when the assembly was not transacting public business".[362] The hall also seems to have served, as Professors Macdonell and Keith affirm, "as a meeting place for social intercourse and general conversation about cows and so forth, possibly for debates and verbal contests".[363]

(i) *Professor Ludwig's Theory*

Professor Ludwig maintained that the *sabhā* was an assembly not of all the people but only of the Brahmans and the Maghavans or rich patrons.[364]

Evaluation of the Above Theories. The authors of the *Vedic Index* maintain that this view of Professor Ludwig "can be supported by the expression *sabheya*, 'worthy of the assembly', applied to a Brahmin, *rayiḥ sabhāvān*, 'wealth-fitting for the assembly', and so on".[365] In addition to this consideration, we might add the following: if Professor Ludwig's interpretation is correct, then, the *sabhā* was made up of two classes of people—the Brahmans and the Maghavans. Now the term Maghavan is "the regular Vedic name for the generous giver of bounties to priests".[366] This being so, we have to presume that the Maghavans were a wealthy class. Since, according to all ancient texts, wealth was associated, not with the priestly or fighting classes, but what came to be called later on the third caste, that is, of the Vaiśyas, we have to imagine that the Maghavans were a section of the people given to vocations that brought them material wealth. They were probably the predecessors of the later Vaiśyas. At any rate their inclusion in the *sabhā* meant that that body was not exclusively a body of priests. In other words, it is reasonable to assume that the *sabhā* was made up of influential people, the most prominent of whom were the Brahmans and the Maghavans.

That the people even in those distant days clamoured for prominence is evident from the term *sabhā-saha,* "eminent in the assembly", occurring in the *Rig Veda.*[367] The eminence of the members which is suggested in the above term was not necessarily attained by members of the assembly by virtue of their skill in playing dice ; it might have also been because of their generous patronage of the assembly, or because of their ability in debating, and the like.

Further, if we agree to the view of the authors of the *Vedic Index* given above that the term *sabhā* was a hall used, in addition to gambling, for the transaction of public business of various kinds, then, the terms *sabhā-sthāṇu,* "pillar of the assembly hall", *sabheya,* and *rayiḥ sabhāvān* receive additional significance in the sense that they help us to postulate the view that the *sabhā* was used for public purposes of various kinds. This assumption receives further support when we note that there were terms like *sabhā-pati.* "lord of the assembly", *sabhā-pāla,* "guardian of the assembly hall", *sabhā-sad,* "sitter in the assembly", and *sabhā-cāra,* "assessors", or "judges" (of the *sabhā*)[368]—all of which lead us to infer that the *sabhā* or hall where the assembly met had assumed greater status since the days of the *Rig Veda,* when only gambling and ordinary conversation might have taken place in it ; and that in the age of the *Samhitas* and the *Brāhmaṇas,* it was the place where more serious business pertaining to the public life of the people was transacted.[369]

Two other details about the *sabhā* may be noted. First, women do not seem to have attended the *sabhā* ; and, second, no evidence of the other kinds of work done by the *sabhā* is traceable in the ancient works.[370]

(ii) Professor Bloomfield's Theory

In the light of the above discussion, Professor Bloomfield's theory that the *sabhā* was used for a domestic purpose, and not as an assembly at all, repeated in the *St. Petersburg Dictionary,* cannot be maintained.[371] Not only is the reference to the *sabhā* as an assembly clear, but, as the authors of the *Vedic Index* rightly affirm, the passages, particularly in the *Samhitas* and the *Brāhmaṇas*, definitely mean the assembly hall, and refer to the king as going to the assembly hall (*sabhā-ga*).[372]

(iii) Professor Heinrich Zimmer's Theory

Professor Zimmer was of the opinion that *sabha* was the meeting place of the village council, presided over by the *grāmaṇi*.[373] The objection to this theory is that in the *Śatapatha Brāhmaṇa*, it is clearly stated that the king went to the *sabhā* just as much as he went to the *samiti*, thus: "Even his (Soma's own) kings come (to him) to attend the assembly (*asya rājñah sabhā-gaḥ*), and he is the first to salute the king, for he is gracious."[374] The evidence of the *Śatapatha Brāhmaṇa* definitely proves that the *sabhā* was an assembly of the highest dignitaries, and that it cannot be equated with a village council. Professor Zimmer's failure to adduce any proof in support of his assertion that the *grāmaṇi* presided over the *sabhā*,[375] violates his theory.

(iv) Professor Alfred Hillebrandt's Theory

Professor Hillebrandt maintained that the *sabhā* and the *samiti* cannot be distinguished, and that the *sabhā* was used for sacrificial purposes. He saw in Agni "of the hall" (*sabheya*) a trace of the fire used in sacrifice on behalf of the assembly when it met.[376]

The first part of the above theory cannot be entertained in view of the statement in the *Atharva Veda* relating to the two daughters of Prajāpati, cited above. As regards the second part of the theory, that the hall might have been used for a sacrificial fire, all that we might say is that that argument does not hold good, in view of the fact that in every house there was a separate place, the central hall, where the sacred fire was lighted, where probably the sacrificial apparatus was kept.[377] It could never have been confounded with the *sabhā* or with any attribute of Indra.

(v) Dr. Jayaswal's Theory

Dr. Jayaswal's theory may be summarized thus: the *sabhā* was a popular body. "It was certainly related to the *Samiti* but its exact relationship is not deducible from the data available. Probably it was a standing and a stationary body of selected men under the authority of the *Samiti*." The *sabhā* had its president called *sabhāpati*, and its Elders. Its function was to act as a National Judicature like our present criminal courts.[378]

The above assumptions of Dr. Jayaswal have been refuted by Professor Ghoshal. In the first place, as Dr. Jayaswal himself admits, it is merely a hypothesis which is not deducible from the available data. This by itself is enough to disprove his theory. Secondly, if, as Dr. Jayaswal asserts, the *samiti* was the sovereign assembly, "it is inconceivable that the binding and inviolable character of its resolutions should be held to be the exclusive attribute of the *sabhā*".[379] Thirdly, Dr. Jayaswal's interpretation of the word *nariṣṭā* occurring in the *Atharva Veda* (*Vidmā te sabhe nāma nariṣṭā nāma vā asi*), in the sense of "not injured", referring to the inviolability of the resolutions of the *sabhā*, is not final in the sense that that word *nariṣṭā* has been rendered into "mirth" by Professor Bloomfield, and into "sport" by Drs. Whitney and Lanman.[379a] And, finally, Dr. Jayaswal's contention that the *sabhā* acted as a national judicature is merely a repetition of the earlier views of Professors Ludwig and Zimmer,[380] which are entirely baseless. To these we might add the objection raised by Dr. Kane that it is extremely doubtful if the *sabhā* was an elective body, and that the assumptions of Dr. Jayaswal are "all conjectural".[381]

(vi) Dr. N. C. Bandyopadhyaya's Theory

In advocating his theory Dr. N. C. Bandyopadhyaya writes that probably the early *sabhās* were of the type of the associations of the kinsfolk but later on the *sabhā* became not only an association of kinsfolk, but of men bound together by ties of blood or of local contiguity. The *sabhā* held a conspicuous place in the political institutions of the country, "which we may designate as the Political Council". It was "a central aristocratic gathering associated with the king". It was an advisory body to the king, and it acted as a judicial assembly.[382]

That the earlier *sabhās* were associations of kinsfolk bound by ties of blood or of local contiguity there can be no doubt, since all over the world, especially in the ancient times, the ties of blood and of residence in a locality seem to have played an important part. But it is not possible to agree to the other views of Dr. Bandyopadhyaya, particularly those relating to the alleged important place which the *sabhā* occupied in the political institutions, because there is no evidence of the exact nature of the work done by the *sabhā*, nor of the political institutions in the early times. The assumptions that the *sabhā* was a central aristocratic gathering around the king, and that it was also an advisory body to the king, are too far-fetched statements which cannot be substantiated by the meagre data relating to the *sabhā* in the ancient works. As regards the last idea of the *sabhā's* being a judicial body, Dr. Bandyopadhyaya merely echoes the views of Professor Ludwig and Dr. Jayaswal without attempting to substantiate them. We shall see below that his description of the *samiti* is equally unconvincing.[383]

(vii) Professor Altekar's Theory

The late Professor Altekar also indulged in much speculation in regard to the nature and functions of the *sabhā*. He started by saying: "The Vedic literature refers to the popular assemblies of the age by three different terms, *vidatha, sabhā,* and *samiti.* The precise meaning of these terms is difficult to determine and it seems not improbable that it may have differed from age to age and locality to locality." He then refers to the theories of Professors Ludwig, Zimmer, Hillebrandt, and Dr. Jayaswal, but without discussing them maintains that the *sabhā* was not the meeting place of the *samiti* but was a separate body. According to him, the *sabhā* "was primarily the village social club, but the few items of the simple village government of the age were also transacted there by its members", like the steps for communal safety, and decisions in the matter of village disputes. In some localities or States, however, the "*sabhā* was associated with the king and was more a political than a social gathering". It is possible to argue, continues the learned Professor, that the status of the members of the territorial *sabhā,* like that of the celestial one (i.e. the one mentioned in the *Atharva Veda,* III. 29. 1 in which the *sabhāsads* or members of the *sabhā* of god Yama were royal in status being entitled to the sixteenth part of the merit accruing to that deity), was also almost as high as that of the king; and that they, too, were entitled to receive a small share of the tithes and tributes that were paid to the ruler. It is not improbable, he continues, that the *sabhā* was the cabinet, the description of a member of the *sabhā* going to it in full paraphernalia seated on a charger or in a carriage, only confirming this hypothesis. His conclusion is: "The balance of available evidence, however, tends to show that the *sabhā* was usually the village assembly, meeting for social as well as political purposes."[384]

Professor Altekar merely tried to improve upon Professor Zimmer's theory which he echoes with a few more embellishments. He started with the view that the *vidatha,* the *sabhā,* and the *samiti* were one and the same, but ended by stating that the *sabhā* was a village assembly which transacted social and political business, without obviously the *grāmaṇi* of Professor Zimmer. And between these two extremes, Professor Altekar would introduce the idea of the *sabhā*'s being a cabinet, and its members having the royal prerogative of receiving a part of the tithes of the people, their status being almost as high as that of the king himself. While there seems to be no objection in treating the *sabhā* as being similar to the *samiti,* it is, as will be pointed out below, doubtful whether both of them could be identified with the *vidatha.* There is no trace of any political business being transacted by the *sabhā* which seems to have dealt with social questions. If the *sabhā* was a village assembly, it cannot be understood how it could have been transformed into a cabinet! As for the members of the *sabhā* possessing the status of the king, and particularly their right to receive a part of the tithes, one cannot help feeling that the learned Professor has imagined more than the ancient works would warrant. Whether the members of a village assembly could ever have claimed equality with the king in status as well as in the matter of the above privilege, is a point which we may not consider seriously, since it rests more on conjecture than on fact. Passages in the *Rig Veda* which refer to the wealthy and well born persons going to the *sabhā*, as has been pointed out by the authors of the *Vedic Index*, may be interpreted in the sense of the wealthier sections of the Aryans, as opposed to the Dāsas, attending the *sabhā*,[385] and need not necessarily be taken as a proof of the political work of the *sabhā*. Professor Altekar's theory, therefore, does not help us to understand either the nature and composition of the *sabhā*.

(viii) Professor Ghoshal's theory

This distinguished historian, who has helped the student not a little in removing the cobwebs that surround some of the theories of modern Indian scholars, has, as noted above, vehemently refuted Dr. Jayaswal's theory. Professor Ghoshal speaks of the deliberative function of the *sabhā* and the *samiti*, and of the *sabhā*'s being a parallel institution to the *samiti*. The former view is based on a passage in the *Atharva Veda* in which it is said how the mystical abstraction *virāja* successively ascended and descended in the *sabhā*, the *samiti*, and the *āmantraṇa*. This passage is insufficient to establish the deliberative functions of the *sabhā*. For, as Professor Ghoshal himself admits, the translators of the passage, Professors Griffith, Whitney, and Lanman, are not agreed as to its exact meaning. While the first one translated it as "consultation personified", the two latter doubtfully translated it as "address".[386] Until more definite and conclusive proof is found of the deliberative function of the *sabhā*, it would be safe not to be positive about it.

There is another suggestion which Professor Ghoshal has made that deserves consideration. He would trace the political activities of a royal pair in the *sabhā* as described in the *Vājasaneyī Saṁhita*, thus:

> The wrong we have done in village or wild,
> In the assembly, in our members,
> The wrong to Śūdra or Aryan
> The wrong contrary to the Law of either,
> Of that Thou art the expiation, Hail![387]

It appears as if we have to construe the above passage, not necessarily in the sense of the king's and the queen's indulging in political activities, but in the sense of their having violated the Common Law of the land. This is suggested in the statements, "the wrong we have done in village or wild", and "the wrong contrary to the Law of either", i.e. of the Śūdra and the Aryan mentioned in the previous sentence. Purely political activities by the royal couple in a village or in the wild (country sides or forest) are inconceivable, but their violation of a customary law in either place is intelligible. What lends support to our assumption is the expiation that is mentioned in the last sentence—it was atonement for some social sin which they had committed, and not for having violated any political principle or agreement relating to the village or the country sides. But it may be argued that the expiation may also refer to a wrong done by the royal couple in the assembly, and to the members obviously of the assembly with which the king and queen were ultimately connected, as is suggested by the words "our assembly". Even here the reference need not be to any political activity of either the royal couple or of the assembly, since the emphasis seems to be placed more on the wrong contrary to the law of either the Śūdra or the Aryan rather than to the political activities of the assembly. In the absence of any definite data relating to the political work of the *sabhā* in those early times, it would be unsafe to attribute any political colouring to the activities of the royal couple in the passage in question. But we may infer the following from it: firstly, that the assembly was a recognized institution; secondly, that the village (assembly) was not the same as the assembly where "our members", that is, those perhaps nearer to the king in rank and wealth, assembled; thirdly, that the ancient usage was recognized by the ruler; and, finally, that the king was in close contact with the villages.

As to what conclusion we shall arrive at concerning the *sabhā* will be mentioned below after we shall have discussed the question of the *samiti*.

(c) *Theories regarding the Samiti*

The same vagueness which surrounds the *sabhā* also envelops the *samiti*. Like the *sabhā*, the *samiti* (*sam-iti*) figures as an assembly from the age of the *Rig Veda* onwards.[388] We have seen above that in the *Atharva Veda* the two bodies have been described as the daughters of Prajāpati. But in the same work they are separately mentioned,[389] thereby suggesting that, while they might have possessed common attributes of origin, they were by no means identical.

(i) *Professor Hillebrandt's Theory*

His theory that the *samiti* and the *sabhā* are much the same, the one being the assembly, and the other primarily the place of the assembly,[390] appears to be incorrect in view of the references to both in the *Atharva Veda*.

(ii) Professor Ludwig's Theory

Likewise improbable is the theory of Professor Ludwig that the *samiti* included all the people, primarily the *viśaḥ*, or subjects, and the Maghavans and the Brahmans, if they desired, though the *sabhā* was the special assembly of the latter two classes of people.[391] If the *samiti* was thus an enlarged *sabhā*, its inclusion of the Brahmanas and the wealthy Maghavans being optional, one cannot understand why there should ever have been a differentiation between the *sabhā* and the *samiti* in the *Rig Veda*, and particularly in the *Atharva Veda*. The explicit difference between the *sabhā* and the *samiti* mentioned in the *Rig Veda* and in the *Jaiminīya Upaniṣad Brāhmaṇa*, the former of which mentions the *samiti* of the gods called *daivi*, or divine, and the latter, which speaks of the *sabhā* of the gods ;[392] and the fact that in the *Rig Veda*, the *samiti* seems to have been no more than a meeting place, or a meeting,[393] as distinct from the meaning given in the same work where, as we have seen above, the *sabhā* appears to mean a gambling hall,[394] conclusively prove that we cannot identify the *samiti* with the *sabhā*. Another consideration which supports our conclusion is the statement in the *Atharva Veda* that the *samiti* does not suit him (or is won over by him) who harasses a Brāhmaṇa,[395] thereby suggesting that a person, who oppressed a member of the priestly class, was not suited for the *samiti*.

(iii) Professor Macdonell's Theory

While delineating the position and powers of the king in the Vedic period, Professor Macdonell wrote thus: "His (the king's) power was by no means absolute, being limited by the will of the people expressed in the tribal assembly (*samiti*). As to the constitution and functions of the latter, we have unfortunately little or no information."[396] In the former statement we have what may be called the general will of the people to which reference has already been made in the earlier pages of this book. Professor Macdonell's supposition in regard to the existence of the general or popular will in the Vedic times is not altogether improbable, especially when we realize that, whether we are dealing with the socio-political condition in ancient India or elsewhere, the ultimate voice in all matters rested with the general body of the people with whose co-operation and obedience alone the king could effectively govern. The second statement of Professor Macdonell will be useful when we shall conclude our remarks on the *sabhā* and the *samiti*. On the whole, concerning his theory, it might be questioned, if the *samiti* were the tribal assembly, then, who composed the *sabhā*? This point is not clear in the above elucidation of the theory by Professor Macdonell.

(*iv*) *Professor Zimmer's Theory*

Professor Zimmer was of the opinion that the *samiti* composed of the *viśaḥ*, could even re-elect the king.[397] This view seems to be accepted by Professor Ghoshal.[398] Professor Zimmer would, therefore, define the *samiti* as composed of the *viśaḥ*, the assembly of the folk in which the king took part.[399] According to that German scholar, the *samiti* was somewhat similar to the assembly in ancient Germany as described by Tacitus—a view with which Professor Ghoshal appears also to be in agreement.[400]

Professor Zimmer's theory is untenable, as was pointed out by the authors of the *Vedic Index* long ago. He was concerned with the question of elective monarchy (Wahlmonarchien). According to him, while the Vedic monarchy was sometimes hereditary, as is undoubtedly proved by several instances in which the descent could be traced, it was also elective in some others, though he seems to admit that it is not clear whether the selection was confined only to the members of all the nobility or only to those who belonged to the king's family.[401] This view seems to have found favour with Professors Weber and Bloomfield.[402] But the authors of the *Vedic Index* wrote thus about his argument: "It must, however, be admitted that the evidence for the elective monarchy is not strong."[403] This, of course, does not disprove Professor Zimmer's theory. It is strange that Professor Macdonell, who was one of the authors of the *Vedic Index*, should have written on this important point relating to the elective nature of the king, in his *History of Sanskrit Literature*, thus:

> The king (*rāja*) was often hereditary. Thus several successive members of the same family are mentioned as rulers of the Triṣṭus and of the Pūrus. Occasionally, however, the king was elected by the districts (*viś*) of the tribes, but whether the choice was then limited to members of the royal race, or was extended to certain noble families does not appear.[404]

In other words, Professor Macdonell, inspite of the qualifying statements he has made in regard to the circle within which the choice of the king was limited, tacitly admits that sometimes the king was elected, thereby lending support to some extent to Professor Zimmer's main contention relating to the importance of the assembly composed of the *viśaḥ*. These considerations may be borne in mind when we shall presently discuss the position of the *viśaḥ* themselves in Vedic polity.

(*v*) *The Theory of the Authors of the Vedic Index* (*Professors Macdonell and Keith*)

They opined: "It is reasonable to assume that the business of the assembly was general deliberation on policy of all kinds, legislation so far as the Vedic Indian cared to legislate, and judicial work. But of all these occupations there is, perhaps as a result of the nature of the text, little or no evidence directly available."[405]

(*vi*) *Dr. Jayaswal's Theory*

In his definition of the *samiti* (*sam-iti*, "meeting together", an assembly), Dr. Jayaswal merely repeats what has been given in the *Vedic Index*. He then relates the following: "The Samiti was the national assembly of the whole people or *Viśaḥ*, for we find the 'whole people' or *Samiti* in the alternative, electing or re-electing the Rājan or King."[406]

This opinion is merely a re-statement of Professor Zimmer's statement mentioned and rejected by the authors of the *Vedic Index*, thus: "That he was elected there (in the assembly), as Zimmer thinks, is as uncertain as whether he was elected at all."[407] It is a pity that Dr. Jayaswal does not refer either to Professor Zimmer or to the authors of the *Vedic Index*. He than defines the *samiti*, again, thus: "The whole people were supposed to be present in the Assembly."[408] We may recall here Dr. Jayaswal's theory regarding the *sabhā* and its relationship to the *samiti* given above. He would then state that the *samiti* was "a sovereign body from the constitutional point of view". He then cites a prayer from the *Atharva Veda* which is a hymn for union and accord, and also a hymn in the *Rig Veda* in which there is a prayer for *"common samiti"* and a "common aim and a common mind", which indicated, according to him, that "matters of State" (*mantra*) were discussed in the *samiti*.[409] It was one of the king's duties, he continues, to allow the *samiti*, as is related in a hymn in the *Rig Veda* which says—"like a true king going to the Samiti". If he did not attend it, "he would be considered 'untrue' ". The *samiti* acted as a sort of a national academy. We may mention here one of Dr. Jayaswal's arguments relating to the antiquity of the *samiti*. "It is noticeable that references to the *Samiti* in the *Rig Veda* are to be found only in portions which are considered to be the latest. We may, therefore, conclude that the *Samiti* was a produce of the developed, not early, Vedic Age." Dr. Jayaswal then discountenances the views of European scholars, who have compared the *samiti* to the German assembly described by Tacitus in the latter's *Germania*, since in the *samiti* there was "a free right of discussion", and "the anxiety of the debater to win over the opinion of others".[410]

There is nothing in the above bundle of suppositions, which can be supported by the available evidence either in the *Rig Veda* or in the *Atharva Veda* or in any of the later texts. Dr. Jayaswal's conclusion that the *samiti* was a product of the later ages partially knocks the bottom of his theory. For if it were so, then, what precisely was the nature of the *samiti* in the early Vedic age? Further, if the *samiti* was a product of the later developed age, how does Dr. Jayaswal reconcile it with his later statement that "it (the *samiti*) must have been, therefore, an ancient institution even then" (i.e.

in the Vedic age when it was regarded as eternal, and when, as he rightly states, it was called a daughter of Prajāpati)?[411] Are we to imagine that there was nothing like an elective principle or discussion in the early times? If the *samiti* was the sovereign body from the constitutional point of view, what exactly was their idea of the constitution in those early times? Are the hymns from the *Rig Veda* and the *Atharva Veda* which Dr. Jayaswal has cited, and which, according to him, refer to the desire for accord and union, and a common aim and a common mind, necessarily to be interpreted in the light given by him ; or is it possible to construe them as ordinary hymns praying for some sort of a harmony among the people which was so vitally needed in those early days when the Aryans had come and settled down in an alien land with unknown problems of great magnitude facing them? Granting that the prayers could be accepted as valid for proving the existence of the *samiti*, do they also prove that it was a sovereign body even on the strength of the translations given by the learned historian? Is not Dr. Jayaswal's statement about the king's attending the *samiti* merely an "inference", as he himself admits? If the *samiti* was a sovereign body and a national academy in one and the same breath, then, on which occasions did it exercise the functions of the former nature, and on which occasions, those of the latter nature? To these questions Dr. Jayaswal's work provides no answer. He has merely erected a superstructure of suppositions which cannot stand scrutiny.[412]

(*vii*) *Professor Altekar's Theory*

This eminent scholar repeated one of the characteristics of the *samiti* as given by the late Dr. Jayaswal (without caring to let the reader know that the latter historian had forestalled him in this detail), basing his conclusions precisely on the same hymn in the *Rig Veda* (96.97.6) on which Dr. Jayaswal had bolstered up his theory. Professor Altekar wrote:

> The concluding hymn of the *Rig Veda* prays that the deliberations of the *samiti* should be harmonious and the minds of its members well disposed towards one another and its conclusions unanimous. It is not impossible to argue that the hope and the desideratum expressed in the hymn refers to the deliberative and administrative activity of a republican State.

But he practically invalidated the assumption thus made when, at the end of the same paragraph, he wrote: "The hymn by itself cannot conclusively prove the existence of a republican State." Immediately in the next paragraph, Professor Altekar wrote of "several kings meeting together in one *samiti*" ; and in the next sentence that he alone became a king whose leadership of the State was assented to by other kings. These latter were probably the *viśpatis* ; and the State contemplated by the *Rig Vedic* hymn in question was one which was the prototype of the later republics already described by the learned Professor. The sovereign power was, of course, not in the populace in general but in the aristocratic leaders of the cantons, which were fairly numerous. In a later context, Professor Altekar affirmed that the "villages had their own popular assemblies known as *sabhās*, and the capital had the Central Assembly for the whole State, which was called a *samiti*".[413]

About the powers of the *samiti*, Professor Altekar wrote: "In the concluding hymn of the *Rig Veda* (x.191.2-3) *samiti* no doubt seems to be referring to a social or learned gathering, but an earlier hymn of the same work refers to the plans of an aspirant for political power, which include the domination of the *samiti*" (Rig Veda, x.166.4).[414]

Before we proceed further, we may note that Professor Altekar has denied two of the major conclusions of Dr. Jayaswal. It was seen above that the latter had maintained that the *samiti* was a sovereign body which Professor Altekar denies, transferring all power to the aristocratic leaders of the *viśaḥ*. Another major conclusion of Dr. Jayaswal that the *samiti* was the product of the later age is demolished by the reference to an earlier hymn in the *Rig Veda* which has been cited above. With the disappearance of these two major planks in the theory of Dr. Jayaswal, we may consider all its other aspects to have simultaneously foundered.

Let us now proceed with Professor Altekar's description of the *samiti* before we reject his theory. "The *Rig Veda* refers to a 'true' king paying visit to his *samiti* and the most important and significant hope expressed in the *Atharva Veda* (vi.88.3) on behalf of an exiled king, who has succeeded in his restoration, is that his *samiti* may for ever be in agreement with him."[415] Professor Altekar continues: "It is quite clear that the *samiti* exercised control over the military and executive affairs of the Central Government ; but how exactly it was exercised and how the *samiti's* powers were co-ordinated with that of the king we do not know." In the next sentence he writes: "We are also completely in the dark as to the constitution of this important body." According to him: "It is rather sad and surprising to find that the *samiti* which exercised so much influence over the king and administration in the days of the *Rig Veda* and the *Atharva Veda*, should completely disappear from view in the period of the later *Samhitas* and the *Brāhmaṇas*."[416]

Professor Altekar's theory of the *samiti* is a conglomeration of ideas some of which are mere repetitions of statements made by earlier historians, while others are self-contradictory. Thus, for instance, his statement that the deliberations of the *samiti* should be harmonious had already been expressed by the learned authors of the *Vedic Index*, which we have cited above. While Professor Altekar is correct in his estimate of the concord between the king and the *samiti*, it is doubtful whether we could agree with his next statement relating to the republican nature of the *samiti*. He contradicts himself when he says that the Rig Vedic hymn cited by him, cannot conclusively prove the existence of a republican State. If several kings met in a *samiti,* it cannot be understood how the leadership of one king could be assented to by the other kings. Further, Professor Altekar would identify the kings with the *viśpatis* which would mean that we have to assign the former to the districts! But this cannot be reconciled with his later statement that the *samiti* was the Central Assembly of the capital! He writes of the exiled king's seeking agreement with the *samiti* after his re-installation, as narrated in the *Atharva Veda,* and cites a passage from the same work in support of his statement. But it is the identical passage (*Atharva Veda,* x.88.3) which Professors Macdonell and Keith would interpret as a proof of the concord between the king and the assembly.[417] Since this passage is capable of more than one interpretation, it is of no avail in proving the political power of the *samiti.* Moreover, if the power in the *samiti,* as the learned Professor maintains, was in the hands of an oligarchical body like the leaders of the *viśaḥ,* one fails to see whether they or the general body of the *viśaḥ* formed the sovereign body. Professor Altekar's edifice of guesses crumbles when he confesses that we have no evidence to prove how the *samiti* exercised the so-called control over the military and executive affairs of the central government ; and that "we are completely in the dark as to the constitution of this important body".

(*viii*) *Professor Ghoshal's Theory*

Professor Ghoshal's theory may be summarized thus: we have seen above that he partially accepts Professor Zimmer's theory that the *samiti* composed of the *viśaḥ* could re-elect its king. He is also inclined to agree with the view "generally held" that "the *samiti* was the Popular Assembly of the Vedic people", and that "it must have come down, to judge by the Greek, Roman and Teutonic analogies, from almost immemorial times".[418] He would base the view that the "*samiti,* evidently as the Popular Assembly *par-excellence,* was a most important asset to the King" on the strength of two passages in the *Atharva Veda* (v.19.15 ; vi.88.3) in one of which it is mentioned, at the end of a long list of imprecations against a Kṣatriya's injuring a Brahman, that the *samiti* does not suit him (*nā smai samitiḥ kalpate nā mitraṁ vayate vaśam*) ; and in the other of which there is a prayer for a consecrated king with a list of blessings on him at the end of which it is stated that the *samiti* may suit him (*dhruvāya te samitiḥ kalpatāmiḥ*).[419]

We may concede to the view that the *samiti* played a significant part in the Vedic age, and that, as is proved by the passages from the *Rig Veda* and the *Atharva Veda* cited above, it was in some manner connected with the king. But it is doubtful whether the passages in question, especially those in the *Atharva Veda,* could be taken as sufficient proof of the great importance of the *samiti.* These passages have also been noticed by other scholars, whose interpretation of the same does not corroborate the view taken by Professor Ghoshal. For instance, the authors of the *Vedic Index* have noticed them but without finding in one of the passages (*Atharva Veda*, v.19.15) any indication of the constitutional or political importance of the *samiti*.[420] Likewise Dr. Kane has noticed the same passage but has no comment to offer on the alleged importance of the *samiti*.[421] The late Professor Altekar, as seen above, after referring to the other passage which we shall mention at once, wrote thus: "Conversely the bitterest curse pronounced upon a king guilty of misappropriating a Brahman's property is that his *samiti* shall never be in agreement with him."[422]

Turning to the other passage in the *Atharva Veda* (vi.88.3), we find that there is likewise no unanimity among scholars in regard to its exact meaning. Professors Macdonell and Keith, as already remarked, interpreted that passage as merely the proof of the concord between the king and the *samiti*.[423] Professor Altekar agreed with this view, although he failed to mention the earlier opinion of the two learned Indologists on this point.[424]

We are thus driven to the conclusion that no significance need be attached to the two passages in the *Atharva Veda* regarding the so-called constitutional and political importance of the *samiti*. Professor Ghoshal next speaks of the "right of control possessed by the Popular Assembly over the distribution of public funds", and refers to a passage in the *Śatapatha Brāhmaṇa* which runs thus:

> The Fathers have prepared this place for him! For Yama is the Kṣatra (nobility, or ruling power), and the Fathers (deceased ancestors) are the clansmen ; and to whomsoever the chief (Kṣatriya) with the approval of the clan, grants a settlement, that (settlement) is properly given: and in like manner does Yama, the ruling power, with the consent of the Fathers, the clan, now grant to this (sacrifice) a settlement on this earth.[425]

In support of his theory that the popular assembly had the right of control over the distribution of public funds, Professor Ghoshal refers us to his earlier statements in his *Agrarian System in Ancient India*, wherein he had written thus: "This passage evidently refers to the public land of the Folk or the State, and it seems to mean that while the King's gift of such land with the consent of the people was in accordance with the tribal or customary law, it was sometimes arbitrarily disposed of by the sole authority of the ruler."[426]

It is difficult to agree with all the conclusions arrived at by the learned historian. His statements seem to point to the following: (*a*) that the public land belonged to the folk ; (*b*) that the king gave as a gift some part of the land in accordance with the tribal or customary law ; but (*c*) that he sometimes arbitrarily disposed of land because of his sole authority. To this we may add the fourth point as based on the passage from the *Śatapatha Brāhmaṇa* given above that the popular assembly had the control over the distribution of lands.

There is no doubt that Professor Ghoshal's conclusion regarding the king's observance of the customary or tribal law, while distributing land, is correct.

On another point, too, Professor Ghoshal seems to receive some support—that relating to the ownership of the land. Opinion among scholars is divided as to whether in the Vedic age the king was the owner of the land. Professor Hopkins strongly maintained that the king was the recognized owner of all land.[427] This view is, on the whole, accepted by Dr. Kane but with this reservation that, where individuals or bodies of persons (by which, we suppose, is meant corporations) had long been in possession of land which they had cultivated, the ownership of the State was qualified and restricted only to the recovery of the tax or a share of the crop. But if the tax was not paid, the State had the right to sell the land.[428] This meant, we suppose, that in the ultimate analysis the right over land was vested in the State. As opposed to the above views are those of Professor Baden-Powell, who asserted that the idea of the king as a landowner was a later one, although he seems to have admitted that the reference to the king's devouring the people might have meant some control over the land.[429] Professors Macdonell and Keith are likewise of the opinion that the position of the king in relation to land is somewhat obscure, particularly in the Vedic age ; and that the idea of the king's being the lord of all the land was only a gradual development. According to them the power of devouring the people was a political power which is to be distinguished from the right of ownership.[430]

Leaving aside the question of the ownership of land which is an intricate one, especially in the Vedic age, let us restrict ourselves to the passage in the *Śatapatha Brāhmaṇa* on which Professor Ghoshal has based his theory relating to the so-called right of the popular assembly to control the distribution of land. According to this theory it would mean that the popular assembly, evidently composed of the *viśaḥ*, was the sovereign body. In other words, the *viśaḥ* were superior to the kṣatra (kṣatriya), who was the king. This is untenable on the strength of the *Śatapatha Brāhmaṇa* itself. The following arguments will prove our contention. Firstly, the kṣatra or the kṣatriya is represented as superior to the *viś*, and as being served by them. Thus in the *Śatapatha Brāhmaṇa*:

> . . . for the *juhū* assuredly is the Kṣatria, and the other spoons (*śruk*) are the *viś*: he thereby makes the Kṣatra superior to the *viś*. Hence the people here serve, from a lower position, the Kṣatriya seated above them: for this reason he places the *juhū* upon (the *prastara*) and the other spoons down below it.[431]

Then, again, in the same work we have the following: "He muttered that (verse) addressed to Indra and referring to the Maruts. Indra indeed is the nobility, and the Maruts are the people ; and the nobility are the controllers of the people."[432]

The inferiority of the *viśaḥ* to the kṣatriyas is proved further when the former are declared to be the food of the latter, and when they are said to be serving the kṣatriyas. ". . . the Soma being the nobility and the other plants, the common people, and the people being the noble man's food. . . ."[433] The subservience of the *viśaḥ* to the kṣatriyas is borne out by the following passage: ". . . Varuṇa, doubtless, is the nobility, and the Maruts are the people ; he thus makes the nobility superior (*uttara*) to the people ; hence people here serve the Kṣatriya, placed above them."[434] Then, again, we have the following: "The cups of milk are taken first, then the cups of *surā*-liquor: he thereby makes the peasantry obedient to the nobility."[435] Then, again, the *Śatapatha Brāhmaṇa* relates: "Therefore the horse alone belongs to the Prajāpati, and the others are sacred to the gods: he thus, indeed, makes the peasantry obedient and subservient to the nobility. . . ."[436] The subordinate position of the people (*viśaḥ*) is again proved by the following: ". . . he makes all the people go down (on their knees) before him ; and hence when a noble approaches, all those subjects, the people, go down before him (Soma, king), crouch down by him on the ground. . . ."[437] These passages conclusively demonstrate the fact that in the age of the *Śatapatha Brāhmaṇa,* the kṣatra or kṣatriya, or the king, was not subordinate to the people but superior to them. If further proof is needed to show that the king was, indeed, all powerful, we may cite the following from the same work: "He then makes (the sacrificer) say that (*Vājasaneyī Samhita*. iv. 34). 'Thou art gracious unto me, go forth, O Lord of the world'—for he (Soma) is, indeed, gracious to him. . . ."[438]

Conclusion. From the above passages we may conclude that, so far as the alleged superiority of the popular assembly over the kṣatriyas is concerned, it is nowhere mentioned: on the other hand, all the available evidence in the *Śatapatha Brāhmaṇa* points to the undoubted superiority of the kṣatra or king over the people. When this is granted, the theory of the control by the popular assembly over the distribution of land becomes not only dubious but untenable. What makes us, therefore, reject the above theory is, in addition to the above evidence from the *Śatapatha Brāhmaṇa,* Professor Ghoshal's own confession that "on the whole, it seems desirable in the complete absence of any data comparable to the Anglo-Saxon charters, laws, and references to historical works, to suspend our judgment regarding the sovereign character of the Vedic *samiti*".[439] If the *samiti* could never have been sovereign, it is doubtful whether we have to construe the king's granting of lands with the approval of people as an evidence of the public approval of certain acts of the king, which had nothing to do with the ownership of the land. We may incidentally mention here that such a custom of the king's or emperor's or state official's granting of land in the presence of the people's representatives continued for centuries in western India without in any way detracting the right over the land which the State possessed.

We may conclude, so far as the *sabhā* and the *samiti* are concerned, with the judicious statement of Dr. Kane, thus: "It is impossible to say how the *sabhā* or *samiti* was constituted in the Vedic period. All that we can say is that it was an assembly of people to which the king, learned men, and others went."[440]

(*d*) *Pariṣad and Vidatha*

(*i*) *Pariṣad*

The above discussion should have led us to the question of the *viśaḥ* with whom the kṣatra or kṣatriya or king was so intimately connected. But we shall continue the topic of the assembly and its synonyms—the *pariṣad* and the *vidatha*. The term *pariṣad* (lit. "sitting around") does not seem to have been common in the Vedic age. But in the *Upaniṣads* it is described as an assemblage of advisers, where intricate questions of philosophy were discussed.[441] This would mean that we have to understand by the term *pariṣad* an assembly of learned men rather than of people of all types. The *Gobhila Gṛihya Sūtra* seems to support our contention in the sense that it refers to a teacher with his *pariṣad* or assembly.[442] Professors Macdonell and Keith maintain that "in the later literature the word denotes a body of advisers on religious topics, but also the assessors of a judge, or the council of ministers of a prince".[443] Their conclusion in regard to the antiquity of this term may be noted: "But in none of these senses is the word found in the early literature, though the institutions indicated by it must have existed at least in embryo."[444]

Meaning of Pariṣad in the Manusmṛiti. The *pariṣad,* according to some scholars, has been equated with the *samiti* ;[445] or considered to be "a body of legal experts called *śiṣṭas*" who were to decide doubtful points of *dharma.*[446] There is little justification for the former, and some for the latter definition in the sense that the term *pariṣad* is used in the *dharmaśāstras* for an assemblage of men learned in the three *Vedas.*[447] It is essentially in this sense that a *pariṣad* is described in the *Manusmṛiti*: "One who knows the *Rig Veda,* one who knows the *Yajur Veda,* and one who knows the *Sama Veda,* shall be known (to form) an assembly consisting of at least three members (and competent) to decide doubtful points of law."[448]This shows that the concept of the *pariṣad* as a body of experts in the Sacred law came to be evolved long after the Vedic times.

Later Connotation of the Term Pariṣad in Kauṭilya. When we come to the age of Kauṭilya, the connotation of the term *pariṣad* is slightly different. It has been seen above how in the matter of the composition of the assembly of ministers (*mantripariṣad*), Kauṭilya did not agree with the opinion of Manu that it should be made of twelve members. According to him it should contain as many members as the needs of the State required (*yathā sāmarthyaṁ iti Kauṭilyaḥ*). In the same context he refers to the one thousand sages that formed Indra's assembly of ministers (*Indrasya hi mantripariṣad ṛṣīṇām sahasraṁ*). In times of emergency, the king shall call both his ministers and the assembly of ministers (*ātyayike kārye mantriṇo mantripariṣadaṁ ca-āhūya brūyāt*).[449] We have here a new idea unknown to the Vedic age, and even to the later ages down till the days of Manu, viz., that the *pariṣad* was no more confined to those who were experts in the sphere of *dharma* but was now meant to cover a different category of persons—those who were experts also in the *nīti-śāstras* or the *daṇḍanīti,* or the science of government. In the same manner, as will be narrated below, Kauṭilya will use the term *sabhā* irrespective of its connotation in the earlier times, thereby suggesting that in this, as well as in other questions, his outlook was not the same as those of others. We shall have to revert to this topic below while discussing the *sabhā* and allied terms.

(*ii*) *Vidatha*: *Theories about Vidatha*

This is another term concerning which there has been divergence of opinion among scholars. It occurs in the *Rig Veda,*[450] but its meaning is not clear.[451] Professor Roth interpreted it in various senses: first in the sense primarily of "order" ; then, in that of a concrete body which gave orders ; and, then, again of an assembly for secular or religious ends or for war.[452] Professor Hermann Oldenberg at first thought it to mean an "ordinance" from *vi-dhā,* "dispose", "ordain", but afterwards thought it meant "sacrifice".[453] Professor Whitney considered the term to be "a council".[454] According to Professor Zimmer, *vidatha* sometimes meant a smaller assembly than a *sabhā* as in *vidatheṣu praśasthaḥ*.[455] Professor Ludwig thought that it was essentially connected with "an assembly", particularly of the Brahmans and the Maghavans, which we have mentioned above in connection with the *sabhā*.[456] He also thought that the word denoted an asylum, like the house of a Brahman.[457] Professor Geldner meant by the word *vidatha* primarily "knowledge", "priestly lore", "sacrifice", and "spiritual authority".[458] Professor Bloomfield was of the firm opinion that *vidatha* referred to the "house" (from *vid,* to "acquire"), in the first instance, and, then, to the "sacrifice", as connected with the house.[459]

The authors of the *Vedic Index,* after stating that the term *vidatha* was one of "obscure sense, confined mainly to the *Rig Veda*", agreed with the view of Professor Bloomfield by saying that "this interpretation, at any rate, appears to suit all the passages. The term *vidathya* (appearing in the *Rig Veda* and the *Atharva Veda*)[460] once applied to the king (*sāmrāṭ*) might seem to be against this view, but it may refer to his being 'rich in homesteads' ; and the connexion of the woman with the Vidatha, as opposed to the Sabhā, tells in favour of Bloomfield's explanation."[461] While commenting on the word *vidathya* occurring in the *Atharva Veda* (xx. 128), they opine that "'having an establishment' seems adequate".[462] They consider doubtful Professor Zimmer's view that the term ever denoted an asylum, like the house of a Brahman, since the *Aitareya Brāhmaṇa* (I. 30. 27. 28), "certainly does not show this clearly".[463]

It is unfortunate that in the face of such divergent opinions on the meaning and nature of the term *vidatha,* further confusion should have been caused by Dr. Jayaswal, who once thought *vidatha* to have been the parent folk assembly from which the *sabhā, samiti,* and *senā* differentiated ;[464] but in a later edition of his book he considered the following to be its meaning: "The religious life was organised through the '*Vidatha*' assembly which had existed even earlier than the *Samiti.*"[465]

Professor Ghoshal, while referring to the first meaning of *vidatha*'s being the parent folk assembly from which the *sabhā* and the *samiti* are alleged to have differentiated, said that Dr. Jayaswal followed Professor Roth ; and that that eminent historian "is completely silent about other interpretations of the term which are contrary to the sense of 'assembly' " Professor Ghoshal then cites the opinions of Professors Ludwig, Zimmer, Oldenberg, Geldner, and Bloomfield, amongst whom, particularly among Professors Ludwig and Roth, there "is room for considerable difference of opinion", and rightly concludes that "in view of these differences of opinion it seems impossible to predicate any certain definite attributes to the Vedic *Vidatha*".[466]

Conclusion. While accepting the above conclusion of Professor Ghoshal, we may note that it is difficult to agree with Professors Macdonell and Keith who, following Professor Bloomfield, maintained that by the term *vidatha* was meant, first, a house, and, then, a "sacrifice" ; and that that interpretation seems to be reasonable in view of the fact that the woman is connected with the *vidatha,* as opposed to the *sabhā.*

In the first place, the terms connoting a house including that meant for the woman, were quite different to the term *vidatha.* This is evident from what Professors Macdonell and Keith themselves have given us in the *Vedic Index.* The house in the Vedic literature was called by the following names: *agāra, āvasatha, gaya, gṛiha, duroṇa, dhāni* (in *dhana-dhāni,* treasure-house), *niveśana, patinām-sadas* (women's quarters), *pastyā, prasāda* (palace), *śālā,* and *harmya.*[467] To this list we may add the term *ocas* given by Professor Max Müller long ago.[468] The absence of the term *vidatha* in this rather long list of terms relating to a house conclusively disproves Professor Bloomfield's theory that that term originally meant a house. Neither can we accept the view that because the woman was (in some indistinct manner) connected with the *vidatha,* it should have meant a house.

And, secondly, the term *vidatha* cannot be denoted to mean a house where a sacrifice was performed, because a house where a sacrifice was to be performed is described in quite a different manner in the *Śatapatha Brāhmaṇa*, thus:

> They (the priests) choose a place of worship. Let them choose (the place) which lies highest, and above which no other part of the ground rises ; for it was from them that the gods ascended to heaven, and he who is consecrated indeed ascends to the gods. He thus sacrifices on a place of worship frequented by the gods ; but were any other part of the ground to rise above it, he would indeed be lowered while sacrificing: let them therefore choose (the place) which lies highest.
>
> While being high, that place should be even ; and being even, it should be firm ; and being firm, it should incline towards the east, since the east is the quarter of the gods ; or else it should incline towords the north, since the north is the quarter of men. It should rise somewhat towards the south, that being the quarter of the Father. Were it to incline towards the south, the sacrifice would quickly go to yonder world ; but in this way the sacrificer lives long: let it therefore rise somewhat towards the south.
>
> Let not the measure of the sacrificial ground be exceeded on the east side, since such an excess would be in favour of his spiteful enemy. It may be so in the south, and also in the north ; but that place of worship is alone thoroughly efficient where the measure of the sacrificial ground is exceeded in the west ; for to him (who possesses such a one) the higher worship of the gods readily inclines. So much as to the place of worship.[469]

There is nothing in the above description of a house where a sacrifice was to be performed, that could justify its association with the *vidatha*, as understood by Professors Bloomfield, Macdonell, and Keith to mean a house, and, then, to mean a house connected with a sacrifice.[470] We may conclude by saying that *vidatha* is a term concerning the nature of which nothing definite may be gathered from the ancient works.

(e) *The Viśaḥ (or Viś), the Senā, the Jana, again, the Parisad, the Pūga, and the Samavāya*

(i) *The Senā*

Dr. Jayaswal's Theory. One of the fallacious theories of Dr. Jayaswal is that mentioned above, which grouped the *senā* with the *samiti* and the *sabhā*. The explanation of the term *senā* and the discussion of the theory of the alleged control which the popular assembly is supposed to have wielded in distributing public lands, brings us to the elucidation of the part played by the *viśaḥ* and by the *senā*. Dr. Jayaswal maintained, as we saw above, that from the parent body of the folk assembly which, according to him, was the *vidatha*, the *senā*, the *sabhā*, and the *samiti* differentiated. The first part of this novel theory relating to the *vidatha* has already been disposed of; it now remains to examine the second part relating to the bifurcation of the *senā* from the *vidatha*. Before we examine this part of the theory, it would be worthwhile to note what Dr. Jayaswal meant by the term *senā*. "The *Senā* or the Army, which was in early times the nation-in-arms, was regarded as a body by itself and evidently as a constitutional unit." He then cites the following passage from the *Atharva Veda*: *tam sabhā ca samitiḥ-ca senā-ca*. He admits in the next sentence that "Much information about the *Senā* is not yet available."[471]

It is true that we know little about Vedic warfare;[472] but even that little is enough to reject the above theory of Dr. Jayaswal. The body of foot soldiers, going together with the charioteers,[473] may lend support to the theory that the *senā* was a corporate body by itself; but it could not be otherwise, since if the foot soldiers (*patti*) were not to be in unison with the charioteers (*rathin*), the army would have ceased to function! But what militates against the first part of Dr. Jayaswal's theory relating to what he called the constitutional side of the army is the fact that, in the *Atharva Veda*, the foot soldiers are represented as being overthrown by the charioteers![474] The authors of the *Vedic Index* have shown that the charioteers (composed of the Kṣatriyas) were opposed to the foot soldiers, especially to the troops (*grāma*) of the infantry.[475] This should dispel any constitutional character of the Vedic army.

Dr. Jayaswal has cited the passage in the *Atharva Veda* relating to the *senā*, the *sabhā*, and the *samiti* which he construed as being the evidence of the constitutional character of the *senā*. The versatile historian has erred here. The passage in question does not prove his point. It would have been better if he had either cited the earlier opinion of Professors Macdonell and Keith on the same passage in the *Atharva Veda*, and on the allied passage in the *Rig Veda*, or at least drawn the reader's attention to it. By not doing so, the late Dr. Jayaswal foisted upon the unwary reader the imaginary constitutional status of the *senā*. In the *Vedic Index* it is rightly stated that those times did not impose the duty of fighting on any particular community. "The Rig Veda evidently knows of no restriction of war to a nobility and its retainers, but the late *Atharva Veda* equally classes the folk with the *bala* 'power', representing the Viś associated with Sabhā, Samiti, and Sena, the assemblies of the people and the armed host." The authors of the *Vedic Index*, while referring to the *Atharva Veda*, cite exactly the same passage, in addition to another one, which Dr. Jayaswal has cited.[476]

In the above citation from the *Vedic Index*, we have not only a satisfactory explanation of the nature of the early society in the Vedic days, but also a possible origin of Dr. Jayaswal's imaginary constitutional status of the *senā* in the association of the *viś* with the *sabhā*, *samiti*, and the *senā*. There is no doubt that in those times the division of society into four castes did not exist ; and that the responsibility of defending the land and of protecting the people was not the privilege of any one particular class. The latter duty devolved upon all—the learned members of the assembly (the Brahmans), the wealthy members of the assembly (the Maghavans), the members of the nobility (the Kṣatras), and the rest of the people living in the rural areas (the *viśaḥ*). In these circumstances, it cannot be understood how the "constitutional status" of the *senā* can be maintained.

Conclusion. What, then, was the *senā*? In the Vedic age, we may be permitted to repeat, there is hardly any trace of a regular army which later on came to be associated with the military class of the land. Professors Macdonell and Keith were of the view that the "*sena* denotes primarily a 'missile', a sense found in the Rig Veda and the Atharva Veda, and then a 'host', or 'army' which is its normal meaning".[477] It will be seen below, while discussing one of the elements of the State, the army, that the concept of the fourfold army was a product of the later ages. Whatever may be our difficulty in ascertaining as to who exactly formed the fighting classes in the Vedic days, it seems evident that one section amongst them, the Kṣatras, had gained predominance.[478] We have already mentioned above their superiority over the *viśaḥ*. This being the case, one cannot understand on what grounds one could construe the constitutional importance of the *senā*, especially when its very nature is uncertain. Perhaps Dr. Jayaswal was inclined to imagine that the *senā* was a body that was always ready for war, on the strength of the word *sangrāma* which, according to Professors Macdonell and Keith, is "the assembly in peace and war", and is joined with the *samiti* in the *Atharva Veda*.[479] Their comment on the term *sangrāma*, used primarily in the sense of on "assembly", is worth noticing. "We might see in this passage, and that cited in note 2 (*Atharva Veda*, iv.24-7), the technical name of the village assembly as opposed to the larger assemblies of the people, but there is no good warrant for doing so."[480] Admitting that the terms *senā* and *samiti* were coupled together in the Vedic times, are we to infer that the people of the rural areas and of the villagers were in a state of perpetual martial readiness, that they had a significance, administrative or constitutional, which marked them off from the rest of the people, and that they formed a class by themselves? If they were a "nation-in-arms", against whom were they constantly fighting? If it is argued that it was the Dasyus, who were their inveterate enemies, against whom they fought, is there valid ground for assuming that the rural and village people had a special constitutional status different to the one enjoyed by the other sections of the people? Since no satisfactory answers to these questions are found in the Vedic literature, the view that the *senā* was a "nation-in-arms" with some special significance of its own may be abandoned. And in order to completely demolish the theory of a "nation-at-arms", the reader may further note that the economically prosperous condition of the villages (*grāma*), mentioned below, altogether precludes any idea of a perpetual military contingency.

(ii) *The Viśaḥ*

There is no doubt that the bulk of the army was composed of the foot soldiers recruited mostly from the people in general. It is while understanding the significance of the people in the ancient socio-political set-up that we come across the term *viśaḥ* or *viś*. This term appears in the *Rig Veda* in more than one sense. It meant a "settlement", or a "dwelling", or a "subject", or a "people", or a "sub-division of the people".[481]

Professor Macdonell had earlier taken the word *viśaḥ* in the sense of "districts",[482] but later on (along with Professor Keith) wrote that "*viś* is an expression of somewhat doubtful significance". And after enumerating its different meanings (which we have cited just above), the authors of the *Vedic Index* wrote that the meaning "a dwelling" is adequate and probable, since the root *viś* means "to enter", or "to settle". But when used in relation to a prince, it meant a "subject", as when the people of Triṇaskanda or of the Triṣṭus are mentioned. They also opined that the term *viś* appeared in a more special sense of a sub-division of the *jana* or the whole people. "This is, however, not common, for in most passages one or other of the senses given above is quite possible." They also doubted whether the *viśaḥ* was a sub-division of the *jana*, and was to be considered as a local sub-division like a canton, or whether it denoted blood relationship equivalent to a class. The relation of the *viśaḥ* to the *grāma* or *gotra* was uncertain. The grouping of the *viśaḥ* along with the *sabandaḥ* or relative in a passage in the *Atharva Veda*,[483] is not enough to draw any definite conclusion.[484] But in an earlier context, while discussing the term *jana*, they stated: "It may be that *Viś* sometimes represents in the older texts what later was known as Gotra." They concluded by saying that in the later period the sense of *viś* was definitely restricted in some cases to denote the third of the classes of the Vedic polity, the people, or clansmen, as opposed to the nobles (Kṣatra, Kṣatriya) and the priests (Brahma, Brahmans).[485]

Professor Zimmer's view that the *samiti* included all the people, primarily the *viśaḥ*, the assembly of the people in which the king took part, has already been cited above. His theory in regard to the *viśaḥ* may be stated thus: basing his statement on a passage in the *Rig Veda* (ii.26.3), he said that the people were divided into cantons (*viśaḥ*), cantons into joint families or clans, or village communities (*grāma, vṛijana*), and these again into single families. He thought that the later four divisions of society are reflected in the *jana, viśaḥ, janman*, and *putra* or sons, and that each village community was originally founded on relationship.[486] Professor Zimmer, however, admitted that neither *grāma* nor *vṛijana* had the special meaning of a sub-division of the *viśaḥ* when used for war, both words only denoting generally an armed host.[487]

The above theory has been questioned by the authors of the *Vedic Index*, who maintain "it is very doubtful whether this precise division of the people can be pressed", although they agree to the view that the division of the *jana* into several *viśaḥs* may be regarded as probable, "for it is supported by the evidence of another passage of the *Rig Veda* (x.84.4), which mentions the *viśaḥs* as a unit of the fighting men.[488] But what definitely violates the theory of Professor Zimmer is the fact that in the *Rig Veda*, there is a clear contrast between the *viśaḥ* and the *jana*.[488a]

We have, therefore, to seek elsewhere for a plausible explanation of the term *viśaḥ*, since its association with the *jana* does not help us. The suggestion that the term *viśaḥ* definitely denotes in some cases the third of the classes comprising the people as opposed to the nobles, made by Professors Macdonell and Keith, is not quite in agreement with another suggestion of theirs that that term may be interpreted to mean the peasantry, which they made on the basis of the later literature comprising the *Brāhmaṇas* and the *Samhitas*.[489] These works, no doubt, refer to the strife between the *viśaḥ* and the Kṣatriyas. But this does not help us to postulate any theory as to the nature of the former. For the *Brāhmaṇas* also declare that the nobility came out of the *viśaḥ*. Thus, in the *Śatapatha Brāhmaṇa*: "And milk is the nobility (chieftains), and *surā*-liquor the peasantry (clan); the milk he purifies after purifying the nobility from out of the peasantry, for the nobility is produced from out of the peasantry."[490] The *viśaḥ* are given here the same importance as the highest class, since in a later context in the same work, it is stated that "he (the Adhvaryu) thus produces the Kṣatra from out of the Brahman, for from out of the priesthood the nobility is produced—the fiery spirit and energy. . . . ."[491] The importance given to the *viśaḥ* is further proved by the statement that both they and the Kṣatriyas were inter-connected. The entire passage, as given by Professor Eggeling, is worth citing:

> Verily, the cups of milk are the nobility (chieftains), and the cups of *surā*-liquor are the peasantry (clan): thus, were he (the priest or Adhvaryu) to draw (the cups) without inter-linking them, he would detach the peasantry from the nobility, and the nobility from the peasantry, and would cause confusion between the higher and lower, and a failure of the sacrifice. He draws them so as to be inter-linked, and thereby combines the peasantry with the nobility, and the nobility with the peasantry, for the prevention of confusion between the higher and lower, and for the success of the sacrifice.[492]

The above passage seems to run counter to the theory that there was always strife between the *viśaḥ* (which term Professor Eggeling has translated in the above passage and elsewhere as peasantry or clans) and the Kṣatriyas, concerning which there is certainly evidence in the *Śatapatha Brāhmaṇa* cited above. It seems more reasonable to suppose that the term *viśaḥ* was used in the *Śatapatha Brāhmaṇa* in a general manner to represent not only the peasantry but all those who lived by trade as well. That is, the *viśaḥ* seem to have possessed a large element of the wealthier classes whose riches might have been responsible for the jealousy of the Kṣatriyas. At any rate, the clear distinction between the priesthood, as represented by the Brahmans, the nobility as represented by the Kṣatriyas, and the people, as represented by the *viśaḥ* in the same *Brāhmaṇa,*[493] proves that the *viśaḥ* formed the third indispensable element in the realm, the first and the second being composed of the priesthood and the nobility respectively. This was evidently the position of the three strata of society in the later times of the *Brāhmaṇas.*

Connotation of the Term Jana. But in the earlier Vedic days, the exact status of the *viśaḥ,* as stated above, is not very clear. There is no evidence to show that that term was used for a clan. This will be clear when we note two things—the contrast between the *viśaḥ* and the *jana* as given in the *Rig Veda* mentioned above, and the connotation of the term *jana.* The latter term was used for a clan or tribe, as in the case of *Pañcajanāḥ* or the five tribes, referred to frequently in the *Rig Veda,* and the *Yādavajanāḥ* or the tribes of the Yadus, etc. The term *jana* was also used collectively for the people, as in the case of the *Yādavāḥ,* or the Yādava people, or the *Bharatajana,* or the Bharata people, or when the king was described as the protector (*gopa*) of the people (*janasya*). Professors Macdonell and Keith, who have given these instances of the use of the term *jana,* are not inclined to agree with the theory of Professor Hopkins that *jana* in these cases, especially in that of the Bharatas, meant a clan or a horde (*grāma*), as distinguished from the people. They admit that the Bharatas are called *gavyan grāmāḥ,* "a horde eager for booty", in the *Rig Veda,* (iii.33.11) but, according to them, *grāma* in this case is "merely a general application".[494] They have suggested in a later context that the *viśaḥ* may be considered as the equivalent of the *curia,* the *jana* being that of the *tribus,* and the *gotra* that of the *gens* of the later Europeans. Notwithstanding these suggestions, one cannot help accepting their own view that "the confusion is increased by the vagueness of the sense of both *Grāma* and *Viś.*"[495]

Concerning the *jana,* the authors of the *Vedic Index* affirm that "the real elements in the state are the Gotra and the Jana, just as ultimately the *gens* and *tribus,* . . . are alone important".[496] But to judge the past from the standpoint of the remnants of a very distant future, and of lands where the socio-political environment was different to the one prevailing in ancient India in the Vedic days, is hardly the proper way of assessing the nature and importance of the institutions of this country. In this connection it is interesting to observe that the term *janatā,* which occurs frequently in the later *Samhitas* and the *Brāhmaṇas,* denoted, according to Professors Macdonell and Keith, "the people as a community, or as a religious unit".[497] This is unconvincing, for if *janatā* meant the people as a community, how was it different from the *viśaḥ* or the *jana*? And if it meant a religious unit, what exactly was its significance? The learned authors of the *Vedic Index* do not enlighten us on these points.

An allied term *janapada* has already been dealt with in connection with the people in general above.

Conclusion. From the conflicting statements of scholars relating to the terms *jana, viśaḥ, samiti, vidatha,* and even *sabhā* occurring in the early Vedic and later *Samhita* and *Brāhmaṇa* literature, we may conclude that those terms are so obscure as not to help us to arrive with certainty at their exact connotation. One thing is certain that, in the case of some terms like *viśaḥ* and the *vidatha,* they disappeared even in early times,[498] the *samiti* sharing their fate some time after. While others like the *jana, grāma, sabhā,* and *pariṣad* survived the impact of Time, although in doing so they underwent some change in their connotation. This is evident when, for instance, we read Pāṇini's *Grammar* and Kauṭilya's *Arthaśāstra.* The terms *samiti, vidatha,* and *viśaḥ* seem to have disappeared by Pāṇini's time (seventh century B.C.), while only *sabhā, sabheya,* and *sabhya* are met with in his work. His use of the term *sabhā* in *sabhā rājamānuṣya pūrva* seems more appropriate to an assembly of ministers and courtiers, rather than to that of learned men, as suggested by Dr. Agrawala.[499] This assumption is supported by the fact that Paṇini, in the same *sūtra* (ii.4.23), mentions the *rājasabhā* as one of the buildings in the capital,[500] where evidently the royal advisers rather than learned men assembled. Further, Pāṇini distinguishes the *rājasabhā* from the *pariṣad* in the same *sūtra,*[501] thereby suggesting that we have to construe the former term as referring more to governmental rather than to academic or learned matters. The Vedic term *sabheya,* meaning "worthy of an assembly", as Dr. Agravala affirms, became *sabhya* in Pāṇini (*sabhāyām sā dhuḥ sabhyaḥ*).[502] Dr. Agrawala, who had earlier identified the *sabhā* with the *pariṣad,* repeats it when he states later on that the ministerial council was *pariṣad,* and that the larger body was called *sabhā.*[503]

Pariṣad in Pāṇini. The linking up of the *pariṣad* with the *sabhā* which is thus done by Dr. Agrawala may be traced to the use of the word *pariṣad* by Pāṇini and by Kauṭilya. Pāṇini gives three kinds of *pariṣad*—the purely learned type which was composed of specialists "within the Charaṇa whose function was to fix the Śākhā text to be adopted by the Charaṇa with special reference to its phonetical and grammatical forms". Pāṇini refers to the *Caraṇa-pariṣad* in his work (*patrādhvaryu pariṣadaś-ca*).[504] That this type of a *pariṣad* was essentially of an academic type is proved by the statement in the *Gobhila Gṛihya Sūtra* that the *ācārya* (or professor) along with his academy (*sapariṣataka ācārya*) greeted the student on the latter's first admission.[505]

The second use of the term *pariṣad* by Pāṇini refers to more of an ordinary socio-cultural type, as in *pāriṣadya* which evidently means a member of a *pariṣad* (*pariṣadaṁ samavaiti*).[506]

The third kind of *pariṣad* in Pāṇini is given thus—*pariṣadadvalo rājā* which Dr. Agrawala has interpreted to mean "a king governing with his council of ministers", that is, as an administrative body. Dr. Agrawala further states that Pāṇini's use of the word *pāriṣadya* in the sense of one's being eligible (*sādhu*) for membership of a pariṣad (*pariṣado ṇyaḥ*) is to be taken in the sense of a *pariṣad's* being an administrative body (*rajaḥ-kṛṣy-āsuti-pariṣado-valaś-ca*).[507] His conclusion that "originally the *pariṣad* began as a body of scholars inside the Vedic schools",[508] appears to be correct, and may be supplemented by saying that the scope of the *pariṣad,* which was restricted generally to the assemblies of learned men in the earlier days, came to be widened in the days of Kauṭilya so as also to include experts in the theory and practice of government. Before passing on to Kauṭilya, it may be added here that the use of the term *pariṣad,* in the administrative sense was continued by the Buddhists, who called it *parisā.*[509]

Kauṭilya on Pariṣad. Kauṭilya mentions the *pariṣad* on many occasions but his theory of the *pariṣad* is best given in connection with the council of ministers which we have described above, while dealing with the composition of the ministerial assembly (*mantripariṣad*). Kauṭilya, as we have noted earlier, uses the technical term *pariṣad* here in a slightly different sense to what it was used by Manu, and also as understood by Pāṇini, when he writes of the king's being surrounded by his assembly of ministers, while receiving his envoys (*mantripariṣadā sāmanta dūtaṁ*).[510] It is interesting to observe that Kauṭilya's concept of the *pariṣad* was different to the one relating to the *sabhā,* as is evident from the statement: "Classmate spies formed as opposing factions shall carry on disputations in places of pilgrimages, in assemblies, in houses, corporations, and amidst congregations of people" (*satriṇo dvandinaḥ-tīrtha-sabhā-śālā-pūga-samavāyeṣu vivādaṁ kuryuḥ*).[511]

Pūga. The three terms used by Kauṭilya in the above passage are all found in Pāṇini—*sabhā, pūga,* and *samavāya.* The *sabhā* has already been disposed of above. *Pūga* is mentioned by Pāṇini as one of the kinds of *āyudhajīvins* or corporations living by the profession of arms. The *pūgas* were organized under their *grāmaṇi.* According to Dr. Agrawala, the *pūga* was less developed than an *āyudhajīvi sangha* but better organized than a *vrāta.* He writes that the *pūga* was organized into some form of a *sangha* government; and that Pāṇini mentions *pūga* along with *sangha* in connection with a quorum, the member whose presence gave completeness to the *pūga* being mentioned as *pūgatitha* (*pūgasya pūrṇaḥ*).[512] We may agree with the same learned scholar when he asserts that there were two kinds of *pūgas*—those governed by the elders (*pūgāññayo' grāmāṇi pūrvāt*), and those consisting of youths (*kumāra pūgas*).[513]

This happy distinction between the *pūgas* composed of the *vriddhas* and of the *yuvans* in Pāṇini's work, which Dr. Agrawala has clearly brought about, helps us to understand a little but interesting detail in Kauṭilya which Dr. Agrawala has already referred to in the same connection. It is when Kauṭilya mentions the *sanghamukyas* as well as *kumārakas* distinctly existing as *sangha* organizations.[514] While explaining how dissensions are caused with particular reference to corporations, whose help was better than that of an army or friend or profits (*saṅghalābho daṇḍa-mitralābhānāṁ uttamaḥ*), Kauṭilya gives the names of two classes of corporations which have figured earlier in this work. These were the corporations of warriors (*kṣatriyaśreṇi*), like those of Kāmbhoja, Surāṣṭra, and other countries which lived by agriculture, trade, and wielding weapons; and those of the Lichchhavikas, Vṛijaka, Mallaka, Madraka, Kukkura, Kuru, Pāñcāla, and others, which lived by the title of *rāja*. Then Kauṭilya continues to state: "Fiery spies may occasion quarrel among the elderly leaders of the corporations by praising youthful leaders in taverns and theatres . . ." (*veśaśauṇḍikeṣu vā pratilomaprasaṁśābhiḥ saṅgha-mukhyamanuṣyāṇām tīkṣṇāḥ kalahān-uttpādayeyuḥ*).[515] The use of the singular (*sanghamukhya*) and of the plural (*kumārakān*) while referring to the elderly and youthful leaders of the corporation, suggests that in the age of Kauṭilya the corporations had either singular or plural executive heads over them.[516]

Samavāya. The term used for congregations of people by Kauṭilya was *samavāya*. It is interesting to note that Pāṇini also refers to assemblies of people under the general name of *samavāya*.[517]

Conclusion. Three points are clear from the study of some of the terms like *pariṣad*, *pūga*, and *samavāya* made above. Firstly, the term *pariṣad*, which was confined originally in the Vedic days only to a congregation or assembly of learned men, seems to have been used in a wider sense of a council or assembly of ministers by the time of Pāṇini. With Kauṭilya the term *pariṣad* ceases to have its Vedic significance; it simply assumes a sort of an administrative importance. Secondly, the two other terms, *pūga* and *samavāya*, do not figure in the Vedic age. The question arises: How and when did these words come into vogue? To this question there is no answer. And, thirdly, the fact that some of the terms, like those mentioned above, are used in an almost identical sense both by Pāṇini and Kauṭilya, is of much significance in understanding the relative position of the two great authors. Pāṇini's use of the terms is, on the whole, simpler; while that of Kauṭilya is what may be called political or administrative, thereby suggesting that in the earlier days of the author of the celebrated *Grammar*, the socio-political conditions were less developed than those of the author of the *Arthaśāstra*.

(f) *The Village or the Grāma*

(i) *Antiquity of the Village*

The village has been the mainstay of rural India throughout the centuries. The term for a village was the *grāma* which is an immemorial unit. Along with it may be grouped the *kṣetra* and *urvarā* which from the Rig Vedic time denoted plough land. The fields or *kṣetra* were carefully measured, according to the *Rig Veda*; while there is also reference to manure in the

Atharva Veda.[518] Intense cultivation by means of irrigation is mentioned in the *Rig Veda* and the *Atharva Veda.*[519]

Ownership of land was on individual basis, there being no evidence of communal or joint ownership of land or of communal cultivation in the Vedic days.[520] Professors Macdonell and Keith affirm that the careful measuring of the fields (*kṣetra*) points "clearly to individual ownership in land for the plough, a conclusion supported by the reference of Apālā, in a hymn of the Rig Veda, to her father's field (*urvarā*), which is put on the same level as his head of hair as a personal possession". The terms "winning fields" (*urvarā-sā, urvarā-jit, kṣetra-sā*) and "lord of fields" (*urvarā-pati*) used for a god, according to the same authorities, are a further evidence in support of the same conclusion. The fact that in the *Cāndogya Upaniṣad* fields and houses (*āyatanāni*) are described as wealth,[521] further substantiates the above conclusion in regard to the individual ownership of land. But in the *Śatapatha Brāhmaṇa,* the bestowing of land as a fee to priests is mentioned with reproof, thereby suggesting that "land was no doubt even then a very special kind of property, not lightly to be given away or parted with". The passage in question is as follows: "It was Kaśyapa who officiated in his sacrifice, and it was concerning this that the Earth also sang the stanza—'No mortal must give me away; thou wast foolish, Viśvakarman Bhauvana: she (the earth) will sink into the midst of water; vain is this thy promise unto Kaśyapa'."[522]

The term *grāma* occurs frequently in the *Rig Veda* meaning a village.[523] The villages were connected with roads as is proved by the following passage in the *Śatapatha Brāhmaṇa*:

> Were he (Prajāpati) to complete (the sacrifice) with tame ones (beasts), the roads would run together, the village boundaries of two villages would be contiguous, and no ogres, man-tigers, thieves, murderers, and robbers would come to be in the forests. By (so doing) with wild (beasts), the roads would run as under, the village boundaries of two villages would be for as under, and there would come to be ogres, man-tigers, thieves, murderers, and robbers in the forests.[524]

From this passage it is not only evident that villages were connected by roads, as stated above, but that villages were contiguous; that there were anti-social elements like thieves, murderers, and robbers; that there was the danger of animals like ogres (by which is meant, as Professor Eggeling says, bears, according to the commentator Harisvāmin); and that the village roads would be blocked by these dangers. We may presume that if thieves and robbers took shelter in the forests adjoining the villages, it meant that there was sufficient wealth in the villages to attract them. This suggests the material prosperity of the villages.

(ii) *Importance of the Village*

Without going further into the question of the ancient Indian villages,[525] we may study their importance under the following heads: the village as an economic centre; the village as a political centre; and the village as a judicial centre.

The Village as an Economic Centre. Mention has already been made above that land was held individually in the Vedic times; and that it could not lightly be given away as a gift to priests. Opinion is divided as to whether the villages were held by clans or by families. Professor Zimmer had maintained that the *grāma* was a clan, standing between the family and the tribe which according to him, was the *viśaḥ*.[526] Professor Hopkins disagreed with this view by pointing out that Professor Zimmer was inaccurate in identifying the tribe with the *viśaḥ*, since a clan was a sub-division below the tribe or *jana*.[527] Professor Macdonnell and Keith were of the view that the *grāma* was perhaps to be regarded "more correctly as an aggregate of several families, not necessarily forming a clan, but only a part of a clan (Viś), as is often the case at the present day.[528] The expression *grāma-kāma* ("desirous of a village"), occurring in the later *Samhitas*, has given rise to some speculation as to whether or not it refers to the bestowing of land by the king on his favourites or whether it refers to the granting of regalia, as in the later Teutonic times.[529] The occurrence of that phrase may as well be taken to mean that those other than the villagers themselves, were anxious to possess lands in a village. It need not be interpreted to mean, as the learned authors of the *Vedic Index* have averred, that such grants of land by the king depressed the actual cultivators and turned them into tenants.[530] If we agree with them that the communal ownership of land did not exist in the ancient times, then, it is clear that there were some who were owners of land, and others, who were merely tenants. There is no evidence to prove that every owner of land was necessarily a tenant. In fact. the learned authors themselves admit that the village included amongst its various members the cultivating owners,[531] which proves that these latter were not the same as tenants.

The material prosperity of the villages is proved by the cattle, horses, and other domestic animals which the villagers possessed, by the wealthy men who lived in the villages, and by the grains which were stored in the villages.[532] Wealth is the result of peace; and the peace that prevailed in the villages is suggested in the statement of the *Rig Veda* that in the evening the cattle regularly returned to the villages from the forests.[533] The existence of large villages (*mahāgrāmāḥ*), mentioned in the *Jaiminīya Upaniṣad Brāhmaṇa*,[534] further proves that prosperous villages of large dimensions existed in the early times. The evidence relating to the material prosperity of the villages should dispel the doubts in regard to the alleged perpetual fear of war which the champion of the "nation-in-arms" theory has advocated, and which we have discussed above.

The Village as a Political Unit. Professors Macdonell and Keith affirm that the village "can hardly be said to have been a political unit".[535] If by the expression "political unit" is meant an administrative unit, it may be doubted whether their opinion is correct. Firstly, if the village were not an administrative unit, it cannot be understood why, as the learned authors themselves admit, the king's share in the village is referred to so early as in the days of the *Atharva Veda*.[536] Further, the careful measuring of the fields and of the village boundaries, both of which are proved by the references given earlier, would have no significance if the villages were not administrative units. Both could have been done only by an authority higher than that of the villagers themselves. The king's share in the villages, however, strongly belies the assumption of the ownership of a whole village by the villagers themselves. Moreover, if, as the learned authors of the *Vedic Index* also themselves admit, the head or leader of the village, the *grāma-nī*, who is met with in the *Rig Veda* and in the later *Samhitas* and the *Brāhmaṇas*,[537] was ranked, as in the following passage in the *Śatapatha Brāhmaṇa*, with the charioteers, as one of the *ratnins* or jewels of the royal establishment, then it is evident that the *grāmaṇi* was either a popularly elected, or self-styled, official, or an officer of the king. The passage in the *Śatapatha Bhāhmaṇa* is the following: "The Sūta, or the Governor, hands it (the sacrificial wooden sword) to the Grāmaṇī (village headman), 'With Indra's thunder bolt: (therewith serve me!' Thereby the Sūta or the Governor, makes the headman to be wealthier than himself."[538] Here the statement "makes the headman to be wealthier than himself" has to be studied along with the previous statement in the same context in which we are informed that, when the Brahman, by means of the thunderbolt, made the king to be weaker than himself, "indeed, the king who is weaker than a Brahman, is stronger than his enemies: thereby he (the Brahman) makes him (the king) stronger than his enemies".[539] On the strength of this assertion it might be said that the *sūta*, by handing over Indra's thunderbolt to the *grāmaṇī*, made the latter stronger than the *grāmaṇī*'s enemies. This passage is enough to prove that the *grāmaṇī* was not only of the same status and importance as the *sūta* or governor, as Professor Eggeling calls him—an official who is described in the *Vedic Index* as a charioteer![540]—but of sufficient importance in the hierarchy of State officials appointed by the king. Professor Macdonell's and Keith's opinion is in support of this assumption. "The Grāmaṇī's connexion with the royal person seems to point to his having been a nominee of the king rather than a popularly elected officer." But the same authorities maintain that the post may have been sometimes hereditary, and sometimes nominated, or elective, there being no evidence in this regard.[541]

And, finally, since the *grāmaṇī* was often connected with the *senānī*, or the royal general—who was one of the *ratnins* of the king[542]—it follows that he was reckoned as one of the State officials. Whether he had only military powers, as Professor Zimmer maintained,[543] or both civil and military powers as head of the village, as Professors Macdonell and Keith affirmed,[544] it is clear that he exercised executive powers on behalf of the king. We shall see below that the village continued to be an administrative unit in the later days of the lawgiver Manu and of Kauṭilya.

The Village as a Judicial Unit. If the *grāmyavādin* was the village judge, as is mentioned in the *Yajur Veda,* and had a *sabhā* or an advisory council of his own, as is given in the *Maitrāyaṇī Samhita,*[545] it means that we have to look upon the village as a unit of the judicial administration of the country. The term *Śatapati,* occurring in the *Samhita* and *Brāhmaṇa* literature,[546] has been understood to mean "Lord of a Hundred Villages", by Professors Macdonell and Keith, rather than to mean "Lord of the Hundred Gods", as was done by the commentator on the *Taittirīya Brāhmaṇa.*[547] The designation of "Lord of a Hundred Villages", we may note by the way, occurs in the later work of the lawgiver Manu, which will be cited at once below. We may, therefore, agree to the view of the authors of the *Vedic Index* that the *Śatapati* was probably a judicial official with the duties of a revenue collector.[548] The existence of this dignitary only adds to the arguments given above that the village was an administrative unit under the king.

(*iii*) *The Village in the Later Ages: In the Manusmṛiti*

The control of the State over the village continued to be maintained in the later days of the *Manusmṛiti* in which the king is enjoined to place a company of soldiers, commanded by a trusted official, in the midst of two, five, or hundreds of villages. The king was likewise to appoint over each village a lord, as well as lords of ten villages, lords of twenty, lords of a hundred, and lords of a thousand villages. And likewise in each town a royal superintendent of all affairs was appointed by the king. We have seen above how closely these State officials of the rural areas were bound to the centre, and how the king appointed a minister to look after these officials. The village headmen were called *grāmikas* or *grāmaṇis* in the days of Manu.[549] The ancient Vedic concept of a *Śatapati,* therefore, seems to have continued in the later times, when Manu improved upon it by introducing the idea of lords of a thousand villages.

In Pāṇini. The *grāma* continued to figure in the *Grammar* of Pāṇini in which a collection of villages was called *grāmatā.*[550] Cultivated lands continued to be called *kṣetra.* The *takṣan* or carpenter in the village, mentioned in the *Rig Veda* and in later literature,[551] figures also in Pāṇini, where he is called *grāma-takṣa.*[552] But in regard to the use of the term *grāmaṇi,* Pāṇini used it in connection with one kind of the corporations we have mentioned earlier, the *pūga* corporation. He would style the *grāmaṇi* constitution of the *pūgas*.[553] These *grāmaṇi* constitutions of warlike people are supposed to be the same which appear in the *Mahābhārata* under the name of *grāmaṇīyas* living on the banks of the Indus, and as having offered stiff opposition to Nakula in his western campaigns.[554] The above shows that the meaning of *grāmaṇi* since the days of Manu and earlier, had changed to connote leaders of warlike communities.

In Kauṭilya. When we reach the age of Kauṭilya, we find greater importance given to the villages than ever before. We had an occasion of mentioning how in regard to boundary disputes between two villages, neighbours or elders of five or twenty villages were to investigate the cases on the evidence to be furnished from natural or artificial boundary marks (*simāvivādaṁ grāmayoḥ ubhayoḥ sāmantāḥ pañcagrāmī daśagrāmī vā*). Then, again, in the same context later on we are informed that disputes concerning fields shall be decided by the elders of the neighbourhood or of the village (*kṣetra-vivādaṁ sāmanta-grāma-vṛiddhāḥ kuryuḥ*).[555] It is thus clear that Kauṭilya had dispensed with the use of the word *grāmaṇi*, while referring to the elders or leaders of the villages. He seems to have replaced it by the term *sāmanta* and *grāmavṛiddāḥ*. He likewise does not use the word *grāmatā* for a collection of villages but calls it *gramakūṭam*, and its superintendent, *gramakūṭa-adhyakṣa*.[556]

Whether we study the condition of the villages as depicted in the *Arthaśāstra* or in the *Manusmṛiti* or even earlier in the age of the Vedic literature, it is clear that the king, as typifying the State, was greatly desirous of being in the closest touch with the people in the rural areas, and of bringing the villages under the central administration. A question that arises in this connection is: Why was the monarch so eager to exercise control over the villages and to look after the welfare of the rural areas? A possible answer is that it was really in the villages and in the country areas that there was, in the last resort, what might be called the general will, that is, the bulk of the people expressing their opinion in regard to certain grave questions of the State like, for example, the removal of a wicked ruler or even an attack by a foreign power. The proxmity of the ruler to the capital and the towns naturally laid them at his mercy; while the distance which separated the rural areas from the capital, and the difficulties which the ruler might have had in reaching them, gave them a peculiar position of advantage which the city and townfolk did not possess. In the final analysis it was undoubtedly the people in the country sides who were reckoned to be of ultimate importance. This perhaps explains why even in the earlier days of the *Śatapatha Brāhmaṇa*, the headman of the village was considered to be of the same importance as the royal officials like the charioteer and the general. A study of this element of the State comprising the people creates the impression that, in spite of all the restrictions which the king placed on the people, he was more concerned with being on good terms with them rather than with the nobles of his own rank, who undoubtedly possessed sufficient strength to coerce him, but whose limited numbers placed them at a disadvantage when contrasted with the people of the towns and of the country sides (the *paurajānapada* of Kauṭilya) we have described above.

CHAPTER VI

THE ELEMENTS OF THE STATE (*Contd.*)

D. THE TERRITORY

1. INTRODUCTION

THE TERRITORY is the next important element in the State. In the description of this element we shall see that, as in the case of others, the ancient Indian political thought was progressive. In an earlier context we had an occasion of mentioning the importance of the term *rājya*. We have also to recall here the discussion that was made above, while instituting a comparative study of the functions and end of the State in Aristotle and Kauṭilya, concerning the happiness of the largest number of the citizens which was the ideal of the ancient Indian State. It was also remarked above that, according to Kauṭilya, the State was to be self-sufficient. Finally, we should also recollect here the remarks made above in regard to the State's not being the growth of a day. All these are essentially concerned with the major question of the territory of the State.

2. THEORIES REGARDING TERRITORY

Two different theories on this vital question have been propounded. These are by Professor Rangaswami Aiyangar and by Dr. Kane.

(*a*) *Professor Rangaswami Aiyangar's Theory*

Professor Aiyangar denies that the territory was an essential element of the State. After rightly stating that "in the most representative political thought of ancient India there is complete agreement on two matters, viz., on the idea of what constitute the essential elements of the State, and on the natural necessity for the State", he writes thus: "In regard to the former, it is usual for our political writers to group the characteristic features as seven, under the heads of Sovereign, Minister, People, Fort, Treasure, Army and Allies." And in support of this assertion, he cites the following statement of Kauṭilya: *svāmi-amātya-janapada-durga-kośa-daṇḍa-mitrāṇi-prakṛitayaḥ.*[557]

In the above list of the element of the State as given by Kauṭilya, which we shall have to comment upon again, Professor Aiyangar has interpreted *janapada* in the sense of people; and he has no place for territory in the constituent elements of the State. In a later context, the distinguished historian affirms that the idea of a fixed territory was the growth of the later times; and that it cannot be expected in the earlier writings. He writes thus:

> The conditions of later times should have somewhat reduced, in practice, the importance of one of the essentials according to the old definition of the State. In the epochs of wide popular and tribal movement represented in the Vedic and Epic periods, it was of course not to be expected that the territorial aspect of the State should be grasped, or stressed, even if understood. Even in the days of Kauṭilya, Powers are referred to by the names of peoples and not by geographical limits. . . . It is, however, clear that in the epochs that followed the disruption of the Mauryan empire, when invasions and immigrations from outside followed one another in an unending procession, frequent unsettlement of the population and of the political boundaries became inevitable, and the State had to be thought of independently of a fixed territory.

Such conditions, according to the distinguished historian, persisted so late as the ninth century A.D.—the age of the rise of the Gurjara-Pratihāra Empire. "Hence the statement that a definite territory constituted an essential feature of the State, as an institution, has to be taken in the light of our history, more as an often-realized idea than as a permanent characteristic of all ancient States."[558]

From the above statements it is clear that Professor Aiyangar has looked at the problem of the territory from the standpoint of the later times; that in the Vedic days and in those of the Epics, there were wide popular and tribal movements; that in those times, the people understood the idea of territory but did not either grasp or stress it; and that it was only in the post-Mauryan days, when the country was inundated with foreign invasions, that the "State had to be thought of independently of a fixed territory".

It is unfortunate that the eminent historian should have postulated the above assumptions none of which is tenable. That in the Vedic days the people certainly understood and grasped the concept of a fixed territory must have been apparent to the reader from the theories relating to the *janapadas* made above. Further proof of the existence of the concept of territory in the Vedic days will be given below. What Professor Aiyangar means by the wide popular and tribal movements not only in the Vedic times but also in the days of the epics one fails to understand. It is not denied that in a vast country like India there were periodical movements of tribes. But this is not equal to saying that the people had no concept of territory as being one of the elements of the State. We shall see at once below that Kauṭilya had a definite theory of territory which, because of its preciseness and comprehensiveness, is perhaps the best we have in the whole range of ancient political thought. The foreign invasions of the post-Mauryan times, no doubt, shattered the frontiers of many a kingdom but this does not mean that the idea of territory, as an element of the State, did not exist. We cannot help remarking that, in his evaluation of the theory of territory, Professor Aiyangar has had recourse to the very criterion which elsewhere he had condemned as being erroneous. This is to judge the past from the happenings of the later times. While editing his monumental work on Bhaṭṭa Laksmīdhara's *Kṛityakalpataru, Rājadharmakāṇḍa*, Professor Aiyangar enunciates this excellent criterion of historical judgment: " . . . to read the present into the past is an admitted defect in historical writing, inspite of the essential unity of human nature, which makes it possible to presume *ordinarily* that the same historic causes will have the same reactions at all times and places, other things being equal."[559] According to his own standard, therefore, it would be incorrect to judge the political condition of the Vedic and epic times, on the basis of either the post-Mauryan or of the Gurjara-Pratihāra times.

(*b*) *Dr. Kane's Theory*

Dr. Kane seems to be of the opinion that the territory was a most important element of the State. He bases his view on the statement of the *Agni Purāṇa* that the territory is the most important element of the State.[560] But the evidence of the *Agni Purāṇa*, a work of the later times, cannot be cited to prove the theory of territory as it existed in the ancient days. But that Dr. Kane is hesitant in ascribing a theory of territory even in the days of Kauṭilya is evident from his statement: "It should be noted that neither Kauṭilya nor Kāmandaka defines *rājya*."[561] We have to trace the concept of territory from the Rig Vedic days which Dr. Kane certainly does with his usual thoroughness. This eminent scholar's view on territory will be mentioned presently.

3. ANTIQUITY OF THE CONCEPT OF TERRITORY

The term *rāṣṭra* meaning territory occurs in the *Rig Veda* in the statement of Trasadasyu: "Mine is the kingdom on both sides (or in both spheres)" (*mama dvitā rāṣṭraṁ kṣatryasya*).[562] The term definitely denoted "a kingdom" or "royal territory" in the *Atharva Veda* and in the later *Samhita* literature.[563] In the *Atharva Veda*, the earth is called mother, and is invoked to impart to the *rāṣṭra* strength and energy.[564] In a famous benedictory passage in the *Taittirīya Samhita*, one of the blessings invoked is the following: "May the king in this kingdom become brave, a skilled archer, and a great warrior!"[565] In the light of this positive evidence in the Vedic literature, it would be incorrect to maintain that the ancient Indians were unaware of the concept of territory.

The supposition that there could ever have been a concept of kingdom without territory is inconceivable. A mere collection of people has never formed a State unless they had a definite territory to claim as their own. Dr. Kane rightly maintains: "The analysis of the elements and nature of the State led ancient Indian writers to hold that a mere conglomeration of people did not by itself constitute a State, but that for a State there must be people who live within certain definite geographical limits (*rāṣṭra*)."[566] If the ancient Indians had not possessed the concept of territory, as some imagine, it is impossible to explain the terms *rājya, sāmrāṭ, sārvabhauma,* etc., which have been discussed in the earlier pages of this book. Even the concept of *janapada* is unthinkable without a definite territory.

4. CHARACTERISTICS OF TERRITORY IN THE MANUSMRITI

When we reach the age of the *Manusmṛiti,* we find that there is an improvement on the earlier concept of territory in the sense that certain characteristics of the kingdom are mentioned in that work. "Let him (the king) settle in a country which is open and has a dry climate, where grain is abundant, which is chiefly (inhabited) by Āryans, not subject to epidemic diseases (or similar troubles), and pleasant, where the vassals are obedient, and his own (people easily) find their livelihood."[567] It may be argued that the above merely suggests the concept of a *rājya* but not that of a definite territory. This objection cannot be entertained because we cannot imagine an undefined kingdom being ruled over by a king. In this connection it is worth while to note that Manu's injunctions that a king should strive to gain what he has not yet gained, and carefully preserve what he has gained,[568] clearly points to a definite territory over which the king ruled. In other words, the terms *rājya* and *rāṣṭra* are inseparable terms.

In Pāṇini. In Pāṇini's *Grammar* we have definitely the term *rājya* given to a monarchical State. The concept of territory is indicated in the king's titles—*sārvabhauma, pārthiva,* and *bhūpati.* Territory was called *bhūmi* and *pṛithvi.*[569] Pāṇini's concept was obviously of the simple type.

In Kauṭilya. But that was not so with Kauṭilya. He does not talk in terms of Manu, who would have the larger part of the population made up of the Aryans, and who preferred an open country with a dry climate in which grain was abundant. The growth in the concept of territory since the days of Manu is apparent in the comprehensive definition of a good country (*janapada-sampat*) given in the *Arthaśāstra,* thus:

> Possessed of capital cities both in the centre and the extremities of the kingdom, productive of subsistence not only to its own people, but also to outsiders on occasions of calamities, repulsive to enemies, powerful enough to put down neighbouring kings, free from miry, rocky, uneven, and desert tracts, as well as from conspirators, tigers, wild beasts, and large tracts of wilderness, beautiful to look at, containing fertile lands,

mines, timber, and elephant forests, and pasture grounds, artistic, containing hidden passages, full of cattle, not depending upon rain for water, possessed of land and waterways, rich in various kinds of commercial articles, capable of bearing the burden of a vast army and heavy taxation, inhabited by agriculturists of good and active character, full of intelligent masters and servants, and with a population noted for its loyalty and good character—these are the qualities of a good country.[570]

It is difficult to come across in ancient texts a more complete and comprehensive definition of territory than the one given by Kauṭilya. The term *janapada* used here by him cannot be taken, as is done by Professor Aiyangar,[571] in the sense of the people, since the numerous attributes mentioned in the description agree only with the territory and the kingdom. This holds good of the opening sentence of the same book dealing with the elements of sovereignty (*prakṛitisampadaḥ*).

If further proof is needed to show that Kauṭilya used the term *janapada* in the sense of the kingdom or *rāṣṭra*, it is found in an earlier context in which one of the duties of the Collector-General is said to have been to divide the *janapada* into four districts (*samāharttā caturthā janapadaṁ vibhajya*).[572] In an earlier context, he uses the term *rāṣṭra* in connection with the same duties of the same high official, in a manner to definitely suggest that, according to him, the *rāṣṭra* was the same as *janapada*. He relates thus: "The Collector-General shall attend to (the collection of revenue from) forts, country parts, mines, buildings, and gardens, forests, herds of cattle, and roads of traffic" (*samāharttā durgaṁ rāṣṭraṁ khaṇiṁ setuṁ vanaṁ vṛijaṁ vaṇikpathaṁ ca-avekṣeta*).[573]

Then, again, Kauṭilya uses the term *janapada* in the sense of the kingdom or *rāṣṭra* when he states: "On all the four quarters of the boundaries of the kingdom, defensive fortifications against an enemy in war shall be constructed on grounds naturally best fitted for the purpose" (*caturdiśaṁ janapadānte sāmparāyikaṁ deva kṛitaṁ durgaṁ kārayet*). In the same context further on he states: "Of these, water and mountain fortifications are best suited to defend populous centres ; and desert and forest fortifications are habitations in wilderness" (*teṣāṁ nadīparvatadurgaṁ janapadārakṣasthānaṁ dhānvanavanadurgamaṭavīsthānaṁ*).[574]

No greater proof is needed to demonstrate the fact that Kauṭilya was aware of the concept of territory than the following statement: "In the opinion of Kauṭilya, no territory deserves the name of a kingdom or country unless it is full of people" (*na hi-ajano janapado rājyaṁ janapadaṁ vā bhavati-iti Kauṭilyaḥ*).[575]

And if still further proof is required to demolish the view that Kauṭilya had no clear idea of territory, we have the following passage in which he describes the extensive empire of his royal patron, thus:

Country means the earth ; in it the thousand *yojanas* of the northern

> portion of the country that stretches between the Himālayas and the ocean form the dominion of no insignificant emperor; in it there are such varieties of land, as forests, villages, mountains, level plains, and uneven grounds (*deśaḥ pṛithivī tasyāṁ Himavat-samudrāntaṁ-udīcīnaṁ yojana-sahasra-parimāṇaṁ-atiryak-cakravarti-kṣetraṁ*). In such lands he should undertake such work as he considers to be conducive to his power and prosperity.[576]

Here we have in this passage not only the concept of a definite territory, bounded on the north by the Himālayas and on the south by the ocean, forming a *rājya* or kingdom but a re-iteration of the nature of that country which was to be conducive to the might and prosperity of the monarch. In the light of these statements in the *Arthaśāstra*, it would be incorrect to maintain that Kauṭilya does not define a *rājya*; and to affirm that we have to come to the post-Mauryan times in order to find a territorial concept of the State.[577] In regard to the concept of territory, Kauṭilya had undoubtedly advanced on the concept of Manu and the earlier writers.[578]

CHAPTER VII

THE ELEMENTS OF THE STATE (*Contd.*)

E. FORTS

1. ANTIQUITY OF FORTS

IN THE elucidation of the elements of the State, we see, again, that the ancient Indian political thought was continuous. When we first come across the term *durga* meaning a fort in the *Rig Veda,* it was used in the sense of a fort, or a stronghold.[579] It was synonymous with *pur,* meaning a rampart, or fort, or stronghold. That even in the Vedic times there were two kinds of forts is clear from the use of the terms *pṛithvī* or broad, and *ūrvī*, or wide forts. Forts of sun-dried bricks or stone (*aśmamāyi*) are mentioned in the *Rig Veda.* That forts in the *Rig Vedic* days were of considerable size is proved by the phrase "with a hundred walls" (*śatabhuji*). Their self-sufficiency is suggested by the term "full of kind" (*gomati*) showing that forts were filled in with cattle, evidently to provide the defendants with food in case of a prolonged siege.[580]

The siege of forts is alluded to in the *Samhitas* and *Brāhmaṇas.* In the *Śatapatha Brāhmaṇa,* we have the following account of a siege: now the gods and the Asuras, both of them sprung from Prajāpati, were contending against each other. The Asuras then built themselves castles in these worlds—an iron one in this world, a silver one in the air, and a golden one in the sky. The gods then prevailed. They besieged them by these sieges (*upasad*) ; and because they besieged (*upa-sad*) them, therefore, received the name *upasads.* They clove the castles, and conquered these worlds. Hence they say: "A castle is conquered by siege" ; for it is, indeed, by beleaguering that one of these human castles is taken.[581]

Although further proof is not available in regard to the nature of the three castles built by the Asuras, yet the fact that the castles are mentioned, and their conquest by beleaguering is likewise described, proves that we have to date the construction of castles to the age of the *Brāhmaṇas.* The explicit reference to one of them having belonged to men is a point that deserves special notice. At any rate the iron castle "in this world" seems to have been a great improvement upon the Vedic castles which were probably built of sun-dried bricks, and which were guarded by palisades and a ditch. Since fire is said to have been used in these sieges in the *Rig Veda,*[582] the assumption is that the palisades were probably of wood.

2. THEORIES ABOUT FORTS

Based on the literature of the Vedic days and after, scholars have propounded three theories about forts which are the following: Professor Zimmer maintained that the palisades were no more than a hedge of thorns or a row of stakes ; that the *pur* may have been sometimes built within the limits of the villages ; and that some of them like the *śaradipur* (autumnal forts) might have been built as a protection against autumnal floods.[583]

The first part of the above theory does not seem to have been probable, since, as noted just above, the evidence is more in favour of wooden palisades than in that of a hedge of thorns or even a row of stakes. There is nothing improbable in the *pur's* being built within the limits of villages, since a *pur* or a fort outside a village would have served no purpose. The suggestion in regard to the autumnal forts is not improbable. The authors of the *Vedic Index*, while repeating Professor Zimmer's view concerning the autumnal forts, affirm that they belonged to the Dāsas ; and that such forts were probably occupied in autumn by the Dāsas against the Aryans.[584] As to why the Dāsas should have occupied the autumnal forts only in autumn is not clear: in fact, a migration from one type of forts to another based on the vagaries of the weather, is both unhistorical and unreasonable.

Professors Pischel and Geldner considered the *purs* (towns) as having had wooden walls and ditches.[585] This is not unlikely when we remember that, even in comparatively later times, the great city of Pāṭaliputra was built of timber.[586]

Professors Macdonell and Keith have favoured the following theory. They say that it would be a mistake to regard the forts with a hundred walls (*śatabhuji*) "as permanently occupied fortified places like the fortresses of the mediaeval barony. They were probably places of refuge against attack, ramparts of hardened earth with palisades and a ditch (like Delhi)." The theory of Professors Pischel and Geldner is possible "but hardly susceptible of proof". On the whole, it is hardly likely that in early Vedic times city life was much developed.[587]

Indian scholars have unfortunately nothing to say on the theories relating to forts. They either ignore this important element,[588] or merely mention the "fort commander",[589] or simply state that the forts were meant for the safety of the king, the people, and the treasury, enumerating, however, the different kinds of forts.[590]

Whatever may have been the exact nature of the ancient castles, it is clear that the Vedic people certainly had the concept of castles. To expect the ancient Indians to have possessed the idea of the mediaeval European type is to pervert history. The later European analogy being useless in this regard, there is no point in saying that the castles mentioned in the ancient texts were merely places of refuge. If it is admitted that the forts in the Vedic days possessed cattle, and that they were made of dried brick and stone, we have to imagine that they were subject to warfare and to long periods of sieges. The theory that they were meant only as places of refuge cannot be sustained.

3. PROGRESS IN THE CONCEPT OF FORTS

(a) *In the Manusmṛiti*

The necessity of framing definite rules for constructing forts seems to have been felt with the progress of Time. This will be evident from the *Manusmṛiti* which speaks of royal fortresses. The king was to build in the country, which has been described earlier, "a town making for his safety a fortress, protected by a desert, or a fortress built of (stone and) earth, or one protected by water and trees, or one (formed by an encampment of armed) men, or a hill-fort. Let him make every effort to secure a hill-fort, for amongst all those (fortresses mentioned) a hill-fort is distinguished by many superior qualities." Of these six kinds of fortresses, the first three are said to be inhabited by wild beasts, animals living in holes, and acquatic animals, the last three by monkeys, men, and gods respectively.[591] In a later context Manu states that the king having duly settled his country, "and having built forts in accordance with the Institutes", should remove those dangerous men who are like thorns to his side.[592] As to when exactly the details about the forts came to be inserted in the *dharmaśāstras* and the *nitiśāstras,* we cannot make out.

(b) *After Manu and before Kauṭilya*

Some progress seems to have been made after the times of Manu and before the age of the *Rāmāyaṇa.* The latter work gives different kinds of forts and how they were equipped. They were well filled with food, grain, money, men, machinery, and water. There were four kinds of forts—those surrounded by sea or river, called *nādeya,* as in the case of Laṅkā ; those surrounded by hills with an entrance that was excavated like Kiṣkindhā ; those surrounded by dense forests, again like Laṅkā ; and those which were surrounded by artificial defences of the type of ramparts, moats, etc., like Ayodhyā. Of all these Laṅkā was an ideal fortress, since it satisfied all conditions: it was protected by the sea, it was located on the top of the hill Trikūṭa, it was surrounded by dense forests, and it was protected by artificial defences. It was surrounded by a deep moat in which were dreadful crocodiles ; and it had four main gates on the four sides, each furnished with iron bolts, and guarded by steel *śataghnis,* huge engines (*iśupālayantra*) for throwing stones and arrows at the enemy.[593]

(c) *In Kauṭilya*

Some time after Manu, one of the predecessors of Kauṭilya called Parāśara seems to have contributed to the history of forts. This is evident from the discussion of the various views relating to the Aggregate of the Calamities of the Elements of Sovereignty in Book VIII, Chapter I of the *Arthaśāstra*. The discussion starts with the opinion of the unnamed teacher of Kauṭilya, who states that of the seven kinds of calamities, viz., the king in distress, the minister in distress, the people in distress, distress due to bad fortifications, financial distress, the army in distress, and an ally in distress—that which is mentioned first is more serious than the next one in the order of enumeration. Bharadavāja's opinion on the above follows in detail but there is no reference in it to forts at all, thereby suggesting that, in the opinion of that political thinker, the problem of forts was not of much consequence, or perhaps, was included in that of the army to which Bharadvāja refers. Kauṭilya replies to the objections of Bharadvāja, and although he, too, does not mention forts at all, yet he has much to say on forts after citing the opinion of Viśālākṣa. This latter political thinker, too, does not mention forts. But Parāśara, who follows, has the following to say: of the distress of the people and distress due to bad fortifications, the latter is a more serious evil, for it is in fortified towns that the treasury and the army are secured. The fortified towns are a secure place for the people ; they are a stronger power than the citizens or country people. And they are a powerful defensive instrument in times of danger for the king.

Kauṭilya's objections to the above arguments of Parāśara are interesting. Forts, finance, and the army depend upon the people ; likewise buildings, trade, agriculture, cattle-rearing, bravery, stability, power, and abundance (of things). In all countries people do not generally reside on fortified mountains and islands owing to the absence of an expansive country. When a country consists purely of cultivators, troubles due to the absence of fortifications (are apparent) ; while in a country which consists of warlike people, troubles that may appear are due to the absence of (an expansive and cultivated) country.[594]

We may comment upon the above before passing on to the next part of Kauṭilya's theory of fortifications which will be in reply to Piśuna's views. In the above passage, Kauṭilya appears, superficially, it may seem, to have rejected Parāśara's theory that bad fortifications are a more serious evil than the distress of the people. But we shall see below that Kauṭilya will himself endorse the major contention of Parāśara. Two new kinds of fortifications are mentioned by Kauṭilya in the above passage: those built on mountains and those on islands. These do not seem to figure in earlier writings. Further, he clearly distinguishes between an agricultural people and a warlike people. The former will have troubles because of a want of fortifications while the latter, of a want of cultivated territory. Thus did Kauṭilya link up what might be called agricultural economy with war economy. Incidentally, we may give some idea of what he meant by an expansive and cultivated country. The answer is given in the manner in which he distinguishes between cultivated lands. The latter may suit for various kinds of agricultural operations ; but cultivated land is adapted for pasture lands, manufacture of merchandise, mercantile transactions of borrowing and lending, and as being attractive to rich merchants.[595] Kauṭilya seems to have made provision in this passage for an expansive economy that was to meet the progressive needs of a growing Empire.

Turning next to Piśuna, we find that that political thinker considered troubles arising from a want of finances more serious than those due to the absence of forts. The reasons were simple: the repairs of fortifications, their maintenance, and their capture by means of intrigue—all these could be done only with the aid of wealth.

It was now, while rejecting Piśuna's theory, that Kauṭilya accepts Parāśara's view in regard to the importance of forts. He now affirms that it is on the fort that the safety of the treasury and the army depends ; and that it is from the fort that secret war (intrigue), the control over one's partisans, the maintenance of the army, the reception of the allies, and the driving out of the enemies and the wild tribes are successfully carried out.[596]

Kauṭilya's theory of forts may be summarized thus: as between forts and the people, the latter were more important ; while as between the fort and the treasury, it was the former that was more important. He would, therefore, in the last resort place reliance upon the people and the fort, and as between these, he would prefer the people. As to why he would prefer the people as against the fort, he says in another context thus:

> Which is better of the two, the tract of land with forts, or that which is thickly populated? The latter is better: for that which is thickly populated is a kingdom in all its senses. What can a depopulated country like a barren cow be productive of? (*durga-apāśrayā puruṣa-apāśrayā vā bhūmih-iti puruṣa-apāśrayā śreyasī puruṣavaddhi rājyaṁ apuruṣā gauḥ vandhyeva kiṁ duhīta*).[597]

While Kauṭilya repeats some of the ideas relating to the location of forts as given in the *Manusmṛiti*, he has his own contribution to give to this side of the problem. We have already seen above the two kinds of forts he has referred to—those on the mountains and those on the islands. To these may be added the following: forts on the plains and those in the centres of rivers. The mountain fort was better than that in the centre of a river, and the latter better than that on a plain.[598] The water fortification in the middle of a river was called *audaka* ; one on the mountain, *pārvata* ; a desert one, *dhānvana,* and a forest one, *vanadurga.* Then, there was the fort on a plain surrounded by low ground. Of these fortifications, the water and mountain fortifications were best suited to defend popular centers ; while desert and forest fortifications were habitations in wildness (*aṭavisthānaṁ*). If Kauṭilya's injunctions reflect in any way the ancient precept and practice in this matter, the fortifications, whether on mountains, in the centre of rivers, or in forests, were not meant as occasional places of refuge but for being permanently inhabited, as was the case with the later fortifications. This explains why they were called *sthānaṁ* (habitations) (*teṣāṁ nadī-parvata-durgaṁ janapadārakṣasthānam dhānvana-vanadurgaṁ aṭavīsthānaṁ*).[599]

In the same connection Kauṭilya gives a very detailed and interesting description of the fortified capital (*sthāniya*) which was to be the seat of the royal treasury (*samudāya-sthānam-sthānīyaṁ*). It was to have three ditches, ramparts, parapets, roads, towers, passage for exit, passage for the movement of troops, an entrance gate, turret, canals, pools, and defensive weapons including explosives (*agnisaṁyoga*), machines (*yantra*), etc.,—all of which are mentioned in detail by him.[600] In the next chapter he enumerates likewise with minute care the many types of buildings which were to be constructed inside the fort.[601] We cannot help concluding that Kauṭilya's genius was fully alive to the needs of constructing a great capital which even in its ruins seems to evoke wonder and admiration. In the following pages of this book we shall see to what extent Kauṭilya's injunctions in regard to the imperial capital were actually put into practice. From what has been stated above, it is clear that he had definitely made much progress since the days of Manu. In the light of all this, it would be incorrect to maintain with Professor Aiyangar that Kauṭilya attached "scant importance to forts (valueless in such great plains)".[602]

F. THE ARMY

1. ANTIQUITY

This element was essentially connected with forts, and, therefore, with the major question of defending the country against aggression. The many references to wars in the *Rig Veda*[603] indicate that the Vedic kings were as much intent on defending their territory as on carrying the war into the enemies' lands. In this connection we may recount the discussion that was made above relating to the term *senā* in order to understand the growth in the theory of the army. It was stated there that the idea of entrusting the duty of defending the country to a caste made up of warriors was a later one. The terms *senā-nī* and *senāpati* occurring in the *Rig Veda*, the *Saṁhitas*, and the *Brāhmaṇas*, prove that the office of a general was one of great antiquity.[604] These terms continued to be used in the same sense in the days of Pāṇini and afterwards.[605]

2. IN THE MANUSMRITI

The earlier ideas of the army and of warfare seem to have undergone a change when we come to the age of the *Manusmṛti*, which describes not only the duties of the Kṣatriyas in the matter of carrying arms for striking and of throwing missiles,[606] but opens a new chapter in the history of inter-state relations by advocating the theory of aggressive designs and of carrying the war into the enemy's territories. Manu states that "of him who is always ready to strike, the whole world is in awe. . . ."[607] Not content with this he enunciates the theory of the Circle of States (*rāja-maṇḍala*), and makes it incumbent upon the monarch to undertake an aggressive war.[608] We lose sight of this theory till we come to Kauṭilya, who will make it the corner-stone of his foreign policy.

3. HISTORY OF THE COMPONENT PARTS OF THE ARMY

Before we pass on to the concept of the army in Kauṭilya, we may briefly mention the progress in the history of the component parts of the army as well as of the kinds of army from the Vedic times onwards. In those distant days, the chariot (*kośa*), the bow (*dhanus*), and the arrow (*paruṣa*) were the commonest forms of martial equipment.[609] There is nothing in the Vedic literature to denote that the Aryans had divided their army into the fourfold division, although there is undoubted proof of the existence of infantry (*patti*), chariots (*ratha*), and horse (*aśva*) in those times. The horses were used for drawing chariots which were then greatly in fashion.[610] Although the elephant is mentioned under the name of *ibha, gaya, nāga varaṇa, śukladanta,* and *hastin,* yet its use in warfare is not apparent.[611] The well-known fourfold division of the army (infantry, horse, chariots, and elephants) appears in the *Manusmṛiti* in which the different components are mentioned in various contexts.[612]

4. IN PANINI

Some improvement upon the concept of the fourfold division of the army in the *Manusmṛiti* is seen in Pāṇini's *Grammar,* which not only repeats the traditional divisions but mentions certain types of specialized branches like the corps of mounted soldiers (*sādi*), of camels (*uṣṭra-sādi*), and of camels and mules (*uṣṭra-vāmi*), thereby suggesting that new units, unknown in the earlier days, were now being introduced in the Indian army.[613]

5. IN THE EPICS

A further picture of the component parts of the army is available in the *Rāmāyaṇa* which, of course, mentions the ancient fourfold division of the army (*caturaṅga-balam, caturanga-sainyaṁ*),[614] and in addition gives different kinds of armies. These were the *mitra-bala,* or soldiers of the allies ; *aṭavī-bala,* or soldiers recruited from the forest and wild tribes ; *maula-bala* or hereditary soldiers (that is, those recruited and maintained by the State from the warrior classes in the realm) ; *bhṛitya-bala,* or mercenary soldiers ; and, finally, *dviṣad-bala,* or soldiers who had deserted from the enemy.[615] These five kinds of armies were evidently improvements since the days of the *Manusmṛiti.*

The definite advance upon the earlier concept of the army is seen in the *Rāmāyaṇa* in the description of those who, in addition to the actual combatants, formed a most essential part of the army. In modern language, they were the miners and sappers, that is, those who prepared the ground for the successful marching of the army. These were the *bhūmi-pradeśa-jña,* or scouts who knew the topography of the country ; *vartma-karma-kovida,* or road-makers ; *mārgin,* or levellers ; *durga-vicāraka,* or surveyors of hills and mountains ; *sūtra-karmaviśārada,* or ground engineers ; *yantraka,* or hydraulic engineers ; *yantra-kovida,* or engineers in charge of missiles (like catapaults, etc.) ; *khanaka,* or diggers ; *sthāpati* or architects and wheel-wrights ; *vṛikṣa-takṣaka,* or wood cutters ; *vardhaki,* or carpenters ; *kūpakāra,* or diggers of wells ; *karmāntika,* or day labourers ; *puruṣa,* or gangmen ; *vaṁśakarmakṛit,* or wickerware makers ; *sudhākāra,* or suppliers of water ; *dṛṣṭa,* or inspectors, and *rakṣin,* or guards.[616] The department of the supply of food and commodities, or the commissariat, as it would be called in the modern times, is likewise described in detail.[617] The camp followers formed a world of their own in those days.[618]

Notwithstanding the above detailed description of the army in the *Rāmāyaṇa,* it is doubtful whether in those days the rulers had a theory of aggressive warfare which we so clearly see in Kauṭilya. This is not strange when it is realized that the great war described in that epic was more of a defensive than of an offensive type. Its objective was not to extend the realm of the conqueror but to set right a great injustice done to all Womanhood. Hence there was no occasion for the author of that epic to have dwelt at length on the theory of *rājamaṇḍala* which was so admirably suited to the needs of the times in which Kauṭilya lived, and to the temperament of a *vijīgiśu* described by him. In the *Manusmṛiti,* no doubt, there was pictured already the portrait of an ambitious and aggressive monarch.[619]

6. IN KAUTILYA

But Kauṭilya's concept of a *vijigīśu* was of an advanced type. His idea of the different kinds of armies was unlike that of the earlier times. No doubt, he was careful to adhere to certain ancient precepts like the one which we have cited above from the *Manusmṛiti,* viz., that the king should daily inspect the armed forces. But Kauṭilya improved upon it by introducing a new idea. While describing the king's routine daily duties, he states that the king, attired in military dress and having mounted on a horse, or a chariot, or an elephant, shall go to see his army drawn up in military array.[620] The army which the king was thus to daily inspect was evidently the standing army which Kauṭilya calls the best army, and which he describes thus:

> Coming down directly from father and grandfather (of the king), ever strong, obedient, happy in keeping their sons and wives well contented, not averse to making a long sojourn, ever and everywhere invincible, endowed with the power of endurance, trained in fighting various kinds of battles, skilful in handling various forms of weapons, ready to share in the weal or woe of the king, and consequently not falling foul of him, and purely composed of soldiers of the Kṣatriya caste, is the best army (*daṇḍasampat*).[621]

In relying thus on the army composed entirely of the Kṣatriyas, it appears as if Kauṭilya had in mind the time-honoured injunction of Manu who, as we have seen earlier, had given the onerous duty of fighting and defending the country only to the Kṣatriyas.

Kauṭilya accepted the five kinds of armies given in the *Rāmāyaṇa* when he wrote thus about the time for recruiting six different kinds of troops: the hereditary troops (*maula*), hired troops (*bhṛitya, bhṛitak*), troops of corporations (*śreṇi*), troops belonging to an ally (*mitra*), troops belonging to an enemy (*amitra*, obviously deserters), and wild tribes (*aṭavī balānām sammuddānakālāḥ*).[621a] It is in connection with the detailed description of every one of these six kinds of troops that we have what might be called the theory of the army in Kauṭilya.

Kauṭilya's Theory of the Army. Briefly stated, it is the following: Kauṭilya gives the precise occasions when the king was to lead the hereditary army, when the hired army was to be put into action, when the army of the corporations (which was a new kind of army that does not figure in the *Rāmāyaṇa*) was to be enlisted, when the army of the friend was to be recruited, when the army of the enemy (deserters) could be utilized, and when the wild tribes could be used in warfare. In this context, he defines a compact body of vast power thus:

> That army which is vast and is composed of various kinds of men and is so enthusiastic as to rise even without provision and wages for plunder when told or untold ; that which is capable of applying its own remedies against unfavourable rains ; that which can be disbanded and which is invincible for enemies ; and that of which all the men are of the same country, same caste, and same training, is (to be considered as) a compact body of vast power.[622]

He elucidates further his theory of the army when he first dwells on the comparative merits of the six kinds of armies, and then, comments on the views of his unnamed teacher. Of the six kinds of armies, "that which is mentioned first is better than the one subsequently mentioned in the order of enumeration". He next gives reasons for this comparative estimate. The hereditary army is better than the hired army inasmuch as the former has its existence dependent upon that of its master, and is constantly drilled. That kind of hired army which is ever near, ready to rise quickly, and is obedient, is better than an army that is made up of soldiers from corporations. The army of a corporation of soldiers, which is native, which has the same end in view as the king's, and which is actuated with similar feelings of rivalry, anger, and expectations of success and gain, is better than the army of a friend. "Even that corporation of soldiers which is further removed in place and time is, in virtue of its having the same end in view, better than the army of a friend. The army of an enemy under the leadership of an Ārya is better than the army of wild tribes. Both of them (the army of an enemy and of wild tribes) are anxious for plunder. In the absence of plunder and under troubles, they prove as dangerous as a lurking snake."

Kauṭilya next cites the opinion of his teacher only to reject it. His teacher had maintained that of the armies composed of Brahmans, Kṣatriyas, Vaiśyas, or Śūdras, that which was mentioned first was, on account of its bravery, better to be enlisted than the subsequent one named in the order of enumeration. In rejecting this opinion, Kauṭilya stated that the enemy may win over to himself the army of the Brahmans by prostration. Hence the army of the Kṣatriyas, trained in the art of wielding weapons, was better; or the army of the Vaiśyas or Śūdras having great numerical strength was better.[623]

Having thus laid down a definite theory of the army, it was only natural that he should have thought of a vast and well-organized military department. It possessed a Superintendent of Armoury (*āyudhāgārādhyakṣa*),[624] a Superintendent of Horses (*aśvādhyakṣa*), a Superintendent of Elephants (*hastyādhyakṣa*), a Superintendent of Chariots (*rathādhyakṣa*), and a Superintendent of Infantry (*pattyādhyakṣa*), the manifold duties of all of whom are given in detail. It is in connection with the last two superintendents that Kauṭilya describes the duties of the Commander-in-Chief (*senāpati*). Kauṭilya's practical sense is seen in one of the duties which he entrusts to the Commander-in-Chief; and that was that after having trained the entire army composed of the fourfold division (*caturaṅgabala*), the Commander-in-Chief was to become "so capable as to order either the advance or retreat of the army (*āyogamayogaṁ ca karmasu*).[625] With the alternative privilege of retreating given to the Commander-in-Chief, it is impossible to charge Kauṭilya with being a visionary.[626]

The huge military department in Kauṭilya was meant for a great purpose—that of enabling Narendra, on whose behalf he had written the book, as we have remarked earlier, to become an ideal *vijigīśu*. Hence almost half of the *Arthaśāstra* is taken up with the vital problem of sovereignty, peace and exertion, sixfold policy, alliances, encampment, war, marches, peace, enemies in the rear, attitude of a conquered king, and very many allied topics which are analysed with such minuteness as to leave the impression that their author was describing the state of affairs, not of an ideal kingdom, but of an empire which was ruled over by his royal master. In fact, in a work consisting of fifteen books, leaving aside the sections on the superintendents mentioned above, ten books (Books V, VI, VII, VIII, IX, X, XI, XII, XIII, and XIV) deal exclusively with the complicated questions arising out of war and peace.[627] This by itself is the greatest tribute that could be paid to Kauṭilya, who may be considered as the most vigorous advocate of the Forward Policy of ancient India. No political thinker before or after him has had either the courage or the wide sweep to champion it, and to make it the fulcrum of the existence of the State.

7. DEFECT IN THE KAUTILYAN WAR MACHINE

We may not close this section without mentioning what may be legitimately considered as a shortcoming in the war machine of the Mauryan times. It may be argued that in the *Arthaśāstra* there is no mention made of the navy. The criticism is not without justification when we observe that Kauṭilya does not refer in detail to this vital side of the armed forces, at least, while describing the various kinds of the army, the military department, and the like. But it would not be correct to maintain that he had no idea of ships at all. Such a charge would be invalidated by the mention of the Superintendent of Ships (*nāvādhyakṣa*), whose duties are mentioned at length. Most of the duties of this high dignitary were directed to peaceful purposes like levying customs duties at the sea ports and port towns, etc. But that Kauṭilya was certainly aware of armed ships is proved by the passage in which he states: "Pirate ships (*hiṁsṛikā*), vessels which are bound for the country of an enemy, as well as those which have violated the customs and rules in port towns shall be destroyed" (*hiṁsrikā nirghātayet amitra-viṣayātigāḥ paṇyapattanacāritropaghātikāśca*).[628] This passage proves that there existed pirate ships in those days against whom the State took drastic action ; that ships carrying contraband goods were liable to be seized and destroyed ; and that foreign ships that violated port laws were likewise destroyed. But no evidence is available in the *Arthaśāstra* about the utilization of ships in war. To what extent this was a defect in the State policy of the Mauryan times is a problem that is outside the scope of our work.

CHAPTER VIII

THE ELEMENTS OF THE STATE (*Contd.*)

G. PUBLIC FINANCE

1. ANTIQUITY OF PUBLIC FINANCE

THE THEORY of public finance in ancient India was intimately bound up with the theory of protection which we have discussed in the earlier pages of this book. It is necessary to repeat here a few details mentioned above in order to get a clear idea concerning this problem. In the Vedic times we see merely the beginnings of the theory of finance. This was but natural because large kingdoms and empires, which alone give rise to problems of magnitude necessitating the growth of finance, do not seem to have existed in the Vedic days. To the smaller kingdoms the question of raising revenue was naturally not one of complications.

2. SOURCES OF PUBLIC FINANCE

(*a*) *Booty in War*

One of the sources of revenue was booty in war. The term *ud-āja* occurring in the *Maitrāyaṇī Samhita*, was taken by Professor Delbrück to mean the share of the booty taken by the king after winning a war (*sangrāmaṁ-jitvā*).[629] Professors Macdonell and Keith were of the opinion that *ud-āja* and *nirāja* were identical terms referring to booty in war.[630]

(*b*) *Bali*

In addition to this there was the offering covered by the term *bali*, a word which occurs frequently in the *Rig Veda*. Many theories have been given of this difficult term. Professor Zimmer maintained that *bali* meant originally voluntary offerings by the subjects.[631] This interpretation was accepted by Professors Geldner and Grassmann, who considered it as the equivalent of presents, gifts, and tribute.[632] But the authors of the *Vedic Index*, while referring to Professor Zimmer's interpretation, altogether deny its accuracy. They say:

There seems to be no ground whatever for this view. No doubt in origin

> the prerogatives of monarchy were due to voluntary action on the part of the tribesmen, but that the Vedic peoples, who were essentially a body of conquering invaders, were in this state is most improbable, and the attitude of the Vedic Indian to his gods was at least as compatible with tribute as with voluntary gifts.[633]

Professor Ghoshal interprets *bali* "as the exclusive designation of the Indo-Aryan king's receipts from his subjects as well as from conquered kings. . . . It is possible that *bali* was from the first of the nature of a customary contribution payable by the subjects, and not depending solely upon their free choice."[634]

The above definition does not help us to understand the exact nature of *bali,* since a compulsory levy or a voluntary contribution from the subjects—if we are to accept Professor Ghoshal's view—could have been given on different occasions. Moreover, it is impossible that the ancient Indians made no distinction between contributions from their own subjects and those from the conquered peoples. We have, therefore, to find out whether the term *bali* had any other significance.

The *Śatapatha Brāhmaṇa* helps us to arrive at the correct nature of *bali*:

> Now when he (the Adhvaryu, or sacrificing priest) offers in the evening after sunset, he does so thinking, 'I will offer to the gods, of this life-giving juice: we subsist on this which belongs to them'. And when he afterwards takes his evening meal, he eats what remains of the offering, and whereof the oblative portions (*bali*) have been distributed all round ; for he who performs the Agnihotra eats only what remains of the offering.

In a note on *bali* occurring in the above passage, Professor Eggeling rightly remarked as follows: "*Bali* is a technical term of the portions of duly consecrated food that have to be assigned to all the creatures."[635] While commenting on the term *ubaḷike kaṭe* occurring in the Rummindei Pillar inscription of Aśoka, Professor Thomas conclusively proved that that term meant "free from *bali*", adding that the term *bali* properly meant a religious cess.[636] The interpretation of Professor W. Thomas helps us to understand the meaning of the term *bali.* It was a cess or a religious tax levied on the performance of some specified religious ceremony.

That *bali* was first taken as a religious offering, and, then, as a tax on religious performances, is proved by Manu, Pāṇini, and Kauṭilya. Manu states the following: "Teaching (and studying) is the sacrifice (offered) to Brahman, (the offerings of water and food called) *tarpaṇa* the sacrifice to the manes, the burnt oblation, the sacrifice offered to the gods, the Bali offering, that offered to the Bhūtas, and the hospitable reception of guests, the offering to men."[637] While explaining in detail the various kinds of offerings like *ahuta, huta, prahuta,* Manu says that "the Bali (is the) offering given to the Bhūtas".[638] In a later context he enjoins that "if another guest comes after the Vaiśvadeva offering has been offered, (the householder) must give him food according to his ability, (but) not repeat the Bali offering".[639] Further on he states that "the remnants (of food) shall be left (where they lie) until the Brahmans have been dismissed ; afterwards he shall perform the (daily) domestic Bali offering ; that is the settled (rule of the) Sacred law".[640] The above statements in the *Manusmṛiti,* therefore, conclusively prove that *bali* meant a religious offering.

Pāṇini uses the term *bali* also as an offering to the different deities, e.g., *mahārāya-bali,* an offering to the *mahārāya* clan of deities like Kubera.[641] It was essentially in the sense of not only an offering to the gods but as a tax on some kinds of religious sacrifices that Kauṭilya used the term *bali,* when he mentions it as one of the sources of revenue from the kingdom (*rāṣṭraṁ*) . We shall mention it along with the other sources below.

(*c*) *Bhāga*

The next source of revenue in the Vedic days was *bhāga.* This word occurs in the compound *bhāgadugha,* meaning "dealer out of portions", "distributor", and is supposed to refer to one of the king's jewels (*ratnins*) in the *Yajur Veda Samhitas* and the *Brāhmaṇas.*[642] The authors of the *Vedic Index* are uncertain as to what exactly were the duties of this official ; but citing the evidence of Sāyaṇa, the famous commentator on the *Vedas* of the early Vijayanagara times, they affirmed that, according to him, the term *bhāgadugha* was either a "tax collector", or "a carver", "thus making this functionary either a revenue officer or a mere court official".[643]

The great mediaeval scholiast obviously had in his mind the following passage in the *Śatapatha Brāhmaṇa* and the *Taittirīya Samhita.* In the former we have the following:

> And on the following day he (the Adhvaryu) goes to the house of the carver (*bhāgadugha*), and prepares a pap for Pūṣan, for Pūṣan is carver to the gods ; and that (officer) is carver to the king: therefore it is for Pūṣan. And he, the carver, assuredly is one of his (the king's) jewels: it is for him that he is thereby consecrated, and him he makes his own faithful follower.[644]

While the nature of the term *bhāga* is thus apparent, it is not clear in what manner it has to be connected with finance. Professor Ghoshal would interpret *bhāga* in its technical sense "as the designation of a special tax on land", and as distinguished from *bali* and *kara* mentioned by Kauṭilya. According to the same scholar, *bhāga* would mean one-sixth of the produce normally levied by the king.[645]

Dr. Agrawala interprets *bhāga* as octroi duty, and refers us to one of the passages in the *Arthaśāstra* which will be discussed at once.[645a]

There is no justification to interpret *bhāga* either as octroi duty or as land tax. In all likelihood it meant the share or portion of the produce payable to the State. This will be evident from the manner in which that term has been used in the *Manusmṛiti*, the *Rāmāyaṇa* and the *Arthaśāstra*. Manu enjoins: "A king who does not afford protection, yet takes his share in kind, his taxes, tolls and duties, daily presents and fines, will (after death) soon sink into hell."[646] In the *Rāmāyaṇa* the term *baliśaḍbhāga* evidently refers to the sixth part of the produce of land.[647] Kauṭilya is more explicit than the author of the *Rāmāyaṇa* when he clearly distinguishes between the many kinds of taxes and *bhāga* thus: *sītā bhāgo baliḥ karo vaṇik*. Dr. Shama Sastry translated these terms correctly thus: produce from crown lands (*sīta*), portion of produce payable to government (*bhāga*), religious taxes (*bali*), taxes paid in money (*kara*).[648]

In the same chapter in a different context Kauṭilya used the term *bhāga* as distinct from capital (*mūla*), fixed taxes (*kḷripta*), premia on coins (*rūpika*), and fixed fines (*atyaya*),[649] thereby proving that *bhāga* was not a land tax but a levy of a particular kind. That he used the term *bhāga* in the sense of a portion of live-stock is clear from a still later context in which he gives the list of demands which the State could make from herdsmen. We are informed that persons rearing cocks and pigs shall surrender to government half of their live stock (*kukkura-sūkaraṁ ardhaṁ-dadyāt*). Those who reared inferior animals were to give one-sixth (*kṣudra-paśavaḥ-ṣaḍbhāgaṁ*). Those that reared cows, buffaloes, mules, asses, and camels were to give one-tenth of their stock to the State (*go-mahiṣā-aśvatara-khara-uṣṭrāḥ-ca-daśabhāgam*).[650] These passages should be enough to prove that *bhāga* was not a special kind of tax but merely a portion of the produce (i.e. a share in kind) to which the State was entitled.

(*d*) *Kara*

The fourth main source of revenue in the ancient times was connoted by the term *kara*. There is more divergence of opinion among scholars about this term than about the two previous terms, *bhāga* and *bali*. *Kara* does not appear in the Vedic literature. When it figures in later literature, it is used so vaguely that no definite interpretation can be given of it. The Jaina literature contains references to its use as a general tax on land as well as on moveables.[651] The commentators on the *dharmaśāstras* like Medhātīthi, Sarvajña Nārāyana, Kullūka, and others do not help us to understand the meaning of the term, because of their conflicting opinions.[652] Professor Meyer, in his translation of the *Arthaśāstra*, agreed with Dr. Shama Sastry's interpretation of *kara* as a tax paid in money.[653] Dr. Ganapati Sastri in his own commentary called *Śrīmūla* on the *Arthaśāstra*, interpeted *kara* as a tax levied on fruit trees.[654] Professor Ghoshal, while rejecting all these as being "not authenticated by independent evidence", cites the evidence of the Girnar Rock inscription of the Mahākṣātrapa Rudradāman in which *kara, viṣṭi,* and *praṇaya* are used together, and affirms: "from this it would seem that *kara* was held like *viṣṭi* and *praṇaya* to be an oppressive tax."[655]

But it is more likely that we have to agree with Dr. Kane and consider *kara* as a tax in general.[656]. It is perhaps in this sense that Kauṭilya had used the term *karada* meaning tax payers, who were to be given land for cultivation for life (*karadebhyaḥ kṛita-kṣetrāṇi-ekapuruṣikāṇi prayachchhet*).[657] Likewise when he says that the king shall protect agriculture from the molestations of oppressive fines, forced labour, and taxes (*daṇḍa-viṣṭi-karābādhaiḥ rakṣet-upahatām kṛiṣim*),[658] he evidently used the term in a general sense. This term will be further discussed below under the sources of revenue in Kauṭilya.

(*e*) *Śulka*

This was another source of revenue since the earliest times. When it first appeared it was in the sense of "price" ; while its inclusion in two passages in the *Atharva Veda* has led to some indecisive controversy.[659] Professor Bühler interpreted *śulka* appearing in the *Manusmṛiti* as a nuptial fee given when a damsel was married.[660] But in a passage cited above, relating to *bhāga*, Manu clearly distinguished between *śulka* from the other kinds of taxes and levies included under the term tolls and duties.[661] It is in the same sense that Pāṇini and Kauṭilya used the term *śulka*.[662]

3. THEORY OF PUBLIC FINANCE

While the above enumeration of the main sources of revenue gives us an idea of their antiquity, it does not help us to arrive at a theory of finance as it was understood in the ancient times. We could study this important problem from the standpoints of general importance attached to finance ; sources of revenue ; rate of taxation ; remissions and exemptions, and taxation in times of economic stringency. These five points may be examined as given in the *Manusmṛiti*, the epics, the *Grammar* of Pāṇini, and the *Arthaśāstra* of Kauṭilya.

(*a*) *Manu's Theory of Taxation*

We get clearer notions of taxation in the *Manusmṛiti* than in any earlier ancient text. The general principle of taxation was laid down in the following ordinances. "After (due) consideration the king shall always fix in his realm the duties and taxes in such a manner that both he himself and the man who does the work receive (their due) reward."[663] This equitable principle of taxation when applied to tolls and duties meant that the king was to make the traders pay duty after having considered the rates of purchase and sale, the length of the road along which the goods had to be carried, the expenses of food and condiments consumed by the members of the staff employed by the traders for the purpose of transporting and selling commodities, and the charges of securing the goods.[664] The king was to draw from his realm moderate annual taxes, just as the leech, the calf, and the bee took their food little by little.[665] While excessive taxation was prohibited, Manu warned the king against levying no taxation at all. "Let him (the king) not cut up his own root (by levying no taxes), nor the root of other (men) by excessive greed; for by cutting up his own root (or theirs) he makes himself or them wretched."[666] In these regulations the importance of taxation is hinted at; but Manu dwells more on the necessity of taxation. This may be borne in mind in tracing the growth of the theory of taxation which will be mentioned below.

In the *Manusmṛiti* the sources of taxation were the produce of land, cattle, trees, meat, honey, clarified butter, perfumes, medicinal herbs, substances used for flavouring food, flowers, roots, fruits, leaves, pot-herbs, grass, (objects) made of cane, skins, earthen vessels, and all articles made of stone. The tolls were levied from the common inhabitants of the realm who lived by traffic. It appears as if no taxes were levied from those who subsisted by manual labour. For it is explicitly stated that mechanics, artisans, and Śūdras, who subsisted by manual labour, were to work for the king for one day in each month.[667]

On the rate of taxation, we have only the following in the same work: a fiftieth part of the increments on cattle and gold; one-eighth, one-sixth, or one-twelfth part of the crops; one-sixth part of the trees, and of all the produce of forest and gardens mentioned above, and of all articles made of stone—these could be levied by the king.[668] There is no evidence of a tax in money; neither of the rate of tolls. But there is an indication of the money economy in a later injunction which refers to the legal tax which could be levied from the Vaiśyas or the trading class. The State could levy one-eighth as a tax on grain, and one-twentieth (on the profits in gold cattle) which amounted to at least one *kārṣāpaṇa*.[669]

Remissions and exemptions were made mostly in favour of the worthy members of the priestly and labouring classes, the latter of whom, as remarked above, were to give their labour for one day in a month. Śrotriyas (i.e. those experts in the great *Śrauta* sacrifices), who were well versed in the Sacred law, (particularly that relating to the *Śrauta Sūtras*)[670] were exempted from taxation.[671] Since, as Professor Bühler rightly stated, it was not even the professional *vaidika*[672]—leaving aside the question of an ordinary Brahman—who could be called a Śrotriya, it follows that the exemptions did not cover the bulk of the Brahmans. Then, the following three categories were exempted from taxation—blind men, idiots, cripples who moved with the help of boards, men who were fully seventy years old, and those who conferred benefits on the Śrotriyas. These could not be compelled by the king to pay a tax.[673]

Taxation in times of financial stringency was not unknown to Manu. He enjoins that if a Kṣatriya (i.e. the king) in times of distress takes even the fourth part of the crops, he is free from guilt, if he protects his subjects to the best of his ability.[674]

Nothing more about the theory of taxation is found in the *Manusmṛiti*. It was suited to the simple conditions in which Manu's State was placed. Excepting the rate of the *bhāga*, or share of the produce, that is, the tax in kind, we have nothing in the above injunctions that could help us to formulate a mature theory of finance. The latitude given to the king to levy a heavier rate of taxation in times of distress, indicates that Manu was aware of the inadequate nature of his peace-time economy.

(*b*) *In the Rāmāyaṇa*

The financial picture remained practically unchanged in the age of the *Rāmāyaṇa*, in which the fixed legal rate was one-sixth of the produce as well as of religious sacrifices (*baliśaḍbhāga*). This was supplemented by the tribute (*upahāra*) from the feudatories. The profits to which the king was entitled were extended to the mines which yielded gems. The labouring class continued to pay their share in the shape of compulsory labour.[675] From the *Rāmāyaṇa* it does not appear that there was any marked development on the financial precept and practice as described in the *Manusmṛiti*.

(*c*) *In Pāṇini*

The same may be said of the age of Pāṇini in whose *Grammar* there is a reference to the two sources of revenue—*āya-sthāna* and *śulka* or tolls. A new idea is introduced in the term *pañcaka* used by Pāṇini in respect of tolls, thereby suggesting that it was levied in terms of an amount of five.[676] From the special mention of the term *śauṇḍika*,[677] a plant used for distilling liquor, used by Pāṇini, it appears as if we are to suppose that much revenue was derived from the sale of liquor. The discovery of several specimens of the *śauṇḍika*, or elongated condenser tubes, at Taxila and its neighbourhood, of the age of the late Kuṣaṇa period,[678] suggests that the sale of liquor continued to be a profitable source of revenue to the State even after Pāṇini's time. Indeed. in the intervening period after Pāṇini and before the Kuṣaṇas, we have the irrefutable evidence of Kauṭilya, which will be cited below, of the profits according to the State from the sale of liquor.

Pānini mentioned other sources of revenue some of which are not met with in the *Manusmṛiti*. Thus, we have a tax on platforms (? *sthaṇḍila*) which Dr. Agrawala supposes to be those let out in market places; on wells (? *udapāna*), stone quarries (*upala*), ferries (*tīrtha*), land (*bhūmi*), grasses (*triṇa*), and dry leaves (*parṇa*).[679] Of these the taxes on platforms and wells were new ones not mentioned in the *Manusmṛiti.* In addition to these there were special taxes, particularly in what was then known as eastern India (*kāranāmni ca Prāçām halādau*). The *Kāśikāvṛitti* gives four examples of these—*sūpeśāṇaḥ*, or the levy of one *śaṇa* coin which Dr. Agrawala thinks was levied on every kitchen or household ; *mukuṭe-kārṣāpaṇam*, or a *kārṣāpaṇa* coin per head ; *drisadimāṣakaḥ* or a *māṣaka* coin per hand-mill in a family ; and *hale-dvipādikā* and *hale-tripādikā,* a levy of two and three *pāda* coins on each *hala* or plough-share of land. These taxes were called *kāra* (which is evidently the same as *kara* of the other authors), and the revenue officer entrusted with the duty of collecting them, *kārakara.*[680] Granting that the evidence of the *Kāśikāvṛitti* belongs to a much later period, yet it is clear that the taxes levied in eastern India seem to have been levied in money, and to that extent were a notable departure from the earlier taxes levied mostly in kind. It would not be wrong if we were to presume that the change-over from what was mostly a barter economy to a money economy, at least so far as the levying of some taxes was concerned, took place in the age of Pāṇini.

(*d*) *In Kauṭilya*

(*i*) *General Theory and Importance of Finance*

The *Arthaśāstra* of Kauṭilya opens a new chapter in the history of Indian finance, as it does in many aspects of the public life of the people. In it we have the most comprehensive, and probably the world's most ancient, theory of public finance. Since Kauṭilya thought of both peace and war economy, we find in his work a clear distinction between what may be called public finance designed for peace time, and public finance designed for war time. Both these two types of finance were governed by the same major principle—the welfare of a strong and powerful State. He expressed it in the following: all undertakings depend upon finance. Hence foremost attention shall be paid to the treasury (*kośapūrvāḥ-sarvārambhāḥ tasmāt-pūrvaṁ kośaṁ-avekṣeta*). What he meant by the increase of treasury, or financial prosperity (*kośavṛiddhiḥ*) is explained by him thus: public prosperity (*pracāra-samṛiddhiḥ*), rewards for good conduct (*caritrānugrihaḥ*), capture of thieves (*coragriho*), dispensing with the service of too many government servants (i.e. economy in public service, *yuktapratiṣedhaḥ*), abundant harvest (*sasyasampat*), prosperity of commerce (*paṇyabāhutyaṁ*), absence of troubles and calamities (*upasarga-pramokṣaḥ*), diminution of remission of taxes (*parihārakṣayo*), and a gold reserve (*hiraṇyopāyanaṁ*)—these are responsible for the prosperous condition of the treasury (*iti kośavṛiddiḥ*).

Kauṭilya's realism is seen when we note the causes which, according to him, were responsible for the depletion of the treasury. Obstruction (*prati-bandhaḥ*), loans (*prayoga*), trading (*vyavahāraḥ*), fabrication of accounts (*avastāraḥ*), causing loss of revenue (*parihāpaṇam*), self-enjoyment (*upabhogaḥ*), barter (*parivartanaṁ*), and defalcation (*apahāraḥ*)—these lead to to the depletion of the treasury (*iti kośakṣayaḥ*). What was meant by obstruction was failure to start an undertaking or to realize its results or to credit its profits to the treasury. A loan is defined by him as lending money of the treasury on periodical interest. Trading was carrying on trade by making use of government money. By fabrication of accounts was meant making unripe the ripe time or, declaring as ripe the unripe time for collecting revenue. Loss of revenue was caused by lessening a fixed amount of income or by enhancing the expenditure. Self-enjoyment is defined as enjoyment when one enjoyed oneself or caused others to enjoy whatever belonged to the State. Barter was the name given to the act of exchanging government articles for similar articles of others. Defalcation of government money took place when a person did not take into the treasury the fixed amount of revenue collected, or when the amount ordered to be spent was not spent, or when the net revenue collected was misrepresented.

Kauṭilya was not content with mere definitions. He provided for the misuse of power by officials. Hence in every one of the above causes that led to the depletion of the State treasury, he recommended the severest penalties by way of fines. For obstruction, it was a fine of ten times the amount in question ; for a loan and trading, a fine in each case of twice the profit earned ; for fabrication of accounts, a fine of ten times the amount (*pañcabandha*) ; for loss of revenue, a fine of four times the loss ; for enjoying gems, it was death sentence ; for enjoying valuable articles, the middlemost amercement ; and restoration of articles together with a fine equal to their value for enjoying articles of inferior value ; for barter, the same punishment as in the case of self-enjoyment ; and for embezzlement, a fine of twelve times the amount embezzled.[681]

"Gold Reserve". The concept of a "gold reserve", as it might be called today, is given in the definition of the best treasury in the *Arthaśāstra*, thus: justly obtained either by inheritance or by self-acquisition, rich in gold and silver, filled with an abundance of big gems of various colours and of gold coins, and capable of withstanding calamities of long duration is the best treasury (*kośasampat*).[682]

The concepts of a treasury filled with gold and gems, and of the financial prosperity (*kośavṛiddhiḥ*) cited above, give us an adequate idea of only one aspect of public finance which Kauṭilya had in mind. The other aspects will be apparent when we shall describe the sources of revenue, rate of taxation, remission and exemptions, and measures to meet financial stringencies.

(ii) *Sources of Revenue*

A stride forward in regard to the sources of revenue since the days of Manu, was taken by Kauṭilya when he delineated them in various contexts. We can only summarize them for the sake of convenience. The main limbs of income (*āyaśarīraṁ*) were the forts (*durga*), the country parts (*rāṣṭra*), mines (*khaṇi*), buildings and gardens (*setu*), forests (*vana*), herds of cattle (*vraja*), and roads of traffic (*vaṇikpatha*). Each of these came in for a detailed examination at his hands. Under the heading forts came the following miscellaneous subjects: tolls, fines, weights and measures, the town clerk (*nāgaraka*), the Superintendent of Coinage (*lakṣāṇadhyakṣa*), liquor, slaughter of animals, threads, oils, ghee, sugar (*kṣāra*), the State Goldsmith (*sauvarṇika*), the warehouse of merchandise, prostitutes, gambling, building sites (*vāstuka*), the corporation of artisans and handicrafts (*kāru-śilpi-gaṇaḥ*), the Superintendent of Gods (*devatādhyakṣa*), and taxes collected at the gates and from the people known as Bāhirikas.

Classified under the heading *rāṣṭra* were the following items of revenue, a few of which have already appeared above under the topics of *bali* and *bhāga*: produce from the crown lands (*sīta*), portion of produce payable to government (*bhāga*), religious taxes (*bali*), taxes paid in money (*kara*), merchants, the Superintendent of Rivers (*nadīpāla*), ferries, boats and ships, towns, pasture lands, road cess (*vartani*), ropes (*rajju*), and ropes to bind thieves (*corarajju*). These may be read along with those also mentioned under the term *rāṣṭra* described below.

Revenue from mines was restricted to gold, silver, diamonds, gems, pearls, corals, conch shells, metals (*loha*), salt, and other mineral extracts from plains and mountain slopes.

Under the heading gardens and buildings were the following: flower gardens, fruit gardens, vegetable gardens, wet fields, and fields where crops were grown by sowing roots from seeds (*mūlavāpaḥ*, e.g., sugar cane, etc.).

The revenue from forests was derived from game, timber, and elephants, all the three having forests of their own ; while that from herds of cattle was secured from cows, buffaloes, goats, sheep, asses, camels, horses, and mules. The income from roads of traffic covered land and water ways. These formed the body of income (*āyaśarīraṁ*).[683]

(iii) *Income and Expenditure Defined*

A mere description of the sources of income did not satisfy the genius of Kauṭilya. He also defined as well what exactly was meant by income and expenditure which had not been done before his time. The general forms of revenue (*āyamukha*, or the mouth from which the income was derived) were made up of capital (*mūla*), share (*bhāga*). premia (*vyāji*), *parigha* (?). *kḷripta* (? fixed taxes), premia on coins (*rūpika*), and fixed fines (*atyaya*).[684]

Before proceeding with the definition of expenditure, it is necessary to explain a term mentioned in the above passage. Dr. Shama Shastry has not interpreted *parigha* in the above list of the forms of revenue but has referred the reader to Dr. Meyer's translation of the word as "gate-duty".[685] This definition does not appear to be correct. Pāṇini mentions the same term *parigha* not in connection with the sources of revenue but while describing the kinds of buildings in a great city. He then mentions parts of a building like *dvāra* (gates), *parikhā* (moats), *kapāṭa* (door leaves), and *parigha* (bolts).[686] It is not improbable that the term *parigha* used by Kauṭilya refers to houses in which bolts were used, that is, to such of the houses of the well-to-do people, who could afford to use them. It may, therefore, be taken as a tax on the houses of the economically prosperous people.

To proceed with Kauṭilya's idea of public finance, we find the following as forming the limbs of expenditure (*vyayaśarīraṁ*): the chanting of auspicious hymns during the worship of gods and ancestors (*devapitṛi-pūjādānārthaṁ*), and on the occasion of giving gifts, the harem, the kitchen (*svastivācanaṁ-antaḥpura-mahānasaṁ*), the establishment of envoys (*dūtaprāvartimaṁ*), the store house (*koṣṭāgāraṁ*), the armoury (*āyudhā-gāraṁ*), the warehouse (*paṇyagṛihaṁ*), the storehouse of raw materials (*kupyagṛihaṁ*), manufactories (*karmānto*), forced labour (*viṣṭih*), maintenance of infantry, cavalry, chariots and elephants (*pattyaśvarathadvipaparigraho*), herds of cattle (*gomaṇḍalaṁ*), the park consisting of deer, birds and snakes (*paśu-mṛiga-pakṣi-vyālavāṭāḥ*), and storeage of firewood and fodder (*kāṣṭatṛiṇa-vāṭaḥ*).[687]

Dr. Shama Sastry translated the word *viṣṭi* here and elsewhere as free labour.[688] This is inadmissible since the word *viṣṭi* was used for forced labour. We may recall here Manu's injunction in regard to the manual labourers, who were forced to do the king's work for one day in the month, which we have cited above. Further, Dr. Sastry used the word "museum" in connection with the beasts, etc. A more appropriate rendering of the word *vāṭaḥ* would be a park in which alone live beasts, deer, and snakes could be preserved.

The details under expenditure mentioned above do not refer to the huge and elaborate administrative machinery of civil servants whose salaries we have noticed in an earlier context. Neither do we find in the list of the items of expenditure the cost of maintaining spies, learned men, public buildings, roads, irrigational works, reservoirs, and judicial courts, all of which must have cost the State vast sums of money. As to why Kauṭilya did not include these items under expenditure cannot be made out.

Further, his description of the body of income (*āyaśarīraṁ*) is inadequate, even from his own standpoint. He has not included under that category at least two items on which he himself had dealt with at some length. These are tolls and fines. One whole chapter is devoted to the duties of the Superintendent of Tolls (*śulkādhyakṣa*).[689] The numerous details mentioned in it, particularly the rate of the tolls, justify our assumption that the revenue from this source must have been immense. From another quarter, too, the State derived uncommon revenue. This was from the innumerable fines which are spread over the whole of the *Arthaśāstra*! Indeed, we may wonder at the number of fines that marked Kauṭilyan State! There was no aspect of the daily life of the people on which the stern hand of the imposer of fines did not fall! We may guess as to why there were so many fines in those days. Perhaps when Kauṭilya, and his royal patron, Narendra, that is, Candragupta Maurya, brought the State into existence, is was financially in an unstable position. It was probably to meet this deficiency that the State had recourse to fines.

Kauṭilya mentions under the head forts three items—liquor, prostitutes, and slaughter house. Every one of them had a superintendent of its own. The Superintendent of Liquor (*surādhyakṣa*) had enormous powers. He controlled the manufacture and sale of liquor throughout the State. And he was entitled to impose fines on the people, and to realize the proceeds from the sale of liquor.[690] The Superintendent of Prostitutes (*gaṇikādhyakṣa*) had likewise vast powers, including those of imposing heavy fines to the extent of 5,000 *paṇas*![691] The Superintendent of Slaughter Houses (*sunādhyakṣa*) was also entitled to levy fines on those who had violated the State regulations.[692] These three officials together must have been responsible for augmenting the State treasury to a considerable extent.

(*iv*) *Other Sources of Revenue*

That Kauṭilya had many more sources of revenue in view is apparent when we note the numerous taxes he mentions in connection with the Superintendent of Store House (*koṣṭāgārādhyakṣa*). These were taxes that were fixed (*piṇḍakaraḥ*), taxes paid in the form of one-sixth of produce (*ṣaḍbhāgah*), taxes paid by the people for the army (*senābhaktaṁ*), taxes levied for religious purposes (*bali*), taxes paid regularly (*kara*), taxes that were specially collected on the occasion of the birth of a prince (*uttsaṅgaḥ*), taxes collected when there was some margin left for such collection (*pārśva*), taxes levied in the shape of grains by way of compensation for any damage done by cattle to crops (*pārihīṇikaṁ*), presentation made to the king (*aupāyanikaṁ*), taxes levied on lands built below tanks, lakes, etc., by the king (*kauṣṭeyakaṁ*)—all these coming under the term *rāṣṭra*.[693]

We have in the preceding passages a staggering number of items on which taxes were levied. Two points are clear from them—that there were taxes in money (*kara*), and that the taxes in kind were paid at the traditional rate of one-sixth of the produce (*ṣaḍbhāgaḥ*). That there was a tax levied for the maintenance of the army, and that it was called by the patriotic term *senābhaktaṁ* (devoted to the army?) is known only from the above passage. It indicates that the mighty war machine of Kauṭilya was run on public funds, and not from the privy purse of the monarch.

Dr. Sastry interpreted the word *kara* as tax or subsidy "paid by the vassal kings and others". This is inadmissible not only on the strength of what has been discussed above concerning the term *kara*, but also on that of the opinion of the commentator of the *Arthaśāstra* whom Dr. Sastry cites. According to the commentator, "such taxes (like *kara*) are collected every year during the month of Bhādrapada or Vasanta under the names of Bhādrapādikā and Vāsantikā."[694] From this we are to infer that *kara* was levied twice every year. We cannot think of vassals paying tribute twice a year; while it is permissible to assume that citizens might have been compelled to pay taxes twice a year, although normally most of the taxes were paid once a year.

(*v*) *Rate of Taxation*

The above passage gives us an idea of the rate of taxation, particularly that in kind, although the exact incidence of taxation in terms of money is not determinable. The rates of tolls are given very minutely, even to the extent of one-twentieth of such articles like cooked rice. They are far too numerous to be mentioned here. Incidentally it may be noted that a single hoofed animal had to pay a *paṇa*, each head of cattle, half a *paṇa*, and a minor quadruped, a quarter of a *paṇa* as toll.[695]

(*vi*) *Remissions*

Remissions and exemptions formed a part of the financial policy of the Kauṭilyan State. The general principle of remission was the following: the king shall bestow on cultivators only such favour and remission (*anugṛihaparihārau*) as will tend to swell the treasury, and shall avoid such as will deplete it.[696] Detailed rules were laid down for the remission of taxes in the case of new lands brought under cultivation. For instance, in regard to land below newly constructed tanks and lakes, the taxes were to be remitted for five years (*pañcavarṣikaḥ parihāraḥ*). For repairing neglected or ruined works of a similar nature, taxes were to be remitted for four years. For improving or extending or restoring water works over grown with weeds, the remission was for three years. In the case of acquiring such newly started works by mortgage or purchase, taxes on the lands below such works were to be remitted for two years. If uncultivated tracts were acquired for cultivation by mortgage, purchase, or in any other way, remission was also for two years. Out of the crops grown by irrigation by means of wind power or bullocks or below the tanks, in fields, parks, flower gardens, or in any other way, so much of the produce (not stipulated) as would not entail hardship on the cultivators, may be given to the State.[697]

Certain sections of the learned professions were exempted from both taxes and fines. These were those who performed the sacrifices (*ṛitvik*).

spiritual guides (*ācāryāḥ*), priests (*purohita*), and those learned in the Śrauta sacrifices (*śrotriyebhyo*). They were endowed with Brahmadeya lands yielding sufficient produce, and exempted from taxes and fines (*adaṇḍakarāṇi*).[698]

Even tolls were remitted, as in the following cases: commodities intended for marriages, or taken by a bride from her parents' house to her husband's (*anvāyanaṁ*), or intended for presentation or taken for the purpose of sacrificial performance, confinement of women, worship of gods. ceremony of tonsure, investiture of sacred thread, gifts of cows (*godāna*) made before marriage, any religious rite (*vṛita*), consecration ceremony (*dīkṣā*), and other special ceremonials. These were to be exempted from the payment of tolls.[699]

(*vii*) *Policy in Times of Financial Stringency*

Kauṭilya's theory of public finance was as much directed to peace times as to those of accute financial crisis. This brings us to the measures advocated by him to replenish the State treasury. We are not told as to how the king, who was to have recourse to the measures of raising revenue in times of stringency, came into "a great financial trouble". If the writing of the chapter on the Replenishment of the Treasury (*kośābhisam-haraṇaṁ*), after the one on the Awards of Punishments (*dāṇḍakarmikaṁ*), is any indication, we may risk the suggestion that the great trouble referred to by Kauṭilya was brought about as much by internal as by external causes. Our surmise is supported by the fact that in the whole book preceding the one on *dāṇḍakarmikaṁ*, and entitled *kaṇṭakaśodhanaṁ* (Removal of Thorns), he has dealt with the measures to remove the thorns of public peace, both in fortified cities and country parts; and he now proceeds, as he informs us in the opening sentences of the chapter on *dāṇḍakarmikaṁ*, to treat of the measures to suppress treason against the king and the realm (*durgarāṣṭrayoḥ kaṇṭaka śodhanaṁ-uktaṁ rājarājyayoḥ-avakṣyāmaḥ*).[700]

Treasury and Treason. Throughout the latter half of the *Arthaśāstra*, there is a strong note of warning against treason which Kauṭilya would suppress by every possible means within his control. One such method is that relating to the replenishment of the State treasury. Four distinct categories of persons are mentioned as being within the kingdom, and as those whose activities would cause troubles to the kingdom. These were chiefs of confederacies living under the king, who were inimical to the ruler, or who sided with the enemy; disloyal courtiers and confederacy of chiefs, who were dangerous to the safety of the king, and who could not be put down in open day light; a seditious minister, and a seditious minister's brother; a seditious Pāraśva (i.e. one who was begotten by a Brahman on a Śūdra woman); a seditious son of a woman servant; and seditious persons conspiring against both the king and his kingdom. Of these the seditious minister appears to have been the worst traitor, since the greater part of the chapter deals with the measures to punish him.[701] This list of traitors around the king was enough to cause a great diversion of public funds in the shape of financial measures which were undertaken to avert danger to the State. It is no wonder, therefore, that the State treasury had to be replenished by means which were of an extraordinary nature.

Sources by which Finance could be Raised. Various measures were advocated by Kauṭilya to augment the financial resources of the realm. Broadly speaking the State could raise revenue in times of financial stringency from eight different sources. First came the country parts which depended solely upon the rains and which were rich in grain. From these the king demanded only one-third or one-fourth of their grain, according to their capacity. The second source referred to the purchase by the king for gold of one-fourth of what remained, after deducting as much of the grain as was required for seeds and the subsistence of his subjects. This could also be done by offering favourable price to the owners. If he failed in the above measures, the Collector-General could prevail upon the peasantry to raise summer crops. The fourth method referred to the demand by the same high dignitary on the cultivators to supply to the State one-fourth of their grain, one-sixth of the forest produce, and of such commodities as cotton, wax, fabrics, barks of trees, hemp, wool, silk, medicines, sandal, flowers, fruits, vegetables, firewood, bamboos. flesh, and dried fish, and one-half of all ivory and skins of animals.

Merchants had to contribute their share to meet financial stringency. Those dealing in gold, silver, diamonds, precious stones, pearls, corals, horses, and elephants had to contribute fifty *karas* (which, according to Dr. Shama Sastry, were equal to ten *paṇas*). Those dealing in cotton threads, cloths, copper, brass, bronze, sandal, medicines, and liquor had to pay forty *karas.* Those who traded in grains, liquids, metals (*loha*), and dealt with carts had to pay thirty *karas.* Merchants trading in glass (*kāca*) and artisans of fine workmanship had to pay twenty *karas.* While artisans of inferior workmanship and those who maintained prostitutes had to pay ten *karas.* Traders in firewood, bamboos, stones, earthen pots, cooked rice, and vegetables paid five *karas.* Dramatists (*kuśīlavā*) and prostitutes had to pay one-half of their wages. The entire property of the goldsmiths was to be confiscated. Kauṭilya was very severe with this class of workers, as we have already remarked earlier. He opined that "no offence of theirs shall be forgiven, for they carry on their fraudulent trade while pretending at the same tune to be honest and innocent". It is doubtful whether this stricture of the otherwise impartial author on the goldsmiths could be either mitigated or improved upon even in our own days!

To continue with the next source of raising revenue, we have to note the demands on herdsmen (*yonapoṣakeṣu praṇayaḥ*). Persons rearing cocks and pigs had to surrender to the government one-half of their livestock; those who reared inferior animals had to give one-sixth of their livestock; those who reared cows, buffaloes, mules, asses, and camels had to give one-tenth of their livestock; and those who maintained prostitutes (*bandhakiposakā*) were to collect revenue (unspecified) with the help of women noted for their beauty and youth in the service of the king. This last regulation may be read in conjunction with the one mentioned above relating to the same class of unfortunate women, who had to pay one-half of their wages.

When such demands were not made by the Collector-General, as mentioned earlier in connection with the theory of *jānapada*, he could raise subscriptions from citizens and country people alike under false pretences of carrying on this or that kind of business (*tasya-ākaraṇe-vā samāharttā kāryaṁ apadiśya paurajānapadān bhikṣeta*). Persons taken in concert were to pay handsome donations, and with their example the king could demand of others similar donations. Spies posing as citizens were to revile those who paid less. Wealthy persons were to be requested to give as much of their gold as they could; and those who of their own accord, or with the intention of doing good, offered their wealth to the king, were to be honoured with a rank in the court, an umbrella, or a turban or some ornaments in return for their gold. Kauṭilya had, indeed, forestalled modern statesmen, who raise loans and reward their supporters, not necessarily in the manner indicated in the above passage, but by means which are agreeable to the sentiments of the present times.

The next category of persons who were required to supply revenue were the spies. Disguised as sorcerers, and under the pretence of ensuring safety, they were entitled to carry away the money, not only of the society of heretics and of temples, but also of a dead man and of a man whose house was burnt, provided it was enjoyable by Brahmans (*pāṣaṇḍasaṅgha-dravyaṁ-śrotriyabhogyaṁ devadravyaṁ vā kṛityakarāḥ pretasya dagdha-gṛihasya vā haste nyastaṁ-iti-upahareyuḥ*). The spies contributed their share to the filling up of the State treasury in ways which are too numerous to be mentioned here. One detail, however, may be mentioned here. They could get themselves merged in the company of merchants only with a view to robbing the latter of their wealth!

The Superintendent of Religious Institutions (*devatādhyakṣa*) also came to the rescue of the State treasury, and adopted methods some of which might perhaps delight the atheist statesmen of our own days. He could collect in one place the various kinds of property of the gods of fortified cities, and of country parts, and then carry them away to the king's treasury! Or having on some night set up a god or an altar, or having opened a sacred place of ascetics or having pointed out an evil omen, the king could collect (through the same official, of course), subsistence under the pretence of holding processions and congregations (to avert calamities). Or else he could proclaim the arrival of the gods, by pointing out to the people any of the sacred trees in the king's garden which had produced untimely flowers and fruits. The Superintendent of Religious Institutions, therefore, could thus play upon the credulity and superstition of the people in order to enrich the State treasury!

Finally, even from seditious persons wealth was extracted by means of prostitute spies, outcastes, ascetics, ordinary female spies, fiery spies, ordinary men spies, and physician spies.

Limitations on Forced Borrowings. While the above methods undoubtedly prove that the State in Kauṭilya did not hesitate every conceivable means of replenishing its treasury, it has to be borne in mind that such State action was strictly circumscribed by two inviolable regulations. The first declared in the clearest terms that "Such demands shall be made only once and never twice" (*sakṛid-eva na dviḥ prayojyaḥ*). We are to presume that such demands were to be made only once in the reign of a monarch, and that was when there was plenty in the kingdom. Repeated demands made every year would have sapped the prosperity of the people. The final warning which Kauṭilya gives towards the end of the chapter proves this: "Just as fruits are gathered from a garden as often as they become ripe, so revenue shall be collected as often as it becomes ripe. Collection of revenue or of fruits, when unripe, shall never be carried on, lest their source may be injured, causing immense trouble."

The second restriction which Kauṭilya put on levying stringent financial aids refers to the wicked and seditious sections of people on whom the burden fell most heavily. "Measures such as the above shall be taken only against the seditious and the wicked, and never against others" (*evaṁ dusyeṣu-adhārmikeṣu ca varteta na etareṣu*).[702] It appears from this that the bulk of the people were not affected by the severe measures adopted by the State to replenish its treasury. But this cannot be reconciled with some of the methods advocated by Kauṭilya which we have mentioned above, and which refer to certain sections of the people like those in the country parts, the herdsmen, and the merchants all of whom cannot be classed along with the seditious and wicked people. We may reconcile this apparent difficulty by noting that most of the measures refer to the seditious persons, while a few refer to the rest of the people as well.

Exemptions from Forced Benevolences. Kauṭilya was not merely content with enacting regulations: he wished to have them enforced. Therefore, in every case where he felt that they might be violated or evaded, he advocated the severest penalties. But where he was sure that the people could not pay the unusual demands, because of unfavourable conditions, or because of public work, he not only exempted them but made provision for State aid. Thus, the king was not to demand benevolences from such subjects who lived in tracts of middle or low quality, nor from people who were of great help in constructing fortifications, gardens, buildings, roads for traffic, colonizing waste lands, exploiting mines, and forming forest preserves of timber and elephants ; nor from people who lived on the borders of his kingdom or who had not enough means of subsistence (*pratyantaṁ-alpa-prāṇaṁ vā*). The king, on the other hand, was to supply grain and cattle to those who colonized waste lands. The property of the forest tribes and of Śrotriyas was exempted from the unusual demands of the State (*araṇya-jātaṁ śrotriyasvaṁ ca pariharet*).[703]

But stern punishment awaited those who circumvented law. If the peasants did not obey the orders of the Collector-General in regard to the raising of summer crops, that high official could warn them that he would levy double the fines (not stated). For evasion of grain returns, a fine of eight times the amount in each kind was imposed. Whoever stole the crops of another person was fined fifty times the amount stolen, "provided the robber belongs to the same community" ; but if he was a foreigner, the latter was put to death (*bāhyasya tu vadhaḥ*).[704]

(*viii*) *Accidental Sources of Revenue*

In addition to the permanent sources of revenue and the abnormal methods of taxation, Kauṭilya mentions a third one called accidental source of revenue. This is in connection with the manifold duties of the Superintendent of Store House. The term used for accidental revenue is *anyajātaḥ* which he defines thus: whatever is lost and forgotten by others and the like form of accidental revenue is called *anyajātaḥ*.[705] This may be likened to the revenue from Lost Property which the State in the modern times may derive from railway stations, steamship offices, air ports, public offices, etc.

Whether we follow the *Manusmṛiti* or the *Arthaśāstra* of Kauṭilya, it is clear that there are two more elements of the State which deserve notice. These are the ally mentioned in both the works, and the enemy referred to only in the *Arthaśāstra*.[706] Since both of them will be discused to some extent under foreign policy below, they are not dealt with here.

CHAPTER IX

LAW AND ORDER

A. INTRODUCTORY: LAW AS A POLITICAL INSTITUTION

THE IMPORTANCE of law and order in the life of the ancient Indians cannot be sufficiently stressed. Justice as one aspect of *dharma* was the pivot upon which the existence of the State as well as of the people depended. In evaluating the part played by it in the history of ancient Indian political thought and institutions, it would be a grievous error to judge the success or failure of law in India by the later standards of the Romans or of the modern Western peoples on the assumption that the originators of the concept of justice in ancient India were in some remote period ethnically the same as the forefathers of the bulk of the Western peoples. A more rational approach to the question of law and order in India would be to view it strictly from the Indian standpoint, since no other section of the Aryan people had ever succeeded in giving to the world the concept of *dharma* from which flowed the idea of justice in ancient India. To trace the long and varied course of either the theory of law as given in the *dharmaśāstras,* or to explain in detail all the aspects of law and of the courts of justice in a work like ours would be to deviate from the main purpose of our study.[707] We may, therefore, consider only such of its salient features as would enable us to get a glimpse of law as one of the political institutions that helped to stabilize the State.

The justification for considering law as one of the political institutions will be apparent when we recall the statements made earlier in this work, while we discussed the theories of protection and assessed its place in the history of ancient Indian political thought. Protection was impossible without the exercise of *daṇḍa* which in its turn implied that there should be an institution that could, while executing the behests of *daṇḍa,* also see whether such orders were within the bounds of equity. It is here that law played an important part. While it served as a support of the State, it also became a restraint on the State. We shall be concerned with these two aspects in this chapter.

B. A SKETCH OF THE HISTORY OF LAW

1. IN THE VEDIC TIMES

The history of law as a support of the State goes back to the Vedic times when the king, in return for the taxes paid to him by the people, performed the duties of a judge.[708] In this sense law may be considered as the reflex of one of the most useful duties of the ruler. In the Vedic times and after law was connoted by the term *dharma* or *dharman*.[709] A regular code of law, as was developed in the later *dharma sūtras,* does not appear to have found favour with the Vedic Indians.[710] It was probably the result of the corresponding importance of the king as one who wielded *daṇḍa* or punishment.[711] The few details about the two kinds of law and procedure detectable in the Vedic literature, enable us to suppose that there was some concept of a court of justice, simple because of its very antiquity. No mention is made in the Vedic literature of a separate body called the court, since the king was himself a court of both criminal and appellate jurisdiction. Justice was the sole concern of the king. We do not find a *sabhā* associated with the king.

The king dispensed with two kinds of cases—criminal and civil. Among the former was included treachery which was punishable with death.[712] The other cases which came within the purview of the criminal court were the slaying of an embryo (*bhrūṇa*), the slaying of a man (*vīra*), and the slaying of a Brahman.[713] The procedure was simple. In case of theft, the ordeal of the red hot axe was prescribed, obviously under the orders of the king,[714] since there was no separate judge to pronounce the sentence. In case of thefts which were detected and proved, the punishment was death ; and when stolen goods were to be returned, it was binding the thieves to posts.[715]

Civil cases were likewise few and simple. Family quarrels leading to a division of property, transfer of chattels, acquisition and sale of land, money lending (*ṛṇa*), and labour questions were some of the civil crimes noticeable in early literature.[716] There is reason to believe that the Vedic Indians knew the concept of the plaintiff, the defendant, and the prosecutor as is evident from the terms *praśnin, abhi-praśnin,* and *praśna-vivāka* occurring in the list of victims at the *puruṣamedha* or horse sacrifice.[717] The phrase *praśnam-eti* means "he asks a person for the decision of a disputed point".[718] The term came to have the definite meaning of "a decision" in the *Aitareya Brāhmaṇa*.[719] The term for a witness was *jñātṛ* which Professor Zimmer interpreted in that sense ; while Professor Roth took it to mean "a surety". Professors Whitney and Bloomfield denied both the interpretations. The authors of the *Vedic Index,* however, agreed with Professor Zimmer.[720] A mediator was called *madhya-śī,* as understood by Professors Roth and Zimmer ; but that term was taken to mean "an adversary" or "preventer" by Professor Lanman. Professor Whitney suggested that it meant "mid-most man", or "chief" as the one around whom his followers camped.[721] In the later *Samhitas,* the word *madhyama-stha,* or *madhyama-ṣṭha,* is supposed to refer to the chief in relation to his followers (*sajāta*).[722] This term has survived in comparatively later history, especially, in that of western India, when the *madhyastha* came to mean "a mediator".[723] The term *prati-praśna* was also used for an arbitrator in the sense of deciding doubts.[724] We may close this brief sketch of civil and criminal law in the Vedic times by observing that even villages seem to have had their own judges, as is evident from the phrase *grāmya-vādin,* meaning a village judge, occurring in the *Yajur Veda.*[725]

2. IN THE MANUSMRITI

The progress in the concept of both law and the courts of justice is visible when we reach the age of the *Manusmṛiti.* The king is no more himself a court of criminal and appellate jurisdiction. The opening verse in the chapter on civil and criminal law in the *Manusmṛiti* relates: "A king, desirous of investigating law cases, must enter his court of justice, preserving a dignified demeanour, together with Brahmans and experienced councillors."[726] That the exclusive monopoly of the king to center in himself the appellate and criminal sides of law had been abandoned by the time the *Manusmṛiti* was composed is further proved by the following injunction in the same work : "When he (the king) is tired with the inspection of the business of men, let him place on the seat (of justice), his chief minister, (who must be) acquainted with the law, wise, self-controlled, and descended from a noble family."[727] Thus, the ground was prepared for the later Kauṭilyan idea of having courts composed of highly qualified councillors.

Another proof that there was progress in the concept of law is seen in the eighteen titles of law as given in detail in the *Manusmṛiti,* which have been cited in an earlier context in these pages.[728] Further, in the number and nature of civil and criminal cases, in the procedure relating to both the types of law, and in the qualifications and nature of witnesses mentioned in detail in the *Manusmṛiti,*[729] there is a considerable progress in the concept of law since the earlier Vedic days. The law court as an adjunct of the State helped to maintain social order as between individual and individual, and between individuals and owners of associations like corporations in a village or a district, or herdsmen.[730] And, as related in an earlier context in this work, not only was the evidence of witnesses taken into consideration but the past usage prevailing in the neighbourhood also taken into account.[731]

3. IN PANINI

The great grammarian continued the connotation of *dharma* in the sense of custom or usage and of religious merit.[732] He would style a judge as a *dharmapati*, a plaintiff as *parivādi*, or *parivādaka*, a witness as *sākṣi*, and an arbiter as *stheya*.[733] The injunction in the *Manusmṛiti* that a Brahman may swear by his veracity,[734] seems to have existed in Pāṇini's days, since one of the two methods of administering an oath was, as in the days of Manu, by using the form *satyaṁ-karoti*, the other being *satya-karoti*, which was used in connection with the payment of earnest money to settle a bargain.[735] A surety was called *pratibha*.[736] Inheritance figures as conspicuously in Pāṇini as it does in Manu.[737] A crime was called *sāhasikya*. The crimes mentioned in Paṇini are almost the same as those described in Manu—theft, robbers, waylaying, murder, infanticide, destroying an embryo, and killing a Brahman.[738] Punishment took the shape of fines, beating with clubs, mutilation of limbs, and death.[739] The concept of law in Pāṇini does not seem to have made much progress since the days of Manu.

4. IN KAUTILYA

When we reach the age of Kauṭilya, we find that a new chapter was opened in the history of law both in regard to its concept as well as procedure. We may be permitted to refer to an earlier context when it was stated that Kauṭilya distinguished between the law courts from the ministerial offices,[740] thereby giving separate status and existence to both. The few ideas we have already mentioned above need a repetition here for the sake of the completion of the subjct.

(a) *How He opens a New Chapter in the History of Law*

Kauṭilya practically shattered the ancient concept of law as it had been understood by Manu, when he defined the four limbs of law, thus: Sacred law, Evidence, History, and Edicts of kings. Of these the one following was superior to the one preceding in the order of enumeration (*dharmah-ca vyavahārah-ca caritraṁ rājaśāsanaṁ vivādārthaḥ-catuśpādaḥ paścimaḥ-pūrvabādhakaḥ*). He defined each term thus: *dharma* is eternal truth holding sway over the world (*atra satyasthito dharmo*) ; *vyavahāraḥ* or evidence, as consisting of witnesses (*vyavahāraḥ-tu sākṣiṣu*) ; *caritra* was the history of the traditions of the people (*caritraṁ sanghe pūṁsāṁ*) ; and *śāsana* was the order of the king (*rājñāṁ-ājña-tu-śāsanaṁ*). In a later context he styles the third source as *saṁsthā* meaning, not history, as Dr. Shama Sastry had understood it, but evidently referring to the usage and custom of the people of the realm. And then he calls the fourth source, not the orders of the king, but *nyāya* which could more appropriately be rendered into equity than edicts of the king, as done by the same distinguished translator of the *Arthaśāstra*. Further down in the same chapter, as already seen above, he calls the law of the king as *dharmanyāya*, and states:

> ". . . whenever the sacred law i.e. (*dharmaśāstra*) is in conflict with rational law (*dharmanyāya*), then, reason shall be held authoritative; for there the original text (on which the Sacred law has been used) is not available (*samsthāyā dharmaśāstreṇa śāstraṁ vā vyāvahārikaṁ yasminarthe virudhyeta dharmeṇārthaṁ viniscayet śāstraṁ vipratipadyeta dharmanyāyena kenacit nyāyaḥ-tatra pramāṇaṁ syāt-tatra pāṭho hi naśyati*).[741]

By adding man-made law to the body of ancient traditional law, and by laying stress on the edicts of the king (*rājaśāsana*), which he had raised to the dignity of *dharmanyāya*, Kauṭilya had gone far beyond the concept of law as given in the *Manusmṛiti*. Nothing proves that Kauṭilya was a radical thinker so much as the manner in which he finally diminished the infallibility of the law when he stated that, in case of a conflict between the latter and the king's law, reason should be held to be authoritative.

(*b*) *The Problem of Law in Kauṭilya*

This could be studied under the following heads: importance placed by Kauṭilya on usage; his concept of justice; kinds of law courts and the procedure adopted in the law courts; the rôle of the judges; and how the law courts served as an adjunct of the State in maintaining law and order.

(*i*) *Importance of Usage*

Although in the passages cited above, Kauṭilya had unequivocally declared the superiority of State law over the *dharmaśāstras*, yet he was fully aware of the importance of maintaining the usage of the castes as well as of corporations. In regard to the various castes of an inferior order like the Rathakāras, he stated: "The king who guides his subjects in accordance with the above rules (custom and avocations which those castes followed from their ancestors) will attain to heaven; otherwise he will fall into the hell." Then, again, concerning partition among mixed castes, he ordained that it should be made in accordance with the custom prevalent in the country, caste, guild, or the village of the inheritors (*deśasya jātyā saṅghasya dharmo grāmasya vā'pi yaḥ ucitaḥ-tasya tenaiva dāyadharmaṁ prakalpayet*).[742] In an earlier context we had cited Kauṭilya's other injunction that boundary disputes were to be settled by the elders among cultivators and herdsmen, who had experience of former possession in the locality,[743] which evidently referred to the previous custom prevailing in the villages. When dealing with conquered territories, he writes thus: "Having conquered the earth with its people of distinct castes and divisions of religious life, he shall enjoy it by governing it in accordance with the duties prescribed to kings" (*jītvā ca pṛithivīṁ vibhaktavarṇāśramāṁ svadharmeṇa bhuñjita*).[744] Since the *svadharma* of each caste was shrouded in ancient usage, it meant that the king had to respect and maintain the usages of the different castes and religious orders. Finally, at the end of the next chapter on the Restoration of Peace in a Conquered land, he, again, asserts the following:

> He (the king) should initiate the observance of all those customs which, though unrighteous and practised by others, are not observed in his own country, and give no room for the practice of whatever is unrighteous though observed by others (*caritraṁ-akṛitaṁ dharmyaṁ kṛitaṁ ca-anyaiḥ pravartayet pravartayet-na ca-adharmyaṁ kṛitaṁ ca-anyaiḥ nivartayet*).[745]

(*ii*) *Concept of Justice : Equity*

The reader must have formed by now some idea of the concept of justice in Kauṭilya. We may reinforce it by a few more considerations. Thus, we have the directive given to the Commissioner (*pradeṣṭṛ*), who was under the Collector-General, in the matter of imposing fines, thus:

> Taking into consideration the (social position of) persons, the nature of the offence, the cause, whether grave or slight (that led to the perpetration of the offence), the antecedent and present circumstances, the time and place, and without failing to notice equitable distinction among offenders, whether belonging to royal family, or to the common people, shall the Commissioner determine the propriety of imposing the first, middlemost, or highest amercement (*puruṣaṁ-ca aparādhaṁ-ca kāraṇaṁ gurulāghavaṁ anubandhaṁ tadāvaṁ ca deśakālau samīkṣya ca uttama-āvara-madhyatvaṃ pradeṣṭā daṇḍakarmaṇi rājñaḥ-ca prakritīnāṁ ca kalpayet-antarānvitaḥ*).[746]

Justice not to be Delayed. Kauṭilya was definitely against delaying justice. This is evident from his regulation relating to the judgement to be given by the presiding officer. "Sentence of punishment shall be passed the very day that a defendant accused of assault fails to answer the charge made against him."[747] The manner in which he defines various kinds of offences and crimes, and the remedial measures which he recommends in every case, in the chapters on Robbery, Defamation, Assault, and Miscellaneous offences, shows how carefully the judicial machinery was planned by him.[748]

Impartiality. Although he was, on the whole, inclined to follow the ancient precepts relating to the sanctity of the person of the Śrotriyas, yet he was not of the opinion that the members of the priestly class could altogether escape the clutches of law. It has already been seen, while discussing the sacredotal theory of the origin of the State, that the only punishment from which the Brahmans were exempted was torture. But a Brahman was subject to fines, disfigurement, and banishment to distant mines for offences ranging from selling or mortgaging lands to heinous crimes like violating the chastity of his *guru's* wife. If a Brahman committed treason, he did not suffer the terrible fate which awaited others, viz., that of being burnt from head to foot, but was simply drowned.[749]

The impartiality of the State in the matter of meteing out justice is seen in the fines imposed on ascetics and atheists. Whenever hermits, etc., had to pay any fines, they could, in the name of the king, perform penance by offering oblations to gods, fire worship, or the ritual called Mahakachhchhavardhana for as many nights as were the number of *paṇas* of their fines. Those heretics called *pāṣaṇḍas,* who had neither gold or gold coin, were similarly to observe their fasts, excepting in the case of defamation, theft, assault, and abduction. "Under these circumstances, they shall be compelled to undergo punishment." This passage proves that under the garb of asceticism or atheism, the citizens could not commit offences of a civil or criminal nature, and escape punishment with impunity. The regulation for the performance of penances on as many nights as the number of *paṇas* of their fines, looks, indeed, novel ; but it is clear that ascetics, like atheists, could not seek exemption from fines. The next injunction of Kauṭilya shows that even in those ancient times, ascetics were never always righteous in their behaviour. "The king shall under penalty of fines, forbid the wilful or improper proceedings of ascetics ; for vice, overwhelming righteousness, will in the long run destroy the ruler himself."[750]

The discharge of justice as a matter of duty and in a most impartial manner is further proved by the following in the *Arthaśāstra*: "As the duty of a king consists in protecting his subjects with justice, its observance leads him to heaven. He who does not protect his people or upsets the social order wields his royal sceptre in vain." In the next passage we have the clearest evidence of Kauṭilya's sense of impartial justice. "It is power and power alone which, only when exercised by the king with impartiality and in proportion to guilt, either over his son or his enemy, maintains both this world and the next" (*daṇḍo hi kevalo lokaṁ paraṁ ca-imaṁ ca rakṣati rājñā putre ca śatrau ca yathādośaṁ samaṁ dhṛitaḥ*).[751] Incidentally it may be remarked here that the impartiality of justice as given above is to be studied along with the problem of protection as one of the most important functions of the State discussed in the earlier pages of this book.

(iii) *Kinds of Law Courts and Procedure : The High Court*

There were three types of law courts, according to Kauṭilya. These were the High Court, if we may use that term, situated in the capital itself ; the Itinerant Courts, again, to use a modern term ; and what may be called the Executive Courts. The existence of the High Court is proved by the passage already cited which refers to the distinction between the court and the offices of the ministers, while dealing with the duties of the Chamberlain (*sannidhātā*). We are informed that "the Court and the offices of the ministers shall be built in a separate locality" (*prathak-dharmasthīyaṁ mahāmatrīyaṁ*). These and other buildings (described in the preceding passage in the *Arthaśāstra*) were to be provided with separate accommodation for men and women, and with a jail and many compartments well guarded.[752] Since this building is called *dharmasthīyaṁ*, and is mentioned along with the offices of the *mahāmātras*, and since we cannot think of these latter being located in distant parts of the Empire, it would not be unreasonable to assume that both the ministerial offices and the High Court were situated in the capital itself.

An objection may be raised against this by saying that in the previous chapter on the buildings within the fort no mention is made of such an important construction like the High Court; that the passage cited above relating to the *dharmasthīyaṁ* has to be studied along with the reference to be cited below relating to the Itinerant Courts in the country sides; and that, therefore, we have to construe the location of the High Court in the country sides.

The above objection is invalidated by two considerations. Firstly, we shall see presently that the Itinerant Courts were located at different parts of the kingdom, and not centered at one place. Secondly, the High Court is coupled with the offices of the ministers. Now we have seen in the previous pages of this book that these latter were of the same cadre as the *amātyas* but for some difference, although it is true that, in the chapter on the buildings in the fort, the residences of the *amātyas* are specifically said to be east by north of the royal palace.[753] But we cannot conceive of one part of the category of ministers, the *amātyas*, living far away from another part of the same category, the *mahāmātras*, unless there is proof in the *Arthaśāstra* that the State differentiated between them even in the matter of residential qualifications. We would be correct in assuming that the residences of the *mahāmātras* were also in the capital; and that consequently the High Court was likewise in the same locality. Finally, the *sannidhātā* or the Chamberlain was entrusted with the construction of the treasure house (*kośagṛihaṁ*), the trading house (*paṇyagṛihaṁ*), the store house (*koṣṭāgāraṁ*), the store house of forest produce (*kupyagṛihaṁ*), the armoury (*āyudhāgāraṁ*), and the jail (*bandhanāgāraṁ*).[754] Of these the *koṣagṛihaṁ*, *paṇyagṛihaṁ*, the *koṣṭāgāraṁ*, the *kupygṛihaṁ*, and *āyudhāgāraṁ* were inside the capital.[755] Since the High Court is mentioned after the store house of grains and of forest produce, and in conjunction with the office of the ministers, and with the jail, which was also located in the capital, we are justified in maintaining that the High Court (*dharmasthīyaṁ*) was in the capital itself. When we realize that, according to Kauṭilya the king was the fountain of justice (*dharmapavartakaḥ*),[756] it is only natural to conclude that the seat justice should have been near him in the capital itself. This would mean that this Court would have to be assigned a separate existence, and that it cannot be confounded with the other two types of courts mentioned below.

The Itinerant Courts. The other two types of courts were the Itinerant Courts established in the country sides, and the courts entrusted with executive powers. While dealing with the major problem of determining the forms of legal agreements in legal disputes, Kauṭilya states: "In the cities of *sangrahaṇa, droṇamukha,* and *sthānīya,* and at places where districts meet, three members acquainted with the Sacred law and three ministers of the king shall carry on the administration of justice" (*dharmasthāḥ-trayaḥ-trayo'amātyā janapadasandhi-sangraha-droṇamukha-sthānīyeṣu vyavahārikān-arthān kuryuḥ*).[757] A *sthānīya* was a fortress in the centre of 800 villages; a *droṇamukha,* a fortress in the centre of 400 villages; a *kharvāṭika,* a fortress in the centre of 200 villages; and a *sangrahaṇa,* a fortress in the midst of ten villages.[758] In a vast Empire like that of Candragupta Maurya, we cannot imagine only a single fortress of the above categories existing. We have to assume that there were many fortresses of each category in the land. This means that the court composed of three *dharmasthas* or judges, well versed in the *dharmaśāstras,* and three ministers of the king, well versed in the *nītiśāstras,* were to go round the different *sthānīyas, droṇamukhas,* and *sangrahaṇas.* The omission of the *kharvāṭikas,* as remarked earlier, in this list is inexplicable. But the itinerant nature of the judges is further proved by the explicit statement in the same passage that they should meet at places where the districts meet—a reference, no doubt, to the many places where they had to go in the discharge of their duties. No other proof is needed to establish the itinerant nature of these judges.

Their jurisdiction covered agreements entered into in seclusion, inside the houses, in the dead of night, in forests, in secret, or in fraud. The procedure they had to follow is given in detail. They had the right to fine the guilty people. The exact relationship between the Itinerant Courts and the High Court in the capital cannot be made out; but since three of the judges were ministers, and since at the end of this chapter describing their composition and duties, Kauṭilya lays great stress on State law, it is not unreasonable to conclude that an appeal lay from these courts to the High Court in the capital.[759]

The Executive Courts. The third kind of courts was made up of three Commissioners (*pradestārāḥ*), or three ministers (*amātyāḥ*), who were to deal with measures to suppress disturbances of peace (*kaṇṭhakaśodhanaṁ kuryuḥ*). These Courts dealt with the guilds (*śreṇi*), artisans (*kārukāḥ*), weavers (*tantuvāyāḥ*), washermen (*rajakaḥ*), goldsmiths (*suvarṇakārāhaḥ*), sweepers and scavengers (*jjharakapāṁśudhāvākaḥ*), physicians (*bhiṣajah*), traders (*vaṇik*), musicians (*kuśīlavā*), dancers (*cārāṇāvāḥ*), mendicants (*bhikṣukāḥ*), cheats (*kuhakāḥ*), and other idlers "who are thieves in effect though not in name" (*corānacorākhyān*), and who were to be restrained from oppressing the country.[760]

The composition and the jurisdiction of the *dharmasthāḥ* and the *kaṇṭakaśodhana* courts reveal that they were two different bodies—the former dealing with the cases in the country parts, the latter, more with those of the towns and cities. Further, the *dharmasthāḥ* courts were composed of six judges, while the *kaṇṭhakaśodhana* courts only of three (i.e. either three commissioners or three ministers). From this it can be deduced that the former were larger courts than the latter. Moreover, the former were to decide cases of contract and tort; the latter, of the oppression (*deśadpīḍanāt*) of the country by the guilds, the craftsmen, the medical practitioners, and the idlers of various types.[761]

(c) *Features of His Legal System: Exemption from being Witnesses*

Without going into the mass of details which Kauṭilya gives about the witnesses,[762] and the procedure to be adopted in the courts in different contexts—which could well form a study by itself, and which definitely points to a considerable improvement since the days of Manu and Pāṇini—we may confine ourselves to one or two features of the legal system in Kauṭilya before passing on to the topics relating to the judges and the relationship between the law courts and the maintenance of social order.

In the history of the legal procedure in Kauṭilya, some points may interest modern students. For instance, there was the question as to who could not become witnesses. While maintaining that, as narrated earlier in these pages, it was obligatory to produce three witnesses who were reliable, honest, and respectable—at least two of whom were to be acceptable to the parties—we are told in the *Arthaśāstra* that the following could not be cited as witnesses: wife's brothers, co-partners, prisoners (*ābaddha*), creditors, debtors, enemies, maimed persons, and persons once punished by the government. Likewise persons legally unfit to carry on transactions, the king, Śrotriyas, persons depending for their maintenance on villages (*grāmabhṛitaka*), lepers, persons suffering from bodily eruptions, outcastes, Cāṇḍālas, persons following mean vocations, the blind, the deaf, the dumb, egoistic persons, females, and government servants. These could not be cited as witnesses excepting in cases of transactions in one's own community. In disputes concerning assaults, thefts, or abduction, persons other than wife's brothers, enemies, and co-partners could be cited as witnesses. In secret dealings, a single woman or a single man, who had stealthily heard or seen them, could be a witness, with the exception of the king or an ascetic. On the side of the prosecution, masters against servants, priests or teachers against their disciples, and parents against their sons, could be witnesses; persons other than these could also be witnesses in criminal cases.[763]

The immunity of the king from appearing as a witness is a point of particular importance to us in the modern days. To what extent Kauṭilya had departed from the injunctions laid down in the *Manusmṛiti* will be evident when we note what Manu says about persons who could not be produced as witnesses: those who had an interest in the suit, those who were familiar friends, companions, or enemies of the parties, men formerly convicted (of perjury), persons suffering from severe illness, those tainted by mortal sin, mechanics, actors, Śrotriyas, a student of the *Vedas*, an ascetic who had given up all connection with the world, one who was wholly dependent upon others, one of bad fame, a Dasyu, one who followed forbidden occupations, an aged man, an infant, a man (living alone), a man of the low castes, one deficient in the organs of the senses, one externally grieved, one intoxicated, a mad man, one tormented by hunger, or by thirst, one oppressed by fatigue, and a thief. Women were to give evidence for women, twice-born men for twice-born men, virtuous Śūdras for Śūdras, and men of the lowest castes for the lowest people. Manu ordained that the king could not be a witness[764]—a rule which Kauṭilya scrupulously followed. There was agreement between Manu and Kauṭilya on most essentials, the points of divergence between the two being the following: Kauṭilya included in the list of persons, who were exempted from being witnesses, wife's brothers, maimed persons, and egoistic persons (*āhamvādinaḥ*), and would not hesitate to recommend that masters could give evidence against servants, teachers against pupils, and parents against children!

Court Fees. The next point in the legal procedure of Kauṭilya that might interest us is the payment of court fees. A general rule is laid down in the *Arthaśāstra* to the effect that in all kinds of fines below 100 *paṇas*, the king should take, in addition to the fine, eight per cent as *rūpa*, and in fines above one hundred, five per cent more as *vyāji*. The justification for levying these court fees is given thus:

> These two kinds of exaction are just, inasmuch as the people are full of sins, on the one hand, and the kings are naturally misguided, on the other (*daṇḍakarmasu sarveṣu rūpam-aṣṭapaṇaṁ śataṁ śatātpare tu vyājīṁ ca vidyāt-pañcapaṇam śataṁ prajānāṁ doṣabāhulyāt rājñām vā bhāvadoṣataḥ rūpavyājyāvadharmiṣṭe dharmyānuprakṛitiḥ-smṛitā*).[765]

One wonders against whom the last part of the sentence was meant: Was the king misguided by his judges?

Torture to elicit Confession: *"The Third Degree"*. Another feature of the legal procedure on the executive side was the use of torture to elicit confession. A whole chapter is devoted to this dismal aspect of law, and another, to the punishments that followed such a procedure. No doubt, certain safeguards are assured before the defendant is subjected to torture (*anyatha karmaprāptaḥ*) ; and no suspected person (*śaṅkitakaḥ*) could be arrested three days after a crime had been committed. Torture that was in vogue was of four kinds (*karmacatuṣkaṁ*) ; punishments were of six kinds (*ṣaṭdaṇḍāḥ*) ; whipping (*kaśa*) was of seven kinds ; suspension from above were of two kinds (*upari nibandhau*) ; and there was the water tube (*udakanāḷikā ca*). In the next passage (which appears to be rather obscure), eighteen kinds of torture are described, which cannot be reconciled with the twenty kinds of torture mentioned above. This list of torture makes woeful reading; and it forms an adverse comment on the administration of justice advocated by Kauṭilya.

The Use of Torture Qualified. But there were some redeeming features in the use of torture. Firstly, there was a category of persons against whom it could not be used, or if used, was not to be used to its full extent. Ignoramuses (*mandāvadhānaṁ*), youngsters, the aged, the afflicted persons (*vyādhitaṁ*), persons under intoxication (*mattaṁ*), lunatics, persons suffering from hunger, thirst, or fatigue from journey, persons who had taken just more than enough of meal, persons who had confessed of their own accord (*ātmakāśitaṁ*), and persons who were very weak—none of these could be subjected to torture (*na karma kārayet*).

As regards women, torture was to be half of the prescribed standard (*śtrīyāḥ-tu ardha karma*). Or women with no exception could be subjected to the trial of cross examination (*vākyānuyogo vā*). No women carrying, or who had not passed a month after delivery, could be subjected to torture.

Those of the Brahman caste and learned in the Vedas, as well as ascetics, could be subjected only to espionage (*Brāhmaṇasya satriparigṛihaḥ śrutavataḥ-tapasvinaḥ-ca*).

Secondly, only those whose guilt was believed to be true (i.e., those whose guilt was established), could be subjected to torture (*āptadoṣaṁ karma kārayet*).

Thirdly, only the king could order the use of toruture. In accordance with the order of the king (*rājavacanāt*), those accused of dacoity, those who had made use of stolen articles, those caught in the very act of stealing, those who had committed culpable crimes, and those who had attempted to seize the king's treasury—these could be subjected once or many times to one or all of the above methods of torture.

And, finally, there was punishment for those who violated the above rules. Those who violated, or caused to violate, the above rules, were punished with the first amercement. The same punishment awaited those who caused death to any one by torture.[766]

It would be erroneous to infer from the discussion made above of the features of the Kauṭilyan legal code that there was no sense of mercy at all. The exemptions from the use of torture mentioned above themselves suggest the better side of the legal system. If further proof is needed we have it in the following passage: Such persons as a pilgrim, an ascetic engaged in penance, a diseased person, any one suffering from hunger, thirst, or fatigue from journey, a villager from country parts, any one that had suffered from physical punishment, and a moneyless pauper, were to be shown mercy.[767]

(*d*) *The Rôle of the Judges*

What was the rôle of the judges in the legal system advocated by Kauṭilya? In an earlier connection we had referred briefly to the judges in the *Artha-śāstra*. If law under Kauṭilya was harsh in the case of law-breakers, it was equally uncompromising in the case of those who administered it. We may be permitted to repeat some of the attributes of the judiciary we had mentioned above, while making a comparative estimate of the same under Aristotle and Kauṭilya. Judges were required to settle disputes free from all kinds of circumvention, with their mind unchanged in all moods or circumstances, pleasing and affable to all (*evaṁ kāryāṇi dharmasthāḥ kuryuḥ-achchhala-dharśinaḥ samāḥ-sarveṣu bhāveṣu viśvāsyā-lokasam-priyāḥ*).[768] This was in regard to their general attitude which even in our own days, would hold good in the case of the members of the judiciary.

Judges not above Law. The judges were not above law. In fact, they were as much subject to it as any ordinary citizen. We have already seen that, if a judge threatened, browbeat, sent out, or unjustly silenced any one of the disputants in his court, he was to be punished, in the first instance, with the first amercement (i.e. a fine ranging from forty-eight *paṇas* to ninety *paṇas*). If he defamed or abused any one of them, the punishment was doubled. If he did not ask what ought to have been asked, or asked what ought not to have been asked, or left out what he himself had asked, or taught. reminded, or provided any one with previous statements, he was to be punished with the middlemost amercement (i.e. a fine ranging from 200 *paṇas* to 500 *paṇas*). When the judge did not inquire into the necessary circumstances, inquired into the unnecessary circumstances, made unnecessary delay in the discharge of his duty, postponed work with spite, caused parties to leave the court by tiring them with delay, evaded or caused to evade statements that led to the settlement of a case, helped witnesses, gave them clues, or resumed cases that had already been settled or disposed of, he was to be punished with the highest amercement (i.e. a fine ranging from 500 *paṇas* to 1,000 *paṇas*). If he repeated the offence, he was to be punished with double the above fine and dismissed.

Further, when a judge or commissioner imposed an unjust fine in gold, he was himself fined either double the amount of the fine, or eight times the amount of the imposition which was either more or less than the prescribed limit. If a judge or commissioner imposed an unjust corporal punishment, he was himself either condemned to the same punishment or made to pay twice the amount of ransom leviable for that kind of injustice. And when a judge falsified what was a true amount or declared as true whatever amount was false, he was fined eight times that amount.[769] While these regulations give an idea of the ignoble part which the judiciary was prone to play in those days, it also indicates the stern measures which the State adopted in controlling the judiciary, and, in particular, in bringing the latter within the ambit of law. In a sense, this may be said to be the

"Rule of the Law", if we could use that modern phrase in regard to the ancient judicial practice, as it prevailed in India.

(e) *Law as an Adjunct of the State*

Law in the socio-political scheme of Kauṭilya was a means to maintain social order and public good. The destruction of the Nandas at home was the first thing that was achieved; and the next was the wresting of the north-western regions from the Macedonian ruler, Seleukos Nikator.[770] A still greater task remained, and that was of reducing the vast country bounded on the north by the Himālayas and on the south by the ocean, to a stable order, so that the fruits of victory might be fully utilized for the good of the people and for the furtherance of the cause of the monarch. In this huge task the State utilized the aid of the law courts which fulfilled their task in five ways, some of which have already figured above. These methods were the following: settling the disputes between citizen and citizen, between citizens and corporations, between citizens and artisans and other professionals, between citizens and merchants, and between citizens and the indigenous "fifth-columnists" and the agents of foreign powers.

Fixing Prices of Daily Commodities. Of these the first three have been dealt with in the previous pages of this work. We might restrict ourselves to the fourth one dealing with citizens and merchants, and with the last one concerning the State and the traitors. The first question of maintaining the relationship between the citizens and the merchants was the duty of the Superintendent of Commerce (*saṁsthādhyakṣa*). His duties consisted in supervising weights and measures, controlling the prices of commodities, and the sale and mortgage of articles, and, in general, in seeing that the merchants were favourably disposed towards the people in selling grains and other commodities. He was empowered to punish with fines ranging from three *paṇas* to 1,000 *paṇas* those who contravened law. He fixed the profits on local and foreign goods. On the former it was five per cent over and above the fixed price, and ten per cent on foreign produce. This was arrived at in the following manner: the Superintendent of Commerce considered the outlay, the quantity manufactured, the amount of toll, the interest on the outlay, and other necessary expenses, and, then, fixed the price on merchandise with due regard to its having been manufactured long ago or imported from a distant country.[771] In this matter Kauṭilya had advanced on Manu, who had merely stated that the king should fix the rates for the purchase and sale of all marketable goods, having only considered whence they came, whither they were to go, how long they have been kept, the probable profit, and the probable outlay.[772]

"Black Marketing". Of special interest to the moderners is the care which the Kauṭilyan State took to prevent what, since the World War II. has unfortunately become almost a daily feature of our commercial life,

the "black marketing" in goods. "Merchants who conspire either to prevent the sale of merchandise or to sell or purchase commodities at higher prices shall be fined 1,000 *paṇas*." We cannot make out what machinery was evolved to detect these anti-social elements in the commercial world. But the above regulation should be read along with that recommending penalties for the adulteration of articles of daily consumption, which consisted of a fine of twelve *paṇas*, and the curb on the middlemen whose income was fixed by the State.[773]

CHAPTER X

THE THEORY OF THE PRĀKRITIS: THE STATE IN RELATION TO OTHER STATES—FOREIGN POLICY AND DIPLOMACY

A. INTRODUCTION

IT WAS seen above, while discussing the theory of the *prākritis* or Elements of the State, that that theory had two aspects—one which considered the State with an individuality of its own, and the other, the State as a unit in a circle of States. We have discussed above the former ; we shall now be concerned with the latter which is involved in the theory of foreign policy as connoted by the term *maṇḍala,* or *cakra,* or *rājamaṇḍala.*

B. HISTORY OF THE THEORY OF RĀJAMAṆḌALA

1. IN THE VEDIC LITERATURE

Although the theory of *rājamaṇḍala* is not found in the *Rig Veda,* yet there is evidence to show that the Vedic Aryans were aware of the rudimentary principles of diplomacy. This is suggested by the description of Agni as a herald or messenger when he is represented as "serving in secret", passing to and fro "between both races", and as "an envoy to mankind". The *Atharva Veda Samhita* marks a stage forward in the concept of foreign relations when Agni is given a political bias, and is said to be a speedy messenger, who was to see the arrival of much tribute. But beyond this there is nothing to suggest that the Vedic Aryans were aware of a well developed theory of *rājamaṇḍala.* It is not improbable that one of the reasons why they never had an occasion of formulating it was perhaps because their kingdoms had not outgrown the size of tribal organizations, although we do come across the names of very many kings in the Vedic literature, and of terms like *sāmrājya,* etc., which we have discussed in the preceding pages of this book.[774]

2. IN THE MANUSMRITI

We do not know when exactly the theory of *rājamaṇḍala* became crystallized, but its first clear picture is found only in the *Manusmṛiti* wherein is stated the following:

> On the conduct of the middlemost (prince), on the doings of him who seeks conquest, on the behaviour of the neutral (king), and (on that) of the foe (let him) sedulously (meditate). These (four) constituents (*prakṛiti*) (form), briefly (speaking), the foundation of the circle (of neighbours); besides eight others are enumerated (in the Institutes of Polity), and thus the total is declared to be twelve. The minister, the kingdom, the fortress, the treasury, and the army are five other (constituent elements of the circle); for, these are mentioned in connection with each (of the first twelve; thus the whole circle consists), briefly (speaking, of) seventy-two constituent parts. Let (the king) consider as hostile his immediate neighbour and the partisan of (such a) foe, as friendly the immediate neighbour of his foe, and as neutral (the king) beyond those two.[775]

Thus was the *rājamaṇḍala* theory laid down in the clearest terms as the foundation of the foreign policy of the rulers. Its relationship to the elements (*prakriti*) of the State, which we have mentioned above, is seen in the inclusion of the minister, the kingdom, the fortress, the treasury, and the army as the five elements in the entire circle of States. Manu had thus completed the theory of the *prakritis*, and ushered in the theory of *rājamaṇḍala*. Another contribution of Manu to the theory of foreign policy was the manner in which he laid stress on a most essential aspect of that theory, viz., the institution of ambassadors which we shall mention presently.

In the Epics. Although Manu had thus laid down the theory on the soundest principles, yet it took centuries for it to develop. There is nothing in the *Rāmāyaṇa* to suggest that the monarchs mentioned in it considered the *rājamaṇḍala* as of vital importance to the State. Neither is there any evidence in the other great epic, the *Mahābhārata*, that the monarchs had recourse to this theory as a matter of State policy. Both the epics, no doubt, describe the ambassadors, as will be mentioned below; but this does not give us an adequate idea of the importance of the *rājamaṇḍala* theory, so far as the two epics are concerned.

In Kauṭilya. We have to come to the stirring times of Kauṭilya in order to understand the vital part the theory of *rājamaṇḍala* played in the life of the State. Kauṭilya made it the corner-stone of the foreign policy of the monarch. No previous author on ancient Indian polity had dwelt at such length on the question of the foreign policy, and no one attached so much importance to it as he did. No doubt he took the theory from where Manu had left it, and perfected it to suit the needs of his own and later times. He elucidated the theory thus:

> The conqueror, his friend, and his friend's friend are the three primary kings constituting a circle of States. As each of these three kings possesses the five elements of sovereignty, such as the minister, the

country, the fort, the treasury, and the army, a circle of States consists of eighteen elements. Thus, it needs no commentary to understand that the (three) circle of States having the enemy (of the conqueror), the Madhyama king, or the neutral king at the centre of each of the three circles, are different from that of the conqueror. Thus, there are four primary circles of States, twelve kings, sixty elements of sovereignty, and seventy-two elements of States.[776]

We may analyse the concept of the *rājamaṇḍala* or *maṇḍala*, or *cakra*, or the circle of States, thus:

Circle I. Consisting of the would-be conqueror (*vijigīśu*) + his friend + his friend's friend (3 rulers).
Circle II. Consisting of the enemy + his friend + his friend's friend (3 rulers).
Circle III. Consisting of the Madhyama king + his friend + his friend's friend (3 rulers).
Circle IV. Consisting of the Udāśīna or neutral king + his friend + his friend's friend (3 rulers).

Since each ruler possessed five elements of sovereignty comprising minister, country, fort, treasury, and army, each circle had 3 rulers + 15 = 18 elements; and, therefore, four circles had $18 \times 4 = 72$ elements. We thus have four primary circles of States, twelve kings, sixty elements of sovereignty, and seventy-two elements of States.[777]

The interdependence of the first part of the theory of the *prakritis* dealing with the independent State (or with the State that had its own individuality), with the second part of the same theory concerning the foreign policy of that State is admirably set forth by Kauṭilya in the next passage thus: "Each of the twelve primary kings shall have their elements of sovereignty." And in the next sentence he epitomizes the end of all State policy in the following cryptic sentence: "Strength is Power; and Happiness is the End." He divides strength into three categories: power of deliberation which is intellectual strength; the possession of a prosperous treasury and a strong army is the strength of sovereignty; and martial power is physical strength. As regards the interrelationship of power and happiness, we are told that the possession of power and happiness in a greater degree makes a king superior to another; in a less degree, inferior; and in an equal degree, equal. "Hence a king shall always endeavour to augment his own power and elevate his happiness."[778]

The circle of States mentioned above was only one of the three main concepts governing the relation between the States, as delineated by Manu and others after. The other two were the policies (*upāya*) and the expedients (*ṣāḍguṇya*). Policy was subdivided into four components—conciliation (*sāma*), concession (*dāna*), sowing dissension (*bheda*), and war (*daṇḍa*) which last, according to Manu, was the last means a ruler could adopt. Expedients were four—co-operation (*sandhi*), hostilities (*vigraha*), marching or mobilization (*yāna*), readiness for attack (*āsana*), division of troops (*dvaidībhāva*), and subordinate alliance (*āśraya*).[779]

Of the three concepts in the theory of foreign relations that which carried the greatest weight with Kauṭilya was the circle of States which he calls merely by the term *maṇḍala*. According to him it was the source of the six-fold policy (*ṣāḍguṇyasya prakritimaṇḍalaṁ yoniḥ*).[780] After elaborating this concept, he says in the end the following: "Thus, a king in the circle of sovereign States shall, by adopting the six-fold policy, endeavour to pass from the state of deterioration to that of stagnation, and from the latter to that of progress."[781] We do not know whether there is any reference in this summing up of the concept of the State policy to Kauṭilya's royal patron Candragupta Maurya's original deterioration in the sense of one who was unwanted in the royal house of the Nandas, his stagnation on his overthrowing them, and his undisputed mastery over the whole land on his having driven the Macedonians out of the north-western regions. Further research alone could enlighten us on this interesting point.

C. THE INSTITUTION OF AMBASSADORS

In the execution and fulfilment of the six-fold policy of the State relating to its foreign affairs, no one played such an important part as the ambassadors. We may study the problem of the institution of ambassadors under the following heads: the term used for ambassadors, their qualifications, kinds of ambassadors, their status, their immunity, their duties, their salary, and their importance.

1. TERM USED FOR AN AMBASSADOR

An ambassador was called a *dūta*.

2. QUALIFICATIONS

From the times of Manu it was laid down that only those could be selected as ambassadors, who were versed in all sciences, who understood hints and expressions of the face, and gestures, who were honest, skilful, of noble families, and loyal, who possessed a good memory, who knew the people, place, and time for action, and who were handsome, fearless, and eloquent. Kauṭilya explicitly states: "Whoever has succeeded as a councillor is an envoy" (*uddhṛitamantro dūtapraṇidhiḥ*).[782]

3. KINDS OF AMBASSADORS

In the next sentences he mentions the three kinds of ambassadors thus: those who possessed ministerial qualifications (*amātyasampat*), and were called *nisṛisṭārthaḥ*, and whom we may style as envoys of class A; those who possessed the same qualifications but less by one quarter, who were called agents with a definite mission (*parimitārthaḥ*), and whom we may style as envoys of class B; and those who possessed the same qualifications but less by one half, and who were styled merely as conveyors of royal writs (*śāsanaharaḥ*),[783] and whom we may call as envoys of class C. In giving thus the three-fold division of ambassadors, Kauṭilya had definitely advanced on the concept of Manu, who made no such provision for three categories of ambassadors. Kauṭilya seemed to imply from the explicit manner in which he laid down the qualifications of the ambassadors, that they could not be selected from amongst the relatives or favourites of the monarch, unless they fulfilled the ministerial qualifications. The only criterion seems to have been the success which one attained as a minister that entitled one to aspire for the post of an ambassador.

The same kinds of ambassadors are mentioned in the *Agni Purāṇa* but in a slightly different order, thus: the envoy entrusted with the management of an affair, according to his own light and discretion, was called *nisrisṭārthaḥ*; he who was charged with the duties of a mission, according to the directions received from his sovereign, was called *mitārthaḥ*; and he whose only duty was to deliver the decisions of his royal master on a particular problem was called *śāsanaharaḥ*.[784]

4. STATUS

From the *Manusmṛiti* it cannot be made out what exactly was the status of an ambassador. But since, according to Kauṭilya, as noted above, the ambassadors were chosen from successful councillors, they were of the status of ministers (*amātyasampat*). The ambassadors enjoyed immunity from arrest, as is gathered from the *Rāmāyaṇa*, but it appears that in Kauṭilya's time, he could pretend to be afraid of imprisonment or even death—a fear which was undoubtedly non-existent in the days of the *Mahābhārata*, so far as death was concerned![785] This will be further evident from what will be described below under the envoy's duties.

5. DUTIES

They were very onerous since Manu's time. The ambassador alone made the king's allies and separated them; and he alone transacted that business by which kings were united or disunited. Kauṭilya enlarged their duties, as given by Manu, when he enjoined that the envoy shall make friendship with the envoy's officers, such as those in charge of wild tracts, of boundaries, of cities, and of country parts. The envoy shall contrast the military stations, sinews of war, and strongholds of the enemy with those of his own master. He was to ascertain the size and area of the forts of the enemy States, as well as the strongholds, of precious things, and of assailable and unassailable points. Having obtained permission, he was to enter the capital of the enemy, and state the object of his mission exactly as entrusted to him, even at the cost of his life! He was not to be puffed up with the respect shown to him by the enemy; but was to stay in the capital of the enemy till he was allowed to depart. He was to ignore the might of the enemy, and to strictly abjure women and liquor, to take to a single bed at night; ascertain through spies the nature and strength of the opposition to, and loyalty for, his own master in the capital of the enemy; and never to disclose to the enemy the strength and means adopted by his royal master.[785a]

6. SALARY

The *Manusmṛiti* does not mention the salary given to an ambassador; but Kauṭilya explicitly states that ambassadors of the middle class were to be paid ten *paṇas* for every *yojana* they travelled; and twice as much when they travelled from ten to 100 *yojanas*. Further, they were endowed with lands which could not be sold or mortgaged by them, and were exempted from paying tolls while crossing rivers. Since these formed envoys of class C, it is evident that those of class A and B were paid higher salaries. Now we have seen above that envoys of class A were of the ministerial cadre. Since the ministers were paid each 2,000 *paṇas*, it follows that class A and B ambassadors were likewise paid the same salary. For like the ministers, "with this they will be loyal and powerful supporters of the king's cause", and "With this amount of subsistence, they will scarcely yield themselves to temptation and hardly be discontended",[786] as Kauṭilya rightly affirmed.

7. IMPORTANCE OF THE AMBASSADORS

Manu wrote thus on the importance of the ambassadors: that the king was to be careful about the details given by the ambassadors. The whole range of the inter-State relations, and, therefore, to a great extent the existence of the State, depended upon the ambassadors.[787] The *Arthaśāstra* of Kauṭilya bears testimony to the vital part played by the ambassadors in the wide range of the foreign policy of the ruler.

CHAPTER XI

THE INSTITUTION OF SPIES

A. ANTIQUITY OF ESPIONAGE: IN THE MANUSMṚITI

As to when exactly the institution of spies was started, it cannot be made out. The spies do not figure in the Vedic literature. When we reach the age of Manu, we find minute regulations laid down by that great lawgiver for the employment of spies in public life. The minister, who was appointed to look after the administration of a group of ten villages, of twenty families, of 100 villages, and of towns, whom we may call in the modern language Minister for Local Government had, among other duties, that of exploring the behaviour of his rural officials through spies appointed over each official.[788] The king was to carefully consider the doings of spies, five classes of whom are mentioned but without being named.[789] This he was to do after having performed his twilight devotions when, well armed, he was to hear in an inner apartment the doings of those who made secret reports, and of his spies.[790] Spies were also used to detect thieves who stole property, who showed themselves openly, and those who lay concealed. Among the rogues who showed themselves openly were the merchants, who traded in marketable commodities; while among those that lay concealed were those who took bribes, gamblers, and those who lived by teaching the performance of auspicious ceremonies, sanctimonious hypocrites, fortune tellers, officials of high rank, physicians who acted improperly, prostitutes, men who lived by showing their proficiency in arts, and those who were non-Aryans but who walked in disguise like the Aryans.[791] Finally, spies were also used to constantly ascertain the king's own and his enemy's strength.[792]

B. IN KAUṬILYA

1. ESPIONAGE IN GENERAL

Manu had set an example which Kauṭilya followed to frightful perfection. The great Mauryan Prime Minister devotes four chapters of his First Book exclusively to espionage, and refers to the part played by spies in judicial and foreign matters. The king was to proceed to create spies with the assistance of the council of ministers, who had themselves been tried under espionage.[793] From this it may be inferred that the ministers were finally appointed only after their character and antecedents had been duly ascertained. This is proved by the opening sentence of the previous chapter on Ascertaining the Purity or Impurity in the Character of Ministers, which states: "Assisted by his prime minister (*mantri*) and high priest (concerning whose appointment there is no reference to spies), the king shall, by offering temptations, examine the character of ministers (*amātya*) appointed in governmental departments of an ordinary nature." Then follow various details relating to the technique of ascertaining by temptations the loyal character of the ministers.[794] A pale reflection of this method still survives in modern governments which ascertain through their Local Intelligence Branches, or similar detective wings, attached to the Police Department, the antecedents and character of persons before the latter are finally admitted into government service.

2. KINDS OF SPIES

But Kauṭilya's was a mere rigorous system of espionage which might find favour with some totalitarian governments of the modern times. There were nine kinds of spies: *kāpaṭika-chhātra,* or he who worked under the guise of a fraudulent disciple, or he who worked in the guise of a *kāpaṭika* (which Dr. Kane would interpret as a bold pupil capable of knowing the mind of others) ; *udāsthita,* or a sham ascetic who, having fallen off from the real duties of asceticism, was still endowed with intelligence and pure character ; *gṛihapatika,* or he who was a householder, who was unable to eke out his livelihood but had intelligence and was of good character ; *vaidehaka,* or a trader who, like the preceding one, being unable to lead the life of a trader, was still intelligent and of good character, *tāpasa,* or he who desired to practise an austere life but could not make a living ; *satrin,* or he who was a classmate or colleague ; *tīkṣaṇa,* or he who was a desperado ; *rasada,* or he who could administer poison ; and, finally, a *bhikṣuki,* or a mendicant woman.

While explaining in detail these spies, Kauṭilya gives an insight into the actual working of the all-embracing espionage under the State. The *kāpaṭika-chhātra* seems to have directed his activities against persons. The *udāsthita* was endowed with cattle and cultivable lands in the province in which he had under him various spies who were paid, clothed, and fed by him, and whose work was to detect crimes committed in connection with the king's wealth. These spies were to send separately their reports to the *udāsthita.* The *gṛihapatika* and *vaidehika* worked in the same manner as the *udāsthita.* The *tāpasa* had a host of spy disciples around him. His area was the city where his subordinates could practise palmistry, and his activities included a forecast of foreign affairs (*videśa pravriti vijñānaṁ*), and even changes in ministerial appointments! And not satisfied with this wide and important field of activity, the *tāpasa* had the unique satisfaction of having the king's minister directing the latter's affairs in conformity with the forecast of the ascetic spy! These five (out of the nine) classes of spies, who formed one class called *pañcasamsthāḥ*, were awarded by the king money and titles![795]

There remain four other types—the *satrin*, the *tīkṣaṇa*, the *rasada*, and the *bhikṣuki*, whose duties have been already mentioned earlier in these pages. The *satrin* was selected from among the orphans maintained by the State. The *satrins* were taught sciences (*lakṣaṇam*), palmistry (*aṅgavidyā*), sorcery (*māyāgata*), legerdemain (*jāmbakavidyā*), the duties of the various orders of religious life (*āśramadharma*), and the reading of omens and augury (*antaracakra*). This class was also called spies working by social intercourse (*samsargavidyā*).

3. PUBLIC LIFE OF OFFICIALS UNDER SCRUTINY

The *tīkṣaṇa* spies or bravadoes were to espy the public character (*bhāyam cāram*) of the following: the movements of the ministers, the priests, the commanders of the army, the heir-apparent, the door-keepers, the officers-in-charge of the harem, the magistrate (*praśastri*), the Collector-General, the Chamberlain, the Commissioner, the City Constable (*nāyaka*), the officer-in-charge of the City (*paura*), the Superintendent of Transactions (*vyavahārika*), the Superintendent of Manufactories (*karmāntika*), the Council of Ministers (*mantripariṣad*), the heads of departments (*adhyakṣāḥ*), the Commissary General (*daṇḍdapāla*), and officers-in-charge of the fortifications, boundaries, and wild tracts. That is, the public activities of all the above highest officials, including the ministers, came under the close observations of well trained spies as well as of the desperadoes. All the information which they collected was transmitted to the king through the Institutes of Espionage (*samsthāvarpayeyuḥ*).

4. PRIVATE LIFE UNDER SCRUTINY

The private life of all the above officials came under the scrutiny of the *rasada* or poisoner spies, whose information was collected by the women mendicants for transmission to the Institutes of Epionage. The information thus collected was tested by the officers of the Institutes (*samsthānāma-antevāsinaḥ*) who, by signs or writing (*samjñā-lipibhiḥ*), verified it through their own spies.

The Institutes of Espionage and the wandering spies did not know each other. When the information received from three different sources (i.e. through the women mendicants, the classmate spies, and the poisoner spies) was found to be exactly the same, it was considered reliable. If the three sources frequently differed, the spies concerned were either punished or dismissed. Incidentally we may note that spies also used *gūḍhyalekhya*, or secret writing to convey their information to the Institutes of Espionage.[796]

5. SPIES IN FOREIGN SERVICE

Spies were used in foreign service as well. They received salaries from foreign kings with whom they lived as servants. If they helped their own and foreign States in catching thieves, they received salary from both the States! Spies were set in motion against kings, who were inimical, or friendly, intermediate, or neutral, and in regard to the eighteen departments of the government.[797] How far these could be compared with their modern counterparts working in similar capacities but under the name of officials of the Foreign and Diplomatic Services of the various governments, is an interesting question which we may not attempt to solve here.[798]

6. CRITICISM OF THE SYSTEM OF ESPIONAGE IN KAUTILYA

We may stop here with the description of the Institutes of Espionage in the *Arthaśāstra,* and recall some of the observations made earlier, while answering the question whether the Kauṭilyan monarch was a tyrant of the Aristotelean type. Well may we wonder how the ancients could have lived under such a widespread, powerful, and well trained system of spies, whose perfidious activities seem to have entered into almost every sphere of the public and private life of the officials and the citizens! When we realize that, as narrated earlier, the king, after having set up spies over his own ministers (*mahāmātras*), proceeded to espy both the citizens and the country people,[799] the picture of the whole country is complete. There was no section of the people that did not come under the preview of the obnoxious system of espiongae which touched every one but the king. The only plausible explanation that could be offered in connection with this terrible system of spying into the character and activities of citizens and officials alike, is that perhaps the age which witnessed the rise to power of Candragupta Maurya was one of disloyalty at home and perfidy abroad. We have already seen above that there were the numerous adherents of the old royal house of the Nandas in Magadha, and the sympathizers of the Macedonians in the north-western parts of the country. Perhaps it was to solve this double danger that faced the new rising Mauryan State that Kauṭilya introduced a system of espionage which had no parallel anywhere in its intricate working, its extensive powers, and its destructive hold on the administration. If, as stated above, the king's minister was to direct his affairs in conformity with the forecast made by the ascetic spy (*tāpasa*), it means that Kauṭilya had enthroned Superstition rather than Common Sense on the seat of Power! Posterity may well ask in dismay: Was it the same Kauṭilya who had so stoutly championed the cause of *ānvikṣakī* or Reasoning at the beginning of his great book?

Part Six

THEORY IN PRACTICE

CHAPTER I

INTRODUCTION

A. POSING A QUESTION

FROM THE foregoing pages it must have been apparent to the reader that, so far as the ancient Indian political thought was concerned, there was nothing in it that was inferior to what obtained in ancient Greece ; and that Kauṭilya, as the most representative of ancient Indian writers on Polity, bears favourable comparison with Aristotle, who is rightly considered to be the greatest exponent of Western political thought. If every theory in the work of that great Greek thinker is not found in Kauṭilya, it was, as is only natural to expect, because the latter lived in an atmosphere that was radically different to the one which had produced Aristotle. The one doubt that comes to our mind in this connection is this: While Aristotle left behind him a profound effect, if not in the immediate ages that followed him, at least centuries afterwards, is there any thing to justify our assumption that the principles laid down by the ancient Indian political theorists, and, in particular, by Kauṭilya, were ever followed by the later generations? In other words, it is worth while asking the question whether the authors of the *dharmaśāstras* and the *nītiśāstras* wrote merely for the sake of argument, or whether they wrote practical guides for statesmen to follow? It is with this question that we shall be primarily concerned in this Part.

B. QUALIFICATIONS TO THE ANSWER

In answering it we have to bear in mind certain considerations. Firstly, we do not propose here to verify every one of the theories that has been enumerated in the previous pages of this book in terms of the actual political practice in the later ages. That would require another dissertation by itself. We shall make a sample survery of such of the political structures spread over the country, as would enable us to assess the practical nature of some of the main theories. Secondly, it may be noted that the ancient writers on Polity did not assert anywhere that they alone should be followed to the exclusion of others. On the other hand, the latitude which they permitted in the application of theory to practical conditions was responsible for a wide difference of opinion on many important questions. Thus, for instance, we have seen the divergence of opinion on such question like the composition of ministers. But this freedom was not to be exercised in cases like the army on the component parts of which there was no difference of opinion among the ancient thinkers. As a result of this freedom of thought a certain amount of flexibility in the application of theory to practice was inevitable. We see this in connection with an important concept like sovereignty which, because of geographical and political considerations, was not exactly the same as that found in the ancient texts. But the introduction of some changes, now and then, did not mean any change in the fundamental principle of the State.

And, finally, the statements that follow will be based mostly on stone and copper plate inscriptions, since these public records are the most reliable witnesses that help us to know to what extent the ancient political theories were actually executed in practice. The evidence gathered from these records will be supplemented by that gleaned from foreign witnesses, numismatics and literature, wherever available, so that the picture thus obtained might be as complete as possible.

C. THE PROBLEMS WHICH WILL BE DISCUSSED IN THIS PART

We shall first deal with the two ancient concepts of *dharma* and *nīti* in general ; then, refer to one of the most important theories discussed in the previous pages, viz., the theory of protection and good government ; next, cite evidence in regard to the forms of government ; further, cursorily glance at the problem of the elements of the State ; and, finally, ascertain to what extent Kauṭilya's theories were followed in practice, especially in the ages immediately following him.

CHAPTER II

THE CONCEPT OF DHARMA

A. UNIVERSAL RECOGNITION OF DHARMA: PROOF IN THE AŚOKAN EDICTS

RULERS OF all persuasions—Hindu, Buddhist, and Jaina—acknowledged the supreme importance of maintaining *dharma*. Emperor Aśoka, who became a Buddhist after the Kalinga war,[1] used the word, as is generally accepted, in the Buddhist sense of being "the sum of moral duties", as Professor E. Senart had suggested long ago.[2] It is defined in the second portion of the Brahmagiri Rock Edict thus:

> Moreover, Devānampriya speaks thus: Obedience must be rendered to mother and father, likewise to elders; firmness (of compassion) must be shown to animals; the truth must be spoken: these same moral virtues (*dharma-guṇa*) must be practised. In the same way the pupil must show reverence to the master, and one must behave in a suitable manner towards relatives. This is an ancient rule, and this conduces to long life. Thus one must act (*esā porāṇā pa(k)itī d(īgh)āvuse ca esa hevaṁ esa kaṭiviye*).[3]

Without controverting the fact that Emperor Aśoka was a Buddhist, we may question whether in the "sum of moral values" which he is supposed to have proclaimed, according to the Buddhist code of conduct, there was anything new which had not been known or propounded by the Hindus centuries before his time. The fact that Aśoka admits that the rule which he proclaimed was an ancient one, suggests that we have to go to the earlier Hindus for the concept of the moral values. There is no need to cite here the numerous authorities in order to show that all that has been said by way of defining the *dhamma* in the Brahmagiri Rock Edict had already been preached and practised by the Hindus for centuries earlier. It thus follows that in the concept of *dharma* which Aśoka preached there was a strong Hindu element which Dr. Hultzsch admits, thus:

> In one important point Aśoka's inscriptions differ from, and reflect an earlier stage in the development of Buddhist theology or metaphysics than, the *Dhammapada*: they do not yet know anything of the doctrine of *Nirvāṇa*, but presuppose the general Hindū belief that the rewards of

the practice of *Dharma* are happiness in this world and merit in the other world.[4]

Dr. Hultzsch's admission of the influence of the Hindu concept of *dharma* in the Edicts of Aśoka should dispel any idea of an exclusively Buddhist concept of *dharma* in the proclamations of that monarch, as some have maintained. There is another consideration which may be mentioned here. Aśoka's impartial attitude to Brahmans and Śramaṇas (Buddhist monks), which is so often publicized in the Edicts, is by itself enough to show that he had not completely abjured his Hindu beliefs. A significant point which seems to have missed the attention of those who unequivocally affirm that Aśoka was a Buddhist is the one relating to the name he assumes in his Edicts. He calls himself in those records *Devānampriya Priyadarśin*, and refers to his *dhamma-lipi* (Rescripts on Morality). But unlike much later Buddhist rulers, for instance, like those of Orissa, he does not style himself a *Parama-Saugata* or a *Parama-Tathāgatha*[5] which, if he had done, would have undoubtedly stamped him as a thorough Buddhist. These considerations point to the possibility of Aśoka's having in his mind the Hindu concept of *dharma* which, as a great monarch, it was his duty to maintain and foster.

Neither the Buddhists nor the Jainas could escape from the fascinating and abiding influence of *dharma*, as it had been understood in ancient India. In a sense, the concept of *dharma* was the precious possession of all—the Hindus, the Buddhists, and the Jainas. This explains why king Khāravela of Kalinga (middle of the second century B.C.), who was a staunch Jaina, is styled in the Hāthigumpha cave inscription as *Dhammarāja* (King of Dharma), even though he is called in the same record *Bhikku Rāja* (King of Monks).[6] We shall see below that his concept of good government was in perfect accordance with that preached in the *dharmaśāstras*.

B. LATER EPIGRAPHIC EVIDENCE

Coming to the first century A.D. we reach the reign of king Gotamīputra Śātakarṇī of western India.[7] In one of the Nāśik Cave inscriptions, it is said of this Śātakarṇī ruler that he was one "who never levied nor employed taxes but in conformity with *dharma*" (*dhamopajitakaraviniyogakarasa*). He sympathised fully with the weal and woe of the citizens (*porajananivisesa samasukhadukhasa*). He was "alien to hurting life even towards an offending enemy", and "stopped the contamination of the four *varṇas*".[8] Evidently king Gotamīputra Śātakarṇī carefully observed the injunctions of the *dharmaśāstras*.

In the second century A.D. was another illustrious ruler, the Mahākṣātrapa Rudradāman, in whose Junāgaḍh inscription dated A.D. 151-52, we have the following: that he was one "who by the raising of his right hand has earned the strong attachment of *Dharma*". Professor Kielhorn, while editing this record, commented on the uncommon description of the raising of the right hand, thus: that it perhaps finds its expression in the precept of Manu, according to which a king, when investigating the cases of law, should do so seated or standing, raising his right hand (*pāṇim-udyamasya-dakṣiṇam*).[9] No better testimony than the above is needed to prove that the ancient rulers carried out the injunctions of the *dharmaśāstras* to the minutest detail!

That the same Great Kṣātrapa Rudradāman ruled according to the precepts of the *dharmaśāstras* is further proved by the same inscription which relates the following: that he ruled "without oppressing the inhabitants of towns and country (*paura-jānapadaṁ janaṁ*) by taxes (*kara*), forced labour (*viṣṭi*), and *praṇaya-kriya*" (which Professor Kielhorn translated as acts of affection); and that by the expenditure of "a vast amount of money from his own treasury", he constructed "not in a long time, a dam three times as strong in breadth and length".[10] We shall have to refer to his able minister Suviśākha, a Pahlava, who helped him to do this, in a later context.

A later royal family also on the western coast of India in Karnāṭaka were the Kadambas of Banavase. They ruled from the third century A.D. till the sixth century A.D.[11] In the undated Nilambūr copper plates of king Ravivarman of the same family, the Kadambas are styled as rulers "who were (like unto) mothers to people (who were) dependent (on them)".[12] The undated Malavaḷḷi pillar inscription inscribed in the cave characters and in the Prakrit language, and discovered in the Shikārpur tāluka, Mysore State, calls an early Kadamba king named Śiva (Skanda) the *Dharma-Mahārāja* of Vaijayantī or Banavasi (in North Kanara). Mr. Lawis Rice had assigned the record to *circa* A.D. 250. One of the interesting statements in this record, which registers a royal gift, is: "This Kadamba and the good Senior Minister (unnamed) may thus have trust. Confirmed by the four *Vedas*, and prescribed in the *Nigamas*. Thus does the Rājā command."[13] The title given to the ruler together with the explicit statement that the gift was made by him in accordance with the four *Vedas* and the *Nigamas*, proves that that Kadamba king ruled according to the precepts of the *dharmaśāstras*.

One of the Tāḷguṇḍa stone inscriptions, Shikārpur tāluka, Mysore State, dated about A.D. 450, praises king Kākusthavarman, also of the Kadamba royal house, thus: "Whose . . . kindness to the needy, just protection of his subjects, lifting up of the humble."[14] King Kākusthavarman's grandson was Mṛigeśavarman. The Hiṭṇahebbāgilu copper plate, assigned by Mr. Rice to *circa* A.D. 450, styles Mṛigeśavarman as the *Dharma-Mahārāja* of the Kadambas, and relates that he was "devoted to well protecting his subjects, a friend of all things living", and "a Yudhiṣṭira in justice".[15] His younger brother was Māndhātṛivarman. The Kūḍagere copper plates call him also by the same title, *Dharma-Maharāja* of the Kadambas.[16] King Mṛigeśavarman's elder son was king Ravivarman who, in the latter's Nilambūr copper plates cited above, is also called *Dharma-Mahārāja*.[17]

Another ancient royal family also of Karnāṭaka was likewise well-known for its observance of the precepts of the *dharmaśāstras*. This was that of the Gangas, who ruled from the second till the eleventh century A.D.[18] One of its early rulers was Mādhava, or Kiriya Mādhava, the son of Daḍiga. The undated Noṇamangala copper plate grant of his great grandson, also called Mādhavavarman, relates that *Dharma-Mahārājādhirāja* Mādhava possessed a character for learning and modesty, "having obtained the honours of the kingdom only for the sake of the good government of his subjects" (*samyak-prajā-pālana mātrādhigata rājya-prayojanasya*); and that he was distinguished for his skill among those who expounded and practised the Science of Politics in all its branches (*viśeṣato'pi anavaśeṣasya nīti-śāstrasya vaktṛi prayokṛi-kuśalasya*).[19] This ruler, according to Mr. Rice, has to be assigned to the beginning of the third century A.D.[20] The Kaḍagattūr copper plates of the Ganga king Durvinīta (A.D. 482-517) bestow the same praise on king Mādhava, and have the following additional information to give about king Durvinīta himself: that the latter possessed the three powers of energy, that he was ever regarded with affection by his subjects, that his punishments were approved of by Vaivasvata Manu, that he was surrounded by a retinue suitable for the maintenance of the *varṇāśramas*, and that he was devoted to *dharma*.[21] One of the Noṇamangala copper plates of king Avinīta of the same line, which was once assigned by Mr. Rice to *circa* A.D. 425 but which is probably to be assigned to A.D. 430, describes that monarch thus—"for protecting his subjects (he was) well prepared"; and confirms the title of *Dharma Mahārāja* given to Mādhava, and refers to the latter's having obtained the kingdom only for the sake of the good government of his subjects, being distinguished among those who expounded and practised the Science of Politics.[22] Later records dated A.D. 517, 797, *circa* 890, and 903 confirm the praise bestowed on Mādhavavarman.[23]

From the south-west we may go to the north-east of the peninsula. Here was the Dabhalarājya comprising the Eighteen Forest Kingdoms (in the erstwhile Chhatisgarh State) of king Saṁṣkobha. As is related in his Betul plates dated only in the (Gupta) era 199 (A.D. 518-19), his father, the Mahārāja Hastin, is described thuś—"One who sought to govern properly the kingdom (*rājyja*)"; while Saṁṣkobha himself is described as one who was intent on establishing the religious duties of the castes and the different orders of life (*varṇāśrama-dharma sthāpanābhiratena*).[24]

Striking westwards across the country we reach the kingdom of Valabhi in Surāṣṭra-Gujarat. Of the fourth ruler, and perhaps the first great sovereign of the Valabhi royal house, Guhasena (A.D. 559-67), it is said in the copper plate of Dharasena II dated A.D. 588, that the former was one whose title to *rājan* was befitting, as he had pleased (*rañjita*) the hearts of his subjects by properly protecting them, according to the rules prescribed in the *smṛitis*.[25]

We may now revert to Karnāṭaka where we have further interesting evidence about the rulers following the *smṛitis* in matters of administration. The Rāmeśvara temple stone inscription found at Āvaṇi, Mūḷbāgaḷ tāluka,

Mysore State, and assigned by Mr. Rice to *circa* A.D. 890, mentions the death of the Noḷamba Pallava ruler Mahendra Noḷamba, who is said to have been a "walker according to Manu" (*Manucaritam*).[26] In the Chikamagaḷūr stone inscription of the Ganga king Rācamalla, assigned by its editor Dr. Fleet to the period ranging from A.D. 989 to 1005, king Rācamalla (evidently the IV of that name) is called *Dharma-Mahārāja*.[27]

C. STILL LATER EPIGRAPHIC EVIDENCE

Even at the risk of transgressing the chronological limits of this work, it is worth while citing the examples of both rulers and their ministers, who scrupulously followed the precepts as given in the *smṛitis*. We have to come to the Hoysala kings, who ruled from Helebid, Hassan district, Mysore State. The chronology of the earlier rulers is still far from being settled.[28] In the Kāṭikere stone inscription, discovered at Arsikere, Hassan district, Mysore State, and assigned doubtfully by Mr. Rice to *circa* A.D. 1100, king Vinayāditya, the father of Eṛeyaṅga Hoysala, is styled as one who was "walking in the path of Manu" (*Manumārggam*).[29] Of a later date is the Govindeśvara temple stone inscription found at Koravangala, Hassan tāluka, in the same State, and assigned by Mr. Rice to *circa* A.D. 1160. The ruler mentioned in it was Hoysala Narasimha, one of whose great officers was Govinda Rāja. The latter is called "the most honourable man in king Narasimha's palace", and "walking according to the laws of Manu" (*aramaneyam mānya-puruṣam Manu-muni-caritam*).[30] He was not the only minister who was famous as one who followed the precepts of Manu. Perhaps a greater name is that of Byāḷike Keśimayya, the *Mahāpradhāna* (Great Minister) of the Yādava king Rāyamurāri Soyideva. In one of the Tāḷguṇḍa stone inscriptions discovered at Tāḷguṇḍa itself, Shikārpur tāluka, Mysore State, and dated A.D. 1169, we have a glowing account of the Great Minister. He was both a commander of the army and the recipient of seventy-two other appointments (not named). He was skilled in administration, counsel, and energy and other modes of policy (*senādi bāhattara niyogādhiṣṭāyakaṁ prabhu-mantrotsāha-pramukha-nīti-niṣṭāyakaṁ*). The king favoured him with orders to administer all the countries attached to the treasury of the south, putting down the evil and upholding the good (*mahā-pasāyitaṁ Byāḷikeya Keśimayya Daṇḍanāyakaraṁ karadu dakṣiṇa-diśāvarada bhaṇḍāravāda deśaṅgaḷ ellavaṁ duṣṭa-nigraha śiṣṭa-pratipālanaṁ mālpud endu kāruṇyam māḍal*).

Before we proceed to cite further evidence from the same record to prove that that Great Minister carried out his sovereign's behest, in accordance with the principles of the *smṛitis*, it is necessary that we should note here that in the phrase *duṣṭa-nigraha śiṣṭa pratipālanam* (putting down the evil and upholding the good), which we meet with in numerous records of this and the earlier periods, we have the essence of the theory of protection which we have discussed at the beginnnig of this book. The same Tāḷguṇḍa stone inscription then continues to narrate that the *Mahāpracaṇḍa Daṇḍanāyaka Keśimayya* accepted the order of the king as a great favour. The inscription narrates thus:

> His (Keśimayya's) practice was that of the Manus, the policy he adopted was the policy of the ancient kings, the good of others was the wealth he accumulated, the promotion of the greatness of his ruler was his own greatness, the satisfaction of his dependents he reckoned as his own satisfaction (*Manu-caya-sevya-vṛitti nija-vṛitti purātana-rājanīti tām tanag aḷvaṭṭa nītiye parārthame tanna bhujārjjitārtthav āḷdana mahimonnatitvame nijonnetiy-āśrita-tuṣṭi tannad endu*).[31]

D. TAXES PAID FOR PROTECTION

The few examples we have given above, which by no means exhaust the list, of the kings and their ministers, are enough to demonstrate the fact that the injunctions laid down in the *dharmaśāstras* in regard to good government were being followed for centuries in historical times. They also prove beyond doubt that the ancient theory of protection was actually carried out in practice throughout the country. We mentioned earlier in connection with this theory, that protection was bound up with the question of paying taxes; and that it was understood that the justification for levying taxes by the king lay in his ability to protect the people. A striking exposition of this theory is found in a comparatively later record. This is one of the many inscriptions discovered in the Cenna Keśava temple at Belūr, Haḷebīḍ, Hassan district, Mysore State. It is dated A.D. 1382, and refers to the reign of the early Vijayanagara king, Harihara II. His minister was Mudda Daṇḍeśa. Of this eminent administrator it is said in that record: "Maintaining the customs of the various castes, he protected all the subjects as if they were his own children. Rejoicing in his protection, which was like that of Bharata, the farmers and merchants resolved to pay him certain dues on account of his protection." And so that all the people may understand the details of this agreement, they were written in the Karnāṭa language (*varṇāśramāṇāṁ anyeṣāṁ maryādāṁ anupālayan paripālayati prītyā yaḥ prajāḥ svā iva prajāḥ Bharatasyeva tasyātha rakṣayā paritoṣitaḥ kriṣīvalavaṇiṅ-mukhyā rakṣā śulkam acīkṭripan ataḥ paraṁ asya viśeṣah sarva-jana vijñānāya Karṇṇāta-bhāṣayā likhyate*).[32] There is nothing in the above account to indicate that a compact was actually entered into between the viceroy, on the one hand, and the farmers and the merchants, on the other. It merely confirms the ancient precept of the *smṛitis* that taxes were paid to the ruler because the latter gave protection to his subjects.

CHAPTER III

THE ARTHAŚĀSTRAS AND THE NĪTIŚĀSTRAS

A. INTRODUCTION

WE HAVE now to see whether in addition to the *dharmaśāstras*, the *arthaśāstras* and the *nītiśāstras* also influnced the life and action of rulers. In this case, too, epigraphic evidence supported by literary references fully supports the view that the principles of the *nītiśāstras* and the *arthaśāstras* were followed by the rulers. The Hāthigumpha inscription of king Khāravela of Kalinga (middle of the second century B.C.), cited earlier, informs us how in his tenth regnal year, adopting the threefold policy of punishment, alliance, and conciliation, he sent out an expedition against Bharatavarṣa and conquered that country (*dasame ca vase daṁḍa-saṁdhi samayo Bharadavasa-paṭhānaṁ mahī-jayanam*).[33] No other proof is required to show that even the Jaina monarchs, amongst whom the greatest undoubtedly was Khāravela, followed the traditional Hindu policy of punishment, alliance, and conciliation.

B. EPIGRAPHIC EVIDENCE

We have already cited the examples of the Ganga king Mādhavarman (third century A.D.), who was reputed to have studied and practised the *nītiśāstras*. Turning to northern India again, we find that, although there is no specific mention of the threefold policy of punishment, alliance, and conciliation in the Allahabad Pillar inscription of Samudra Gupta the Great, yet there cannot be any doubt that he had scrupulously followed that policy as well as the precepts of the *smṛitis* both in his conquests and in his administration. That he was a strict adherent of the *dharmaśāstras* is clear from the following eulogy bestowed on him in the same inscription: that he was "the supporter of the real truth of the scriptures", "of whom it used to be said, 'the building of the pale of religion . . . the path of the sacred hymns . . . all these are his,' " "who put to shame (Kaśyapa) the preceptor of (Indra), the lords of the gods, and Tumburu, and Nārada. and others by his sharp and polished intellect", "whose . . . some people (were accustomed to) taste with affection . . . whose protection (of) other people . . . sought", "whose mind busied itself with the support and the initiation, etc., of the miserable, the poor, the helpless, and the afflicted; who was the glorified personification of kindness to mankind. . . ."[34] His diplomatic dealings with the various rulers mentioned in the same inscription fully support our assumption that he was an adept in statecraft. These different rulers, it may be noted, ranged from the western parts of India to Ceylon.[35] Reverting again to western India, we find that the Ganga king, Avinīta (A.D. 430-82), as is related in his Mallohaḷḷi copper plates dated A.D. 459, was in kingly policy equal to Bṛihaspati (*narendranītau Bṛihaspati tulyasya*).[36]

C. LITERARY EVIDENCE

1. BUDDHIST

Turning to literature we find striking corroboration of the practise of State policy both in Buddhist and Hindu literature. In the *Mahāvāstu* in the story of the Final Defeat of Mara, it is related that, while the Bodhisattva was seated under the tree, he won the five kinds of awareness, namely, that of the past, that of calm, that of ease, that of the impossible, and, finally, that he would that day awaken to the unsurpassed perfect enlightenment. "He also mastered the four rules of polity, namely, those relating to conciliation, punishment, dissension, and gifts."[37] Professor E. Senart considered the latter statement as an interpolation, comparing it with the statement in the *Yājñavalkyasmṛiti*.[38] But we need not suppose that the concept of State policy was unknown to the Buddhists, although, like the Jainas, they gave just a twist to the earlier Hindu ideas on statecraft, as must have been evident to the reader from what has been already said of the Buddhist idea of kingship in the earlier pages of this work. In the *Mahāvāstu* itself we have enough proof of this. In an interesting earlier context, the parrot relates to king Brahmadatta of Banaras, the following:

> O Lord of Men, a five-fold power is desirable for a king. Be attentive, and hearken to my words. The first power is innate in him ; the second is the power of his sons ; the third that of the relations and friends ; the fourth, O king, is that of his army ; and regard as the fifth the matchless power of wisdom. Whosoever, O king, has this five-fold power, his kingdom is firm, prosperous, rich, and populous.[39]

Although in the list of the five powers, that relating to the king and to the army are common to the Buddhists and the Hindus, yet it shows that the former were aware of the concept of friends, or, allies, as they were called in the Hindu concept, and of the power of the king. Since the power of friends and of the army could not have been utilized except in terms of the concept of statecraft, we have to assume that the Buddhists were aware of the Science of Polity.

2. HINDU

(a) *Pañcatantra*

In Sanskrit literature we have a more admirable corroboration of the sixfold policy of the State. In the *Pañcatantra* which has been assigned to 200 B.C., we have a collection of fables written in prose with an admixture of interesting aphoristic verses which were meant to teach princes political wisdom. This work popularized the intricate questions of diplomacy both in India and in the foreign lands in a manner which no book on Polity has ever done. The fact that it was ordered to be translated into Pahlavi, the court language of Persia, by the Persian monarch Khusru Anushirvān (A.D. 531-79), proves that by the middle of the sixth century A.D., the Indian theory of diplomacy had already gone beyond the Indian shores westwards to enrich the diplomatic theory of the foreign lands. As Dr. Shama Sastry has shown, the *Pañcatantra* was based on Kauṭilya's *Arthaśāstra,* borrowing from the latter not merely subtle ideas but even phrases and sentences.[40]

(b) *Daśakumāracarita*

(i) *Sixfold Policy*

The wide popularity of the sixfold policy enunciated by Kauṭilya is further corroborated by Daṇḍin in the latter's *Daśakumāracarita.* Puṇya-varman, the king of Vidarbha, is described thus in that work. He was fully conversant with the sacred lore and with Political Science. He at once removed calamities human as well as divine ; he was an expert in the employment of the six expedients of foreign policy. He himself led (i.e. maintained in order) the four castes according to the path laid down by Manu (*nediṣṭho dharmārthasaṁhitāsu . . . sadyaḥ pratikartā daiva-mānuṣīṇāṁ-āpadaṁ ṣāḍguṇya-upayoga-nipuṇaḥ Manumārgeṇa praṇetā cāturvarṇasya*). While in the above we have an indirect reference to Kauṭilya's *ṣāḍguṇya* or sixfold policy, which Daṇḍin has elaborated at great length in connection with the king's foreign policy, the passage directly referring to Kauṭilya is found later on in the same Uchchhvāsa. The licentious and unscrupulous royal favourite, Vihārabhadra, who was an expert in the art of receiving bribes even from ministers, relates thus to the king Anantavarman:

> There are some who will inform the king. 'We can convert even a single cowrie into a lakh of coins, destroy all foes without weapons, or make even a single bodied mortal an Emperor, if only one is ready to follow the path we shall show.' And when the king asks them what that path was, they reply, 'There are four branches of royal knowledge, viz., the three *Vedas,* the practical arts (such as agriculture, commerce,

etc.), logic with metaphysics (*ānvīkṣiki*), and the Science of Government (*daṇḍanīti*). Of these the first three are vast and bear fruit slowly, let them alone, therefore ; study only the fourth ; it has been recently composed by the learned Viṣṇugupta in six thousand stanzas for the use of the king, Maurya (Candragupta), which, when well studied, and put into practice, yields the desired fruit' (*nanu catasro rājavidyāḥ trayī vārtā ānvīkṣikī daṇḍanītiḥ-iti tāsu tisraḥ-trayī-vārtā-ānvīkṣikyo mahatyo mandaphalāḥ-ca tāḥ-tāvadāsatām adhīṣva tāvad-daṇḍanītiṁ iyaṁ-idānīṁ-ācārya Viṣṇuguptena Mauryārthe ṣaḍbhiḥ ślokasahasraiḥ saṁkṣiptā sā-eva-iyam-adhītyā samyak-anuṣṭīyamānā yathokta-karmakṣamā*).[41]

(ii) Ṣāḍguṇya and Ānvīkṣikī

Before we proceed to note further evidence of the permanent effect of Kauṭilya's principles as revealed in the same famous classic, it may be observed that Daṇḍin's use of the terms *ṣāḍguṇya* and *ānvīkṣikī* exactly in the sense used by the Mauryan Prime Minister, is highly important in the sense that, by the age of Daṇḍin (seventh century A.D.), those terms, and along with them, we may add, the concept of foreign policy, and even the idea of the daily duties of the king, as described in the *Arthaśāstra,* had become a part of the routine programme and policy of monarchs. Daṇḍin's explicit reference to the king's following the path laid down by Manu, in regard to the welfare of the four castes (*catur-varṇa*), is likewise an additional proof to show that the precepts of the *dharmaśāstras* were meant not for mere reading but for being practised.

(iii) Espionage

Incidentally we may add that Daṇḍin's sarcastic eulogy of the Science of Government as taught by Kauṭilya, was well deserved. The author makes the same person, who had advised the king to study Viṣṇugupta's (i.e. Kauṭilya's) Science of Government, remark thus: "(For) that *śāstra* is connected with others ; unless all are read, nothing is thoroughly known! Let its principles be grasped after a short or long time (i.e. let the question stand apart) ; when this *śāstra* is learnt, the first lesson taught is—Not to trust one's wife or child!" (*adhighata śāstreṇa cādāveva putradāram-api na viśvāsyaṁ*).[42] In this passage there is a direct reference to the wide-spread and deep laid espionage of the Kauṭilyan State some aspects of which have been described above.

(iv) Rājamaṇḍala

The unscrupulous Vihārabhadra, who seems to have epitomized in himself some of the worst qualities of the relentless administrator described in the *Arthaśāstra,* had the satisfaction of seeing the foolish king follow his advice with the result that Vasurakṣita, the old and wise counsellor of the king, bemoans the evil ways into which his royal master has fallen, and reflects thus: "Surely this kingdom will fall into the hands of Vasantabhānu, the ruler of Aśmaka, who is an adept in policy" (*sarvathā-nayajñasya Vasantabhānoḥ-Aśmakendrasya haste rājyam idaṁ patitaṁ*).[43] The Aśmaka ruler's diplomacy was forthwith put into execution with such success that the army of king Anantavarman was reduced to great straits. The whole picture described by Daṇḍin appears to visualize the dangers described by Kauṭilya of foreign spies in one's own country. King Vasantabhānu then instigated Bhānuvarman, the king of Vanavasi on the border, to invade the territory of Anantavarman. One cannot help feeling that this part of the narrative reflects the actual practice relating to the *rājmaṇḍala* theory that has been discussed above.[44]

(*v*) *Nītiśāstra*

King Anantavarman's kingdom was conquered by Vasantabhānu, but his queen and the young prince Bhāskaravarman escaped. It is in connection with the latter's thread ceremony by the family priest that we learn that the youth was taught Politics, and that his benefactor mused thus:

> A kingdom, as is well-known, is maintained by three kinds of powers: these powers are diplomacy, authority (or regal power), and personal energy (activity) ; these mutually assisting each other dispatch all affairs. Diplomacy determines the objects, authority commences them, and energy effects their attainment. For this reason the tree of Policy serves an administrator a great deal ; it has counsel consisting of five elements for its root ; the twofold authority is its stem, the fourfold *utsāha* (personal energy) forms its main branches ; the seventy-two *prakṛitis* are its leaves, the six expendients of royalty its blossoms, power, its flowers, and success, its fruit ; and as the tree is of a complex nature i.e. depends upon many supports), it is very hard to make it yield fruit (lit. to turn it into account) by any one who has no one to back him up (*rājyaṁ nāma śaktitrayāyattaṁ śaktayaḥ-ca mantraprabhāvaḥ-utsāhāḥ paraspara-anugṛihītāḥ kṛityeṣu kramante mantreṇa-hi viniscayo' arthānām prabhāveṇa prārambhaḥ utsāhena nirvahaṇaṁ ataḥ pañcāngamantramūlo dvirūpaprabhāvaskandhaḥ-caturguṇaḥ-utsāhaviṭapo dvisaptati-prakṛitıpatrah ṣaḍguṇakisalayaḥ śakti-siddhi-puṣpaphalaḥ-ca nayavanaspatirneturupakaroti*).[45]

The concluding portion of the same Uchchhvāsa VIII in the *Daśakumāracarita* is a further proof of the popularity of the principles taught in the *nitiśāstras*. The same saviour of the kingdom, who described the above simile, won over the devoted and upright ministers and spies under various guises, and inspired a sense of duty among the people, tormented the heretics, "cleared out all those who stood like thorns in the way of the prosperity of the State, thwarted the secret plans of the foes, and firmly established the four castes in their respective spheres and duties (*cāturvarṇyaṁ ca svadharma karmasu sthāpayan*) since all undertakings based on policy emanate from wealth (*arthamūlā hi daṇḍaviśiṣṭhakarmārambhāḥ*), and no sin would be worse than showing weakness in adhering to the principles of policy".[46]

(*vi*) *Daily Royal Programme*

Not only were the main principles of policy as enunciated in the *nītiśāstras* and *arthaśāstras* thus portrayed in the *Daśakumāracarita* but even the daily royal routine as given in detail by Kauṭilya. Since this passage in that work is the best testimony to the prevalence of the Kauṭilyan principles of policy, we may cite it in full:

> Now (as regards a king's daily course of life), a king, on rising, when he has scarcely washed his mouth fully, must devote the first watch of the day to the examination of the day's receipts and expenditure, admitting (i.e. taking into account) a handful or half a handful (*muṣṭiṁ-ardhamuṣṭiṁ vā*) (of anything); and yet even when he hears, the clever superintendents (*te' adhyakṣadhūrtāḥ*) will defraud him of twice as much. By the force of their own ingenuity, they multiply a thousandfold the forty modes of defrauding set forth by Cāṇakya. In the second watch, the prince, with his ears painfully assailed by the squabbles of contending subjects, lives a most wretched life. Even therein, the judges and others, disposing of the suits favourably or unfavourably to the litigants as they please, join their sovereign with sin and infamy, and, indeed, themselves with money. In the third watch, he finds leisure to bathe and eat; but, until his food is digested, he lives in dread of poison. In the fourth, he rises to stretch forth his hands to receive gold (presents). In the fifth, he has to suffer great mental strain on account of the consideration of political schemes. In presenting these, too, the counsellors, appearing to be neutral, enter into mutual agreement, and pervert at will merits and defects, mis-state the reports of the ambassadors and spies, misrepresent possibilities and impossibilities, confound all distinctions of place and time, and live upon (seek their own ends through) the friends of their own partisans or enemies; and secretly stirring up internal and external factions, and then appearing to allay these openly, they bring their helpless master into their power.
>
> In the sixth, the king is to divert himself as he likes or to consult his ministers (about amusement); and the time thus allotted for self-amusement is an hour and a half! In the seventh watch, he has the troublesome task of reviewing his troops. In the eighth, he has to worry himself with ambitious projects in the company of generals.
>
> In the evening, in the first watch of the night, after the performance of

the evening *sandhyā* (twilight prayers), he must receive his secret emissaries, and through their medium instruct their extremely cruel hearted agents entrusted with the work of using the sword or fire or administering poison (where necessary). In the second, after eating, he must begin, like a Brahman, to con his portion of study. In the third, with the sounds of trumpets he is sent to sleep, which he may enjoy in the fourth and fifth (watches) ; but how possibly can the poor man get any repose, his mind being distracted by constant, anxious thought? In the sixth, he must begin to prepare for the duties prescribed by the *śāstras* and the business to be attended to. In the seventh, he must consult with the ministers regarding the dispatch of agents and emissaries ; and these fellows, as is well-known, increase the money obtained from both sides by saying sweet things, by trading on the road, being free from the fear of having to pay taxes ; and making work even in a slight degree where there is none, they wander about at all times. In the eighth, the *purohita* (chaplain) and others, assembling, relate to the king—'Last night we saw a bad dream ; the planets are not favourably situated ; besides the omens are evil ; so (to avert the threatened misfortune) let propitiatory rites be performed. Let all the sacrificial implements be made of gold ; when this is done, the rites are prolific in their effect'. And with these and many other seemingly soothing words, persuade the king to confer rich donations upon them, and thereby secretly enrich themselves through such means.[47]

The above full picture of the routine duties of a king, bears a close resemblance to that given in Kauṭilya cited earlier, barring the sarcastic, and perhaps the justifiably correct, estimate of the superintendents, the judges, the counsellors, the secret agents like the spies, and the priests. If Daṇḍin is to be relied upon, the daily programme of a prince in his age was exactly on the model laid down in the *Arthaśāstra*. The cumulative evidence available in the *Daśakumāracarita* clearly demonstrates the fact that, centuries after the days of the Mauryan Prime Minister, the latter's principles of Polity had come to stay in the country. Granting that the exact date of *Daṇḍin* is still one of the many unsolved problems in Sanskrit literature,[48] we may agree with the general Indian view that he flourished in *circa* A.D. 650.[49] This would mean that in the second half of the seventh century A.D., Kauṭilya's theories had attained such celebrity as to receive a detailed treatment at the hands of one of the greatest Indian prose writers. When we add to this the testimony of the *Pañcatantra* cited earlier, we may unequivocally maintain that, from the early centuries B.C. till the seventh century A.D., the principles of Polity as embodied in the *Arthaśāstra* had already crystallized themselves in the minds of the people. No greater tribute can be paid to the practical utility of the theories of Kauṭilya than their detailed exposition as given in the *Pañcatantra* and the *Daśakumāracarita*.

D. THE THEORY OF ṢĀḌGUNYA AND RĀJAMAṆḌALA IN RELATION TO THE DATE OF THE ARTHAŚĀSTRA

A digression may be permitted here, since it has some bearing on the popularity of Kauṭilya as a practical statesman for centuries after his time. This leads us to examine the observations of Dr. V. A. Smith on the nature of the principles of government described by Kauṭilya, and to a repetition of a few statements made earlier in these pages. Dr. Smith wrote thus:

> The author (Kauṭilya) assumes that the principles propounded by him are to be applied in the government of a small kingdom, surrounded by other small kingdoms, all either actually or potentially hostile. The rules of the text-book do not provide for the needs of an extensive consolidated empire, and it is obvoius that the work deals with the state of things as existing before the Mauryas had acquired paramount power.[50]

Dr. Smith in this instance committed an error similar to the one which Professor Winternitz had made when the latter had not only discounted the *rājamaṇḍala* theory as a sort of geometrical problem but gone to the limit of disbelieving the statements in the *Arthaśāstra* and even its authorship![51] Professor Winternitz's arguments have been ably and convincingly disposed of by Dr. Narendra Nath Law, who also refers to the error made by Dr. Smith in the latter's earlier edition of his work.[52] We are concerned here with Dr. Smith's arguments that Kauṭilya's diplomacy referred to a small kingdom ; and that the *Arthaśāstra* refers to a state of things as existing before the Mauryans came to power. The second argument is not intelligible. Apart from the fact that it fails to explain why Kauṭilya should have written a large work referring to a state of things with which he was not at all concerned, there is the other question as to why he should have eulogized any one of the Nandas by describing him as a *vijigīśu* which he does of his royal patron, Candragupta Maurya. Further, as we have already stated earlier in these pages, Kauṭilya specifically refers to Narendra, a title which he would never have used in connection with the Nandas, whom he hated, and whose downfall he had carefully planned. Finally, the explicit statement at the end of his work, which also we have cited earlier, that he wrote it in order to rescue the scriptures, the science of weapons, and the earth which had passed on to the Nanda king, makes it impossible for us to agree with the view that the book could ever have been meant for the pre-Mauryan times.

The argument relating to the alleged smallness of the extent of the kingdom adduced by Dr. Smith is not a new one: almost all the previous scholars who disbelieved in Kauṭilya's authorship of the work either stated, or referred to it, without proving what they maintained. Dr. Ganapati Sastri and Professor Rangaswami Aiyangar have rejected this objection but, in our opinion, their arguments are insufficient to disprove the contention of those who have upheld the view that Kauṭilya has described a small kingdom in his work. The two eminent Indian scholars maintain (*a*) that the theories in the *Arthaśāstra* were intended to apply as much to a small as to a large kingdom ; and (*b*) that the mutual duties of an emperor and subjects are dealt with in the Seventh Book, Chapters XV and XVI of the *Arthaśāstra*.[53] The two learned Indian historians as well as others seem to have missed a passage in the *Arthaśāstra* which we have cited earlier, while discussing the concept of territory, which refers in unmistakable terms to the largest kingdom that could have been thought of in northern India in those days ; and which we may be permitted to repeat here, since it has a significant bearing on the entire theory of *rājamaṇḍala* and *ṣāḍguṇya*. In Book IX styled the Work of an Invader (*abhiyāsyatkarma*), Kauṭilya writes thus: "Country (space) means the Earth, in it the thousand *yojanas* of the northern portion of the country that stretches between the Himālayas and the ocean form the dominion of no insignificant emperor. . . . In such lands he should undertake such works as he considers to be conducive to his power and prosperity."[54]

The above passage is important from the following points of view: firstly, it demonstrates beyond doubt that Kauṭilya had a very large Empire in view—an Empire bounded by the Himalayas and the ocean, in which there were mountains, plains, etc. The reference here could not have been to the kingdom of the Nandas which was limited to Magadha, and which was never of such extensive limits. A striking proof of the assertion of Kauṭilya that the southern limit of the Mauryan Empire was the ocean is afforded in the Gīrnār rock inscription of the Mahākṣātrapa Rudradāman which is cited below, and which affirms that Candragupta Maurya had built a dam on the Sudarśana lake in the neighbourhood of the place where the inscription was inscribed. This definitely proves that Kathiawad was under that Mauryan Emperor, and that the southern limit of his Empire was, indeed, the ocean. And, secondly, it helps us to assign the age in which the *Arthaśāstra* was written. Since in the above passage Kauṭilya clearly states that in such a wide Empire, the monarch could undertake works conducive to his own power and to the prosperity of the people, it is obvious that he referred to a *fait accompli*, and not to an imaginary achievement, or to one that was desirable. Now we have shown elsewhere that Candragupta Maurya, the Narendra of Kauṭilya, first subverted the Nandas of Magadha, and proclaimed himself Emperor in 320 B.C. It was only after his victory over the Nandas that he could think of liquidating the Macedonian danger which he did by signing a treaty with Seleukos Nikator in 303-02 B.C.[55] When he had thus made himself master of the whole of northern India with an Empire stretching from Gāndhāra till the eastern confines of Magadha, he could think of undertaking the construction of public works conducive to his own power and to the welfare of his subjects. That is, since the *Arthaśāstra* reflects the final consolidation of power by Candragupta Maurya, we are justified in assuming that that work was written in 303-02 B.C.

The subversion of the Nandas, who had ruled for about a hundred years,[56] and the wresting of the north-western provinces from the Macedonians was not without its own troubles. We may be permitted to repeat that there was the question of the loyal adherents of the old royal family in Magadha itself ; and that there was the other equally dangerous problem of the foreigners and their indigenous sympathisers. The former could be understood in terms of a small kingdom, but the latter cannot certainly be understood as having been confined to a small kingdom. It is here we see the significance of the many pointed references to the large number of foreigners in the *Arthaśāstra*. These foreigners formed an external danger (*bāhyatabhyantara*). That Kauṭilya definitely refers to the wresting of the foreign territory is evident from his definition of external dangers thus: "The provocation of the chief of a district, the officer in charge of the boundary, the chief of the wild tribes, and a conquered king is what is termed external danger (*rāṣṭra-mukhya antapāla-āṭavika-daṇḍopanatānām-anyatamakopo bāhyakopaḥ*). This should be overcome by setting one against the other" (*tam-anyonya-ena-avagrāhayet*).[57] Since the king is classified with foreign dangers, it may be assumed that the reference here is to a foreign king ; and that it points to the signal success which Candragupta Maurya had won over Seleukos Nikator not by war but by diplomacy. Future research alone may enlighten us as to what part Candragupta Maurya played in joining hands with Seleukos' enemies against that Macedonian ruler, in accordance with the principle of setting up one against the other mentioned in this connection.

But it cannot be gainsaid that the removal of the Macedonian danger is referred to in the above passage. That that menace left behind it its adherents is apparent from the many references to the foreigners (*bāhyā*), who were in league with disloyal local persons.[58] They again figure in the chapter on External and Internal Dangers.[59] We cannot help noting the direct reference to the withdrawal of the Macedonians from the north-western regions in the following objection which Kauṭilya brings forward to his teacher's opinion that foreign rule, which depends upon its winning the affection of the people, is for the enjoyment of others in its own condition. Rejecting this opinion, Kauṭilya states thus: "But foreign rule brought into existence by seizing the country from its king still alive thinks that the country is not its own, impoverishes it and carries off its wealth, or treats it as a commercial article ; and when the country ceases to love it, it retires, abandoning the country."[60] Is it too much to see in this passage a direct reference to the foreigner (Seleukos, really, his royal master Alexander the Great), who had seized the country from its king still alive (Porus the Senior) ; who thought that the country was not his own (because it was so different to the Greeco-Macedonian land from which he had hailed) ; who impoverished it and carried off its wealth (as Alexander the

Great did when he had carried off the finest Indian oxen to Macedonia, and after him, perhaps Seleukos) ; or who treated it as a commercial article ; and who, when the country ceased to love him (evidently because of the atrocities which the Macedonian Conqueror had committed in the course of his campaigns), retired abandoning it (as Seleukos certainly did)?[61]

From what has been narrated above, it is clear that the inclusion of the theory of *rājamaṇḍala* and of *ṣāḍguṇya* in the *Arthaśāstra* is perfectly justifiable ; and that, therefore, we could well assume that the theory of diplomacy as expounded by its author was one of national importance in the sense that it directly dealt with the wiping out of a foreign danger which had threatened to engulf the coutnry. It is this which explains its popularization in the two famous Sanskrit works mentioned above.

E. EPIGRAPHIC EVIDENCE (*Contd.*)

We may now continue with the epigraphic evidence in further support of what has already been given in this section, in regard to the above conclusion of ours. While explaining the attitude of a conquered king, Kauṭilya writes thus: "He (the conqueror) may reinstate kings who are spirited and who can strengthen his army ; likewise he may reinstate those who are possessed of a good treasury and army, and who can therefore help him with money, as well as those who are wise, and who can therefore provide him with lands."[62]

Two famous examples are sufficient to prove that it was not idle advice which Kauṭilya had given in his work. The first refers to the illustrious Mahākṣātrapa Rudradāman about whom the Girnar inscription relates the following: that he was one "who reinstates deposed kings", and "who day by day is in the habit of bestowing presents and honours and eschewing disrespectful treatment", evidently of the conquered kings.[63] About five centuries later the great Samudra Gupta did the same, as is narrated in his Allahabad Pillar inscription:

> Whose (i.e. Samudra Gupta's) great good fortune was mixed with, so as to be increased by (his) glory produced by the favours shown in capturing and then liberating Mahendra of Kośala, Vyāghrarāja of Mahākāntara, Maṇṭarāja of Karāḷa, Mahendra of Piṣṭapura, Svāmidatta of Koṭṭūra on the hill, Damana of Eraṇḍapalla, Viṣṇugopa of Kañci, Nilarāja of Avamukta, Hastivarman of Vengi, Ugrasena of Palakka, Kubera of Devarāṣṭra, Dhanañjaya of Kuṣṭalapura, and all other kings of the region of the South.[64]

One of the kings of Karnāṭaka in western India was Mahendra Noḷamba, who has already figured as one who was a walker in the path of Manu. In the Baragūr stone inscription discovered in the Sīra tāluka, Mysore State, and dated A.D. 878, it is related that that ruler was in his camp at

Baragūr, "having succeeded in his scheme of sowing dissensions among those outside his frontiers dependent on his original territory, rejoiced to have increased the kingdom, and in being a supreme king" (*Śrī Mahendrādhirājan . . . pṛithvī rājyaṁ geyyuttaṁ Baragūroḷ bīḍaṁ biṭṭalli tanage bāhyābhyantara-prakṛiti-maṇḍalādhina tantrāvāpa-kāryya sampannav appa rājyad abhivṛiddhige karaṁ santuṣṭan āgi tāṁ parama Maheśvaran appudaṟiṁ*).[65]

Of the Ganga king Śrīvikrama, the father of king Bhūvikrama (A.D. 670), it is related in the later Gaḷigekere copper plates assigned by Mr. Rice to *circa* A.D. 890, that he was distinguished for his skill among those who teach and practise the Science of Politics in all its branches (*viśeṣato' navaśeṣasya nīti-śāstrasya vaktṛi-prayoktṛi-kuśalo*).[66] The same praise is bestowed on him in the later Narsāpūr copper plate record dated A.D. 903.[67]

CHAPTER IV

FORMS OF GOVERNMENT

A. EMPIRES

We have now to see how far some of the theoretical forms of the State like an empire, a republic, and a confederacy actually existed in ancient India. In this context the reader may recall the statements made earlier in Part Three above under the Forms of Government, particularly those concerning the alleged republican nature of some of the self-governing clans mentioned in Buddhist literature. But in regard to the first one, there is no difficulty since, as is well known, Aśoka the Great had fulfilled the requirements of a *cakravartin* or emperor, while before him Candragupta Maurya had likewise legitimate claims to an imperial title. The *Mahāvāstu* mentions a Bodhisattva, who was a universal king ruling over four continents, possessing the seven treasures of a king, and was a ruler of righteousness, pursuing the path of ten virtues. The seven treasures were, of course, of the Buddhist colouring, viz., the wheel, the elephant, the horse, the precious stone, the woman, the householder, and the counsellor.[68] Of these the elephant, the horse, and the counsellor may be likened to their Hindu counterparts of the army and the ministers, the others being Buddhist concepts. The wheel like the king was irreparably bound up with the *dharma*. It is this which made Lord Buddha say, as is related in the *Salesutta* of the *Mahāvagga*: "I am a king, an incomparable, religious king (*dharmarāja*), with justice (*dhammeṇa*) I turn the wheel, a wheel that is irresistible."[69]

When we come to the second century B.C., we find the concept of *cakravartin* both among the Buddhists and the Jainas. Thus, for instance, in one of the Nānāghaṭ inscriptions (*circa* 200 B.C.) occurs the word *apratihata-cakrasya*;[70] while in the Hāthigumpha inscription of Emperor Khāravela, the latter is styled the Great King of Kalinga (*Kalingādhipati*), meaning an "Overlord".[71] But in the Mañcapuri inscription of his queen, Khāravela is called a Kalinga Emperor (*Kalinga-cakravartin*).[72] The term *adhipati* in the Hāthigumpha inscription, therefore, as rightly suggested by the Editors of that record, is to be understood in the sense of an Emperor.

B. ELECTIVE MONARCHIES

While discussing the theory of kingship under the Forms of Government in Part Three above, it was stated that the principle of election was known to the ancient Indians. The Junāgadh inscription of the Mahākṣātrapa Rudradāman enlightens us on this interesting point. It relates that "he (Rudradāman) who, because from the womb was distinguished by the possession of undisturbed consummate Royal Fortune, was resorted to by all castes and chosen their lord to protect them" (*ṇā ā garbhāt prabhṛitty-avahita-samud (i) tā(?)-rājalakṣmī-dhāraṇā guṇatas-sarva-varṇair-abhig-haṁmya rakṣaṇārtha*).[73] The statement that all the castes chose him unmistakably refers to a popular election. In the modern sense, it was a democratic choice. That the elective principle had already taken firm roots in some parts of the country is proved by the many examples in the Buddhist *Jātakas* of bad kings who were expelled, and of others who were elected in their place, by the people.[74]

C. MILITARY CORPORATIONS, REPUBLICS, AND OLIGARCHIES

1. SELF-GOVERNING COMMUNITIES FROM THE SEVENTH TILL THE FOURTH CENTURY B.C.

Pāṇini's evidence of the existence of republics or corporations of warriors called by him *āyudhajīvins*, has already been cited in Part Three above, while describing the Forms of Government. In the same context the testimony of the Greek writers, who had accompanied Alexander the Great in the course of the latter's Indian conquests, was cited to prove that there were self-governing clans like the Ossadians, the Ambastanes (*Ambaṣṭhas*), the Xanthrians (Cathaeans), the Malloi (Malavas), and others. The Yaudheyas have also figured in the same connection. Likewise have we mentioned that, according to the Buddhist literature, there were clans like the Lichchhavīs, the Vajjians, the Śakyas, the Moriyas, the Mallas, etc., in whose constitutions some Indian scholars have seen elements of a modern type.[75]

2. SOME BUDDHIST CLANS RE-EXAMINED

In addition to the remarks already made in Part Three above in regard to these clans, we would like to examine a statement made by Dr. Vincent Smith concerning the Lichchhavīs. These, as is well-known, have figured most in Buddhist literature, because of the important part they played in history for over a thousand years. They lived in the land of the Vajjians in the region now called Muzaffārpur district of Bihar to the north of the Ganges. Their capital was the well-known city of Vaiśāli, a wide city nine miles in extent, now represented by the village and ruins in the neighbourhood of Basārh, twenty miles north of Hājipur, and on the northern side of the river about twenty-seven miles distant in a direct line from Patna (Pāṭaliputra). Dr. Smith, who has given us these details, obviously following the direction given by Mr. Stephenson in 1834,[76] next writes thus: "The Lichchhavīs were governed by an assembly of notables, presided over by an elected chief (*nāyaka*)." The same distinguished historian continues to give their Mongolian origin with which we are not concerned.[77]

The above estimate of the Vaiśāli constitution needs to be examined. We may recall here the remarks already made in Part Three above regarding the form of government obtaining among the Lichchhavīs. The location of this clan in the land of the Vrijjis (Vajjians), which Major Cunningham was the first to point out,[78] and which Dr. Smith merely repeats, raises an initial difficulty. Was the Lichchhavī oligarchy a distinct unit by itself or a part of the larger Vajjian confederacy? No satisfactory answer has been given by the advocates of the so-called republican or oligarchical government of the Lichchhavīs. On the other hand, we may doubt whether the seven conditions laid down in the *Mahāparinirbbāṇa Sutta,* and cited in Part Three above, were ever meant for a political purpose. In the same *Sutta,* in the *Book of the Great Decease,* we have first the determination of king Ajātaśatru of Magadha to root out the Vajjians; next his sending the Brahman Vassakāra as a messenger to the Exalted One, who was then at the Vulture's Peak; the meeting of Vassakāra with the Venerable Ānanda, the summoning of the Vajjians by the Exalted One, and the laying down of the seven conditions "which would ensure the welfare of the Vajjian Confederacy".[79] Here are seven conditions of social welfare which have been interpreted to mean the republican constitution of the Lichchhavīs! The whole passage embodying the seven conditions as laid down by the Exalted One undoubtedly laid stress on the concord existing in the Vajjian confederacy, by reaffirming that nothing was to be re-enacted which had not already existed, nothing was to be abrogated that had already been enacted, and acting in accordance with the ancient institutions. These regulations, we may be permitted to repeat, could as well be applied to any guild, corporation, or a monarchical government anywhere. They do not necessarily imply a republican constitution but merely suggest a corporate existence which we notice in the life of many associations and corporations. To read in the above regulations much more than what they contain is to distort their significance. If the Vajjians formed a larger confederacy within which the Lichchhavīs lived,[80] the same remark regarding their corporate existence may be said to be applicable to the Lichchhavīs themselves.

3. WERE ALL THE LICHCHHAVIS AN OLIGARCHY?

That there is some confusion among scholars, who have repeated one another's statements regarding the wholesale oligarchical nature of the Lichchhavīs, will be evident when we shall further examine the history of that clan. There is no doubt that they had an assembly of their own, but they had leaders who were not members of it, as the following will show. In the story of *Buddha's Visit to Vesali* (Vaiśāli) as given in the *Mahāvāstu,* a great demonic plague which struck the people of Vaiśāli is described. The ravages of the plague could not be stopped by any means. So the people of Vaiśāli sought the aid of Tomara, the Lichchhavī, who "had a great following and retinue", requesting him to go to Rājagriha to meet the Exalted One (Buddha), where the latter was staying at the invitation of king Bimbisāra. Tomara obeyed, and with a fitting escort riding in carriages left the city of Vaiśāli and set out for Rajagriha. That he was not one of the assembly of the Lichchhavīs is proved by the fact that, when Bimbisāra told him that the latter would escort the Exalted One to the boundary of his kingdom, provided the Lichchhavīs marched out in a procession as far as the boundary of their own territory, Tomara duly communicated Bimbisāra's message to the assembly of the Lichchhavīs.[81] Here, therefore, we have a leader among the Lichchhavīs who was not a member of the Lichchhavī assembly.

In the course of the same story, we have some details about their organization. They had 168,000 chariots; and there were among them Lichchhavīs with at least seven different kinds of horses, chariots, whips, etc., which all suggest different clans.[82]

Even if it is argued that the above do not definitely mean clans, yet the existence of separate chiefs, which is proved by the reference to a leader like Tomara, is further corroborated by other instances. Thus, for instance, in the story of the *Wooing of Yaśodhara,* in the description of the exhibition given by Prince Sarvārthasiddha, it is stated that "all the Śakyan princes tried, the Koliyan princes tried, the Lichchhavī princes tried, and other princes also tried, but no one was able to draw".[83]

Another example of a chieftain among the Lichchhavīs is given in the *Mahāli Sutta* which mentions Hare-lip, the Lichchhavī, who came to the Great Wood (which stretched from Vaiśāli northwards to the Himālayas) with a retinue of his clan to pay homage to the Blessed One, who was then in that place.[84]

These few instances of the chieftains amongst the Lichchhavīs given above will dispel any generalization of the republican character, or of a single general assembly,. of the Lichchhavīs as a whole. They help us to risk the suggestion that, while there might have been corporations among the Lichchhavīs, they had different clans which had leaders of their own, thereby justifying the statement of Kauṭilya cited earlier that the corporations of warriors (*kṣatriyaśreṇi*) of Lichchhavika, Vrijika (Vajjian), Mallaka,

Madraka. Kukkuru, Kuru, Pāñcala, and others lived by the title of *rāja*.[85]

4. THE MALLAS

About the Mallas of Kuśīnara, we learn in the *Mahāparinirbbāṇa Sutta* that in the night of the final passing away of the Tathāgatha, the Venerable Ānanda allowed them to pay homage to the Exalted One in groups—each family in a group, each Malla with his children, his wives, his retinue, and his friends. This was just after they had finished some public affair in their Council Hall.[86] And when Ānanda again went to the Council Hall of the Mallas to convey to them the sad news of the passing away of the Exalted One, the Mallas, again, in the same order, clan after clan, wept and expressed their grief.[87] Eight chieftains of the Mallas are said to have carried the body of the Exalted One.[88]

5. THE SAKYAS

As to the Śākyas, they, too, had their own assembly of about five hundred persons, who used to come together "on some business". In the *History of the Deer Park*, as narrated in the *Mahāvāstu,* it is said that when the young and beautiful Śākyas, who were the children of a lovely Śākyan maiden by the royal sage Kola, came to the assembly of the Śākyas in Kapilavastu, the latter were delighted. "Now their grand father, a chieftain of the Śākyans, and a large number of their relatives will still be living."[89]

6. THE YAUDHEYAS

From the brief sketch of the main Buddhist clans given above, it is clear that we are not justified in attributing to them either a republican constitution or a general organization, as has been assumed by some scholars. But there is no gainsaying the fact that they enjoyed some kind of an autonomy which was perhaps similar to the one enjoyed by the Yaudheyas, who also have figured above in Part Three. These latter are said to have been destroyed by the Mahākṣātrapa Rudradāman (A.D. 151-52). His Junāgaḍh inscription relates that he "by force destroyed the Yaudheyas who were loath to submit, rendered proud as they were by having manifested their title of heroes among all Kṣatriyas".[90] But the Yaudheyas managed to survive, since their subjugation by Samudra Gupta the Great is mentioned in his Allahabad Pillar inscription.[91] The fact that their leader Mahasenāpati is called a Mahārāja,[92] proves that they were also a clan with a king of their own.

7. CAUSES OF THE FALL OF THE SELF-GOVERNING COMMUNITIES

A question that arises at this stage is: when and how did these corporations, self-governing communities, and oligarchical States disappear? Dr. Kane writes on this point thus: "From about the 5th or 6th century A.D. the oligarchic States or Republics became rare and disappeared."[93] While the learned scholar helps us to assign the age when the oligarchical States disappeared, he has not enlightened us on the reasons which explain their disappearance. The reader may recall here the causes of the disappearance of the Indian and Greek City States made above in Part Three, when we made a comparative study of the Indian and Greek self-governing communities.

Two causes may be given that explain their extinction. In the first place, we may assume from the little information available from their coins, and from the fragmentary notices of them in literature and inscriptions that while, in the earlier ages, the Yaudheyas seem to have had a self-governing constitution, in the later times they appear to have eschewed it for a monarchical constitution, as is evident from the example of Mahāsenāpati given above. This by itself was detrimental to the progressive well-being of the Yaudheyas. It clearly shows that they had a tendency to give up their own constitution which, more than any thing else, paved the way for their ultimate disappearance. For when once they had taken to the monarchical form of government, they invited disaster at the hands of more powerful monarchical States.

This will be evident from the facts we have cited above. First came the attack on them by the Mahākṣātrapa Rudradāman, when they appear to have retained their earlier self-governing character. This is inferred from the fact that no ruler of the Yaudheyas is mentioned in the Junāgaḍh inscription of Rudradāman, which merely refers to them as proud Kṣatriyas. Then came the attack on them by the great Gupta Monarch cited above. This could have had no other effect but of subverting their principality and their constitution which latter by this time appears to have been monarchical.

As to where exactly the Yaudheyas were spread, and where they were overwhelmed will be evident by recounting a few facts about their habitat as revealed in their coins. On the basis of the find-spots of their coins, Major Cunningham had shown that the Yaudheyas had inhabited originally the eastern Punjab as far as Sonepat between Delhi and Karnāl.[94] This fact may be studied along with that referring to the wide extent of their first great imperial enemy, Rudradāman. Dr. Bhagavanlal Indraji, basing his statements on the epigraphic evidence, correctly gave the limits of the wide empire of that Mahākṣātrapa, thus: ". . . roughly the country from Bhilsā in the east to Sindh in the west and from about Abu in the north to North Konkan in the south including the peninsulas of Cutch and Kathiawad."[95] The same scholar rightly maintained that Ujjain was the capital of that Mahākṣātrapa ruler.[96] We are concerned with two facts—the one relating to the capital of that Mahākṣātrapa ruler, and the other, to the extension of his empire to Bhilsā. Both these localities are in eastern Rajasthan not very far from the region of Delhi and Sonepat. Rudradāman's conquest of the Yaudheyas would suggest that we have to look for them in the region of Malwa.

The above surmise is supported by the evidence of the Allahabad Pillar inscription in which the Yaudheyas are mentioned next to the Ārjunāyanas, who are preceded by the Mālavas. That is, when Samudra Gupta subverted the Yaudheyas, they were in the region of Malwa. Now he was followed by Candra Gupta II who, as pointed out by Dr. Indraji long ago, seems to have passed from Allahabad through Bundelkand to Bhilsā and thence to Malwa.[97] Since it was in the region of Bhilsā that the Mahākṣātrapa Rudradāman had evidently conquered the Yaudheyas, it would not be wrong to assume that they succumbed to the Guptas under Skanda Gupta (A.D. 454-70), when the latter conquered the region of Malwa.[98]

Whatever remnants of their once-independent State had survived even after the westward drive of Skanda Gupta, the Yaudheyas lost them beyond hope in the new, and a greater, danger that faced them in the reign of the same Gupta monarch. This was that of the Huns, who were the next cause of the disappearance of the Yaudheyas. The Huns appeared precisely in the same province of Malwa, first under Toramāna, and then under his son Mihirakula. The father and son between themselves covered the period from A.D. 450 to A.D. 520.[99] We can only assume that the policy of aggrandizement of Mihirakula could not have tolerated the existence of any self-governing communities like those of the Yaudheyas, whose greater territory had already been absorbed by the Guptas.

The final stroke that fell on the Yaudheyas, if they survived the imperialistic designs of the Huns, seems to have come in the reign of king Yaśovarman of Kanouj soon afterwards (A.D. 533-34). His empire stretched from the Himālayas to the ocean.[109] Whether he himself belonged to any one of the Yaudheya clans or to Ujjain is question that is outside our purview. His powerful sway made it impossible for any military corporations or clans to exist. We have in the changing nature of the Yaudheya constitution itself, and in the successive waves of imperial conquests—first, of Rudradāman, next of the Guptas, then, again, of the Huns, and, finally, of Yaśovarman—the causes that explain the complete disappearance of the Yaudheyas and similar military clans from history.

D. CONFEDERACIES

Evidence about the existence of confederacies is available in epigraphs ranging from the second century B.C. to the first quarter of the ninth century A.D. In the Hāthigumpha cave inscription of Emperor Khāravela, that monarch is said to have thoroughly broken "the confederacy of the Tramira (Dramira) countries of one hundred and thirteen years which has been a source of danger to his people" (*janasa dabhāvanaṁ ca teresa-vasa-satikaṁ ābhi(ṁ)dati T(r)mira deṣa-sanghātaṁ . . . vitāsayati*).[101] In the unsettled chronology of the reign of Emperor Khāravela, and, indeed, of the other rulers of that period, it is uncertain as to who exactly were the kings who had formed themselves into a confederacy which was broken by king Khāravela. Whether the much disputed word *samghāta,* as the Editors of the Hāthigumpha cave inscription had understood, necessarily meant a confederacy of Tamil kings, or of a Tamil king and of his allies to the north of the Tamil land, it is too premature to affirm. But the existence of a confederacy may not be doubted, since the Hāthigumpha record explicitly mentions it.

A more positive proof of a confederacy of kings is afforded in the history of the Rāṣṭrakūṭa king Govinda III (A.D. 783-815). As is related in his Maṇṇe copper plates, on his father's death he had to contend against a confederacy of twelve kings.[102] From other inscriptions it is known that the confederacy was led by a monarch called Stambha whom Mr. Rice correctly identified with Kambha, the elder brother of Govinda III himself. Kambha was also called Kambharasa or Kambhaiya. The reason why Kambha rose in revolt against his younger brother was because their father Dhruva, Nirūpama Dhārāvarṣa, had set aside his claims in favour of his younger brother Govinda. The confederacy was easily put down, and the elder brother was reconciled to the younger, as is proved by the fact that Kambha continued to administer as viceroy of the large province of Gangavāḍi 96,000 under his younger brother.[103] The identity and fate of the other members of the confederacy are not known.

CHAPTER V

THE ELEMENTS OF THE STATE

A. THE KING'S DUTIES AND ACHIEVEMENTS

1. THE BUDDHIST SOURCES EXAMINED

IN THE Story of the Three Birds as given in the *Mahāvāstu*, the Owl enumerates to king Brahmadatta the following duties of a king: that the latter should not fall into the power of wrath, pay equal attention to both parties in a dispute and decide accordingly, should not act out of favouritism, hatred, or folly, should not take delight in sensual pleasures, should administer all the affairs of his city and his provinces in righteousness, should give largesse to the worthy, so that they may not be alienated from him, maintain his influence with his court, should dispense justice to all while keeping an eye on the State affairs, restrain those who might do violence, show that it is righteousness that brings reward, should admit large bodies of immigrants into his realm, should always show favour to the poor and protect the rich, should not gamble with his wealth or love the wives of others, because then he "becomes hateful to his subjects and soon loses his life", should cultivate ties of friendship with neighbouring kings, "for other people honour kings who are steadfast in friendship", should not talk at great length on all sorts of topics, but give his judgements at the appropriate time and make them bear on the point at issue, should keep his counsel secret, for "princes who reveal their counsel come to great harm", while those who keep their counsel to themselves will not fall into the power of their enemies, should not be confused in his judgement or lose in talk, but should be full of purposefulness, should not excite the anger of enemies, should give protection to those who live justly, for "the wheel of power turns in dependence on the wheel of justice", should see that his acts are just, and should be circumspect in all things.

2. HINDU ELEMENT IN THE BUDDHIST ACCOUNTS

There is nothing in the above list of duties of the king as given in the *Mahāvāstu* which has not been dealt with by the earlier Hindu authors on Polity. Indeed, the Buddhists merely echoed the Hindu concept of *dharma* when they said (in the words of the Owl, one of the sons of king Brahmadatta of Banaras), the following:

> Always, O king, give your protection to those who live justly. For the wheel of power turns in dependence on the wheel of justice. By the power of those who live righteously, all ills are assuaged. The *devas* send them rain in season, and then the corn crops grow. It is this, O king, that the deeds done by the virtuous men are a source of blessing in this world and of happiness in the world beyond.[104]

Does not the last sentence reflect the Hindu concept of doing good in this world with corresponding result in the next world? If further proof is wanted to show that the Buddhists only continued the Hindu ideas, we have it in the following opening lines of the *Śārika* bird's description of the duties of a king:

> This world, Father, rests on two foundations. The acquisition, without avarice, of wealth, and the conservation of what is gained. Therefore, O Lord of Men, acquire wealth and conserve what you have gained, make firm efforts within the bounds of righteousness. Sire, the realm of that king, who rules unrighteously, becomes weakened and rent on all sides. But, Sire, the realm of the king who rules righteously is strong, prosperous, flourishing, and populous.

There is an element of the Kauṭilyan statecraft in the further enumeration of the duties of the king by the same *Śārika* bird:

> A kingdom where insidious enemies are at work becomes split up into five realms. Do not trust them, and do not be led astray by them. The noble who is led astray and obeys the will of others, falls into the power of his enemies. . . . To win power for yourself, and out of regard for your kingdom, examine all matters yourself, even though you thus incur the displeasure of your foes.[105]

The above may be compared with what has been cited from the *Artha-śāstra,* and with what Manu has enjoined, concerning the duties of the king, which we shall not cite here.[106]

3. EXAMPLES

The greatest example of a monarch who fulfilled most of the duties mentioned above was Emperor Aśoka. We shall deal at length with him below. When we reach the second century B.C., we come across another example of a great ruler, whose education and duties were in accordance with the ancient precepts. This was the great Jaina Emperor Khāravela. The Hāthigumpha cave inscription relates the following about him: for fifteen years he had played youthsome sports ; after that he had mastered the royal correspondence, currency, finance, civil and religious laws, and all branches of learning. This was probably when he was the *yuvarāja* or crown prince for nine years. On the completion of his twenty-fourth year, he was crowned Emperor. In his first regnal year he caused to be repaired the gates, walls, and buildings of the capital which had been damaged by storm. In the city of Kalinga he caused embankments to be constructed on the lake called after Ṛishi Khabīra, and other tanks, and cisterns and the restoration of all the gardens. The whole work cost him 3,500,000. All this he did in order to gratify the people (*pakatiyo ca raṁjayati*). In the third regnal year he, who was well versed in the science of the Gandharvas (i.e. music), entertained the capital with the exhibition of the *darpa*, dancing, singing, and instrumental music ; and caused to be held festivals and assemblies (*samājas*). In the fifth year he caused the canal excavated 103 yars ago by king Nanda, to be brought into the capital from the road of Tanasuliya (or the canal called Tanasuliya). Having been re-anointed, while celebrating the *rājasūya*, he remitted all tithes and cess, and bestowed many privileges amounting to hundreds and thousands on the city and rural people (*pōraṁ-jānapadaṁ*). Since the inscription is a little defaced in this particular place, and since the above follows immediately Emperor Khāravela's achievements in the fifth year, we are to assume that his remission of tithes, etc., and his celebration of the *rājasūya* took place in his sixth regnal year. In the eighth regnal year he gave the Kalpa-wishing tree with foliage and with elephants, chariots with drivers, houses, residences, and rest houses to Brahmans, exempting them from taxes, at the end of a sacrifice. Probably in the twelfth regnal year he built excellent towers with carved interiors, and he created a settlement of a hundred masons, granting them exemption from land revenue. And he likewise created a wonderful and marvellous enclosure of stockade for driving in elephants. And from the Pāṇḍya land he caused jewels, rubies, and pearls in hundreds to be brought to his capital.

We learn that the wheel of *dharma* was not an exclusive monopoly of the Buddhists from a reference in the same record to his thirteenth regnal year, when on the Kumāri Hill, where the wheel of conquest had been made to revolve well (*supavata-vijaya-caka*, meaning that the Jaina religion had been well established), he offered respectfully royal maintenance, China clothes (*silks*), and white cloths (of the Śvetāmbaras) to the monks who, by their austerities, had extinguished the round of lives, and who were preachers on the religious life and conduct at the Relic Memorial (*kāya-nisīdayāya*). Emperor Khāravela then summoned a Council (*saṁghayana*) of the wise ascetics (*śamaṇas*) and sages from hundreds of quarters, of good deeds and who fully followed (the faith), on the top of the hill, and near the Relic Depository of the Arhat. He then got up four columns inlaid with beryls at a cost of seventy-five hundred thousand ; and caused to be compiled expeditiously the text of the seven-fold *Angas* of the sixty-four letters.[107]

Emperor Khāravela had more than justified his title to greatness as a *cakravartin* by his avidity for studying the sciences, by his solicitude for the welfare of his subjects, by his construction of many public works of utility, by his celebration of the religious rites, including that of the *rājasūya,* and even by the observation of the minutest details of holding festivals when the dance called *darpa* was exhibited. It is interesting to note that the dance called *darpa* was, as pointed out by the late Professor Beni Madhav Barua, a sport conducted along with a drinking bout (*madya krīḍa*) which, according to the *Arthaśāstra,* ladies of good society were not permitted to witness on pain of a fine of three *paṇas* (*pratiṣiddhā strī darpamadyakrīḍāyāṁ tripaṇaṁ daṇḍaṁ dadyāt*).[108] Jaina by persuasion, Emperor Khāraveda had scrupulously adhered to the precepts as enunciated by Kauṭilya.

A later example of an illustrious ruler who followed the classical precepts is that of the Mahākṣātrapa Rudradāman. The Junāgaḍh inscription of that ruler gives many details about him, although not so complete as those in the case of Emperor Khāravela, which enable us to affirm that Rudradāman carefully maintained the principles of the *dharmaśāstras.* He, too, rebuilt the ancient Sudarśana lake in an excellent manner for the benefit of the people ; granted protection of life to people who sought shelter under him of their own accord, and who prostrated themselves before him ; attained wide celebrity by the study and practise of grammar, music, logic, and other great sciences (*śabdārtha-gāndharvva nyāyādyānāṁ vidyānāṁ-mahatīnāṁ*) ; attained proficiency in the management of horses, elephants, and chariots, and in the use of the sword, the shield, and in the pugilistic combat, in (the science of) the acts of quickness and efficiency of opposing forces ; bestowed daily presents and honours and eschewed disrespectful treatment ; rightfully obtained his treasury by the impositions of taxes like *bali,* tolls (*śulka*), and share (*bhāga*), which overflowed with an accumulation of gold, silver, diamonds, beryls, and other precious stones ; and mastered the use of clear, agreeable, sweet, charming, and beautiful prose and verse which were marked by the proper use of words.[109]

In still later times we come across a magnificent monarch who scrupulously adhered to the ancient precepts. This brings us to the Gupta age. Although the materials on this royal family are, on the whole, not very exhaustive, yet the famous Allahabad Pillar inscription enables us to affirm that in Samudra Gupta were embodied many qualities that were the synthesis of the ideals of a Hindu monarch. That record describes his attainments in different capacities—as a dutiful son, as a learned man, as a poet, as a ruler, as a promoter of the *dharma,* and a great conqueror.

(a) *As a Dutiful Son*

In the words of the Allahabad Pillar inscription, Samudra Gupta on "being looked at (with envy) by the faces, melancholy (through the rejection of themselves), of others of equal birth, while the attendants of the court breathed deep sighs (of happiness) was bidden by (his) father (Candra Gupta I)—who, exclaiming, 'Verily (he is) worthy!', embraced (him) with the hairs of (his) body standing erect (through pleasure), (and thus) indicative of (his) sentiments, and scanned (him), with an eye turning round and round in affection, (and) laden with tears (of joy), (and) perceptive of (his noble), nature (to govern of a surety) the whole world".[110] That Samudra Gupta should have been thus selected (*tat-parigrihīta*) from amongst his brothers, because of his great qualities, even when he was a youth, is by itself a tribute to his genius which he fully justified in the course of his extraordinary career both as a soldier and a statesman.

(*b*) *As a Learned Man*

The same record continues to relate the following:

> Whose (Samudra Gupta's) happy mind was accustomed to associate with learned people—who was the supporter of the real truth of the scriptures . . . firmly fixed . . . who, having overwhelmed with (the force of the) commands of the collective merits of (his) learned men, those things which obstructed the beauty of excellent poetry, (still) enjoys in the world of the wise, the sovereignty of the fame (produced) by much poetry . . . and of clear meaning, ... (of whom it used to be said)—'The building of the pale of religion ; fame as white as the rays of the moon (and) spreading far and wide ; wisdom that pierced the essential nature of things . . . calmness . . . the path of the sacred hymns, that is worthy to be studied ; and even poetry, which gives free vent to the power of the mind of the poets ; (all these are his)' ; (in short) what (virtue) is there that does not belong to him, who alone is a worthy subject of contemplation for those who can recognise merit and intellect?[111]

(*c*) *As a Poet*

What is referred to above as efficiency in poetry is further elucidated in the same record thus:

> Who (Samudra Gupta) put to shame (Kaśyapa), the preceptor of (Indra), the lord of the gods, and Tumburu, and Nārada, and others, by (his) sharp and polished intellect and choral skill and musical accomplishments ; who established (his title of 'King of Poets' (*pratiṣṭita kavirāja-śabdasya*) by various poetical compositions that were fit to be the means of subsistence of learned people ; whose many wonderful and noble deeds are worthy to be praised for a very long time.[112]

In proof of the statement that the monarch excelled in the use of musical instruments, he issued the lyrist type of gold coins in which he is represented as sitting on a high-backed couch and playing on the *vīṇā*.[113]

(d) *As a Ruler*

The same pillar inscription continues to narrate, thus: "Whose (Samudra Gupta's) . . . some people (unaccustomed to) taste with affection, displaying exceeding great joy when they beheld (his) many actions that resembled nothing of a mortal nature ; (and) whose protection other people, affected by (his) prowess sought, performing obeisance." Then, again, we have the following in the same record:

> Whose mind busied itself with the support and the initiation, etc., of the miserable, the poor, the helpless, and the afflicted ; who was the glorified personification of kindness to mankind ; who was equal to Dhanada and Varuṇa and Indra and Antaka ; whose officers were always employed in restoring the wealth of the various kings who had been conquered by the strength of his arms.[114]

(e) *As a Promoter of the Dharma*

In addition to what has been said in the above passages relating to Samudra Gupta's having been one who built the "pale of religion", and one who followed "the path of the sacred hymns", it is stated in the same inscription that he was one "who was the giver of many hundreds of thousands of cows", obviously to the Brahmans, according to the *smṛitis,* after performing sacrifices, and one who promoted the dharma (*śāstra-tattvārtha bhaṛtṛiḥ*).[115]

(f) *As a Great Conqueror*

The same record continues to relate that he was one "who was skilful in engaging in a hundred battles of various kinds ; whose only ally was the prowess of the strength of his own arm ; who was noted for prowess ; whose most charming body was covered with all the beauty of the marks of a hundred confused wounds, caused by the blows of battle axes, arrows, spears, pikes, barbed darts, swords, lances, javelins for throwing, iron arrows, *vaitastikas,* and many other (weapons)". The long list of monarchs whom he subjugated, or, when they proved to be turbulent, killed, or reinstated, and of the many rulers of the frontier lands and of the distant islands with whom he had either cordial or diplomatic relations, are an abundant proof of his achievements as India's greatest conqueror.[116] That he was a generous foe is referred to in the same inscription, thus: "Whose tranquil fame, pervading the whole world, was generated by establishing (again) many royal families, fallen and deprived of sovereignty

. . . who, being fully of compassion, had a tender heart that could be won over simply by devotion and obeisance." And in proof of this eulogy, the scribe gave the names of kings whc were reinstated by Samudra Gupta, whom we have cited in detail earlier.[117]

B. MINISTERS

1. AN IDEAL MINISTER: SUVISAKHA

We shall see below that there was much similarity in regard to the ministers and other dignitaries mentioned in the *Arthaśāstra* and in the Edicts of Aśoka. The remarks made here may be studied along with those that follow in order to obtain the continuity of the subject.

An example of an exceptionally able minister is given in the Junāgaḍh inscription of Rudradāman (A.D. 150), which has been so often cited above. The part which this minister played in the history of the public works of that age is narrated in the record in connection with the reconstruction of the huge dam which cost the Mahākṣātrapa "a vast amount of money from his own treasury". The record relates thus:

> When in this matter the Mahākṣātrapa's councillors and executive officers who, though fully endowed with the qualifications of ministers, were averse to a task (regarded as) futile on account of the enormous extent of the breach, opposed the commencement of the work ; and when the people in their despair of having the dam built were loudly lamenting, the work was carried out by the minister Suviśākha, the son of Kulaipa, a Pahlava, who, for the benefit of the inhabitants of the towns and country, had been appointed by the king in this government to rule over the whole of Ānartta and Surāṣṭra, (a minister) who by his proper dealings and views on things temporal and spiritual increased the attachment (of the people), who was able, patient, not wavering, not arrogant, upright (and) not to be bribed, (and) who by his good government increased the spiritual merit, fame, and glory of his master (*asminnarthe Mahākṣātrapasya matisativa-karma-sacivaiḥ amātyaguṇa samudyuktaiḥ-api-atimahatavād bhedasya-ānutsāha vimukha matibhiḥ pratyākhyāt ārambhaṁ punaḥ-setubandhanaiḥ āsyād-hāhābhūtāsu prajāsu iha-ādhiṣṭhāne paura-jānapadajan ānugraḥ pārthivena kṛitsā-nāṁ Ānartta-Surāṣṭrānām pālanārthan-niyuktena Pahlavena-Kulaipa-putreṇa āmātyēna Suvaśākhena yathāvad artha-dharma-vyavahāra-darśanaiḥ anurāgaṁ abhivarddhayatā śaktena dāntena ācapalena āvis-mitena āryyeṇa āhāryyeṇa svadhitiṣṭhatā dharma-kīrtti yaśāṁsi bhartur-abhivarddhayat-ānuṣṭitaṃ iti*).[118]

2. CONCLUSION ABOUT HIM

From the above, we may deduce the following: that the monarch had around him fully qualified ministers (*mantrisacivaiḥ*) and executive officers ; that he used to consult them on matters of importance like the construction of dams and other public works ; that they were not afraid to tell him frankly their views, particularly about the undertaking of a work at an enormous cost ; that they opposed the commencement of the work ; that the king was sorely troubled became of the loss that was caused to the people, who loudly lamented, evidently when they heard of the attitude of the ministers, who were opposed to the repairing of the dam ; that there was a capable, honest, firm, and humble minister, who was prepared to go against the wishes of his colleagues—for he, too, was an *amātya* (minister)—if thereby he could do some good to the people ; and that that minister, the Pahlava Suviśākha, was resolute, humble, and incorruptible. Whether the pointed reference to Suviśākha's upright, honest, and resolute character had any reference to the irresolute attitude of his colleagues, and how far their remonstrance was genuine or guided by monetary considerations are problems which will remain a mystery. At any rate, the middle of the second century A.D. witnessed the construction of a work of great public utility by a minister, who undoubtedly approached some of the ideal standards described in the *Arthaśāstra* of Kauṭilya.

C. RĀṢṬRA: THE REALM

1. CONCEPT OF THE RASTRA OR JANAPADA

We may now see to what extent the concept of the *rāṣṭra*, or the *janapada* existed in ancient India. It has been noted already that to Kauṭilya the term *jānapada* meant the realm which he sometimes also rendered by the term *rāṣṭra*.[119] This is precisely the sense in which the term *jānapada* was used in the Edicts of Aśoka. Thus in the VIII Rock Edict of Girnar, we have the following: *etayaṁ hoti bāmhaṇa samaṇānāṁ dasaṇe ca dāne ca thairānaṁ dasaṇe ca hiraṁṇa-paṭivadhāno ca jānapadasa ca janasa dasapanaṁ dhammānusasṭī ca dhamma—paripuchhā ca tadopayā* (on these tours the following takes place, (viz.), visiting the Brāhmaṇas and the Śramaṇas and making gifts (to them), visiting the aged and supporting (them) with gold, visiting the people of the country, instructing (them) in morality, and questioning (them) about morality, as suitable for this occasion).[120] .

The officers who were directly concerned with the people of the country or of the realm were called *rājukas*, who will figure again below. The statement in the IV Rock Edict at Delhi-Topra that "My *Lajūkas* (*rājukas*) are occupied with the people, with many hundred thousands of men" (*sata-sahasesu-janasi āyatā*) clearly proves that it was the people of the country that the great Emperor had in view. The same record continues to narrate thus: "I have ordered that either rewards or punishments are left to their discretion, in order that the *Lajūkas* should perform (their) duties confidently (and) fearlessly, that they should bestow welfare and happiness on the people of the country, and that they should confer benefits (on them)" (*janasa jānapadasā hita sukhaṁ*). This record proves that Emperor Asoka's ideal was that of the ancient Hindu type, viz., that of a father protecting his children. It states thus: "For, as one feels confident after having entrusted (his) child to an intelligent nurse, (thinking): 'The intelligent nurse will be able to keep my child well', so the *Lajūkas* were appointed by me for the welfare and happiness of the country-people" (*jānapadasa hita-sukhāye*).[121] We need not add further proof from the Rock Edicts in order to demonstrate the fact that by the term *jānapada* was meant the country sides in the age of Emperor Aśoka.

2. RASTRA AND PROVINCES

There was no uniformity in the ancient times about the exact divisions into which the *rāṣṭra* or country was divided.[122] In the Rock Edicts there was a clear division of the Mauryan Emperor into provinces in which there were chief towns. The main provinces were four, which were in the charge of royal princes. These were Ujjain, Tośali, Suvaṇṇagiri, and Surāṣṭra. Of the three princes, who were in charge of the first three provinces, two were probably the sons of the Emperor himself, called merely *kumāras* or princes, while the third was perhaps a near relative of his, called likewise by the title *āryapāla*. The fourth provincial viceroy was the Yavana Rāja Tuṣāspa.[123]

Quite different to the above arrangement was the Buddhist concept of provinces as given in the *Mahāvāstu*, which refers to sixteen great provinces or countries, which were called *mahājānapadas*. They were the Aṅgas, Magadhas, Kāśis, Kośalas, Vajjis, Mallas, Cetis (Cedis) Vaṁsas (Vatsas?), Kurus, Pāñcālas, Matsyas, Surasenas, Aśmakas, Avantis, Gāndhāras, and Kāmbhojas.[124] This list is as ambiguous as the one found in the *Purāṇas* and other Hindu works.[125]

3. FAMINE POLICY AND RELIEF

A major problem closely connected with the country parts, or the realm as a whole, was that of famine. In the Mauryan times, as is related in the undated Sohgaurā copper plate of the pre-Aśokan times, the *mahāmātras* of Śrāvasti ordered that the *dravya* storehouses of Triveṇi, Mathurā, Chañcu, Modāma and Bhadra were to be spent only in case of drought.[126] Emperor Khāravela's great example of bringing into the capital from the road of Tanasuliya the canal (or the Tanasuliya canal), which had been earlier constructed by king Nanda, has already been noticed above. Likewise we have also referred to the unique example of the repairing of the Sudarśana lake by the Mahākṣātrapa Rudradāman, which had originally been constructed by Puśyagupta, the provincial governor (*rāṣṭriyena*) under Candragupta Maurya, and then adorned by Tuṣāpa, the viceroy (*adhiṣṭaya*) of Surāṣṭra under Emperor Aśoka. But a breach of 420 cubits long, just as much broad, and seventy-five cubits deep, had caused all water to escape. By spending "a vast amount of money from his own treasury, and in not too long a time (he) made the dam three times as strong in breadth and length".[127] The magnificent achievement of Rudradāman is an example for modern statesmen to follow, so far as the expeditious manner in which the huge engineering feat was accomplished. We can only presume that its construction must have been not a little responsible for warding off the evil efffects of the famine-ridden regions in its neighbourhood.

Nowhere do we get such a graphic picture of famines as in Kalhaṇa's *Rājatarangiṇī* (begun in A.D. 1148, and finished in A.D. 1150),[128] which mentions them on many occasions. In the reign of an early Kashmir king called Tuñjīna, there occurred a terrible famine when, as a result of the sudden snow-fall, the autumn crop in the month of Bhādrapada suddenly withered, and in the snow that fell deep "the rice crop sank together with the people's hope of famine". Tormented by hunger, men forgot the love of wife, the affection of the son, the kindness for the parent, modesty, pride, and high birth. Fathers abandoned sons, sons, fathers. At the grim condition all round, the king alone was seen melting with compassion. He utilized his own wealth and the accumulated treasures of the ministers to buy food, "and accompanied by his wife (Vākpuṣṭā), day and night, restored human beings to life". When his treasure was exhausted, being unable to find any means of giving success to his suffering people, he contemplated committing suicide. But his queen prayed to Heaven which sent aid to men in the shape of pigeons, and gradually the famine came to an end.[129]

In A.D. 917-18 there occurred another terrible famine when Kashmir was in utter chaos following the death of the ambitious queen-mother Sugandhā in prison, and the rise to power of the Tantri military clique. Inundations ruined the entire autumn crop causing a great famine. Dead bodies filled the river Vitastā, and there was no limit to those who suffered and died. The ministers and the Tantris became rich by selling stored rice at high price. The people whom Candrāpīḍa and others had so carefully protected, "were sent to perdition in this manner by these ghoulish kings".[130]

The year A.D. 1099-1100 witnessed a continuous famine in Kashmir. The villages were submerged by floods, and food and articles of daily consumption were sold at exorbitant rates. King Kalaśa added to the torments of the people by imposing a heavy tax "depriving them of breath like a big boulder on an old bullock worn out by the plough". He squeezed the people through the officials by means of organized repressions, and not a clod remained in their fields in the towns, the country, or elsewhere".[131]

While the examples of king Kalaśa and of the Tantri military clique undoubtedly illustrate the type of the wicked monsters who ruled the country of Kashmir, against whom Kauṭilya, for instance, as already seen above, had warned, such perverted kings were by no means the usual rule in that land. There was a great famine in Kashmir in the reign of king Avantivarman (A.D. 856-83), due to the inundations of the waters of the Mapāpadma lake. The king placed at the disposal of the engineer Suyyu his own money out of which the latter constructed new channels from the Vitastā, and brought the waters of the Mahāpadma lake under control. He then founded all types of villages on the land thus reclaimed, and had them irrigated in a systematic manner so that the whole land was enriched with splendid crops.[132]

D. TREASURY

1. A FULL TREASURY

Under this detail we shall see the concept of a full treasury, the existence of exemptions, and the nature of the tax called *bali* about which we have already remarked earlier. About the first point, it has already been narrated, on the strength of the Junāgaḍh inscription of Rudradāman, that his treasury overflowed with the taxes, tolls, and shares obtained in a just manner, and with the accumulation of gold, silver, diamonds, beryls, etc. This was in the middle of the second century A.D.

About five centuries earlier, as is related in the Rummindei Pillar inscription of Asoka, that great Emperor made the village of Lummini, or Lumbinī, modern Rummindei, the birth place of Buddha, free of taxes, and paying only one-eighth share of the produce to the State.[132a] We shall see below, while discussing the major question whether Kauṭilya was an idealist, that Aśoka merely followed the great Mauryan Prime Minister in this as well as in other respects.

2. REMISSIONS OF TAXES

Remissions of taxes were not made to any one particular community. We have cited above the evidence of the Hāthigumpha cave inscription of Emperor Khāravela how that great Jaina monarch gave at the conclusion of the *rājasūya* sacrifice gifts to the Brahmans (*Bamhaṇānām jātim parihāram dadāti*).[133] These gifts were of various kinds (which are enumerated). In order that they might be acceptable, they were exempted from taxation. The epigraphic evidence about the remission of taxes is so great as to merit a study by itself. It may merely be said here that exemptions from taxation under certain specified conditions are noticeable in the history of India under the Hindu rulers for centuries after the times of Emperor Khāravela.

3. THE TAX ON RELIGIOUS CEREMONIES

The third detail that calls for some comment by way of substantiating what has already been stated is that of the tax called *bali*. It was stated earlier in these pages that that term signified a tax on religious sacrifices or performances. Later usage was in conformity with the earlier practice in regard to the levying of such taxes and tolls. The Kotavumachgi stone inscription of the later Western Cālukya ruler Vikramāditya V dated A.D. 1012, which will be cited in more detail below, relates that the following permanent taxes could be levied according to usage: one *gadyāṇa* for a Vedic sacrifice, two *paṇas* for a marriage, one *paṇa* on the occasion of the *upanayanaṁ* or thread ceremony, one *gadyāṇa* severally on the three *parvas* of *Bādube*, *Kārapuṇṇime* and *Dīpāḷige*.[134]

E. LOCAL GOVERNMENT

1. CARE OF THE COUNTRY

We may note here such of the few aspects of the local government during the period under review, as would enable us to understand the influence of political theory on the country in general. From what has been narrated in the previous pages of this work, it is clear that the ancient Indian State was careful in maintaining the welfare of the country sides. Indeed, the country parts have been the Heart of India on the prosperity of which ultimately the success and prestige of the State has always depended. The great care which the State bestowed on the safety of the country sides is proved by the Junāgadh inscription of Rudradāman so often cited above, in which it is related that that distinguished ruler was the lord of the eastern and western Ākarāvanti, the Anūpa country, Ānartta, Surāṣṭra, Śvabhra, Maru, Kachchha, Sindhu, Sauvīra, Kukkura, Aparānta, Niśādha, and other countries gained by his own valour, the towns, marts, and rural parts (*nagara-nigama-janapada*) of which were never troubled by robbers, snakes, wild beasts, diseases, and the like, where all subjects were attached to him, and where through his might the objects of religion, wealth, and pleasure were duly attained.[135] The first part of this passage appears to have been in conformity with Kauṭilya's injunction: "He (the king) shall protect agriculturists from the molestation of oppressive fines, forced labour, and taxes (*daṇḍaviṣṭikarābādhaiḥ*), herds of cattle from thieves, tigers, poisonous creatures, and cattle disease."[136]

2. USE OF THE KAUTILYAN TERMS

A glimpse of the local administration in the Pallava territory in the south-eastern part of the peninsula is afforded in the Pikira copper plate grant of the Pallava king Simhavarman, evidently the II of that name. It is dated only in his sixth regnal year which cannot be determined,[137] the chronology of the early Pallavas being still in an unsettled condition. Perhaps the record under discussion is to be referred to the sixth or seventh century A.D. What is of significance to us is the manner in which it describes the importance of the country sides. The record relates that king Simhavarman, King of Righteousness (*Dharma Mahārāja*), of the family of the Pallavas, addressed the royal order (which is contained in the record) to the villagers in the village (named) Pikira in Muṇḍarāṣṭra and to the Chief Superintendents (*sarvādyakṣa*), courtiers (*vallava*, i.e. *vallabha*), and the carriers of royal writs (*śāsana-sañcārin*), who were appointed to this district The order was to this effect:

> This village has been given by us, having made it a *Brahmadeya* (i.e. an endowment village) to Vilāsaśarman of the Kaśyapa *gotra*, and of the Taittirīya *sākhā*, accompanied by all immunities (*sarvapārihara-opeto*), with the exception of the cultivated land enjoyed by the temples (*deva-bhoga-hala varjjam*), for the increase of the length of (our) life, power, and victory.

Further the record states: "Therefore, this village must be exempted and caused to be exempted with all immunities. And that wicked man who will transgress against this our edict is liable to corporal punishment" (*asmat-śāsanaṁ atikramet sa-pāpas'-sarīram-daṇḍam-arhati*).[138]

We have in the above epigraph some of the terms like *sarvādhyakṣa* and *vallabha* which are reminiscent of similar terms used in the *Arthaśāstra.* The penalty for transgressing the royal decree was corporal punishment which was severer than the one imposed by Kauṭilya, who was more in favour of fines, although he sometimes speaks of other modes of punishment as well.

3. CONTROL BY THE CENTRE

A feature of the local administration of those ages as of the times afterwards was the one referring to the control exercised by the State over the guilds in towns and over the city council. The Paharpur copper plate grant dated in the (Gupta) year 159 (A.D. 479) enlightens us on this point. The name of the ruler is not mentioned in the record, but its learned editor, the late Rao Bahadur K. N. Dikshit, conjectured it to be Budhagupta of Puṇḍravardhana (Bengal). The inscription records that a certain Brahman named Nāthaśarman and his wife Rāmi approached the District Officers (*āyuktakas*) and the City Council (*adhiṣṭhāna-adhikarṇaṁ*), headed by the Mayor (*nagara-śreṣṭhin*) at Puṇḍravardhana, with a request to donate, in accordance with the procedure prevalent in the locality, a certain specified sum of money for offerings to the *Arhats.* The City Council in the first instance consulted with the Board of Records Keepers (*akṣaya-nīvisamudāya*) presided over by Divākaranandin, who pointed out that there was no objection to the transaction, especially as, besides bringing in some revenue to the treasury, it would entitle the king to one-sixth share of the religious merit accruing from the endowment. The Council, therefore, decided to accept the offer of the Brahman couple, and recorded the transfer of the land to the Jaina temple. The village elders of the respective villages, in which the lands in question were situated, were then asked by the Council to mark out the lands thus granted and to maintain them in perpetuity.[139] The procedure followed here was much the same in western and southern India, as attested to by numerous epigraphs which recorded gifts made in perpetuity in the presence, and with the concurrence, of the royal officers and the villages. These are too numerous to be cited here.

The importance of the above Paharpur copper plate grant lies in the fact that, firstly, it proves that the central government exercised control even in regard to the grant of lands in a village for religious purposes; secondly, that the concurrence of the State officials like those placed over the district and of the City Council headed by the Mayor of the City, was needed for the transfer and for making a gift of land; thirdly, that there were Record Keepers even in villages; and finally, that there was communal concord, as is evident from the gift made by a Brahman couple to the Jaina *Arhats.*

4. WOMEN'S ROLE IN LOCAL GOVERNMENT

In the history of local government, particularly of western India, women have played a significant part. One of the most important rural offices was that of the *nāḍ-gāvuṇḍa*, or *nāḷ-gāvuṇḍa,* Head of the District. The term *gāvuṇḍa* (from which is derived the modern *gauḍa*), meaning a village headman, is rightly supposed to have been derived from *grāmakūṭa* (village assembly).[140] The stone inscription found at Bandaṇike, Shikārpur tāluka, Mysore State, and dated A.D. 912, is of special interest in this connection. It relates that in the reign of the Rāṣṭrakūṭa king Kannara Deva (Kṛṣṇa II, A.D. 884-913),[141] when the viceroy over the Banavase 12,000 Province was Kalivittarasa, the Nāḍ-gāvuṇḍa of the Nāgarakhaṇḍa Seventy division, which was a part of the larger Banavase Province, was Sattarasa Nāgārjuna. The latter died under orders of Kalivittarasa, i.e. obviously in a fight against some one whose name is not mentioned in the record. At this the king conferred the rank and title of *Nāḍ-gāvuṇḍa* on Sattara's wife Jakkiyabbe under whom served the Perggaḍe Nandāvūra Kaliga. The inscription eulogizes this woman administrator thus: skilled in ability for good government, faithful to the Jinendra-śāsana, rejoicing in her own beauty (*uttama prabhu-yukte Jinendraśāsana-bhakte, kānti-ātta-vibhrame*). Jakkiyabbe received the Nāgarakhaṇḍa Seventy division as a charge, which she protected well, "though a woman, in the pride of her own heroic bravery" (*Nāgarakhaṇḍaṁ elpattumaṁ vadhuvāgiyuṁ nijavīra-vikrama-garbbadiṁ pettavaṁ pratipālisutt osad iḷdaḷ iḷd avasānadoḷ tanu rūjeyaṁ pudaṅguḷise*).

But an incurable bodily disease having overtaken her, and being convinced that the worldly enjoyments were insipid, she resigned her office with the intention of ending her life in the orthodox Jaina manner.[142] This is one of the earliest examples of a woman administrator in the history of Local Administration in India.[143]

5. EDUCATIONAL CENTRES IN THE RURAL AREAS

An example of a thriving rural educational centre is given in the Kotavumachgi stone inscription of the later Western Cālukya ruler Vikramāditya V mentioned above. It is dated A.D. 1012, and it mentions that that monarch appointed the *Daṇḍanāyaka* Keśavayya as the viceroy over the Belvola 300 and the Puligere 300 provinces. Receiving the permission of his suzerain, Keśavayya made Ummachige (i.e. Kotavumachgi, fourteen miles north-east of Gadag, Dharwar district) into an *agrahāra* (i.e. a Brahman locality), and granted it with the usual exemptions and honours to Maunara Śrīdhara Bhaṭṭa of Roṇ. The latter made it over to 104 *mahājanas* on condition that the gift was to be enjoyed by himself, the *mahājanas,* and the people of the village.

While specifying the details of the gift, we learn a good deal about the educational activities of that village. To the teacher (unnamed), who performed the *bhaṭṭavritti* (i.e. the duties of a priest), fifty *mattars* of land and one house-site were to be given. He had to perform the duties of expounding *Nyāya* and *Prabhākara.* Twenty-five *mattars* of land were to be given to the pupils ; twenty-five *mattars* together with one house-site to the teacher called Nāgadeśiga, as *akkarigavṛitti,* for composing and expounding the works on mathematics, astronomy, prosody, and the knowledge of sounds (i.e. philology and grammar). The *mattars* were to be utilized for his daily requirements in virtue of his services as a teacher, for feeding his pupils once a day, and for supplying them with a cloth every year. Twelve *mattars* and one house-site were to be given to the person who supplied tender cocoanuts (evidently for worship) ; six *mattars* and one house-site were to be given to the person who supplied vessels for *abhiṣekha.* The barbers were to receive eight *mattars* and a house-site each ; the drummers, twelve *mattars* and a house-site each ; while 100 *mattars* and two house-sites were to be granted to the feeding house of those that managed by *guṇaśāsana* (? royal quality). Thus, in all 300 *mattars* of land were set apart for charitable and educational purposes.

The Administrator of the Rural Areas (*ūroḍeyar*) was likewise given a sumptuous gift of 200 *mattars* of land as *mānya* along with three house-sites each of which was eight hands broad and twenty-five hands long. Moreover, the *ūroḍeyar* was to levy permanently the following tolls (*śāsvata sunkaṁ*): a *kūṇḍe* for the open space of an oil press ; the reaper of a door frame for every set of wooden materials for (building purposes) ; one *gadyāṇa* for a Vedic sacrifice ; two *paṇas* for every marriage ; one *paṇa* on the occasion of an *upanayanam* ; one *gadyāṇa* severally on the three *parvas* of *Bādube, Kārapuṇṇime,* and *Dīpālige.* These three were, as they are today, religious festivals. *Bādube* is that festival which falls in Vaiśākha bahuḷa Amāvāsya, i.e. on the first new moon in May; *Kārapuṇṇime* is the full moon festival in June ; while *Dīpāḷige* is the famous Dīpāvaḷi which falls on the new moon of Āśvina in October-November.[144] The significance of these taxes on religious festivals has already been cited above in this chapter, while dealing with the question of the royal treasury.

6. SOCIAL LEGISLATION IN THE VILLAGES

Much more interesting than the above details are those dealing with the social legislation in the village of Ummachige. There was a tank called Deyiṁgere in that village. For the up-keep and repairs of that tank certain taxes were set apart. These were the income derived from the following fines: a fine of two *paṇas* for abusing one another ; twelve *paṇas* for beating ; three *gadyāṇas* for drawing out a dagger ; twelve *gadyāṇas* for stabbing (which fines in all cases could be changed on considerations of the distinctions of caste) ; three *gadyāṇas* in the case of a bachelor committing adultery ; and three *gadyāṇas* on the occasion of the purification ceremony (except where a *māṇi* got up a processional *maṇḍapa* with weapons). In addition to these were the spoils obtained after a raid ; the *daśavanda* or one-tenth of the property of persons dying inestate ; and the *paṇas* (not specified) imposed as tolls on the musical instruments like the *kaḷe* (the horn) and the *maddaḷe* (a drum).

Before we proceed with the other details of the public gift, we may observe, that even in the matter of levying fines, the people were careful to observe the injunctions of the *smṛitis.* It was seen above that fines for abusing one another, for beating, for drawing out the dagger, and for stabbing were to be imposed on considerations of the distinctions of caste (*jāti-bhedav-aridu daṇḍavaṁ viśesaṁ māḷpar*). This was in accordance with the *Manusmṛiti* wherein it is stated as follows:

> . . . I will next propound the (manner of) deciding (cases of) defamation. A Kṣatriya, having defamed a Brāhmaṇa, shall be fined one hundred (*paṇas*) ; a Vaiśya, one hundred and fifty or two hundred ; a Śūdra shall suffer corporal punishment. A Brāhmaṇa shall be fined fifty (*paṇas*) for defaming a Kṣatriya ; in (the case of a) Vaiśya the fine shall be twenty-five (*paṇas*) ; in (the case of a) Śūdra twelve. For offences of twice-born men against those of equal caste (*varṇa,* the fine shall be) also twelve (*paṇas*) ; for speeches which ought not to be uttered that (and every fine shall be) double.[145]

To continue with the Kotavumachgi record, we may note that the above gift-deed was made for the welfare of the highest as well as the lowest sections of the people. Those who kept a cowpen (*koṭṭa*), the *gāmuṇḍas*, and the chief men of the low caste got each a house-site.

As in the case of other public charters, one of which we have cited above under the date A.D. 479, all the gifts comprising the 500 *mattars* of land and all the house-sites attached to them, which were presented as a *mānya* gift, for the purpose of the feeding house, charity, etc., were to be preserved under the joint protection of the 104 *mahājanas*, who were to protect and enjoy them permanently, "however adverse the times might be". Imprecatory verses at the end of the gift deterred any one who might fail to carry out the clauses of the gift-deed.[146]

7. CONCLUSIONS IN REGARD TO LOCAL GOVERNMENT

From the skeleton survey made above of some of the features of the local administration in ancient India, certain conclusions may be deduced. These are the following: (*i*) the local administration was under the control of the king. (*ii*) The ruler bestowed careful attention on the welfare of the rural areas, protected the people of the country from oppressive fines, and from the depradations of robbers and wild beasts. (*iii*) The rural areas had their own organizations of a corporate nature over which, too, the State exercised some control. (*iv*) The villages were benefited from the remissions of taxes made by the king. (*v*) In western India the rulers made history by appointing women to the highest administrative posts in the district. (*vi*) The villagers managed their own educational institutions making due provision for the maintenance of not only the students and teachers but also of all those who were concerned with the daily well-being of those institutions. The provision was in the shape of money payment, lands, and house-sites. (*vii*) The villagers were entitled to raise their own tithes by way of tolls and duties, evidently after having received the previous sanction of the king. Such tolls were raised even from religious festivals. (*viii*) The villagers had the further right, at least in western India, of enacting such social legislation as was conducive to their general well-being. It referred to crimes like beating, stabbing, and adultery. (*ix*) The amounts raised from fines were utilized for the common good of the village, viz., the repair and the upkeep of the village tank. (*x*) The welfare of the entire village and the responsibility of maintaining the public gift were the concern of all the people, especially of the *mahājanas*, who were the recipients of such gifts. These facts should suffice to show that the country sides were not only a vital part of the whole kingdom but were animated with a public spirit which manifested itself in various acts of charity and social legislation.

CHAPTER VI

WAS KAUṬILYA AN IDEALIST?

A. INTRODUCTION

1. DR. VINCENT SMITH ON KAUTILYA

A STUDY of the principles which Kauṭilya expounded in the *Arthaśāstra* reveals that that work, like the earlier works on Polity and the *dharmaśāstras,* was not meant as a mere compendium of theoretical dogmas unrelated to practical needs but was a guide for statesmen to follow, particularly in regard to the great political experiment which he himself had helped to establish, and to the later ones which those who came centuries after him might think of bringing into existence. But in passing this judgment on the great Mauryan Prime Minister, we have to examine the views of Dr. V. A. Smith, who was imbued sometimes with that inveterate bias towards certain aspects of Indian life which perhaps came into conflict with the imperial achievements of his own great people, and who might be taken to be the representative of that section of Western thought that has always been as chary of praise as it has been enthusiastic in condemnation of the thoughts and achievements of the ancient Indians. He shares this defect with the late Professor M. Winternitz and the late Dr. Aurel Stein, at least so far as this part of our study is concerned.

Dr. Smith wrote thus on Kauṭilya in general:

> It is not desirable to amalgamate the rules laid down in the *Arthaśāstra* with the descriptions recorded by the Greek, because the latter present to us the impression made upon foreign observers of institutions actually existing at a particular date, 300 B.C., in round numbers, after the foundation of the Maurya Empire; whereas the former expresses arrangements favoured by Brahman ministers, as suitable for any independent kingdom at any time. The *Arthaśāstra* text-book cites the opinion of many earlier authors of unknown antiquity, and treats of the political state of India prior to the establishment of a paramount power by the Mauryas. We may accept it as an authoritative account of political and social conditions in the Gangetic plain in the age of Alexander the Great, 325 B.C.[147]

In a later context the same distinguished British historian wrote thus:

> The author (Kauṭilya) assumes that the principles expounded by him are to be applied in the government of a small kingdom surrounded by other smaller kingdoms, all either actually or potentially hostile. The rules of the text-book do not provide for the needs of an extensive consolidated empire, and it is obvious that the work deals with the state of things as existing before the Mauryas had acquired paramount power.[148]

Dr. Smith's inherent weakness as a Western critic of the Indian institutions is further apparent when in a still later context in the same work he writes thus:

> Although many of the rules in Chānakya's treatise are puerile, and some merely theoretical, the book on the whole was intended to be a practical manual of statecraft and administration, and as such it is well worth reading. Books like the so-called *Laws of Manu* and *Dharmaśāstras* set forth the Brahmanical ideal—the treatise of Chandragupta's minister openly discards ideals and presents a plain unvarnished statement of the immoral practice of kings and Brahman ministers in the fourth century before Christ, prior to the realization of the novel idea of a great empire extending over nearly all India.[149]

2. DR. SMITH'S ARGUMENTS ANALYSED

Dr. Smith's arguments may be analysed thus: that the Greek accounts cannot be amalgamated with the Indian account as given in Kauṭilya's *Arthaśāstra*. because the Greeks were more precise, referring as they did to a particular age (300 B.C.), while the Indian account is vague ; that the *Arthaśāstra* was a mere Brahmanical production meant for any age and any set of rulers ; that Kauṭilya treats of the political condition before the rise of Candragupta Maurya to power ; that he deals with a small kingdom as existing before the Mauryans had become paramount rulers ; that many of the statements in the *Arthaśāstra* are puerile, some theoretical, but that, on the whole, it was a practical manual on statecrafts ; and that Kauṭilya discards the Brahmanical ideals and presents a picture of the immoral practices of kings and Brahman ministers as prevailing in the fourth century B.C., before the novel ideal of a great empire extending over the whole of India was realized.

3. EVALUATION OF DR. SMITH'S ARGUMENTS

We may examine the above in detail, although in doing so we may have to repeat a few ideas already discussed above. That the Greeks should have recorded their impressions about institutions actually existing in a particular year is only natural, since we cannot credit them with a knowledge of either institutions or men before or after their own time. But the main consideration is whether all such Greek accounts are infallible, and to what extent they actually reflected the nature and number of institutions which they are supposed to have seen. This will lead us to a close study of the statements made by one such Greek eye-witness, which we shall make at once below, in order to see how far he was trustworthy. It will be shown that the account of the Mauryan capital as left by that foreign eye-witness is by no means dependable.

The contention that the *Arthaśāstra* was a Brahmanical production, meant for any time and for any independent kingdom, is not denied. Indeed, it is precisely in its being a manual on statecraft, not only for the Mauryan times but for all time and for any kingdom, that its supreme importance lies. Its universality is exactly one of its greatest merits. But what one cannot understand is why the eminent British historian should have partially condemned the work because it was a Brahman's production. We cannot help feeling that Dr. Smith in this particular instance seems to have been influenced, unconsciously though, by the Missionaries to whom, on the whole, the Brahmans, their ways of life, and their intellectual achievements have always been, as they are, a perpetual anathema! If, as custodians of learning and tradition, and as expounders of the principles of the *dharmaśāstras* and the *nītiśāstras* for over a millennium, the Brahmans had not written on those subjects—although there is no evidence that every one of the authors of the *dharmaśāstras* and the *nītiśāstras* belonged necessarily to the priestly class—one would like to know who else was competent both by training and tradition to write on them? This side of Dr. Smith's argument is far too trivial to be seriously considered.

Dr. Smith contradicts himself when in one place in the passages cited above, he asserts that the *Arthaśāstra* was a theoretical production, and in another affirms that, inspite of its being puerile, it was, on the whole, a practical manual of statecraft. Evidently the learned historian could not himself decide as to which parts of the *Arthaśāstra* were childish, which, theoretical, and which, meant to be followed. Dr. Smith would have been more correct if he had stated—as has been shown in the earlier pages of this work—that, since certain statements of Kauṭilya are bordering on the superstitious, and a few left unexplained, his work is not worthy of a practical statesman! But to condemn that Mauryan Prime Minister on this score would be as unjust as to condemn Aristotle on the ground that, as stated above in these pages, on the authority of the editor of the *Politics* himself, because that Greek thinker has given clear evidence of many lapses in thinking, and in particular, of his inveterate hatred of all things Asiatic, he should be considered as being unfit for serious study!

Coming to the next contention of Dr. Smith that Kauṭilya wrote of the political conditions before the rise to power of the Mauryas, the reader may recall the statements made in this Part under the heading the theory of *ṣāḍguṇya* and of *rājamaṇḍala* in relation to the date of the *Arthaśāstra* discussed above. All that we may affirm in regard to this point is that we could charge Kauṭilya with any other shortcoming—and we have done so in regard to some of his institutions in the previous pages of this book—but we cannot accuse him of having written about the conditions as existing in the pre-Mauryan times, since that would have been an achievement which was as base as it was unbecoming. Whatever else Kauṭilya was, he was certainly not a renegade. This side of the argument of Dr. Smith, therefore, that the *Arthaśāstra* refers to the pre-Mauryan times has no cogency in it.

We have also dealt with in the same context Dr. Smith's statement that Kauṭilya refers to a kingdom, small in extent, amidst other small kingdoms. Dr. Smith evidently did not study thoroughly the *Arthaṣāstra* ; if he had done so, such a premature judgment on the extent of the Empire described in the *Arthaśāstra* would not have been passed by that eminent historian.[150]

One of the main points of criticism levelled at Kauṭilya by Dr. Smith relates to the former's being a theorist, who openly discarded the earlier ideals and presented a plain unvarnished account of the immoral practices of kings and Brahman ministers in the fourth century B.C. We cannot help affirming that the distinguished historian fell a victim more to sentiment than to rationalism when he laid this defect at the door of Kauṭilya. As to how far the latter accepted the ideals of his predecessors, and to what extent he deviated from them has already been shown in the previous pages of this work. Kauṭilya's rejection of the theories of his predecessors, including those of his own teacher, far from being a serious defect in him, points to his independence as a political thinker. Indeed, it is this, more than any thing else, which gives great worth to his work. Kauṭilya as much presented a picture of the immoral practices of the kings and Brahman ministers in the fourth century B.C. as Machiavelli did of the immoral rulers and Christian statesmen in the fifteen century in his *Prince*. The statement that the ancient Indian kings and their ministers indulged in a career of immoral practice in the fourth century B.C., or afterwards, is both injustifiable and unhistorical, betraying as it does the learned scholar's utter lack of knowledge of the *dharmaśāstras* and of the actual historical practice as gathered from epigraphs of those and of the later times.

B. AN EVALUATION OF THE ARTHAŚĀSTRA: EXTERNAL EVIDENCE: KAUṬILYA AND MEGASTHENES

This does not mean that we have refuted the main charge against Kauṭilya that he was merely a *paṇḍit*, a theorist, and an idealist. We have disposed of the first point relating to Kauṭilya's being a *paṇdit* in the earlier pages of this book.[151] In this section we shall be concerned with the major question of the realism in the Arthaśāstra which can be solved in two ways: first, by noticing the evidence that is available in the account of a foreign witness, which will be styled external evidence ; and, second, that which is found in the epigraphs of the greatest Indian monarch of the early times, which we shall call internal evidence. To this double sided evidence the reader may add that of literature which has already been cited above.

1. MEGASTHENES: INTRODUCTION

The external evidence centres round the well-known name of Megasthenes. Before we examine his evidence, we have to acquaint ourselves with (*a*) a few facts relating to his official career ; (*b*) the dates of his stay at Pāṭaliputra ; and (*c*) the nature and importance of his book which has been made—unsuccessfully, though—to serve as a counterblast to Kauṭilya's *Arthaśāstra*.

(*a*) *His Official Career*

Dr. Smith wrote:

> Soon after the conclusion of peace in or about 303 B.C., Seleukos had sent as his envoy to the court of Chandragupta an officer named Megasthenes, who had been employed under Sibyrtios, satrap of Arachosia. The envoy resided for a considerable time at Pātaliputra (now Patna), the capital of the Indian empire, and employed his leisure in compiling an excellent account of the geography, products, and institutions of India, which continued to be the principal authority on the subject until modern times.[152]

Professor V. R. R. Dikshitar wrote thus on the same ambassador: "Megasthenes was the representative of Seleukos at the Court of Sibyrtius, Satrap of Arachosia. He was sent to Pāṭaliputra, Candragupta's Court, as King's ambassador. . . . Hence Megasthenes must have visited the Indian Capital some time between 302 and 288 B.C. We cannot with any certainty fix exactly the year when he visited Candragupta."[153]

(*b*) *The Dates of His Stay at Pāṭaliputra*

Neither of the eminent scholars helps us to arrive at any definite conclusion regarding the official career of Megasthenes. Unless we decide this point, we shall not be able to appreciate the evaluation that will follow of his official account. We have shown elsewhere, on the strength of the narratives of the Greek writers, who had accompanied Alexander the Great, that the above statement of Dr. Smith and others that Megasthenes stayed at Pāṭaliputra for a considerably long time is incorrect. Megasthenes first came to India as the ambassador of Sibyritius between 320 B.C. and 316 B.C. He came again as the ambassador of Seleukos Nikator in 303-02 B.C..[154] A few facts relating to Candragupta Maurya and to his son Bindusāra Amitraghāta will help us to fix the dates of the stay of Megasthenes at Candragupta Maurya's court. Now Chandragupta Maurya reigned from 320 B.C. till about 296 B.C., when his son Bindusāra succeeded him. The latter ruled from 296 B.C. till 268 B.C.[155] We know that Seleukos sent another ambassador called Deimachos to the court of Bindusāra Amitraghāta in 296 B.C.[156] Beyond these facts there is nothing in the Greek accounts that could enable us to arrive at any definite conclusion about Megasthenes' stay at Pāṭaliputra. Since he first came as the ambassador of Sibyritius from 320 B.C. till 316 B.C., and again came as the ambassador of Seleukos in 303-02 B.C., we are justified in concluding that his stay in India did not, on the whole, exceed five or six years. He cannot be credited with a considerably long stay at Pāṭaliputra, as maintained by Dr. Smith.

In this connection it may be realized that the diplomatic convention of replacing one ambassador by another, immediately after the former has relinquished his office, is a modern one which might not have existed in the ancient times, when diplomatic conventions were still in their infant stage. As to whether Megasthenes continued to be Seleukos' ambassador at Pāṭaliputra from 303-02 B.C. till 296 B.C., when that ruler sent Deimachos to the same court, is highly doubtful. Since a continued stay of an ambassador at a foreign court in those ancient times was improbable, we may reasonably conclude that Megasthenes' stay at Candragupta's court was only for a short period of one or two years.

If the above conclusion in regard to the total length of Megasthenes' stay at Pāṭaliputra was limited to about five or six years is accepted, it is extremely doubtful whether he could have written such a detailed and excellent account of the products and institutions of India, which was to become a source of admiration for posterity. The fragments in his account which have come down to us, no doubt, contain valuable details some of which we shall examine below. But we may doubt whether, in those ancient times, during the stay of five or six years, Megasthenes had all the leisure, and in particular, the facilities which were needed for compiling an exhaustive account of India. We have to remember a few considerations in this connection. To have written a faithful and detailed account of the institutions, and even products, of India, we have to presuppose that Megasthenes knew the principal Indian languages of the time. Although we are in the dark as to what exactly was the official language of the Mauryan court, yet we may presume that Sanskrit and Pali were in vogue at the Mauryan capital. One would like to know whether there is any evidence of the Greek ambassador's having mastered either of the two or other Indian languages, so as to have been able to have understood the institutions of the people.

A more weighty consideration comes in our way of crediting Megasthenes with freedom of movement in the Mauryan capital. We have seen that there was a wide-spread system of espionage from which even the highest officials like the ministers could not escape. Would Megasthenes have had access to all the sources of information relating to the different topics described by him in his book, with innumerable spies hovering round him and shadowing him in all places and at all times? Finally, if we are to give any credence to Kauṭilya's contempt for, and hatred of, a foreigner, concerning which there is ample evidence in the *Arthaśāstra*, could we imagine an agent of a foreign ruler—for that was more or less the status of an ambassador—moving about freely in the Mauryan capital with a view to securing all kinds of information on the people, products, and institutions of the land? Until these questions are satisfactorily answered, it is unsafe to depend either upon the exhaustiveness or the trustworthiness of the account of Megasthenes.

(*c*) *Nature and Importance of His Work*

Western scholars are, on the whole, naturally prone to evaluate the *Indika* of Megasthenes in rather exaggerated terms. We have cited above Dr. Smith's opinion that it continued to be the principal authority on the products and institutions of India until the modern times. The same scholar wrote further: "Although often misled by erroneous information received from others, Megasthenes is a veracious and trustworthy witness concerning matters which came under his personal observation, and his vivid account of Chandragupta's civil and military administration may be accepted without hesitation as true and accurate."[157]

As opposed to the above was the opinion of the late Professor Dikshitar who, after examining many aspects of the work of Megasthenes, wrote that it was "vitiated by discrepancies of a glaring character and this has considerably reduced its intrinsic character as a source of information for an important period of Hindu India. The evidence of Megasthenes could not be looked upon as something positive and conclusive."[158] In a later context Professor Dikshitar characterizes the account of Megasthenes "as either drawn from imagination or from hearsay information".[159] And, finally, the same eminent scholar says: "Bereft of mythological, geographical, and legendary details, the useful portion of Megasthenes' report is very meagre and its authority cannot be taken as absolute."[160]

The *Indika* of Megasthenes cannot be accepted as perfectly authentic; neither can it be dismissed as being entirely useless. It contains some statements which prove those in the *Arthaśāstra*. Indian historians have, of course, rejected the claims put forward by Western scholars on behalf of Megasthenes for outright infallibility and exhaustiveness. Perhaps one of the best attempts in this direction is that of Dr. Narendra Nath Law, who has rejected the erroneous assumptions of Professor Winternitz. The latter scholar, basing his remarks on Dr. Stein's *Megasthenes und Kauṭilya*, had stated that the agreements between Megasthenes' account of India and the description of the same as found in Kauṭilya's *Arthaśāstra* are of such a nature that they hold good in regard to the condition of India at all times, and that their differences relate to the most essential details. Dr. Law, in examining these and other mistaken assumptions of Professor Winternitz, laid down four criteria which may be borne in mind:

(*i*) Since Megasthenes' work has come down to us only in fragments, "we would be mistaken in drawing such inferences as could only have been drawn if the whole work had been before us". Professor Winternitz, therefore, is in error for this reason when he thinks that it is a matter for surprise that Megasthenes does not mention Kauṭilya.[161]

(*ii*) As admitted by Professor Winternitz himself "the description of Megasthenes may in some cases be inaccurate or coloured for tendencious purposes".[162] Therefore, as Professor Macdonell and Keith have rightly remarked, it would be "dangerous to put much trust" in them, "since they were collected by observers who were little used to accurate investigations on such matters, and whose statements were based on inadequate information, vary in their statements". The learned authors of the *Vedic Index* referred in particular to the status of the king as landowner on which the Greek accounts are unreliable.[163]

(*iii*) The authors on whose testimony Megasthenes wrote his *Indika*, "do not at times hesitate to alter the quoted passages to suit their liking".

(*iv*) Dr. Schwanbeck (who was the first German scholar to have acquainted the world of the work of Megasthenes),[164] stated that, though Megasthenes wrote portions of his work from personal observation, yet he had to depend for the rest upon hearsay and report.[165]

2. INACCURACIES IN MEGASTHENES' INDIKA

Five major inaccuracies in the *Indika* are enough to prove that its author is unreliable.

(*a*) *No Written Laws in Ancient India*

Megasthenes wrote that there were no written laws in ancient India, and that the people were ignorant of writing, and that they trusted to memory in all the business of life.[166] He has altogether erred here. Not only was writing known to the Indians but written laws were likewise known to them.[167] Three centuries before Megasthenes, Pāṇini mentions *grantha, lipikāra, Yavanāni lipi,* and the numerals marked on the ears of cattle to indicate their owners.[168] Kauṭilya's testimony is even more emphatic in rejecting the erroneous statement of Megasthenes. He has a whole chapter on the duties of the Records Keepers with clerks sitting apart and with shelves for accounts books well arranged, which we have cited in an earlier context.[169] Then, there is another complete chapter on the Procedure of Forming Royal Writs, at the beginning of which he defines a writer (*lekhaka*) thus:

> "Hence one who is possessed of ministerial qualifications, acquainted with all kinds of customs, smart in composition, good in legible writing, and sharp in reading shall be appointed as a writer". Then, again, at the end of the same chapter, Kauṭilya states that "Having followed all sciences and having fully observed forms of writing in vogue, these rules of writing royal writs have been laid down by Kauṭilya in the interest of the king".[170]

We may also recall here the high place which Kauṭilya gave to written laws, while discussing the relative merits of Sacred law, usage, and State law, cited elsewhere in these pages. In the light of Pāṇini's and Kauṭilya's evidence, Megasthenes' statement that the people were ignorant of writing may be dismissed as a fabrication.

(*b*) *Division of the People into Seven Castes or Classes*

Megasthenes divides the people into seven castes or classes. These were the sophists, the agriculturists, the herdsmen, the shepherds and graziers, the artisans and traders, the military, the overseers, and the councillors.[171] Dr. Smith admits that Megasthenes has erred here.[172] No authority is needed to refute the statement of Megasthenes that the people were divided into seven classes, and that the Brahmans formed a separate class of philosophers or sophists. Megasthenes here is as unreliable as when he says, like Strabo, that no private person was permitted to keep either a horse or an elephant, the possession of either animal being a royal privilege. Dr. Smith has likewise admitted that this "is undoubtedly inaccurate", and is corrected by the statements of Arrian.[173]

(*c*) *The King's Share of the Land Revenue was One-fourth*

Dr. Smith has tried to justify this statement of Megasthenes by saying that in practice the normal share of the gross produce varied from province to province, and that, therefore, Megasthenes' information is correct.[174] But Megasthenes did not write an account of the whole of India ; and his statement relating to the king's share of the land produce is entirely disproved both by the legal codes and by the actual practice prevailing in the country which limited the king's share to one-sixth (*ṣaḍbhāga*).[175]

(*d*) *There was no Slavery in India*[176]

Megasthenes seems, in this instance, as well in some others, to be merely repeating the statements of Strabo, who had never come to India. Dr. Law attempts to reconcile the categorical statement of Megasthenes with the assertion of Kauṭilya that no Aryan could be made a slave (*na-tu-eva Āryasya dāsabhāvaḥ*).[177] But there is no need to justify slavery in the days of Kauṭilya in this manner: the whole chapter from which the above sentence is taken is styled *dāsakalpaḥ*, and refers to slaves and labourers. It opens with the statement that the selling or mortgaging by kinsmen of the life of a Śūdra, who is not a born slave, and has not attained majority, but is an Ārya by birth, is punishable with a fine of twelve *paṇas*.[178] In an earlier context he states: "Those who do not heed the claim of their slaves (*dāsa*), hirelings (*āhitaka*), and relatives shall be taught their duty by the king" (*dāsa-āhitaka-bandhūn aśraṇvato rājā vinayaṁ grāhayet*).[179] He also imposed a heavy fine of twenty-four *paṇas* on those who committed adultery with slave women.[180] Professor Dikshitar, while citing the first piece of evidence given above, puts pertinently the following question in regard to Megasthenes: "In this particular Megasthenes' report is decidedly incorrect and if such portions of the report are not correct, one is tempted to ask, what amount of credit can be given to the other portions of the same report?"[181]

In addition to the testimony of Kauṭilya concerning the existence of slavery in India, we may add that available in the Buddhist literature which mentions slaves even in the days of Buddha. The *Brahmajāla Sutta*, the *Sāmaññaphala Sutta*, the *Ambaṭṭha Sutta*, and the *Mahāvāstu* definitely mention slavery.[182]

(*e*) *There were no Contracts and Money Lending, etc.*

The Greek eye-witness writes the following:

> "The Indians neither put out money at usury, nor know how to borrow. It is contrary to established usage for an Indian either to do or suffer wrong, and therefore they neither make contracts nor require securities. Among the Indians one who is unable to recover a loan or a deposit has no remedy in law. All the creditor can do is to blame himself *for trusting a rogue*."[182a] In an earlier context he wrote thus: "They (the Indians) have no suits about pledges or deposits, nor do they require either seals or witnesses, but make their deposits and confide in each other."[182b]

Megasthenes is altogether unreliable here. Lending money, contracting debts, usury, witnesses, and recovery of debts—all these were known to the ancient Indians. In the *Manusmṛiti* adequate provision was made in respect of all these features of the transactions of the people. Manu's regulations relating to the lending of money, non-payment of debts, witnesses, and usury are too numerous to be mentioned here. He made provision even for the kinds and rate of interest. "A money lender," according to the *Manusmṛiti*, "may stipulate as an increase of his capital, for the interest, allowed by Vasiṣṭha, and take monthly the eightieth part of a hundred. Or remembering the duty of good men, he may take two in the hundred (by the month), for he who takes two in the hundred becomes not a sinner for gain."[182c] A usurer was excluded from participating in a *śrāddha* ; a Brahman was forbidden to take the food of a usurer ; and there were even liberal and niggardly Śrotriyas who had taken to usury.[182d]

If the above evidence is not enough to completely disprove the statements of Megasthenes, we may turn to Kauṭilya, who has minute details to give on *vyāji* (rate of interest), the different forms of legal agreements, valid and invalid transactions, witnesses, sealed and unsealed deposits, and securities. The standard rate of interest, we may add by the way, was a *paṇa* and a quarter per month, which was called just (*sapādapaṇā dharmyā māsavṛiddhiḥ paṇaśatasya*). He laid down that ten *paṇas* per cent prevailed among forest (i.e. among those who worked in forests) ; and twenty *paṇas* per month prevailed among sea traders (*sāmudrāṇām*). Persons who exceeded, or caused to exceed, the above rate of interest, were punished with the first amercement ; and hearers of such transactions were to pay half of the above fine. The detailed regulations which Kauṭilya has given in connection with the lending and borrowing of money, and which are mentioned in this context, and those which are described in Part Four above, under economic rights and styled the right to receive deposits, altogether invalidate the superficial statements of Megasthenes regarding the lending of money and deposits.

We could have gone to the length of condemning all that Megasthenes has stated in his account but for the fact that in some contexts he helps us to substantiate the statements of Kauṭilya.[183]

3. KAUTILYA AND MEGASTHENES: VERACITY OF THE ARTHASASTRA

We shall be concerned in this section with the question of ascertaining how far Kauṭilya's assertions are borne out by those of Megasthenes.

(*a*) *King's Duties*

The reader may recall here the rigorous time-table of the daily routine of the ruler, as given in the *Arthaśāstra,* and as confirmed by the *Daśakumāracarita,* cited above. What is evident from the detailed account given by Kauṭilya about the daily duties of the ruler is that the latter was engaged in the business of the State throughout the day and for the greater part of the night. Both Strabo and Megasthenes confirm, on the whole, the severity that marked the daily life of the monarch. Strabo affirms that the king did not sleep during day time;[184] while Megasthenes states that the king remained in the court throughout the day.[185] Megasthenes explicitly writes that the king of the Indians was Sandrakottas.[186] This has rightly been taken to mean the Narendra of Kauṭilya,[187] that is, Candragupta Maurya.

(b) *Heads of the Departments*

Kauṭilya writes that each department was officered by several temporary heads, in addition, obviously, to the permanent head called the *adhyakṣa* (*bahumukhyaṁ-anityaṁ ca-adhikaraṇaṁ sthāpayet*).[188] These "temporary heads" refer to purely civil departments. Turning to the army, he states: "Elephants, cavalry, chariots, and infantry shall each be officered with many chiefs, inasmuch as chiefs, when many, are under the fear of betrayal from each other and scarcely liable to the insinuations and intrigues of an enemy."[189]

Now Megasthenes speaks of two kinds of boards—one referring to the capital city of Pāṭaliputra, and the other, to the army. The administrator of the city was entrusted to thirty members divided into six boards or committees of five members each.[190] Dr. Law tried to reconcile this information with that relating to the allocation of duties among the various departments;[191] while Professor Dikshitar has accepted as historical all that Megasthenes has stated, and has given what he imagines to be their parallels in the *Arthaśāstra*.[192] This is rather strange in view of the fact that the learned Professor has repeatedly condemned Megasthenes as being untrustworthy! The proper way is not to institute a comparison between the duties of the artisans, the protection to be given to foreign merchants, etc., and the boards, as is done by Dr. Law, but to see whether there was anything in the *Arthaśāstra* that could be made to agree with what Megasthenes says. We believe the temporary heads, referred to above, formed, as suggested by Dr. Shama Sastry, precisely the boards, since the members of the boards held office only for a short period. But Dr. Sastry did not go beyond the suggestion made above. Our assumption that the many chiefs (*bahumukhyaṁ*) formed themselves into boards will be clear when we note that in the case of civil as well as military departments of government, each department had a superintendent (*adhyakṣa*) over it. This was also true of the departments of elephants, cavalry, chariots, and infantry, each of which had its own *adhyakṣa*. We are, therefore, justified in maintaining that, when Megasthenes meant by the boards of civil and military departments, he referred to the civil and the military departments as described in the *Arthaśāstra*.

(*c*) *Duties of Superintendents*

Dr. Law has conclusively shown that the duties of the Superintendents of Rivers, Commerce, Forest Produce, and Markets, as given by Kauṭilya, are precisely those given by Megasthenes. In this category are to be included the other miscellaneous duties of measuring land, controlling huntsmen, collecting taxes, recording births and deaths, repairing buildings, regulating prices, and looking after temples which Kauṭilya enumerates in detail, and which are substantiated by Megasthenes.[193]

(*d*) *Penal Code*

There can be no doubt that the penal code, and, in particular, the drastic punishments and the use of torture recommended by Kauṭilya, were very harsh. This is borne out by Megasthenes, who refers to the severity of the law.[194] The attempt made by Professor Dikshitar to extenuate the nature of law and punishments, especially of torture,[195] is as unnecessary as it is unconvincing. The needs of the age, we may be permitted to repeat, necessitated the imposition of the severest penalties ; and Kauṭilya did not hide this fact in any apologetic language.

(*e*) *Irrigation*

Kauṭilya has devoted an entire chapter to the duty of the king to save the kingdom, as we have already seen, from the national calamities among which figure floods. While explaining Recruitment of Lost Power, he writes that irrigational works (*setubandha*) are the source of crops ; and that the results of a good shower of rain are ever attained in the case of crops below the irrigational works.[196] That the construction of the major irrigational works was the duty of the State is proved by the injunction: "He (the king) shall also construct reservoirs (*setu*), filled with water either perennial or drawn from some other source. Or he may provide with sites, roads, timber, and other necessary things those who construct reservoirs of their own accord."[197] The second sentence evidently refers to private enterprise aided by the State in regard to irrigational works.

In the Chapter on the Duties of the Superintendent of Agriculture (*sītādhyakṣa*), he refers to differential taxation. Those who cultivated irrigating by manual labour (*hasta-prāvartimaṁ*) were to pay one-fifth of the produce as water rate (*udakabhāgaṁ*) ; those who cultivated by carrying water on shoulders (*skandaprāvartimaṁ*), one-fourth of the produce ; those, by water lifts (*srotoyantraprāvartimaṁ*), one-third of the produce ; and those, by raising water from rivers, lakes, tanks, and wells (*nadī-saras-taṭāka-kūpa-udghāṭaṁ*), one-third or one-fourth of the produce. In this context he speaks of three crops—wet crops (*kedāra*), winter crops (*haimana*), and summer crops (*graiṣmika*), raised according to the supply of workmen and water.[198]

Kauṭilya mentions the measurement of land when he describes the measurements of space and time in a separate chapter. Fifty-four *angulas* formed one *hasta* used in measuring timber forests ; forty-two *angulas* were equal to one *kikṣu* used in measuring the grounds for the encampment of the army, for forts, and for palaces ; 108 *angulas* were equal to one *gārhapatya dhanus* for measuring roads and fort walls ; the same number of *angulas* but equal to one *pauruṣa* being used as a measure in building sacrificial altars ; six *kamsas* or 192 *angulas* were equal to one *daṇḍa* used in measuring such lands as were gifted to Brahmans ; ten *daṇḍas* were equal to one *rajju* ; two *rajjus* were equal to one *paridesa* (square measure) ; three *rajjus* equal to one *nivartane* (square measure) ; and three *rajjus* plus two *daṇḍas* on one side only were equal to one *bāhu* or arm.[199] The *rajjus* (ropes) were obviously to be used by the officials who were in charge of land measurement.[200]

Megasthenes corroborates the statements of Kauṭilya concerning the irrigational works and the crops raised, but shows some ignorance in regard to the number of crops raised. He writes that the greater part of the soil of India in his day was under irrigation, and consequently bore two crops. There were Superintendents of Rivers ; land was measured as in Egypt ; and sluices were inspected so that every one could have an equal share of them.[201] Megasthenes has erred when he writes of only two crops. This part of his narrative, as Professor Dikshitar rightly says, was obviously based on hearsay, since there is no evidence that the Greek ambasador ever went to the country side to verify his statements.[202]

(*f*) *Espionage*

We have seen that the *Arthaśāstra* recommends a wide-spread and rigorous system of espionage controlled by the State. The overseers, described by Megasthenes as moving about the country and reporting to the king or to the officers immediately higher than themselves, could only have been one type of spies mentioned by Kauṭilya.[203]

(*g*) *Army*: *Elephants*

Kauṭilya does not give an exact estimate of the army under the Mauryan State. But he has many things to say about its organization, divisions, arrays, and maintenance. The reference to the War Boards in the *Fragments* of Megasthenes, mentioned earlier, merely helps us to corroborate the general impression created by the account of Kauṭilya that the organization of the army was a complicated affair.[204]

One vital part of the army was composed of elephants concerning which

Kauṭilya has detailed information to give. Dr. Stein, on a close examination of the accounts of Kauṭilya and Megasthenes on this particular point, admitted that there was almost complete agreement between the two writers on the following points: places where the elephants were caught, their height, age, hunting, stalls, size, feeding, training, diseases, and remedies. The only difference in the accounts was in regard to their longevity. Kauṭilya refers to elephants aged forty, thirty, and twenty, while Megasthenes writes of elephants which were 300 and 200 years old, evidently on hearsay.[205]

Kauṭilya mentions an *āyudhāgāra* or armoury where all weapons were deposited only after they had been marked with the king's seal. Persons with weapons were not allowed to move about unless they were permitted by a passport. When weapons were lost or spoilt, the Superintendent of the Armoury had to pay double their value. An account of the weapons that were destroyed was maintained.[206]

Megasthenes confirms this when he writes: "There are royal stables for horses and elephants, and also a royal magazine for the arms, because the soldier has to return his arms to the magazine, and his horse and elephant to the stables."[207]

(*h*) *Superintendent of Ships*

In his enumeration of the duties of the Superintendent of Ships (*nāvādhyakṣa*), Kauṭilya makes provision for the hiring out of the State ships for passenger and merchandise traffic in the following passage: "Those (who make use of the king's boats in) fishing out conch shells and pearls shall pay the requisite amount of hire (*naukāhāṭakaṁ*), or they may make use of their own boats." "In those large rivers which cannot be forded even during the winter and summer seasons, there shall be launched larger boats (*mahānāvaḥ*) provided with a captain (*śāsaka*), a steerman (*niyāmaka*), and servants to hold the sickle and the ropes and to pour out water." We have cited earlier the passage referring to the free ferrying of Brahmans, ascetics, children, the aged, the afflicted, royal messengers, and pregnant women at State expense.[208]

Megasthenes confirms the two major ideas in the above passages, viz., provision for passenger and commercial traffic, when he writes that the Admiral of the Fleet (by which he evidently meant the *nāvādhyakṣa*) was "letting out ships on hire for the transport of both passengers and merchandise".[209]

(*i*) *Marriage*

Six kinds of marriage are described in the *Arthaśāstra*, obviously after the model of the *Manusmṛiti*. The giving in marriage of a maiden for a couple of cows was called *ārṣa*. The giving in marriage of a maiden to an officiating priest in a sacrifice was called *daiva*. The voluntary union of a maiden with her lover was called *gāndharva*. Giving a maiden after receiving plenty of wealth (*śulka*) was called *āsura*. The abduction of a maiden while she was in sleep and in intoxication was called *paiśāca*. Of these six kinds of marriages, the first four (*ārṣa, daiva, gāndharva,* and *āsura*) were ancestral customs of old, and were valid, when they were approved of by the father of the maiden. The rest had to be sanctioned both by the father and the mother, for it was only they who received the money (*śulka*) paid by the bridegroom for their daughter. In case of the absence by death of either the father or the mother, the survivor was to receive the *śulka*. If both of them died, the maiden herself was to receive it. Any kind of marriage was considered as approved only when it pleased all those that were concerned in it.[210]

Like any foreigner ignorant of the full implication of a local problem but acquainted with some of the customs of the people, and desirous of selecting only the sensational element out of a more reasonable mass of materials, Megasthenes knows only one out of the six kinds of marriages, confounds it with another detail, and makes capital out of it, giving the impression that he has been a close observer of the society around him! He writes: "They (the Indian people) marry many wives, whom they buy from their parents,.giving in exchange a yoke of oxen. Some they marry hoping to find in them willing helpmates; others for pleasure and to fill their houses with children."[211] The second part of his statement relating to wives' being helpmates, etc., is applicable to the Indians as well as to the Greeks, and is in conformity both with custom and the injunctions of the *dharmaśāstras*. The first part of the statement concerning the buying of maidens from their parents in exchange for a yoke of oxen is evidently the result of confusion on the part of Megasthenes of the *ārṣa* with the *āsura* form of marriage. Nevertheless the Greek ambassador's testimony is useful in proving, not that the *ārṣa* form of marriage was universal, but that it existed in the country and that, at the same time, the *āsura* form also prevailed.[212]

(j) *Personal Safety of the King*

Concerning one of the measures to be taken for the personal safety of the ruler, Kauṭilya writes thus: "With a view of acquiring efficiency in the skill of shooting arrows at moving objects, he shall engage himself in sports only in such forests as are cleared by hunters and hound-keepers from the fear of high way robbers, snakes, and enemies." Then, again, while dealing with the king's going out of the capital, he writes thus: "On the occasion of going out of, and coming into (the capital), the king's road shall on both sides be well guarded by staff-bearers and free from the presence of armed persons, ascetics, and the cripple (*vyaṅga*)."[213]

Megasthenes confirms the measures taken for the personal safety of the monarch but, as is usual with foreigners, confounds the details which he might have only got from indifferent informants with those which he might have perhaps seen himself. The *Indika* relates that whenever the king went a-hunting, the roads were blocked by ropes ; and when he was leaving the city, portions of the streets reserved for the king were cleared of dangers and dangerous persons. Megasthenes also writes that the king was accompanied by women.[214] The Greek ambassador has confused three items—one relating to the measures taken in regard to the king's leaving the capital, concerning which his statement is in agreement with that given by Kauṭilya, since he might have had occasions of seeing the king's going out of the capital. The second item is in regard to the king's going a-hunting which he might never have had an occasion of witnessing, since those times were unlike our own, when special hunting excursions are got up for distinguished foreign royal guests. And the third item concerns the function of the armed women in the palace which he could gather only from hearsay, since it is extremely doubtful whether he could ever have been inside the palace. The reference to the king's going a-hunting as given by Megasthenes is incorrect ; likewise that referring to the women accompanying the king. Obviously he must have heard of the royal custom about which Kauṭilya writes thus: "On getting up from the bed, the king shall be received by troops of women armed with bows."[215] Inspite of this defect, Megasthenes confirms the measures advocated by Kauṭilya in regard to the personal safety of the king while going out of and coming into the capital.[216]

(*k*) *Care of Foreigners*

Kauṭilya includes, among the other duties of the Superintendent of the Capital City, that concerning the managers of charitable institutions, who were to send information to the *gopas* or *sthānikas* about any heretics and travellers (*pāthika*), who wished to reside in the institutions ; the masters of the houses who were to make a report of strangers arriving at, or departing from, their houses ; the wayfarers who were to be on the look out for strangers ; and the spies who were to make a search for suspicious persons.[217] While enumerating the duties of the Superintendent of Commerce, he says that foreigners importing merchandise shall be exempted from being sued for debts unless they are (local) associations and partners.[218] The State, therefore, not only kept a strict watch over the movements of foreigners but, in regard to trade, gave foreign merchants sufficient guarantee against legal compensation.

It is obviously these regulations which Megasthenes had in mind when he wrote that there was a board to look after the foreign visitors, which duty Dr. Smith equated with the duties of modern European consuls.[219] Megasthenes corroborates Kauṭilya when he states that all foreigners were closely watched by officials, who provided them with suitable lodgings, escorts, and, in case of need, medical attendance. Deceased strangers were decently buried, and their estates were administered by the Commissioners, who forwarded their assets to the person entitled.[220]

The account of Megasthenes is in substantial agreement with that of Kauṭilya regarding the care bestowed by the State on foreigners, and the close watch kept on the latter. In this connection we have to recall the great danger which Kauṭilya saw in the foreigners, particularly about the safety of the State, and about which he has dealt with in connection with the major question of the sovereignty of the State. The danger of foreign envoys against whom the king was to send counter envoys, spies, visible and invisible watchmen,[221] which Kauṭilya mentions, only further strenghtens our suspicion that the State kept a strict watch over them, while granting them some commercial immunities. It is not surprising, therefore, that all foreigners were watched by the spies. But when Megasthenes definitely refers to a special board to look after the foreigners, he magnifies a detail concerning them which we have seen above. He evidently constituted the managers of institutions, the masters of houses, and the Superintendent of Commerce into a board about which there is no evidence in the *Arthaśāstra.* Neither is there any specific statement in that work relating to the assets of the deceased foreigners, whose obsequies were performed at State expense, according to Megasthenes, who relates that they were to be returned to their legal claimants abroad. Dr. Law, while noticing this detail as well as the one which refers to the escorting of foreigners, writes both these details are not found in the *Arthaśāstra,* but that the other details referring to the legal immunity of the foreigners, show that the foreigners "used to get a good treatment".[222]

It is possible that Megasthenes, while writing about the assets of the deceased foreigners, had in mind certain regulations mentioned in the *Arthaśāstra* which unmistakenably point to the minute rules relating to pledges, property, entrusted to another for delivery to a third person, and deposits in general which bespeak the great solicitude of the State for returning to the owners the property belonging to them.[223]

(*l*) *Pāṭaliputra*

Some Western scholars have denied that the *Arthaśāstra* was written by Kauṭilya because he does not mention Pāṭaliputra by name in his work.[224] This argument is as untenable as the one relating to the anonymity of the author himself, or that relating to the name of the kingdom where the work was composed, or that concerning the monarch on whose behalf it was written. We shall show in this section that the description of the capital as given by Kauṭilya agrees very well with that given by Megasthenes.

(i) Professor Dikshitar's Theory Evaluated

Here it is necessary to examine the validity of the identification of Pāṭaliputra made by Professor Dikshitar with that described by Megasthenes. The eminent scholar refers the reader to Book II, Chapters I till IV in the *Arthaśāstra,* which deal with the Formation of Villages, the Division of Land, the Construction of Forts, and the Buildings within the Fort respectively,[225] and in the same connection informs us that there were four compartments leading to the public hall.[226] This is both vague and confusing. In a still later context the same scholar, while attempting to refute Dr. Stein's objection that Kauṭilya does not mention Pāṭaliputra by name, is at pains to explain the construction of the capital in stone and wood, and to justify its location.[227] These arguments are inadequate to prove that the capital described by Kauṭilya possessed many of the attributes mentioned by Megasthenes. Indeed, historians who have advocated the view that Kauṭilya has referred to the capital city of Pāṭaliputra as described by Megasthenes, have been, on the whole, concerned more with the wooden structure of the palace than with the general agreement of the capital as described in the *Arthaśāstra* with that given in the *Indika.*

(ii) Kauṭilya's Description of the Capital

Admitting the fact that Kauṭilya does not mention Pāṭaliputra by name, let us see whether he describes it at all. In Chapter III entitled the Construction of Forts, in Book II, he describes the fortified capital. After saying that water and mountain fortifications are best suited to different populous centres, and that desert and forest fortifications are inhabitations in wilderness, he writes thus:

> Or having no refuge in times of danger, the king may have his fortified capital (*sthāniya*) as the seat of his treasury (*samudāyasthānaṁ*) in the centre of his kingdom: in a locality naturally best fitted for the purpose, such as the bank of the confluence of rivers, a deep pool of perennial water, or of a lake, or tank, a fort, circular, rectangular, or square in form, surrounded with an artificial canal of water, and connected with both land and water paths (may be constructed). (Here follows the description of the wide moat.)
>
> At a distance of four *daṇḍas* (twenty-four feet) from the (innermost) ditch, a rampart, six *daṇḍas* high and twice as much broad, shall be erected by heaping mud upwards and by making it square at the bottom, oval at the centre, pressed by the trampling of elephants and bulls, and planted with thorny and poisonous plants in bushes. Gaps in the rampart shall be filled up with fresh earth.
>
> Above the rampart, parapets in odd or even numbers and with an intermediate space of from twelve to twenty-four *hastas* from each other shall be

built of bricks and raised to a height of twice their breadth. (Here follows the description of the passage for chariots.) Towers, square throughout, and with moveable staircase or ladder equal to its height, shall also be constructed. (Here follows the description of a broad street.) Between the tower and the broad street shall be constructed an Indrakośa, which is made up of covering pieces of perforated wooden planks affording seats for the archers. (Here follow the description of roads for the gods, paths to ascend the parapet,. a passage for flight, a door for exit.) Having made on both sides the rampart bulge out to the extent of a *daṇḍa*-and-a-half, an entrance gate (to the fort) one-sixth as broad as the width of the street shall be fixed. (Here follow the details of squares and pillars.) On the first floor, five parts (are to be taken) for the formation of a hall (*śālā*), a well, and a boundary house. (Here come the details of two platforms); carvings of images (here follow details of storeys and secret stair case); a top-support of ornamental arches (*torṇa-śiraḥ*) projecting as far as two *hastas.* (Here follow the details of the door panels, cross-bars, iron bolt, a boundary gate, and four beams to shut the door against elephants, and turrets (*hastinakha*) (outside the rampart) raised to the height of the face of a man, removable or irremovable, or made of earth in places devoid of water.) A turret above the gate, and starting from the top of the parapet shall be constructed, its front resembling an alligator up to three-fourths of its height.

In the centre of the parapets, there shall be constructed a deep lotus pool; a rectangular building of four compartments, within the other; an abode of the goddess Kumārī (*Kumārīpuram*), having its external areas one-and-a-half times as broad as that of its innermost room; a circular building with an archway; and in accordance with available space and materials, there shall be constructed canals (*kulyā*) to hold weapons, and three time as long as broad. (Here follow the details of the weapons of war stored in those canals.)[228]

While describing in detail the buildings inside the fortress, Kauṭilya again refers to the king's harem (*antaḥpuraṁ*) which should occupy one-ninth of the whole site of inside the fort.[229] In an earlier context he had stated that the king was to construct his own residential palace (*vāsa-griham*) after the model of the treasury house (*kośagṛiha-vidhānena vāsa-gṛiham*); while his harem (*antaḥpuraṁ*) was to consist of many apartments, one within the other, enclosed by a parapet and a ditch, and provided with a door.[230] Since the author uses the word *vāsagṛiha* distinctly from *antah-pura,* and since both are used in the same context, it is to be presumed that the *vāsagṛiha* was the main palace, and that the *antaḥpura* was the residential quarter of the royal ladies.

(iii) *Kauṭilya's Description Analysed*

It is necessary to observe a few points before we analyse the above description of the capital as given in the *Arthaśāstra*. The first is that, as Professor Dikshitar rightly stated, Kauṭilya wrote a book on Polity for all time, and for all kings, and for all places. Hence he could not have prescribed only one standard by way of a model fortress at Pāṭaliputra.[231] Secondly, it is generally overlooked by historians that Candragupta Maurya did not establish a kingdom on a barren soil: his predecessors were the imperial Nandas ; and there is reason to believe that Pāṭaliputra had already been founded in the fifth century B.C. long before the rise to power of the Mauryas.[232] We have, therefore, to suppose that there was already a great capital before the time of Candragupta Maurya, which he could only have enlarged and strengthened on the lines laid down in the *Arthaśāstra*. Thirdly, we have to note, as already suggested earlier, that Kauṭilya wrote his book soon after the liquidation of the Macedonian power in the north-western regions, say in 303-02 B.C. This considerably strengthens our presumption that the new Mauryan capital could have arisen only as an improvement on the old one constructed by the earlier kings of Magadha. Fourthly, it is futile to find every detail mentioned by Kauṭilya echoed in the narrative of Megasthenes, since, we may repeat, as a foreigner, inspite of his ambassadorial status, he had no chance of inspecting in detail the great fortress. And, finally, it should be remembered that in those ancient times the fortress had a larger construction inside which was the royal palace. The whole palace was not the same as the entire fortress.

The above description of the capital as given by Kauṭilya may be analysed, from our point of view, thus:

Location: It was to be in the centre of the kingdom, and on the bank of a river.

Shape: It was to be rectangular or square in form.

Ditches: It had to possess three ditches or moats.

Building Materials: It was to be built of stone bricks.

Rampart: It was to have a rampart of mud.

Towers: It was to have square towers and turrets.

Seats for Archers: It was to have seats in the *Indrakośa* meant each for three archers.

Gate: It was to have an extensive gate.

Images: It was to have possessed carvings of images and ornamental arches.

Lotus Pool: It was to have a lotus pool.

Area: The king's palace was to occupy one-ninth of the entire area of the fortress.

(iv) Comparison of the Arthaśāstra with the Indika

Now to turn to Megasthenes in order to see how far the above details agree with those mentioned in the *Indika*. The Greek ambassador informs us that the great city which lay on the confluence of the Son with the Ganges, stretched in the inhabited quarters to an extreme length on each side of eighty *stadia*, that its breadth was fifty *stadia*, and that a ditch encompassed it all round. The moat was six hundred feet in breadth and thirty cubits in depth ; and the wall was crowned with 570 towers and had forty-six gates. It was a parallelogram surrounded by a wooden wall with holes for discharging arrows.[233]

In the above account Megasthenes confirms the location and size of the capital on the bank of the Son ; its shape which was—not exactly a rectangle, as Kauṭilya would put it—but a parallelogram, according to Megasthenes ; its rampart, as Kauṭilya calls it, or a wall, as Megasthenes terms it ; its ditch which, according to Megasthenes, was sixty feet in breadth, and thirty feet in depth, and which probably comprised all the three ditches mentioned by Kauṭilya ; its towers and its wooden wall with holes for discharging arrows which are undoubtedly the *Indrakośa* of Kauṭilya ; and its gates which, according to Megasthenes, were many, but which, according to common sense, could have been only one, as Kauṭilya rightly states. Even in regard to the detail of the gate we may reconcile the evidence of Megasthenes with the statement of Kauṭilya by saying that the former perhaps refers to the main gate as well as to the passage for flight (*pradhāvitikāṁ*) and the door for exit (*niṣkuradvāraṁ*), mentioned by Kauṭilya.

We are now left with the stone-brick mortar work, the parapets, the carvings of images, and the lotus pool. Let us take the first item of the stone-brick and wooden work. Scholars, who have argued against the contemporaneity of Kauṭilya with Megasthenes, and especially against the view of the *Arthaśāstra's* having been the work of Kauṭilya, have adduced the evidence of the Greek ambassador in regard to the construction of houses in wood as violating the evidence of Kauṭilya, who writes of stone structure. Here it is necessary to bear in mind three facts: the construction of houses in cities on the banks of rivers or on the sea coast ; the construction of the fortress wall ; and the construction of the royal palace. There seems to be some confusion among modern scholars, who have taken all the three types of construction to be one and the same. A little consideration would show that there is no justification for such a confusion. Megasthenes refers to the first and the third, i.e. to the houses in general and to the royal palace but does not seem to refer to the construction of the fortress wall. He relates:

> . . . such cities are situated on the banks of rivers or on the sea coast are built of wood instead of brick, being meant to last only for a time— so destructive are the heavy rains which pour down, and the rivers also

> when they overflow their banks and inundate the plains—while those cities that stand on commanding situations and lofty eminence are built of brick and mud.[234]

This general description cannot be applied to Pāṭaliputra, especially to the great royal palace, as has been assumed by some, who speak of Kauṭilya's being posterior to Megasthenes.[235]

We have to see whether Megasthenes has described the fortress wall and the royal palace. Both these were, of course, visible to people, and could have come under the observation of the foreign witness as well. Since the great city was inside the fortress, it is presumable to think that when Megasthenes described the city he meant also the fortress. Only in this way can we identify the city with the fortress. Megasthenes states that the wall of the fortress-city had 570 towers and sixty-four gates.[236] This wall has been taken by Dr. Smith to be a massive timber palisade[237] which, however, does not appear to be correct. Dr. Smith seems to refer here to the *Indrakośa* mentioned above. There appears no doubt that the fortress-city had a stone wall around it comprising parapets in the manner laid down by Kauṭilya. In the detailed description of the fort, Kauṭilya writes: "Above the rampart, parapets in odd and even numbers and with an intermediate space of from 12 to 24 *hastas* from each other shall be built of bricks and raised to a height of twice their breadth."[238] It is clear that the brick-wall of Kauṭilya must have been so perfectly done as to leave the impression that it was built of stone. Incidentally it may be noted that the fact that the fortress wall was built of stone is confirmed even by the later evidence of Fa Hien (A.D. 399-414), who wrote of the city built of stone in the midst of which were the royal palace and the halls which were so grand as to create the impression that they were built by spirits.[239]

Now in regard to the palace structure. Megasthenes relates that it was constructed of timber, and was considered to excel in splendour and magnificence the palaces of Susa and Ekbatana. It was adorned with golden pillars clasped all round by a vine embossed in gold, while images of birds in silver charmed the eye.[240] There were parks in which peacocks and domesticated pheasants were kept. There were cultivated plants some of which were attended to by the king's servants with special care, "for there are shady grounds and pasture grounds planted with trees, and branches of trees which the art of the woodsman has deftly interwoven". Parrots kept hovering round the king.[241] The extensive park was studded with fish ponds and furnished with a great variety of ornamental trees and shrubs.[242]

When Megasthenes refers to the various kinds of plants, he proves the statements of Kauṭilya who, while describing the king's duty to the harem, writes: "Poisonous snakes will not dare enter such buildings as are provided with *jīvanti* (*faederia foetida*), *śveta* (*aconitum ferox*) *muṣkakapuṣpa* (?), and *vandāka* (*epidendrum tesselatum*), and as are protected by the branches of *pejāta* (?) and of *aśvattha*" (*ficus religiosa*).[243]

Megasthenes' reference to peacocks confirms the measures which, according to Kauṭilya, the king had to take in guarding against poison being administered to the ruler. "Cats, peacocks, mongooses, and the spotted deer eat up snakes. Parrots, *mainas* (*śārika*), and Malabar birds (*bhṛiṅgarāja*) shriek when they perceive the smell of snake poison." That there were other domesticated birds, including the pheasants, is evident from the next passage in the same context. "The heron (*crauñca*) swoons in the vicinity of poison ; the pheasant (*jīvanjīvaka*) feels distress ; the youthful cuckoo (*maṭṭakokila*) dies ; the eyes of the patridge (*cakora*) are reddened."[244] Since all these were measures which were daily taken against poison and fire, it follows that the many birds and animals mentioned by Kauṭilya were preserved in the royal palace, as suggested by Megasthenes.[245]

There is one detail which seems to have escaped the notice of scholars, who have rightly upheld the view that Megasthenes, on the whole, only substantiates what Kauṭilya has stated in regard to the royal palace. The Greek ambassador asserts that the extensive royal park was studded with fish pond. He merely proves what is given in the *Arthaśāstra,* wherein it is stated: "In centre of the parapets, there shall be constructed a deep pool" (*prākāramadhye kṛitvā vāpīṁ puṣkaraṇīṁ*).[246]

CHAPTER VII

WAS KAUṬILYA AN IDEALIST? (*Contd.*)

AN EVALUATION OF THE ARTHAŚĀSTRA: INTERNAL EVIDENCE: KAUṬILYA AND AŚOKA

A. INTRODUCTION

THE EVIDENCE from the *Indika* of Megasthenes only demonstrates the fact that the statements in Kauṭilya, in regard to various important questions, were not those of a pedantic *pandit*, who wrote for the edification of his royal patron. On the other hand, they were of practical utility, and were actually put into practice by the rulers. A study of the Edicts of Aśoka will further corroborate the fact that the precepts of Kauṭilya were carried out in practice by that great Mauryan Emperor.

B. KAUṬILYA AND AŚOKA—A COMPARISON OF THE CONCEPT OF DHARMA

1. THE PRACTICAL ASPECT OF DHARMA

The most conclusive proof that the *Arthaśāstra* was not a work embodying mere theory but was one which was meant as a practical guide on statecraft, is afforded in the Edicts of Aśoka, which enlighten us on the interesting question as to what extent that famous Mauryan Emperor followed the injunctions of the great Mauryan Prime Minister.[247] The one important fact that emerges from a study of the Edicts is the great prominence which Aśoka gave to the preservation and propagation of *dharma*. As Professors Mookerjee and Dikshitar have rightly stated, Aśoka's concept of *dharma* had two aspects—the practical and the doctrinal.

(*a*) *Eleven Main Ideas*

The former comprised eleven ideas which were the following: dutifulness to parents; reverence to the elders and teachers; dutifulness to superiors (*agrabhūti*); regard for the Brahmans, the Śramaṇas and the ascetics; kind treatment of slaves and servants; kindness to the poor and the suffering; regard for friends, relatives, and others; gifts to the Brahmans, and the ascetics; gifts to friends, acquaintances, and relatives; gifts of wealth to the aged ; and non-violence to all living creatures, including abstention from injuring or killing animals. These eleven virtuous qualities were both positive and negative in the sense that they embodied rules for doing good things, and for abstaining from doing bad deeds (*aparisravaṁ*).[248]

The practical aspect of the concept of Aśoka's *dharma* was nothing but a faithful reflection of the principles on the same subject as enunciated in the *Arthaśāstra*. This side of the question seems to have missed the attention of historians. Emperor Aśoka dwelt at greater length on some points than was done by Kauṭilya, who was crisp and clear in his injunctions. But in essence there was no deviation from the main principles as laid down by Kauṭilya. Thus, in his Chapter on the End of Sciences (*vidyāsamuddeśaḥ*), he states: "Harmlessness, truthfulness, purity, freedom from spite, abstinence from cruelty, and forgiveness are duties common to all i.e. to the king, the Kṣatriyas, the Brahmans, the Śūdras, the householders, the *Brahmacārins* or students, the *Vānaprasthas* or forest recluses, and the ascetics."[249] We have in this general law of Kauṭilya, governing the public conduct of all sections of the people, the precursor of the practical code of Aśoka's *dharma*.

Of the eleven ideas comprising Aśoka's code of *dharma*, we have in the above passage dispensed with the last but one relating to abstinence from cruelty to living beings which Kauṭilya laid down as one of the duties of all sections of the people, including the king, but which Aśoka magnified as the main plank of his moral code.

(i) *Duty to the Parents, Elders, and Superiors*

The remaining ten ideas may be grouped thus: dutifulness to parents. elders, teachers, and superiors ; regard for the Brahmans and the Śramaṇas, kindness to the poor and the afflicted ; and regard for friends, relatives, and others. Of these we may dispense with the last as being indefinite in the sense that it cannot be made out whether Aśoka in his Edicts refers to his personal friends and relatives, in the ordinary non-political sense of the term, or whether he refers to friends in the political context. In the III Rock Edict at Girnār, it is stated: "Meritorious is obedience to mother and father. Liberality to friends, acquaintances, and relatives, to Brāhmaṇas and Śramanas is meritorious" (*sādhu mātari ca pitari ca susrūsā mitra saṁstuta-ñātīnaṁ bāhmaṇa samaṇānam sādhu dānam*).[250] The use of the terms *mitra, saṁstuta,* and *ñātīnaṁ* used in the above context leaves no doubt in our mind that they connoted persons of a personal nature than of public political import. If this assumption is correct, it may be observed that the inclusion of the word *mitra* in the Edicts might not have had the same significance which is given to it in the *Arthaśāstra* where it had a political connotation, particularly in the context of the *rājamaṇḍala* theory.[251] No parallel need be drawn between Kauṭilya's regulations and those of Aśoka in regard to the favour that had to be shown to the personal friends of the ruler who, then as now, were, as they unfortunately are, an indispensable and a not-too-respectable an element of administrative adjustments of a country.

(ii) Duty to Teachers

As regards dutifulness to parents, elders, teachers, and superiors, we need not prove that this ideal had already been inculcated in the *Manusmṛiti.*[252] Aśoka's solicitude for observing dutifulness to teachers is evidently to be traced to Kauṭilya's injunction that the royal prince (the future ruler), with a view to maintaining efficient discipline, was invariably to keep company with the aged professors of science, since in them alone discipline had its firm root.[253] Teachers were to be respected, as also ministers, because both of them were to keep the king within bounds of proper decorum, and to warn him of his careless proceedings even in secret.[254]

(iii) Duty to Priests

As for Aśoka's solicitude for the Brāhmaṇas and the Śramaṇas, it may be observed that here, too, the great Mauryan Emperor seemed to have had the precepts of Kauṭilya before him. For in the *Arthaśāstra* it is stated that those who performed Vedic sacrifices (*ṛitvik*), spiritual guides, priests, and those learned in the Vedas shall be granted *Brahmadeya* lands, yielding sufficient produce and exempted from taxes and fines (*ṛitvik-ācārya-purohita-śrotriyobhyo Brahmadeyāni adaṇḍakarāṇi-abhirūpadāyakāni prayachchhet*).[255] Aśoka does not mention, of course, the *Brahmadeya* lands, but his gifts to the Brāhmaṇas and the Śramaṇas obviously came within the above general regulation of Kauṭilya.

(iv) Compassion on Slaves

The Rock Edicts contain abundant proof of the consideration that was shown by Aśoka to slaves and servants. But in this detail, too, the great Emperor was not enunciating a new principle in his domestic policy. On the other hand, he merely followed the earlier ordinances of Kauṭilya, which we have cited earlier, and which said: "Those who did not heed the claims of their slaves (*dāsa*), hirelings (*āhitaka*) and relatives shall be taught their duty."[256] That there was nothing new in the Mauryan Emperor's anxiety for the welfare of the slaves is apparent when we observe that every provision had been made by Kauṭilya for the State's looking after the welfare of the slaves. Kauṭilya devotes two chapters to the question of slaves, labourers, and servants,[257] thereby proving that, long before the days of Aśoka, the Mauryan State was fully alive to the need of protecting the interests of slaves and servants.

(v) Restoring Peace in a Conquered Country

Kauṭilya's broad policy in regard to the great question of restoring peace in a conquered country may now be seen, since it has an important bearing on the question of Aśoka's policy of *ahiṁsā,* which the latter publicized in his Edicts. After stating that the king should, through his spies, bring home to the leaders of the conquered people and of corporations his own esteem and concern in their well-being, as contrasted with the evils of the enemy, Kauṭilya relates the following:

> He should please them (the leaders of provinces, villages, castes, and corporations) by giving gifts, remitting taxes, and providing for their security. He should always hold religious life in high esteem. Learned men, orators, charitable and brave persons should be favoured with gifts of land and money and with remissions of taxes. He should release all the prisoners, and afford help to miserable, helpless, and diseased persons. He should prohibit the slaughter of animals for half a month during the period of *cāturmāsya* (from July to September), for four nights during the full moon, and for a night on the day of the birth-star of the conqueror or of the national star (*rājadeśanakṣatra*). He should also prohibit the slaughter of females and young ones (*yonibāla-vadham*) as well as castration. Having abolished those customs or transactions which he might consider either as injurious to the growth of his revenue or army, or as unrighteous (*kośadaṇḍa-upaghātikaṁ-adharmiṣṭaṁ vā*), he should establish righteous transactions (*tad-apanīya dharma vyavahāram sthāpayet*).[258]

An analysis of the above regulations reveals the following important ideas: that of remitting taxes, that of holding religious life in high esteem, that of helping the miserable, the helpless, and the destitute, that of releasing prisoners, and that of prohibiting the slaughter and castration of animals. Of these something has already been said above about holding religious life in high esteem. As regards helping the destitute, the Rock Edict V at Girnār says that the Emperor had appointed Mahāmātras of Morality who had many duties amongst which was this—that they were to be occupied in "supporting prisoners (with money) (?) . . . (if one has) children, or with those who are bewitched, (i.e., incurably ill?), or with the aged".[259] In the Rock Edict VIII at Girnār, he undertook tours of morality. In the course of these tours the following took place: visiting the Brahmans and the Śramaṇas and making gifts to them, (exactly in the spirit of Kauṭilya, who had stated that the king should hold religious life in high esteem), "visiting the aged and supporting (them) with gold", etc.[260] In the Rock Edict V at Kālsi, it is clearly stated that the Mahāmātras of Morality were occupied with many duties (which are enumerated), and "with the destitute and with the aged" (*anathesu vudhesu*).[261]

About the idea of releasing prisoners, we shall have to examine it in detail in order to see to what extent the practice followed by Aśoka was in conformity with the precepts promulgated by Kauṭilya. Likewise we shall note the agreement between Kauṭilya and Aśoka in regard to the prohibition of the slaughter of animals. We have to see whether the general policy of restoring peace in a conquered country, as enunciated by Kauṭilya, was followed by Aśoka. The Rock Edict XIII at Girnār, Kālsi, and Shahbazgarhi gives an account of the settlement of Kalinga after the great war against that province. Of the three versions, those at Kālsi and Shahbazgarhi contain a full account of the settlement of the country, while that at Girnār is mutilated. In this record there is no direct reference to the main points in the general ordinance of Kauṭilya mentioned above. But it is clear that the great monarch considered deplorable any injury to the Brāhmaṇas, the Śramaṇas, and the members of other sects (like the Pāṣaṇḍas), who were inhabitants of Kalinga, and who were accustomed to practise certain virtues (enumerated in detail). The Edict mentions that the monarch desired towards all beings abstention from hurting, self-control, and impartiality in case of violence. It relates that he considered that "even (to one) who should wrong (him) what can be forgiven is to be forgiven".[262] These statements are, on the whole, in accordance with the general policy of Kauṭilya of showing favour to the conquered people. But the specific methods of releasing prisoners, remitting taxes, and preventing cruelty and slaughter of animals are missing in it. Of these we shall have to say something about the first and third methods, while that relating to the remission of taxes is not met with in the Rock Edicts.

Belief in Heaven. Before we pass on to see how far Aśoka followed Kauṭilya in the above and other important details, we may mention that the Rock Edicts prove that Aśoka, perhaps before he finally became a Buddhist, believed in the earlier Hindu concept of happiness in this and the next world. The Separate Rock Edict II at Jaugaḍha relates that the borderers, who were to be taught morality, "may attain (happiness) both (in) this world and (in) the other world" (*dhaṁmam caleyūti hidalogaṁ ca palalogamca*).[263] In the Delhi-Topra Pillar Edict III we have the following: "This (action conduces) to my (happiness) in this world, that other (action) to my (happiness) in the other (world)" (*iyam me hidatikāye iyaṁmana me pālatikāye*).[264] The idea of attaining heaven for good work done in this world is given in the Separate Rock Edict I at Dhauli, when the Emperor addresses the judicial officers of Tosalī, thus: "But if (you) observe this, you will attain heaven, and you will discharge the debt (which you owe) to me" (*sampaṭi-pajamīne cu etaṁ svagaṁ ālādhayisatha mama ca ānaniyaṁ*).[265] This is repeated in the orders given to the judicial officers at Samāpā, as given in the Separate Rock Edict I at Jaugaḍha.[266] Aśoka had extended the principle of Kauṭilya who, while dealing the question of the end of sciences, and of the king's duty of restricting the people to their own sphere of work, writes thus: "The observance of one's own duty leads one to *svarga* and infinite bliss" (*svadharmaḥ-svargāya-ānantyāya-ca*).[267]

(vi) Cruelty to and Slaughter of Animals

Emperor Aśoka put forward in Rock Edict IV at Girnār and in its different versions a claim on behalf of himself concerning two major subjects—abstention from cruelty to animals, and abstention from discourtesy to priests. It opens thus:

> In times past, for many hundreds of years, there had ever been promoted the killing of animals and the hurting of living beings, discourtesy to relatives, discourtesy to Brāhmaṇas and Śramaṇas. . . . Such as they had not existed before for many hundred of years, thus there are now promoted, through the instruction in morality on the part of king Devānampriya Priyadarśin. abstention from killing animals, abstention from hurting living beings, courtesy to relatives, courtesy to Brāhmaṇas and Śramaṇas, obedience to mother (and) father, (and) obedience to the aged.[268]

The statement that for hundreds of years before Emperor Aśoka's time there had prevailed an unqualified policy of injury to living beings and discourtesy to parents, Brāhmaṇs, and Śramaṇas, is evidently a monarchical exaggeration which is pardonable in the case of a ruler, who has given such splendid proof of his earnestness as a pious Buddhist, but who obviously did not know that, so early as the days of Manu, righteous conduct, dutiful behaviour to parents and priests, and non-injury to living beings had already been preached as the general pattern of social behaviour.[269]

Kauṭilya's injunctions in regard to the duty of all castes to observe certain general principles, in which abstention from cruelty and observance of truthfulness are included, have already been cited under the practical aspect of *dharma* mentioned above. Likewise his ordinances relating to abstention from killing and hurting animals, including the castration of animals, have appeared above under the caption of restoring peace in the conquered country.

An almost exact reproduction of the injunctions of Kauṭilya in regard to the days when the slaughter and castration of animals were prohibited, is met with in the Delhi-Topra Pillar Edict V to the following effect:

> When (I had been) anointed twenty-six years, the following animals were declared by me inviolable, viz., parrots, mainas, the *aruṇa*, ruddy geese, wild geese, the *nandīmukha*, the *gelāṭa*, bats, queen-ants, terrapins, boneless fish, the *vedaveyaka*, the *Gangā-pupuṭaka*, skate-fish, tortoises,

and porcupines, squirrels (?), the *sṛimara*, bulls set at liberty, iguanas (?), the rhinoceros, white doves, domestic doves, (and) all the quadrupeds which are neither useful nor edible. Those (she-goats), ewes, and sows (which are) either with young or in milk, are inviolable, and also those (of their) young ones (which are) less than six months old. Cocks must not be caponed. Husks containing living animals must not be burnt. Forests must not be burnt either uselessly or in order to destroy (living beings). Living animals must not be fed with (other) living animals. Fish are inviolable, and must not be sold on the three Cāturmāsīs (and) on the Tiṣyā (i.e. Pauṣya) full moon, during three days, (viz.,) the fourteenth, the fifteenth, (and) the first (*tithi*), and invariably on every fast day. And during these same days also no other classes of animals which are in the elephant-park (and) in the preserves of the fishermen, must be killed. On the eighth (*tithi*) of (every) fortnight, on the fourteenth, on the fifteenth, on Tiṣyā, on Punarvasu, on the three Cāturmāsīs, (and) on festivals, bulls must not be castrated, (and) he-goats, rams, boars, and whatever other (animals) are castrated (otherwise), must not be castrated (then). On Tiṣyā, on Punarvasu, on the Cāturmāsīs, (and) during the fortnight of (every) Cāturmāsī, horses (and) bullocks must not be branded.[270]

While in the above ordinance we have full details of the animals and the birds that were not to be killed, and of the animals that were not to be castrated—which are naturally lacking in the general order passed by Kauṭilya in connection with the same subject—it cannot be denied that that ordinance of Aśoka was, in spirit and in some details, modelled on the one laid down by Kauṭilya. In other words, it appears as if we have to construe the Delhi-Topra ordinance as a vindication of the Moral Code as set forth in the *Arthaśāstra*.

C. THE EXECUTIVE IN THE ARTHASĀSTRA AND IN THE ROCK EDICTS: THE KING

Under this head we shall see to what extent Aśoka's practice was in conformity with the principles of Kauṭilya in regard to the ideal of duty, the king's pleasures, and the mode of counting years from the time of the king's coronation.

1. THE KING: THE IDEAL OF DUTY

(a) *Similarity in Ideals*

Kauṭilya ordained that all urgent matters were to be heard by the king atonce and never put off. In an earlier context he wrote: "In works of emergency, he (the king) shall call both his ministers and the assembly of ministers and tell them of the same" (*ātyāyike kārye mantriṇo mantri-pariṣadaṁ ca-āhūya brūyāt*).[271] In a later passage, while describing the duties of the king, the *Arthaśāstra* relates the following:

> He (the king) shall, therefore, personally attend to the business of the gods, of heretics (Pāṣaṇḍas), of Brahmans learned in the Vedas, of cattle, of sacred places, of minors, the aged, the afflicted, and the helpless, and of women—all this in order (of enumeration), or according to the urgency or pressure of those works. All urgent calls he shall hear atonce (*sarvaṁ-ātyayikaṁ kāryaṁ śraṇuyāt-na-atipātayet*), but never put off ; for when postponed, they will prove too hard or impossible to accomplish.[272]

Kauṭilya had thus laid down an Administrative Code which Aśoka implicitly followed both in regard to the consultation with the council of ministers and the prompt disposal of State business. The Girnār Rock Edict VI enlightens us on this double aspect of the vital question, thus:

> In times past neither the disposal of affairs nor the submission of reports at any time did exist before. But I have made the following arrangement. Reporters are posted everywhere, (with instructions) to report to me the affairs of the people at any time, while I am eating, in the harem, in the inner apartment, even at the cowpen, in the palanquin, and in the parks. And everywhere I am disposing of the affairs of the people. And if in the council (of Mahāmātras) a dispute arises, or an amendment as moved, in connexion with any donation or proclamation which I myself am ordering verbally, (or in connexion with) an emergent matter which has been delegated to the Mahāmātras, it must be reported to me immediately anywhere, (and) at any time (*ya ca kiṁci mukhato āñapayāmi svayaṁ dāpakaṁ vā srāvāpakaṁ vā ya vā puna mahāmātresu ācāyike* (*atiyāyike* in Kālsi) *aropitaṁ bhavati tāya athāya vivādo nijhatī va saṁto parisāyaṁ ānaṁtaraṁ paṭivedetavyaṁ me sarvatra sarve kāle*).[273]

The only difference between Kauṭilya's ordinance regarding the prompt disposal of the business of the State and Aśoka's arrangement about the same is that the latter gives the various places where his agents were to keep him informed of the urgent work ; while Kauṭilya merely formulates a general rule when he says that "all urgent calls he (the king) shall hear atonce", with a possible clause for conducting expeditiously the work which is not met with in the Rock Edicts. What is interesting is that Aśoka uses the very same term *ātyayika* for urgent State work, which was used by Kauṭilya. But in regard to the claim put forward by the great Emperor that "in times past neither the disposal of affairs nor the submissoin of reports at any time did exist before",[274] all that may be said is that it is without foundation. For in addition to the testimony

Kauṭilya cited above, we have that of Pāṇini, who definitely refers to the *aṣadakṣīṇa* business of the State of an important nature, and uses the term *ātyayika* exactly in the same sense of work of an urgent nature,[275] proving beyond doubt that so early as the seventh century B.C.,[276] the concept of disposing of the urgent business of the State was known in the country. In regard to one of the main duties of the king, therefore, Aśoka only followed the precept which had already been set forth by Kauṭilya.[277]

(*b*) *Royal Pleasures*

The Rock Edict VI of Girnār cited above states that the Emperor was accustomed to be in the parks (*uyānesu*).[278] Evidently this was exactly according to the rules of Kauṭilya, who provided for *mṛigavana* and *vihāra*, where the king could have his sports and hunts (*vihārārthaṁ*).[279] Pleasure grounds were both external and internal, and were placed under the *mahāmātras*, whose character had been tested under love allurements.[280] Hunting was, we may incidentally note, a desirable pastime which Kauṭilya defended against the opinion of Piśuna.[281] Since the precedent had already been set in the earlier days for the monarch to be in the parks, it is not surprising that it should have been followed in the days of Aśoka.

(*c*) *Method of Counting Years*

The method of dating the Edicts from the year of Emperor Aśoka's coronation which is expressed, for instance, in the terms *dbādasa-vāsābhisitena, duvāḍasa* (*dbādasa*) *vasābhisetena* (when I had been anointed these twelve years), found in the Rock Edict III at Girnār, Kalsi,[282] etc., is to be traced to the precedent set by the earlier rulers, and expressed in the term *rāja-varṣa*, or the King's Year, which evidently was counted from the coronation of the king, as given in the *Arthaśāstra*.[283]

2. MINISTERS

(*a*) *Terms Used*

The terms used in general for ministers and a council of ministers in the Edicts were in accordance with those in the *Arthaśāstra*. The ministers under Aśoka were called *mahāmātras*, who either had judicial functions in cities, or controlled the borders of the Empire. A special class of *mahāmātras* controlling women were called *strī-adhyakṣa-mahāmātras*.[284] In addition to these were the high officials called *rājukas* or *lajūkas*, who were in charge of many hundreds of men, and who could mete out rewards or punishments at their discretion. They were perhaps entrusted with executive duties, one of which was "holding the rope", i.e. for measuring the fields of farmers, as revenue officers.[285] Then, there were the *prade-śikas, yuktas,* and *dūtas.* The *yuktas, pradeśikas,* and the *rājukas* are mentioned in the Rock Edict III at Girnār, which ends by saying that the *yuktas* were to register (the rules embodied in the Edict) "both with (the addition of) reasons and according to the letter".[286] The same Rock Edict XIII at Girnar mentions the *dūtas* or envoys.[287]

(*b*) *Official Hierarchy*

The titles of most of the members of the official hierarchy under Aśoka were the same as those under Kauṭilya. We have seen above that the *mahāmātras* are mentioned in the *Arthaśāstra* as ministers of high rank.[288] We have likewise seen the use of the term *adhyakṣa* in the sense of Superintendents by Kauṭilya.[289] The *strī-adhyakṣa-mahāmātras* of Aśoka, however, were probably an innovation of the later ages, since they are not met with under that designation in Kauṭilya. Perhaps that term was the equivalent of the *aṁtarvaṁśika* or officer in charge of the harem, mentioned by Kauṭilya.[290] The *rājukas* of the Edicts may be traced to the *cora-rajjukas* and *rajjūḥs* mentioned in the *Arthaśāstra* as revenue officials connected with the survey, land settlement, and irrigation in the country parts.[291] But in the Aśokan times, the *rājukas* seem to have had also executive powers. The *pradeśikas* of the Edicts were, as pointed out by Dr. Thomas long ago, the *pradeṣṭārāḥ* or Commissioners of Kauṭilya.[292] The same eminent scholar pointed out that the *yuktas* of the Edicts were no other than the *yuktas* and the *upayuktas* of the *Arthaśāstra.*[293] The *dūtas* of the Edicts could have been no other than the *dūtas* or envoys or ambassadors mentioned in the same work.[294]

(*c*) *Mantripariṣad*

This was a political institution known to Pāṇini, who mentions the king and his council of ministers (*rajaḥkṛiṣy-āsuti-pariṣado-valach*).[295] Kauṭilya, as we have already seen, mentions the functions of the *mantripariṣad.*[296] Aśoka continued the concept of the *pariṣad,* as will be evident from the work that was entrusted to it in the Edicts. In the Rock Edict III at Girnār, it is stated that the council of *mahāmātras* "also shall order the *Yuktas* to register (these rules) both with the addition of) reasons and according to the letter" (*parisā pi yute āñapayisati gaṇanāyaṁ hetuto ca vyaṁjanato ca*).[297] In the Rock Edict VI at Girnār we are informed, as already seen earlier, that "if in the council (of *Mahāmatras*), a dispute arises, or an amendment is moved, in connexion with any donation or proclamation which I myself am ordering verbally, or (in connexion with) an emergent matter which has been delegated to the *Mahāmatras,* it must be reported to me immediately, any where (and) at any time".[298] The discussion of urgent matters in the *mantripariṣad,* as revealed in the Edicts, was in perfect agreement with the injunction of Kauṭilya that, in the case of an emergent matter, the king should summon both his ministers and assembly of ministers and tell them atonce of the same.[299]

(d) *Transfer of Officials*

Emperor Aśoka refers to the movement of officials every five years in his Rock Edict III at Girnār, thus: "Every where in my dominions the *Yuktas*, the *Rājukas*, and the *Prādeśikas* shall set out on a complete tour (throughout their charges) every five years for this very purpose, (viz.,) for the following instruction in morality as well as for other business."[300] The principle of transfer which is involved in the movement of officials is obviously the same which Kauṭilya mentions, but in a different context, thus: "Government servants shall not only be confiscated of their ill-earned hoards, but also be transferred from one work to another, so that they cannot either misappropriate government money or vomit what they have eaten up."[301] Kauṭilya refers in the above ordinance perhaps to the continual transfer of dishonest officials ; but Aśoka obviously has in his mind the transfer of hardworking and honest officials. But the principle of transfer in both is obviously the same.

D. THE JUDICIARY

1. A HARSH CODE

The Edicts of Aśoka contain interesting details of the judicial system of that great monarch which, on the whole, were in general agreement with the framework of the judiciary as described in the *Arthaśāstra*. When one thinks of Aśoka one is inclined to imagine that that monarch was a humane and kind-hearted ruler from the beginning of his reign. Such an assumption is dispelled when we learn from what the later Chinese traveller, Yuan Chwang, had to say, and from what is recorded in the Edicts themselves. According to Yuan Chwang, Aśoka in his early career was a most cruel ruler, who had constructed a jail that was called Hell-Prison of Aśoka.[302] The Edicts bear witness to the earlier rigour of the judicial system of the Emperor, as the following remarks will show.

2. JUDICIAL PROCEDURE IN ASOKA

We may first give a brief outline of the judicial procedure as gleaned from the Edicts, and, then, refer to the use of torture and to the jails in those times. The Separate Rock Edict I of Dhauli contains an account of the judiciary under Aśoka. The record commences with the statement: "At the word of Devānampriya, the *Māhāmatras* of Tosalī (in Orissa), (who are) the judicial officers of the city (*nagalaviyohālokā*), have to be told (thus)." Then follows the theory of Protection which will be cited below. The Emperor then states thus:

> For you (the *Mahāmātras* of Tosalī) are occupied with many thousands of men, with the object of gaining the affection of men. . . . And you do not learn how far this (my) object reaches. Some single person only learns this, (and) even he (only) a portion, (but) not the whole. Now you must pay attention to this, although you are well provided for. It happens in the administration (of justice), that a single person suffers either imprisonment or harsh treatment (torture) (*nityam eka-pulise pi athiye baṁdhanam vā palikilesaṁ vā pāpunāti*). In this case (an order) cancelling the imprisonment is (obtained) by him, accidentally, while (many) other people continue to suffer. In this case you must strive to deal (with all of them) impartially. But one fails to act (thus) on account of the following dispositions: envy, anger, cruelty, hurry, want of practice, laziness, (and) fatigue. You must strive for this, that these dispositions may not arise to you. And the root of all this is the absence of anger and the avoidance of hurry. He who is fatigued in the administration (of justice), will not rise; but one ought to move, to walk, and to advance (*nityaṁ e kilaṁte siyānate ugachchha saṁcalitaviye tu vaṭitaviye etaviye vā*). He who will pay attention to this must tell you: 'See that (you) discharge the debt (which you owe to the king); such and such is the instruction of Devānampriya'. . . . And if you act thus, you will be able to fulfil (this duty). For the following purpose has this rescript been written here (viz.,) in order that the judicial officers of the city may strive at all times, (for this), (that) neither undeserved fettering nor undeserved harsh treatment are happening to (men). And for the following purpose, I shall send out every five years (a *Mahāmātra*) who will be neither harsh, nor fierce, (but) of gentle actions, (viz., in order to ascertain) whether (the judicial officers), paying attention to this object, . . . are acting, thus, as my instruction implies.

The Rock Edict then continues to narrate that from Ujjain the provincial governor, who was a prince, will send out a deputation for the same purpose every three years. For the same purpose an officer will be deputed from Takṣaśīlā. And these *Mahāmātras,* while thus on tour, without neglecting their own duties, will ascertain whether the judicial officers were carrying out their duties, as instructed by the Emperor.[303]

From the above the following may be deduced about the judicial procedure under Aśoka:

(*a*) That the highest ministers called the *mahāmātras* in their judicial capacity were called the *nagara-viyohātaka* ;
(*b*) That they dealt with many thousands of men;
(*c*) That their duty was to execute the Emperor's orders ;

(*d*) That they were well provided for (*suvihitā*);
(*e*) That they administered according to *nīti* (*nitiyam*, i.e. *daṇḍanīti*);
(*f*) That they consequently decided cases, but, in doing so, sometimes with reference to an individual and not to the larger body of litigants;
(*g*) That in the course of the administration of justice, a single person suffered either imprisonment or torture,[304] while the others escaped, that is, in the course of the administration of justice, there was a chance of a single innocent man's being punished, while the many who were guilty, escaped punishment;
(*h*) That the judges had to be impartial;
(*i*) That they were not to fall victims to the many dispositions enumerated or to anger or to hurry;
(*j*) That they were not to be fatigued while conducting their duties;
(*k*) That they were implicitly to carry out the orders of the Emperor;
(*l*) That they were not to impose punishments involving undeserved fettering and harsh punishment; and
(*m*) That their work was supervised every five years by imperial superintendents of the rank of *mahāmātras*, and every three years by provincial superintendents (also of the same rank) from Ujjain and Taxila, who were to see that the judicial *mahāmātras* carried out the Emperor's orders to the letter.

3. A COMPARISON BETWEEN ASOKA AND KAUTILYA

Let us now see how far the judicial procedure of Emperor Aśoka was in conformity with that laid down by Kauṭilya. For the sake of brevity, we might center this part of our study around the following eight items: the basis of the judicial system of Aśoka; the technical name of the judges; the pecuniary position of the judges; the necessity of the judges to be impartial; the use of torture and imprisonment in the judicial proceedings; the need to eschew undeserved fettering and harsh treatment; the supervision of judges; and the release of prisoners.

(*a*) *The Basis of the Judicial System*

Aśoka's judicial system was based on *nīti* which has been understood by Professors Lüders and Hultzsch to be *daṇḍanīti*.[305] This is enough to show that that Emperor merely followed the principles of the *daṇḍanīti* which Kauṭilya had elaborately treated in the *Arthaśāstra*. It does not mean, however, that Aśoka followed the Kauṭilyan *daṇḍanīti* to the letter. But in so far as the judicial procedure is concerned, the Separate Rock Edict I at Dhauli definitely proves that it was based on the pattern of the *daṇḍanīti*.

(*b*) *The Technical Term for the Judges*

These dignitaries were called, as remarked above, *nagala-viyohālaka* which Professor Lüders equated with the *paura vyāvahārikas* of Kauṭilya.[306]

(*c*) *The Pecuniary Position of the Judges*

When Aśoka ordered that the *nagara-vyavahārikas* were to pay attention to what he said, "although you are well provided for", it is clear that he was following the principles of Kauṭilya, according to whom the *paura-vyavāhārikas* were paid each 12,000 *paṇas*.[307] It may not be wrong to assume that the judges under Aśoka continued to be paid high salaries.

(*d*) *The Judges to be Impartial*

Emperor Aśoka's ordinances in this regard are nothing but a feeble echo of the severe injunctions laid down in the *Arthaśāstra* about the impartiality of the judges. All that the great Emperor could do was to exhort his judges to deal with all men impartially, and not to fail in this matter because of the various dispositions mentioned in detail in the Rock Edict. Here he was undoubtedly following the rules of the iron discipline which Kauṭilya had laid down concerning the behaviour, speech, and action of the judges, and which we have cited already in the earlier pages of this work. These severe regulations made it impossible for any judge to swerve from the path of justice. Emperor Aśoka had evidently a similar intention in mind, when he ordered the Separate Rock Edict I to be inscribed, although in the clarity of expression and comprehensiveness of details, he does not reach the expectations of Kauṭilya.

We may recall here the careful and impartial manner in which the commissioners or *pradeṣṭārāhs* were to administer justice, which we have cited earlier. When Kauṭilya ordered that "without failing to notice equitable distinctions among offenders, whether belonging to royal family or to common people, shall the Commissioner determine the propriety of imposing the first, middle-most, or highest amercement",[308] he had laid down the principle which Emperor Aśoka faithfully ordered in his Pillar Edict IV at Delhi-Topra, when he ordered the *lajūkas* (*rājukas*) to perform their duties fearlessly, confidently, and unperturbed, and when he stated the following: "For the following is to be desired, (viz.) that there should be both impartiality in judicial proceedings and impartiality in punishments."[309]

(*e*) *Imprisonment, Torture, and Death Penalty*

While there is no doubt that there was not only imprisonment but even death penalty imposed on prisoners, opinion is divided among scholars on the use of torture. In the different versions of the Rock Edict V occur the terms *bandhana*, *vadha*, and *palibodha* which are interpreted by Professors Lüders, Mookerjee and Dikshitar as imprisonment, execution, and torture respectively; but which Professor Hultzsch has interpreted as "supporting prisoners (with money), in causing their fetters to be taken off, and in setting them free, etc.".[310] The latter interpretation does not help us to understand the passage so much as the former which, in the general context of Aśoka's liberal policy, would suggest that that monarch was anxious only to mitigate the rigour of the three kinds of punishments inflicted on prisoners, and not to abolish the death penalty which continued to exist. This assumption of ours is proved by the Separate Rock Edict I of Dhauli in which, as noted above, the Emperor states that that ordinance was written "in order that the judicial officers of the city may strive at all times (for this), (that) neither undeserved fettering nor undeserved harsh treatment are happening to men".[311]

That the extreme penalty of death was not abolished but, like imprisonment and torture, was reduced in severity, for some time, is proved by the Pillar Edict IV of Delhi-Topra:

> And my order, (reaches), even so far, (that) a respite of three days is granted by me to persons lying in prison on whom punishment has been passed; (and) who have been condemned to death. (In this way) either (their) relatives will persuade those (*Lajūkas*) to (grant) their life, or if there is none who persuades (them), they will bestow gifts or will undergo fasts in order to (attain happiness) in the other (world). For my desire is this, that, even when the time (of respite) has expired, they should attain (happiness) in the other (world).[312]

There is nothing in the above Pillar Edict and in its versions to suggest that the death sentence was altogether abolished by Aśoka. We thus reach the conclusion that, so far as punishments were concerned, the Emperor continued the precedent set by Kauṭilya, who had advocated the death penalty only in specified cases, while he made more ample use of imprisonment and torture.[313]

(*f*) *Solicitude for the Welfare of Prisoners*

The few citations from the Rock Edicts given above tend to prove that Emperor Aśoka was definitely against undeserved harsh treatment and imprisonment of prisoners. In this, too, he only followed in the footsteps of Kauṭilya, who even made provision in the jails for halls (*śālā*), pits (*khāta*, privy?), water wells, bath rooms, remedies against fires and poison, equipping them with cats and mongooses, and even with the necessary means to worship the guardian gods appropriate to each.[314] Kauṭilya's solicitude for the welfare of prisoners is almost modern in spirit. When an officer let out or caused to be let out offenders from the lockup (*cāraka*), or caused to obstruct prisoners in such of their daily avocations as sleeping, sitting, eating, or excreting, he was to be punished with fines ranging from three *paṇas* upwards. The regulations relating to the proper conduct of the Superintendent of Jails were so carefully laid down so as to prevent that official from misusing his powers and from ill-treating the prisoners in his charge.[315] These details are certainly not available in the Rock Edicts, which seem merely to follow the general principle of mitigating the hardships of prisoners, as advocated by Kauṭilya.

(g) *Respite to, and Release of, Prisoners*

The above assumption could be better appreciated in terms of the provision Emperor Aśoka made for the respite that was given to, and for releasing periodically, prisoners. The periodical release of prisoners by the Emperor was not a novel feature introduced by him. It had already existed in the days of Kauṭilya. Thus in the *Arthaśāstra*:

> On such of the days to which the birth star of the king is assigned, as well as on full moon days, such prisoners as are young, old, diseased, or helpless (*anātha*), shall be let out from the jail (*bandhanāgāra*) ; or those who are of charitable disposition or who have made any agreement with the prisoners may liberate them by paying an adequate ransom. Once in a day, or once in five nights, jails may be emptied of prisoners in consideration of the work they have done, or of whipping inflicted upon them, or of an adequate ransom paid by them in gold. Whenever a new country is conquered, when the heir apparent is installed on the throne, or when a prince is born to the king, prisoners are usually set free.[316]

Of the many occasions on which the great Prime Minister recommended that prisoners should be released, only one, in a slightly different form, seemed to find favour with the Mauryan Emperor who, as we saw above, in his Pillar Edict IV at Delhi-Topra, granted a three days' respite to persons lying in prison on whom the death sentence had been passed. The ending of the Pillar Edict V at the same place proves that he had ordered the release of prisoners many times. "Until (I had been) anointed twenty-six years, in this period the release of prisoners was ordered by me twenty-five (times)."[317] In the Rock Edict V, too, it is stated that the prisoners were set free,[318] although it cannot be made out on which occasion the jail delivery took place. Aśoka had understood the spirit underlying the principle of releasing the prisoners ; and adapting one of the occasions for effecting their freedom recommended by Kauṭilya, namely, when an heir apparent was installed on the throne, converted it into the day when he was anointed as a ruler. This slight change did not materially alter the principle laid down by the Mauryan Prime Minister regarding periodical jail delivery.

(*h*) *Supervision over the Judges*

The Rock Edicts make it clear that Aśoka was very careful in seeing that every five years his own high officials called the *yuktas, rājukas,* and *pradeśikas,* and every three years, those from Ujjain and Taxila, went round the country to see that the judges carried out their duties properly.[319] There was nothing new in this promulgation of Aśoka. It was merely dents and their subordinates" ; and that the king shall "with adequate by the Collector-General shall first check (the proceedings of) Superintendents and their subordinates" ; and that the king shall "with adequate punishments, test first the conduct of government servants, and then shall, through those officers of approved character, examine the conduct of the people both in towns and villages".[320] When it is realized that the Commissioners had the duty of dispensing with justice and of meting out punishments,[321] and that over them was the Collector-General, we may presume that the principle of supervising the judicial and executive work of the Commissioners had already been established for Aśoka to follow. The only innovation which that monarch introduced was a time limit of five and three years for imperial and provincial supervisors respectively, which is not met with in the *Arthaśāstra.*

E. THE STATE SHARE OF REVENUE

When Emperor Aśoka on visiting Lumbini, (Lummini, mod. Rummindei), the birth-place of Buddha, declared it free of taxes, and ordered that it should pay only one-eighth share of the produce,[322] he had merely given vent to views already expressed on tax-free villages by Kauṭilya. Dr. Thomas has shown that the term *ubalika* used in the above Rock Edict for a rent-free village was the same as *uchchhulka* in the *Arthaśāstra.*[323] As regards the State demand of one-eighth, it had already been laid down by Manu, who had ordained that the king could take one-eighth, or one-sixth, or one-half of the crops.[324] The share of one-eighth mentioned in the Rummindei Edict was not in accordance with the rate of one-sixth advocated by Kauṭilya ; but the term *bhāga* used in the Edict was precisely the same technical term used for the State demand in the *Arthaśāstra.*[325]

F. THE END OF THE STATE

1. DHARMAVIJAYA IN ASOKA AND KAUTILYA: INTRODUCTION

It was stated in the earlier pages, while describing the practical aspect of Aśoka's *dharma,* that he made as the pivot of his policy the general duties which Kauṭilya had enjoined in regard to all the castes, viz., harmlessness, truthfulness, purity, freedom from spite, abstention from cruelty, and forgiveness.[326] We shall further elucidate this subject, since it is intimately related to the question of the end of the State.

The first point that may be noticed in regard to the end of the State in the concept of Aśoka is that it was based on righteousness, and that it stood for the maintenance of *dharma.* In the words of the Edicts, his reign was one of the conquest of *dharma (dhammavijaye).*[327] Here, again, Aśoka only extended further the theory propounded by Kauṭilya, who describes three kinds of conquerors: *dharmavijayī,* who was satisfied with the mere obeisance of the conquered; the *lobhavijayī,* who was satisfied only with the surrender of territory and treasury; and the *āsuravijayī,* who was satisfied not merely with the surrender of territory and treasure but with the sons and wives of the conquered, and even with the life of the latter.[328] The concept of the *dharmavijayī,* as given in the Edicts, is in accordance with that mentioned in the *Arthaśāstra.*[329] But it is necessary here to observe the manner in which Aśoka had enlarged the concept of Kauṭilya in regard to the *dharmavijayī.* This brings us to the different interpretations of *dharmavijaya* as given by modern scholars like Professor Hultzsch, Mr. Manohan, and Professor Dikshitar.

2. THEORIES ON DHARMAVIJAYA

(a) Dr. Hultzsch on Dharmavijaya

Dr. Hultzsch following M. Senart would include in *dharma* the sum of moral duties.[330] The reader may recall here the remarks made earlier on the comparison of the concept of *dharma* in Kauṭilya and in Aśoka. The word *dharma* was first used by Aśoka in the Maski Rock Edict, but its definition was given in the Brahmagiri Rock Edict, thus:

> Moreover, *Devānampriya* speaks thus: Obedience must be rendered to mother and father, likewise to elders; firmness (of compassion) must be shown towards animals; the truth must be spoken; these same moral virtues (*dhammaguṇa*) must be practised. In the same way the pupil must show reverence to the master, and one must behave in a suitable manner towards relatives. This is an ancient rule, and this conduces to long life. Thus one must act.

The other Rock Edicts merely amplify this definition.[331] The virtues thus preached center round the following: obedience to elders and parents; respect to the Brahmans and the Śramaṇas; courtesy to servants and slaves; charity and liberality; and abstention from killing or injuring living beings. Emperor Aśoka's *dharmavijaya,* it may be added, was first conceived of after his war with Kalinga, when he issued his proclamation of morality (*dharma śrāvaṇa*). It was essentially a conquest by morality.[332]

When applied to the forest tribes and the kings, who were his neighbours, the *dharmavijaya,* as is clear from the Rock Edict XIII, meant the following: "And even the inhabitants of the forests which are (included) in the dominions of *Devānampriya,* even those he pacifies (and) instructs. And they are told of the power (to punish them) which *Devānampriya* (possesses) inspite of (his) repentance, in order that they may be ashamed (of their crimes), and may not be killed. For *Devānampriya* desires towards all beings abstention from hurting, self-control, and impartiality in (case of) violence." This was the conquest by morality (*dharmavijaya*) which Aśoka substituted for the conquest by arms, and which he claims to have won even among his neighbours.[333] In this conquest by morality, the part played by Aśoka's envoys is given thus in the Rock Edict XIII: "Even those to whom the envoys of Devānampriya do not go, having heard of the duties of morality, the ordinances, (and) the instruction in morality, of Devānampriya, are conforming to morality and will conform to it."[334]

What exactly was expected of the borderers is given in the Separate Rock Edict II of Dhauli thus:

> It might occur to my unconquered borderers (to ask): 'What does the king desire with reference to us?' (This) alone is my wish with reference to the borderers (*antānaṁ*), that they may learn that Devānampriya desires this, (that) they may not be afraid of me, but may have confidence in me; (that) they may obtain only happiness from me, not misery; (that) they may learn this, (that) the king will forgive them what can be forgiven; (that) they may (be induced) by me (to) practise morality; (and that) they may attain (happiness) both (in) this and (in) the other world.[335]

The above precepts, on which the conquest of morality was based, may be reduced to the following: pacification in regard to the wild tribes; forgiveness of their wild habits and crimes; instruction to be given to them in morality; and persuasion concerning the borderers and neighbouring kings. This is all that the Edicts contain regarding the conquest by morality the exact lines along which it was effected being left rather vague in the records.

(*b*) *Mr. Manohan on Dharmavijaya*

While commenting on the above, Mr. Manohan writes:

> As to the precise nature and effects of this 'conquest', we are left in the dark ; it is unfortunate that the Greek records are silent on the subject. From the edict we gather that 'conquest' was made through envoys (*dūta*). They were sent to the various countries to preach, not Buddhism, but 'dhamma', and in Aśoka's view, as we know, 'dhamma' was compatible with adherence to various creeds. We may infer that the envoys were politely received.[336]

Mr. Manohan is correct in doubting about the nature and effects of the conquest of *dharma*. But the conquest was effected not only through the envoys, who were no doubt, sent to the neighbouring lands, but through the *mahāmātras, pradesikas, anta-mahāmātras,* (i.e. those in charge of the border areas), and *dharma-mahāmātras.*[337] Moreover, the Edicts are clear as to the principles on which the *dharmavijaya* was based, and the officers who were entrusted with the duty of executing them. The Pillar Edict VII at Dhauli gives us an idea as to what the officers did in this matter. The *lajūkas* were ordered "In such and such a manner" to exhort the people who were devoted to morality ; pillars of morality were set up ; the *mahāmātras* of morality were appointed ; and proclamations of morality were issued.[338]

There seems to be no doubt that the sum of moral values which Aśoka had in mind were inculcated in the minds of the forest people as well in the lands of the neighbouring and foreign kings in a manner to suggest that he was more concerned with their acquiescence in the principle of morality than in recognizing him as their political suzerain. Even here one cannot help suspecting that the Emperor was not entirely in a conciliatory mood when dealing with the forest tribes. The Rock Edict XIII cited above amply proves this, for it says that "they (the inhabitants of the forests within his dominions) are told of the power (to punish them) which Devānampriya (possesses) inspite of (his) repentance, in order that they may be ashamed (of their crimes) and may not be killed" (*anutape pi ca prabhave Devānaṁpriyasa vucati teṣa kiti avatrapeyu na ca haṁñeyasu*).[339] In the above there is a latent threat to the use of force against the forest people, in case they persisted in their evil ways, which has to be taken into account when we consider the measures which he took to promulgate the principles of his *dharmavijaya.* That is, in addition to the positive means of inculcating them, he held in reserve the use of *daṇḍa* by which the wild tribes could be brought to reason. We cannot help feeling that, inspite of his being a confirmed pacifist, Aśoka had not altogether abjured the essence of the Kauṭilyan theory, viz., a belief in the efficacy of punishment.

(c) Professor Dikshitar on Dharmavijaya

While rejecting Mr. Manohan's view cited above, and what Professor Dikshitar calls "the old interpretation of *dhammavijaya*" (by which, we suppose, he meant that advocated by Professor Hultzsch), the learned historian writes thus: :

> What Aśoka aimed at was not to make known to the conquered States, as well as to neighbouring States through ambassadors or special messengers (*dūtas*) that the king had given up *lobhavijaya* and *āsuravijaya* in which he had indulged in the early part of his rule, and had taken his stand at the pedestal of *dharmavijaya.* In other words, the emperor informed his subjects and the kings of other States that he would be satisfied with mere obeisance from them and that he expected them at the same time to follow the *śāstric* (*śāstrānugama śāstritaṁ*) injunctions without recourse to any rebellion or war. Any other meaning will have no legs to stand on.

Professor Dikshitar then proceeds to say that the above "forms an unimpeachable evidence to demolish the theory that Aśoka was a Buddhist".[340]

We are not concerned so much with the conclusion of Professor Dikshitar relating to the religion which Aśoka professed, as with his earlier statement that the Emperor had made it clear to the conquered States as well as to the neighbouring kings that he would be satisfied with mere obeisance from them, and that he expected them to follow the *śāstric* injunctions without having recourse to war or rebellion. While Professor Dikshitar is right in assuming that Aśoka wished to make it clear to his people as well as to the neighbouring kings that he had given up war and conquest—that is, in the language of the *Arthaśāstra,* that he had eschewed *lobhavijaya* and *āsuravijaya*—he does not seem to be correct when he maintains that that monarch wanted mere obeisance and an assurance from his subjects as well as from the neighbouring kings that both would follow the *śāstric* injunctions. There was no need for Aśoka to seek any assurance from his own subjects about their allegiance: it was taken for granted that they owed unqualified allegiance to him. As regards the kings of other States, the assumption of Professor Dikshitar is untenable. There is nothing in the Rock Edicts to suggest that the Emperor had in his mind the question of the allegiance of the neighbouring rulers: all that he was concerned with was that they might conform to his high ideal of moral virtues and practise them.

A careful examination of the Edicts reveals that there were two types of borderers: one comprising tribes within Aśoka's Empire (*iha-rāja-viśaye*), like the Yonas, who were associated with the Kāmbhojas and Gāndhāras, and who were quite distinct from the Yona kings of distant lands to whom also the Emperor had sent his emissaries ;[341] and the other composed of the forest tribes whom we have mentioned just above. In the case of all excepting the forest tribes, the method used was one of persuasion ; while in the case of the wild tribes it was coloured with a tinge of admonition. But as regards the neighbouring and distant rulers, as we have shown elsewhere, Aśoka's message of morality was more recommendatory than persuasive, since the distant Western rulers were already aware of some of the main principles underlying Aśoka's concept of *dharma*.[342] To assume therefore, along with Professor Dikshitar that the Mauryan Emperor in extending the influence of the latter's *dharmavijaya*, also wished to secure the obeisance of the rulers of the other States, would be to violate the facts as given in the Edicts.[343]

(*d*) *Conclusion*

Emperor Aśoka's concept came nearest to that of the *dharmavijayī* described in the *Arthaśāstra*, when, firstly, he publicly proclaimed that he had given up war ; and secondly, when he insisted, not on his conquered subjects' (who, excepting in the case of the people of Kalinga, were nil) doing obeisance to him, which as a matter of necessity they had to perform, but, when, in addition to it, they conformed to his principles of morality, and lived up to them. In other words, Aśoka completed the concept of a *dharmavijayī* as given in the *Arthaśāstra* by laying down rules as to what his conquered subjects were to do after they had done him obeisance. It is only in this manner that we can interpret the concept of *dharmavijaya*, as given in the Edicts, with that described in the *Arthaśāstra*, in relation to the end of the State.

3. SOCIAL GOOD IN ASOKA AND KAUTILYA

Turning to the other great end of the State, social good, let us see how far the concept of Aśoka approached that of Kauṭilya. This aspect of the question may be studied from the following points of view: protection, medical relief, *samāja*, aid to the destitute, and *ahiṁsā*. Since enough has been already said about the last point, we shall restrict ourselves to the other four main ideas underlying Aśoka's concept of social good.

(*a*) *Protection*

The maintenance of *dharma* which Aśoka had made the cardinal principle of his government was one of the duties of the State, while the other was that which guaranteed protection to all the subjects.[344] We have seen in the earlier pages of this book the importance of the theory of protection in the works of Manu and Kauṭilya. Aśoka's theory of protection was modelled on that of the ancient Hindus. Dr. Hultzsch in this connection wrote thus: "As a pious Hindu he acknowledged the debt (*ṛiṇa*) which every king owes to his subjects in return for the revenue (*ṣaḍbhāga*) levied from them, and which consists in affording them protection (*pālana*)."[345] This is clear from the Rock Edict VI which states the following: "And whatever effort I am making (is made) in order that I may discharge the debt (which I owe) to living beings, (that) I may make them happy in this (world), and (that) they may attain heaven in the other (world)."[346]

In the same Rock Edict the Emperor clarifies his theory of protection in these words: "For I consider it my duty (to promote) the welfare of all men." And in the Separate Rock Edict I at Jaugaḍha, he proclaims the following: "All men are my children. As on behalf of (my own) children I desire that they may be provided by me with complete welfare and happiness in this world and in the other world, even so is my desire on behalf of all men." That there was no ambiguity in his mind is proved by the fact that he directed the *dharma-mahāmātras* to busy themselves with all sections—the Brahmans, the Ibhyas (or Vaiśyas), the ascetics, the householders, the Buddhist clergy, the Ājivikas, the Nirgranthas (or Jainas), and the other sects, so that there might be concord (*samavāya*) among all of them.[347]

Without entering again into the theory of protection concerning which enough has been said in the earlier pages of this work, it may merely be noted that Kauṭilya had already laid down the broad policy of protecting all castes, and of looking at the general prosperity of the whole society in the following ordinance, which we may be permitted to repeat: "Hence the king shall never allow people to swerve from their duties; for whoever upholds his own duty, ever adhering to the customs of the Āryas, and following the rules of caste and the divisions of religious life, will surely be happy here and hereafter."[348] That Kauṭilya was not an advocate of orthodoxy of any type is proved by the statement which we may, again, repeat, viz., that "the king bent on doing good to all the people (*sarva bhūta hite rataḥ*) will enjoy the earth unopposed."[349]

(*b*) *Social Good*

If the State wished to realize the above end, it could not but move in the direction of social good. The welfare of all the sections of the people (*yogakṣema*), which the Edicts mention as one of the great objectives of Aśoka, was precisely the *hitasukhaṁ* of Kauṭilya which we have described above.[350] Social good was attained by Aśoka through six means the first of which was by insisting on a proper treatment of all sections of people—relations, friends, acquaintances, dependants, and slaves.[351] The injunctions of Kauṭilya in regard to the impartiality of the judges to all classes of people, and of the king to all his subjects, may be recalled in this connection, as also Emperor Aśoka's insistence on the impartiality of his judges to all sections of the people.

The second method which aimed at social welfare was the one concerning benevolent works constructed for the good of all. These consisted of planting banyan trees on the road sides, raising mango groves, digging up wells at a distance of eight *kos*, with steps for descending into the water, and numerous drinking places.[352] Aśoka seems to have had in mind the earlier injunction of Kauṭilya in regard to the construction of places for drinking water, and groves, although he had undoubtedly improved upon them. Kauṭilya had stated that the king should construct, among other things, roads, reservoirs (*setu*) filled with water, and groves,[353] but he did not lay down the exact distance at which the wells were to be constructed.

The third method by which social welfare was achieved by Aśoka refers to medicinal plants. We have discussed elsewhere the significance of the exact plant which, along with others, was imported by Aśoka.[354] Here, too, Aśoka extended Kauṭilya's injunction which said that certain specified commodities were exempted from paying toll. Among these were those intended for presentation, or taken for the purpose of sacrificial performance, confinement of women, worship of gods,[355] etc. Medicines were subject to tolls ranging from one-twentieth to one-twentififth (of their cost price?).[356] Emperor Aśoka not only accepted the principle of Kauṭilya of exempting certain necessities like medicines from tolls but went a step further in importing medicinal plants from the distant lands of the Mediteranean Sea, obviously with the view of naturalizing them in the country. Truly did the great Emperor confer one of the greatest boons on suffering humanity by this benevolent measure of his which is only hinted at in the regulations of Kauṭilya.

The fourth method by which Aśoka added to social good was by declaring certain items as either good or harmful to society. In the Rock Edict I he differentiates between festivities which were permissible and those which were prohibited without naming them. "And no festival meeting (*samāja*) must be held. For king Devānampriya Priyadarśin sees much evil in festival meetings."[357] The *samāja* referred to here is to be traced to the first kind which comprised occasions of festivals, fairs, and pilgrimages, when the right of manufacturing liquor for four days was permitted (*utsava-samājā-yātrāsu-caturaḥ-sauriko deyaḥ*). On these occasions, according to the commentator of the *Arthaśāstra*, there was "Liberty to drink liquor without limit".[358] These were evidently the objectionable *samājas* referred to in the Edicts. As regards the other type of *samājas*, we find them mentioned by Kauṭilya in connection with the work of a conqueror in the territory subjugated by him. "He should follow the people in their faith with which they celebrate their national, religious, and congregational festivals or amusements" (*deśa-daivata-samājotsava-vihāreṣu ca bhaktiṁ-anuvarteta*).[359]

The fifth method by which social good was secured by Aśoka was by giving State aid, through the *dharma-mahāmātras*, to the destitute and the aged (*anathesu vudhesu*).[360] We have already seen above that, according to Kauṭilya, it was the duty of the king to provide the orphans, the aged, the infirm, the afflicted, and the helpless with maintenance (*bāla-vṛidaha-*

vyādhita-vyasani-anāthān-ca rājā vibhṛiyāt). Aśoka's relief measures were on lines already prescribed by Kauṭilya.

In regard to the sixth method which consisted in the observance of non-injury to living animals, or *ahiṁsā*, as we might call it in the modern days, it has already been seen above that Aśoka only followed and extended the policy laid down by Kauṭilya. The cursory comparative study of the principles promulgated in the *Arthaśāstra* of Kauṭilya and of the practice as described in the Edicts of Aśoka, only proves one of the major subjects that has been discussed in the previous pages of this work, namely, that the great Mauryan Prime Minister was a realist, whose one great object was the concentration of all power in the State with a view to achieving the maximum of social good.

NOTES

PART ONE

INTRODUCTORY

1. Manu, *The Laws,* II. 10-11, p. 31 (Georg Bühler's trans. in the *Sacred Books of the East,* Vol. XXV, Oxford, 1886) ; Jones, Henry, *The Institutes of Hindu Law* or *The Ordinances of Menu,* II. 10-11, p. 21 (Calcutta, 1799).
2. Keith, A. B., *A History of Sanskrit Literature,* pp. 498-99 (Oxford, 1928).
3. Toynbee, Arnold, *A Study of History,* I. pp. 43-44 (Oxford, 1948, 4th impression).
4. Aiyangar, Rangaswamy, K. V., *Some Aspects of Ancient Indian Polity,* p. 62 (Madras, 1935, 2nd ed.).
5. Professor K. V. Rangaswamy Aiyangar is an advocate of the view that Manu came after Kauṭilya (Read Aiyangar, *ibid.,* pp. 27-34). After a detailed study of the resemblances and differences between Manu and Kauṭilya, he came to the following conclusion: "They (the resemblances and differences) tend to show that, as regards the date of composition, so far as it may be judged from their subject-matter, the *Mānavadharma Śāstra, in its present form,* belongs to a much later age than the *Arthaśāstra* and stands between it and the *Śukranītisāra*" (Aiyangar, *ibid.,* p. 34). I do not think this view is tenable, although it has been upheld by other scholars as well. In the present work I have accepted the common view that Manu preceded Kauṭilya—a fact which is amply borne out by the frequent references to Manu himself in the *Arthaśāstra.*
6. Macdonell, A. A., and Keith, A. B., *Vedic Index of Names and Subjects,* II. p. 129 (Delhi reprint, 1958).
7. Ghoshal, U. N., *The Beginnings of Indian Historiography and Other Essays,* p. 123 (Calcutta, 1944). See *ibid.,* page, n. (2) for the reference to *Kāṭhaka Saṁhita,* the *Taittirīya Brāhmaṇa,* and the *Śatapatha Brāhmaṇa.*
8. *Manu,* II. 7, p. 30 (Bühler) ; II. 8, p. 21 (Jones).
9. *Ibid.,* I. 2, p. 1 (Bühler) ; I 2, p. 9 (Jones).
10. Macdonell, A. A., *Sanskrit Literature,* p. 62 (London, 1925). Mahamahopadhyaya Dr. P. V. Kane has ably discussed the question of the dates of Manu and other ancient lawgivers (P. V. Kane, *The History of the Dharmaśāstras,* I. pp. 135-58 ; 168-90. Poona, 1930). Professor Bühler assigned Manu to a period ranging from the beginning of the second century B.C. to the second century A.D. (Bühler, *Manu, op. cit.,* Intr. pp. cxiv-cxvii). Dr. Kane and Professor Aiyangar seem to agree to this view (Aiyangar, *op. cit.,* p. 26, n. 46). Dr. A. C. Burnell's earlier view that the *Manusmṛiti* was composed in the Deccan in about A.D. 500 (Burnell, A. C. in his Introduction, p. xxvii to his translation of Manu's *Code,* edited by E. W. Hopkins (1891) is rightly rejected by Professor Aiyangar as being unacceptable (Aiyangar, *ibid.,* p. 26, n. 42).
11. Macdonell, *Skt. Lit.,* p. 102. In the Vedic age the name Bṛihaspati was given to a god (Macdonell-Keith, *Vedic Index,* II, p. 72). But it was also borne by men, as is proved by the name Bṛihaspatigupta Śayasthi, who is mentioned in the *Vaṁśa Brāhmaṇa* (II. 7, 1, 2) as the pupil of Bhavatrāta Śayasthi (*Vedic Index,* II. p. 72). Bṛihaspatigupta's pupil, we may note by the way, was Su-pratīta Auluṇḍya, himself a teacher, as mentioned in the same *Vaṁśa Brāhmaṇa* (*Vedic Index,* II, p. 456).
12. Keith, *ibid.,* pp. 451-52.

13. Bühler, *op. cit.*, p. cxviii ; Jolly, *Hindu Law and Custom*, pp. 33, 44, 48, 56 (Eng. trans., 1928) ; Kane, *op. cit.*, I. pp. 123, 126, 207-13.
14. Macdonell, *Skt. Lit.*, p. 429.
15. Kane, *ibid.*, I. pp. 190-96.
16. *Vedic Index*, I. pp. 87-88. On Śvataketu, read *ibid.*, I. pp. 88, 89 ; II. 89, 409, 410. On the earlier teacher Yājñalkya, read *ibid.*, I. pp. 72, 88, 117, 397, 479, 484 ; II, pp. 87, 90, 102, etc. Read also Macdonell, *ibid.*, p. 214 ; Ghoshal, *op. cit.*, pp. 31-32, 40-49.
17. Macdonell, *ibid.*, p. 429 ; Aiyangar, *op. cit.*, pp. 26, and *ibid.*, n. (42) ; 34-37 ; Kane, *ibid.*, I. pp. 168, 190. Read Kane, *ibid.*, I. p. ix where Dr. Kane has rejected Dr. R. G. Bhandarkar's date of Yājñavalkya,—not earlier than the sixth century A.D.—(*Vaiṣnavism and Śaivism*, p. 148) as being too late. On the complicated question of the dates of Manu and other lawgivers, as given by Dr. Meyer, read the discussion by Professor Keith (*Skt. Lit.*, Preface, pp. xix-xx) which is as vague as it is cursory.
18. The literature on Kauṭilya is legion. A good summary of the views of scholars, who have maintained that Kauṭilya was of a later date, is given by Professor Aiyangar (*ibid.*, pp. 149-64) who has adequately disproved their objections. Dr. Narendra Nath Law's learned study in this connection is of particular significance, since he has successfully refuted professor Winternitz's arguments for a late date for Kauṭilya. Read Law, N. N., *Studies in Indian History & Culture*, pp. 209-66 (London, 1925). I follow Dr. Shama Sastry's date (fourth century B.C.), which Professor Aiyangar also adopts, for Kauṭilya. Read Sastry, Shama, *Arthaśāstra*, Preface, p. vii ff. (Mysore, 1929, 3rd ed.). Dr. Keith's arguments for placing Kauṭilya before A.D. 300 (Keith, *The Age of the Arthaśāstra* in the *Dr. B. C. Law Commemoration Volume I*, pp. 477-95, Calcutta, 1945) do not seem to be convincing. The reader may also refer to my *India's Diplomatic Relations with the West*, p. 27, and note (47) on p. 325, (Bombay 1959) in this connection.
19. Macdonell, *ibid.*, p. 260.
20. Aiyangar, *ibid.*, p. 83.
21. Dr. Keith citing Professor Meyer in the former's *Skt. Lit.*, Preface, xviii, xix, and n. (3) ; Bata Krishna Ghosh, *Indian Historical Quarterly*, III. pp. 607-11 ; Keith, *ibid.*, p. xix, n. (4).
22. Aiyangar, *ibid.*, p. 83. On the earlier Vasiṣṭha, read Macdonell, *op. cit.*, p. 155.
23. Keith, *ibid.*, Preface, p. xix.
24. Jolly in S. B. E. (Oxford, 1880) cited by Macdonell, *ibid.*, p. 428.
25. Aiyangar, *ibid.*, p. 89. Dr. Keith does not seem to refer to Viṣṇu.
26. Macdonell, *ibid.*, p. 429 ; Aiyangar, *ibid.*, p. 75.
27. See, for instance, Kane, *op. cit.*, III. pp. 3, 9, 17, 23, ff.
28. Macdonell, *ibid.*, p. 435 ; Keith, *ibid.*, p. 75.
29. Professor Keith assigned him to about A.D. 700 (*Skt. Lit.*, p. 463). Professor Aiyangar states that the age of Kāmandaka ranges from the first century A.D. to the sixth century A.D. (Aiyangar, *ibid.*, p. 14. and note, 23, where a reference is given to Professor Hermann Jacobi, who assigned that ancient teacher to the third century at the latest. Jacobi, H., *Indian Antiquary* for 1918, p. 159.) See Aiyangar, *ibid.*, p. 26 for the views of Dr. Kane and Dr. Ganapati Sastri.
30. Bhandarkar, R. G., *Early History of the Deccan*, p. 207. On the Rāṣṭrakūta Kṛṣṇa's dates, read Rice, Lewis, *Mysore and Coorg from the Inscriptions*, p. 67 (London, 1909).
31. Aiyangar, *ibid.*, pp. 10, 16 where Somadeva is rightly assigned to *circa* A.D. 959. Professor Keith comments on Somadeva's work *Nītivākyāmṛita* but does not enlighten us on his date (Keith, *op. cit.*, pp. 463-64).
32. Zimmer, H., *Altindischen Leben*, p. 180 (Berlin, 1879).

33. As, for instance, with Rudolph von Jhering, *The Evolution of the Aryan*, p. 50 (Translation by A. Drucker, London, 1897).
34. On Ṛta, read *Rig Veda*, I. 123. 9 ; IV. 7. 7 ; VII. 36. 5 ; X. 124. 3 ; see also *Vedic Index*, I. p. 399.
35. Zimmer, *op. cit.*, p. 181.
36. Ājīgarti after having been bought by Rohita, the son of Hariscandra, was actually tied to three stakes before being released through Rohita's supplications. On *drupada*, read *Rig Veda*, I. 24, 13 ; IV. 32. 23. On Śunaḥśepa, whose story is given in the *Aitareya Brāhmaṇa* (VII. 13-18), and in the *Śāṅkhāyana Śrauta Sūtra* (XV. 20. 1 ff ; XVI. 11. 2) ; *Rig Veda*, I. 24 ff ; V. 2. 7. See also *Vedic Index*, I, p. 384 ; II. p. 385.
37. Jhering, *ibid.*, pp. 51-54.
38. Winternitz, M., "Kautilīya Arthaśāstra" in the *Calcutta Review* for April, 1924, (*op. cit.*), p. 23.
39. *Vedic Index*, I. pp. 390-98. In a later context, Professor Macdonell writes that the word *dhāman* occurring in the *Rig Veda* in the sense of "house", or its intimates, (*Rig Veda*, I. 144, I ; II. 3. 2, etc. ; *Atharva Veda*, IV. 25. 7, etc.), is also found in the sense of "ordinance", or law, expressing much the same as *dharman* (*Vedic Index*, I. p. 399).
40. Macdonell, *Skt. Lit.*, p. 37.
41. Keith, *Skt. Lit.*, pp. 92, 450, 451, 455, 467.
42. Keith, *ibid.*, p. 451.
43. Kielhorn, F., *Epigraphia Indica*, IX. p. 113, n. (7).
44. Kane, *op. cit.*, I. p. 1.
45. Aiyangar, *op. cit.*, pp. 39, 54, 89-90.
46. Read Aiyangar, *ibid.*, p. 89, and *ibid.*, p. n (159) where the citation from Vijñāneśvara is given.
47. Aiyangar, *ibid.*, p. 101. Cf. Dr. Kane, who writes that the term *dharma*, according to the ancient texts, meant religious merit, religious ordinances, or rites, fixed principles or rules of conduct, the peculiar duties of the *āśramas* (or the orders), privileges and duties, and instruction in the *dharmas* of all the *varṇas* and *āśramas* (Kane, *ibid.*, I. pp. 1-3). In the light of the discussion I have made in these pages, the elucidation of the term *dharma* by Professor Dr. H. N. Sinha, (*Sovereignty in Ancient Indian Polity*, pp. 27-30, 326, and *passim*, London, 1938) does not appear to be adequate. On p. 27 the learned author writes thus: "Now Dharma may bear the interpretation of customs and usage, both sacred and secular in society." He then merely refers to the verses in the *Rig Veda* citing their numbers but not mentioning them in detail, in which *dharma* is used in the sense of custom, moral laws, duties in general, and "of duties or what is right". But after this and other discussions, Professor Sinha writes that *dharma* was public law! (*ibid.*, p. 326). Evidently the learned historian is not sure as to what exactly was connoted by the term *dharma*.
48. Aiyangar, *ibid.*, pp. 79-80.
49. Read *Manu*, I. 2, and II, III, VI, and IX ; on the *anuloma* and *pratiloma* castes, read *ibid.*, X. Cf. *Kauṭilya*, as regards the mixed castes, Bk. III. Ch. VII., p. 184 ff. That these regulations were meant for all subjects is proved by the following injunction of Kauṭilya: "The king who guides his subjects in accordance with the above rules will attain to heaven ; otherwise he will fall into the hell" (*ibid.*, p. 188). Cf. *Yājñavalkya*, I. 1. Read also Kane, *op. cit.*, I. p. 3.
50. In the earliest days, as is related in the *Manusmṛiti*, the political jurisdiction of the rulers seems to have been limited to the region called Brahmāvarta lying between the Sarasvatī and the Dṛṣadvatī ; to the region called Brahmarṣī which comprised Kurukṣetra, Maṭsya, Pāñcala, or Kānyakubja, and Sūrasena or Mathurā ; to the Madhyadeśa which lay between the Himālayas and the Vindhyas ; that is,

to Āryāvarta in general which was the land bounded by the eastern and western oceans, and lying between the Himālayas and the Vindhyas; and to the land inhabited by the Mlechchhas (*Manu*, II. 17-23, pp. 32-33). But in the days of Kauṭilya (fourth century B.C.) the boundaries of the Mauryan Empire had exceeded those limits. Neither Manu nor Kauṭilya mentions the southern and western regions which with the gradual widening of the political and cultural horizons, came to be included under the general designation of Bharatavarṣa. I do not wish to cite the eprigraphic evidence in this connection.

51. Aiyangar, *op. cit.*, p. 54.
52. Professor Aiyangar admits this when he writes thus, while discussing the difference between the *dharmaśāstras* and the *nītiśāstras*: "Rules of law and conduct on the other hand, like those contained in a *Dharmasūtra*, are of interest to all *classes* of men equally. . ." (Aiyangar, *ibid.*, pp. 18-19). Professor Keith was correct when, as remarked above, he included "righteous conduct" as one of the components of *dharma*.
53. Read Kane, *op. cit.*, III. pp. 4-5 for the various meanings of the science of government.
54. *Vedic Index*, I. p. 337, n. (2) where full references are given to the different meanings of the term in the *Rig Veda, Atharva Veda*, the *Aitareya Brāhmana*, and the *Śatapatha Brāhmaṇa*.
55. Winternitz, *Calcutta Review*, *op. cit.*, for a full account of this eminent German Indologist's view on the subject. See also Law, N.N., *op. cit.*, pp. 256-57.
56. Kane, *ibid.*, I. pp. 9, 87.
57. Law, *ibid.*, pp. 257-58. The term *sūtra* means books of rules for the guidance of sacrificers, etc. Read *Vedic Index*, II, p. 463. The *sūtras* were treatises which were compiled "solely to meet practical needs" (Macdonell, *Skt. Lit.*, p. 244).
58. On the *sūtra* literature read Macdonell, *ibid.*, pp. 244-63. On page 263, *ibid.*, the reader will find evidence of the prejudiced mind of Professor Macdonell, who wrote that the *sūtra* literature "was entirely the conscious work of an idle priesthood, invented to enslave and maintain in spiritual servitude the minds of the Hindu people". This is an instance of inherent prejudice persisting inspite of deep learning!
59. An objection may be raised here by saying that the *Baudhāyana Dharma Sūtra* deals also with the duties of kings and with criminal justice. But, as Professor Macdonell states, this work is of southern India (Macdonell, *ibid.*, pp. 259-260), and cannot be taken to be typical of all *dharmasūtras*.
60. Kane, *ibid.*, I. pp. 8, 9.
61. Eggeling, J., *Śatapatha Brāhmana*, I. Intr. p. xxiii (S.B.E. Vol. XII. Oxford, 1882).
62. Keith, *op. cit.*, p. 451.
63. *Kauṭilya*, Bk. I. Ch. I. 6, p. 5. This is confirmed by Daṇḍin, *Daśakumāracaritra*, Uchchh. VIII, p. 137 (M. R. Kale's trans. 3rd ed. revised. Bombay, 1926).
64. Kane, *ibid.*, I. p. 246. See *ibid.*, p. 8 where Dr. Kane would date the extant works on the *dharmasūtras* of Gautama, Baudhāyana, and Āpastamba to the period from 600 to 300 B.C.
65. *Manu*, VII. 14, p. 218.
66. Dr. Kane has given enough evidence to show that the *Arthaśāstra* was called *dṛṣṭārtha smṛiti* (Kane, *ibid.*, III. pp. 7, 840) which would seem to imply that that body of knowledge could not lay pretentions to equality with the *smṛitis* proper, at least in regard to their nature and importance. In a later context, the same authority mentions the *arthaśāstras* as a branch of the *upavedas*; while, in the same connection, he would, following the Vedic *śiṣṭas*, classify the *daṇḍanīti* apart from the *upavedas* but under the fourteen or eighteen *vidyās* (Kane, *ibid.*, III. p. 843, and note, 1638). Dr. Law differentiates between the *daṇḍanīti* and the *arthaśāstras* by saying that the former refers to polity, and is a part and parcel

of the *arthaśāstra*, both referring to the ideal of the State (Law, *op. cit.*, p. 258). The learned author, I am afraid, is not quite clear here.

67. Aiyangar, *op. cit.*, pp. 53-54.
68. Aiyangar, *ibid.*, p. 52.
69. Keith, *op. cit.*, p. 451.
70. Keith, *ibid.*, p. 243.
71. Keith, *ibid.*, p. 451, *op. cit.*
72. Keith, *ibid.*, p. 450.
73. Keith, *ibid.*, p. 451, *op. cit.*
74. Keith, *ibid.*, p. 405.
75. Macdonell, *op. cit.*, p. 29.
76. Macdonell, *ibid.*, p. 35.
77. *Manu*, II. 6, 7, 12, pp. 30-31.
78. *Manu*, VII 43, p. 222.
79. *Manu*, VII 18, p. 219. Mr. Jones gave a slightly different version of this passage: "Punishment governs all mankind ; punishment alone preserves them ; punishment wakes, while their guards are asleep ; the wise consider punishment as the perfection of justice" (Jones, *op. cit.*, p. 123).
80. *Kauṭilya*, Bk. I. Ch. II, 7, p. 6 ; Shama Sastry, *ibid.*, text, p. 6 (Mysore, 1924).
81. *Kauṭilya*, Bk. III. Ch. I. 150, p. 171 ; text, p. 150. See also Aiyangar, *ibid.*, p. 54, and note (100).
82. *Yājñavalkya*, II. 21 cited by Kane, *op. cit.* I. pp. 87, 179 ; see also Aiyangar, *ibid.*, p. 179.
83. Eggeling, *op. cit.*, V. 4. 4. 7. p. 108 (Oxford, 1894).
84. Macdonell, *ibid.*, pp. 31, 32.
85. Macdonell, *ibid.*, p. 212.
86. Macdonell, *ibid.*, p. 217. See *ibid.*, p. 203 where Professor Macdonell states that it is posterior to the *Jaiminīya Brāhmaṇa* (which, according to him, was the oldest), the *Kauśītakī Brāhmaṇa*, and the *Aitareya Brāhmaṇa*. The latest of all the *Brāhmaṇas* was the *Gopatha Brāhmaṇa* of the *Atharva Veda* and the *Short Brāhmaṇas* of the *Sāma Veda*.
87. Macdonell, *ibid.*, p. 202.
88. *Mahābhārata*, XII. 59. 28 ff ; Keith, *op. cit.*, p. 451.
89. *Kauṭilya*, Bk. I, Ch. I. p. 1.
90. Macdonell, *ibid.*, p. 34. See *ibid.*, p. 263 for the one-sided and ill-considered view of the same Indologist on the authors of the *sūtras*.
91. *Bṛihadāraṇyaka Upaniṣad*, I. 4. 11-12 cited by Professor Aiyangar, *op. cit.*, p. 105, and note (188).
92. On Pindar's concept of law as the order of the universe, read Sir T. E. Holland, *Jurisprudence*, p. 19 (London, 1880), cited by Professor Aiyangar, *ibid.*, p. 106, and note (189). Professor Aiyangar states that the idea of *dharma* was the same as that of Pindar. I beg to differ from him.
93. Read Aiyangar, *ibid.*, pp. 52, 53 where the learned Professor rightly rejects the erroneous ideas of Sir Henry Maine.

PART TWO

THE MAIN SCHOOLS OF POLITICAL THOUGHT

1. Macdonell, *op. cit.*, p. 211 ; *Vedic Index*, II, pp. 88, 236 for further references. Professor Max Müller had already given complete lists of these teachers in his *History of Ancient Sanskrit Literature*, p. 438 ff.
2. Eggeling, *op. cit.*, I. Intr. pp. xxxi-xxxiii, and note (1) on p. xxxiii.
3. *Kauṭilya*, Bk. I. Ch. I, 1 ; Bk. XV. Ch. I. 427, pp. 1, 459 ; text, pp. 1, 427.
4. *Kauṭilya*, pp. 17, 71.
5. Professor Aiyangar correctly estimated the schools as eighteen excluding that of Kauṭilya himself (Aiyangar, *op. cit.*, pp. 50, 51, and note (52). He would identify Bharadvāja with Kaṇika (Kaṇiṅka) Bharadvāja. According to Dr. Kane's calculation, there were only five schools and seven individual teachers. Kane, *op. cit.*, I. p. 99 ; III. p. 2.

5a. Cf. Kane, *ibid.*, III. p. 2.

6. *Mahābhārata, Anuśāsanaparvan*, Ch. 39, 8 ; *Śantiparvan*, Ch. 58, 1-3 ; 31-32, 102, cited by Dr. Kane, *ibid.*, III. p. 2, and *ibid.* n. (1). In the *Śrīmat Bhāgavata*, Kāvya is the name of Śukrācarya. *Bhāgavata Purāṇa*, Bk. VII. 5. p. 31 (Gorakhpur, 1955).
7. *Mahābhārata, Śantiparvan*, Ch. 22, 59, cited by Keith, *op. cit.*, p. 451, *op. cit.*
8. In a later work called *Nītiprakāśa*, ascribed to one Vaiśampāyana, the following authors on Polity are mentioned—Brahma, Rudra, Subrahmaṇya, Indra, Manu, Bṛihaspati, Śukra, Bharadvāja, Gauraśiras, and Vyāsa (Aiyangar, *ibid.*, p. 9, and note 11). If this work is the same as the *Nītiprakāśa* noticed by Professor Keith (*Skt. Lit.*, p. 464), it seems to have been a work of a later date which "is of no value whatever as evidence for early Indian usage or philosophy" (Keith, *ibid.*). Daṇḍin in the *Daśakumāracaritra*, mentions the following authors on the *śāstras* and on practical government: Śukra, Āngīrasa, Viśāla, Akṣabāhu, Dantiputra, Parāśara, and others (Daṇḍin, *ibid.*, Uchch. VIII. p. 139). In this connection I may add that Kauṭilya performs obeisance to Śukra and Bṛihaspati at the beginning of his work (p. 1). Since Śukra mentioned here, who is not to be confounded with his namesake of a later date, and who was the author of a *Nītisāra* (cf. Keith, *ibid.*, p. 464), is not explicitly stated by Kauṭilya as being the exponent of a school of Politics, I have not included the earlier Śukra in the general list of authors on the *arthaśāstras*. If he is to be included, the total number of ancient authors would be at least twenty-five.
9. *Vedic Index*, I. p. 534.
10. Professor Jolly cited in Aiyangar, *op. cit.*, p. 153. See also Law, *op. cit.*, pp. 226-27. On Bharadvājīputra, read *Vedic Index*, I. p. 241 ; II. pp. 101, 102, 221, 502. See also Eggeling, *op. cit.*, I. Intr. pp. xxxiii, *op. cit.*
11. *Mahābhārata* cited in Keith, *Skt. Lit.* pp. 451, *op. cit.*, 457.
12. Jolly, J., and Schmidt, R. *Kauṭilīya Arthaśāstra*, I. Intr. pp. 69, 73, 74, 91 (Punjab Skt. Series, 1923) ; Aiyangar, *ibid.*, p. 50, note (96).
13. Ganapati Sastri, *Arthaśāstra*, Intr. q.v. (Trivandrum, 1924) ; cited in Law, *ibid.* pp. 227-28 where Keśavasvāmin is also cited. See also Aiyangar, *ibid.*, p. 123, see also Jolly, J. *Feitschrift für Indologie und Iranistrik*, 1927, pp. 216-21.
14. *Kauṭilya*, Bk. I. Ch. XIII. 23, p. 23 ; text, p. 22.

15. *Kauṭilya*, pp. 5, 28, 62, 199, 216.
16. *Śat. Brah.* I. pp. 216-18. See *ibid.*, p. 216, n. (1) for further versions of this celebrated legend as given by Professors Weber, Max Müller, and Muir. The legend of the Deluge is repeated in the *Mahābhārata, Vanaparvan*, 12747-12802. To assert, as Professor Jhering did, that the Indians borrowed this from the Babylonians (Jhering, *op. cit.*, p. 184) is preposterous. I do not wish to elaborate this detail here. It would require a separate dissertation by itself. Professor Macdonell seems to agree to its Semitic origin (*Skt. Lit.*, p. 216).
17. Manu of the legend procreated the human race through his own daughter Iḍā (*Śat. Brāh.* I. p. 219ff.). Just as Manu of the Deluge was not the same as Manu Vaivasvata, so also Manu Prajāpati was, it seems, not the same as Manu Vaivasvata. The *Śat. Brāh.* refers to the non-earthly nature of Manu Prajāpati (*Śat. Brāḥ.* III. p. 250 ; V. 460).
18. *Śat. Brāh.* V. p. 361.
19. It is not possible here to discuss the question of the age of the *Rig Veda*,—a subject on which there is a vast literature. Those who have assigned a later age to the *Rig Veda* than the one proposed above (e.g., Professor A. B. Keith, *Woolner Comm. Vol.*, pp. 137-56), have advanced the stereotyped arguments which are not convincing. I would rather agree with Professor Jacobi, who would assign the antiquity of the *Vedas* to the period between 4500 B.C. and 2500 B.C. (Jacobi, *Ind. Ant.* XXIII. p. 154). B. G. Tilak's *Orion*, etc., may also be consulted in this connection. See also R. Shama Sastry, *Drapsa—The Vedic Cycle of Eclipses*, Intr. pp. 2 ; 130. Jogesh Chandra Ray, *The Vedic Antiquity* (which, according to him, ranged from 6000 B.C. to 3000 B.C.) in *Indian Culture*. I. (1939) pp. 77 ff. Read also Winternitz, *History of Skt. Lit.*, I. pp. 304-05 where, on the basis of the clay tablets discovered by Hugo Winckler in Boghazköi in Asia Minor in 1907, and of the names like Mitra, Varuṇa, Indra, Professor Winternitz arrived at the date fourteenth century B.C. for the *Vedas*. The Mohenjo Daro finds afford ample scope to maintain the antiquity of the *Vedas*. But I desist from discussing this question here. On Manu's being considered as one of the heroes and priests in the *Rig Veda*, read Macdonell, *Skt. Lit.*, p. 108.
20. *Taitt. Sam.* III. 1, 9, 4-6 ; *Aitareya Brāhmaṇa* V. 14.
21. Nābhā-Nediṣṭa Mānava received the cows from the Āngīrasas, through his father's advice. Read *Vedic Index*. I, p. 442. His story may be read in conjunction with Śaryata Mānava, who was also called "a descendant of Manu" in the *Jaimīni Upaniṣad Brāhmaṇa* (*Vedic Index*, II. p. 365).
22. *Manu*, I. 36, p. 14.
23. *Manu*, *ibid.*, 60-63, p. 19.
24. *Manu*, *ibid.*, 102, p. 26.
25. Professor Bühler maintained that the internal evidence of the *Manusmriti* seems to point to an older legal literature of the nature of a *dharmasūtra* (Bühler, *Manu*, Intr. p. xxiii). This fact should also be borne in mind in our estimate of the antiquity of Manu, the lawgiver, although, it must be confessed, the precise age of the *dharmasūtras* themselves is still an unsettled question.
26. *Manu*, I. 83, p. 23. In a later context the following is stated in the same work: "A man who follows the conduct of the virtuous, has faith and is free from envy, lives a hundred years, though he be entirely destitute of auspicious marks" (*ibid.*, IV. 158, p. 153).
27. *Mahābhārata* cited in Keith, *Sk. Lit.*, pp. 450, 451, *op. cit.*
28. Keith, *Skt. Lit.*, pp. 438-39.
29. Kane, *op. cit.*, I. pp. 110-16.
30. On page 202 Professor Macdonell gives *circa* 800-500 B.C. as the date of the *Brāhmaṇas* ; but on page 217 he states that the "Internal evidence shows it to belong to a late period of the *Brāhmaṇa* age" (Macdonell, *ibid.*, pp. 202, 217).

30a. Fleet, J. F., *Journal of the Royal Asiatic Society*, 1911, p. 675 ; Smith, *The Early History of India*, p. 27, n. (1) (Oxford, 1914).
31. *Vedic Index*, I. pp. 131, 147, 189, 335, 519.
32. Macdonell, *op. cit.*, pp. 178, 191, 245, 267, 273, 274.
33. Macdonell, *ibid.*, p. 431 ; Bhandarkar, R. G. *Early History of the Deccan*, pp. 139, 140-41.
34. Kane, *op. cit.*, III. p. 1041.
35. Kane, *ibid.*, I, pp. 99, 117, 217-18.
36. Read Keith's pertinent remarks on the Vedic Indians' being given not only to reflection and religious practices but to practical life as well (Keith, *Skt. Lit.*, p. 450). But Professor Keith's views on Kauṭilya's *Arthaśāstra*, which will be cited below, cannot unfortunately be entertained.
37. Aiyangar, *op. cit.*, pp. 51-52. See also *ibid.*, pp. 58-61 in this connection.
38 & 39. Keith, *ibid.*, p. xviii.
40. I agree with the judgment of the late Professor V. R. Ramachandra Dikshitar, who wrote on this point thus: "Though the *Arthaśāstra* was for the time being intended for Candragupta, it was a text book on Polity for all time, and for all kings, and for all places" (Dikshitar, V. R. R., *The Mauryan Polity*, p. 334. Madras, 1932).
41. Dr. R. Shama Sastry translated the passage thus: "In the interest of kings" (*Kauṭilya*, p. 75). But Professor Rangaswami Aiyangar rightly interpreted the same as "in the interest of Narendra", i.e. king of men (Aiyangar, *ibid.*, pp. 39, 42, n. (73), 79 (n. 135). The reference in Professor Aiyangar's book is evidently to Dr. Ganapati Sastri's *Arthaśāstra*, (Trivandrum). Dr. Kane is also of the same opinion as that of Professor Aiyangar, that is, that Kauṭilya wrote his work for the sake of the king (Kane *ibid.*, I. p. 88, and notes 161 and 162).
42. Read my *India's Relations with the West*, pp. 82 ff. (Bombay, 1958) for an account of Alexander the Great's relations with the Indian tribes.
43. *Kauṭilya*, Bk. XV. Ch. I. 431, p. 463 ; text, p. 431.
44. *Kauṭilya*, Bk. I. 1, p. 1 ; text, p. 1 ; Bk. XV. Ch. I. 427, p. 459 ; text, p. 427.
45. *Ibid.*, Bk. XV, Ch. I. 431, p. 463 ; text p. 431 (*evaṁ śāstram-idaṁ yuktaṁ etābhiḥ-tantrayuktibhiḥ avāptau pālane ca-uktaṃ lokasya-asya parasya ca dharmam-arthaṁ ca kāmaṁ ca pravartayati pāti ca adharma-anartha-avidveṣāni-idaṁ śāstraṁ nihanti ca*).
46. *Ibid.*, Bk. XV. Ch. I. 427, p. 459 ; text, p. 426.
47. Cf. Aiyangar, *op. cit.*, p. 53.
48. Read the pertinent remarks of Professor Aiyangar in this connection (Aiyangar, *ibid.*, pp. 43, 48, 161-63). Dr. N. N. Law's work may also be read with profit in this context (Law, *op. cit.*, pp. 229 ff.).
49. Read my *I. R. D. West*, pp. 110-11, 116-19, 131-32, 134-36. On some points of similarity between the account of Megasthenes and Kauṭilya, read *ibid.*, pp. 204-07. I shall deal with the latter point more elaborately in Part Six below.
50. Aiyangar, *ibid.*, pp. 62-63.
51. *Kauṭilya*, Bk. XIV, Ch. I. pp. 441 ff. There is nothing surprising in Kauṭilya's belief in the supernatural when we observe that even in the twentieth century, Western historians are prone to interpret history in terms of the Unseen. Thus, Professor H. A. L. Fisher writes in his *History of Europe*, while dealing with a predetermined pattern in history: "I can see only one emergency following upon another as wave follows upon wave, one great fact with respect to which, since it is unique, there can be no generalisations, only one safe rule for the historian: that he should recognise in the development of human destinies the play of the contingent and the unforeseen" (Cited by A. L. Rowse, *The Use of History*, pp. 19-20, London, 1948, 4th impression). Centuries ago Kauṭilya recognized the unforseen when he admitted the rôle of the supernatural in State action.
52. Aiyangar, *op. cit.*, pp. 62-63, *op. cit.*
53. *Kauṭilya*, Bk. III. Ch. VII. 165, p. 188 ; Bk. XI. Ch. I. 378, p. 407 ; text, pp. 165,

378. The relevant passages are—*deśasya jātyā saṅghasya dharmo grāmasya vā'pi yaḥ ucitaḥ-tasya tenaiva dāya-dharmaṁ prakalpayet*. Then again—*sanghalābho daṇḍamitra-lābhānaṁ-uttamaḥ*. See also Aiyangar, *ibid.*, p. 63.

54. Read *Manu*, I. 108, p. 27 ; II. 6, 12, 18, pp. 30-32 ; VII. 41, 42, 46, pp. 260-61.

55. Macdonell, *op. cit.*, pp. 428-29 ; Keith, *Skt. Lit.*, p. 463 ; Bhandarkar, R. G., *E. H. D.* p. 207 ; Aiyangar, *ibid.*, pp. 10, 16. The chronology of the political thinkers, excepting in the case of Somadeva Sūri, is by no means settled. But I have found it convenient to follow it as given by Professors Macdonell and Keith, and to arrange them in the manner done by me rather than to select them at random and study them without reference to the ages in which they lived as, for instance, is done by the eminent historian, Professor U. N. Ghoshal. According to him Yājñavalkya agrees with Kauṭilya—which is not quite improbable, if we assume that there was only one Yājñavalkya, and that of the post-Kauṭilyan age ; while Manu and Bhīṣma follow Kauṭilya, particularly in regard to the pattern of government, which, however, is improbable (Ghoshal, U. N. *A History of Indian Political Ideas*, pp. 297, 300 (Oxford, 1959). Likewise it is difficult for me to agree with Professor Ghoshal in his statement that Manu was the reputed founder of the *Arthaśāstra* School (*ibid.*, pp. 83, 90). There is no evidence in the extant versions of the *Manusmṛiti* to uphold this theory. Perhaps Professor Ghoshal's view is to be traced to the fact that the earliest author on *arthaśāstra*, as I have explained in detail, was Manu, according to Kauṭilya. But as against this may be noted also the fact that Manu was essentially connected with the great problem of the delineation of *dharma* ; and that, according to the *Manusmṛiti*, *daṇḍa* was quite a different subject, of great antiquity but distinct from the *dharmaśāstra* associated with the name of that lawgiver. These considerations make it difficult for one to agree to the above view of the learned Professor in regard to Manu.

56. Aiyangar, *ibid.*, p. 16.

57. Fleet, J. F., *Dynasties of the Kanarese Districts* (in the *Bombay Gazetteer*), p. 407 (Bombay, 1896).

PART THREE

POLITICAL THOUGHT ANALYSED

1. Garner, James, Wilford, *Introduction to Political Science,* pp. 38-42 (New York, no date). The definitions of the State are innumerable.
2. Read Gettell, Raymond, Garfield, *Introduction to Political Science,* pp. 24-25 (Revised ed., Calcutta, 1950).
3. MacIver, Robert, *The Modern State,* pp. 12-13, 487 (Oxford, 1946).
4. MacIver, *ibid.,* pp. 487 ff.
5. Cf. Aiyangar, *op. cit.,* pp. 69-70, 108-109.
6. Professor MacIver very graphically explains the relationship between religion and the State in the distant past when he writes that "the interpretation of the unknown became itself a lore, and the secret of man's powerlessness itself a power" (MacIver, *ibid.,* pp. 169-80, where he dwells on the relations between the Church and the State in Europe. See also Jhering, *op. cit.,* p. 45).
7. *Atharva Veda,* III. 4. 2 ; IV. 8. 1 ; XI. 6. 15 ; XII. 3. 31 ; XVIII. 4.31 ; *Taittirīya Samhita,* II. 1. 3. 4 ; VII. 5. 8. 3 ; *Aitareya Brāhmaṇa,* VII. 23, etc. See also Roth, *Journal of the American Oriental Society,* 16, p. ccxliii where Professor Roth has amended the text of the *Jaiminīya Upaniṣad Brāhmaṇa.*
8. *Vedic Index,* II. p. 221.
9. *Śat. Brah.* V. 1. 1. 12-14, p. 4 (S. B. E. XLI).
10. *Śat Brāh.* XIII. 9. 4. 1 (S.B.E. XIV).
11. Eggeling in *ibid.,* p. xv.
12. Eggeling, *ibid.,* p. xv, and note (1) for references to the *Taittrīya Brāhmana* (III. 8. 9. 4) and the *Āpastamba Sūtra* (1. 1).
13. *Śat. Brāh.* XIII. 1. 9. 9. p. 29 (S. B. E. XIV) ; *Rāmayāṇa,* Canto I. cited by Eggeling in *ibid.,* p. xxiv, note (2). See *Bālakāṇḍa,* Ch. 8, pp. 14-15 (*Ayodhyākāṇḍa,* ed. by T. Krishnamacharya. Madras, 1929).
14. Rāmāyaṇa, *Ayodhyā Kāṇḍa,* 13. p. 129. See also *ibid.,* 14 till 34, pp. 130 ff., where Daśaratha is called merely a *rāja,* and not a *cakravartin.*
15. *Ibid., Bālakāṇḍa,* 13. 20 ; *Ayodhyakāṇḍa,* 10. 35, pp. 20, 123. From the latter it appears that the different kings were subservient to him.
16. See *Vedic Index, passim* for their names. Some of them were the following: Khila, Āyavasa, Bharata, Citraratha, Hariscandra, Pṛithu, Punarvasa, Riṇacaya, Sudās, Vṛiśanva, etc.
17. *Taitt. Āraṇyaka,* I. 31. 6.
18. Cf. Gettell, *ibid.,* p. 60.
19. *Manu,* VII. 3, p. 216.
20. *Ibid.,* VII. 15, p. 218.
21. *Ibid.,* VII. 20-21, p. 219. The late Professor A. S. Altekar, while trying to explain the origin of the State in ancient India, would make us believe that the State was brought into existence by a divine agency ; that for a long time after the creation of society, there was a golden age of harmony and happiness ; that society flourished for a long time without a king or law court but "somehow there was a moral degradation" ; and that Brahmā created an asexual king called Virajas whom he appointed as king and whom men agreed to obey. This conjecture of society in remote antiquity is supposed to be based on the *Śantiparvan* (Ch. 58)

of the *Mahābhārata* and on the later Buddhist work called *Dīgha Nikāya*. (Altekar, A. S., *The State and Government in Ancient India from the Earliest times to c. 1200 A.D.*, pp. 12-13 (Banaras, 1949). I cannot understand why we should depend upon the *Mahābhārata* and the *Dīgha Nikāya* for a picture of the remotest period of society when we have earlier works which give us some idea of the same. Granting, for argument's sake, that the account given in that epic is trustworthy, in the sense that it depicts the nature of society in the hoary past, it does not invalidate what has been stated above by me. On the other hand, it supports my conetntion that protection against the evil nature of man was a prime factor in the origin of the State.

22. *Śat. Brāh.* XI. 1. 6. 24, p. 18 (S.B.E. XIV).
23. *Kauṭilya*, I. 9. p. 8 ; text, p. 9.
24. *Manu*, VII. 22, p. 219.
25. *Śantiparvan*, 15. 34 ; *Yājñavalkya*, I. 361 ; *Kāmandaka*, II. 40, 42-43 ; *Śukranītisāra*, I. 23. See also Kane, *op. cit.*, III. p. 238.
26. *Vedic Index*, I. p. 441, under *nātha* for full references on this point.
27. *Ibid.*, II. p. 218 for further references. The learned authors further state that "possibly the later plan of associating the king's son in the monarchy prevailed in the earlier times also". This is inadmissible, as they themselves have shown that the very term for a *yuvarāja* was unknown in those early ages, although the term *rājaputra*, meaning a king's son, or prince, was certainly known (*ibid.*, II. p. 218). As regards Professor Hopkins' view on this point, see *Journal of the American Oriental Society*, 13, p. 139.
28. *Rig Veda*, I. 178. See also *ibid.*, I. 32, 34, 295, 552 where he is said to have pardoned the sins of the penitents.
29. *Vedic Index*, I. p. 441.
30. *Manu*, VII. 35, p. 221.
31. *Ibid.*, 80, p. 229.
32. *Ibid.*, VIII. 172, p. 285.
33. *Ibid.*, 304, p. 307.
34. *Kauṭilya*, Bk. IV. Chs. I, II, III, IX, pp. 227-54. Professor J. J. Anjaria maintains the view that the championing of the *varṇāśaramadharmas* by the king in ancient India, as much iniquitous as the social order itself for which it was meant (Anjaria, J. J., *The Nature and Ground of Political Obligation in the Hindu State*, pp. 175-88. London, 1935). This view, based on modern standards. seems to pervert the ancient principles. Professor Altekar rightly observes that this is an instance of misunderstanding the factors that promoted the development of the Hindu social institutions (Altekar, *op. cit.*, p. 30). On the Hindu social institutions, read Dr. Pandhari Nath Prabhu, *The Hindu Social Organization* (Bombay, 3rd ed).
35. *Kauṭilya*, Bk. I. Ch. IV. 9, p. 9 ; text, p. 9. See also Aiyangar, *op. cit.*, p. 88, note (157).
36. Cf. *Manu*, VII. 35, p. 221.
37. Somadeva Sūri, *Nītivākyāmrita*, pp. 17, 66, 105 (Grantharatnamālā, Bombay, no date. See also Aiyangar, *ibid.*, p. 108, notes 191-93.
38. See Part Five, Chapter III below.
39. See Part One, Chapter IV above.
40. Salmond, *Jurisprudence*, p. 65 cited by Kane, *op. cit.*, III, p. 238.
41. Taylor cited in Kane, *ibid.*
42. Machiavelli, *Discourses*, I, 3 ; quoted by H. Butterfield, *The Statecraft of Machiavelli*, p. 111 (1940). Cited in Kane, *ibid.*
43. MacIver, *op. cit.*, p. 227, and *ibid.*, note (1) for further references.
44. *Śāntiparvan*, Ch. 58, *op. cit.* Professor Altekar also dealt with this question. But his treatment is far too diffused to be accurate. He bases his account on

the origin of the State as given in the *Mahābhārata* and the *Dīgha Nikāya* (see note 21 above in this work), connects it with the theories of Greece and Rome (which are not named or cited), and with those of Hobbes, Locke, and Rousseau—evidently in support of the view that there was anarchy at the beginning of human history!—reverts to the families, *viśas*, and *janas* as given in the Vedic books, and concludes thus: "The available evidence thus shows that as among Indo-Aryan communities, State was evolved in India also in pre-historic times out of the institution of joint family. The patriarch of the family was instinctively revered and obeyed; and social traditions and atmosphere inspired a similar respect for, and evoked a similar obedience to the head of the village and tribe, who generally acquired the status of chiefs and king" (Altekar, *op. cit.*, pp. 12, 18, 19). Professor Altekar, one cannot help feeling, has failed to understand the question of the origin of the State. Whatever may be the truth of the last statement relating to the kings' growing out of the village chiefs—which, so far as Vedic India is concerned, is hardly borne out by the Vedic texts!—it cannot be accepted as a universal axiom to explain the origin of the State. Professor Altekar's book contains much evidence of his erudite learning but as an attempt to understand the State in ancient India, it is so confused, involved, and speculative that it fails to solve the major problems dealt with by him.

45. Read MacIver, *op. cit.*, pp. 19, 223.
46. MacIver, *ibid.*, pp. 14-15, 162-63.
47. *Kauṭilya*, Bk. I. Ch. I. 9, p. 8; text, p. 9. The student may read Professor Rangaswami Aiyangar's comments on the State as an institution of correction (Aiyangar, *op. cit.*, pp. 79, 80). But it is not merely as an institution of correction that we have to view the State: it was also as an institution of encouragement to further social good that we have to study it.
48. Green, T. H., *Lectures on the Principles of Political Obligation*, pp. 99-101 (ed. Bosanquet, London, 1901). See also Aiyangar, *ibid.*, p. 68.
49. Read Maine, Sir Henry, *Early Law and Custom* (ed. Pollock, 1906).
50. Aiyangar, *ibid.*, pp. 68-69.
51. Read Tod, *Antiquities of Rajasthan, passim*; Malcolm, Sir John, *Central India*, Chapters 12 and 13; Hodgson, B. H., *System of Law in Nepal* in the *J.R.A.S.* (O.S.), I. pp. 45-57; 258-80. See also Aiyangar, *ibid.*, p. 59, and note (106).
52. Read *Manu*, I. 93-101; II. 135; IX. 245; 313-22; X. 3; XI. 31-35, etc. The late Professor Altekar has also tackled this problem of the so-called theocratic nature of the ancient Indian State. But his arguments, I am afraid, are not cogent, and his analogies not quite relevant. For instance, he writes thus: "Under theocracy (by which he means, as he writes in the same paragraph, the State's being 'under the influence of theology'!) the head of the church is himself the king, as was the case with the early Khalifas in Islam or as is still the case with the Vatican kingdom under the Pope. Or the king may be a mere agent or instrument of the church, as was the case for some time in Europe during the 8th and 9th centuries A.D." (Altekar, *op. cit.*, pp. 31-34). The examples of the Khalifas, the Pope, and the kings of Europe are partially correct in so far as the two former claimed to have received their powers from God. From this standpoint the theocratic theory is merged into the divine right theory but that does not help us to solve the theocratic nature of the Indian State. When we say that a State is theocratic, we mean that its government is administered by God directly or through a sacredotal class. The best example of a theocratic State in history is the Jewish State (which was really a commonwealth) from Moses to the monarchs, which believed in God's direct intervention in human affairs, and in His revelation in the government of society. From these points of view, neither the government of the Khalifas nor that of the Popes can be strictly called theocratic governments, although, as stated above, the Khalifas claimed, as the Pope still does claim, that they alone received their

(political and) spiritual authority from God. But there is no proof of their having invoked God's direct intervention in the purely political affairs of their governments. Moreover, when we think of the Pope—not merely the Pope in the Vatican City to whcih he was confined in comparatively recent times!—we forget their political counterparts were the Holy Roman Emperors. Professor Altekar was obviously not aware of the facts of European history. His citation of the European monarchy is not to the point.

53. Read *Manu*, VII. 2, 144, pp. 217, 238 ; IX. 322, p. 399 ; X. 84, 447. I do not wish to cite the evidence in *Manu* in regard to the equality of all before the law. See *ibid.*, VIII. 88, p. 269, etc.
54. Professor Aiyangar, while describing the position of the Brahmans, correctly states it thus: "The function of the Brahman in these cases was only that of *expounder* and not *legislator*" (Aiyangar, *op. cit.*, p. 107).
55. *Manu*, VIII. 123, 268, 378, 383, 385, pp. 278, 301, 320, 321.
56. *Kauṭilya*, Bk. III. Ch. X. 171, p. 195 ; text, 171. On the explanation of the three types of amercements, first, middlemost, and highest, read *ibid.*, p. 217 (trans.).
57. *Ibid.*, Bk. III. Ch. X, 173, p. 197 ; text, p. 173.
58. *Ibid.*, Bk. III. Ch. XI. 176, p. 199 ; text, p. 176.
59. *Ibid.*, Bk. III. Ch. XX. 200, p. 204 ; text, p. 200.
60. *Ibid.*, Bk. III Ch. IV. 159, p. 180 ; text, p. 159.
61. *Ibid.*, Bk. III. Ch. XX. 198, p. 223 ; text, p. 198.
62. *Ibid.*, IV. Ch. VIII. 222, p. 250 ; text, p. 222.
63. *Ibid.*, IV. Ch. XI. 229, p. 257 ; text, p. 229. See Aiyangar, *ibid.*, p. 34, where the learned Professor says that the Brahmans were not exempted from the law against suicide. Kauṭilya, of course, believed in the laws relating to social purity, as is clear from his regulations on the *pratiloma* and *anuloma* castes (Book III. Ch. VII. 163, pp. 185-186 ; text, p. 163) ; but this did not mean that his regulations were either partial to the priests or dictated by religious motives. See also Aiyangar, *ibid.*, p. 39.
64. Bandopadhyaya, N. C., *Development of Hindu Polity and Political Theories*, Part I, pp. 83-87 ; see also U. N. Ghoshal, *The Beginnings*, p. 123. On pp. 123-27, 135, Professor Ghoshal rejects this theory on similar grounds.
65. Radha Kumud Mookerjee, *Chandra Gupta Maurya and His Times*, pp. 79-84 cited by Professor U. N. Ghoshal, *Beginnings*, pp. 136-42, where Professor Mookerjee's theory is refuted.
66. Dicey, A. V., *Introduction to the Study of the Law of the Constitution*, pp. 183-91.
67. *Śat. Brāh.* V. 4. 4. 5, p. 106 (S.B.E. XLI).
68. Professor Ghoshal has rejected Professor Mookerjee's theory on different grounds. See his *Beginnings*, pp. 136-42.
69. Jayaswal, K. P., *Hindu Polity: A Constitutional History of India in Hindu Times*, pp. 184-91, 211 (Bangalore, 1955, 3rd and enlarged ed.).
70. Ghoshal, *ibid.*, pp. 104-14.
71. Ghoshal, *ibid.*, pp. 105-06. The eminent historian elaborates this in his *A History*, pp. 27-29. The reference to Viśvarūpa is *Yājñavalkya*, I. 30, where the long passage from the *Vedas* is quoted.
72. *Manu*, VII. 3, p. 216.
73. Kane, *op. cit.*, III. pp. 32-33. The reference to the *Brāhmaṇas* is to the *Śat. Brah.* V. 1. 3. 4 ; V. 1. 4. 2 ; V. 2. 2. 14 ; as given by Dr. Kane on page 32, *ibid*
74. Ghoshal, *A History*, p. 28.
75. Figgis, J. N., *The Divine Right of Kings*, pp. 5-6 (London, 1914).
76. *Manu*, I. 58, p. 19.
77. *Śāntiparvan*, Ch. 67. See also *ibid.*, Ch. 59 ; Kane, *ibid.*, III. p. 34.
78. *Manu*, I. 58, 87-90, pp. 19-24.

79. *Manu*, I. 118, p. 28.
80. *Ibid.*, II. 18, p. 32.
81. Dr. Kane has also discussed this problem but from a slightly different standpoint, Kane, *op. cit.*, III, p. 35.
82. See note (31) above in this Part.
83. *Kauṭilya*, Bk. II. Ch. I. 47, p. 46 ; text, p. 47.
84. Aiyangar, *op. cit.*, pp. 116-17, and note (208) on page 116, where the relevant citation from Kauṭilya is given.
85. *Manu*, VII. 205, p. 249.
86. *Śat. Brāh.* V. 4. 4. 11, p. 109 (S.B.E. XLI). Cf. *Maitrāyaṇī Samhita*, II. 1. 8 ; III. 8 ; IV. 4. 3 ; *Taittirīya Samhita*, II. 6. 5 ; *Vedic Index*, II. p. 213, and note (20).
87. Professor Aiyangar writes thus of the socialistic theory: "The aim of the ancient Indian State was less to understand an improved *social* order, than to act in conformity with the established *moral* order of the *Universe*. The State again felt no obligation, as a modern State does, to tax the rich to feed the poor, and to regard it as one of its duties to equalize burdens by taxation, and to equalize incomes or rewards through the State control of the production and the distribution of wealth" (Aiyangar, *op. cit.*, pp. 117-18). Professor Aiyangar is, on the whole, correct when he writes that the aim of the ancient State was to act in conformity with the established moral order of the universe. But how the idea of a socialistic State could be made to fit in with the principles of Polity as laid down by the ancients, is difficult to understand. The universe which the ancients had in their mind was the one limited by the geographical frontiers of India. They were not concerned with the universe as a whole. There is no evidence in the ancient texts of any attempt by the rulers or statesmen to utilize the machinery of government to bring about an improved type of society.

    In this connection I am unable to follow Professor Ghoshal's characterization of the paternal rule of the king as beneficent and authoritarian, and its historical application, as given in his *A History*, pp. 120-29, 134, 179, 293, 446, and 587. What the learned Professor describes on pp. 120-29 is the importance of the king's functions, the measures taken by him to ward off internal danger, his education, etc., which have little bearing on the question of the paternal aspect of the theory discussed by me.
88. Gettell, *op. cit.*, p. 110.
89. *Manu*, IX. 322, p. 399.
90. *Ibid.*, XI. 84, p. 447.
91. *Ibid.*, IX. 327, p. 400.
92. *Ibid.*, X. pp. 401 ff, and in particular verse 124, p. 429, which deals with the maintenance of the Śūdras by the Brahmans.
93. *Kauṭilya*. Bk. I. Ch. III. 7, p. 7 ; text, 7.
94. *Ibid.*
95. *Ibid.*
96. *Ibid.*, Ch. II, 6, p. 5 ; text, p. 6.
97. *Manu*, X. 63, p. 416.
98. Sarkar, B. K., *Positive Background of Hindu Society*, Bk. II. pp. 34-39 (Allahabad, 1914) ; Jayaswal, *Hindu Polity*, p. 9 ; Bhandarkar, D. R. *Some Aspects of Ancient Indian Polity*, pp. 66-69 ; Kane, *op. cit.*, III. p. 20. My treatment of the organismic theory is slightly different to the one given by the learned Indian authors, particularly Professor Rangaswami Aiyangar (*op. cit.*, p. 71). This erudite historian maintains that the ancient Indian State was organic because it had a history of internal growth ; that it had fully developed organs and functions ; and that it was responsive to its environment. Hence the State was organic. The existence of the developed functions and organs may be admitted ; but what is meant by the history of internal growth and the State's being responsive to its environment cannot be

understood. Probably by the former, the learned Professor meant that the ancient State was a living organism; and by the latter, that it was developed in its environment. He seems to have missed the two essential points I have referred above—the specialized functions of the organs and their interdependence.

As against the other Indian scholars, who have accepted the organismic theory, Professor Anjaria has vehemently denied its existence (Anjaria, *op. cit.*, Chapter IV). His arguments are the following: there is no finality among scholars in regard to the nature of the organic theory; the Hindu thinkers did not regard the State as a moral organism; they attached a permanent stigma of inferiority to a large number of people; and the Hindu concepts did not harmonize the authority of the State with the liberty of the individual.

I am afraid Professor Anjaria has altogether misunderstood the ancient Indian theory of the *varṇāśramadharmas*, the theories of the ancient Greeks, and of the modern Western thinkers as well. The argument that there is no finality among modern thinkers about the nature of the organic theory is only an excuse not to understand it. The second argument that the Hindu thinkers did not regard the State as a moral organism is a clear proof that Professor Anjaria has not understood the organismic theory at all. It is not only as a moral organism but as a political one that both ancient and modern thinkers have conceived of the State. The statement that the ancient Hindus did not think of the State as a moral organism is historically erroneous. The *saptānga-rājya*, as will be shown in the following pages, was as much a moral organism as it was material, governed as it was by the *dharmaśāstras*. The other statement that the ancient Hindus attached a permanent stigma of inferiority to a large section of the people is, as seen above, likewise erroneous, since both Manu and Kauṭilya, not to speak of others, definitely assigned a place of respect to the vast bulk of the people. Professor Anjaria forgets, when he thus charges the ancient Hindus with a crime which they never committed, that the relegation of some sections of the people to a place of inferiority was the accepted standard of social conduct, even in ancient Greece where, as is proved by Aristotle's *Politics* (I. 4. 6, and *passim*), slavery is described an institution of social necessity. Professor Anjaria has misjudged the past from the present standpoint of ethics. His statement that the authority of the State did not harmonize with the liberty of the individual is likewise erroneous, since the *dharmaśāstras* give sufficient freedom to the individual within the framework of his social status. His theory has rightly been rejected by Dr. Kane as being one-sided. But Dr. Kane dismisses it only from the points of view of slavery and democracy (Kane, *op. cit.*, I. p. 20).

99. Aristotle, *Politics*, IV. 4-9, pp. 153-54 (Trans. by Benjamin Jowett; with an Introduction, Analysis, and Index by H. W. C. Davis, Oxford, 1948).
100. Cf. Gillette—Reinardt, *Problems of Social Order*, p. 651 (American Book Co., 1942).
101. Cf. MacIver, *op. cit.*, pp. 185-86.
102. Read *Kauṭilya*, Bk. VIII. pp. 399-465. See also Aiyangar, *op. cit.*, pp. 109-10, where the learned Professor briefly refers to this side of the question.
103. *Kauṭilya*, Bk. XIII. Ch. V. 409, 410, pp. 438, 439; text, pp. 409, 410.
104. Cf. Aiyangar, *ibid.*, p. 109.
105. *Kauṭilya*, Bk. III. Ch. I. 150, p. 171; text, p. 150.
106. *Manu*, VIII. 304-05, p. 307. See also the next verse (306, p. *ibid.*), in which the following is stated: "A king, who protects the created being in accordance with the sacred law and smites those worthy of corporal punishment, daily offers (as it were) sacrifices at which hundred thousands (are given as) fees."
107. *Ibid.*, VIII. 307, p. 307. In the light of these statements, Professor Ghoshal's view that taxes were the price paid for the services of the people (*History of Hindu Political Theories*, pp. 17-18, 1st ed. 1927) cannot be maintained.

108. Somadeva Sūri, *Nītivākyāmrita*, p. 18, cited by Aiyangar, *op. cit.*, p. 109, note (198).
109. Cf. MacIver, *op. cit.*, p. 17 ff., 184 ff., 230-31.
109a. Professor Aiyangar rightly maintains that the promulgation of laws was one of the most important functions of the ancient State (Aiyangar, *ibid.*, pp. 93, 100 ff.).
110. *Manu*, VII. 170, pp. 243-44, *op. cit.*
111. *Mahābhārata, Rājadharmaparvan*, cited in Aiyangar, *ibid.*, p. 85, note 150.
112. *Kauṭilya*, Bk. I. Ch. XIX. 39, p. 38 ; text, p. 39. See also Aiyangar, *ibid.*, p. 85, and note (151).
113. *Kauṭilya, ibid.*
114. Read Aiyangar, *ibid.*, p. 86 where the learned author comments on this.
115. *Kauṭilya*, Bk. VI, Ch. II. 261, p. 291 ; text, p. 261.
116. The statement of Somadeva Sūri that the subjects find their roots in the sovereign, cited by Professor Aiyangar (*ibid.*, p. 84, and note 148), merely means that the strength of the king was not in himself but in his people. It does not refer to the complicated relations of the State with the individual, as understood by modern writers on Politics.
117. Read *Manu*, VII. 155-203, pp. 240-49.
118. Read *Kauṭilya*, Bk. VI, VII, VIII, IX, X, XI, XII, XIII, pp. 287-439.
119. Read *Manu* under various heads like adoption, law, judiciary, Aryan, assault, boundary disputes, castes, Brahman, father, daughter, and the various topics relating to the daily life of the individual.
120. In particular, *Kauṭilya*, Books III & IV, pp. 167-265, may be of special significance in this connection.
121. Read *Manu*, I, 89, p. 24 ; VII. 77-79, p. 228.
122. Read my *I. D. R. West*, pp. 92-93. Dr. Smith (*E. H. I.*, p. 79) merely refers to the murmurings of the Macedonian soldiers. Was it mere home sickness that made them murmur?
123. Read *Kauṭilya*, Bk. II. Chapters on the Superintendents of Horses, Elephants, Chariots, Infantry, and Commander-in-Chief, pp. 146-57 ; and on the revenue administration, Chapters on tolls, revenue collectors, etc. In fact, Bk. II, pp. 45-160 gives a comprehensive account of the costly and elaborate administrative machinery of the Mauryans. Book X which is related to war (pp. 391-405) describes the details of warfare from the time of encampment till action against an enemy. Books XII and XII continue the same topic in greater detail. These references hardly convey an adequate idea of the large machinery of war and peace which Kauṭilya has described. For some estimate of the same, read Dikshitar, V. R. R., *The Mauryan Polity* ; Law, N. N., *Studies in Indian History and Culture* (1925), and his *Aspects of Indian Polity* (1921). On the police force as we now know it, we have no information that would enable us to form some idea of the Mauryan police system. The chapters on robbery (*Kauṭilya*, Bk. III. Ch. XVII. pp. 216-17), on assaults (*ibid.*, Ch. XIX, pp. 219-22), and on gambling (*ibid.*, Ch. XX, pp. 222-25) seem to suggest that adequate provision was made by the Mauryan State to detect crimes under those heads. But nothing more than this can be said about the police system.
124. Read in particular *Kauṭilya, ibid.*, Book VIII. pp. 349 ff ; Bk. IX. pp. 367 ff.
125. Read Gettell, *op. cit.*, pp. 384-85.
126. Read MecIver, *op. cit.*,pp. 160-61.
127. Gettell, *ibid.*, p. 385.
128. Gettell, *ibid.*, pp. 191-92.
129. Gettell, *ibid.*, p. 194.
130. Gettell, *ibid.*, p. 193.
131. Read G. Jellenek, *Recht des Modernes Staates*, Chapter XX ; J. W. Burgess, *Political Science and Comparative Constitutional Laws*, I. Ch. III. See also Gettell, *ibid.*, p. 193, and note (1).

132. Aristotle, *Politics*, III. 15-17, pp. 135-43.
133. MacIver, *op. cit.*, p. 339. Read also *ibid.*, p. 70, where Professor MacIver writes thus, while contrasting the progress of the Greek City States with the rest of the world: "Religion too sat less heavily upon this people (the Greeks), as compared with the superstition dominated peoples of the Orient." Although the learned Professor does not explicitly apply his class theory to India, yet it is obvious that, while writing about the Orientals, he had the people of India also in view. If this presumption is correct, his statement is as unsympathetic as it is unhistorical.
134. As to whether citizens even in the modern Western world are guided by the herd instinct, read Lasky, Harold, *A Grammar of Politics*, pp. 19, 42 (London, 1934); Bryce, Lord, *Modern Democracies*, II. p. 600 ff. I have discussed this aspect of the question in my *Principles of Civics*, pp. 141-42 (2nd ed. Ahmedabad, 1960).
135. Bryce, *op. cit.*, I. pp. 165-66.
136. *Manu*, VII. 1-2, p. 216. Read also *ibid.*, 87, 94, 98, etc., pp. 230-32.
137. *Rig Veda*, IV. 12. 3; 42. 1; V. 69. 1; VII. 64.2; VIII. 25.8; 56. 1; X. 109. 3; Cf. *Vājasaneyī Samhita*, IV. 19; X. 4; *Taittirīya Brāhmaṇa*, II. 4. 7. 7. See also *Vedic Index*, II. p. 203, and note (7); and *ibid.*, p. 216 for Professor Zimmer's view.
138. Aristotle writes thus in his *Politics*, while describing monarchies: "But since this (i.e. that once for all one class should rule and the others serve) is unattainable, and kings have no marked superiority over their subjects, such as Scylax affirms to be found among the Indians, it is obviously necessary on many grounds that all citizens alike should take their turn of governing and being governed" (*Aristotle*, VII. 14-3, p. 286). Scylax mentioned here was obviously Skylax of Karyanda in Karia, who in *circa* B.C 500 undertook a voyage from the waters of the Punjab rivers in Gāndhāra down the Indus to the sea, and thence across the ocean to the Red Sea. The particulars of his voyage have been lost but his voyage was included by Herodotus in the latter's work (Smith, V. A., *E.H.I.*, p. 40, and note (1). It is clear that, in addition to Herodotus, Aristotle also utilized the work of Skylax. The statement of the latter merely points to the regal but not the social superiority, which the ancient Indian kings attained among their people, assuming that Skylax's statement (which ignores quite a number of self-governing communities during his time) refers only to kings. But it does not invalidate the observations made by me in regard to the king's being one of the members of the Kṣatriya class.
139. *Manu*, VII. 133-35, p. 237.
140. Professors Macdonell and Keith observe that "Taxation would not normally fall on Kṣatriya or Brahman" (*Vedic Index*, II. p. 213). This is incorrect. Manu clearly states that only blind men, idiots (or cripples) who moved with the help of boards, elderly men seventy years old, and those who conferred benefits on Śrotriyas were exempted from the payment of taxes (*Manu*, VIII. 394, p. 322). Nowhere is it stated in the *Manusmṛiti* that the Kṣatriyas were free from paying the taxes.
141. *Manu*, VII. 123, p. 236.
142. *Ibid.*, IV. 2, 3, 5, 6, pp. 128-29.
143. Cf. Gettell, *op. cit.*, pp. 195-99.
144. *Vedic Index*, II. 211, and note (6). On Divodosa, read *ibid.*, I. p. 363; on Sudās, *ibid.*, II. p. 454; on Pijavana, *ibid.*, I. p. 524; but see *ibid.*, I. p. 363, note (2) where Pijavana is also an epithet of Sudās; on Kuruśravana, *ibid.*, I. p. 170; on Mitrātīthī, *ibid.*, II. p.165; on Upamaśravas, *ibid.*, I. p. 93.
145. Macdonell, *Skt. Lit.*, p. 158.
146. On *adhirāja*, read *Vedic Index*, I. pp. 19-20, and note (1) for further references. On *ekarāja*, read *ibid.*, I. p. 119, and notes (1)-(3) for further references.
147. *Śat. Bhāh*. I. 4-28, p. 97 (S.B.E.XLI).

148. *Ibid.*, XII. 9-1, p. 269 (S.B.E.XLIV).
149. *Vedic Index*, I, pp. 377-78 and notes (4)-(6) on page 378 for further references to the *Mahābhārata*. The reference to Yāska is to his *Nirukta*, II. 10. See also *Vedic Index*, I. p. 377, note (2).
149a. Macdonell, *Skt. Lit.*, p. 158.
150. Why the learned authors of the *Vedic Index* (II. p. 211) doubt about the "character and validity" of this story cannot be understood, especially when they admit that, so far as the evidence of that legend in regard to the elective principle is concerned, "the value of which, as evidence of contemporary views, is not seriously affected. . . ." They have adduced no reason whatsoever for doubting either the character or validity of the story. See also *ibid.*, I. pp. 335, 336, 463, 542.
151. Fleet, *D.K.D.* p. 395.
152. Altekar, *op.cit.*, p. 22.
153. Altekar, *ibid.*
154. *Diodorus*, XVII, cited by Smith, *E.H.I.*, p. 91, n. (1).
155. Agrawala, V.S., *India as known to Panini*, pp. 409, 468 (Lucknow, 1953).
156. Gettell, *op.cit.*, p. 471.
157. Smith, *op. cit.*, p. 99.
158. MacCrindle, *India during Alexander's Invasion* ; see also Smith, *ibid.*, p. 99.
159. Read my *I.D.R. West*, pp. 94-95 for an account of these two clans and of their struggle with Alexander the Great.
160. Read Gettell, *ibid.*, pp. 471-73.
161. If more proof is wanted to substantiate the statement that the king was one of the many, the reader may turn to the *Śatapatha Brāhmaṇa*, VII. 1·1·4, p. 299 (S.B.E.XLI), where the king (Kṣatriya), with the approval of his clan, makes a grant of a settlement. Then, again, in the same work (XII. 8. 3. 19, p. 259. S.B.E.XIV), it is stated that a Kṣatriya is the consecrator of a Kṣatriya, thereby proving beyond doubt the fact that all Kṣatriyas, including the king, were, for certain purposes, perfectly equal. See also *Vedic Index*, II. p. 207.
162 & 163. *Vedic Index*, II, p. 216.
164. *Śat. Brāh.* XIII. 4.2.17, pp. 359-60 (S.B.E. XLIV) ; see also *Vedic Index*, II. p. 216.
165. *Rig Veda*, IV. 12,3 ; 42,1 ; V. 69·1 ; VII. 64·2 ; VIII. 25·8 ; 56,6 ; X. 109·3 ; see also *Vedic Index*. I. p. 203, and note (7) for further references.
166. *Taittirīya Samhita*, I. 8. 14. 2 ; *Vājasaneyī Samhita*, X. 17 ; *Taittirīya Brāhmaṇa*, I. 7·8·5 ; *Śatapatha Brāhmaṇa*, V. 4·2·2. See also *Vedic Index*, I. p. 200, and note (7).
167. Professor Altekar's indecisive reasoning is apparent when we note his remarks on the so-called republican form of government in the Vedic age. While referring to the last hymn in the *Rig Veda*, which concerns the unanimous decision of the *samiti*, he writes thus: "It is not impossible to argue that the hope and the desideratum expressed in the hymn refers to the deliberative and administrative activity of a republican State." But in the next sentence he admits that the *samiti* was only a check upon the king's powers, and that it is doubtful whether it denoted the Central Assembly of a republican State. "The hymn itself cannot conclusively prove the existence of a republican State" (Altekar, *ibid.*, p. 76). If it cannot prove the existence of a republican State, then, why speak of the so-called deliberative and administrative activities of a republican nature in the *samiti*?
168. Altekar, *ibid.*, p. 77, where he has cited the *Mahābhārata*, XII. 67, 54, and Sāyaṇa's interpretation of *vairāja*.
169. *Aitareya Brāhmaṇa*, VIII. 23 ; *Vedic Index*, II. pp. 16-17, 84, 283.
170. Professor Altekar rejects Sāyaṇa's meaning of the term *vairājya*, the evidence of the *Mahābhārata*, and the interpretation of *vairājya* as given in the *Vedic*

Index, II. p. 221. His explanation that *vairājya* can be taken to mean a State devoid (*vi*) of king, on the analogy of *virāṭ*, *viśeṣeṇa-rāja* (Altekar, *ibid.*, p. 77, and note 4) is too farfetched to be convincing.

171. Aiyangar, *op. cit.*, p. 46.
172. Aiyangar, *ibid.*, p. 42, and note (85).
173. Hopkins, *J.A.O.S.* 13, pp. 73 ff., 184 ff., 190 ; Fick *Die Sociale Gliederung im nordostlichen Indien zu Buddhas Zeit*, pp. 52, n. (2).
174. MacIver, *op. cit.*, p. 347.
175. Read Saletore, *I.D.R. West*, pp. 82-84, 89.
176. Saletore, *ibid.*, p. 85.
177. Agrawala, *op. cit.*, pp. 453, 454.
178 & 179. Agrawala, *ibid.*, pp. 426-27.
180. *Paṇini*, IV. 1·137 ; Agrawala, *ibid.*, p. 428.
181 & 182. Saletore, *ibid.*, pp. 97-98.
183. Agrawala, *ibid.*, pp. 53, 80, 425.
184. Pāṇini, VIII. 3·97 ; Agrawala, *ibid.*, p. 80, *op. cit.*
185. Bhandarkar, R.G., *E.H.D.* p. 135.
186. Saletore, *ibid.*, pp. 93, 343.
187. Agrawala, *ibid.*, p. 445.
188. Cunningham, Major, Arthur, *Coins of Ancient India*, p. 77 (London, 1891).
189. Cunningham, *ibid.*, p. 78.
190. *Kauṭilya*, Bk. I. Ch. XVII. 35, p. 34 ; text, p. 35.
191. *Ibid.*, Bk. XVI. 312. p. 339 ; text, p. 312.
192. Saletore, *ibid.*, pp. 84-101.
193. Agrawala, *ibid.*, p. 434.
194. Agrawala, *ibid.*, pp. 429-32 ; Dr. Agrawala also cites Vaidya, P.L., *Antagaḍadāsao*, p. 4 ; *Mahāvagga*, IX. 4·1.
195. Jayaswal, *op. cit.*, pp. 25-165. (1955 ed.) ; D. R. Bhandarkar, *Some Aspects of Ancient Indian Polity*, pp. 121-25 (Calcutta, 1919). This fantastic theory has been restated by Professor Altekar, *op. cit.*, pp. 82-91.
196. *Kauṭilya*, Bk. XI. Ch. I. pp. 407-10 ; text, pp. 378-81.
197. Altekar, *ibid.*, p. 88. *op. cit.*
198 & 199. *Pāṇini*, V. 2·52 ; *Mahāvagga*. III. 3·6. Both cited by Agrawala, *ibid.*, p. 433.
200. Jayaswal, *op. cit.*, pp. 103-17 ; Bhandarkar, D. R., *ibid.*, pp. 121-25. For a detailed account of the Buddhist theory of government, read Mehta, R.N., *Pre-Buddhist India*, Ch. II. pp. 79. ff (1939).
201. Bhandarkar, D. R., *ibid.*, pp. 148-50. See Majjhima Nikaya, I. 231.
202. Bhandarkar, D.R., *ibid.*, p. 154.
203. Bhandarkar, D.R., *ibid.*, pp. 154-55.
204 & 205. Bhandarkar, D.R., *ibid.*, p. 156. The reference to the *Jātakas* is obvious to *Jātaka*, I. p. 105. Professor Altekar would, however, reject Professor Bhandarkar's opinion, thus: "Dr. Bhandarkar's view that this statement (in the *Jātaka* relating to the *uparājas, senāpatis*, etc.) suggests that the Lichchavi State was a confederation of 7707 principalities, each having full authority under its *rāja*, *uparāja*, etc., does not seem probable. . . .Such a big confederation is impracticable" (Altekar, *ibid.*, p. 82, note (1). I am afraid Professor Altekar, while referring to what Professor Bhandarkar said in the latter's *Carmichael Lectures*, p. 135 (1918 ed.), missed what that learned historian said later on in the same work, which I have cited.
206. *Dīgha Nikāya*, III. 92 ff. ; Cf. *Jātaka*. II. (*Ulūka Jātaka*), p. 352 ; Bhandarkar, D.R., *ibid.*, 121, n. (1).
207. Bhandarkar, D.R. *ibid.*, p. 121.
208. *Mahābhārata*, *Śāntiparvan*, Ch. 59, v. 125 ; Bhandarkar, D.R. *ibid.*, p. 121, n. (2).

209. *Manu,* X. 79, p. 419 ; VII. 2. p. 216.
210. Altekar, *op. cit.,* p. 85.
211. *Mahāvagga,* X. 3. pp. 264 ff ; (S.B.E. XVII) ; *Cūlavagga,* IV. 9, pp. 24-27 (S.B.E.XX) ; *Mahāparinirbbāṇa Sutta,* XI. Ch. 1. pp. 3-81 (S.B.E.XI). On the internal constitution of the Buddhist *sanghas,* read the excellent account as given in Beni Prasad, *op. cit.,* pp. 321-27.
212. Rhys Davids, *Buddhist India,* p. 26 (1903).
213. Rhys Davids, *ibid.,* p. 26 ; see also *Mahāvāstu,* I. p. 271 (Senart's ed.).
214. After conjuring up an attractive but imaginary picture of the constitution of the republics, Professor Altekar wrote thus: "Want of adequate reliable data handicaps the historian perhaps in no other sphere so much as in the case of the republics. We get only a dim and blurred picture of their constitutions and their working" (Altekar, *ibid.,* p. 91). And yet in the previous seven pages of the same book, the learned Professor ventured to draw this "dim and blurred picture" of the constitution of the republics! The limitation which he admits in the above statement, and which faces the historian, is by itself enough to discount his attempts at visualizing that picture. On the *gaṇa* or republican type of constitutions in ancient India, read Thomas, F.W., *J.R.A.S. for 1915,* p. 535 ; Bhandarkar, D. R., *op. cit.* ; Majumdar, R.C., *Corporate Life in Ancient India* (Calcutta, 1918) ; Smith, *E.H.I.* p. 145, and note (2). I might add here that the technical term *gaṇa,* in the sense of a republic, does not occur in the *Vedic Index.* Perhaps it was evolved long after the age of the *Mahābhārata.*
215. Dr. P. V. Kane, while giving a very useful list of the *gaṇas* in literature and history, rightly states that we have no information at all on the most important points in connection with the republics, viz., who were entitled to vote, and what were the qualifications for membership, etc. Read Kane, *op. cit.,* III. pp. 87-91. Dr. Kane has correctly characterized the theory of Dr. Jayaswal and Dr. Bhandarkar, thus "This is to say the least a gratuitous assumption" (Kane, *ibid.,* III. p. 90). He rejects the evidence of the Buddhist literature which he has given in detail, as being of no help in solving the most important points relating to voting and membership. In this connection it may be noted that Professor Rangaswami Aiyangar has cited the reference to the Vajjian (Vrijjian) republic in Rhys Davids' *Buddhist India.* pp. 17-41, in a manner to suggest that the passage in the *Mahānirbbāṇa Sutta* refers to the possible dangers of anarchy (Aiyangar, *op. cit.,* p. 78). I do not agree with the learned Professor's interpretation. The seven conditions are positive injunctions, which do not indicate anarchy at all.
216. *Vedic index* II, p. 431, and notes (12 & 14).
217. *Pāṇini,* II.1.59. *Śreṇyādayaḥ kritādibhiḥ.* Agrawal, *op. cit.,* p. 437.
218. Professor Agrawala has attempted to give fourteen variants of the term *śreṇi* on the basis of the statements of Pāṇini. These may also be applied, according to him, to the terms *pūga* and *eka* forms of government (Agrawala, *ibid.,* pp. 489-90). I must confess that "the constitutional variety and gradation" which he has thereby suggested, makes little or on sense. In the absence of corroborative evidence either of contemporary or even later times, the interpretations given by him may be characterized as being doubtful.
219. *Kauṭilya,* Bk. XI. Ch. I. 378, p. 407 ; text, p. 378.
220. *Ibid.,* p. 410 ; text, p. 381.
220a. *Ibid.,* Bk. III. Ch. XIX, 196, p. 221 ; text, p. 196.
221. *Ibid.,* Bk. IV. Ch. I. 201, p. 227 ; text, p. 200 ; see also *ibid.,* Bk. III. Ch. XIV. 185, p. 209, text, p. 185.
222 & 223. Agrawala, *ibid.,* pp. 434-37. Professor H. N. Sinha's definition of some of these terms may be noted. He writes thus: ". . . a Śreṇi is a corporation of persons belonging to different castes but of the same calling ; the Pūga is the corpora-

tion of men of different castes and calling; the Vrāta is the association of the kith and kin, while a Gaṇa is a federation of all of these" (Sinha, *op. cit.*, p. 98). On what texts the above definitions are based, cannot be made out. On the same page, the learned author would style Pāṇini's *pūga* and *vrāta* as definitely bearing "the import of a trade guild, while the Āyudhajīvi Saṃgha is also a guild where men took up the calling of arms" (*ibid.*, p. 98). I am afraid this is mere speculation.

224. See *Vedic Index*, I. p. 534 ; II. pp. 415-17 where the two terms do not figure.
225. *Rig Veda*. V. 53. 11 ; III. 26.2, where the third term *śardha*, which is given in the preceding reference, is not mentioned. See also *Vedic Index*, II. p. 341.
226. *Taittirīya Samhita*. IV. 5.4.1 ; *Kāṭhaka Samhita*, XVII. 13 ; *Maitrāyaṇī Samhita*, II. 9.4 ; *Vajasaneyī Samhita*, XVI. 25 ; see also *Vedic Index*, II. p. 342.
227. Altekar, *op. cit.*, p. 75.
228. Agrawala, *op. cit.*, p. 477.
229. Cf. Fowler Warde, *The City State of the Greeks and Romans*, p. 26 (London, 1910).
230. Cf. Fowler, *ibid.*, pp. 36-37.
231. MacIver, *op. cit.*, p. 339.
232. Cf. Gettell, *op. cit.*, p. 82.
233. Fowler, *ibid.*, p. 50.
234. Fowler, *ibid*, pp. 45-46.
235. Fowler, *ibid*, p. 52. For a full account of a Greek City State, read A. E. Zimmern, *The Greek Commonwealth*.
236. Bryce, Lord, *Modern Democracies*, I. p. 187 ; Cf. Fowler, *ibid.*, pp. 163, 177-78.
237. Read Fowler, *ibid.*, pp. 152, 163-68 for further information.
238. Agrawala, *ibid.*, pp. 477-91.
239. It is interesting to observe here that the Professor Altekar summarily rejected Dr. Jayaswal's theory of *Paura-jānapada* assemblies on precisely the same grounds, namely, that literary evidence does not help to prove the existence of a governmental body! (Altekar, *op. cit.*, p. 107). And yet the same eminent historian has built up the fantastic edifice of Central Assemblies, etc., on the basis of the Buddhist literary sources!
240. Agrawala, *ibid.*, pp. 48-61.
241. Agrawala, *ibid.*, p. 482.
242. Fowler, *ibid.*, pp. 40-46.
243. Cunningham, *op. cit.*, p. 67.
244. Cunningham, *ibid.*, p. 71.
245. Cunningham, *ibid.*, p. 76.
246. See Saletore, *I.D.R. West*, p. 88.
247. Agrawala, *ibid.*, p. 476.
248. *Kauṭilya*, Bk. II. Ch. III. pp. 50-53 ; text, pp. 51-54.
249. Fowler, *ibid.*, pp. 45, 90.
250. Fowler, *ibid.*, pp. 42-47.
251. Agrawala, *ibid.*, p. 482.
252. Fowler, *ibid.*, p. 40.
253. MacIver, *op. cit.*, p. 70.
254. Duncker cited in Fowler, *ibid.*, p. 46, and note (1).
255. MacIver, *op. cit.*, p. 70, *op. cit.*
256. Read *The Cambridge Ancient History*, V. Athens, pp. 375-97 (4th impression, Cambridge, 1953).
257. Read Fowler, *ibid.*, pp. 245-72.
258. Fowler, *ibid.*, p. 52, *op. cit.*
259. Agrawala, *ibid.*, pp. 194-97.
260. *Kauṭilya*, Bk. II. Ch. II. pp. 48-50 ; see also pp. 323-26. For fuller details, read

Kane, *op. cit.*, III. pp. 139, 142, 152, 497, etc. On page 139, Dr. Kane affirms that grants of land could be made only by the king, and not by a district officer.

261. Fowler, *op. cit.*, p. 100.
262. Aristotle, *Politics*. II. 9·14, p. 84.
263. Read Kane, *ibid.*, II. pp. 490, 574-81, 636-40, 700.
264. Fowler, *ibid.*, p. 101.
265. *Aristotle*, II. 5·7, p. 62. On Aristotle's criticism of Plato's concept, read *ibid.*, pp. 61-62.
266. *Aristotle*, VI. 5·11, p. 248.
267. *Kauṭilya*, Bk. VII. Ch. XVI. 312, p. 339; Bk. XI. Ch. I. pp. 407-10.
268. Fowler, *ibid.*, p. 112.
269. Fowler, *ibid.*, pp. 137-38, 154.
270. Fowler, *ibid.*, pp. 154-57.

270a. *Avadānaśataka*, II. p. 103. On the date of this Buddhist work, read Keith, *Skt. Lit.*, p. 65. See also Altekar, *op. cit.*, 71, note (1) where this passage has been cited, but where the learned author translates *gaṇa* as a democratic government. It had, however, earlier been cited by Professor Bhandarkar, who was perhaps the first to bring it to the notice of the scholars. But Professor Bhandarkar, however, would date the *Avatadānaśataka* to *circa* 100 B.C., Bhandarkar, *Carmichael Lectures* for 1918, of p. 147. But it is not clear on what grounds the age to which he assigns the *Avadānaśataka* rests.

270b. Cunningham, *op. cit.*, p. 77.

271. Read Fowler, *ibid.*, pp. 252-59, 281-94.

271a. Dr. Jayaswal correctly stated that the Indian republics fell victims to intrigues and dissensions, and cited the evidence of the *Mahābhārata* (*Sāntiparvan* LXVI. vv. 6-7, 10-12) and the Buddhist tradition relating in the Lichchhavīs (*J.A.S.B. for 1838*, pp. 994-95) in order to prove this point (Jayaswal, *op. cit.*, 168, and *ibid*, notes 16-18).

272. Read Saletore, *I.D.R. West*, pp. 82-102 for an account of Alexander the Great's conquest of the various Indian tribes. Dr. Jayaswal perhaps referring to the lesser Porus, mentioned by the Greek writers, wrote thus: "It is significant that young Porus, King or President of Gāndhāra, when faced with the foreign invaders, looked towards the imperial power of Magadha, and that Kauṭilya, a man of Taxila, should advocate their abolition in his Science of Commonwealth" (Jayaswal, *ibid.*, p. 168). I am afraid this is an instance of confusion of thought and wrong inference. I have shown on the authority of the Greek writers themselves, in my work cited above, that the king of Taxila, which was the capital of Gāndhāra, was Taxiles. He was quite different to the lesser Porus, although both were traitors, who sided with Alexander the Great against the magnanimous Porus of the Punjab. Therefore, to call the lesser Porus king of Taxila is an error. Dr. Jayaswal is correct when he stated that Kauṭilya belonged to Taxila. Kauṭilya's birth place was Śalatūra, mod. Lahur, a small town four miles north-west of Ohind, in the angle where the Kabul river meets the Indus (Cunningham, *Ancient Geography of India*, pp. 66-67; *A.S.R.* II. p. 95. Read also Agrawala, *op. cit.*, pp. 9-11). But this is not equal to saying that Kauṭilya had ever an invitation from the lesser Porus to wipe out the democratic republics! There is no evidence at all about the traitor Porus' ever having asked Kauṭilya to do away with the Indian republics; and, what is important, the Mauryan State of which Kauṭilya was to be the greatest Prime Minister was yet to be born! (Read in this connection my *I.D.R. West*, pp. 104-21 for a discussion of the question as to when Candragupta Maurya established himself as a power in Magadha). Dr. Jayaswal has, in this passage as elsewhere in his interesting book, merely manipulated facts in order to suit his fantastic theories!

272a. *Kauṭilya,* Bk. VIII. Ch. IV. 333, p. 359, text, p. 333.

272b. Cunningham, *Coins,* pp. 77, 78.

272c. *Kauṭilya,* Bk. I. Ch. XVII. 35, p. 34 ; text, p. 35. While analysing the causes of the disappearance of the Hindu republics, Dr. Jayaswal wrote that their smallness "was the very weakness of the polity" ; and that intrigues and dissensoins were the other causes of their disappearance (Jayaswal, *op. cit.,* pp. 167-68). While I agree with the latter, it is doubtful if the former was really a valid cause of the break-up of the republican polity. The example of the Yaudheyas, again, is enough to disprove this as a general cause. The coins of the Yaudheyas were found in "the Eastern Punjab, and all over the country between the Satlej and Jumna rivers. Two larger finds have been made at Sonpath, between Delhi and Karnal" (Cunningham, *Coins,* p. 76). The Yaudheya republican State was certainly not a small State! And yet it disappeared!

273. *Atharva Veda,* III. 3. 4 ; *Kāṭhaka Samhita,* XXVIII, I ; *Taittirīya Samhita,* II. 3. 1 ; *Maitrāyaṇī Samhita,* II. 2. 1 ; *Pañcaviṁśa Brāhmaṇa,* XII. 12. 6 ; *Kauśika Sūtra,* XVII. 30.

274. *Vedic Index* I, p. 258.

275. *Śat. Brāh.,* XII. 3. 1-4, 13, 269, 273. (S.B.E. XLIV).

276. The Śriñjayas figure very often in Vedic literature. They were closely associated with the Kurus and the Triṣṭus. At one time the Śriñjayas and the Kurus had a common priest called Devabhāga Śrautarṣa. Read *Vedic Index,* I. pp. 29, 166, 316, 322, 376, 380, 521 ; II. 6, 63, etc.

277. *Taittirīya Brāhmaṇa,* I. 5. 9. 1 ; *Aitareya Brāhmaṇa,* I. 14. 6. See *Vedic Index,* II. 215, note (38) for further references to *arājatā* in the later works.

278. *Manu,* VII. 27-28, p. 220. Dr. Kane, while commenting on this particular topic (Kane, *op. cit.,* III. p. 26) also refers to *Manu,* VII. 3, 4, which, in my opinion, refers more to the decline of a king's fame rather than to the latter's being punished by the people.

279. *Manu,* VIII. 111, p. 233.

280. *Anuśāsanaparvan,* Ch. 61. vv. 32-32 ; see also Kane, *op. cit.,* III. p. 26.

281. *Śāntiparvan,* Ch. 92. v. 6. Yājñavalkya endorses the earlier view that a bad king could be deposed and killed by the people. *Yājñavalkya,* I. 356.

282. *Rāmāyaṇa, Ayodhyākāṇḍa,* Ch. 67, pp. 218-19. For a good English rendering, read Hari Prasad Sastri, *The Ramayana of Valmiki,* I. pp. 307-309 (London, 1952).

282a. *Rāmāyaṇa, ibid.,* Ch. 68, p. 219.

283. *Rāmāyaṇa, ibid.,* Ch. 67, vv. 3. 31, p. 219, *op. cit.* See also *ibid.,* v. 16. p. 218. See also Aiyangar, *op. cit.,* p. 82, note (140).

284. *Mahābhārata, Śāntiparvan,* Chs. 59, 67, and 68. See also *ibid.,* Ch. 92, vv. 6-9 ; *Kāmandaka, Nītisara,* II. 40 ; *Matsya Purāṇa,* Ch. 225, vv. 8-9.

284a. *Jātaka,* VI. p. 39 ; see also Altekar, *op. cit.,* p. 14, and note (3).

284b. Rhys. Davids, *Buddhist Suttas,* pp. 3-6 (S.B.E. XI) ; see also Aiyangar, *ibid.,* p. 78.

285. Jacobi, *The Jaina Sūtras, Ācaranga Sūtra,* II. 3.1.10 ; p. 138. See also Jayaswal, *op. cit.* p. 84, and note (35) ; Aiyangar, *ibid.,* p. 77, and note (133) ; Altekar, *ibid.,* p. 71, and note (2).

286. Jacobi, H. *The Jaina Sūtras,* Part II, p. xi, (S.B.E. XLV, 1894).

286a. Professor Aiyangar would interpret *arāja-vyasānabādhaḥ* as an *interregnum* (Aiyangar, *ibid.,* p. 49, and note 92). There is no justification for this in view of what Kauṭilya himself says relating to anarchy, as I have shown here.

287. *Kauṭilya,* Bk. I. Ch. X, 16, pp. 15-16 ; text, p. 16.

288. *Ibid.,* Bk. III. Ch. XVI. 191, p. 215 ; text, p. 190. Dr. Shama Sastry translated the word *rājyavibhrama* as national disturbances (*Kauṭilya,* p. 215) ; while Professor Aiyangar understood by it an *interregnum* (Aiyangar, *ibid.,* pp. 83, 84, and note (146) on page 84). But the learned Professor does not appear to be correct

in interpreting it as an *interregnum*. Dr. Sastry's interpretation is more plausible. I would, however, take it as civil war.

289. *Kauṭilya*, Bk. V. Ch. V. 253, p. 282 ; text, p. 253.
290. Jayaswal, *op. cit.*, pp. 82, 83, 84, 164-68.
291. Kane, *op. cit.*, III. pp. 30-31. It appears as if we are to construe from the comments of Dr. Kane that *arājatā* was not really a state of chaos and the negation of any constitution but just a condition where there was no king or ruler. There is some truth in this interpretation. What is to be noted is that it was precisely the condition where there was no king that led to all misery. But I cannot understand the significance of all the examples given by the eminent Jurist, viz., Yuan Chwāng's description of the election of Harṣavardhana, the election of the successor to the Pallava king Paramésvaravarman II,—which latter is mentioned in one of the inscriptions of the Vaikunṭha Perumāḷa temple, as is known to students of the history of southern India,—and the selection as king of the once-poor man Vāsaskara as described in the *Rājtaraṅgiṇī*.

    Professor Aiyangar states that Dr. Jayaswal's theory is ingenious but opposed to the traditional connotation of the term *arājatā* as given in the *Ayodhyākāṇḍa* of the *Rāmāyaṇa*, Ch. 67 (Aiyangar, *op. cit.* p. 49, and note 92).

    Professor U. N. Ghoshal's condemnation of Dr. Jayaswal's theory is more vehement. He writes that it "is a brilliant example of the author's ingenuity in discovering the hidden meaning of familiar facts" ; that it is a novel interpretation ; that Dr. Jayaswal has invoked "an imaginary *Arājaka* constitution 'based on the rule of the law' ", and fathers "on its exponents an equally imaginary theory of the basis of the State" ; and that a portion of a text in the *Śāntiparvan* torn off its context, as is done by Dr. Jayaswal, can hardly be attributed to a class of the so-called *arājaka* democrats "whose existence is unknown to history" (Ghoshal, *The Beginnings*. pp. 107-08).
292. *Manu*, VII. 3, p. 216.
293. *Mahābhārata, Śāntiparvan*, Ch. 59. vv. 106-08 ; Ch. 66 of the Bombay ed. ; Ch. 67 of the Calcutta ed. See also *Kane, op. cit.*, III. 31, and note (41) for the citations of the references to *Śāntiparvan*. This theory is repeated in the *Śukranītisāra*, I. ll. 125-40.
294. Kauṭilya, Bk. I. Ch. IV, 9. p. 8 ; text, p. 9.
295. *Ibid*, Bk. I. Ch. XIII. 23, p. 22 ; text pp. 22-23.
296. See, for instance, Professor Aiyangar, *op. cit.*, p. 39 and note (65), where the learned Professor compares it with the account given in the *Śāntiparvan*, Chapter 59.
297. Bhandarkar, *Carmichael Lectures*, pp. 119, 122-24, *op. cit.* I am afraid this eminent historian had a poor idea of the origin of the social contract theory. On page 119 of the same book, he states that "the theory in Europe was, as we know, originated by Hobbes, and further developed or altered by Locke and Rousseau". Professor Bhandarkar was evidently not aware of the fact that it was a very ancient theory which had originated with the Greeks. Professor Aiyangar, on the other hand, rightly compared the social contract as given by Kauṭilya with that of Epicurus and his school "in which modern writers have *hitherto* seen the germ of the idea of the origin of the State in a compact" (Aiyangar, *op. cit.*, p. 81).
298. *Kauṭilya*, Bk. I. Ch. XIII. 23 pp. 22-23 ; text, pp. 22-23.
299. Aiyangar, *ibid*, p. 81, op. cit.
300. *The Bible*, Samuel, Book II. Ch. V, 3, p. 348 (London. no year).
301. Read Gettell, *op. cit.*, pp. 112-13.
302. I am glad to observe that Professor Ghoshal comes to the same conclusion. But my treatment of this subject relating to a comparison between the Indian and Western versions of the social contract theory is different to his approach

to the same subject in his revised edition of *A History of Hindu Political Theories* (1923) published in 1959 under the title of *A History of Indian Political Ideas* (etc.), which I have very often cited in my book. I agree with Professor Ghoshal when he asserts that the theory of Hobbes presents the strongest contrast to the Indian theories, since Hobbes "is the author of a comprehensive system of political philosophy which deserves to rank among the greatest of its kind". While, according to the same authority, "the Indian exponents of the contract theory are nothing if not unsystematic. Hobbes's (sic!) method of precise definition and logical deduction is not paralleled in the Indian theories. . . .Hobbes's idea of the will of the State as forming the source of moral as well as legal right constitutes an important landmark in the advance of European rationalism. We look in vain in the Indian theory of contract for such examples." With these views one may be in agreement but what one cannot understand is what the same authority says earlier on the same page, thus: "Again, while the European thinkers attribute the origin of Society and the State respectively to man's social instinct and his deliberate act of will based upon contract, their Indian counterparts *hold the State along with property to have been produced by popular agreement* and conceive the social organization to have arisen out of a process of the division of labour based upon the norm (*dharma*) of the classes concerned" (*Italics mine*). He continues to state that "the fundamental difference between the Indian and Western theories is that the former fail to rise to the level of a philosophical theory of the State attained by the latter" (Ghoshal, *History of Indian Political Ideas*, p. 539).

The statement that the State along with property came to be produced by popular agreement, as maintained by Professor Ghoshal, is controvertible. If this is admitted, we have also to agree to the view that the ancient Indians were aware of some kind of technique of popular agreements which were precedent to the establishment of the State. This may be doubted. The reader, however, would do well to carefully go through the analysis of this question by Professor Ghoshal, since it refers to the same topic but from another point of view.

I have not included in the discussion of the social contract theory the Buddhist and Jaina contribution to the same theory because, in the final analysis, neither the Buddhists nor the Jainas had any substantial theory to give to the world. I may repeat here the Buddhist concept, as gathered from the Buddhist canonical works like the *Dīgha Nikāya* and the Tibetan versions of the Buddhist thought as preserved in the fifth volume of the Tibetan *Dulva*, a *Vinaya Pīṭaka* compilation in thirteen volumes, in the following manner. According to the *Dīgha Nikāya*, there was a stage of perfect happiness which lasted for ages, but which finally gave place to an age of decline when differences in sex, colour, property, etc., arose. Along with these new problems came when men gathered together, and chose a man who could maintain social order and inflict just punishment. In return they gave him a share of their paddy. He was called the *mahāsammata* or Great Elect, the *rājan*.

The Tibetan *Dulva* has an equally interesting account to give, but the chief who was selected was the handsomest and the largest among the people, who became a regular king, and as he was the lord of the fields, he received the name of Protector of the Fields or *kṣrtriya*. He also became the lord of the law (*Dīgha Nikāya*, III. Sec. 27. P.T.S. London, 1890-1911 ; W. W. Rockhill, *The Life of the Buddha derived from Tibetan works in the Bkah-Hgyur and Bstan-Hgyur*, pp. 1-8). Professor Beni Prasad's opinion that the Buddhists borrowed the theory from the Brahmanical thinkers but that they later on developed it on their own lines, is, I think, reasonable. The learned Professor's elaborate description of the Buddhist and Jaina theories (Beni Prasad, *op. cit.*, Ch. VIII. pp. 202-42) makes interesting reading. His opinion on the Jaina contribution to the social contract theory may be noted. "In the Jaina account, government is not instituted by any definite contract. Pre-eminence on one side and need of guidance on the other establish a certain relationship. In course of time, as necessity demands, this informal relationship is converted into one of rulers and ruled" (Beni Prasad, *ibid*, p. 225). This is a correct estimate of the Jaina contribution with which I agree.

PART FOUR

A COMPARATIVE STUDY

1. Childe, Gordon, V., *Man makes Himself*, pp. 189, 215 (London, 1936). Professor Ralph Turner, however, assigns Hammurabi to *circa* 1940 B.C. (Turner, Ralph, *The Great Cultural Traditions*, I. p. 140, New York and London, 1941. First ed. 2nd impression). Both these dates are hypothetical, the less reliable being those of Professor Turner, whose date of Manu, *circa* A.D. 100 (*ibid.*, II. p. 762) is altogether erroneous. On page 133 of his I volume, Professor Turner says that he has used the dates as given in William L. Langer's *An Encyclopaedia of World History* (1940) in some cases, and in some others as those given in the publications of the Oriental Institute, University of Chicago. As regards dates, Professor Turner's statements are unreliable.
2. On Hammurabi, there is an ever-growing literature, particularly on the Continent. The following may be read in this connection: Kohler, J., Peiser, F. E., Ungnand, A., *Hammurabis Gesetz* (6 vols. 1904-23); Ulmer, Friedrich, *Hammurabi sein Land und seine Zeit* (1907); Eilers, Wilhelm, *Die Gezesetsstele Chammurabis in Die Alte Orient* (1932); Cruveilhier, Pierre, *Introduction au code d 'Hammurabi* (1937); Cuq. Edouard, *Etudes sur le droit babylonien les lois assyriennes et les lois hittites* (1927); Johns, C. H. W., *The Oldest Code of Laws in the World*, etc. (1903); Harper, Robert, F., *The Code of Hammurabi*, etc. (1904).
3. Childe, *ibid.*, p. 156.
4. For a full account of the finds in Mohenjo Daro and Harappa, read Sir John Marshall, *Mohenjo Daro and the Indus Valley Civilization*, 3 vols. (London, 1932); Ernst Mackay, *Further Excavations at Mohenjo Daro* (New Delhi, 1936); Pigott, *Prehistoric India* (London, 1950); Ernst Mackay, *Chanchu Daro Excavations*, 1935-36 (New Haven, Connecticuct, 1943); Madho Swarup Vats, *Harappa* (New Delhi, 1940); Wheeler, Sir Mortimer, *Ancient India*, III, 1947, pp. 61-76. For a succinct account of the urban civilization at Mohenjo Daro and Harappa, read Childe, Gordon, V., *New Light on the Most Ancient East*, pp. 174-85 (London 1952, rewritten).
5. *Manu*, VII. 70, p. 227; VIII. 237, p. 296; IX. 289, p. 393.
6. *Ibid.*, VII. 29, p. 220.
7. *Ibid.*, I. 2, p. 9. (Jones). Dr. Bühler calls him "Divine One" (*Manu*, I. 2, p. 1), which is less befitting than the epithet "sovereign ruler" used by Jones.
8. *Manu*, VII. 42, p. 221 (Bühler); 42, p. 125 (Jones).
9. *Ibid.*, II. 18, pp. 18-23 (Bühler); 19-23, p. 22 (Jones). In the former Madhyadeśa is located to the east of Prayāga and to the west of Vinaśanā; while in the latter, it is located to the west of Prayāga and to the east of Vinaśanā (or the land where the Sarasvatī disappeared). I think Dr. Bühler is correct.
10. Professor Childe says the same about Hammurabi's code. Childe, *op. cit.*, p. 156.
11. *Manu*, Chs. XI, XII. 1-103, pp. 430-507.
12. Turner, *op. cit.*, I. p. 141.
13. *Manu*, X. 115, p. 426.
14. *Ibid.*, VIII. 145-49, p. 279.
15. The whole concept of property as given in Manu and Hammurabi is worthy of a separate study which when made would be more in favour of the great Indian

lawgiver than in that of the Babylonian. In this connection, Dr. Kane's opinion on the law of limitations and the law of judicial procedure, is worth citing: "A careful perusal will convince any unbiassed reader that the Dharmaśāstras evolved during the course of centuries an indigenous system of judicial procedure of a high order.... This system compares most favourably with any system of judicial procedure prevalent anywhere in the West up to the 18th century A.D." (Kane, *op. cit.*, III. p. 410).

16. Turner, *ibid.*, I. p. 141.
17. *Manu*, VII. 125-26, p. 236.
18. *Ibid.*, VIII. 5, p. 253.
19. *Ibid.*, VIII. 215-19, p. 293. Read *ibid.*, 231, p. 295 for the wages of a hired herdsman, who is permitted to milk with the consent of the owner the best cow out of ten, and to take the milk thus got as his hire, "if no other wages are paid to him".
20. Turner, *op. cit.*, I. p. 140.
21. *Manu*, VIII. 415, p. 326.
22. *Ibid.*, VIII. 416-17, p. 326.
23. *Ibid.*, VIII. 65-68, pp. 265-66.
24. *Ibid.*, VIII. 70, p. 266.
25. *Ibid.*, IV. 180, 185, pp. 157-58. Read *ibid.*, 363, p. 317 for punishment for sexual intercourse with a female slave maintained by another man.

25a. Turner, *ibid.*, 5. pp. 141-42.

25b. *Manu*, VIII. The whole of this chapter (pp. 255-327) deals with civil and criminal law. On the restrictions put on the Śūdras, read *ibid.*, 20-23, pp. 255-57.

25c. *Ibid.*, VIII. 1, p. 253.

25d. *Ibid.*, VIII. 4-11, p. 254.

26. Johns, C. H. S., *The Oldest Code of Laws in the World,* Sections 196 and 200, p. 43 (Edinburgh, 1905); Kane, *op. cit.*, III. p. 389; Turner, *ibid.*, I. p. 142.
27. *Manu*, VIII. 334, p. 312.
28. *Ibid.*, VIII. 280, p. 303; Kane, *ibid.*, III. p. 389.
29. *The Bible*, Leviticus, XXIV. 20, p. 143. See also *ibid.*, p. 21 where the universality of law is proclaimed thus: "Ye shall have one manner of law, as well for the stranger, as for one of your own country: for I am the Lord your God."
30. *The Bible*, Deut. XIX. 21, p. 224.
31. On the Twelve Tables, read Liddell, Henry, G. A., *A History of Rome*, etc., pp. 114-16 (ed. by P. V. M. Benécke. London, 1902).
32. Ortolan, *History of Roman Law*, p. 114 (Trans. by Pritchard and Nasmyth, 1871), cited by Kane, *ibid.*, III. p. 389, and note 617.
33. Turner, *ibid.*, I. p. 142. Cf. Johns, *op. cit.*, Sects. 1, 8, 14, 22, 129, 130, 154-58; pp. 1, 3, 5, 6, 24, 25 31.
34. *Manu*, VIII. 279, p. 303.
35. Turner, *ibid.*, I. p. 142.
36. *Manu*, VIII. 352-53, p. 315.
37. *Ibid.*, VIII. 364, p. 317.
38. *Ibid.*, VIII. 378, p. 320.
39. *Ibid.*, VIII. 379, p. 320.
40. *Ibid.*, VIII. 323-24, p. 310.
41. *Ibid.*, VIII. 325, p. 311.
42. *Ibid.*, VIII. 326-34, pp. 311-12.
43. *Ibid.*, VIII. 40, p. 260.
44. *Ibid.*, VII. 88, p. 230.
45. *Ibid.*, VII. 89, p. 230.
46. *Ibid.*, VII. 94, p. 231. Read *ibid.*, 90-93, pp. 230-33, for laws regarding the actual conduct of wars.

47. *Manu*, VIII. 203, p. 290.
48. *Ibid.*, VIII. 286, p. 393. An adulterer was known by his redundant limbs, says Manu, while describing the various categories of socially wicked men. See *ibid.*, XI. 50, p. 490.
49. *Ibid.*, IX. 290, pp. 393-94.
50. Bühler, *ibid.*, Intr. pp. ci. cii ; VIII. 109-16, pp. 273-74.
51. *Manu*, VIII. 335-36, p. 313.
52. *Ibid.*, VIII. 337-38, p. 313.
53. *Ibid.*, VIII. 129-30, p. 276.
54. *Ibid.*, VII. 16, p. 218.
55. *Ibid.*, VIII. 126, p. 276.
56. *Ibid.*, VIII. 318, p. 309. Read Kane, *op. cit.*, III. pp. 338-406. Dr. Kane has interesting details to give on the punishments inflicted on Brahmans (Kane, *ibid.*, p. 397).
57. *Manu*, VIII. 14-15, p. 255. Cf. the instructions given to the judges by the Egyptian Emperor Thutmol III. The judges should act alike to all, regarding him whom they know as well as him whom they do not know ; and him who was near to the judges as well as him who was far away from the judges (Turner, *op. cit.*, I. p. 308). But here is nothing of the grand Indian concept of equity and sacredness in the Egyptian idea of justice.
58. Stephens, *History of Criminal Law*, I. p. 471, cited by Kane, *ibid.*, III. p. 390.
59. Hart, *Way of Justice*, p. 94, cited by Kane, *ibid.*
60. Brew, J.M., *In the Service of Youth*, p. 208 ; Kane, *ibid.*, p. 391.
61. Turner, *op. cit.*, I. p. 142. For further details, read Johns, *op. cit.*, on dowry, Sects., 138, 139, 159-61, 163, 164 ; on divorce, Sects., 137, 138 ; on wife, Sects., 127, 128, 133-42, 144, 145, 148-51, 153 ; on debt, Sects. 48, 113, 117, 151.
62. *Manu*, V. 148, p. 195. In the next sentence, Manu confirms this stricture passed on a woman: "She must not seek to separate herself from her father, husband, or sons ; by leaving there she would make both (her own and her husband's) families contemptible" (*Manu*, V. 149, p. 195, Cf. *ibid.*, IX. 3, p. 328). Read also *ibid.*, V. 150-56, pp. 195-96.
63. *Manu*, IX. 3, p. 328.
64. *Ibid.*, IX. 4, p. 328.
65. *Ibid.*, IX. 11, p. 329.
66. *Ibid.*, IX. 18, p. 330.
67. *Ibid.*, IX. 96, p. 344.
68. *Ibid.*, IX. 101-02, p. 345.
69. *Ibid.*, IX. 275, p. 302.
70. *Ibid*, VIII. 389, p. 32.
71. *Ibid.*, IX. 46, p. 335.
72. *Ibid.*, IX. 19-25, pp. 330-31.
73. *Ibid.*, IX. 59-80, pp. 337-42.
74. *Ibid.*, IX. 59, p. 337.
75. *Ibid.*, IX. 81, p. 342.
76. *Ibid.*, IX. 82, p. 342.
77. *Ibid.*, IX. 87, pp. 342-43. I do not wish to cite the many references to this side of the question.
78. *Ibid.*, IX. 98, p. 345.
78a. *Ibid.*, IX. 100, p. 345.
79. *Ibid.*, IX, 194, p. 370-71. For a definition and full account of *Strīdhana*, read Kane, *op. cit.*, III. pp. 772-78.
80. Professor Jhering called the Babylonian law commercial. Jhering, *op. cit.*, pp. 185 ff.
81. Professor Georg Bühler, while commenting on the *dharmasūtras* and the

dharmaśāstras, wrote that the latter were typified by *Manusmṛiti* and the digest of *Yājñavalkya* ; and that the *dharmaśāstras* "are free from all signs of sectarian influence, or of having been composed, like many of the later Digests, at royal command" (*Manu,* Intr. p. liv). This is an admission on the part of the learned Western critic, who was otherwise by no means sympathetic to the regulations of Manu.

82. Turner, *op. cit.,* I. p. 306.
83. Turner, *ibid.,* I. pp. 136-37, 313.
84. Turner, *ibid.,* I. p. 137.
85. Turner, *ibid.,* I. p. 136.
86. Read Saletore, B.A., "A Sumerian Custom and its Historic Indian Parallels" in the *Journal of the Assam Historical Research Society,* IV. (1936) pp. 1-11.
87. Turner, *ibid.,* I. pp. 310-11.
88. *Manu,* VII. 58-59, p. 225.
89. *Ibid.,* VII. 59-62, p. 225.
90. Read Saletore, *I.D.R. West,* pp. 60-62, 69.
91. *Manu,* VII. 114-18, p. 234.
92. *Ibid,* VII. 119, p. 235.
93. *Ibid.,* VII. 82, p. 229.
94. *Ibid.,* VII. 120-21, p. 235.
95. *Ibid.,* VII. 123, p. 235.
96. *Ibid.,* VII. 124, p. 235. Cf. *ibid.,* VIII. 231, p. 382.
97. *Ibid.,* VIII. 34, p. 259.
98. *Ibid.,* IX. 273, p. 390.
99. *Ibid.,* IX. 275, p. 391.
100. Turner, *ibid.,* I. pp. 309-10.
101. *Manu,* VII. 80, p. 229.
102. *Ibid.,* VII. 127-28, p. 236.
103. *Ibid.,*VIII. 398, 401, pp. 323-24.
104. *Ibid.,* VII. 129, p. 236.
105. *Ibid.,* VII. 139, p. 238.
106. *Ibid.,* VII. 130-32, pp. 236-37.
107. Turner, *ibid.,* I. p. 309.
108. *Manu,* VII. 120, pp. 427-28.
109. *Ibid.,* VII. 137, p. 237.
110. *Ibid.,* VII. 138, p. 238.
111. Turner, *ibid.,* I. pp. 309-10.
112. *Manu,* VII. 133, p. 237.
113. *Ibid.,* VII. 133, p. 237 ; VIII. 392-93, p. 322. The equivalents of a *māṣa* in silver and gold are given in *ibid.,* VIII. 133-36, p. 277.
114. *Ibid.,* VIII. 159, p. 282.
115. *Ibid.,* VIII. 398, 401, 407, pp. 323-25.
116 & 117. Turner, *ibid.,* I. pp. 311-12.
118. *Manu,* VII. 87-94, 164-67, 170-71, 187-99, pp. 230-31, 242-48.
119. *Ibid.,* VII. 201-03, pp. 248-49.
120 & 121. *Ibid.,* II. 17-22, pp. 32-33.
122. *Ibid.,* VIII. 159-211, pp. 240-50. On an ambassador, see *ibid.,* VIII. 63, pp. 225-26.
123. See Saletore, *I.D.R. West,* pp. 33-42.
124. MacIver, *op. cit.,* pp. 16, 162-64, 224, 226.
125. *Manu,* VII. 19, p. 219. See also *ibid.,* 124-25, p. 275-76, 306, where, while describing to what extent physical punishment could be inflicted on criminals (VIII. 124-25, pp. 299-300),—from which the Brahmans were exempted, their punishment being banishment—Manu gives only ten places on which it could be inflicted.

126. This is Professor MacIver's assessment of ancient society. See MacIver, *ibid.*, p. 224.
127. *Manu*, II. 6, 9-12, pp. 30-31.
128. MacIver, *ibid.*, p. 226.
129. Read *Manu*, VIII. 20-21, p. 255 ; X. 4, etc., for the disabilities on the Śūdras.
130. MacIver, *ibid.*, p. 185.
131 & 132. MacIver, *ibid.*, p. 186.
133. *Manu*, VII. 22, 24, pp. 219-20.
134. *Ibid.*, VIII. 172, p. 285.
135. *Ibid.*, VIII. 172, 303-06, pp. 285, 307 ; IX. 253, p. 386.
136. MacIver, *ibid.*, p. 184.
137. MacIver, *ibid.*, p. 185.
138. On the duties of the Brahmans, read *Manu*, I. 88, 102-10 ; IV. 2-13 ; X 1-2, 74-76 ; on those of the Kṣatriyas, I. 89 ; X. 77-79, 115 ; VII. 87-95, 114 ; VIII. 411-12 ; X. 83, 95, 117 ; on those of the Vaiśyas, I. 90 ; VIII. 410, 418 ; IX. 326-33 ; X. 78-80 ; X. 98 ; on those of the Śūdras, I. 91 ; VIII. 410, 418 ; IX. 333-35 ; X. 99-100 ; 121-29. The references in this note are only to the verses, and not to the pages.
139. *Manu*, X. 63, p. 416.
140. *Ibid.*, I. 107, p. 27.
141. MacIver, *ibid.*, pp. 186-87.
142. It would be tedious to give all the references to these three topics in the *Manusmṛiti*. But the following may be read: *Manu*, III. 67, 153, etc. ; II. 108, 176, 185-87, etc. ; III. 70-121, etc., all the references being to verses.
143. *Kauṭilya*, Bk. I. Ch. I, 1, p. 1 ; text, p. 1.
144. *Ibid.*, Bk. XV. Ch. I. 427, p. 459 ; text, p. 427.
145. *Manu*, I. 2, 116, pp. 2, 28 ; II. 1, p. 29 ; VII. 1, p. 216.
146. *Kauṭilya*, Bk. I. Ch. III. 7, p. 6 ; p. 7.
147. *Ibid.*, Bk. I. Ch. V. 10, p. 10 ; text, p. 10.
148. & 149. *Ibid.*, Bk. I. Ch. II. 7, pp. 5-6 ; text, pp. 6-7. Kauṭilya seems to have used the term *ānvikṣakī* in the sense of logical process. This is clear from his definition of the term in which there is no reference to the rejection of the soul and the materialistic concept of existence which came to be associated with *ānvikṣaki* in later literature. Read Kane, *op. cit.*, III. pp. 46, (and note 56), 47, (and note 58). Kauṭilya is definitely more intelligible in his insistence on the study of *ānvikṣakī* than the author of the *Bārhaspatyasūtra*, who stated that the king was to follow the *Laukāyatī* doctrines at the time of securing material wealth (*artha*), and the *Kāpālikaśāstra* at the time of securing sexual and similar desires (*Bārhaspatyasūtra*, II. 5-6, cited by Kane, *ibid.*, p. 48, note 59). Even if we take *ānvīkṣakī* in the latter sense of atheism, it is clear from Manu's condemnation of the atheists that atheism had no place in that great lawgiver's political philosophy. See *Manu*, II. 11 ; III. 150 ; IV. 163 ; VIII. 22, IX. 67, pp. 31, 103, 154, 256, 443-44.
150. *Kauṭilya*, Bk. I. Ch. II. 6, p. 5 ; text, p. 6.
151. *Ibid.*, Bk. I. Ch. III. 8, p. 7 ; text, p. 8. See also *ibid.*, 9, p. 8 ; text, p. 9.
152. *Ibid.*, Bk. I. Ch. IV. 9, p. 8 ; text, p. 9
153. *Ibid.*, Bk. I. Ch. IV. 8, p. 8 ; text, p. 8.
153a. *Ibid.*, Bk. IX. Ch. VII. pp. 385-90 ; text, pp. 358-63.
154. & 155. *Ibid.*, Bk. III. Ch. I. 150, p. 171 ; text, p. 150. I am afraid I cannot agree with Dr. Shama Sastry's interpretation of *nyāya* as king's law. It is nearer equity, while *saṁsthā* probably meant that which had existed or which was established in the sense of precedent.
156. *Ibid.*, Bk. I. Ch. XV. 29, p. 28 ; text, p. 29. The number twelve given by Kauṭilya, as referring to Manu, does not agree with the printed versions of the *Manusmṛiti*, but with *Kāmandakīya Nītiśāstra*, XI. 67 (Cf. Bühler, *Manu*, p. xxxviii). In the

available versions of the *Manusmṛiti*, the number is either seven or eight (*Manu*, VII. 54, p. 224). It is possible that Kauṭilya here refers to an old *Mānavadharma-śāstra* which is lost (Cf. Bühler, *ibid.*, p. xxxvi). Kauṭilya's continual reference to Manu, I may reiterate, definitely points to Manu's having lived long before Kauṭilya, whatever may be the fate of the *dharmaśāstra* attributed to Manu.

157. *Kauṭilya*, Bk. II. Ch. VII. 63, p. 62 ; text, p. 63. Here, too, I think Kauṭilya refers to an earlier Manu. The punishment attributed to Manu by Kauṭilya, cannot be traced in the *Manusmṛiti*, where we have spies supervising the work of government officials (VII. 122, p. 235) ; and the confiscation of the property of those government servants, who marred the business of suitors in law suits (IX. 231, p. 283 ; see also *ibid.*, 259, p. 388). But this is not the same which is mentioned by Kauṭilya.
158. *Kauṭilya*, Bk. III. Ch. XI. 177, p. 201 ; text, p. 177. As the late Dr. Shama Sastry wrote (*ibid.*, p. 201, note 1), this rule is not included in the extant *Manusmṛiti*. On perjury, read *Manusmṛiti*, VIII. 119-23, 257, 263, pp. 273, 299-301.
159. *Kauṭilya*, Bk. III. Ch. XVII. 192, pp. 216-17 ; text, p. 192. This citation is, again, not traceable in the extant *Manusmṛiti*, where the severest punishments are prescribed for thieves. *Manu*, IX. 275-80, pp. 391-92.
160. *Manu*, VII. 63-68, 155-59, pp. 225-26, 240-41. See also Saletore, *I.D.R. West*, pp. 22-23.
161. *Kauṭilya*. Bk. VI. Ch. I. 259, p. 289 ; text, p. 289.
162. *Ibid.*, Bk. XV. Ch. I. 431, p. 463 ; text, p. 431.
163. *Ibid.*, Bk. II. Ch. X. 75, p. 75 ; text, p. 75. The late Dr. Shama Sastry had translated this passage thus: "Having followed all sciences and having fully observed forms of writing in vogue, these rules of writing writs have been laid down by Kauṭilya in the interest of kings" (*ibid.*, p. 75, trans.). This is inadmissible, since the text clearly states *Narendrārthe* which, as Professor Rangaswami Aiyangar rightly said, means "for the sake of Narendra" (Aiyangar, *op. cit.*, pp. 13, and note (21), 79, and note (135) which unmistakenably points to Candragupta Maurya.
164. Professor Aiyangar is correct in maintaining that the State in the *Arthaśāstra* was not a small one but an empire (Aiyangar, *ibid.*, pp. 158, 169).
165. Manu certainly dealt with purely materialistic questions like agriculture, inheritance, trade, defamation, drinks, etc. But even here the great lawgiver's sole concern was more ethical than materialistic. I do not wish to cite the references in Manu to the various topics mentioned above.
166. As in the case of Manu, the numerous references in the *Arthaśāstra* are not given. The reader, if he fights shy of wading through the translation of the *Arthaśāstra*, may at least see its Index in order to verify the number of problems given by me.
167. *Manu*, VII. 5, 9, 13, pp. 217, 218.
168. On *rājatva*, read *Kauṭilya*, Bk. I. Ch. VII. 13, p. 12 ; text, p. 13 ; on *prakṛitiḥ*, text, pp. 257, 259, 321.
169. *Ibid.*, Bk. VI. Ch. II. 261, p. 291 ; text, p. 261.
170. Professor U. N. Ghoshal (*History of Indian Political Ideas*, pp. 153-55) following Professor G. B. Bottazzi (*Precursori di Nicolo Machiavelli in India ed in Grecia, Kauṭilya ed Thucidide*, p. 21), and Professor A. Hillebrandt (*Altindische Politik*, p. 36), have compared Kauṭilya with Machiavelli. The first point of comparison between Kauṭilya and Machiavelli is that which refers to the wide range of subjects. Here we may agree with Professor Ghoshal that the Indian thinker's concept of a single branch of knowledge is not seen in Machiavelli. The second point of comparison is the method used by them. Machiavelli's was the empirical method, that is, a method based on observation and experiment, and not on theory. Kauṭilya's was to a great extent an empirical method, as Professor Ghoshal main-

tains (p. 155). I shall discuss this important point relating to method towards the end of my comparative study of Aristotle and Kauṭilya.

The third point of comparison between Machiavelli and Kauṭilya refers to the former's application of history to point a moral which Kauṭilya certainly does at the beginning of the latter's work, while discussing the need to restrain the organs of the senses, when he cites twelve examples of earlier rulers, who had come to grief in this connection (Bk. I. Ch. VI. 12, p. 11), and again in a later context (Bk. I. Ch. XX. 41, p. 40).

The fourth point of comparison is said to be the similarity in the main head of discussion in the work of the two great thinkers. Machiavelli dwells on the preservation and increase of dominion in his *Prince* ; and Kauṭilya also dwells on the acquisition and preservation of dominion.

The fifth point of comparison relates to the rules and principles adopted by both who, while sympathizing with the aspirations of the subjects, advocate the use of force and fraud to consolidate the interests of the State.

To these we may add that both the Italian and the Indian thinkers championed the cause of a centralized and autocratic monarchy against all other forms of government.

The points of contrast between Machiavelli and Kauṭilya are the following: Machiavelli heralded a new age of political philosophy in Europe ; while Kauṭilya was practically the last link in the chain of great political thinkers. In this connection I find it difficult to agree with Professor Ghoshal when he states that the individual authors and schools which preceded Kauṭilya introduced a number of modernist political ideas into the stock of our ancient political thought (Ghoshal, *History*, etc., p. 154). If at all any one was responsible for introducing what may be termed revolutionary ideas, which to some extent seem modern, it was Kauṭilya, and not his predecessors about whom we know so little, and who live mostly in the work of Kauṭilya himself. The works of Kauṭilya's predecessors are not extant ; and from what few details are available about some aspects of some theories, it would be hazardous to postulate the view that they were modern in their outlook.

Secondly, in Machiavelli we do not have the detailed treatment of the machinery and working of government which is met with in Kauṭilya.

Thirdly, Machiavelli pours his wrath upon the aristocrats ; while Kauṭilya does not single out any class or clan or caste in the country for criticism. On the other hand, he is most severe with traitors—an attitude which is perfectly justifiable on account of the treachery of not less than three Indian royal renegades, who had sided with Alexander the Great against their own country (Read Saletore, *I.D.R. West*, pp. 84-85).

And, finally, in Machiavelli there was an intense patriotism which was made the corner-stone of his whole policy of freeing his motherland from foreign rule. The closing chapter of his *Prince* indicates to us the depth of his feeling in regard to the deliverance of his land which took place only 300 years after him. No such patriotic aim is noticeable in Kauṭilya. There was no patriotism with the latter but there was an equally powerful feeling and urge which in those distant ages served the same purpose as patriotism, namely, the desire to preserve the ancient scriptures and the ancient usage, etc. It is this which, as we have already noticed in this work, is mentioned at the end of the *Arthaśāsrta*.

Professor Ghoshal has not given any reason why this "fundamental difference", as he rightly calls it, existed in their objectives. We may explain it thus: when Machiavelli lived he saw his country (Italy) passing under the dominion of foreigners. This was as a result of the treaty of Cateau Cambrésis (1559) by which Spain retained her hold over Italy, particularly over Milan and Naples, while the French controlled some other parts of Italy. A few years earlier Machiavelli had written that Italy "was without head, without order, beaten, despoiled, torn, over-run" ; that "she had endured every kind of desolation" ; and that "to all of us the barbarous dominion stinks" (Grant, A. J., *Europe*: *The History of the Last Five Centuries*, p. 480, London, 1949).

But the situation in India was quite different. Kauṭilya's royal patron had already uprooted the vile Nandas, and had planned to overthrow the foreigners from the north-western parts of the Mauryan dominion. The "barbarous dominion" in the homeland of Magadha had been liquidated, while that outside was in the process of being wiped out. And now there remained the sole question of consolidating the Empire both against internal and external enemies—the followers of the Nandas and the hirelings of the Macedonians. There was also the equally great question of preventing a repetition of the history of treachery associated with the three traitors mentioned above. Here we have, therefore, a fundamental difference in the objectives of the policies of the two great writers which has been missed by historians.

171. Aristotle, *Politics*, Intr. p. 2.
172 & 173. Cf. Saletore, *I.D.R. West*, pp. 105-07, 325.
174 & 175. Davis, *Aristotle*, Intr. pp. 1-2.
176. Davis, *ibid.*, p. 3.
177. Davis, *ibid.*, pp. 3, 9, 10.
178. Professor Davis admits that Aristotle was not the founder of Political Science. Read Davis, *ibid.*, p. 3. As for Kauṭilya, enough has been said in this book of his many predecessors and the antiquity of Political Science in India.
179. *Aristotle*, III. 14. 4, p. 133.
180. *Ibid.*, III. 14. 14, p. 135.
181. *Ibid.*, VII. 6. 7, pp. 270-71.
182. *Ibid.*, VII. 13. 3, p 286.
183. Read Sir Henry Maine, *Early History of Institutions*, Lecture, XIII ; T. H. Green, *Principles of Political Obligation*, pp. 99-100 (With an Introduction by Lord Lindsay, London, 1948). Professor Rangaswami Aiyangar has rightly rejected the observations of both Sir Henry Maine and Professor Green as being one-sided and erroneous (Read Aiyangar, *op. cit.*, pp. 11, 52, 53, 68).
184. *Kauṭilya*, Bk. III. Ch. XIII. 182, p. 206 ; text, p. 181.
185. *Ibid.*, Bk. VII. Ch. XIV. 307, p. 335 ; text, p. 307.
186. Davis, *ibid.*, p. 6.
187. Davis, *ibid.*, pp. 1-2. See *ibid.*, VII. 3-4, pp. 265-68 for conditions of a perfect State wherein Aristotle imposes limitations on population and territory.
188. *Aristotle*, I. 11. 12, p. 49.
189. *Ibid.*, I. 5. 7, p. 38.
190. *Ibid.*, I. 13, p. 51.
191. See above notes (62) and (63) in this Part.
192. *Kauṭilya*, Bk. III. Ch..III. 154, p. 175 ; text, p. 154.
193. *Aristotle*, I. 2. 16, pp. 29-30.
194. *Ibid.*, II. 5, 12, p. 63.
195. *Ibid.*, III. 15. 16, p. 138.
196. *Ibid.*, IV. 12, p. 171.
197. *Ibid.*, I. 8. 12, p. 40.
198. *Ibid.*, II. 7. 14, p. 75.
199. *Ibid.*, II. 6. 7, p. 68.
200. *Kauṭilya*, pp. 283-365 (trans.).
201. & 202. *Aristotle*, I. 2. 8, p. 28.
203. *Ibid.*, I. 12, p. 29.
204. Cf. Davis—"It is often difficult to follow his (Aristotle's) discussions of these and cognate subjects" (Davis, *ibid.*, Intr. p. 5).

205. Read Gettell, *op. cit.*, pp. 59-62.
206. *Kauṭilya*, Bk. V. Ch. I. 238, p. 267 ; text, p. 237.
207. *Ibid.*, Bk. V. Ch. II. 246, p. 275 ; text, p. 246. Read also Law, *Studies*, p. 223.
208. *Aristotle*, I. 1. 1. ff., pp. 25-26.
209. *Ibid.*, I. 2. 6 ff., pp. 27-28, *op. cit.*
210. *Kauṭilya*, Bk. II. Ch. I. 46 ff., pp. 45-48.
211. See *Kauṭilya*, pp. 46-47, where it is stated that the king shall bestow on cultivators only such favours and remissions as would tend to swell the treasury ; that the lands will be given for cultivation or otherwise by the king ; that the king shall exercise the right of ownership with regard to fishing, ferrying, and trading in vegetables, reservoirs, and lakes, and shall maintain at State expense the orphans, the aged, the infirm, the afflicted, the helpless, and the helpless women.
212. *Aristotle*, VII. 4 ff., pp. 265-72.
213. *Kauṭilya*, Bk. II. Ch. IV. pp. 53-55 ; text, pp. 54-57.
214. *Ibid.*, Bk. II. Ch. XXXVI. pp. 160-65 ; text, pp. 143-47.
215. *Aristotle*, VII. 3. 4 ff., pp. 265-70.
216. *Ibid.*, IV. 4. 8-11, pp. 152-53.
217. *Ibid.*, V. 3. 6, pp. 192-93.
218. *Ibid.*, II. 9. 22, p. 86.
219. *Kauṭilya*, Bk. VI. Ch. I. 258, p. 287 ; text, p. 257.
220. *Ibid.*, Bk. I. Ch. VII. 13, p. 12 ; text, p. 13.
221. *Ibid.*, Bk. I. Ch. VIII. p. 12-14 ; text, pp. 13-14.
222. *Ibid.*, Bk. VIII. Ch. I. 325, p. 352 ; text. pp. 324-25.
223. *Ibid.*, Bk. VI. Ch. I. 259, p. 289 ; text, p. 259.
224. Cf. Gettell, *op. cit.*, p. 191.
225. *Aristotle*, III. 6. 7-8, pp. 114-15. See also pp. 143-45, 147, 164.
226. *Kauṭilya*, Bk. XI. Ch. I. 378, p. 407 ; text, p. 378.
227. Some of these republican communities figure in Buddhist literature. We have mentioned a few details about them in this work.
228. *Aristotle*, III. 13. 3. till 14. 9, pp. 132-34.
229. *Ibid.*, III. 14. 6, p. 133 ; *op. cit.*
230. *Ibid.*, III. 13. 14, p. 132.
231. *Ibid.*, I. 12. 3, p. 50.
232. *Ibid.*, I. 13. 3, p. 51.
233. Cf. *Manu*, VII. 26, p. 220. "They declare that king to be a just inflicter of punishment, who is truthful, who acts after due consideration, who is wise, and who knows (the respective value of) virtue, pleasure, and wealth." This is by no means the only statement of Manu on this point.
234. *Kauṭilya*, Bk. I. Ch. V. 10, p. 9 ; text, p. 10.
235. *Ibid.*, Bk. I. Ch. VI. 12, pp. 10-11 ; text, pp. 11-12.
236. *Ibid.*, Bk. I. Ch. VII. 13, pp. 11-12 ; text, pp. 12-13.
237. *Aristotle*, VII. 13. 21-22, p. 290. See also *ibid.*, p. 260.
238. & 239. *Ibid.*, III. 16. 5, p. 140.
240. *Ibid.*, II. 28. 24, p. 81.
241. *Ibid.*, III. 15. 14-15, p. 138.
242. *Ibid.*, IV. 4. 31, p. 157.
243. *Ibid.*, III. 9. 8, p. 118.
244. *Ibid.*, VII. 14. 8, p. 288.
245. *Ibid.*, III. 16. 8, p. 140.
246. *Ibid.*, II. 8. 21, p. 81.
247. *Ibid.*, III. 16. 3-4, p. 139.
248. *Ibid.*, III. 13. 14, pp. 129-30.
249. *Kauṭilya*, Bk. III. Ch. I. 150, p. 170.
250. *Ibid.*, Bk. III. Ch. VII. 165, p. 188 ; text, p. 165.

251. *Aristotle*, III. 16, p. 140.
252. *Ibid.*, III. 5. 4, p. 158.
253. *Kauṭilya*, Bk. III. Ch. I. 150, p. 171, *op. cit.*
254. *Ibid.*, Bk. III. Ch. IX. 168, p. 191 ; text, p. 168. Cf. Aiyangar, *op. cit.*, pp. 63, 91-93.
255. *Kauṭilya*, Bk. III. Ch. I. 150, p. 171, *op. cit.*
256. *Ibid.*, p. 170.
257. *Ibid.*, trans. p. 170 ; text, p. 150.
258. *Aristotle*, I. 6. 3 ff., pp. 35-36.
259. *Ibid.*, I. 2. 12, p. 29.
260. *Ibid.*, I. 2. 16, p. 29.
261. *Ibid.*, III. 9. 1-3, p. 117.
262. *Ibid.*, III. 12. 1-2, p. 125.
263. *Kauṭilya*, Bk. I. Ch. II. 6, p. 5 ; text, p. 6.
264. *Ibid.*, Bk. I. Ch. IV. 9, p. 8 ; text, p. 9.
265. *Aristotle*, VI. 8. 9, p. 253.
266. *Ibid.*, VII. 13. 6, p. 284.
267. *Kauṭilya*, Bk. I. Ch. IV. 9, p. 8 ; text, p. 9.
268. *Aristotle*, III. 16. 8, p. 140, *op. cit.*
269. *Ibid.*, IV. 16. 3. 4, p. 185.
270. *Ibid.*, IV. 16. 5-6, pp. 185-86.
271. *Ibid.*, II. 8. 13, p. 79.
272. *Ibid.*, II. 9. 25, p. 86.
273. *Ibid.*, VI. 3. 6, p. 242.
274. *Ibid.*, VI. 8. 8-11, p. 253.
275. *Kauṭilya*, Bk. III. Ch. XX. 200, pp. 224-25 ; text, p. 200.
276. *Aristotle*, IV. 15. 1-4, pp. 179-80.
277. *Ibid.*, IV. 15. 5-7, p. 180.
278. *Ibid.*, IV. 15. 8-13, pp. 181-82.
279. *Ibid.*, IV. 15. 1, p. 179.
280. & 281. *Ibid.*, IV. 15. 14-19, pp. 182-83.
282. *Ibid.*, IV. 15. 11-13, p. 182.
283. *Ibid.*, VI. 8. 3-20, pp. 251-55.
284. *Ibid.*, VI. 8. 22, p. 255.
285. *Kauṭilya*, Bk. I. Chs. IX & X. pp. 14-17 ; text, pp. 15-18.
286. *Ibid.*, Bk. II. Ch. IX. 68, p. 68 ; text, p. 68. On the qualifications of ministers, read *ibid.*, Bk. I. Ch. IX. pp. 14-15, *op. cit.*
287. *Ibid.*, Bk. II. Ch. IX. 69, p. 70 ; text, p. 69.
288. The reader may consult Professor V. R. Ramachandra Dikshitar's *Mauryan Polity*, for a fuller treatment of this subject. It is not exhaustive, and not quite accurate in some places, but it gives a sufficiently good picture of the machinery of administration of the Mauryans. I do not wish to cite quite a number of books which deal with some specialized aspects of this topic.
289. While translating the word *akṣapaṭalaḥ* in Bk. II. Ch. VII, the late Dr. Shama Sastry interpreted that term to mean "Keeping of Accounts" (*Kauṭilya*, p. 61). This is incorrect. The word *akṣapaṭala* can refer only to Records Keeping. Even so late as A.D. 1128-29 there was an *akṣapaṭalaka* under king Govindacandra of Kanouj. (*Ep. Ind.* XI. pp. 24-25).
290. *Kauṭilya*, Bk. II. Ch. VII. 64, p. 63 ; text, p. 64.
291. *Kauṭilya* mentions the *amātyas* in a different context earlier in Bk. I. Ch. VIII. entitled the Creation of Ministers (*Kauṭilya*, pp. 12-14), and again in the next Chapter IX on the Creation of Councillors (*Ibid.*, pp. 14-15). See text, pp. 13-14. In neither context does he confound the *amātyas* and the *mantris* with the *mahā mātras*.

292. *Kauṭilya*, Bk. IV. Ch. I. 201, p. 227 ; text, p. 200.
293. *Ibid.*, Bk. II. Ch. IV. 59, p. 57 ; text, p. 59.
294. *Ibid.*, Bk. IV. Ch. IX. 222, p. 250 ; text, p. 222.
295. *Ibid.*, Bk. II. Ch. XXXV. 143, p. 160 ; text, p. 143.
296. *Ibid.*, Bk. IV. Ch. I. 200, p. 227, *op. cit.* The late Professor Ramachandra Dikshitar in his *Mauryan Polity*, pp. 171-72, associated the *pradeṣṭārāḥ* with what he calls the *dharmādhikārin*, or, as he called, the Judge of the High Court of Justice. According to him, "the *pradeṣṭārāḥ*, were commissioners, who occupied somewhat lower status, (than the *amātyas* who formed a panel of councillors to assist the *dharmasthas* or the judges), and answer perhaps to our modern District Judges and District Magistrates". The learned author has, I am afraid, imagined more than what the text of the *Arthaśāstra* would permit. In fact, there is a good deal of speculation in this otherwise scholarly work, which detracts its value. In my elucidation of the Executive in the *Arthaśāstra*, I have tried to follow Kauṭilya rather than most of his modern exponents.
297. *Kauṭilya*, Bk. II. Ch. VII. 63, p. 62 ; text, p. 63.
298. *Ibid.*, Bk. II. Ch. IX. 69, p. 69 ; text, pp. 64, 69.
299. *Ibid.*, Bk. II. Ch. VII. 65, 67, pp. 63, 67 ; text, pp. 64, 67, 224.
300. *Ibid.*, Bk. II. Ch. VIII. 67, p. 67 ; text, p. 67.
301. *Ibid.*, Bk. II. Ch. VIII. 67, p. 68 ; text, p. 67. On espionage, Kauṭilya states thus: "Also his (Collector-General's) subordinates, constituting his various establishments of espionage, shall along with their colleagues and followers, attend to their duties likewise" (Bk. II. Ch. XXXV. 143, p. 160 ; text, p. 143).
302. *Ibid.*, Bk. I. Ch. XIX. 38, p. 37 ; text, p. 38.
303. See *ibid.*, Bk. V. p. 267, and *passim*.
304. *Ibid.*, Bk. I. Chs. VIII, XV. pp. 12-14 ; 26-29 ; text, pp. 13-14, 26-29.
304a. *Ibid.*, Bk. I. Ch. IX. 15, p. 15 ; text, p. 15.
305. *Ibid.*, Bk. I. Ch. IV. 9, p. 9 ; text, p. 9.
306. *Ibid.*, Bk. I. Ch. XIX. 39, p. 38 ; text, p. 39.
307. *Ibid.*, Bk. I. Ch XII. 20, p. 19 ; text, p. 20.
308. *Ibid.*, Bk. II. Ch. I. 47, p. 46 ; text, p. 47.
309. *Ibid.*, Bk. II. Ch. I. 49, p. 48 ; text, p. 48.
310. *Ibid.*, Bk. III. Ch. IX. 168, p. 191 ; text, p. 168. See also Bk. III. Ch. VIII, which opens with the statement that "Disputes concerning *vāstu* are dependent for settlement on the evidences to be furnished by people living in the neighbourhood". As to the definition of *vāstu*, it is given in the next sentence, thus: "Houses, fields, gardens, buildings of any kind (*setubandah*), lakes, and tanks are each called *vāstu*" (Bk. III. Ch. VIII. 166, p. 188 ; text, p. 166). This makes it clear that Kauṭilya laid great emphasis on usage.
311. *Aristotle*, VII. 6. 6, pp. 269-71.
312. *Kauṭilya*, Bk. III. Ch. XXVIII. pp. 139-42 ; text, pp. 126-28.
313. *Ibid.*, Bk. II. Ch. I. 46, p. 45 ; text, p. 45.
313a. *Ibid.*, Bk. V. Ch. I. 239, p. 268 ; text, p. 239.
314. *Ibid.*, Bk. I. Ch. XIX. 38, p. 37 ; text, p. 37, *op. cit*.
315. *Ibid.*, Bk. II. Ch. XVIII. 100-01, pp. 107-09 ; text, pp. 99-101.
316. *Ibid.*, Bk. I. Ch. VII. 12, p. 12 ; text, p. 12.
317. *Ibid.*, Bk. II. Ch. VI. 60-62, pp. 57-61 ; text, pp. 59-62. The word *nāgaraka* in this context has been translated by Dr. Shama Sastry as Town Clerk. But in an earlier context he had translated it as Superintendent of the Capital City (see above note 214 for reference). I follow his earlier interpretation.
318. *Ibid.*, Bk. II. Ch. XXV. 142-43, pp. 158-60 ; text, pp. 141-43.
319. *Ibid.*, Bk. II. Ch. VII. 63-65, pp. 61-64 ; text, pp. 62-64.
320. *Ibid.*, Bk. III. Chs. XIII & XIV. pp. 197-208 ; text, pp. 174-81. See also Bk. III. Chs. XV & XVL. pp. 212-16 ; text, pp. 181-87.

321. *Aristotle*, VI. 8. 11-12, p. 253.
322. *Kauṭilya*, Bk. IV. Ch. IX. 225, p. 253 ; text, p. 225.
323. *Ibid.*, Bk. IV. Ch. XIII. pp. 261-65 ; text, pp. 233-37.
324. *Ibid.*, Bk. IV. Ch. IX. 222, p. 250 ; text, p. 222 ; Bk. V. Ch. I. 238, p. 268 ; text, p. 238.
325. *Aristotle*, VI. 14, p. 254.
326. *Kauṭilya*, Bk. II. Ch. XXXVI. 144-47, pp. 161-65 ; text, pp. 143-47.
327. *Aristotle*, VI. 8. 16, p. 254.
328. *Kauṭilya*, Bk. II. Ch. VI. 61, p. 59 ; text, p. 61.
329. *Kauṭilya*, Bk. II. Ch. VII. 62, p. 61 ; text, p. 62, *op. cit*.
330. *Aristotle*, VI. 8. 18-19, p. 255.
331. *Kauṭilya*, Bk. I. Ch. XIX. 39, p. 38, *op. cit*.
332. *Ibid.*, Bk. III. Ch. I. 150, p. 170 ; text, p. 150, *op. cit*.
333. *Ibid.*, Bk. V. Ch. II. 244, p. 273 ; text, p. 244.
334. *Ibid.*, pp. 69, 71, 86, 89, 94, 99, 104-06, 109, 125, 127, 131, 135-36, 140, 142, 147, 155, 157, 232, etc., (trans.).
335. *Aristotle*, V. 5. 3 ; 15 ; 12-14 ; pp. 199, 211, 234-35.
336. *Kauṭilya*, Bk. II. Ch. VIII. pp. 65-68 ; text, pp. 65-67.
337. *Aristotle*, VII. 8. 6, p. 273.
338. *Ibid.*, VII. 8. 7-9, pp. 273-74.
339. *Kauṭilya*, Bk. II. Ch. XV. pp. 99-106 ; text, pp. 93-97.
340. *Ibid.*, Bk. II. Ch. XXXVI. 141, p. 161 ; text, p. 144.
341. *Ibid.*, Bk. IV. Ch. I. pp. 227-31 ;text, pp. 200-04.
342. *Ibid.*, Bk. IV. Ch. II. pp. 232-34 ; text, pp. 204-07.
342a. *Ibid.*, Bk. III. Ch. XII. 180, p. 204 ; text, p. 180.
342b. *Ibid.*, Bk. IV. Ch. I. 200-01, p. 227 ; text, pp. 200-01.
342c. *Aristotle*, I. 13, 13-14, p. 52.
342d. *Ibid.*, III. 5. 5, p. 111.
342e. *Ibid.*, VI. 4. 12, p. 245.
342f. *Ibid.*, VII. 9. 3, p. 274 ; cf. *ibid.*, 9. 7, p. 275.
343. *Ibid.*, VII. 15. 1, p. 291.
344. *Ibid.*, VII. 2. 16 ; 3. 8-10, pp. 262, 264-65.
345. *Ibid.*, VII. 2. 2 ; 14-14-22 ; pp. 260, 289-90.
346. *Ibid.*, I. 13. 15, p. 53.
347. *Ibid.*, II. 7. 8, pp. 73-74.
348. *Ibid.*, V. 9. 11-12, p. 215.
349. *Ibid.*, VIII. 1-2, p. 300.
350. *Kauṭilya*, Bk. I. Ch. V. 11, p. 10 ; text, p. 11.
351. *Ibid.*, Bk. I. Ch. III. 8, p. 7 ; text, p. 8.
352. *Ibid.*, XIV. Ch. I. 431, p. 463 ; text, p. 431.
353. *Bāṇabhaṭṭa*, *Kādambarī*, I. p. 109 (ed. by P. Peterson, Bombay, 1889) cited in full in Aiyangar, *op. cit.*, p. 14 (n. 25).
354. *Aristotle*, VII. 14. 3, p. 286.
355. *Kauṭilya*. Bk. III. Ch. I. 150, p. 171 ; text. p. 150.
356. *Aristotle*, III. 9. 8, p. 118.
357. *Kauṭilya*, Bk. I. Chs. VI and VII. pp. 10-12 ; text, pp. 11-13.
358. *Aristotle*, II. 5. 27, pp. 66-67.
359. *Ibid.*, VII. 9. 7, p. 275.
360. *Kauṭilya*, Bk. XIX. 39, p. 38 ; text, p. 39.
361. *Ibid.*, Bk. VII. Ch. V. 275-77, pp. 304-06 ; text, pp. 284-85.
362. *Aristotle*, III. 6. 3-6, pp. 112-13.
363. *Ibid.*, I. 2. 8, p. 28.
364. *Ibid.*,III. 9. 12, p. 119.
365. *Kauṭilya*, Bk. I. Ch. V. 11, p. 10, *op. cit*.

366. *Kauṭilya*, Bk. I. Ch. IV. 9, p. 9, *op. cit.*
367. *Aristotle*, III. 4-5 ; III. 5-10, pp. 106-07. Cf. *ibid.*, III. 3. 4, p. 105 where he again reverts to this subject.
368. *Ibid.*, III. 1. 10, p. 102.
369. *Ibid.*, III. 1. 12, p. 102.
370. *Ibid.*, III. 2. 3, p. 103 ; cf. *ibid.*, III. 2. 5, page *ibid.*
370a. *Ibid.*, VII. 7. 1, p. 270.
371. Cf. Saletore, *I. D. R. West*, p. 76.
372. *Aristotle*, VII. 7, 1-3, pp. 270-71. See also *ibid.*, VII. 14. 3, p. 286.
373. *Ibid.*, VII. 2. 3, p. 260 ; cf. *ibid.*, VII. 14, 12-22, pp. 288-90.
374. *Ibid.*, VII. 14. 15, p. 289.
375. *Thucydides*, I. p. 24 ; II. 82, 83 (Benjamin Jowett's trans. 1st ed.), cited by Fowler, Warde, W., *The City State of the Greeks and the Romans*, pp. 250, 255 (London, 1910).
376. *Thucydides*, I. p. 222 cited by Fowler, *ibid.*, p. 256.
377. *Ibid.*, I. p. 223 ; cited by Fowler, *ibid.*, p. 256.
378. Fowler, *ibid.*, p. 258.
379. Fowler, *ibid.*, p. 257.
380. Fowler, *ibid.*, p. 258, and *ibid.*, n(1).
381. *Aristotle*, III. 1. 4-5, p. 100.
382. *Ibid.*, III. 2. 1-3, p. 103.
383. *Ibid.*, III. 1. 5, p. 101.
384. *Ibid.*, III. 1. 5-12, pp. 100-01 ; Cf. *ibid.*, 2. 2, p. 103.
385. *Ibid.*, III. 4. 10-11, pp. 107-08 ; Cf. *ibid.*, III. 13. 12, p. 129.
386. *Ibid.*, III. 4. 9, p. 107, *op. cit.*
387. *Ibid.*, III. 4. 5, p. 106.
388. Altekar, *op. cit.*, p. 38.
389. Gettell, *op. cit.*, pp. 375-89.
390. Laksi, Harold, *Grammar of Politics*, p. 57 (London and New York, 1934).
391. Green, T. H., *Political Obligation*, pp. 37-38.
392. MacIver, *op. cit.*, p. 21.
393. *Ibid.*, pp. 154-60. Read also Gettell, *ibid.*, pp. 186-87, for a clear and able discussion of this problem.
394. *Kauṭilya*, Bk. VIII. Ch. II. 326, p. 353 ; text, pp. 325-26.
395. *Manu*, VIII. 8, p. 217.
396. See note (289) of Part Three above.
397. *Kauṭilya*, Bk. IV. Ch. III. pp. 234-37 ; text, pp. 207-10 ; Bk. VIII. Ch. II. pp. 352-54 ; text, pp. 325-27.
398. *Ibid.*, Bk. XV. Ch. I. 431, p. 463 ; text, p. 431.
399. *Manu*, XII. 52-72, pp. 496-99.
400. Ghoshal, *A History*, pp. 54, 207-08, 425-26, 481, 550-51, 564. On page 61, note (8), Professor Ghoshal does not accept Professor V. P. Varma's views (*J.B.R.S.* XXXIX, p. 74) that there was no room for the concept of rights in the theory of *dharma* of the Hindus, by saying that the texts utilized by Professor Ghoshal contradict Professor Varma's contention. On page 567, note (23), Professor Ghoshal again refers to Professor Varma's opinion, and again rejects it as being "negatived by the clear evidence of the *Śmṛti* texts from first to last as explained above".
401. Gettell, *ibid.*, p. 154.
402. *Manu*, VIII. 411, p. 325.
403. *Ibid.*, X. 83, 85, pp. 420-21. See also 86-95, pp. 421-22.
404. *Manu*, X. 98, p. 423.
405. *Ibid.*, X. 116, p. 427.
406. *Ibid.*, X. 115, p. 426.
407. *Ibid.*, VIII. 339, p. 313.

408. Gettell, *ibid.*, p. 150.
409. *Ibid.*, p. 152.
410. *Kauṭilya*, III. Ch. II. pp. 172-75 ; text, pp. 152-54.
411. *Manu*, IX. 192, p. 370.
412. *Ibid.*, IX. 194, pp. 370-71.
413. *Manu*, IX. 199, p. 372.
414. *Ibid.*, V. 160-64 ; X. 65, pp. 197, 339. On the marriage of virgin widows, *ibid.*, IX. 69-70, 176, pp. 339-40, 363.
415. *Kauṭilya*, Bk. III. Ch. II. pp. 173-74, *op. cit.*
416. *Ibid.*, Bk. III. Ch. III. 155, pp. 175-76 ; text, p. 154.
417. *Ibid.*, p. 177 ; pp. 155-57.
418. *Ibid.*, Bk. IV. Ch. IV. 159, pp. 180-81 ; text, pp. 158-59.
419. Read my *India's Diplomatic Relations with the West* (1958) and *India's Diplomatic Relations with the East* (1960) for the numerous examples of Indians, who went to the foreign lands either on political or commercial missions.
420. *Kauṭilya*, Bk. IV. Ch. III. 155, pp. 177-78 ; text, pp. 155-56.
421. *Ibid.*, Bk. IV. Ch. VIII. 221, p. 249 ; text, p. 221.
422. *Manu*, VII. 149, p. 279.
423. *Kauṭilya*, Bk. III. Ch. XIII. 182, p. 207 ; text, pp. 182-83.
424. *Ibid.*, 190-91, pp. 215-16 ; text, p. 191.
425. *Ibid.*, 190, p. 215 ; text, p. 190.
426. *Ibid.*, Bk. II. Ch. I. 46, pp. 45-46 ; text, p. 46.
427. *Ibid.*, Bk. II. Ch. I. 47, p. 47 ; text, p. 47.
428. *Ibid.*, Bk. II. Ch. XXVIII. 127, p. 140 ; text, p. 127.
429. *Manu*, VIII. 27-28, p. 258.
430. *Kauṭilya*, Bk. IV. Ch. I. 203, p. 231 ; text, p. 203. Of the three kinds of amercements, first, middlemost, and highest, we have defined the first two. The highest amercement ranged from a fine of 500 *paṇas* to 1,000 *paṇas*. *Kauṭilya*, Bk. III. Ch. XVII. 192, p. 217 ; text, p. 192.
431. *Ibid.*, Bk. II. Ch. I. 47, p. 47 ; text, p. 47.
432. *Ibid.*, Bk. II. Ch. XXIX. 128-31, 142-46 ; text, pp. 128-31.
433. *Ibid.*, Bk. II. Ch. XXXVI. 146, pp. 163-64 ; text, p. 146.
434. *Ibid.*, Bk. II. Ch. XXXIV. 141, p. 157 ; text, pp. 140-41. On the measure *māṣa*, see *ibid.*, pp. 113 ff.
435. *Ibid.*, Bk. II. Ch. XXV. 119-21, pp. 131-34 ; text, pp. 119-21.
436. *Ibid.*, Bk. II. Ch. XXXVI. 146-47, p. 164 ; text, pp. 146-47.
437. *Ibid.*, Bk. III. Ch. XIII. 182, p. 207 ; text, pp. 182-83.
438. *Ibid.*, Bk. II. Ch. XVI. 98, pp. 104-05 ; text, p. 98 ; Bk. II. Ch. XXVIII. 127, p. 141 ; text, p. 127. Reference may also be made to Bk. II. Ch. XXI on the duties of the Superintendent of Tolls (*śulkādhyakṣa*), pp. 121-23, in order to see the restrictions on merchants and the movements of goods.
439. *Kauṭilya*, Bk. II. Ch. XXIII. 114, 115, pp. 125-27 ; text, pp. 113-15.
440 & 441. *Ibid.*, Bk. III. Ch. XIII. 184, p. 208 ; text, p. 184. From one of these rules it appears that twelve *paṇas* were equal to four times the amount of wages. It cannot be made out whether the wages in this case were three *paṇas* ; if so, whether they were wages for a month or for a year. Perhaps the wages were for a month. But we are in the dark as to what exactly a *paṇa* connoted. The description of the weights and measures given in Bk. II. Ch. XIX. pp. 113-18 helps us to know what they were but not in terms of modern weights and measures.
442 & 443. *Ibid.*, Bk. III. Ch. XIV. 185, p. 209 ; text, p. 185.
444. *Ibid.*, 186, p. 210 ; text, p. 186.
445. *Ibid.*, Bk. V. Ch. III. 247-49, pp. 276-79 ; text, pp. 247-49.
446. *Ibid.*, Bk. III. Ch. XII. and in particular 180, p. 204 ; text, p. 180.

447. *Kauṭilya*, Bk. IV. Ch. I. 200, p. 227 ; text, p. 200. Read *ibid.*, p. 227 ; text, p. 180 for the regulations about the work done by, and the wages to be paid for the artisans.

448. *Ibid.*, Bk. V. Ch. II. 242, p. 271 ; text, p. 242.

448a. *Manu*, VII. 133 ; VIII. 394, pp. 237, 322.

449. *Kauṭilya*, Bk. III. Ch. I. 148, pp. 167-71 ; text, pp. 147-51.

450. Kauṭilya had far advanced on Manu in regard to the attempts made by the judges to hush up a case (*Manu*, VIII. 43, p. 260), cases which could be declared as void (*Manu*, VIII. 163-68, pp. 283-84), and judges who were fined for improperly deciding cases (*Manu*, IX. 234, p. 383).

451 & 452. *Kauṭilya*, Bk. II. Ch. VIII. 67, pp. 67-68 ; text, pp. 67-68.

453 & 454. *Ibid.*, Bk. IV. Ch. VI. 216, p. 243 ; text, pp. 215-16.

455, 456 & 457. *Ibid.*, Bk. IV. Ch. VIII. 220, pp. 247-48 ; text, p. 220.

458. *Ibid.*, Bk. IV. Ch. IX. 225, p. 253 ; text, p. 225.

459. *Ibid.*, Bk. III. Ch. XI. 175, p. 199 ; text, p. 175.

460. *Ibid.*, Bk. III. *ibid.*, 177, p. 201 ; text, p. 177.

461. *Ibid.*, Bk. III. *ibid.*, 175, p. 199 ; text, p. 175.

462. *Manu*, IX. 104, 156-57, p. 185 ; pp. 345, 358, etc.

463. *Kauṭilya*, Bk. III. Ch. V. 160, p. 181 ; text, p. 160.

464. *Ibid.*, Bk. III. Ch. V. 161, p. 183 ; text, p. 161.

465. *Ibid.*, Bk. III. Ch. VII. 165, p. 188 ; text, p. 165.

466. *Ibid.*, Bk. III. Ch. IX. 170, p. 193 ; text, p. 170.

467. *Ibid.*, Bk. III. Ch. IX. 168, p.190 ; text, p. 168.

468. *Ibid.*, Bk. III. Ch. XI. 174, p. 197 ; text, p. 175. Cf. *Manu*, VIII. 140-41, p. 278.

469. Kautilya, Bk. III. Ch. XI. 175, p. 199 ; text, p. 175.

470. *Manu*, VIII. 312, p. 308.

471. *Kauṭilya*, Bk. III. Ch. XX. 199, p. 223 ; text, p. 199.

472. *Ibid.*, Bk. IV. Ch. VIII. 222, p. 250 ; text, p. 222.

473. *Ibid.*, Bk. IV. Ch. XI. 229, p. 257 ; text, p. 229.

474. *Aristotle*, I. 6. 7, p. 68, *op. cit.*

475. *Ibid.*, II. 7. 14, p. 75 ; Cf. *ibid.*, 7. 15-17 ; *ibid.*, page ; III. 10. 15, p. 92.

476. *Ibid.*, III. 12. 9, p. 127.

477. Read *Kauṭilya*, pp. 43, 54, 109-12, 288, 303, 317, 319, 362, 370-73, 396-97, 400-03, 455. Relevant pages of the text are not given by me.

478. Read *ibid.*, pp. 293-407. Dr. N. N. Law defines a *vijigīśu* as one who desired to become the centre of the deliberations of the politicians regarding the Inter-State relations (Law, *Studies*, p. 197). But I would agree with Professor K. V. Rangaswami Aiyangar's definition of a *vijigīśu* (see my *I. D. R. West*, 37 and *passim*) as a conqueror but restrict the term to the future or would-be conqueror. There is no point in a sovereign's being the centre of international deliberations without the necessary military power behind him, and without his having already attained the position of a conqueror. A conference of great military in peace times is a need and a reality now-a-days, but even then they meet at conferences because they have the requisite military sanction behind them. We have, therefore, to presume that it is an ambitious conqueror, who is connoted by the term *vijigīśu*, and not a mere politician.

479. *Aristotle*, III. 12-9, p. 127, *op. cit.*

480. *Kauṭilya*, Bk. I. Ch. II. 7, p. 6 ; III. 8, p. 7, *op. cit.*

481. *Aristotle*, I. 2. 8 ; II. 2. 8 ; VII. 4. 11, 5. 1 ; 8. 8, pp. 28, 56, 267, 268, 273.

482. *Kauṭilya*, pp. 45 ff., 57 ff., 227 ff., 271 ff., and *passim*.

483. *Aristotle*, III. 9. 8, p. 118.

484. *Ibid.*, IV. 13. 9, p. 285 ; Cf. *ibid.*, IV. 7. 4, p. 161.

485. Read Saletore, *I. D. R. West*, pp. 85, 91.

486. That there were still adherents of the Nandas, and perhaps of Seleukos Nikator,

even when the *Arthaśāstra* was written, is evident from Kauṭilya, pp. 349 ff. (trans.).

487. *Kauṭilya*, Bk. II. Ch. VIII. 65, p. 65 ; text, p. 65.
488. *Ibid.*, Bk. I. Ch. III. 8, p. 7 ; text p. 8. See also *ibid.*, Bk. I. Ch. XXIX. 39. p. 38 ; text, p. 39.
489. *Ibid.*, Bk. I. Ch. XIX. 39, p. 38 ; text, p. 39, *op. cit.*
490. *Aristotle*, VII. 9. 7, p. 275. Cf. II. 5. 27, p. 66.
491. *Kauṭilya*, Bk. I. Ch. IV, 9 ; Ch. V. 10, pp. 6, 9, 10.
492. *Aristotle*, I. 13. 15, p. 53.
493. *Ibid.*, II. 7. 9. p. 74, where he says, while criticising Phalaeas' theory of property, "that there is no use in having one and the same (type of education) for all" ; while in VIII. 1. 3. p. 300, he affirms that it should be one and the same for all!
494. *Ibid.*, VIII. 1. 2, p. 300.
495. *Ibid.*, VIII. 1. 1, p. 300.
496. *Kauṭilya*, Bk. I. Ch. V. 10, p. 10 ; text, p. 11. We would not be justified in literally interpreting *yoga* mentioned here as referring exclusively to the practice of "self-contrôl", for in that case it would reduce Kauṭilya's book to the position of a treatise on philosophy! What he meant was perhaps steady application by the people in regard to the many principles of public and private life, all of which were aimed at the maintenance of a strong and efficient government.
497. *Ibid.*, Bk. II. Ch. VII. pp. 61-65, *op. cit.*
498. *Ibid.*, Bk. II. Ch. X. 71, p. 71 ; text, p. 70.
499. *Ibid.*, Bk. I. Ch. IX, 15, pp. 14-15 ; text, pp. 15-16.
500. *Ibid.*, Bk. V. Ch. III. 248, p. 277 ; text, p. 248.
501. *Ibid.*, Bk. I. Ch. IX. 15, p. 14 ; text, p. 15.
502. *Aristotle*, II. 11. 15, p. 95 ; cf. *ibid.*, VII. 3. 9, p. 285.
503. Read *Kauṭilya*, Books IV, V, VI, VII, VIII, IX.
504. *Aristotle*, V. 3. 11. p. 194.
505. *Ibid.*, V. 6-13, p. 203.
506. *Ibid.*, II. 9. 22, p. 86.
507. *Ibid.*, IV. 9. 10, p. 166.
508. *Ibid.*, IV. 11. 12, p. 171 ; cf. *ibid.*, V. 8. 5, pp. 208-09.
509. *Kauṭilya*, Bk. VI. Ch. I. 261, p. 289 ; text, p. 261.
510. *Aristotle*, VII. 2. 16, p. 262.
511. *Ibid.*, VII. 3. 8-10, pp. 264-65.
512. *Kauṭilya*, Bk. VII. Ch. XIII. p. 329 ff. See also Saletore, *I. D. R. West*, p. 27 ff., where the theory of *rājamaṇḍala* as given by Kauṭilya is given in detail.
513. *Aristotle*, VII: 14. 14-22, p. 289.
514. *Ibid.*, III. 3. 4. 7, p. 104.
515. *Ibid.*, VII. 4. 5. 1, p. 266.
516. *Ibid.*, VII. 15. 1, p. 291.
517. Davis, *Aristotle*, p. 4.
518. *Aristotle*, II. 1. 1, p. 54.
519. *Ibid.*, I. 2, pp. 25-26.
520. *Ibid.*, II. 5-27, pp. 66-67.
521. *Ibid.*, I. 2. 13, p. 29.
522. *Ibid.*, II. 5. 2, p. 61.
523. *Ibid.*, II. 5-8, p. 62. See also *ibid.*, I. 8, p. 38 where he states that he would analyse the question of property according to his method of resolving the whole into its parts.
524. *Ibid.*, II. 1. 2, p. 54.
525. *Ibid.*, I. 13. 2-10, pp. 50-51.
526. *Ibid.*, I. 13. 8, p. 51.
527. *Ibid.*, I. 13. 4, p. 50.

528. *Aristotle*, I. 1. 13. 15, p. 53.
529. *Ibid.*, III. 12. 1-8, pp. 125-26.
530. *Ibid.*, III. 13. 1, p. 127.
531. *Ibid.*, II. 7. 9-14, pp. 74-75.
532. *Ibid.*, IV. 1. 1-3, pp. 145-46.
533. *Ibid.*, II. 6-12, pp. 73, 79.
534. *Ibid.*, II. 5. 19, p. 65 for the example of Crete.
535. Cf. Strayer, Joseph, R., *The Interpretation of History*, pp. 8-9 (in collaboration with Jacques Barzun, Haji Holborn, Herbert Heaton, Dumas Malone, George La Piana. Edited by Joseph, R. Strayer, New York, 1950).
536. Acton, Lord, *A Lecture on the Study of History*, p. 40 (London, 1896).
537. Holborn in Strayer, *op. cit.*, pp. 64-65. The reference to Thucydides is to the latter's Chapter XXI. On the date of Thucydides, read Couch, H. N., *Classical Civilization*, p. 407 (General Editor: Geer Russell, M., New Jersey, 1956).
538. Acton, *ibid.*, p. 53.
539. Davis, *Aristotle*, p. 5, *op. cit.*
540. Aiyangar, *op. cit.*, p. 62.
541. Ghoshal, *A History*, p. 82. See also *ibid.*, pp. 111-12 on the plan and purpose of *Kauṭilya's* work. See also *ibid.*, pp. 154-56 for a repetition of the arguments in regard to Kauṭilya and Machiavelli. On Kauṭilya and Machiavelli, see above note (170) of this Part.
542. *Kauṭilya*, Bk. I. Ch. I. 6, p. 5 ; text, p. 5. See also *ibid.*, Bk. XV. Ch. I. 431, p. 463 ; text, p. 431.
543. *Ibid.*, Bk. I. Ch. II ; 7, Ch. III. 8 ; Bk. XV 431, pp. 6, 7, 463 ; text, pp. 6, 8, 431, *op. cit.*
544. Ghoshal, *A History*, pp. 55, 82, 112, 428 where the learned author cites the opinion of Medhātīthi, who states (VII. 43) that *ānvikṣaki* is the science of reasoning beneficial to one's soul, allaying mental anxieties in adversity as well as in prosperity but adopted by the Buddhists, the materialists, and others.
545. Kāmandaka, *Nītisāra*, II. ii.
546. Aiyangar, *op. cit.*, p. 39, n. (63), where the reference to Kāmandaka is also given.
547. Law, *Studies*, pp. 80, 84.
548. Kane, *op. cit.*, III. pp. 46-48.
549 & 550. *Kauṭilya*, Bk. I. Ch. II. 7, pp. 5-6 ; text, pp. 6-7.
551. *Aristotle*, VII. 5. 1 ff., p. 268 ff.
552. Read Plato, *Republic*, Pat III. Bk. V. 471 c-vii, ff., pp. 171-78 (Edited and translated by F. M. Conford, Oxford, 1951).
553. *Kauṭilya*, Bk. I. Ch. I. 9, p. 8 ; text, p. 8.
554. *Kauṭilya*, Bk. I. Ch. VII. 12, p. 12 ; text, p. 12.
555. *Ibid.*, Bk. III. Ch. I. 150, p. 171 ; text, p. 150.
556. *Ibid.*, Bk. XIV. p. 441, *op. cit.*
557. *Ibid.*, Bk. I. Ch. VI. 12, p. 11 ; text, pp. 11-12.
558. *Ibid.*, Bk. I. Ch. XVIII. 33, p. 33 ; text, p. 33.
559. *Ibid.*, Bk. I. Ch. XX. 41, p. 40 ; text, p. 41.
560. *Ibid.*, Bk. VIII. Ch. III. 329, p. 356 ; text, p. 329
561. *Ibid.*, Bk. IX. Ch. VII. 360, p. 387, text, p. 360.
562. *Ibid.*, Bk. V. Ch. VI. 257, p. 286 ; text, p. 257.
563. *Ibid.*, Bk. I. Ch. XVII. 35, p. 34 ; text, p. 35.
564. *Ibid.*, Bk. VII. Ch. XVI. 312, p. 339 ; text, p. 312.
565. *Ibid.*, Bk. XI. Ch. I. 378, p. 407 ; text, p. 378.
566. *Ibid.*, pp. 350-52, 357-60, 367.
567. Davis, *op. cit.*, p. 4.
568. On Aristotle's verdict on Political Science, read *ibid.*, III. 12. 1, p. 125. Cf. *Kauṭilya*, Bk. I. Ch. IV. 9, p. 8, *op. cit.*

569. Davis, *op. cit.*, p. 4.
570. Shama Sastry, *Kauṭilya*, p. 5, note (1).
571. Ghoshal, *A History*, pp. 147-48.
572. *Kauṭilya*, Bk. XI. Ch. I. 378, p. 407 ; text, p. 407.
573. & 574. Kāmandaka, *op. cit.*, I. 5. 7, cited by Aiyangar, *op. cit.*, p. 13, note (22). See also Aiyangar, *ibid.*, pp. 14-15, 20, 23-26. See *ibid.*, pp. 64-65 for the difference between Kauṭilya, Kāmandaka, and others.
575. Aiyangar, *ibid.*, pp. 16-17, and p. 17, note (31) where Professor Aiyangar has given identical passages in Kauṭilya and in Somadeva Sūri's *Nītivākyāmrita*. See also *ibid.*, pp. 25-26 for another later author Vaiyśampāyana, who borrowed freely from Kauṭilya's *Arthaśāstra*. It is a sad comment on our scholarship that the history of Indian plagiarism can be dated to the tenth century A.D. and after!
576. That no detailed study of the principles of Aristotle and Kauṭilya in the manner done by me in these pages, has ever been attempted will be evident when the reader will turn to Professor Aiyangar's book cited already in which he just refers to the similarity in the views of the two great thinkers on the nature and end of the State, giving a few references to Aristotle's *Politics*. See Aiyangar, *ibid.*, p. 70, and note (117). But nothing further was attempted by the learned historian. My friend and colleague, Mr. G. S. Dikshit, Reader in History at the Karnatak University, has kindly brought to my notice Professor Dr. M. V. Krishna Rao's book entitled *Studies in Kauṭilya* (Mysore, 1953). It adds to the already long list of Kauṭilyan studies by Indian and Western scholars which I have abstained from citing in my work. Professor Krishna Rao certainly makes a good study of Kauṭilya and Machiavelli, and Kauṭilya and Aristotle. But his approach to the subject is quite different to the one adopted by me. Moreover, there is an idealistic tone in it which I do not think is applicable in the case of Kauṭilya, who was anything but an idealist.

PART FIVE

POLITICAL INSTITUTIONS

(ELEMENTS OF THE STATE)

1. Gettell, *op. cit.*, pp. 19-20.
2. MacIver, *op. cit.*, p. 6.
3. Griffith, *Hymns of the Rig Veda*, I, pp. 695-96 ; Macdonell, *Vedic Mythology*, p. 89 ; Macdonell—Keith, *Vedic Index*, II, pp. 424-25.
4. *Śat. Brah.*, I. 8. 1. 24, p. 223. (S. B. E. XII).
5. *Śat. Brah.*, IX. 5. 2. 8, p. 277 (S. B. E. XLIII). Cf. *ibid.*, X. 2. 4. 4. and 5, p. 314.
6. Professor Ghoshal admits that there is no reference to the elements of the State, or, as he calls them, the structure of the State, earlier than the Arthaśāstra works. "Of a scheme of State structure such as is mentioned in the early Arthaśāstra works, there is in the older Dharmasutras no trace." He then refers to the seven elements as given in *Viṣṇu*, and in the later works like the *Gautamasūtra* and the *Dharmasūtra* of Sumantu quoted in the *Sarasvatīvilāsa Vyavahārakāṇḍa* (Ghoshal, *A History*, p. 55). Professor Ghoshal, as narrated by me below, included among the Arthaśāstra works Manu's *Dharmaśāstra*. I am afraid I cannot agree with the learned historian in classifying Manu's work among the *Arthaśāstras* ; nor in citing the evidence of the *Viṣṇusmṛiti* and the later works to prove his contention.
7. *Manu*, VII. 156-57, p. 241. Dr. Kane (*op. cit.* III, p. 17), who cites this reference to Manu, evidently has confounded the theory of the seven elements of the State with the theory of foreign policy which we shall discuss below.
8. *Manu*, IX. 294-96, p. 395.
9. *Ibid.*, IX. 297, p. 395.
10. *Śantiparvan*, 69. 64-65 ; Kane, *ibid.*, III, p. 181, and note (21).
11. *Śukranītisāra*, I. 61-62 ; Kane, *ibid.*, III, p. 18. For those who have defended the organismic theory, read Jayaswal, *op. cit.*, p. 9 ; Bk. Sarkar, *Positive Background of Hindu Sociology*, Bk. II, pp. 34-39 ; D. R. Bhandarkar, *op. cit.*, pp. 66-89 ; Kane, *ibid.*, III, p. 20.
12. *Yājñavalkya*, I. 353 ; *Viṣṇu*, III. 33 ; *Gautama*, as cited in the *Sarasvatīvilāsa*, p. 45 ; *Śāntiparvan*, 69. 64-65 ; *Agni Purāṇa*, 233, 12 ; *Kāmandaka*, I. 16 ; IV. 1-2. See Kane, *op. cit.*, III, p. 18, and note (2) where Aparārka's interesting elucidation of the term *prakriti* is given.
13. *Kauṭilya*, Bk. VI. 257, p. 287 ; text, p. 257. Dr. Shama Sastry calls them "the elements of sovereignty". It is more correct to interpret them as elements of the State. Dr. Law has commented on the seven constituent elements of the State, as given by Kauṭilya, and has refuted Professor Winternitz's unfounded statements. Read Law, *op. cit.*, pp. 213-19.
14. *Kauṭilya*, VI. 259, p. 289 ; text, p. 259. Here again I am interpreting *prakriti* as referring to the State, and not as sovereignty, as is done by Dr. Shama Sastry.
15. *Ibid.*, Bk. VIII, pp. 348-52 ; text, pp. 257-59. In the light of this discussion, it would not be correct to agree with Dr. Kane that Kauṭilya almost unequivocally agreed to the view of Manu in this respect (Kane, *ibid.*, III, p. 17). Professor Aiyangar, while referring to Kauṭilya's order of preference, writes that it "would

not only be an indication of the possibility of conceiving of more or less complete types of polity in which one or other of these essentials may be absent (e.g., settled territory as in the Vedic State, international position as in the Vassal State), but also of the features of the epochs in which they were conceived". He then proceeds to describe those features like the ceascless internecine warfare, oppressive taxation, disorganisation and insolvency, external enemies, and capricious and irresponsible personal rule ; which "*were* some of the conditions that actually prevailed in North India during the period intervening between the conquests of Darius and Alexander" (Aiyangar, *op. cit.*, pp. 70-71). I must confess that it is rather difficult to follow the learned Professor when he asserts that Kauṭilya's order of preference indicates a type of polity in which one of the essentials is absent, and likewise reflects the feature of the epochs in which those essentials were conceived. Is it not possible that there is too much of speculation in these surmises of the distinguished historian?

16. *Kāmandaka,* IV. 1-2 ; Kane, *ibid.*, III, p. 18.
17. *Kauṭilya,* Bk. VIII. Ch. II. 325, p. 352 ; text, p. 325. Dr. Kane interprets this passage by saying that "the king is the State (Kane, *op. cit.*, III, p. 18). He then cites the earlier passage in the *Arthaśāstra* as given in Chapter I of the same book, and states that "Kauṭilya makes his position clear (in VIII. 1) by saying that it is the king who appoints ministers and servants and superintendents, etc.". This interpretation is not justifiable on the following grounds: (*a*) Kauṭilya's reference to the king's being the aggregate of all the people is in connection with the discussion of the relative importance of the king and his ministers as given by Bharadvāja, and not in connection with the point with which Kauṭilya opens the next chapter, namely, the troubles of the king. We cannot think of Kauṭilya's confounding the question of the relative importance of the two elements mentioned above with the troubles of the kingdom. (*b*) The interpretation given by Dr. Shama Sastry is more correct in the sense that Kauṭilya is rightly resolving all the elements of the State in the manner suggested above. And (*c*) granting that, for argument's sake, Dr. Kane is correct, Kauṭilya's reduction of the elements to one, viz., the king, would make no sense. If the king alone were the sole element, over whom would he rule? And how could he stabilize himself?
18. Gettell, *op. cit.*, pp. 19-20.
19. The word *prakriti* has also been used in the sense of ministers by *Śukra* (*Śukranītisāra*, II. 70-73), and in that of subjects as in one of the inscriptions of king Khāravela (*Ep. Ind.* XX, p. 79. See also Kane, *ibid.*, III, p. 17). To these we may add the views of a few commentators like Medhātīthi (on *Manu*) and Aparārka (on *Yājñavalkya*). According to the former, the technical term *prakriti* meant either the operating cause (*kāraṇa*), so as to make the elements of the State components in the sense the potsherds were to the jar, or else it refers to their nature (*svabhāva*), so as to make the State partake of their characteristics. Aparārka defines it as that whereby a product is made, fixed, and brought into shape in the sense of gold being the *prakriti* in an ear-ring (Kane, *ibid.*, III, p. 17, note (20) where Aparārka's passage (as given in the latter's work) page 588) is given in full. See Ghoshal, *A History*, p. 427 where Medhātīthi is cited only with Aparārka.

Professor Ghoshal, while explaining the same Chapter in Kauṭilya, speaks of a longer list of the seven constituent elements, and of a smaller one of two units, meaning thereby that Kauṭilya thought of a twofold concept of the State (Ghoshal, *A History*, p. 119). I am afraid I cannot agree with the distinguished historian. In the first place, it is unsafe to talk of the structure of government in this context, when we are describing the elements of the State. The term structure of government would be more appropriately used in connection with the legislature, the judiciary, and the executive which make up the State, rather than with the king, the territory, the army, etc., which form the elements of the State. What is discussed by Professor Ghoshal in this particular context is the theory of elements, and not the question of the separation of powers which did not exist in ancient Indian thought. Secondly, there is no justification for stating that Kauṭilya's reduction of the seven elements of the State to two involves a twofold concept of State structure, one comprising a larger list of seven, and the other, two smaller units. It would be better to remember here that Kauṭilya never theorizes, as Aristotle did, and, therefore, had no occasion for dividing the so-called structure of the State into the two types imagined by Professor Ghoshal. In an earlier context, the same eminent historian describes the seven constituent elements which he would render thus—the sovereign ruler, the official class, the rural area, the fortified (or urban) area, the permanent residence, the standing army, and the permanent foreign ally. (Ghoshal, *ibid.*, p. 89). It cannot be made out in what manner this enumeration differs from the usual ones given by other scholars, excepting that, in the place of minister, Professor Ghoshal would have "the official class". But this does not seem to improve matters, since the whole of the official class, if that is intended to be covered by the words "official class", did not constitute an element of the State. If it did, then, we should take the larger body of all those attached to the Revenue Department also as forming an element, and should style them "the permanent revenue staff"! Moreover, the whole of the official class, comprising quite a number of court and palace officials, who had no place in government, would also form another element of the State! This classification, therefore, appears to be redundant.

Professor Ghoshal in a later context affirms that Manu's arguments about the relative importance of the elements, "being derived wholly from Kauṭilya" (Ghoshal, *ibid.*, p. 427). Proof in support of the borrowing by Manu from Kauṭilya would be welcome here.

20. *Kauṭilya*, pp. 9-10, 12, 15, 36, 46, 123, 387, etc.
21. *Ibid.*, Bk. VII. Ch. X. 294, p. 323 ; text, p. 294.
22. *Ibid.*, Bk. II. Ch. XXII. 112, p. 123 ; text, pp. 111, 112.
23. Smith, *E. H. I.*, p. 44.
24. *Kauṭilya*, Bk. I. Ch. XXI, pp. 41-44 ; text, pp. 42-45.
25. *Ibid.*, Bk. I. Ch. XIII. 23, p. 23 ; text, p. 23.
26. *Ait. Brāhmana*, VIII. 14. 4 ; 19. 2. In view of the analysis of the concept of kingship made in these pages, it is needless for me to state that statements like the following occurring in Dr. Vishwanath Prasad Varma's book, are incorrect. "In the *Aitareya Brāhmaṇa* occurs the first reference to the creation of a king" (Varma, V. P., *Studies in Hindu Political Thought and its Metaphysical Foundations*, p. 170 ff. Delhi-Varanasi-Patna, 1959, 2nd ed.). See *Vedic index*, I, p. 28 ; II, p. 141 for further references in the *Brāhmaṇa* literature.
27. *Vedic Index*, I, p. 28. The following describe the famous ritual of coronation. *Taittirīya Samhita*, I. 8. 11 ; *Kāṭhaka Samhita*, XV. 6 ; *Maitrāyaṇī Samhita*, II. 6 ; *Vājasaneyī Samhita*, X. 1-4 ; *Śatapatha Brāhmaṇa*, V. 3. 5 ; 10-15 ; XII. 1. 4 ; 2. 17. For *puruṣamedha* read *Vājasaneyī Samhita*, XXX. 12 ; *Taitt. Sam.* III. 4. 8. 1 ; on *rājasuya*, read *Vedic Index*, II, pp. 219-20 for further references.
28. This summary is based on Dr. N. N. Law's excellent account of the coronation as given in his *Studies*, pp. 33-66, where detailed references to the *Brāhmaṇas* are also given. See also Aiyangar, *op. cit.*, pp. 72, and note (120). See also Jayaswal, *op. cit.*, pp. 192-213 for another detailed study of the ceremony of coronation.
29. Law, *ibid.*, pp. 35-36.
30. *Kauṭilya*, Bk. I. Ch. V. 10-11, pp. 9-10 ; text, pp. 10-11.
31. *Manu*, II. 31-32, p. 35.
32. *Ibid.*, II. 37, p. 36.
33. *Ibid.*, II. 42, p. 37.
34. *Ibid.*, II. 44, p. 38.
35. *Ibid.*, II. 46, p. 38.

36. *Manu*, II. 49, p. 39.
37. *Ibid.*, II. 65, p. 42.
38. *Ibid.*, VII. 2, p. 216.
39. *Ibid.*, VII. 37, p. 221.
40. *Ibid.*, VII. 43, p. 222.
41. *Ibid.*, VII. 44-51, pp. 222-23.
42. *Ibid.*, VII. 54-58, pp. 224-25.
43. *Ibid.*, VII. 145-47, pp. 238-39.
44. *Kauṭilya*, Bk. I. Ch. III. 8, pp. 6-7 ; text, pp. 7-8.
45. *Ibid.*, Bk. I. Ch. V. 10, p. 9 ; text, p. 10.
46. *Ibid.*, Bk. I. Ch. V. 10, pp. 9-10 ; text, pp. 10-11.

47 & 48. *Ibid.*, Bk. I. Ch. XIX. 3, 7, 38, pp. 36-38 ; text, pp. 37-38. On the *nāḷikā*, read Dr. Fleet's note on p. 37, note (1) of the translation of the *Arthaśāstra*.

49. The late Professor V. R. R. Dikshitar has also given the time-table of the king. (*Mauryan Polity*, pp. 106-11). He writes thus: "Days and nights were divided into eight periods respectively and a fixed time-table was drawn up. The king went to bed at 9 P.M., and got up at 3 A.M. accompanied by music on both occasions." The learned author then goes on to narrate the duties as given by the king. He seems to have erred here for, as was pointed out by Dr. Shama Sastry, it was sixteen parts in all, that is, eight parts per day and eight parts per night, according to the *nāḷikas* or the length of the shadow (*nāḷikābhiḥ-ahar-aṣṭadhā-rātṛim ca vibhajet chchhāyāpramāṇena vā*). Further, how Professor Dikshitar came to arrive at 9 P.M. as the time when the king went to bed, cannot be made out, since Kauṭilya explicitly states the duties of the king at night began with the reception of secret emissaries. There is nothing in the *Arthaśāstra* to justify the division of the day and night, as done by Professor Dikshitar, particularly in view of the specific statement that the king enjoyed sleep during the fourth and fifth parts of the night. A good deal of speculation mars the significance of Professor Dikshitar's otherwise valuable book.

50. *Manu*, VII. 2, 35, pp. 216, 221.
51. *Ibid.*, VII. 111-12, p. 233.
52. *Ibid.*, VIII. 172, 304, 306, pp. 285, 307.
53. *Ibid.*, VII. 14, p. 218.
54. *Ibid.*, VIII. 27-29, pp. 257-58.
55. *Ibid.*, VIII. 1-2, 9-19, 41-43, pp. 253-55, 260-61.
56. *Ibid.*, VIII. 25-26, 44-46, 52-55, 61-123, pp. 257, 261, 263-75.
57. *Ibid.*, IX. 234, p. 383.
58. *Ibid.*, IX. 270, p. 390.
59. *Ibid.*, VIII. 312, p. 308.
60. *Ibid.*, VIII. 3, p. 253, *op. cit.*
61. *Ibid.*, VIII. 108-15, pp. 509-11.
62. *Ibid.*, VII. 54, 60, pp. 224-25.
63. *Ibid.*, VIII. 30-44, 403, pp. 258-61.
64. *Ibid.*, VII. 78-79, pp. 228-29.
65. *Ibid.*, VII. 145, p. 239.
66. *Ibid.*, VII. 128-29, p. 236.
67. *Ibid.*, VII. 80, p.229.
68. *Ibid.*, VIII. 394, p. 322.
69. *Ibid.*, VII. 69-76, pp. 227-28.
70. *Ibid.*, VII. 87-95, pp. 230-31.
71. *Ibid.*, VII. 96-97, p. 231.
72. *Ibid.*, VII. 222, p. 252.
73. *Ibid.*, VII. 37-8, p. 221.
74. *Ibid.*, VII. 133, p. 237.
75. *Ibid.*, XI. 4, p. 431.

76. *Manu*, VII. 43, p. 222, *op. cit.*
77. *Kauṭilya*, Bk. I. Ch. V & VI, pp. 9-13 ; text, pp. 10-13.
78. *Ibid.*, Bk. II. Ch. I. 47, p. 47, *op. cit.*
79. *Ibid.*, p. 234, *op. cit.*
80. *Ibid.*, Bk. IV. Ch. IV. 210-12, pp. 237-39 ; text, pp. 210-12.
81. *Ibid.*, p. 252, *op. cit.*
82. Cf. Gettell, *op. cit.*, p. 170.
83. Professor Aiyangar, for instance, in his work already cited (pp. 102-103). His account of the duties of the king (*ibid.*, pp. 73-76) differs from that given by me in many respects. He refers to the king's tours (*ibid.*, p. 73) which I am unable to trace in Kauṭilya. Professor Ghoshal discusses the functions of the king as "a principle of authority of the temporal ruler in the sense of his dues for protection" ; and in that of the "equivalence of his functions to those of deities" (Ghoshal, *A History*, etc., pp. 49, 116, 164, 198, 273, 316. 329-90, 491). This analysis does not help us in ascertaining what exactly were the functions of the king. The third author, who has dealt with the subject of the functions of the king, is Professor Dikshitar, who wrote of the following duties of the king—enforcing *svadharma*, protection of life and property, promotion of trade and commerce, proper administration of justice, looking after the *sanyāsins*, protection against calamities, foreign policy, and promoting arts and education (*Mauryan Polity*, pp. 115-19). This is both inadequate and misleading.
84. *Kauṭilya*, Bk. I. Ch. VIII. 13-14, pp. 12-14 ; text, pp. 13-14.
85. *Ibid.*, Bk. II. Ch. IX, pp. 68-71 ; Bk. IV. Ch. IX, pp. 250, 254 ; text, pp. 68-70. 222-26.
86. *Ibid.*, Bk. I. Ch. IX. 15, p. 15 ; text, pp. 15-16.
87. *Manu*, II. 143, p. 56.
88. *Ibid.*, VII. 78, p. 228.
89. *Kauṭilya*, Bk. XIV. Chs. I. II. III. & IV, pp. 441-57 ; text, pp. 410-26.
90. *Ibid.*, Bk. II. Ch. I. 47, p. 46 ; text, p. 47.
91. *Ibid.*, Bk. II. Ch. VI, pp. 57-61, *op. cit.*
92. *Ibid.*, Bk. II. Ch. V. 59, p. 57 ; text, p. 59.
93. *Ibid.*, Bk. V. Ch. III. 247, p. 276 ; text, p. 247.
94. *Ibid.*, Bk. I. Ch. XVIII. 38, p. 37, *op. cit.*
95. *Ibid.*, Bk. I. Ch. XX. 40, p. 39 ; text, p. 40.
96. *Ibid.*, Bk. X. Ch. III. 369, p. 397 ; text, p. 369.
97. Read *Manu*, VII. 164-200, pp. 242-48.
98. *Kauṭilya*, Bk. VI, p. 287 ff.
99. *Ibid.*, Bk. I. Ch. XIX. 39, p. 38 ; text, p. 39.
100. *Ibid.*, Bk. II. Ch. I. 46, p. 45 ; text, p. 46. Whether the experts in witchcraft were also given rent free lands is not clear.
101. *Kauṭilya*, Bk. II. Ch. IV. 55, p. 54 ; text, p. 55.
102. *Aristotle*, V. 4-10, pp. 225-26.
103. *Kauṭilya*, Bk. VII. Ch. V. 277, p. 306 ; text, p. 277.
104. *Ibid.*, Bk. I. Ch. XIII. 23, pp. 22-24 ; Bk. II. Ch. XXXV. 142, pp. 158-60 ; text, p. 142 ; on the work of the spies, see *ibid.*, pp. 25, 342, 374, 384, 423-25, etc. (trans.).
105. *Ibid.*, Bk. I. Ch. XIII. 24, p. 24 ; text, p. 24.
106. *Ibid.*, Bk. III. Ch. X, pp. 194 ff ; see also *ibid.*, pp. 99 ff.
107. *Ibid.*, Bk. II. Ch. XV, pp.104 ff ; see also *ibid.*, pp. 121-27.
108. *Ibid.*, Bk. I. Ch. II, p. 5. See also *ibid.*, pp. 8-9.
109. *Ibid.*, Bk. II. Ch. XVI. 98, pp. 105-06 ; text, pp. 98-99.
110. *Ibid.*, Bk. VII. Ch. V. 277, p. 306 ; text, p. 277.
111. *Ibid.*, Bk. V. Ch. II. 243, 244, pp. 271-73 ; text, pp. 242-46.
112. *Ibid.*, Bk. I. Chs. VI. & VII, pp. 10-12 ; text, pp. 11-13.
113. *Ibid.*, Bk. I. Ch. XIX. 38, p. 36 ; text, p. 38.

114. *Kauṭilya*, Bk. I. Ch. XIX. 39, p. 39 ; text, p. 39, *op. cit.*
115. Aiyangar, *op. cit.*, p. 43. Professor Aiyangar gives no reference to his statements excepting in one instance where, I am afraid, he has erred.
116. *Kauṭilya*, Bk. I. Ch. XIX. 38, 39, pp. 37-38, *op. cit.*
117. *Ibid.*, Bk. I. Ch. X. 16, p. 15 ; text, p. 16.
118. *Ibid.*, Bk. V. Ch. VI, pp. 283-84 ; text, pp. 254-57.
119. Cf. *ibid.*, Bk. I. Ch. IV, pp. 8-9, *op. cit.*
120. *Ibid.*, Bk. III. Ch. I. 148, p. 167.
121. *Ibid.*, Bk. III. Ch. I. 150, pp. 170-71 ; text, p. 150.
122. *Ibid.*, Bk. IV. Ch. X. 228, pp. 255-56 ; text, p. 228. On the definitions of the amercements, read *ibid.*, p. 217 (trans.).
123. *Ibid.*, Bk. IV. Ch. XIII. 236, p. 265 ; text, p. 236. The reason why the expatiation was to be done in honour of god Varuṇa is given in the next sentence "By this act the king will be free from the sin of unjust imposition ; for king Varuṇa is the ruler of sinners among men" (*ibid.*, p. 265 ; text, p. 237).
124. Read *ibid.*, pp. 228, 233 ff, 289, 291, 304-06, 350.
125. *Ibid.*, Bk. VIII. Ch. X. 322, p. 350 ; text, p. 322. An example of looking at the Kauṭilyan kingship from the metaphysical point of view is Dr. Vishwanath Prasad Varma's interpretation of the theory of kingship in Kauṭilya in terms of the "Philosophy and Sociology of Karma" (Varma, *op. cit.*, pp. 185-98). Whatever may be the value of this work from the metaphysical point of view, it hardly helps us to get a correct idea of the Kauṭilyan theory of kingship.
126. These details about the Buddhist contribution to the theory of kingship are based on Professor Beni Prasad's very learned and comprehensive study of the subject as given in his *Theory of Government in Ancient India*, pp. 202-20.
127. For the earlier date of this collection, read Rhys Davids, *Dialogues of the Buddha* (Sacred Books of the Buddhists, Vol. II.), pp. ix-xxi ; Rhys Davids and Oldenberg. *S. B. E.* XI, p. x ; Vol. XIII, p. xxiii. On the later date, read G. K. Nariman, *History of Sanskrit Buddhism from Winternitz, Sylvani Levi, and Huber*, p. 9. (Bombay, 1920). See also Beni Prasad, *ibid.*, p. 204, and note (1).
128. Keith, A. B., *Buddhist Philosophy*, p. 22, cited in Beni Prasad, *ibid.*, p. 210, and note (2), Dr. Beni Prasad wrote Malinda which is obviously an error for Mahinda. *i.e.*, Mahendra.
129. Beni Prasad, *ibid.*, pp. 214-15, 217.
130. W. W. Rockhill, *The Life of Buddha . . . derived from Tibetan works*, etc., pp. 1-7. Beni Prasad, *ibid.*, pp. 207-208.
130a. Beni Prasad, *ibid.*, pp. 202, 205, 208.
131. *Dīgha Nikāya*, III. Sec. 27 (Rhys Davids and J. E. Carpentier, Pali Text Society, 1890-1911) ; see also Beni Prasad, *ibid.*, pp. 205-06, and p. 206, note (1) ; Ghoshal, *A History of Hindu Political Theories*, p. 119 (Oxford, 1923).
132. Rockhill, *op. cit.*, pp. 1-8 ; Beni Prasad, *ibid.*, pp. 207-08.
133. Beni Prasad, *ibid.*, p. 208.
134. *Kauṭilya*, Bk. I. Ch. II. 6, p. 5 ; text, p. 6, *op. cit.*
135. Aśvaghoṣa, *Saundara Nandam Kāvyam*, Canto. I. pp. 7-8 ; Canto. II, p. 9. (Ed. by M.M. Hara Prasad Shastri, Bib. Indica, N. S. No. 1251). See also Beni Prasad, *ibid.*, p. 217.
136. Aśvaghoṣa, *Buddha Carita. The Śāriputra Prakarana and Other Fragments of Plays.* I. 12, 14 ; II. 24, 42, 44 (Heinrich Lüder's ed.) ; see also Beni Prasad, *ibid.*, pp. 217-18.
137. Ārya Śūra, *The Jātakamala*, Story II, pp. 8-14 ; Story III, p. 20 ; Story VIII, p. 56 ; Story IX, pp. 71-92 (trans. by J. S. Speyer. Sacred Books of the Buddhists, Vol. I.).
138. Beni Prasad, *op. cit.*, p. 215.
139. Śūra, *ibid.*, Story II, pp. 8-14, *op. cit.*, Beni Prasad, *ibid.*
140. Śūra, *ibid.*, Story VIII, p. 56, *op. cit.*, Beni Prasad, *ibid.*, p. 216.

141. Śūra, *op. cit.*, Story X, pp. 93-104 ; Beni Prasad, *ibid.*, p. 126.
142. Śūra, *ibid.*, Story XI, pp. 71-92 ; Beni Prasad *ibid.*, p. 126.
143. Beni Prasad, *ibid.*, pp. 209, 211.
144. Beni Prasad, *ibid.*, p. 215.
145. Cf. Beni Prasad, *ibid.*, pp. 202, 220. On Jainism read Shah, Chimanlal, J., *Jainism in North India* (London, 1932) ; Saletore, B.A., *Mediaeval Jainism with special reference to the Vyayanagara Empire* (Bombay, 1938) ; Desai, *P. B.*, *Jainism in South India and Some Jaina Epigraphs* (Sholapur, 1957).
146. Jacobi, Hermann, *Jaina Sūtras*, Part II. Intr., p. xl. (S.B.E. XLV, 1895. Part I of the same was edited by the same eminent scholar in 1885 as S.B.E. Vol. XXII). On the date of the Council at Valabhi, see also Duff, Miss Mabel, C., *The Chronology of India*, p. 33.
147. Beni Prasad, *ibid.*, p. 229.
148. On the date of the ruler, read Rice, Lewis, *Mysore and Coorg from the Inscriptions*, p. 67 (London, 1909). On Jinasena, read Bhandarkar, *Early History of the Dekkan*, p. 200 (in the *Bombay Gazetteer*). Fleet, J. F., *Dynasties of the Kanarese Districts*, p. 407 (*Bombay Gazetteer*, 1896). See also Beni Prasad, *ibid.*, p. 221, note (1)where Dr. Prasad gives the other works of Jinasena.
149. Fleet, *ibid.*, pp. 407-08.
150. Cf. the other Jaina works that have referred to some aspect or other of Political Science. Mention may be made of *Harivaṁśapurāṇa*, ascribed to a Jinasena, who is different to the one mentioned above and the *Padma Purāṇa* and *Pradyumna Carita* by *Mahāsenācārya*. The *Harivaṁśapurāṇa* ascribes the foundation of all social and political institutions of Ṛṣabha. Dr. Beni Prasad commenting on them rightly maintains that, "It is interesting that the Jainas have their Purāṇas which betray deep Brāhmaṇic influence" (Beni Prasad, *ibid.*, p. 228). The *Pradyumna Carita* has been edited by Manoharlal Sastri and Ram Prasad Sastri in the Manik Chand Digambara Jaina Granthamala, No. 8, Bombay Vikrama Samvat 1973.
151. Jacobi, Hermann. *The Jaina Sūtras*. Part II, IX, 17-49, pp. 37-40 (S.B.E. XLIV).
151a. Cf. *Manusmriti*, I. 89, p. 24 ; VII. 87-95, 144, pp. 230-31, 238 ; X. 77-79, 115, pp. 419, 423.
151b. Jacobi, *ibid.*, XVIII. 33-51, pp. 85-88.
151c. See above under Part Three. On the basis of the details gathered from the *Jaina Sūtras*, we may reject Dr. Beni Prasad's statement that they touch on government "in a rather left-handed way" (Beni Prasad, *op. cit.*, p. 228) as being incorrect.
152. Jinasena, *Ādipurāṇa, Prastāvana*, 55-58. Text published with a Hindi translation by Lala Ram Jain in the *Syādvāda Granthamāla*, No. 4. Guṇabhadra's *Uttara Purāṇa* was also published in the same series, both appearing under the title of *Mahāpurāṇa*.
153. The *Manusmriti* defines Āryāvarta thus: "But (the tract) between those two mountains (the Himālayas and the Vindhyas) which (extends) as far as the eastern and the western oceans, the wise call Āryāvarta (the country of the Āryans)." Since in the preceding verse (no 21), Manu has described the Madhyadeśa or the central region as lying between the Himālayas and the Vindhyas to the east of Prayāga and to the west of Vinaśanā (the place where the Sarasvatī disappeared, *Manu*, VII. 21-22, p. 33), Professor Ghoshal's equation of Āryakṣetra, as given by Jinasena, with the middle region of Bharatavarṣa (*A History*, etc., p. 457) does not seem to be correct. But Professor Ghoshal's treatment of the Jaina theory of the cycles is very exhaustive.
154. *Ādipurāṇa*, III. 214-16. Professor Ghoshal would make the last group of patriarchs five (Ghoshal, *ibid.*, p. 457) ; but this would make them in all fifteen, when he himself states in para one of the same page, that there were only fourteen patriarchs beginning with Pratiśruti! Evidently he has included Bharata whom he would style a Kuladhara on the same page.

155. *Ādipurāṇa,* III. XV. 130-90, 240-45, 255-57 ; Beni Prasad, *ibid.*, pp. 222-24. Professor Ghoshal makes Ṛṣabhadeva the last but one, and Ṛṣabha's son Bharata, the last successor in the list of patriarchs (Ghoshal, *ibid.*, p. 457).
156. *Ādipurāṇa,* IV. 106-98 ; XVI. 254 ; XXV-XXVI ; XLIII. Read also Beni Prasad, *ibid.*, p. 224-27. Professor Ghoshal gives a full account of Jinanesa's views (Ghoshal, *ibid.*, pp. 464-66).
156a. *Ādipurāṇa,* XVI. 241-46 ; Beni Prasad, *ibid.*, p. 225.
157. *Manu,* VII. 114, 115, p. 234.
158. *Ibid.*, VII. 13-14, pp. 218-21, etc., *op. cit.*
159. *Ibid.*, 126-30, p. 276, *op. cit.*
160. *Ibid.*, VII. 35, p. 221.
161. *Ibid.*, VII. 158, p. 241 ; *Kauṭilya,* Bk. VII. Ch. VIII. 288, p. 317 ; text, p. 288. The reader may also refer to my *I.R.D. West,* pp. 36-45.
162. Beni Prasad, *ibid.*, p. 224.
163. *Ādipurāṇa,* XVI. 271-75.
164. Professor Ghoshal has much to say about Jinasena's work (*ibid.*, pp. 457-58). I am afraid I cannot agree with the learned historian when he writes about the revolutionary theory of man and of the social institutions alleged to be found in Jinasena's work *Ādipurāṇa.* But for Jinasena's idealism, in which he has, like a devout Jaina, turned topsy-turvy some ideas of the Hindu mythology, there is hardly anything new in the theory of kingship as enunciated by him.
165. Fleet, *D.K.D.* 402.
166. Rice, *Mysore and Coorg,* pp. 70-71.
167. Peterson, Professor, *Report on Skt. Mss. for 1883-84,* p. 48 ; Bhandarkar, *E.H.D.*, p. 207, and note (2). *Nītivākyāmrita* was first published in the Bombay Granthamāla Series (1887) ; and then by Pandit Pannalal Soni, but edited by Nathuram Premi, Bombay, 1923. The *Yaśastilaka* was published in the Bombay Kāvyamāla, No. 70, 1901. It contains the commentary of Śrutasāgara. Professor K. K. Handiqui's *Yaśastilaka and Indian Culture* is a very good work.
168. Beni Prasad, *op. cit.*, p. 230, n. (1).
169. Beni Prasad, *ibid.*, p. 242.
170. Somadeva Sūri, *Nītivākyamrita,* pp. 1-26 ; Beni Prasad, *op. cit.*, p. 230. The commentator Haribala on *Nītivākyāmrita* states that Somadeva, instead of saluting The Tīrthankaras, preferred to imitate Śukra, the author of the now lost *Auśānasa Arthaśāstra* which began with a salutation of the State, thus: *namo-astu rājya-vrikṣāya ṣāḍguṇyāya praśākhine* (Jayaswal, *op. cit.*, p. 10. On pp. 8-10, Dr. Jayaswal has a useful critique on the *Nītivākyāmrita*).
171. Somadeva, *Nītivākyāmrita,* pp. 26-56.
172. *Kauṭilya,* Bk. VIII. Ch. II. 326, p. 353 ; text, p. 326.
173. Somadeva, *ibid.*, p. 17 ; see also Aiyangar, *op. cit.*, p. 108.
174. Somadeva, *ibid.*, p. 105.
175. Somadeva, *ibid.*, p. 66.
176. Cf. also Ghoshal, *A History,* p. 486.
177. Beni Prasad, *ibid.*, pp. 233-35.
178. Somadeva, *Yaśastilaka,* III. pp. 367-74 ; Ghoshal, *ibid.*, p. 468.
179. On the ministers, read *Nītīvākyāmrita,* pp. 62-135 ; on Kauṭilya, Bk. I. Chs. VIII, IX, X, & XIV. pp. 12-17, 26-29.
180. Somadeva, *ibid.*, pp. 136-37.
181. Somadeva, *ibid.*, pp. 207-15.
182. Somadeva, *ibid.*, pp. 324-44.
183. Somadeva, *ibid.*, pp. 216-20.
184. Somadeva, *ibid.*, pp. 221-71.
185. *Kauṭilya.* Bk. I. Ch. XVII, pp. 32-35 ; text, pp. 32-35.
186. Somadeva, *Nītivākyāmrita,* pp. 18, 251-71. See also Aiyangar, *op. cit.*, p. 109.

187. Somadeva's commentator Haribala admits this. Haribala's commentary with the text was published by Mr. Soni in 1923, as mentioned above. See *ibid.*, pp. 6-7 (1923 ed.) ; Aiyangar, *ibid.*, p. 17 and note (31) ; Beni Prasad, *ibid.*, p. 242.
188. Cf. Beni Prasad, *ibid.*, pp. 241-42. Professor Ghoshal gives an elaborate account of Somadeva's theory. Read Ghoshal, *A History*, pp. 476-89.
189. Read Hegel, G.W.F., *The Philosophy of Right* (1821) ; read also Beni Prasad, *ibid.*, p. 345.
190. Beni Prasad, *ibid.*, p. 227.
191. Hemacandra, *Triṣaṣṭhiśalākapuruṣacaritra*, Bk. I. *Ādīśvaracaritra*, pp. 93-99, 148-55 (Trans. by Dr. Helen N. Johnson, Baroda O.S. 1931). (Text published in Devanāgari, in 1906). See also Ghoshal, *ibid.*, pp. 459-60.
192. Law, *op. cit.*, pp. 260-61.
193. Hemacandra, *Laghu Arhannīti*, II. 11. 66-68 (Ed. with a Gujarati commentary, Ahmedabad, 1906) ; see also Ghoshal, *ibid.*, p. 492.
194. *Kauṭilya*, Bk. XIII. Ch. V. pp. 437-39 ; text, pp. 408-10.
195. Indraji, *Hist. of Gujarat*, pp. 192-93.
196. *Kauṭilya*, Bk. I. Ch. VIII. p. 14 ; text, p. 14. Dr. Kane, who has given a comprehensive account of the ministers, affirms, while citing the same passage, that "it follows that *mantrins* were regarded by Kauṭilya as of a higher grade than *amātyas* in general" (Kane, *op. cit.*, III. p. 105). Dr. Kane's exhaustive note in this connection (*ibid.*, pp. 104-11) should be read by all students. The justification for styling the *mantris* superior in official status to the *amātyas*, which is not very clear in the above conclusion arrived at by Dr. Kane, is given below in this work on the sub-section on Public Service.
197. *Manu*, VII. 55, p. 224.
198. *Kauṭilya*, Bk. I. Ch. VII. 13, p. 12 ; text, p. 13.
199. *Manu*, VII. 54, 58, pp. 224-25 ; see also *ibid.*, 60-61, 141, pp. 225, 238.
200. *Kauṭilya*, Bk. I. Ch. IX. 15, p. 14 ; text, p. 15, *op. cit.*
201. *Ibid.*, Bk. I. Ch. XV. 29, p. 28 ; text, p. 29, *op. cit.*
202. *Manu*, VII. 57, p. 225.
203. *Ibid.*, VII. 59, p. 225.
204. *Ibid.*, VII. 146-47, p. 239.
205. *Ibid.*, Bk. I. Ch. XV, pp. 26-29 ; text, pp. 26-29. On the council of ministers, see Kane, *ibid.*, III. pp. 91, 107, 108 ; Aiyangar, *op. cit.*, pp. 44, 45 ; Ghoshal, *ibid.*, pp. 90, 123-24.
206. *Kauṭilya*, Bk. II. Ch. VII. 64, p. 63 ; text, p. 64.
206a. *Ibid.*, Bk. I. Ch. XV. 29, p. 29 ; text, p. 29.
206b. *Ibid.*, p. 28 ; text, p. 29.
207. *Ibid.*, Bk. V. Ch. III. 247, p. 276 ; text, p. 247.
208. Law, *I.H.Q.* 1929, p. 283 ; Aiyangar, *ibid.*, p. 45, and *ibid.*, note (82) ; Shama Sastry, *Kauṭilya*, p. 276.
209. Professor Aiyangar wrote in this connection, thus: "It is further indicated, perhaps, by the significant rule that 'the king should give only gold and not villages.' " And he refers to the following statement in *Kauṭilya—hiraṇyaṁ-eva dadyāt na grāmaṁ* (Aiyangar, *op. cit.*, p. 45, and note 83, where the reference is given to *Kauṭilya*, V. 3).

But this is misleading. There is no reference here to the ministers at all: the whole passage from which Professor Aiyangar has taken the above citation relating to the payment in gold, refers to the monetary expediency of the sovereign when in financial difficulties, with particular reference to the colonization of waste lands. Kauṭilya plainly states the following: "When wanting in money (*alpa kośaḥ*), the king may give forest produce, cattle, or fields, along with a small amount of money. If he is desirous of colonizing waste land, he shall make payment in money alone ; and if he is desirous of regulating the affairs of all villages equally, he shall give no village to any (of his subjects) (*alpakośaḥ kupya-puśu-kṣetrāṇi dadyāt alpaṁ ca hiraṇyam śūnyaṁ vā niveśayituṁ abhyuthito hiraṇyam-eva dadyāt na grāmaṁ grāmasajāti-vyavahārasthāpanārtham*) (*Kauṭilya*, Bk. V. Ch. III. 249, p. 278 ; text, p. 249).

210. *Ibid.*, Bk. II. Ch. V. 58, p. 56 ; text, p. 58.
211. *Ibid.*, Bk. III. Ch. I. 148, p. 167 ; text, p. 147.
212. *Ibid.*, Bk. II. Ch. I. 46, p. 45 ; text, p. 46.
213. *Manu*, IX. 234, p. 383.
214. *Ibid.*, VII. 123-24, pp. 235-36. Cf. *ibid.*, IX. 231, 259, pp. 382, 388.
215. *Ibid.*, VIII. 34, p. 259.
216. *Kauṭilya*, Bk. IV. Ch. IX. 224-25, pp. 250-52 ; text, pp. 222-24. On the punishment of the judges, read *ibid.*, p. 224 (transl.).
217. *Ibid.*, Bk. III. Ch. XX. 200, pp. 224-25 ; text, p. 200.
218. *Manu*, VII. 113-23, pp. 234-35. Cf. *Mahābhārata*, XII. Chs. 87. 3-11 ; Bühler in *Manu*, p. xxxiii.
219. *Kauṭilya*, Bk. II. Ch. VII. 63, p. 62 ; text, p. 63. The statement that payment, according to the quantity of work done, was to be made at the end of the month of *Āṣādha* (middle of July), strongly suggests that the salaries, too, were paid at the same time. This would justify the assumption made by historians that the salaries mentioned in the *Arthaśāstra* were annual, and not monthly.
220. *Ibid.*, Ch. VII. 64, p. 63 ; text, p. 64.
221. *Ibid.*, Bk. I. Ch. VII. 64, p. 64 ; text, p. 64.
222. *Ibid.*, Bk. II. Ch. VI. 60, p. 59 ; text, p. 60. Kauṭilya's solicitude for every detail in regard to the division of time, is seen in the manner in which he describes the divisions of time. "The royal year, the month, the *pakṣa*, the day, the new years's day on Śrāvaṇa (*vyuṣṭa*), the third and the seventh *pakṣas* of (the seasons such as) rainy season, the winter season, and the summer short of their days, the rest complete, and a separate intercalary month are (the divisions of time)" (*Kauṭilya, ibid.*, page). In this connection, the reader would do well to read the explanation of the 354 days as given by Dr. Shama Sastry and Dr. Fleet in the *Arthaśāstra*, p. 59, notes (1) & (2), and also *ibid.*, p. 63, note (1). Professor Aiyangar refers to the submission of yearly administrative reports "in the month of Āṣāḍha" (Aiyangar, *op. cit.*, p. 45). But this is rather vague in view of the explanation given above.
223. If we count all the departments mentioned their number appears to be twenty-eight (Cf. Kane, *op. cit.*, III. p. 142), although in one context Kauṭilya speaks of only eighteen departments, thus: "Thus with regard to kings, who are inimical, friendly, intermediate, of low rank, or neutral, and with regard to their eighteen government departments (*aṣṭādaśa-tīrtha*), spies shall be set in motion" (*Kauṭilya*, Bk. I. Ch. XII. 21, p. 21 ; text, p. 21).

223a. *Ibid.*, Bk. II. Ch. VII. 62, p. 61 ; text, p. 62.
224. *Ibid.*, Bk. II. Ch. X. 71, p. 71 ; text, p. 70.
225. *Ibid.*, Bk. V. Ch. III. 248, p. 277 ; text, p. 248.
226. *Ibid.*, Bk. II. Ch. VII. pp. 61-64 ; text, pp. 62-65.
227. *Ibid.*, Bk. II. Ch. IX. 69, p. 70 ; text, p. 69.
228. *Ibid.*, Bk. V. Ch. III. 247-48, pp. 276-77 ; text, pp. 247-48.
229. *Ibid.*, Bk. II. Ch. XXXVI, pp. 160-65 ; text, pp. 143-47.
230. *Ibid.*, pp. 222, 245, 276 ; text, p. 197 (for the Superintendent of Gambling).
231. All these details are gathered from the same chapter on the City Superintendent mentioned in note (229) above.
232. *Ibid.*, Bk. I. Ch. IX. 15, pp. 14-15, *op. cit.*
233. *Ibid.*, Bk. I. Ch. X. pp. 15- ; text, pp. 16-18.
234. *Ibid.*, Bk. II. Ch. IX, pp. 68-70 ; text, pp. 68-70. In more than two contexts Kauṭilya uses the term *yukta* for government servants (Bk. II. Ch. VIII. and Ch.

IX), but in another context, he uses the term *bhṛitaka*. Thus, in the previous chapter, he writes that if a government servant (*bhṛitaka*) gives information to the State about embezzlement, he shall get one-twelfth of the amount (*dvādaśa-aṁśaṁ bhṛitakah*) (Bk. II. Ch. VIII, 67, p. 68 ; text, p. 67). It is not unlikely that, while the word *yukta* stood for a government official in some higher capacity, the term *bhṛitaka* perhaps covered the lower cadres of government servants. We have seen above under Part Four, Ch. V.H. (5) (b) that *yukta* was the designation of a certain higher type of officials called chief officers.

235. *Kauṭilya*, Bk. V. Ch. IV. 251, p. 280 ; text, p. 251.
236. *Manu*, VIII. 262-63, pp. 300-01.
237. On the definition of an *aratni* or *prajāpatya hasta*, read Kauṭilya, p. 117 ff. and p. 117 notes (1)-(3).
238. *Ibid.*, Bk. III. Ch. VII. pp. 188-90 ; text, pp. 166-67.
239. *Ibid.*, Bk. IV. Ch. XIII. 234, pp. 261-62 ; text, p. 234.
240. Read *Vedic Index*, I. pp. 2-5 for full details. See also Kane, *op. cit.*, III. p. 541.
241. *Manu*, IX. 223-24, pp. 380-81.
242. *Ibid.*, VII. 47, 50, p. 223.
243. *Ibid.*, IV. 74, p. 140.
244. *Ibid.*, IX. 227, p. 383.
245. *Mahābhārata*, *Udyogaparvan*, Ch. 37. 19 ; see also Kane, *ibid.*, III, pp. 538-42 for a succinct account of gambling.
246. *Kauṭilya*, Bk. III. Ch. XX. 198, pp. 222-23 ; text, pp. 197-98.
247. *Ibid.*, Bk. VIII. Ch. III. 329, p. 356 ; text, p. 329.
248. *Manu*, IV. 209, 219, pp. 161, IX. 259, p. 388.
249. *Kauṭilya*, Bk. II. Ch. XXVII, pp. 136-39 ; text, pp. 123-25.
250. *Manu*, IX. 259, p. 388.
251. Read *Kauṭilya*, pp. 126, 138, 177, 207-08, 224, 254-59, 259, 262, 264-65. The chapter on Sexual Intercourse with Immature Girls (pp. 258-61) is a very sad reflection on the depraved morals of the times which the State evidently tried to rectify.
252. *Ibid.*, Bk. I. Ch. XII. 20, p. 19 ; text, p. 20.
253. *Ibid.*, Bk. II. Ch. I. 47 ; text, p. 47, *op. cit.*
254. *Manu*, IX. 259, p. 388, *op. cit.* ; *ibid.*, 284, pp. 392-93.
255. *Kauṭilya*, Bk. II. Ch. XXXVII. 144, p. 161, *op. cit.*
256. *Ibid.*, Bk. X. Ch. III. 369, p. 397 ; text, p. 369, *op. cit.*
257. *Ibid.*, Bk. V. Ch. III. 247, p. 277 ; text, p. 247.
258. *Ibid.*, Bk. II. Ch. IV. 55, p. 54 ; text, p. 55.
259. *Ibid.*, Bk. IV. Ch. I. 203, p. 231 ; text, p. 203, *op. cit.*
260. *Ibid.*, Bk. IV. 229, p. 257 ; text, p. 229. Read *ibid.*, p. 224 (trans.) for regulations for the prevention of abortion among female slaves.
261. *Ibid.*, Bk. II. Ch. XV, pp. 99-104 ; text, pp. 93-97.
262. *Ibid.*, Bk. II. Ch. XII. 84, p. 88 ; text, p. 84.
263. *Ibid.*, Bk. II. Ch. XXVI. 123, p. 136 ; text, p. 123.
264. *Ibid.*, Bk. IV. Ch. II. 206, p. 233 ; text, p. 206.
265. *Ibid.*, Bk. II. Ch. XXIV, pp. 127-31 ; text, pp. 115-18.
266. *Ibid.*, pp. 144, 189, 257 (trans.).
267. *Ibid.*, Bk. II. Chs. I & II, pp. 45-50 ; text, pp. 45-50. Here, too, the word *viṣṭi* (*daṇḍaviṣṭikarābādhaiḥ*) is rendered by Dr. Shama Sastry as "free labour" which I interpret as "forced labour".
268. *Ibid.*, Bk. II. Ch. I. 47, p. 46 ; text, p. 47.
269. *Ibid.*, Bk. II. Ch. XXXVI. 146, p. 164 ; text, p. 146.
270. *Ibid.*, Bk. VII. Ch. XIV. 307, p. 334 ; text, p. 307.
271. *Ibid.*, Bk. II. Ch. I. 47, p. 46 ; p. 47.
271a. *Ibid.*, Bk. III. Ch. X. 173, p. 196 ; text, p. 173.
271b. *Ibid.*, Bk. III, p. 197 ; text, p. 173.

272. *Kauṭilya*, Bk. III. Ch. XIV. 184, p. 209 ; text, p. 184.
273. *Ibid.*, Bk. III. Ch. X. 171, p. 195 ; text, p. 171.
274. *Ibid.*, Bk. III. 186, p. 210 ; text, p. 186.
274a. The detailed rules regarding labourers are given in *ibid.*, Bk. III. Ch. XIV. 185-87, pp. 209-11 ; text, pp. 184-87.
274b. *Ibid.*, pp. 210-11 ; text, pp. 185-86.
274c. *Ibid.*, Bk. III. Ch. X. 173, p. 197 ; text, p. 173.
275. *Manu*, IX. 271, p. 391.
276. *Ibid.*, IX. 282, p. 392.
277. *Ibid.*, IX. 264-66, p. 389.
278. *Kauṭilya*, Bk. II. Ch. I. 49, p. 48 ; text, pp. 48-49.
279. *Ibid.*, Bk. II. Ch. IV. 55, p. 53 ; text, pp. 54-55.
280. *Ibid.*, Bk. III. Ch. X. 171, p. 194 ; text, p. 171.
281. *Ibid.*, Bk. VII. Ch. XIV. 307, p. 334 ; text, p. 307.
282. *Ibid.*, Bk. II. Ch. XXXVI. 144, p. 161 ; text, p. 144.
283. *Ibid.*, Bk. IV. Ch. XIII. 234, p. 263 ; text, p. 234. The Superintendent of Pastures (*vivītādhyakṣa*) mentioned here is not to be confounded with the Superintendent of Agriculture (*sītādhyakṣa*) cited earlier.
284. Read Kane, *op. cit.*, III, pp. 181, 197 for some notices of roads in the other classical works on Polity.
285. *Kauṭilya*, Bk. IV. Ch. III. 207, p. 234 ; text, p. 207.
286. Like those given in *ibid.*, Bk. XIV, pp. 441 ff, too numerous to be cited.
287. *Ibid.*, Bk. II. Ch. XXIX. 129, p. 143 ; text, 129.
288. *Ibid.*, Bk. IV. Ch. III. 208, p. 235 ; text, pp. 207-08.
289. *Ibid.*, Bk. II. Ch. XXVIII. 126, p. 140 ; text, p. 126.
290. *Ibid.*, Bk. VIII. Ch. IV. 331, p. 357 ; text, p. 331.
291. *Candogya Upanisad*, I. 10. 1-3 ; Kane, *op. cit.* III, pp. 163-64.
292. *Rāmāyaṇa*, *Bālakāṇḍa*, Ch. 9, 8, p. 15. The drought is ascribed to the oppression and evil ways of king Romapāda of Anga (*Ibid.*, vv. 7-8, p. 15).
293. *Nirukta*, II. 10, cited by Kane, *ibid.*, III, p. 164.
294. *Kauṭilya*, Bk. IV. Ch. III. 208, pp. 235-36 ; text, pp. 207-08.
295. The late Dr. Shama Sastry translated the word *nāgarika pratinidhi* in this context as Superintendent of Villages (*Kauṭilya*, p. 234). This is inadmissible. In the first place, the first part of the term *nāgarika* evidently refers to a citizen in a town where the danger of fire was greater than in a village or in country side. And, secondly, *pratinidhi* is an observer, a spy, an emissary (Apte, *Skt. Eng. Dicty.*, p. 644), and not a Superintendent for whom the technical term used by Kauṭilya is *adhyakṣa*. Probably the next technical term *niśāntapratinidhi*, in the same context, is to be used also in the sense of Observers at Night.
296. *Kauṭilya*, Bk. IV. Ch. III, pp. 234-37 ; text, pp. 207-10.
297. Read *Ibid.*, Bk. VIII, on the calamities facing the Elements of Sovereignty, etc., pp. 349-65 ; text, pp. 321-38, in order to get an adequate idea of this great problem.
298. Read *Vedic Index*, I, p. 273 where the references to the *Aitareya Brāhmaṇa* are given in detail.
299. *Śat. Brah.*, XIII. 4. 2. 17, pp. 359-60 ; see also *Vedic Index*, I, p. 273.
300. *Śat. Brah.*, V. 4. 4. 11, p. 109 ; see also *Vedic Index*, I, p. 213.
301. *Maitrāyani Saṃhita*, II. 1. 8 ; III. 8 ; IV. 4. 3 ; *Taittirīya Brāhmaṇa*, II. 6. 5.
302. *Atharva Veda*, III. 19, 1 ; IX. 7. 9 ; XV. 2. 3. See also *Vedic Index*, II, p. 251.
303. *Rig Veda*, VIII. 35, 16-18 ; I. 113-16 ; see also *Vedic Index*, II, p. 250-51.
304. *Manu*, VIII. 41, p. 260. Dr. Bühler translated the word *jānapadān* as districts. But I think it is more appropriate to interpret it as country parts. Dr. Jayaswal refers to this verse in Manu (Jayaswal, *op. cit.*, p. 232, and note 20), and would interpret the word *jānapadān* as a corporate institution. There is no justification for this, as will be shown below in our discussion of Dr. Jayaswal's theory.

305. *Rāmāyaṇa, Ayodhyakāṇḍa*, Ch. II. 19, 49. Ch. IV. 1 ; Ch. III. 24, 27, pp. 106, 110, 282.
306. *Kauṭilya*, Bk. I. Ch. XIII. 22, p. 22 ; text, p. 22, *op. cit.* Dr. Shama Sastry's interpretation of *Mahāmātya* or, as he corrects it, *mahāmātra*, into prime minister is inadmissible, since there could not have been two or more prime ministers, and since in a previous context (Bk. I. Ch. X. 16, p. 15) he himself has translated *mantri* as prime minister.
307. *Ibid.*, Bk. II. Ch. XXXV. 141, p. 158 ; text, p. 141.
308. *Ibid.*, Bk. VI. Ch. I. 258, p. 288 ; text, p. 258.
309. *Ibid.*, Bk. VIII. Ch. IV. 334, p. 360 ; text, p. 334.
310. *Ibid.*, Bk. IX. Ch. I. 340, p. 368 ; text, p. 340.
311. Jayaswal, *op. cit.*, p. 3.
312. *Ibid.*, p. 43.
313. & 314. *Ibid.*, p. 231.
315. *Ibid.*, p. 320.
316. Jayaswal, *Ep. Ind.* XX, p. 71 , Hirananda Sastri, *ibid.*, XXI, p. 27 ; Jayaswal, *Polity*, p. 235, and note (29).
317. Jayaswal, *Polity*, pp. 232-42.
318. *Rāmāyaṇa, Ayodhyakanda*, Ch. II. 19, p. 106 when it is stated following: *tasya dharmārtha viduṣo bhāvaṁ-ājñāya sarvaśaḥ Brāhmaṇa janamukyās-ca paurajāna padaih saha.* In the same chapter in verse 26, we have the following: *te tamūrcuhu-mahātmānām paurajānapadaiḥ saha bahavo nṛipa kalyāṇā guṇah putrasya santi te.* Further on in verse 49, we have *āśaṁsate janaḥ sarvo rāṣṭre puravare tathā abhyantaras-ca bāhyas-ca paurajānapado janaḥ*, etc.
319. Jayaswal, *Polity*, p: 231.
320. See note (318) above.
321. Dr. (Miss) P. C. Dharma has attempted to connect what she calls the various corporations in the *paura* and *janapada* bodies but this is, I am afraid, all conjecture (Read Dharma, *The Ramayana Polity*, p. 37, Madras, 1941).
322. Jayaswal, *Polity*, p. 231.
323. *Ibid.*, p. 238.
324. For the earlier translation of this page by Dr. Jayaswal, read *Ep. Ind.* XX. pp. 78-79. On the former page is the translation, and on p. 79, ll. 6-7 is the sentence in question from the inscription. For his later reading of the same sentence, read the *Journal of the Bihar and Orissa Research Society*, III, pp. 425-507. This may be compared with what he said in *Ep. Ind.* XX, p. 71.
325. Read Barua, B. M., *I. H. Q.* XIV, pp. 464-77 ; Kane, *op. cit.*, III. p. 94.
326. Jayaswal, *ibid.*, p. 231.
327. *Ibid.*, pp. 231, 251, and n. (24) where the citation from the *Divyāvadāna* (pp. 407-08) is given.
328. Jayaswal, *ibid.*, p. 237.
329 & 330. *Ibid.*, pp. 240-41 ff.
331. Kane, *ibid.*, III, p. 544.
332. Keith, *Hist. of Skt. Lit.*, p. 449.
333. Jayaswal, *ibid.*, p. 239, and note (49) citing Vasiṣṭha XVI, 20, and *Bṛihaspati* from *Vīramitrodaya*.
334. Jayaswal, *ibid.*, pp. 245-53.
335. *Ibid.*, p. 248.
336. *Ibid.*, p. 249.
337. *Kauṭilya*, Bk. I. Ch. XIII, pp. 22-24 ; text, pp. 22-24.
338. See note (306) above.
339. *Mahābhārata Śantiparvan*, LXXXIII, 45-46. *Tasmai mantraḥ prayoktavyo daṇḍam —ādhistathā nṛipā paurajānapadā yasmin—viśvāsaṁ dharmato gataḥ.* Cited by Jayaswal, *ibid.*, p. 250, note (20).

340. Jayaswal, *ibid.*, p. 250.
341. *Manu*, VII. 54, 58, pp. 224-25, *op. cit.*
342. *Kauṭilya*, Bk. I. Ch. IX. 15, p. 14 ; text, p. 15, *op. cit.*
343. Jayaswal, *ibid.*, p. 250. The citation from *Śantiparvan* (LXXXV. 11-12) given by him on the same page, note (21), does not help to improve matters.
344. Read the pertinent remarks of Dr. Kane (*op. cit.*, III, pp. 106-07) on the king's consulting with his ministers.
345. Jayaswal, *ibid.*, p. 252.
346. *Kauṭilya*, Bk. V. Ch. II. 242, p. 271 ; text, p. 242.
347. The word *sangrahaṇa* also means accepting, receiving, but not in the sense of begging. See Apte, *Skt. Eng. Dicty.*, p. 948.
348. *Kauṭilya*, Bk. II. Ch. XXXV, pp. 158-60 ; text, pp. 141-43.
349. *Ibid.*, Bk. II. Ch. I. 47, p. 46 ; text, p. 47.
349a. *Ibid.*
350. *Ibid.*, Bk. II. Ch. I, p. 45 ; text, p. 45.
351. *Ibid.*, Bk. II. Ch. I. 48, p. 47 ; text, p. 48.
352. *Ibid.*, Bk. V. Ch. II. 244, p. 273 ; text, p. 244.
353. *Ibid.*, p. 273, n. (1).
354. *Ibid.*, Bk. V. Ch. II. 244, p. 273 ; text, p. 244.
355. Jayaswal, *ibid.*, p. 235, *op. cit.* The references given on the same page are to his own editing of the seals in the *Ep. Ind.* XX, p. 71 ; Hirananda Sastri, *ibid.*, XXI, p. 72 ; and the latter's *Memoir on the Nalanda Seals* (A.S.I.).
356. Cunningham, *Coins.*, p. 77, *op. cit.*
357. On the rejection of the theory by Professor Altekar, read his *State and Govt.*, pp. 101-08, where he has adduced different arguments to disprove Dr. Jayaswal's theory. See also Kane, *op. cit.*, III, pp. 93-96. Professor U. N. Ghoshal has correctly taken *janapada* to mean rural areas (*A History*, p. 125). Dr. (Miss) Dharma likewise correctly understood the term *paura* as denoting represesntatives of the capital, and *janapada*, as those of the country excluding the capital (Dharma, *op. cit.*, p. 36).
358. Kane, *op. cit.*, III, p. 95. Another untenable interpretation of the term *paura-jānapada* was given by the late Professor Dikshitar, who said it meant the organized body of citizens, who attended to the local administration of the city (Dikshitar, *Hindu Adm. Institutions*, pp. 156-57). It was refuted by Dr. N. N. Law, *I.H.Q.* II, p. 407, and particularly in *I.H.Q.* V. 184.
359. *Atharva Veda*, VII. 12 ; 1 ; VIII. 10. 5. 6 ; XIII. 1. 56 ; XV. 9. 2. 3 ; see also *Vedic Index*, II, p. 430.
360. *Atharva Veda*, VII. 12. 1, *op. cit.* See also Kane, *ibid.*, III, p. 92.
361. *Rig Veda*, VI. 28. 6 ; VIII. 4. 9 ; X. 34. 6. See *Vedic Index*. II, p. 426, note (2) for further reference in the *Samhitas* and the *Brāhmanas*.
362 & 363. *Rig Veda*, X. 34. 6 ; *Atharva Veda*, V. 31. 6 ; XII. 46 (where *dyūta* replaces *sabhā*) ; *Vedic Index*, II, p. 426, and notes (3) and (6). See also Kane, *ibid.*, III, pp. 92-93, where the *sabhā* is described as a gambling hall of the Rig Vedic times
364. Ludwig, *Translation of the Rig Veda*, pp. 3, 253-56 ; *Vedic Index*, II. p. 426. Professor Ludwig's citations from the *Rig Veda* (VIII. 4. 9 ; X. 71, 10), in support of his view, have been characterized by Professors Macdonell and Keith as vague (*Vedic Index*, p. II. 426), note (7).
365. Macdonell—Keith, *Vedic Index*, II, pp. 426-27.
366. *Vedic Index*, II, p. 118.
367. *Rig Veda*, X. 71. 10.
368. *Vedic Index*, II, pp. 427-28 for further references.
369. That there is some justification for this supposition of ours is evident when we note that the term *sabhāpāla*, "guardian of an assembly", occurring in the *Taittirīya Brāhmaṇa* (III. 7. 4. 6), is different from *sabhāvin*, "keeper of a gambling hall",

also occurring in the same work (*Taitt. Brah.* III. 4. 16. 1). This meaning is, of course, according to the great mediaeval scholiast, Sāyaṇa (*Vedic Index*, II, p. 428). But it helps us to observe that the *śabhā* in course of time had ceased to be a mere gambling hall.

370. *Maitrāyaṇī Samhita*, IV. 7. 4 ; *Vedic Index*, II, p. 426.
371. Bloomfield, M., *J.A.O.S.*, 19, p. 13 ; *Vedic Index*, II, p. 42).
372. *Vedic Index*, II, p. 427, and note (11).
373. Zimmer, Heinrich, *Altindisches Leben*, p. 174 (Berlin, 1879). See also *Vedic Index*, II, p. 427.
374. *Śat. Brah.*, III. 3. 4. 14, p. 79. Cf. *Candogya Upaniṣad*, V. 3. 6 ; see also *Vedic Index*, II, p. 427, note (12).
375. *Vedic Index*, II, p. 427, note (12).
376. Hillebraṇdt, Alfred, *Vedische Mythologie*, pp. 2, 123-25 ; *Vedic Index*, II. p. 427, note (15).
377. On *agniśālā*, read *Vedic Index*, I, pp. 9-10.
378. Jayaswal, *Polity*, pp. 17-20.
378a. See also *Vedic Index*, II. p. 426, and note (5).
379. Ghoshal, *Beginnings*, p. 150.
380. Ghoshal, *ibid.*, pp. 151-52.
381. Kane, *op. cit.*, III. pp. 92-93.
382. Bandyopadhyaya, Narayan Chandra, *Development of Hindu Polity*. Part I, pp. 110 ff. See also Ghoshal, *Beginnings*, p. 154.
383. For a detailed refutation of Dr. Bandyopadhyaya's theory, relating to the *sabhā*, read Ghoshal, *Beginnings*, pp. 154-56.
384. Altekar, *op. cit.*, pp. 97-98.
385. *Vedic Index*, II. p. 427.
386. *Atharva Veda*, VIII. 10. 5-6 ; Ghoshal, *Beginnings*, p. 148, and note (12).
387. *Taitt. Samhita*, XX. 7, p. 115 (Trans. by A. B. Keith. Harvard Or. Series). Cited by Ghoshal, *Beginnings*, p. 152, note (23). The inherent bias of Western scholars, while dealing with Indian questions—barring a few illustrious examples—is seen in Professor Zimmer's wild conjectures like the following: the public hall (*sabhā*) was the rendezvous of gamblers. *Sabhāsthanu* was the game of the village. "No vice was so universal as deceit and gambling. Perjury was not uncommon, and there was no lack of robbers and thieves" (Zimmer, *op. cit.*, pp. 117-80). Professor Von Jhering, another biassed and uncharitable critic of the Indians, and particularly of the Hindus, not only cites the above statement of Professor Zimmer but adds the following: "As to the alleged honesty and strict morality of the people, we may gather their state from the fact that gambling and cheating were regarded as equivalent" (Jhering, *The Evolution of the Aryan*, p. 63. n. 1). I do not wish to make any comment on these and other statements of Professor Jhering. I may rest content with the fact that, so far as his work relating to India is concerned, it long ago fell into that detestable limbo from which it has never recovered! The only reason which has prompted me to give him a chance of emerging from it is just to show how, beneath his scholarship, lay a deep layer of pride and hatred which he shared with Professor Zimmer.
388. *Rig Veda*, I. 95. 8 ; IX. 92. 6 ; X. 97. 6 ; 166. 4 ; 191. 3 ; *Atharva Veda*, V. 19. 15 ; VI. 88. 3 ; VII. 12. 1 ; XII. 1. 56 ; see also *Vedic Index*, II. p. 430, and notes (1) & (2).
389. *Atharva Veda*, XV. 9. 2 ; see also Kane, *op. cit.*, III. p. 92.
390. Hillebrandt, *Vedische Mythologie*, pp. 2, 124, n. (6) ; see also *Vedic Index*, II. p. 430.
391. Ludwig, *Rig Veda*, pp. 3 ; 253 ff. (trans.) ; see also *Vedic Index*, II. p. 430.
392. *Rig Veda*, X. 11. 8 : *Jaimīnya Upaniṣad Brāhmaṇa*, II. 11. 13. 14 ; see also *Vedic Index*, II. p. 431.

393. *Rig Veda*, X. 191. 3 ; see also Kane, *ibid.*, III. p. 92.
394. *Rig Veda*, II. 24. 13.
395. *Atharva Veda*, V. 19. 15 ; see also Kane, *ibid.*
396. Macdonell, *Skt. Lit.*, p. 158.
397. Zimmer, *op. cit.*, p. 175.
398. Ghoshal, *Beginnings*, p. 148, and note (10) where he cites the statement of Professor Zimmer, thus: "In Wahlmonarchien fand Zweifelsohne durch die vereinigten Vis in der *Samiti* die Erkürung des Herrschersstatt."
399. Zimmer, *op. cit.*, p. 174, cited by Ghoshal, *ibid.*, p. 143, and note (1), when the statement from the learned German Professor's work is given as follows: "Die Versammlung des Stammes heisst *Samiti*, an ihr nimmt der Konig Antheil" (the last word should be Anteil).
400. Ghoshal, *Beginnings*, pp. 143-44.
401. Zimmer, *ibid.*, pp. 167 ff.
402. Weber, *Indische Studien*, pp. 17, 188 ; Bloomfield, *Hymns of the Atharva Veda*, p. 336. See also *Vedic Index*, II. p. 211, note (1).
403. *Vedic Index*, II, p. 211.
404. Macdonell, *Skt. Lit.*, p. 158.
405. *Vedic Index*, II. p. 431.
406. Jayaswal, *Polity*, p. 12.
407. *Vedic Index*, II, p. 431 citing Zimmer, and citing the following references *Atharva Veda*, VI. 88. 3 ; Roth, *St. Petersburg Diety.*, q.v.
408. Jayaswal, *ibid.*, p. 12, *op. cit.*
409. Jayaswal, *ibid.*, p. 13 citing *Atharva Veda*, VI. 64 ; *Rig Veda*, X. 191-3.
410 & 411. Jayaswal, *ibid.*, pp. 14, 16.
412. Read Ghoshal, *ibid.*, pp. 144-47 for a different refutation of Dr. Jayaswal's theory.
413. Altekar, *op. cit.*, pp. 76, and *ibid.*, note, 95-97.
414. Altekar, *ibid.*, p. 98.
415. Altekar, *ibid.*, citing *Atharva Veda*, VI. 88. 3.
416. Altekar, *ibid.*, pp. 98-99.
417. *Vedic Index*, II. p. 431, and note (9), *op. cit.*
418. Ghoshal, *ibid.*, p. 146.
419. Ghoshal, *ibid.*, p. 148, note (13) citing *Atharva Veda*, V. 19. 15 ; VI. 88. 3.
420. *Vedic Index*, II. p. 430.
421. Kane, *op. cit.*, III. p. 92, *op cit.*
422. Altekar, *op. cit.*, p. 98, *op. cit.*
423. *Vedic Index*, II. p. 431.
424. Altekar, *ibid.*, p. 98, *op. cit.*
425. *Śat. Brah.*, VII. I. 1. 4. p. 299 (S. B. E. XLI). Professor Ghoshal (*Beginnings*, p. 149) cites only a sentence in this passage, thus: "To whomsoever the Kṣatriya with the approval of the *viś* grants a settlement, that is properly given" ; and informs us that it is Professor Eggeling's translation. The reader will find that there is some difference in the version of Professor Eggeling, as cited by me, and that given by Professor Ghoshal.
426. Ghoshal, *ibid.*, p. 149, note (13a).
427. Hopkins, *India, Old and New*, pp. 221 ff ; *Vedic Index*, II. p. 214.
428. Kane, *op. cit.*, III. pp. 495-96. See also *ibid.*, II. pp. 865-69 for a full discussion of the theory of the ownership of land.
429. Baden-Powell, *Village Communities in India*, p. 145 ; *Indian Village Community*, p. 207 ff ; *Vedic Index*, II. p. 214.
430. *Vedic Index*, II. p. 215.
431. *Śat. Brah.* I. 3. 4. 15, p. 94 (S.B.E. XII).
432. *Ibid.*, II 5. 2. 27 (S.B.E. XII).
433. *Ibid.*, III. 3. 2. 8 (S.B.E. XXVI).

434. *Śat. Brah.*, II. 5. 2. 7, p. 393.
435. *Ibid.*, XII. 7. 3. 12, p. 227 (S.B.E. XLIV).
436. *Ibid.*, XIII. 2. 2. 15, p. 303 (S.B.E. XLIV).
437. *Ibid.*, III. 9. 3. 7, p. 228.
438. *Ibid.*, III. 3. 4. 14, p. 39.
439. Ghoshal, *Beginnings*, p. 149.
440. Kane, *op. cit.*, III, p. 92. Dr. Kane's remarks on the "frantic efforts" made by scholars like Dr. Jayaswal and others to prove that India had elective bodies, in order to "counteract the sinister propaganda of many English writers that East is East and West is West", may be read in this connection. Kane, *ibid.*, III, p. 93. In the light of the detailed discussion we have made of the terms *sabhā* and *samiti*, we may dismiss the following explanation of the same by Professor Sinha as being too general and arbitrary. "Of these two, the Sabhā seems to be a council of the influential men and the elders, while the *Samiti* was an assembly of the people meeting on special occasions" (Sinha, *op. cit.*, p. 22). I cannot make out on what grounds the definition of these terms rests.
441. *Brihadāraṇyaka Upaniṣad*, V. 1. 1 ; see *Vedic Index*, I. p. 449. The story of the proud youth Śvataketu illustrates the nature of a *pariṣad* (Br. Up. VI. 2. 1 ff ; Cf. *Cān. Upan.*, V. 3. 1 ff.). Professor Ghoshal gives this story, *Beginnings*, p. 47.
442. *Gobhila Gṛihya Sūtra*, III. 2. 40 ; *Vedic Index*, I. p. 497.
443. *Vedic Index*, I. p. 497, and note (3) where there is a reference to Professor Hillebrandt's work.
444. *Vedic Index*, I. p. 497.
445. Ghoshal, *Beginnings*, p. 47.
446. Mookerjee, Radha Kumud, *Local Government in Ancient India*, p. 79 ; Ghoshal, *ibid.*, p. 47. Read Professor Ghoshal's criticism of Dr. Mookerjee's description of the *pariṣad* on the same page, note (9).
447. Kane, *op. cit.*, III. pp. 100-01.
448. *Manu*, XII. 112, p. 510.
449. *Kauṭilya*, Bk. I. Ch. XV. 29, pp. 28-29 ; text, pp. 28-29.
450. *Rig Veda*, I. 31, 6 ; 117, 25 ; III. 1. 18 ; 27. 7 ; IV. 38. 4 ; VI. 8. 1 ; X. 85. 26 ; 92. 2 ; *Atharva Veda*, IV. 25. 1 ; V. 20. 12 ; XVIII. 3. 70.
451. *Vedic Index*, II. p. 296.
452. Roth cited in the *Vedic Index*, II. p. 296, notes (1)-(4).
453. Oldenberg, H., *Sacred Books of the East*, XLVI, p. 26 ff. See also *Vedic Index*, II. p. 296, note (5) for further references to Professor Oldenberg's reversion to the meaning of "Sacrifice".
454. Whitney, W. D., *Atharva Veda*, I. 13. 4 (Har. Or. Series No. VII. Edited by C. R. Lanman. Harward, 1905). See also *Vedic Index*, II. p. 296, note (2).
455. Zimmer, *Alt. Ind.*, p. 177. See also *Vedic Index*, II. p. 297.
456. Ludwig, *Rig Veda* (trans), pp. 3, 259 ; *Vedic Index*, II. p. 296, note (6).
457. Ludwig, *ibid.*, p. 3, 261 ; *Vedic Index*, II. p. 297.
458. Geldner, *Vedische Studien*, I. p. 147 ; *Rig Veda Glossar*, p. 161 ; *Zeitschrift der Morgenländischen Gesellschaft*, 52, p. 757 ; *Vedic Index*, II. p. 296.
459. Bloomfield, M., *J.A.O.S.*, 19, p. 12 ff ; *Vedic Index*, II. p. 296.
460. *Rig Veda*, I. 91. 20 ; 167. 3 ; IV. 27. 2 ; *Atharva Veda*, XX. 128. 1 ; *Vedic Index*, II. p. 296, n. (10).
461. *Vedic Index*, II. pp. 296, n. (10), 297, note (11). The authors refer to *Atharva Veda*, VII. 38. 4 ; *Maitrāyaṇī Samhita*, 10. 7. 4.
462. *Vedic Index*, II. p. 296, note (10).
463. *Ibid.*, II. p. 297, note (14). See also *Rig Veda*, I. 31. 6 ; V. 62-6.
464. Jayaswal, *Polity*, I. pp. 11-20, cited by Ghoshal, *Beginnings*, p. 143.
465. Jayaswal, *ibid.*, p. 20 (3rd ed., 1955).
466. Ghoshal, *ibid.*, p. 153, and note (25). I only wish Professor Ghoshal had done

sufficient justice to the learned authors of the *Vedic Index*, who were the first, as pointed out by me, to bring out cearly the difference of opinion amongst all the preceding scholars.

467. *Vedic Index*, II. p. 580, and *q.v.* for various other references.
468. Max Müller, *Chips from a German Workshop*, IV. p. 424 (London, 1875).
469. *Śat. Brah.*, III. 1. 1-3 ff., pp. 1-2 (S.B.E. XXVI).
470. As Dr. Kane has pointed out on the strength of the *Rig Veda*, I. 91. 20, it appears that we have to consider the *sabhā* "in some ways different from *vidatha*", since in that passage in the *Rig Veda*, Soma is said to confer a son who is *sādanya, vidathya*, and *sabheya* (Kane, *op. cit.*, III. p. 92).
471. Jayaswal, *ibid.*, p. 20.
472. *Vedic Index*, II. p. 417 ; Macdonell, *Skt. Lit.*, pp. 165-66.
473. *Rig Veda*, II. 12. 8 ; *Vedic Index*, II. p. 417.
474. *Atharva Veda*, VII. 62. 1 ; *Vcdic Index*, II, p. 417.
475. *Rig Veda*, I. 100-10 ; *Atharva Veda*, VII. 62-1 ; *Vedic Index*, II, pp. 168-69.
476. *Atharva Veda*, XV. 9. 2 ; III. 19. 1 ; IX. 7. 9 ; *Vedic Index*, II. p. 251, n. (35). Read also *ibid.*, note (34) for references to the *Rig Veda*.
477. *Vedic Index*, II. p. 472. Read *Rig Veda*, I. 66. 7 ; 116-1, where the term *senā-jū*, according to the authors of the *Vedic Index*, means "swift as an arrow". See also *Atharva Veda*, VIII. 8. 7 ; XI. 10.
478. According to Dr. Kane, in the Vedic age soldiers other than the Kṣatras or Kṣatriyas were not known (Kane, *op. cit.*, III, p. 202). In view of what he has said above relating to the responsibility of defending the country, it is difficult to agree with the view of the learned author that the Kṣatriyas were the only soldiers known in the Vedic age.
479. *Atharva Veda*, XII. 1. 5. 6.
480. *Vedic Index*, II, p. 416, note (1).
481. *Rig Veda*, IV. 4. 3 ; 37. 1 ; 50. 8 ; V. 3. 5 ; VI. 8. 4 ; 21. 4 ; 48. 8 ; VI. 56, 22 ; 61. 3 ; 70. 3 ; 104. 18 ; X. 91. 2 ; 124. 81 ; 173. 6 ; *Atharva Veda*, III. 4. 1 ; IV. 8. 4 ; 22 ; 1. 3. 1. See *Vedic Index*, II, p. 306, note (2) for further references.
482. *Macdonell, Skt. Lit.*, p. 158.
483. *Atharva Veda*, XV. 8. 2. 3 ; XIV. 2. 27 ; *Rig Veda*, X. 91. 2 ; *Vedic Index*, II, p. 306.
484. *Vedic Index*, II, p. 306.
485. *Ibid.*, II, pp. 271, 305-07.
486. Zimmer, *op. cit.*, pp. 159 ; *Vedic Index*, I, p. 269.
487. *Zimmer, ibid.*, p. 161 ; *Vedic Index*, I, p. 269.
488. *Vedic Index*, I, p. 269.

488a. *Rig Veda*, X. 91. 2 ; *Vedic Index*, I, p. 269, note (8).

489. *Vedic Index*, II, p. 307, and note (12) in which references are given to the *Brāhmaṇas* and the *Samhitas*, where the strife between the *Viśaḥ* and the *Kṣatriyas* is described.
490. *Śat. Brah.*, XII. 7. 3. 8, p. 225. (S.B.E., XLIV).
491. *Ibid.*, XII. 7. 3. 12, p. 227. (S.B.E., *ibid.*).
492. *Ibid.*, XII. 7. 3. 15, p. 228. (S.B.E., *ibid.*).
493. *Ibid.*, XI. 2. 7. 14-16, p. 41. (S.B.E., *ibid.*).
494. *Vedic Indcx*, I, p. 269, and notes (1) till (5) ; Hopkins, *Religions of India*, pp. 26, 27.
495. *Vedic Index*, I, pp. 269-70. Read *ibid.*, p. 270 where the authors have compared the Indian *viś, jana*, and *gotra* with the *viś, zantu*, and the *daqyu* found in the Iranian world. Is it possible that the *daqyu* were the Iranian counterpart of the Indian *dasyu*?
496. *Vedic Index*, I, p. 271.
497. *Ibid.*, I, p. 273, and notes (1) and (2).
498. *Ibid.*, I, p. 271, *ibid.*, 11. 431. The *samiti* is not mentioned either in the Buddhist works, or in the Epics or in the law-books.

499. *Pāṇini*, II. 4-23 ; Agrawala, *op. cit.*, p. 21.
500. Agrawala, *ibid.*, p. 133
501. Agrawala, *ibid.*, p. 403.
502. *Pāṇini*, IV. 4. 105 ; Agrawala, *ibid.*, p. 404.
503. Agrawala, *ibid.*, p. 408.
504. *Pāṇini*, IV. 3. 123 ; Agrawala, *ibid.*, p. 297.
505. *Gobhila Gṛihya Sūtra*, III. 4. 25, *Drahyāyana Gṛihya Sūtra*, III. 1. 25 cited by Professor Agrawala, *ibid.*, p. 297. Professor Agrawala gives further proof in this connection on the same page from Caraka and Patañjali.
506. *Pāṇini*, IV. 4. 41 ; Agrawala, *ibid.*, p. 297.
507. *Pāṇini*, V. 2. 112 ; Agrawala, *ibid.*, pp. 297, 399.
508. Agrawala, *ibid.*, pp. 297-98.
509. *Jataka Stories*, VI, pp. 405, 431 (Fausböll).
510. *Kauṭilya*, Bk. I. Ch. XX. 45, p. 43 ; text, p. 45.
511. *Ibid.* Bk. I. Ch. XIII. 23, p. 22 ; text, p. 22.
512. *Pāṇini*, V. 2. 52 ; Agrawala, *ibid.*, p. 437.
513. *Pāṇini*, VI. 2. 28 ; Agrawala, *ibid.*, pp. 436-39.
514. Agrawala, *ibid.*, p. 439 where the reference to *Kauṭilya* is cited but without explaining the context.
515. *Kauṭilya*, Bk. XI. Ch. I. 378, p. 407 ; text, p. 378. The late Dr. Shama Sastry interpreted *sanghamukhyamanuṣyāṇām* as "leaders of corporations", and *kumārakān* as "inferior leaders". In the light of Pāṇini's distinction between *yuvan* and *vṛiddha* members of the *pūgas*,—which, as Professor Agrawala informs us, adopted a type of *sangha* government—these can be better interpreted as elderly leaders and youthful leaders of the *sanghas*.
516. *Kauṭilya*, Bk. XI. Ch. I. 379, 380, 381, pp. 408-10 ; text, pp. 378-81. On the *sanghamukhya*, read also Majumdar, R. C., *Corporate Life in Ancient India*, p. 104 (2nd ed.) ; Ghoshal, *Beginnings*, p. 67.
517. *Pāṇini*, IV. 4. 43 ; Agrawala, *ibid.*, p. 157.
518. *Rig Veda*, I. 110. 5 ; *Atharva Veda*, III. 14. 3. 4 ; XIX. 31. 3 ; *Vedic Index*, I, p. 99.
519. *Rig Veda*, VII. 49. 2 ; *Atharva Veda*, I. 6. 4 ; XIX. 2. 2 ; *Vedic Index*, I, p. 99.
520. *Vedic Index*, I, p. 100.
521. *Candogya Upanisad*, VII. 24. 2 ; *Vedic Index*, I, p. 100.
522. *Vedic Index*, I, p. 100 ; *Śat. Brah.*, XIII. 7. 1. 13. 15 ; p. 421 (S.B.E., XLIV). The authors of the *Vedic Index*, (I. p. 100) refer to the same *kāṇḍa* but *adhyāya* 6, *Brāhmaṇa* 2, 18, as a further proof of this point. The passage runs thus: "Now to the sacrificial fees. What there is towards the middle of the kingdom other than the land and the property of the Brāhmaṇa, but including the men, of that eastern quarter belongs to the Hoṭri, the southern to the Brahman, the western to the Adhvaryu, and the northern to the Udgāṭri ; and the Hotrakas share this along with them" (*Śat. Br.*, *ibid.*, p. 412). The evidence of this passage in regard to the special nature of land as property is not clear.
523. *Rig Veda*, I. 44. 10 ; 114. 1 ; X. 146. 1 ; 149. 4 ; *Atharva Veda*, IV. 36. 7. 8 ; V. 17. 4 ; VI. 40. 2 ; *Vedic Index*, I, p. 244.
524. *Śat. Brah.*, XIII. 2. 4. 2, pp. 306-07 (S.B.E., XLIV) ; *Vedic Index*, I, p. 244.
525. *Baden-Powell's Indian Village Community* (1896), and *Village Communities in India* (1899) are the most substantial contributions to this subject.
526. Zimmer, *op. cit.*, pp. 159, 160 ; *Vedic Index*, I, p. 245.
527. Hopkins, *Religions of India*, p. 27 ; *Vedic Index*, I, p. 245, note (16).
528. *Vedic Index*, I, p. 245, and read *ibid.*, note (17) for further clarification.
529. *Ibid.*, I, p. 246.
530 & 531. *Ibid.*, I. 246.
532. *Atharva Veda*, IV. 22-2 ; VIII. 7. 11 ; *Bṛihadāranyaka Upanisad*, VI. 3. 13 ; *Vedic Index*, I, p. 244.

533. *Rig Veda*, X. 149, 4. Cf. *Maitrāyaṇi Samhita*, IV. 1. 1 ; *Vedic Index*, I, p. 244.
534. *Jaiminīya Upaniṣad Brāhmaṇa*, III. 13. 4 ; *Vedic Index*, I, p. 245.
535. *Vedic Index*, I, p. 246.
536. *Atharva Veda*, IV. 22, 2 ; *Vedic Index*, I, p. 247.
537. *Rig Veda*, X. 62. 11 ; 107. 5 ; *Atharva Veda*, III. 5. 7 ; XIX. 31. 12 ; *Taittirīya Samhita*, II. 5. 44 ; *Vedic Index*, I, p. 247, note (26) for further references.
538. *Śat. Brah.*, V. 4. 4. 18, p. 111 (S.B.E., XLI). See also *Vedic Index*, I, p. 247. On the *grāmaṇī*, read Eggeling, *Śat. Brah.*, V, p. 60, n. (1) ; Zimmer, *Alt. Leben.*, p. 171.
539. *Śat. Brah.*, *ibid.*, 4. 4. 15, p. 110. I have added the words "Brahman" and "king" in this context.
540. *Vedic Index*, I, p. 247.
541. *Ibid.*, I, p. 247.
542. *Rig Veda*, VIII. 20. 5 ; IX. 96. 1 ; X. 84. 2 ; *Vedic Index*, II, p. 472. On the *senānī's* being one of the *ratnins* of the king, read *Vedic Index*, II, p. *ibid.*, note (5) for further references.
543. Zimmer, *ibid.*, p. 171.
544. *Vedic Index*, I, p. 247.
545. *Taittirīya Samhita*, II. 3. 1. 3 ; *Kāṭhaka Samhita*, XI. 4 ; *Maitrāyaṇī Samhita*, II. 2.1 ; *Vedic Index*, I, p. 248. I do not accept the interpretation of *sabhā* as "court" given by the learned authors of the *Vedic Index*.
546. *Maitrāyaṇī Samhita*, IV. 14. 12 ; *Taittirīya Brāhmaṇa*, II. 8. 4. 2, see also *Vedic Index*, II, p. 351.
547 & 548. *Vedic Index*, II, p. 351.
549. *Manu*, VII. 114-21, pp. 234-35, *op. cit.*
550. *Pāṇini*, IV. 2. 43 ; V. 2. 1 ; Agrawala, *op. cit.*, pp. 63, 141, 142.
551. *Rig Veda*, IX. 112. 1 ; *Vedic Index*, I, p. 297.
552. *Pāṇini*, V. 4. 95 ; Agrawala, *ibid.*, p. 230.
553. *Pāṇini*, V. 3. 112 ; Agrawala, *ibid.*, p. 438.
554. *Sabhāparvan*, Ch. 32. 9 ; Agrawala, *ibid.*, p. 438.
555. *Kauṭilya*, Bk. III. Ch. IX. 168. 169, p. 191 ; text, pp. 168-69.
556. *Ibid.*, Bk. IV. Ch. IV. 211, p. 238 ; text, p. 211. On the village government, read Sinha, *op. cit.*, pp. 317-26.
557. Aiyangar, *op. cit.*, p. 69. The citation from the *Arthaśāstra* is in *Kauṭilya*, Bk. VI. Ch. I. 257, p. 287 ; text, p. 257.
558. Aiyangar, *ibid.*, pp. 78-79.
559. Aiyangar, *Krityakalpataru*, *Rājadharmakāṇḍa*, Preface, p. viii. (Gaekwad Oriental Series, No. C).
560. Kane, *op. cit.*, III. p. 132.
561. Kane, *ibid.*, p. 19.
562. *Rig Veda*, IV. 42. 1 ; VII. 34. 11 ; 84. 2 ; X. 109. 3 ; 124. 4 ; *Vedic Index*, II, p. 223 ; see also Kane, *ibid.*, III. p. 132.
563. *Atharva Veda*, X. 3. 12 ; XIII. 1. 35 ; *Vājasaneyī Samhita*, IX. 23 ; XX. 8 ; *Taittirīya Samhita*, 1. 6. 10 ; III. 5. 7. 3 ; V. 7. 4. 4 ; see *Vedic Index*, II, p. 223, note (2) under *rāṣṭra* for further references.
564. *Atharva Veda*, XII. 1. 8. and 10 ; see also *Vedic Index*, II, p. 223 ; Kane, *ibid.*, III. p. 132.
565. *Taitt. Sam.*, VII. 5. 18 ; Kane, *ibid.*, III. p. 132, n. (175) where the passage in the *Taitt. Sam.* is cited in full.
566. Kane, *ibid.*, III. p. 19.
567. *Manu*, VII. 69, p. 227. See also Kane, *ibid.*, III. p. 132, note (176).
568. *Manu*, VII. 99, p. 232.
569. *Pāṇini*, VI. 2. 130 ; VI. 2. 18 ; 2. 19 ; II. 3. 39 ; V. I. 41-42 ; Agrawala, *op. cit.*, pp. 398-99.

570. *Kauṭilya*, Bk. VI. Ch. 1. 258, p. 288 ; text, p. 258.
571. Aiyangar, *op. cit.*, p. 69, where he has interpreted *janapada* as people, while referring exactly to the same opening sentence in Book VI of the *Arthaśāstra*.
572. *Kauṭilya*, Bk. II. Ch. XXXV. 142, p. 158 ; text, p. 141.
573. *Ibid.*, Bk. II. Ch. VI. 59, p. 57 ; text, p. 59.
574. *Ibid.*, Bk. II. Ch. III. 51, p. 50 ; text, p. 51.
575. *Ibid.*, Bk. XIII. Ch. IV. 404, p. 433, text, p. 404.
576. *Ibid.*, Bk. IX. Ch. I. 340, p. 368 ; text, p. 340.
577. That Professor Aiyangar contradicts himself is evident when, as seen above, he says in one context that, "Even in the days of Kauṭilya, Powers are referred to by the names of peoples and not by geographical names", and almost immediately afterwards states that "an ambition" (i.e., of universal dominion that transcended the limits of the kingdom of the Nandas) was realized even in "Candragupta's own life time, when he ruled from the hills of Assam to the Paropanisus" (Aiyangar, *ibid.*, pp. 78-79). If Candragupta Maurya realized his ambition, are we to imagine that his illustrious Prime Minister, who had been instrumental in Candragupta's uprooting the Nandas, was not aware of the concept of a definite territory over which his royal master was to rule? If Kauṭilya was ignorant of the concept of a definite territorial extent of the Mauryan Empire, how could he give us the details of the boundaries of such an Empire? These questions are not answered by Professor Aiyangar. Incidentally I might mention here that the statement of the learned Professor that Candragupta Maurya ruled over an Empire stretching from Assam to the Paropanisus is an exaggeration. Paropanisus was the name given to the Caucasus which was never conquered by that Mauryan ruler (see Saletore, *I.D.R. West,* pp. 83, 103-10, 113-14, etc.). The incongruity in Professor Aiyangar's statements is evident when he affirms that Kauṭilya's concept of the State was larger than that of the earlier times! (Aiyangar, *ibid.*, pp. 73-74).
578. The assertion of Professor Ghoshal that Kauṭilya mentions the *rājya* as the second important element of the State (*Beginning*, p. 119) is not correct. The reader may refer to the elucidation of the theory of the Constituent Elements of the State given above in this work, in order to see how carefully Kauṭilya distinguishes between the relative importance of the respective Elements of the State. The reader may refer to Professor Sinha's conjectures on the origin and development of the *rāṣṭra* (Sinha, *op. cit.*, pp. 14-15, 18-19, 21, 25-26, 29-30, 58-59, etc.). His equation of *rāṣṭra* with *rājya*, however, is correct.
579. *Rig Veda*, V. 34. 7 ; VII. 25. 2 ; *Vedic Index*, I, p. 369.
580. On *aśmamāyī*, read *Rig Veda*, IV. 30. 20 ; on *śatabhuji*, read *Rig Veda*, I. 166, 8 ; VII. 15. 14 ; *Vedic Index*, I, 538, 539.
581. *Śat. Brah.*, III. 4. 3. 4, pp. 105-06 (S.B.E. XXVI). Professor Eggeling states (*ibid.*, p. 105, n. 3) that this account is found also in the *Aitareya Brāhmaṇa*, I. 23 , *Taittiriya Brāhmaṇa*, VI. 2. 3. *Vedic Index*, I, p. 538, n. (2) gives further reference to the same legend in the same works.
582. *Rig Veda*, VII. 5. 3 ; *Vedic Index*, I, p. 539.
583. Zimmer, *op. cit.*, pp. 143-45. As regards the hedge of thorns, etc., it was corrected by Professor Roth (*Zeitschrift den Deutschen Morgenländischen Gesellscheft*, 48, p. 109). See *Vedic Index*, I, 539.
584. *Vedic Index*, I, pp. 538-39.
585. Geldner, *Vedische Studien* (*op. cit.*), I, pp. xxii, xxiii ; see also *Vedic Index*, I, p. 339.
586. Rhys Davids, *Buddhist India*, p. 262. Cf. *Mahāparinirbbāṇa Sutta*, p. 12 ; see also *Vedic Index*, I, p. 539. For a short account of the capital, read Smith, *O.H.I.*, pp. 77-78.
587. *Vedic Index*, I, p. 539.
588. As is done by Dr. Jayaswal.

589. As is done by Prof. Altekar, *op. cit.*, pp. 145-46.
590. As is done by Dr. Kane, *op. cit.*, III, pp. 178-79. Dr. Kane begins with Manu and practically ends with *Nītrivākyāmrita*, with the *Pañcatantra*, the *Purāṇas*, the *Rājanītiprakāśa*, etc., coming between them!
591. *Manu*, VII. 70-72, p. 227.
592. *Ibid.*, IX. 252, p. 386.
593. For a detailed account, read the *Rāmayaṇa*, *Bālakāṇḍa*, 5-10 ff., 70-3 ; *Ayodhyākāṇḍa*, 100-53 ; *Sundarakāṇḍa*, 3-10 ff., 43-13 ; *Yuddhakāṇḍa*, 3-20 ; *Uttarakāṇḍa*, 5-22.
594. *Kauṭilya*, Bk. VIII. Ch. I. 322-23 ; pp. 349-51 ; text, pp. 321-23.
595. *Ibid.*, Bk. VII. Ch. XI. 297, p. 324 ; text, pp. 296-97.
596. *Ibid.*, Bk. VIII. Ch. I. 323, pp. 350-51 ; text, pp. 321-23.
597. *Ibid.*, Bk. VII. Ch. XI. 297, p. 325 ; text, p. 297.
598. *Ibid.*, Bk. VII. Ch. XII. 299, p. 327 ; text, p. 299.
599. *Ibid.*, Bk. II. Ch. III. 51, p. 50 ; text, p. 51.
600. *Ibid.*, pp. 51-52 ; text, pp. 51-54.
601. *Ibid.* Ch. IV, pp. 53-55 ; text, pp. 54-57.
602. Aiyangar, *op. cit.*, p. 48. I am afraid Professor Aiyangar never cared to go through the other passages in the *Arthaśāstra* regarding the forts. If he had done it, he would not have passed this incorrect judgment on Kauṭilya.
603. *Rig Veda*, III. 33. 53 ; VII. 18. 33. 83, etc.
604. *Rig Veda*, VII. 20.5 ; IX. 96. 1 ; X. 84. 2. See *Vedic Index*, II, p. 472 for further reference.
605. *Pāṇini*, V. 1. 128 ; IV. 1. 84. Cf. *Aśvapati* in the same work. See also Agrawala, *op. cit.*, pp. 404, 408, 420. In view of this evidence stretching from the Vedic times till those of Pāṇini, it is incorrect to say, as Dr. Jayaswal does, that the term *ṣenāpati* was not a military commander but a Minister for War! (Jayaswal, *op. cit.*, p. 291).
606. *Manu*, X. 79, p. 419 ; Cf. VII. 87, p. 231.
607. *Ibid.*, VII. 103, p. 232.
608. *Ibid.*, VIII. 158-65, pp. 241-42. See below on ambassadors and foreign relations.
609. On *kośa*, read *Vedic Index*, I, p. 189. The references to the chariot, the bow, and the arrow are far too many to be given. The reader may refer to the *Vedic Index* for an exhaustive account of them.
610. See *Vedic Index*, I, pp. 42, 43 ; see also under *dāna*, *ibid.*, I, p. 351.
611. *Vedic Index*, I, pp. 79, 218, 440 ; II. 288, 384, 501, 502.
612. *Manusmṛiti*, VII. 96, 172, 193, 222, pp. 231, 244, 247, 252.
613. *Pāṇini*, II. 4. 2 ; VI. 2. 40 and 41 ; Agrawala, *op. cit.*, p. 419.
614. *Rāmāyaṇa*, *Bālakaṇḍa*, Ch. I. 69. 3 ; *Yuddhakāṇḍa*, 3. 25.
615. *Ibid.*, *Yuddhakāṇḍa*, Ch. 17-24. Read Kane, *op. cit.*, III, pp. 202-04 for a good account of the different kinds of the army.
616. *Rāmāyaṇa*, *Ayodhyakāṇḍa*, Ch. 80, pp. 236-37.
617. *Ibid.*, *Uttarakāṇḍa*, Ch. 64. 3 ff ; *Ayodhyakāṇḍa*, Ch. 83-16, 19.
618. *Ibid.*, *Ayodhyakāṇḍa*, Ch. 36-2 ff, Ch. 83-15, Ch. 91-63.
619. *Manu*, VII. 102-03, 155-61, pp. 232, 240-41.
620. *Kauṭilya*, Bk. I. Ch. XX. 45, p. 43 ; text, p. 45.
621. *Ibid.*, Bk. VI. Ch. I. 258, p. 288 ; text, p. 258.
621a. *Ibid.*, Bk. IX. Ch. II. 342, p. 370 ; text, p. 342.
622. *Ibid.*, Bk. IX. Ch. II. 344, p. 372 ; text, p. 344.
623. *Ibid.*, Bk. IX. Ch. II. 345, pp. 372-74 ; text, p. 344-45.
624. *Ibid.*, Bk. II. Ch. XVIII. pp. 109-13 ; text, pp. 101-02.
625. *Ibid.*, Bk. II. pp 146-55, 157 ; text, pp. 132-40.
626. Professor Aiyangar merely states that, "In the military department much stress is laid on elaborate organization and discipline, the retention of a standing army, and

the possession of a strong elephant corps, victory being supposed to incline to the side which is strong in elephants". The learned Professor compares the reference to the contingent of elephants in Kauṭilya with that given by Megasthenes (Aiyangar, *op. cit.*, p. 45). This is doing scant justice to the great Mauryan statesman whose detailed account of the military department is not only not examined by Professor Aiyangar but is dismissed in a sentence!

627. *Kauṭilya*, pp. 267-459 ; text, pp. 237-431.
628. *Ibid.*, Bk. II. Ch. XXVIII. 126, p. 140 ; text, p. 126.
629. *Maitrāyaṇi Samhita*, I. 10. 16 ; IV. 3. 1 ; Delbrück, *Festgruss an Böhtlingk*, p. 25 cited in *Vedic Index*, I, p. 86.
630. *Vedic Index*, I, p. 86.
631. Zimmer, *op. cit.*, pp. 166-67.
632. *Geldner, Der Rig Veda in Auswah, Erster Teil*, q.v. ; Grassmann, *Wörterbuch Zum Rig Veda, q.v. bali.*
633. *Vedic Index*, II, p. 62.
634. Ghoshal, *Beginnings*, p. 167.
635. *Śat. Brah.*, II. 3. 1. 11, p. 329 (S.B.E. III).
636. Thomas, F. W., *J.R.A.S. for 1909*, p. 467.
637. *Manu*, III. 70, pp. 87-88.
638. *Ibid.*, III. 74, p. 88.
639. *Ibid.*, III. 108, p. 95.
640. *Ibid.*, III. 265, p. 124.
641. *Pāṇini*, III. 1. 36 ; Agrawala, *op. cit.*, p. 386. Dr. Kane (*op. cit.*, III, p. 190) interprets *bali* as the one-sixth part of the produce of land. This I feel, is inadmissible in view of what has been said above.
642. *Taittirīya Samhita*, I. 8. 9. 2 ; *Kāṭhaka Samhita*, XV. 4 ; *Maitrāyaṇī Samhita*, II. 6. 5 ; IV. 3. 8 ; *Vājasaneyī Samhita*, XXX. 13 ; see *Vedic Index*, II, p. 100 for further references. See also Ghoshal, *Beginnings*, p. 171, and note (21).
643. *Vedic Index*, II, p. 100.
644. *Śat. Brah.*, V. 3. 1. 9, pp. 62-63 (S.B.E. XLVI).
645. Ghoshal, *Beginnings*, p. 171.
645a. Agrawala, *ibid.*, p. 242.
646. *Manu*, VIII. 307, p. 307.
647. *Rāmāyaṇa*, *Ayodhyakāṇḍa*, 75. 25 ; *Uttarakāṇḍa*, 74. 29. Dr. Miss Dharma is not correct when she interprets *baliṣaḍbhāga* as one-sixth of the profits (Dharma. *op. cit.*, p. 58).
648. *Kauṭilya*, Bk. II. Ch. VI. 60, p. 58 ; text, p. 60.
649. *Ibid.*, p. 58 ; text, p. 60.
650. *Ibid.*, Bk. V. Ch. II. 243, p. 272 ; text, p. 243.
651. *Abhidhānarājendra*, cited by Ghoshal, *Beginnings*, p. 173, and note (29).
652. Read Ghoshal, *ibid.*, p. 173 for their opinions.
653. Meyer, *Arthaśāstra*, II, p. 81, and note.
654. Ganapati Sastri, *Arthaśāstra*, cited by Ghoshal, *ibid.*, p. 174, and note 33.
655. Ghoshal, *ibid.*, pp. 174-75.
656. Kane, *op. cit.*, III, p. 190.
657. *Kauṭilya*, Bk. II. Ch. I. 47, p. 46 ; text, p. 47.
658. *Ibid.*, Bk. II. Ch. I. 49, p. 48 ; text, p. 48.
659. Read *Vedic Index*, II, p. 387.
660. *Manu*, VIII. 304 ; IX. 100, pp. 291, 345.
661. *Ibid.*, VIII. 307, p. 307, *op. cit.*
662. *Pāṇini*, V. 1. 47. Agrawala, *op. cit.*, p. 414 ; *Kauṭilya*, Bk. II. Ch. XXI where the duties of the Superintendent of Tolls are given. pp. 121-27 ; text, pp. 109-12.
663. *Manu*, VII. 128-29, p. 236.
664. *Ibid.*, VII. 127, p. 236.

665. *Manu*, VII. 129, p. 236.
666. *Ibid.*, VII. 139, p. 238.
667. *Ibid.*, VII. 138, p. 238.
668. *Ibid.*, VII. 130-32, pp. 236-37, *op. cit.*
669. *Ibid.*, X. 120, pp. 427-28.
670. Bühler, *ibid.*, Intr. pp. xlviii-xlix.
671. *Manu*, VII. 133, p. 237.
672. Bühler, *ibid.*, p. xlviii, *op. cit.*
673. *Manu*, VIII. 394, p. 322.
674. *Ibid.*, X. 118, p. 427.
675. *Rāmāyaṇa, Bālakāṇḍa*, Ch. 5. 14 (tribute) ; *ibid.*, Ch. 53. 9. (gems) ; *Ayodhyākāṇḍa*, Ch. 10. 35 ; 82. 8 (tribute) ; Ch. 100. 45 (mines) ; Ch. 100. 29 (light tax etc.). *Uttarakaṇḍa*, 39, 8 (tribute).
676. *Pāṇini*, IV. 3. 75 ; V. 1. 47 ; Agrawala, *op. cit.*, p. 413-14.
677. *Ibid.*, IV. 3. 76 ; Agrawala, *ibid.*, p. 414.
678. Agrawala, *ibid.*, p. 414.
679. *Pāṇini*, IV. 3. 76, *op. cit.* ; Agrawala, *ibid.*, p. 414, *op. cit.*
680. *Ibid.*, VI. 3. 10 ; III. 2. 21 ; Agrawala, *ibid.*, pp. 414-15.
681. *Kauṭilya*, Bk. II. Ch. VIII. 66, pp. 65-66 ; text, pp. 65-66.
682. *Ibid.*, Bk. VI. Ch. I. 258, p. 288 ; text, p. 258.
683 & 684. *Ibid.*, Bk. II. Ch. VI. 60, pp. 57-58 ; text, p. 60.
685. *Ibid.*, p. 58, note (2).
686. *Pāṇini*, VIII. 2. 22 ; Agrawala, *ibid.*, p. 133.
687. *Kauṭilya*, Bk. II. Ch. II. 60, p. 58 : text, p. 60.
688. *Ibid.*, p. 48 ; text, p. 48, *op. cit.* Dr. Kane translated the word *viṣṭi* merely as labourers (Kane, *op. cit.*, III. p. 208).
689. *Kauṭilya*, Bk. II. Ch. XXI. pp. 121-23 ; text, pp. 109-12.
690. *Ibid.*, Bk. II. Ch. XXV. pp. 131-35 ; text, pp. 126-28.
691. *Ibid.*, Bk. II. Ch. XXVII, pp. 136-39 ; text, pp. 123-25.
692. *Ibid.*, Bk. II. Ch. XXVI. pp. 135-36 ; text, pp. 122-23.
693. *Ibid.*, Bk. II. Ch. XV. 94, p. 99 ; text, p. 93.
694. *Ibid.*, p. 99, note (6).
695. *Ibid.*, Bk. II. Ch. XXI. 111, p. 123 ; text, p. 111 ; Ch. XXII. pp. 124-25 ; text, pp. 112-13.
696. *Ibid.*, Bk. II. Ch. I. 47, p. 46 ; text, p. 47.
697. *Ibid.*, Bk. III. Ch. IX. 170, p. 193 ; text, p. 170.
698. *Ibid.*, Bk. II. Ch. I. 46, p. 45 ; text, p. 46. Dr. Sastry translated the word *Śrotriya* as "one learned in the Vedas" (*Ibid.*, p. 45). This is inadmissible in view of Professor Bühler's more correct rendering of the same word which I have cited above.
699. *Kauṭilya*, Bk. II. Ch. XXI. 111, p. 122 ; text, p. 111.
700. *Ibid.*, Bk. V. Ch. I. 237, p. 267 ; text, p. 237.
701. *Ibid.*, Bk. V. Ch. I. pp. 267-71 ; text, pp. 237-42.
702. *Ibid.*, Bk. V. Ch. II. 271-76 ; text, pp. 242-46.
703. *Ibid.*, p. 271 ; text, p. 242.
704. *Ibid.*, pp. 271-72 ; text, p. 242.
705. *Ibid.*, Bk. II. Ch. XV. 94, pp. 99-100 ; text, pp. 93-94.
706. *Manu*, IX. 294, p. 395 ; *Kauṭilya*, Bk. VI. Ch. I. 257, p. 287 ; text, p. 257, *op. cit.*
707. The reader may refer to the account of land as given in Dr. Kane's most useful work on the *History of the Dharmaśāstras* which I have so often cited in these pages.
708. *Vedic Index*, II. p. 213 where the authors admit that, in return for the payment of taxes like *bali*, etc., the king performed the duties of a judge.
709. *Rig Veda*, I. 22. 18 ; 164, 43, 50 ; III. 3. 1 ; 17. 1 ; 60. 6 ; V. 26. 6 ; 63. 7 ; *Atharva*

Veda, XI. 7. 17 ; XII. 5. 7 ; XIV. 1. 51 ; *Vājasaneyī Samhita*, X. 29 ; XV. 6 ; XX. 9 ; XX. 6 ; *Taittirīya Samhita*, III. 5. 2. 2. See also *Vedic Index*, I. p. 390

710. *Vedic Index*, I. p. 391.
711. *Ibid.*, I. pp. 391-92.
712. *Pañcaviṁśa Brāhmaṇa*, XIV. 6. 8.
713. *Vedic Index*, I. p. 391, and notes (4)-(6) for further references.
714. *Candrogya Upaniṣad*, VI. 16 ; Weber, *Indian Literature*, pp. 72-73 ; *Vedic Index*, I, p. 392.
715. *Vedic Index*, I. p. 392, and notes (13)-(14) for further references.
716. *Ibid.*, I, p. 392, and notes (16)-(19) for further references.
717. *Vājasaneyī Samhita*, XXX. 10 ; *Taittirīya Brāhmaṇa*, III. 4. 6. 1. See also *Vedic Index*, I. p. 393. It cannot be that *praśna-vivāka* was the judge or the arbiter, as the authors of the *Vedic Index* maintain, since the king was himself the judge. The *praśna-vivāka* was perhaps the prosecutor. He could not have been the arbiter, since the latter was known as *madhyama-śī*, as admitted by the learned authors. (*Vedic Index*, I, p. *ibid.*).
718. *Vedic Index*, II. pp. 41-42, and p. 42, note (1).
719. *Aitareya Brāhmaṇa*, X. 8. 8 ; Whitney, *Trans. of the Atharva Veda*, p. 597 ; *Vedic Index*, II. p. 42.
720. *Atharva Veda*, VI. 32. 3 ; VIII. 8. 21 ; Keith, *Śānkhyana Āraṇyaka*, p. 66, n. (4) ; Zimmer, *op. cit.*, p. 181 ; *Vedic Index*, I. p. 290.
721. *Rig Veda*, X. 97. 12 ; *Atharva Veda*, IV. 9. 4 ; *Vājasaneyī Samhita*, XII. 86 ; Zimmer, *ibid.*, p. 180 ; Lanman in Whitney's *Trans. of the Atharva Veda*, p. 159. But see *Vedic Index*, II. p. 127, note (4) for Professor Roth's another article overlooked by Professor Lanman. See *Vedic Index*, II, pp. 127-28 for another view by Professor Geldner.
722. *Vedic Index*, II. p. 128.
723. I do not wish to cite the many references in epigraphs and literature to this term in the early and later mediaeval ages.
724. *Vedic Index*, II. p. 31.
725. *Taittirīya Samhita*, II. 3. 1. 3 ; *Vedic Index*, I. p. 248, *op. cit.*
726. *Manu*, VIII. 1, p. 253, *op. cit.* Read also Kane, *op. cit.*, III. p. 268 for further remarks on this point.
727. *Manu*, VII. 141, p. 238.
728. *Ibid.*, VIII. 3-7 pp. 252-53, *op. cit.*
729. Read *Manu*, VIII. pp. 253-327. On every one of the specified points raised by me, the reader could profitably consult Dr. Kane's masterly work. (Kane, *op. cit.*, q.v.).
730. *Manu*, VIII. 219, 232, pp. 293, 295.
731. *Ibid.*, VIII. 259, p. 300.
732. *Pāṇini*, VI. 4. 41 ; Agrawala, *op. cit.*, p. 416.
733. *Pāṇini*, I. 3. 23 ; III. 2. 142 ; and 146 ; IV. 1. 84 ; V. 2. 91 ; Agrawala, *ibid.*, pp. 416-17.
734. *Manu*, VIII. 113, p. 274.
735. *Pāṇini*, V. 4. 66 ; Agrawala, *ibid.*, p. 417.
736. *Pāṇini*, II. 3. 39 ; III. 2. 179 ; Agrawala, *ibid.*
737. *Pāṇini*, VI. 2. 5 ; Agrawala, *ibid.* For the similarity of some terms like *aṁśam āari*, co-share, see *Manu*, IX. 150-53, pp. 357-58. Cf. *Pāṇini*, V. 2. 69.
738. *Pāṇini*, I. 3. 32 ; III. 2. 87 ; 2. 155 ; IV. 4. 36 ; V. 1. 125 ; VI. 4. 174 ; Agrawala, *ibid.*, p. 418.
739. *Pāṇini*, V. 1. 65, 66 ; 4. 2 ; VI. 1. 64 ; Agrawala, *ibid.*
740. *Kauṭilya*, p. 56, *op. cit.*
741. *Ibid.*, Bk. III. Ch. I. 150, pp. 170-71 ; text, p. 150.
742. *Ibid.*, Bk. III. Ch. VII. 165, p. 188 ; text, p. 165.

743. *Kauṭilya*, p. 191, *op. cit.*
744. *Ibid.*, Bk. XIII. Ch. IV. 408, p. 437 ; text, p. 408.
745. *Ibid.*, Bk. XIII. Ch. V. 410, p. 439, text, p. 410.
746. *Ibid.*, Bk. IV. Ch. X. 228, pp. 255-56 ; text, p. 228.
747. *Kauṭilya*, Bk. III. Ch. XIX. 196, p. 221 ; text, p. 196.
748. *Ibid.*, Bk. III. Chs. XVII-XX. pp. 216-25 ; text, pp. 191-200.
749. *Ibid.*, Bk. IV. Ch. XI. 229, p. 259 ; text, p. 229.
750. *Ibid.*, Bk. III. Ch. XVI. 191, p. 216 ; text, p. 191. Obviously the learned translator has taken *upekṣitaḥ* as "destroyed", perhaps in the sense of being "disregarded completely".
751. *Ibid.*, Bk. III. Ch. I. 150, p. 171 ; text, p. 150.
752. *Ibid.*, Bk. II. Ch. V. 58, p. 56 ; text, p. 58.
753. *Ibid.*, Bk. II. Ch. IV. 55, p. 53 ; text, p. 55, *op. cit.*
754. *Ibid.*, Bk. II. Ch. V. 57, p. 55 ; text, p. 57.
755. *Ibid.*, Bk. II. Ch. IV. 55, p. 53 ; text, p. 55, *op. cit.*
756. *Ibid.*, Bk. III. Ch. I 150, p. 170 ; text, p. 150.
757. *Ibid.*, Bk. III. Ch. I. 147, p. 167 ; text, p. 147.
758. *Ibid.*, Bk. II. Ch. I. 46, p. 44 ; text, p. 46.
759. *Ibid.*, Bk. III. Ch. I. pp. 167-71 ; text, pp. 147-51.
760. *Ibid.*, Bk. IV. Ch. I. pp. 227-31 ; text, pp. 200-04.
761. Professor Aiyangar also comments on these courts thus: "According to him (Kauṭilya) there were to be several courts of justice in the kingdom. They were to be of two classes: viz., *Dharmasthīya* (common and canon law courts), *Kaṇṭhakaśodhana* (administrative and police courts),—presided over respectively by officers, in panels of three bearing the style of *Dharma-amātyāḥ* (ministers of law), and *Pradeṣṭarāh* (*Directors*). The first took note of all causes between subject and subject, while the second had to form (1) standing commissions for the examinations of serious crimes like treason, murder, violence, etc. ; (2) preventive organizations with wide jurisdiction and summary powers of overriding the ordinary law in the interests of equity and promptness of disposal ; and (3) special courts for investigating cases of official oppression, misconduct, and malversation." Professor Aiyangar has nothing more to say about these courts (Aiyangar, *op. cit.*, p. 74).

    I am afraid it is not possible to agree with the learned historian either about the interpretation of the composition or the duties of both the types of courts. (*a*) There is no justification for calling the *dharmasthīya* courts as common law courts. The latter term is misleading, since all courts had to administer common law or usage as embodied in the *dharmaśāstras*. (*b*) It is incorrect to state that both were presided over by panels of three judges. It was only the *kaṇṭhakaśodhana* courts that were presided over by three commissioners or by three ministers. (*c*) The *kaṇṭhakaśodhana* courts were not standing commissions for trying serious crimes like treason, for there is no reference to treason at all in the whole chapter dealing with the various organizations. (*d*) There is nothing to show that the artisans, etc., who came within the purview of the *kaṇṭhakaśodhana* courts, had wide jurisdiction and summary powers to override the ordinary law. Professor Aiyangar, I cannot help feeling, has missed the main point in this regard: it refers to the *pīḍanam* or oppression which the various bodies caused to society. We cannot think of either the guilds or the sweepers or the scavengers having wide jurisdiction! And (*e*) as regards the *dharmasthīya* courts, there is nothing to show that they decided all kinds of cases: their jurisdiction was limited to contract and tort. Professor Aiyangar has nothing to say on the High Court in the capital.
762. Already cited in connection with the comparative study of the judiciary in Aristotle and that in Kauṭilya.
763. *Kauṭilya*, Bk. III. Ch. XI. 175-76, p. 199 ; text, pp. 175-76.
764. *Manu*, VIII. 64-68, pp. 265-66.

765. *Kauṭilya*, Bk. III. Ch. XVII. 193, p. 217 ; text, p. 193.
766. *Ibid.*, Bk. IV. Ch. VIII, pp. 247-50 ; text, pp. 220-22. On punishments of death with or without torture, read *ibid.*, Bk. IV. Ch. XI, pp. 256-58 ; text, pp. 228-30.
767. *Ibid.*, Bk. III. Ch. XX. 199, p. 224 ; text, p. 199.
768. *Ibid.*, Bk. III. Ch. XX. 200, pp. 224-25 ; text, p. 200, *op. cit.*
769. *Ibid.*, Bk. IV. Ch. IX. 225, p. 252 ; text, pp. 224-25.
770. Read Saletore, *I.D.R. West*, p. 108 ff.
771. *Kauṭilya*, Bk. IV, pp. 232-34 ; text, pp. 204-07.
772. *Manu*, VIII. 401, p. 324.
773. *Kauṭilya*, Bk. IV. Ch. II. 206, p. 233 ; text, p. 206.
774. Read Saletore, *ibid.*, pp. 17-39 for a fuller account. This part of the chapter is based on that work of mine.
775. *Manu*, VII. 155-58, pp. 240-41.
776. *Kauṭilya*, Bk. IV. Ch. II. 261, p. 291 ; text, p. 261.
777. See note (774) above. The reference here is to pages 38-39 of the same work.
778. *Kauṭilya*, Bk. VI. Ch. II. 261-62, p. 291 ; text, pp. 261-62.
779. Read Saletore, *I.D.R. West*, p. 33.
780. *Kauṭilya*, Bk. VII. Ch. I. 263, p. 293 ; text, p. 263.
781. *ibid.*, Bk. VII. Ch. I. 266, p. 296 ; text, p. 266. The reader may also refer to my *West*, pp. 22-35, 57-58, 62-68.
782. *Manu*, VII. 63-64, pp. 225-26 ; *Kauṭilya*, Bk. XVI. 30, 29 ; text, p. 30. See also Saletore, *ibid.*, pp. 22-35. That scholars have not done any justice to this side of the State's activities will be evident if we take any work on ancient Indian Polity, as, for instance, Altekar, *op. cit.*, pp. 222-23, where the learned Professor is doubtful about the existence of such an institution like that of the ambassadors! On page 222, para 2nd, of the same he confounds an ambassador with a licensed and open spy which, to say the least, is to distort facts.
783. *Kauṭilya*, Bk. I. Ch. XVI. 30, p. 29 ; text, p. 30, see also Saletore, *ibid.*, p. 28.
784. Cf. Saletore, *ibid.*, pp. 53-57.
784a. Cf. Saletore, *ibid.*, pp. 62-63.
785. Cf. Saletore, *ibid.*, pp. 62-64.
786. *Kauṭilya*, Bk. V. Ch. III. 247, p. 276 ; text, p. 247. Dr. Kane is of the opinion that the salaries mentioned here could have been mostly in terms of copper coins. According to him, a *yojana* was equal to about nine to ten miles. (Kane, *op. cit.*, III, pp. 123-25).
787. Cf. Saletore, *ibid.*, pp. 22-23.
788. & 789. *Manu*, VII. 122. 153-54, pp. 235, 240.
790. *Ibid.*, VII. 223, p. 252.
791. *Ibid.*, IX. 256-60, pp. 387-88.
792. *Ibid.*, IX. 298, p. 396.
793. *Kauṭilya*, Bk. I. Chs. X-XIII, pp. 15-25 ; text, pp. 16-24. Bk. I. Ch. XI. 18, p. 17 ; text, p. 18.
794. & 795. *Ibid.*, Bk. I. Ch. XI. 18-19, pp. 17-19 ; text, pp. 18-19. See Kane, *ibid.*, III, p. 129.
796. & 797. *Ibid.*, Bk. I. Ch. XII, pp. 19-22 ; text, pp. 20-22. Dr. Shama Sastry here and elsewhere translated *tīkṣṇa* as a firebrand. But I think Dr. Kane's interpretation of the same term as a desperado is better (Kane, *ibid.*, III, p. 129). Dr. Agrawala has connected the term *viṣya*, occurring in *Pāṇini*, according to whom it denoted a person marked out for administering poison (*viṣeṇa vadhyaḥ*) (*Pāṇini*, IV. 4. 91), with the nefarious practice of the *rasada* mentioned by Kauṭilya (Agrawala, *op. cit.*, p. 413).
798. Dr. Kane cites the *Encyclopaedia Britannica* which says that an ambassador is "an honourable spy acting under the law of nations" (Kane, *op. cit.*, III, p. 129). But in addition to the ambassadors are various other officials of the diplomatic corps

of the respective governments, who might be performing the same duties as those performed by the spies in the foreign service of Kauṭilya but suited to modern conditions.

799. *Kauṭilya*, Bk. I. Ch. III, p. 22 ; text, p. 22, *op. cit.*

PART SIX

THEORY IN PRACTICE

1. Hultzseh, E., *Corpus Inscriptionum Indicarum*, I: *Inscriptions of Aśoka*, Intr., pp. xliii-xlvii for an account of Aśoka's conversion to Buddhism. But we are not enlightened by the eminent Indologist as to which religion he had professed before the Kalinga War.
2. Senart, E., *Ind. Ant.*, XX, p. 260 ; Hultzsch, *ibid.*, p. xlix.
3. Hultzsch, *ibid.*, Intr., p. 1 ; 176-77.
4. Hultzsch, *ibid.*, Intr., p. xliii, and references given therein.
5. Ray, H. C., *Dynastic History of Northern India*, I, p. 415.
6. Jayaswal, K. P. and Banerjee, R. D., *Ep. Ind.*, XX, pp. 80, 89.
7. Read Bhandarkar, R. G., *E.H.D.* (in the *Bombay Gaz.*), pp. 149-51.
8. Senart, *Ep. Ind.*, VIII, p. 61.
9. Kielhorn, *Ep. Ind.*, VIII. 48, note (2). The reference is to *Manu*, VIII. 2, p. 253 where the verse runs thus: "There (in the court of justice) either seated or standing, raising his right hand, without ostentation in his dress and ornaments, let him examine the business of suitors."
10. Kielhorn, *ibid.*, p. 49.
11. Rice, Levis, *Mysore and Coorg from the Inscription*, p. 21 (London, 1909).
12. Gopinath Rao, T. A., and Venkoba Rao, *Ep. Ind.*, VIII, p. 148.
13. *Epigraphia Carnatica*, VII. Sk. 262, pp. 142-43.
14. *Ibid.*, Sk. 176, p. 114. The same record was re-edited by Professor Kielhorn in *Ep. Ind.*, VIII, pp. 24 ff, 35-36.
15. *Ep. Car.*, IV. Hs. 18, pp. 84-85.
16. *Ibid.*, VII. Sk. 29, p. 45. Mr. Rice assigned this record to *circa* A.D. 400. But this is inadmissible on the strength of the date A.D. 450 which he himself has given to Māndhatṛivarman's elder brother Mṛigeśavarman.
17. *Ep. Ind.*, VIII, p. 148, *op. cit.*
18. Rice, *My. & Coorg*, p. 29. I follow, on the whole, Mr. Rice in the generalogy of the Gangas, and not Dr. Fleet, who disbelieved in the existence of this line.
19. *Ep. Car.*, X. Mr. 73, p. 172.
20. Rice, *My. & Coorg.*, p. 49. See *Ep. Car.*, X. Intr., p. VIII where he calls him Taḍangala Mādhava. But in *My. & Coorg*, p. 49. Taḍangala Mādhava is assigned by him to *circa* A.D. 357-70. Evidently there is some confusion here.
21. *Ep. Car.*, XII. Mi. 110. pp. 115-16.
22. *Ep. Car.*, X. Mr. 72, p. 172. While editing this record Mr. Rice gave the date *circa* A.D. 425 but in his *My. & Coorg*, he assigned king Avinīta to A.D. 430 to 482 (*My. & Coorg*, p. 49). The date A.D. 430 is confirmed in *E. C.*, IX.
23. *Ep. Car.*, IX. D.B. 68, p. 72, Nl. 60, p. 39 ; IV. Yd. 60, p. 62 ; X. Kl. 90, p. 25. But IX. D.B. 67, p. 71, dated A.D. 459, does not bestow this praise on king Mādhava.
24. Hira Lal, *Ep. Ind.*, VIII, pp. 287-88.
25. Fleet, *Corpus Inscriptionum Indicarum, Gupta Inscriptions*, p. 31 ff. I am eiting this without verifying it. See also Diskalkar, D. B. *Selections from Inscriptions*, I. P. I., pp. 112-13. On the dates of Guhasena, read Bhagavanlal Indraji, *History of Guj* (Bombay Gaz., I. P. I.), p. 85.
26. *Ep. Carn.*, X. Mb. 38, p. 78.

27. Fleet, *Ep. Ind.*, VIII, p. 58. On Racamalla, IV, see Rice, *My. & Coorg*, p. 49.
28. Mr. Rice, Lewis, and Dr. Fleet, J. F. are still the best authorities on the Hoysalas. Professor William Coelho's *Hoyśalavaṁsa* (Bombay) is a praiseworthy attempt at writing a general history of the Hoysalas. Dr. J. Duncan Derrett's *The Hoysalas* (Oxford, 1957) is a recent contribution to the subject which does not carry in anywhere either in the field of chronology or in that of the elucidation of events.
29. *Ep. Car.*, V. A.K. 102 (*a*), p. 151.
30. *Ep. Carn.*, V. Hn. 72, p. 23.
31. *Ibid.*, VII. Sk. 92, pp. 59-60 ; text, p. 174. In another stone inscription, also found in the same locality, but dated A.D. 1181, the Great Minister Keśimayya is praised in the same manner (*ibid.*, VII. Sk. 119, p. 89). He is said to have been the grandson of Keśavadeva and Paṁpāmbikā. It cannot be made out whether he was identical with Byāḷike Keśimayya. Perhaps he was but then the question arises—Did he have two royal masters, one in A.D. 1108, and, again, in A.D. 1181?
32. *Ep. Car.*, V. Bl. 75, pp. 62-63 ; translit., p. 147.
33. Jayaswal-Banerjee, *Ep. Ind.*, XX, pp. 79, 88.
34. Fleet, *Ins. of the Guptas*, pp. 11, 12, 14.
35. Fleet, *ibid.*, p. 8. See also Kane, *op. cit.*, III, pp. 71-72.
36. *Ep. Car.*, IX. D.B. 67, p. 71 ; text, p. 159. In this record the ruler is called Koṅgaṇi Mahārāja which, as its learned Editor, Mr. Lewis Rice said, was the name of Avinīta. Read Mr. Rice's remarks also on the date of the record. (*Ep. Car.*, *ibid.*, Intr., p. 1).
37. *Mahāvāstu*, II, p. 360 (London, 1952).
38. *Ibid.*, p. 360, note (5). Cf. *Yājñavalkya*, I, 345.
39. *Ibid.*, I, pp. 232-33.
40. For a full discussion, read my *I.D.R. West*, pp. 42-47
41. & 42. Daṇḍin, *Daśakumāracarita*, Uchchh. VIII. Trans., pp. 133, 135 ; text, pp. 187, 191.
43. *Ibid.*, p. 139 ; text, p. 195.
44. *Ibid.*, pp. 139-44.
45. *Ibid.*, pp. 150 ; text, p. 208. Mr. Kale translated the word *prakritiḥ* as "subjects". obviously missnig the point that the term seventy-two *prakritis* refer to the seventy-two elements discussed in the *rājamaṇḍala* theory which has been discussed in this book.
46. *Ibid.*, p. 151 ; text, pp. 209-10.
47. *Ibid.*, pp. 135-37 ; text, pp. 191-93.
48. Professor Keith with characteristic indefiniteness in regard to chronological details, merely writes that the date of Daṇḍin is still open to dispute. He would place him anterior to Subandhu and Bāṇa (Keith, *Skt. Lit.*, pp. 296-97). This does not help us very much. Professor Macdonell had earlier written that the *Daśakumāracarita* "probably dates from the sixth century A.D." But while writing about Daṇḍin's *Kavyādarśa*, he would assign the latter work to the "end of the sixth century"! (Macdonell, *Skt. Lit.*, pp. 332, 434). This would give Daṇḍin an age of about a century which is incredible!
49. Professor M. R. Kale's discussion of the date of Daṇḍin is more helpful than that of the Western scholars. He would assign that author to *circa* A.D. 650. (Kale, *op. cit.*, Intr., p. xxii).
50. Smith, *E.H.I.*, p. 146.
51. Read Winternitz, M., *Calcutta Review*, April, 1924.
52. Law, *Studies*, pp. 209-66. See *ibid.*, p. 216, note (1). The arguments adduced by Professor Jolly and Dr. Otto Stein have been summed up by Professor Rangaswami Aiyangar (Aiyangar, *op. cit.*, App. VI, pp. 149-64). Dr. Pran Nath was another scholar who said that the *Arthaśāstra* was composed in the sixth century A.D. Among Western scholars, mention must be made in this connection of Professor Hermann

Jacobi (*Sitzungen Köenigliche Preussiche Akadamic für 1912*, pp. 834-39 ; *Indian Antiquary*, 1924, pp. 128-36 ; 141-46) and of Professor J. J. Meyer (*Arthaśāstra*, 1926). Among Indian scholars, who have held the other view referring to the authorship of the *Arthaśāstra* mention may be made of Dr. N. N. Law, Professor Rangaswami Aiyangar, Dr. Ganapati Sastri, and Dr. Shama Sastry, who have all upheld the theory that Kauṭilya was the author of that work. References to all these will be found in Aiyangar, *ibid.* Dr. Jayaswal also discusses the date of Kauṭilya (Jayaswal, *op. cit.*, pp. 366-78). See also Ghoshal, *Beginnings*, p. 105, note (1).

53. Aiyangar, *ibid.*, pp. 158-59.
54. Kauṭilya, Bk. IX. Ch. I. 340, p. 368 ; text, p. 340, *op. cit.*
55. Read my *I.R.D. West*, pp. 108-31.
56. Smith, *E.H.I.*, pp. 42-43.
57. *Kauṭilya*, Bk. IX. Ch. II. 347, p. 375 ; text, p. 347.
58. *Ibid.*, Bk. IX. Ch. III. 348, p. 376 ; text, p. 348.
59. *Ibid.*, Bk. IX. Ch. V. pp. 379-81 ; text, pp. 352-53.
60. *Ibid.*, Bk. VIII. Ch. II. 325, p. 353 ; text, p. 325.
61. On the atrocities committed, and on the wealth carried away, by Alexander the Great, read my *I.D.R. West*, pp. 83-93, and in particular, p. 86. That Poros the Senior was still alive is proved by Megasthenes, who relates that he visited Candragupta, called by him Sandrakottos, "the greatest king of the Indians, and Porus, still greater than he". Arrian (Arrianus) also writes that Megasthenes visited Poros the Senior (E. A. Schwanbeck, *Fragments of the Indika of Megasthenes,* Edited by J. W. McCrindle, *Ancient India as described by Megasthenes and Arrian*, p. 13 (Calcutta, 1926). According to Diodorus (XIX. 14), Poros died in 317 B.C. (McCrindle, *ibid.*). But this need not invalidate Megasthenes' statement that he visited Poros, since the date 317 B.C. would fall within the reign of Candra Gupta Maurya (320-296 B.C.).
62. *Kauṭilya*, Bk. VII. Ch. XVI, 311, p. 339 ; text, p. 311.
63. Kielhorn, *Ep. Ind.* XX, pp. 47-48.
64. Fleet, *Ins. of the Guptas*, pp. 12-13. On page 8, l. 23 the statement referring to them is—*aneka bhṛṣṭarājyotsanna-rājyavaṁśa pratiṣṭāpana*. See also Kielhorn, *ibid.*, p. 48, n. (1).
65. *Ep. Car.*, XII. Si. 38, p. 95 ; text, pp. 274-75.
66. *Ibid.*, IV. Yd. 60, p. 63 ; text, p. 183.
67. *Ibid.*, X. Kl. 90, p. 25 ; translit., p. 26.
68. *Mahāvastu*, I. 41 (trans. J. J. Jones, London, 1949).
69. *Mahāvagga*, p. 102 (S.B.E.X.). See also Kane, *op. cit.*, III. p. 66.
70. *Archaeological Survey of India*, V. p. 50 ; Kane, *ibid.*, p. 66.
71. *Ep. Ind.*, XX. p. 86.
72. *Ibid.*, p. 82, n. (1) ; Kane, *ibid.*, p. 66.
73. *Ep. Ind.*, VIII. pp. 43, 47.
74. Fick, Richard, *Die Sociale Gliederung im nordöstlichen Indien zu Buddhas Zeit* (*Social Organisation in North-East India in Buddha's Time*), pp. 103-04 (Trans. by S. Maitra, Calcutta, 1920). See also Kane, *op. cit.*, III, p. 36.
75. For another kind of confused thinking, read Jayaswal, *op. cit.*, pp. 54, 183, 185 where Dr. Jayaswal has read more than what the Greek accounts would warrant.
76. See Cunningham, *Archaeological Survey of India*, I, pp. 55-63.
77. Smith, *O.H.I.*, pp. 46-47.
78. Cunningham, *ibid.*, XVI, p. 34. Read also *ibid.*, pp. 6, 8, 12, 90 for further notices.
79. *Dialogues of Buddha*, Part II, pp. 78-80 (Sacred Books of the Buddhists, reprinted in London, 1959).
80. The Lichchhavīs are said to have "formed a part of the Vajjian confederacy, being often referred to as Vajjis" (D.P.N.'s note in the *Mahāvastu*, I. p. 209, note (2).

81. *Mahāvastu,* I. pp. 209-12.
82. *Ibid.,* I. p. 214, note (2) where it is doubtfully asked whether the reference is to clans. See also *ibid.,* pp. 215-16.
83. *Ibid.,* II. p. 73.
84. *Dialogues of Buddha,* Part I, p. 198.
85. *Kauṭilya,* p. 407, *op. cit.*
86. *Dialogues of Buddha,* Part II, pp. 162-64.
87. *Ibid.,* p. 179.
88. *Ibid.,* p. 187.
89. *Mahāvastu,* I. p. 300.
90. *Ep. Ind.,* VIII, p. 47.
91. Fleet, *Ins. of the Guptas,* p. 14.
92. Fleet, *ibid.,* p. 251.
93. Kane, *op. cit.,* III. p. 89.
94. Cunningham, *Coins,* p. 76.
95 & 96. Indraji, *Hist. of Guj.,* p. 36.
97. Indraji, *ibid.,* p. 65.
98. Indraji, *ibid.,* pp. 69-70.
99. Indraji, *ibid.,* pp. 73-76.
100. Indraji, *ibid.,* p. 77.
101. *Ep. Ind.,* XX. pp. 79, 88. It cannot be understood how the learned Editors have introduced the word *janapada* in their translation on page 88, when it does not occur in the text. On Khāravela's conquest, read Smith, *E.H.I.,* p. 219, note (1).
102. Fleet, *D.K.D.,* p. 395.
103. Rice, *My. & Coorg,* p. 69.
104. *Mahāvastu,* I. pp. 228-30.
105. *Ibid.,* I. p. 231.
106. Cf. *Manu,* VII. 143-49, pp. 238-39 ; *Yājñavalkya,* I. 327-33. See also Kane, *ibid.,* III. pp. 160-61.
107 & 108. *Ep. Ind.,* XX. pp. 79-80, 87-89. Some of the terms translated by the learned Editors of this inscription (Dr. Jayaswal and Prof. Banerjee) are doubtful. On the word *dapa,* which they took to be *drava,* meaning a dance, (*Ep. Ind. ibid.,* p. 87, note (1), the late Professor Beni Madhav Barua wrote that it was *darpa* which is mentioned by Kauṭilya as a sport and pastime along with *madya-krīḍā* which ladies of good society were not to witness on pain of a fine of three *paṇas.* (*Kauṭilya,* Bk. III. Ch. III, 155, p. 177 ; text, p. 156). The late Professor Barua's is probably the most exhaustive note on Khāravela which I have seen. His readings are more appropriate than those of the learned Editors of the Hāthigumpha inscription (Barua, B. M., *Kharavela's Personal History: Three Points. Proceedings of the V Indian Oriental Conference,* 1928, pp. 364-85).
109. Kielhorn, *Ep. Ind.,* VIII. pp. 43-44, 47-49. On page 48 Professor Kielhorn translated the word *bali* as tribute but I think "tax" is a more appropriate rendering, in view of the discussion of this term in this book. The reference to *śulka* (tolls) and *bhāga* (share) is significant. The prevalence of these taxes fully justifies my statement that they were sources of revenue, made in the earlier pages of this book.
110 & 111. Fleet, *Ins. of the Guptas,* pp. 11-12.
112. *Ibid.,* pp. 14-15.
113. Allan John, *Catalogue of the Coins of the Gupta Dynasties and of Śaśānka, King of Gauḍa,* p. lxxv. (London, 1914).
114-117. Fleet, *ibid.,* pp. 12, 14.
118. *Ep. Ind.,* VIII. pp. 44, 45, 49. Dr. Kane calls the council of ministers an advisory body, and others, executive councillors. Kane, *op. cit.,* III. p. 105.
119. *Kauṭilya,* pp. 22, 57 ; text, pp. 22, 59, *op. cit.*

120. Hultzsch, *Ins. of Aśoka*, pp. 14, 15.
121. Hultzsch, *ibid.*, pp. 123, 124.
122. Fleet, *J.R.A.S. for 1912*, p. 707 ; Kane, *J.B.B.R.A.S.*, XXIV, pp. 648-53 ; Kane, *Hist. of Dharmaśāstras*, III, pp. 138-39.
123. Hultzsch, *ibid.*, Intr. p. xxxix-xl.
124. Rhys Davis, *Buddhist India*, p. 23 citing *Anguttaranikāya*, I. p. 213, II. p. 252 ; *Dīghanikāya*, II. p. 200. See also *Mahāvāstu*, I. p. 157, and *ibid.*, n. (2) ; 140, and note (2) ; II. pp. 2, 393.
125. For details, read Kane, *op. cit.*, III. pp. 135-36.
126. *Ep. Ind.*, XXII. p. 1. The interest of this record lies in the fact that it refers to the pre-Aśokan times. Dr. Fleet assigned it to a period ranging from 320 to 180 B.C., or even earlier (Fleet, *J.R.A.S.*, 1907, p. 509). Dr. Jayaswal assigned it to Candragupta Maurya's reign when, according to the Jaina canonical works, there were many famines. (Jayaswal, *Ep. Ind.*, XXII, pp. 1, 3). The record is also interesting from another point of view: it refers to a decision of far-reaching consequence, since it covered the *dravya* store houses of four important cities ; and it was one which was taken by the council of *mahāmātras* of Śrāvasti (*Sāvasṭīyāna Mahāmātan*), thereby suggesting that they transcended the injunctions of Kauṭilya, who did not make provision for such a noble line of action on the part of ministers, while dealing with the measures to be taken in times of drought.
127. *Ep. Ind.*, VIII. pp. 47-49.
128. Kalhaṇa, *Rājataranginī*, Translator's note, p. xv. (Trans. by Ranjit Sitaram Pandit, Allahabad, 1935).
129. *Ibid.*, II. vv. 17-53, pp. 44-47.
130. *Ibid.*, V. vv. 270-78, pp. 178-79.
131. *Ibid.*, VII. vv. 1218-25, pp. 305-06. The date of king Kalasa is based on Ray, *D.H.N.I.*, I. p. 182.
132. Rajatarangini, V. vv. 72-115, pp. 164-66 ; Ray, *ibid.*, p. 182.
132a. Hultzsch, *Ins. of Aśoka*, p. 165.
133. *Ep. Ind.*, XX. p. 88, *op. cit.*
134. *Ibid.*, pp. 68, 70. Dr. Kane (*op. cit.*, III, p. 198) notices them but without enumerating them.
135. *Ep. Ind.*, VIII. pp. 43, 47.
136. *Kauṭilya*, Bk. I. Ch. I. 48, p. 48 ; text, p. 48.
137. On the early Pallavas, read Fleet, *D.K.D.*, pp. 320-22 ; Gopalan, R., *The History of the Pallavas of Kanchi* (Madras, 1928).
138. Hultzsch, *Ep. Ind.* VIII. pp. 162-63. Dr. Hultzsch translated the term *sarvādhyakṣa* as "general overseers" which, in view of what has been stated in these pages on the authority of Kauṭilya's *Arthaśāstra*, is less suggestive than "Chief Superintendent". The same scholar translated *vallabha* as a "court favourite" which, for the same reason, may be better rendered into "courtier", as done Dr. Shama Sastry.
139. Dikshit, K. N., *Ep. Ind.* XX, pp. 62-64.
140. *Ep. Ind.* VII, p. 183.
141. Rice, *My. & Coorg*, p. 67.
142. *Ep. Car.*, VII. Sk. 219, p. 130 ; text, p. 289. Mr. Rice assigned this record to A.D. 918. This is inadmissible in view of the date Śaka 834 (A.D. 912) given the record itself, which fell within the reign of Kannara II. The year A.D. 918 witnessed Jakkiyabbe's death in the Jaina manner.
143. On the local administration under the Guptas, read R. N. Saletore, *Life in the Gupta Age*, pp. 294-303.
144. I am indebted to Mr. S. B. Purohit, Assistant in the Kannada Research Institute in the Karnatak University, for the information on *bādube* and *kārapunnime*. See

also Panchamukhi, R. S., *Ep. Ind.* XX. (*op. cit.*) 65, n. (3). But Mr. Panchamukhi has not attempted to explain these terms. On the full moon and new moon festival days in Karnāṭaka, read Fleet, *Ep Ind.* V. pp. 11 ff.

145. *Manu*, VIII. 266-69, p. 301. Cf. *Yājñavalkya*, Ch. II. 220-24. See also Panchamukhi, *Ep. Ind.* XX, p. 67, n. (1).

146. Panchamukhi, *ibid.*, pp. 67-70. I am unable to accept all the interpretations of the terms given by the learned Editor of this record. For instance, Mr. Panchamukhi interprets *suṅka* as tax, whereas it is more properly intelligible as tolls. He does not explain the difficult term *guṇaśāsana* which I think perhaps meant "the qualities laid down in the orders of kings", or *śāsanas*, referring to the officials of the feeding house. That is, it was probably a sort of a code of conduct for guiding that institution. Mr. Panchamukhi says in a note that the exact significance of the word *guṇaśāsana* is not clear (Panchamukhi, *ibid.*, p. 70, note (3). He would translate *ūroḍeyar* as a village officer (*ibid.*, p. 66). This is inadmissible. The *ūroḍeyar* was a dignitary of much higher status and powers than a mere village officer. I would have equated the *ūroḍeyar* with a district officer but the *nād-gavuṇḍa* comes in the way. The only alternative is to imagine that, in addition to a district officer, whose duties were in some cases specified, there was another State official called *ūroḍeyar*, whose duties are, however, not clear in the epigraphs. The word *māṇi* is translated by Mr. Panchamukhi as a bachelor which is not entirely incorrect. But it does not bring out the precise significance of the term. I may add that that term is still used among the Madhva Brahmans of South Kanara for denoting a youth who has just undergone initiation and is still in his teens.

147. Smith, *E.H.I.*, p. 145.

148. Smith, *ibid.*, p. 146, *op. cit.*

149. Smith, *ibid.*, p. 152.

150. It is strange that Dr. Smith should have brought forward the novel theory that Kauṭilya wrote of the pre-Maurya times when, as he himself admits, Kauṭilya or Cāṇakya or Viṣṇugupta speaks with contempt of the Nandas in the *Mudrārākṣasa*, Act I (Smith, *ibid.*, p. 43, note 2). Dr. Smith is not the only scholar who has missed the passage in the *Arthaśāstra* relating to the wide extent of Candragupta Maurya's Empire. The late Professor V. R. R. Dikshitar, whose *Mauryan Polity* is one of the most dependable books on the subject, does not refer to the extent of the Empire of Candragupta Maurya. Two objections may be raised against Kauṭilya's statement relating to the extent of the Mauryan Empire. First, that he does not mention it by name. This might be interpreted to mean that he was merely thinking in the abstract of an ideal Empire. The same argument might be used in connection with his teacher, who is never mentioned by name, and with Narendra, whom he likewise does not mention by name. These arguments are an article of faith with the die-hards, who have always disbelieved in the authenticity of the *Arthaśāstra* and in the historicity of Kauṭilya himself! It would be as erroneous to decry the historicity of Narendra or the Mauryan Empire as given in that work, or of Kauṭilya's teacher,—because none of these is mentioned by name—as it would be, for instance, to doubt the historicity of most of the ancient works in Sanskrit because they do not contain the names of their authors, or refer to the regions where they were composed!

And, secondly, it might be argued that the extent of the Empire as given by Kauṭilya, namely 1,000 *yojanas*, would be too great for the Empire of Chandragupta Maurya. According to Dr. Shama Sastry (*Arthaśāstra*, pp. 118, note (6), 149, n. (14), a *yojana* is equal to 55/44 miles, or roughly five miles. Dr. Kane rightly states that the *yojana* has various meanings (Kane, *op. cit.*, III. p. 145, note 185). Dr. Fleet calculated a *yojana* as equal to four-and-a-half miles. (Fleet, *J.R.A.S.* for 1912, pp. 234, 237, 462-63). According to Dr. Sastry's calculation of five miles per *yojana*, Kauṭilya's explicit statement that the northern portion of the country, which stretched between the Himālayas and the Ocean was 1,000 *yojanas*, was about 5,000 miles. If we accept Dr. Fleet's computation, the extent of the Empire would be 4,500. When we realize that, as related above, the southern limit of the Empire was Surāṣṭra, and that the north-western regions of India were also under Candragupta Maurya, it is not impossible to agree with Kauṭilya about the wide extent of that monarch's Empire, although its exact extent in terms of miles will remain an unsolved problem until more proof is available on the subject.

151. As stated earlier, Professor Winternitz's assertion that Kauṭilya was only a *paṇḍit* has been ably dealt with by Dr. N. N. Law (*op. cit.*, pp. 211-14, 221). An equally unsympathetic and erroneous estimate of Kauṭilya was by Professor A. B. Keith, which also we have disposed of earlier. Professor Keith (*Sk. Lit.* p. xviii, *op. cit.*) seems to have judged the Mauryan Prime Minister from the standpoint of the excellence of the Sanskrit language. Dr. Otto Stein (*Megasthenes und Kauṭilya*, 1912) is no better study in this respect! One wonders whether accepting Professor Keith's criterion one could judge Aristotle by the high standards of Homer, or Machiavelli by those of Dante! Would any Western author, we wonder, condemn either Aristotle or Machiavelli because neither possesses poetic expression or ennobling thoughts?
152. Smith, *E.H.I.*, pp. 126-27.
153. Dikshitar, *op. cit.*, p. 34.
154. Saletore, *I.D.R. West*, pp. 133-34.
155. Saletore, *ibid.*, p. 107. I follow Dr. Fleet's chronology of the reigns of the two Mauryan rulers.
156. Saletore, *ibid.*, p. 133. I am afraid Dr. Smith has made much of a detail relating to the stay of Megasthenes. The Greek sources say that that Greek ambassador was sent by Seleukos "not once, but frequently" to Candragupta Maurya. The construction put on the word "frequently" put by Dr. E. A. Schwanbeck and by Professor McCrindle, (McCrindle, *Ancient India as described by Megasthenes and Arrian*, pp. 13-14) makes it very doubtful whether we could accept Dr. Smith's opinion that Megasthenes lived at the court of the Mauryan ruler for a considerable time. I do not see any justification for extending his stay at Pāṭaliputra for more than five or six years.
157. Smith, *ibid.*, p. 127.
158. Dikshitar, *ibid.*, p. 36.
159. Dikshitar, *ibid.*, p. 40.
160. Dikshitar, *ibid.*, p. 373.
161. Winternitz, *Calcutta Review*, April, 1924, (*op. cit.*), p. 19.
162. Winternitz, *ibid.*, p. 22.
163. *Vedic Index*, II. p. 214. Cited also by Law, *op. cit.*, p. 230.
164. Dr. Schwanbeck edited the *Indika* and published it at Bonn, in 1846. It was translated into English by Professor McCrincle in 1877.
165. Law, *ibid.*, pp. 230-31.
166. *Megasthenes*, Fragment 27 ; McCrindle, *Ancient India*, p. 68.
167. Professor Dikshitar calls this a distorted version of the actual condition obtaining in the land. He treats this subject in a slightly different way (Dikshitar, *ibid.*, pp. 342-43).
168. *Pāṇini*, III. 2. 21 ; VI. 3. 115 ; Agrawala, *op. cit.*, pp. 311-12 for a useful discussion on this point. According to Professor Godstücker, Vedic literature was available to Pāṇini even in Mss. (Goldstücker, *Pāṇini*, pp. 11-47 ; Agrawala, *ibid.*, p. 311).
169. *Kauṭilya*, Bk. II. Ch. VII. pp. 61-65, *op. cit.*
170. *Ibid.*, Bk. II. Ch. X. pp. 71-75 ; text, pp. 70-75.

171. *Megasthenes,* Fragment XXXII : McCrindle, *Ancient India,* pp. 83-86, Smith, *E.H.I.*, p. 140, note (2).
172. Smith, *ibid.*, p. 140.
173. Smith, *ibid.*, p. 141. Dr. Law has likewise drawn attention to this error in Megasthenes (Law, *op. cit.*, pp. 233-34).
174. Smith, *ibid.*, p. 138. The confusion in the mind of Dr. Smith in regard to this detail is apparent when on page 135 of his work, he speaks of one-sixth value of the gross produce, and on page 138, of one-fourth!
175. Professor Dikshitar (*Maur. Polity*, pp. 142-43) cites in this connection the opinion of Professor Hopkins (*J.A.O.S.*, 13, p. 88), who rightly rejects this statement of the Greek ambassador, as being erroneous.
176. Megasthenes in Arrian, *Indika*, Ch. 10 ; Smith, *ibid.*, p. 105, n. (1). See also McCrindle, *Ancient India*, p. 211.
177. Law, *op. cit.*, pp. 235-36.
178. *Kauṭilya*, Bk. III. Ch. XIII. pp. 205-08 ; text, pp. 181-84.
179. *Ibid.*, Bk. II. Ch. I. 47, p. 47 ; text, p. 47.
180. *Ibid.*, Bk. IV. Ch. XII. 232 ; p. 260 ; text, p. 232.
181. Dikshitar, *ibid.*, p. 350.
182. *Dialogues of the Buddha*, Part I, pp. 5, 19 ; 76-77, 84, 101, 103, 128, (S. B. Pali, Vol. II) ; *Mahāvastu*, Vol. II. pp. 2, 34, 55, 164-65 (Jones, J. J., London, 1952) ; Vol. III. pp. 20 ff., 40, 49, 57, 173, 374, 379, 389, 404, 442 (same translator, London, 1956).
182a. *Megasthenes*, Frags. XXVII B and C. in McCrindle, *Ancient India*, p. 72.
182b. *Ibid.*, pp. 68-69.
182c. *Manu*, VIII. 140-41, p. 278.
182d. *Ibid.*, III. 153, 180 ; IV. 210, 220, 224-25 ; pp. 103, 109, 161-64. See also under money lending *ibid.*, I. 90. IX. 326 ; X. 115. These references are only to verses and not to pages.
182e. On *vyāij*, see *Kauṭilya*, Bk. II. Ch. VI. 60, p. 58 ; text, p. 60 ; Ch. XII. 84, p. 87 ; text, p. 84 ; Bk. III. Ch. I. 148-50, pp. 167-70 ; text, pp. 148-50.
182f. *Ibid.*, Bk. III. Ch. XI. 174-77, pp. 197-201 ; text, pp. 174-77 ; Ch. XII. 177-81, pp. 201-05, text, pp. 177-81. See also note (223) below.
183. For an exhaustive study of Kauṭilya and Megasthenes, read Dr. Otto Stein, *Megasthenes und Kautilya* (*op. cit.*) (Wien, 1921). Dr. Stein has been effectively answered by Dr. Bernhard Breloer in the latter's *Kauṭilyan Studien. I. Das Grundeigentum in Indien* (Bonn, 1927) ; *II. Altindisches Privatrecht bei Megasthenes und Kautilya* (Bonn, 1928). Dr. Shama Sastry has referred to this useful work of Dr. Breloer (Shama Sastry, *Kauṭilya,* Preface, p. xxxi, note (1).
184. McCrindle, *Ancient India as described in Classical Literature*, p. 55. See also *ibid.*, p. 107.
185. *Megasthenes*, Frag. XXVII ; in McCrindle, *Ancient India*, p. 70. Dikshitar, *ibid.*, p. 107.
186. Arrian, *op. cit.*, V ; Dikshitar, *ibid.*, p. 351, note (3).
187. Dikshitar, *ibid.*, p. 351, n. (3).
188. *Kauṭilya*, Bk. II. Ch. IX. 69, p. 20 ; text, p. 69. Dr. Law comments on the text by saying that the several heads were transferable from one department to another (Law, *op. cit.*, p. 246). This is not borne out by the text where *anityam* is probably to be understood in the sense of "temporary", as Dr. Shama Sastry rightly says.
189. *Kauṭilya*, Bk. II. Ch. IV. 57, p. 55 ; text, p. 57. See also Sastry, *ibid.*, (Eng. trans.), Intr. p. xxxi ; Law, *ibid.*, p. 246.
190. Smith, *E.H.I.*, pp. 132-34.
191. Law, *ibid.*, pp. 244-46.
192. Dikshitar, *ibid.*, pp. 228-35.

193. Law, *op. cit.*, pp. 240-42.
194. Smith, *op. cit.*, pp. 137-51. Dr. Law does not seem to refer to this aspect of the question.
195. Dikshitar, *op. cit.*, pp. 165-66.
196. *Kauṭilya*, Bk. VII. Ch. XIV. 307, p. 334 ; text, p. 307.
197. *Ibid.*, Bk. II. Ch. I, 47, 46 ; text, p. 47.
198. *Ibid.*, Bk. II. Ch. XXIV. 117, p. 129 ; text, p. 117. Dr. Law refers to *kulyā-vapaṇam ca kālatāḥ*, to the agriculturists making their own arrangements for the raising of water, and to the different water rates (*udakabhāgam*) payable to the State (Law, *op. cit.*, pp. 233-34). It is only the commentator who explains the term waterlift by saying that it means channels (*kulyā*). See Shama Sastry, *ibid.*, p. 129, n. (3).
199. *Kauṭilya*, Bk. II. Ch. XX. 106, pp. 117-18 ; text, pp. 106-07.
200. Cf. Dikshitar, *op. cit.*, pp. 365-66.
201. *Megasthenes*, Fragments I and XXXIV ; McCrindle, *Ancient India*, pp. 30, 86 ; see also Kane, *op. cit.*, III. pp. 162-63. Dr. Law does not refer to these details.
202. Dikshitar, *ibid.*, p. 332. Here in note (3) reference is given to *Megasthenes*, Frag. II.
203. Dikshitar, *ibid.*, p. 358. See also Smith, *E.H.I.*, p. 147.
204. For further details, read Smith, *ibid.*, pp. 132-33.
205. *Megasthenes*, Fragment, XXIX ; *Kauṭilya*, Bk. III. Chs. XXXI-XXXII, pp. 151-55. Stein, *op. cit.*, p. 41 ff. See also Dikshitar, *ibid.*, pp. 333-34. Megasthenes describes the army of Sandrakottas or Candragupta Maurya as having been composed of 400,000 or 600,000 men, 30,000 cavalry, 9,000 elephants (Frags. XXVII ; XLVI ; MacCrindle, *Ancient India*, pp. 68, 141). See also Kane, *op. cit.*, III. p. 204. There are no means of verifying the details given by Megasthenes. But is it possible that in those times, when the foreigners were disliked, Megasthenes could have had any occasion of even visiting the Army Headquarters of the Mauryan Government?
206. *Kauṭilya*, Bk. V. Ch. III. 249, p. 278 ; text, p. 249.
207. Megasthenes cited by Law, *op. cit.*, p. 244. The reference is to *Megasthenes*, Frag. XXXIV ; McCrindle, *Ancient India*, p. 88. Professor Dikshitar does not mention this. (See Dikshitar, *ibid.*, pp. 335-36).
208. *Kauṭilyya*, Bk. II. Ch. XXVIII. 127, pp. 139-40 ; text, p. 126-27.
209. *Megasthenes*, Frag. XXIII. See also Law, *ibid.*, p. 243 where he rightly rejects Professor Winternitz's assertion that the Admiral of the Fleet performed only fiscal and commercial duties.
210. *Kauṭilya*, Bk. III. Ch. II. 152, p. 172 ; text, pp. 151-52. Cf. *Manu*, IX. 196, p. 371.
211. *Megasthenes*, Fragment, XXVII. See also Stein, *op. cit.*, p. 64.
212. Read Dikshitar, *ibid.*, pp. 340-41 for a slightly different treatment of the subject.
213. *Kauṭilya*, Bk. I. Ch. XX. 45, p. 43 ; text, p. 45.
214. *Megasthenes*, Fragment XXVII ; McCrindle, *Ancient India*, p. 71.
215. Kauṭilya, Bk. I. Ch. XXI. 4,2 p. 41 ; text, p. 42.
216. Read Dikshitar, *op. cit.*, pp. 347-48 for a slightly different treatment of this topic.
217. *Kauṭilya*, Bk. II. Ch. XXXVI, 144-45, pp. 160-62 ; text, pp. 143-45.
218. *Ibid.*, Bk. II. Ch. XVI. 98, p. 105 ; text, p. 98.
219 & 220. Smith, *op. cit.*, p. 134, and note (1). The reference is to *Megasthenes*, Frag. XXXIV ; McCrindle, *Ancient India*, p. 87.
221. *Kauṭilya*, Bk. I. Ch. XVI. 32, p. 32 ; text, p. 32.
222. Law, *op. cit.*, pp. 240-41.
223. *Kauṭilya*, Bk. III. Ch. XII, pp. 201-05 ; text, pp. 177-81. See notes 182 (e) and 182 (f) above.
224. Winternitz cited by Law, *op. cit.*, pp. 231-32 ; Stein, *op. cit.*, p. 28.
225. Dikshitar, *ibid.*, p. 109.

226. Dikshitar, *op. cit.*, p. 110.
227. Dikshitar, *ibid.*, pp. 333-34.
228. *Kauṭilya*, Bk. II. Ch. III, pp. 50-52 ; text, pp. 51-54.
229. *Ibid.*, Bk. II. Ch. IV. 55, p. 53 ; text, p. 55.
230. *Ibid.*, Bk. I. Ch. XX. 40, p. 39 ; text, p. 40.
231. Dikshitar, *ibid.*, p. 334.
232. Smith, *ibid.*, p. 127.
233. McCrindle, *Ind. Ant.*, VI, p. 136 ; Hultzsch, *Ins. of Aśoka*, Introd., pp. xxxviii ; *Megasthenes*, Frags. XXV-XXVI ; McCrindle, *Ancient India*, pp. 65-68. See also Kane, *op. cit.*, III, p. 183. Dr. Kane has cited the evidence of Patañjali, who frequently refers to Pāṭaliputra in his *Mahābhāṣya*. See also Smith, *ibid.*, p. 127.
234. *Megasthenes*, Fragments, XXVI ; McCrindle, *ibid.*, p. 67.
235. Dr. Law has rightly rejected this superficial argument of Professor Winternitz as being "wide of the mark" (Law, *op. cit.*, p. 232).
236. McCrindle, *Ind. Ant.*, VI, p. 131 ; Hultzsch, *ibid.*, p. xxxviii.
237. Smith, *ibid.*, pp. 127-28.
238. *Kauṭilya*, Bk. II. Ch. III. 52, p. 51 ; text, p. 52.
239. Fa Hien in Legge, *A Record.*, etc., p. 77 ; see also Kane, *op. cit.*, III, p. 183.
240. McCrindle, *The Invasion of India by Alexander*, p. 189 ; see also Dikshitar, *ibid.*, p. 109.
241. McCrindle, *Ancient India as described in Classical Literature*, Aelian, Bk. XIII. C. xviii, cited by Dikshitar, *op. cit.*, p. 109, note (4).
242. Smith, *op. cit.*, p. 128.
243. *Kauṭilya*, Bk. I. Ch. XX. 40, p. 39 ; text, p. 40.
244. *Ibid.*, Bk. I. Ch. XX. 40-41, pp. 30-40 ; text, pp. 40-41.
245. Pofessor Dikshitar also refers to these passages but the reference given by him to the *Arthaśāstra*, Bk. I. Ch. XXII (Dikshitar, *ibid.*, p. 110) should be to Ch. XX.
246. *Kauṭilya*, Bk. II. Ch. III. 54, p. 52 ; text, p. 54. A good study of the remains of the great Mauryan royal palace is found in Lt.-Col. L. A. Waddell's *Report on the Excavations at Pāṭaliputra* (Patna), (Calcutta, 1903) ; while the further exeavations on the site of that capital are described in the *Annual Report of the Archaeological Survey, Eastern Circle, for 1912-13*, pp. 55-61.
247. Among the scholars who have in smaller or larger measure dealt with this aspect of the question may be mentioned Professor Rangaswamy Aiyangar, Dr. Kane, Professor Dikshitar, Dr. Agrawala, and Professor Radha Kumud Mookerjee. The last named historian's is the most exhaustive of the studies in this connection. But by styling it *Parallelisms between Aśokas' Edicts and Kauṭilya's Arthaśāstra* (*Proceedings of the V Indian Oriental Conference* I, pp. 329-47, Lahore 1930), Professor Mookerjee seems to create the impression that we have to judge Kauṭilya by the standards of Aśoka. His treatment of the subject of referring first to Aśoka and, then, to Kauṭilya seems to confirm this.

The opening sentence of this learned paper seems to dispel that fear but creates another one. "The purpose of this paper is to bring together the parallel passages in the Arthaśāstra of Kauṭilya and inscriptions of Aśoka so as to show to what extent they throw light upon each other and may be considered as contemporary documents" (*ibid.*, p. 329). The first part of the statement may be conceded but the second appears doubtful, if not inadmissible. Kauṭilya, as is commonly accepted, was the Prime Minister of Candragupta Maurya, whose son was Bindusāra Amitraghāta, whose son was Aśoka. The dates of the Mauryan monarchs are still a matter of uncertainty. Following Dr. Fleet, they may be assigned to these dates—Candragupta Maurya, 320-296 B.C. ; Bindusara, 296-68 B.C. ; and Aśoka 264 B.C. accession. (See Saletore, *I. D. R. West*, p. 107). If we agree with the view of Professor Mookerjee, we have to make Kauṭilya a contemporary of three monarchs—Candragupta Maurya, Bindusāra, and Aśoka, that is, make him live a life of fifty-six years only as a Prime Minister. This, when added to the unknown factor of his earlier life before he became Prime Minister, would give him a long period of not less than seventy-five or eighty years. There is, of course, nothing improbable in an Indian statesman's living such a long span of life ; but in the case of an aggressive statesman like Kauṭilya, it is doubtful whether we could assign to him such a long life.

Further, although, as will be pointed out below in the text, Aśoka's earlier life as a ruler appears to have been severe, if not cruel, yet it is again doubtful whether it was due to the personal influence of Kauṭilya, or to the effect of the latter's state manual, or to the inherent nature of the ruler himself. I agree with the view of the late Dr. Shama Sastry that Kauṭilya lived long before Aśoka (Cf. Saletore, *ibid*., p. 150). The assumption of Professor Mookerjee that Kauṭilya's book and Aśoka's Edicts were contemporary documents is untenable.

Moreover, Professor Mookerjee's comparison between the Aśokan precepts in regard to all sects and those given in the *Arthaśāstra* do not seem to be relevant. He writes that the passage in the Rock Edict VII that Devānampriya Priyadarśin Rāja desires that in all places should reside diverse sects is the same as Kauṭilya's injunction that *Pāṣaṇḍas* and *Cāṇḍālas* should dwell near the cremation ground (beyond the city) ; that no Pāṣaṇḍas could be accommodated in a *dharmaśālā* without the permission of the City Officer, Gopa ; and that their abode should be searched for suspicious characters. (Mookerjee, *ibid*., 336-36. Cf. *Kauṭilya*, Bk. II. 144, p. 161 ; text, p. 144.

I am afraid that is a wrong parallel. In the first place, the crisp Rock Edict VII opens with the statement that King Devānampriya Priyadarśin "desires (that) all may reside everywhere". (*Devānam Piye Piyadasi lājā savatā ichhati sava-pāsaṁḍa vasevu*). The next sentence is "For all these desire self-control and purity of mind" (*save hi te sayamaṁ bhāvasuddhi cā ichhaṁti*). The rest of the short Rock Edict refers to men possessing various desires and passions, their fulfilling the whole or only a portion of their duties ; and to any one who, while practising great liberality, does not possess self-control, being a very mean man (Hultzsch, *Ins. of Aśoka*, p. 36). Here we have, therefore, the Emperor's desire that the Pāṣaṇḍas or heretics may live like other sects anywhere, so as to fulfil their duties. That is, it is an Edict of Freedom.

But the references to the Pāṣaṇḍas in the *Arthaśāstra*, as given by Professor Mookerjee, form an Edict of Prevention! In the first citation from the *Artha-śāstra*, it is an explicit order in these terms: "Heretics and Cāṇḍālas shall live beyond the burial grounds" (*Pāṣaṇḍa-cāṇḍālānāṁ śmaśānānte vasaḥ*) (Bk. II. Ch. IV. 56, p. 54 ; text, p. 56). That this is a prohibitory order which gave no option to the Pāṣaṇḍas and Cāṇḍālas is clear from the preceding injunction which states that the rule regarding the cremation grounds, if violated, would entail a fine equal to the first amercement. Here, therefore, we have a contrast between Kauṭilya's precept which is prohibitory, and that of Aśoka, which is permissive.

Professor Mookerjee's second citation from Kauṭilya is wide of the mark. The contexts from which it is taken do not warrant its interpretation in the sense of freedom that was to be given to the Pāṣaṇḍas. On the other hand, it is incriminatory. This will be made clear when we note the contexts in which the references to the Pāṣaṇḍas occur. The first reference is in the chapter on the duties of the City Superintendent, to the following effect: "Managers of charitable institutions shall send information (to Gopa or Sthānika) as to any heretics (*pāṣaṇḍa*) and travellers arriving to reside therein. They shall allow ascetics and men learned in the Vedas to reside in such places only when those persons are known to be of reliable character." (*Kauṭilya*, Bk. II. Ch. XXXVI 144, p. 166 ; text, p. 144). Here it is not the City Officer, whom Professor Mookerjee confounds with the Gopa (who, by the way, as is narrated in the beginning of the same chapter, was an officer in charge of the accounts of ten, twenty, or forty households), who is the officer concerned, but either the Sthānika or the Gopa to whom the managers of charitable institutions had to send the requisite information about the heretics. And that information was about the movements of the latter.

In a later context in the same chapter, Kauṭilya writes that any wayfarers going along a high road shall catch hold of certain types of people ; and then he says that, as we have already seen, "(Spies) shall also make a search for suspicious persons in the interior of deserted houses, in the workshops or houses of vinters and sellers of cooked rice and flesh, in gambling houses, and in the above of heretics". (*Kauṭilya, ibid.*, pp. 161-62 ; text, p. 144, *op. cit.*).

It is not the above references, therefore, that could be made to agree with the ordinances of Aśoka, as Professor Mookerjee would make us believe, but a statement of Kauṭilya which seems to have escaped the learned historian's notice. It occurs in the chapter on the Resumptions of Gifts, Sale Without Ownership, and Ownership, and runs thus: "Ascetics and heretics shall, without disturbing each other, reside in a large area" (*āśramiṇaḥ pāṣaṇḍa vā mahatyavakāśe paras-paraṁ-abādhamānā vaseyuḥ*) (*Kauṭilya*, Bk. III. Ch. XVI. 191, p. 216 ; text, p. 191). But even this injunction did not give any freedom to the heretics to live as they liked: they were to live without disturbing others, not in the persuasive manner of Aśoka but in the peremptory way of Kauṭilya. From whatever angle we view the references to the Pāṣaṇḍas in the *Arthaśāstra*, they cannot be equated with those mentioned in the Rock Edicts.

In another place, too, Professor Mookerjee's attempts to draw a parallel between the *Arthaśāstra* and the Rock Edicts is unconvincing. He writes that Aśoka's concern for the Ājīvikas as described in Pillar Edict VII, and also in the granting of cave dwellings to them, may be likened to Kauṭilya's Brahmanical prejudice against them, when the Mauryan Prime Minister classifies them along with the Śākyas (Buddhists) "as being unworthy of attainment at any ceremony connected with the gods or ancestors" (Mookerjee, *op. cit.*, p. 346).

There is some confusion in the comparison drawn by Professor Mookerjee. Rock Edict VII of Delhi—Topra mentions the Ājīvikas in the following context: "Some (*Mahāmātras*) were ordered by me to busy themselves with the affairs of the Samgha ; likewise others were ordered by me to busy themselves also with the Brāhmaṇas (and) Ājīvikas ; others were ordered by me to busy themselves with the Nirgranthas ; others were ordered by me to busy themselves also with various (other) sects ; (thus) different *Mahāmātras* (are busying themselves) specially with different (congregations)" (Hultzsch, *op. cit.*, p. 136). This Rock Edict describes the Emperor's concern not only for the Ājīvikas but for all—the Brahmans, the Nirgranthas or Jainas, and various other sects.

Professor Mookerjee's statement referring to the grant of cave dwellings given by Emperor Aśoka to the Ājīvikas is perhaps to be traced to II Cave Inscription on the Barabar Hill which contains the following single sentence: "By King Priyadarśin (when he had been) anointed twelve years, this cave in the Khalatika mountain was given to the Ājīvikas" (Hultzsch, *ibid.*, p. 181).

Even according to the learned historian's own citations from the *Arthaśāstra*, the two passages from the Rock Edicts cannot be considered as being parallel to those in that work. The Delhi-Topra Rock Edict refers to Emperor Aśoka's solicitude for the welfare of the Ājīvikas ; and the Barabar Hill inscription confirms it by mentioning the gift of a cave dwelling to them. While the passages in the *Arthaśāstra* prove that Kauṭilya, instead of showing any compassion or sympathy for them, imposed a penalty on those who might be inclined to consider the Ājīvikas in a charitable manner. The benevolent attitude of Aśoka cannot be compared with the malevolent disposition of Kauṭilya in regard to the Ājīvikas.

Professor Mookerjee states on the same page (p. 346) that the term *Devīkumālānaṁ* in Pillar Edict VII is identical with *devī* used by Kauṭilya for the queen (*Artha-śāstra*, I. 10) and with *kumāra* used for a prince (*Arthaśāstra*, I. 20).

This comparison likewise cannot be sustained. It requires no proof to show that the word *devī* meant a queen, and the word *kumāra*, a prince. But the parallel, if accepted would be misleading. In Rock Edict VII Delhi-Topra we have the statement that the chief officers (*mukhya*) were occupied with the gifts of the Emperor and of the queens, and of those of his sons and of the queens' sons (Hultzsch, *op. cit.*, pp. 131, 136). In the latter context the term *devīkumālānaṁ* occurs which Dr. Hultzsch translated as sons of the queens.

One fails to see how it could be made to agree with the passage in the *Artha-śāstra* where it is stated as follows: "Never, in the view of Kauṭilya, shall the king make himself or his queen an object (*lakṣaṇam*, butt) of testing the character of his councillors, nor shall he vitiate the pure, like water with poison" (Bk. I. Ch. X. 17, p. 17 ; text, p. 17).

There is another reference to the queen (*devī*) in the Chapter on the King's Duty towards the Harem, wherein it is stated that the king, when in the interior of his harem, shall see the queen only when her personal purity is vouchsafed for by an old maid servant. (*Kauṭilya*, Bk. I. Ch. XX. 41, p. 40 ; text, p. 41). In the same Chapter we are informed that the residences of the princes and the princesses shall be located in a particular quarter (*Ibid.*, p. 40 ; text, p. 41). In the light of this glaring difference between the references to the queens and the princes in the *Arthaśāstra* and in the Rock Edicts, we cannot understand how they could be considered as being the same! These shortcomings in the article of Professor Mookerjee do not detract its worth. Indeed, Professor Mookerjee has considerably lightened the task of scholars working on this aspect of the problem by giving us a very exhaustive study of the parallelisms in the *Arthaśāstra* and the Rock Edicts.

Perhaps in this connection I might dispose of another view relating to Kauṭilya and Aśoka. Professor Sinha writes thus: "It was this living example of Aśoka that might have supplied Kauṭilya his ideals of kingship. The king of Kauṭilya is the Aśoka devoid of his too great love for Buddhistic ways of life" (Sinha, *op. cit.*, pp. 148, 149, 191, 192, 193). Professor Sinha postulates in this statement the theory that Kauṭilya had before him the living example of Aśoka. The learned author seems to go a step further that Professor Mookerjee in affirming that Aśoka supplied Kauṭilya with the pattern of kingship. We need not cite here again the mass of evidence available in the *Arthaśāstra* to show that such a theory cannot be maintained at all. The very purpose of Kauṭilya's writing his book would be unintelligible if we were to suppose that he composed it either during or after Aśoka's reign!

248. Mookerjee, Radha Kumud, *Aśoka*, p. 194 ; Dikshitar, *op. cit.*, pp. 250-52. I cannot agree with Professor Dikshitar's characterization of *prāṇānām anāraṁbha* (*praṇārambho*) *pāṇesu-sayamo, vihiṁsā bhūtānām*, and *svabhūtānām achhatiṁ* as referring to three different negative qualities (Dikshitar, *ibid.*, p. 251). They are three aspects of the same major problem of non-injury to living beings, or, *ahiṁsā*, as we might now-a-days call it.
249. *Kauṭilya*, Bk. I. Ch. III. 8, p. 7 ; text, p. 8.
250. Hultzsch, *op. cit.*, pp. 4-5.
251. See *Kauṭilya*, pp. 282, 315-18.
252. On dutifulness to teachers, read Manu, II. 71-73, p. 43 ; on dutifulness to parents, *ibid.*, II. 145-48, 225-37, pp. 56-57, 71 ; IV. 162, 179-80, 182, pp. 154, 157.
253. *Kauṭilya*, Bk. I. Ch. V. 10, p. 9 ; text, p. 10, *op. cit.*
254. *Ibid.*, Bk. I. Ch. VII. 13, p. 12 ; text, p. 13. The text runs thus: *maryādāṁ sthāpayet-ācāryān-amālyān-vā*. Dr. Shama Sastry had translated it as, "Those

teachers and ministers who keep him (the king) from falling a prey to dangers". The word *maryādām* admits of a more appropriate interpretation in the sense of "bounds of morality" or "propriety" than that of danger, as understood by the learned translator. See Apte, *Sanskirt-English Diety.*, p. 745.

255. *Kauṭilya*, Bk. II. Ch. I. 46, p. 46 ; text, p. 46.
256. *Ibid.*, Bk. II. Ch. I. 48, p. 47 ; text, p. 47, *op. cit.*
257. *Ibid.*, Bk. III. Chs. XIII-XIV, pp. 205-11 ; text, pp. 181-87. See *ibid.*, Bk. IV. Ch. XII. 232, p. 260, for a penalty on a servant who took under his protection the wife of the absentee husband!
258. *Ibid.*, Bk. XIII. Ch. V. 409, p. 438 ; text, p. 409.
259. Hultzsch, *ibid.*, p. 10, and *ibid.*, notes (6)-(8).
260. *Ibid.*, p. 15.
261. *Ibid.*, p. 33. Cf. VIII Rock Edict at Kalsi, *ibid.*, p. 37. Cf. its versions at Girnar, etc.
262. Hultzsch, *op. cit.*, pp. 24-25, 47-49 ; 68-69.
263. *Ibid.*, pp. 116-17.
264. *Ibid.*, pp. 121-22.
265. *Ibid.*, pp. 94-97.
266. *Ibid.*, p. 118.
267. *Kauṭilya*, Bk. I. Ch. III, 8, p. 7 ; text, p. 8.
268. Hultzch, *ibid.*, pp. 7-8.
269. *Manu*, IV. 246, p. 167 ; V. 43-47, 56, pp. 175-77. On *dharma*, which Professor Bühler interpreted as justice, read *Manu*, VIII. 15-16, p. 255. Professor Aiyangar merely refers to the prohibition of the castration of animals in the *Arthaśāstra* (III. 10). (Aiyangar, *op. cit.*, p. 42, and note (71). I am unable to find the reference to castration in the *Arthaśāstra* in Book III, Ch. 10. But see note (258) above for the proper reference to this point.
270. Hultzsch, *op. cit.*, pp. 127-28. See also Mookerjee, *Proceedings*, p. 345.
271. *Kauṭilya*, Bk. I. Ch. XV. 29, p. 29 ; text, p. 29.
272. *Ibid.*, Bk. I. Ch. XIX, 39, p. 38 ; text, p. 39.
273. Hultzsch, *ibid.*, pp. 12-13. For Kalsi, *ibid.*, pp. 34-35 ; for Shahbazgarhi, *ibid.*, p. 58 for Manshera, *ibid.*, p. 76. Jaugadha, *ibid.*, p. 107, etc. Cf. Mookerjee, *ibid.*, p. 333.
274. Hultzsch, *ibid.*, p. 12, *op. cit.*
275. *Pāṇini*, V. 4. 34 ; Agrawala, *op. cit.*, p. 403. Read *ibid.*, p. 412 for further remarks on the transaction of business.
276. Read Saletore, *I.D.R. West*, p. 337 for a short discussion of the date of Pāṇini.
277. Professor Mookerjee has also noticed the readiness of Aśoka for transacting public business as given in Rock Edict VI but the parallels which he gives from Kauṭilya do not, in my opinion, seem to meet the point, although he certainly cites from the same book and chapter in the *Arthaśāstra*. Professor Mookerjee's comparison of Aśoka's readiness with the list of duties mentioned by Kauṭilya (which the learned Professor refers us to Book II Ch. XXX,—which should be to Book I Chapter XIX, since Book II. Ch. XXX refers to the Superintendents of Chariots and Elephants and the duties of the Commander-in-Chief) is not relevant. Likewise his reference to the king's inspection of the horses, elephants, etc. as given in Bk. I. Chapter XIX, is beside the mark.
278. Hultzsch, *op. cit.*, pp. 12, *op. cit.*
279. *Kauṭilya*, Bk. II. Ch. II, 49, p. 48 ; text, p. 49.
280. *Ibid.*, Bk. I. Ch. X. 17, p. 17 ; text, p. 17.
281. *Ibid.*, Bk. VIII. Ch. III. 329, p. 556 ; text, p. 329.
282. Hultzsch, *ibid.*, pp. 4, 29, etc.
283. *Kauṭilya*, Bk. II. Ch. VI. 60, p. 59 ; text, p. 60. Cf. Mookerjee, *Proceedings*, p. 332. Professor Mookerjee's parallel of *Devanampiye evam āha* or *āñapayati* with

Kauṭilya's formula mentioned in connection with royal writs (Mookerjee, *ibid.*, p. 330 ; Kauṭilya, Bk. II. Ch. X, pp. 71-72) is not convincing. Kauṭilya's explicit statement that *iti* is used to indicate the completion of a writ, while an oral message is indicated by the phrase *vācikamasyeti* (an oral message along with this writ) (*Kauṭilya*, pp. 72-73), is not exactly in conformity with Aśoka's formula. Is it possible that Aśoka preferred, in this instance, to imitate the Iranian monarchs? See Dr. Hultzsch's comments on Aśoka's preamble—"*Devānampriya Priyadarśin* speaks thus!" in Hultzsch, *ibid.*, p. xliii.

284, 285, 286 & 287. Hultzsch, *op. cit.*, pp. xi-xli, pp. 5, 25.

288. *Kauṭilya*, Bk. I. Ch. XIII, p. 22, *op. cit.*

289. Professor Dikshitar's attempt to equate the *mahāmātras* of the Edicts with the *adhyakṣas* of the *Arhtaśāstra* (Dikshitar, *op. cit.*, p. 210), is unconvincnig.

290. *Kauṭilya*, Bk. I. Ch. XII. 20, p. 20 ; text, p. 20 ; Bk. I. Ch. XX. 41, p. 40 ; text, p. 41.

291. *Ibid.*, Bk. II. Ch. VI. 60, p. 58 ; text, 60. See also Dikshitar, *ibid.*, pp. 216-17, F. W. Thomas in *C.H.I.*, I. pp. 487, 508.

292. Kauṭilya, Bk. I. Ch. XII. 20, p. 20, p. 20. Dr. F. W. Thomas was the first to point that the term *pradeśika* in the Edicts was the same as the term *pradeṣṭri* in Kauṭilya (Thomas, F. W., *J.R.A.S. for 1914*, p. 383 ; *ibid. for 1915*, p. 112. Dr. Hultzsch doubted its accuracy (Hultzsch, *Ins. of Aśoka*, p. 5, note (3), although he would equate the *pradeśikas* of Aśoka with the *pradeśikeśvaras*, provincial chiefs of Kalhaṇa (*Rājataranginī*, IV. 126). But there is no reason to doubt Dr. Thomas' interpretation since, in this as well as in other matters, Aśoka would have followed naturally the example of Kauṭilya ; and unless there are valid grounds for maintaining that he had introduced radical administrative reforms, particularly in the nomenclature of officials, it may be presumed that he continued the practice as it had prevailed in the reign of his illustrious grand-father, whose great Prime Minister was Kauṭilya.

293. *Kauṭilya*, Bk. II. Ch. V. 59, p. 57 ; text, p. 59 ; *ibid.*, Ch. IX, pp. 68-71 ; text, pp. 68-70 ; Thomas, *Ind. Ant.*, XXXVII, p. 21, *J.R.A.S. for 1909*, p. 467 ; *ibid.*, 1914, p. 387 ff. See also Dikshitar, *op. cit.*, pp. 224-25. The term *yuktas* continued to exist in the form of *āyuktaka* and *viniyuktaka* in the Valabhi inscriptions. Fleet, *Ins. of the Guptas*, p. 169, and notes (4) and (5) ; Hultzsch, *Ins. of Aśoka*, p. 5, note (1).

294. *Kauṭilya*, Bk. I. Ch. XVI, pp. 29-32 ; text, pp. 30-32. Read also Dikshitar, *op. cit.*, p. 213.

295. *Pāṇini*, V. 2. 112 ; Agrawala, *op. cit.*, p. 399.

296. *Kauṭilya*, Bk. I. Ch. XV. pp. 26-28, *op. cit.* Dr. Agrawala's reference to *Kauṭilya* (Agrawala, *ibid.*, p. 400) should be to Bk. I. Ch. XV, and not to Bk. I. Ch. XI which deals with the Examination of Gems.

297. Hultzsch, *ibid.*, pp. 4, 5, and notes (7) & (8) on p. 5.

298. Hultzsch, *ibid.*, pp. 11, 13, *op. cit.*

299. *Kauṭilya*, Bk. I. Ch. XV, p. 29, *op. cit.* Dr. Jayaswal was the first scholar to point out the exact similarity between Kauṭilya's regulations and the practice under Aśoka (Jayaswal, *Ind. Ant.*, XLII. p. 283, cited by Hultzsch, *ibid.*, p. 13, and note (1). On Aśoka's *mantripariṣad* read Dikshitar, *op. cit.*, pp. 158-59. Professor Mookerjee institutes a comparison between the *dāpaka* mentioned in the *Arthaśāstra*, as fining and collecting the amount of fines, with the *dāpakam* mentioned in the VI Rock Edict (Mookerjee, *Proceedings*, p. 335). He also equates the officer called *vracabhūmika* mentioned in XII Rock Edict with the officer under the Department of Live Stock, who worked under the *samāhartā* mentioned in the *Arthaśāstra* (Mookerjee, *ibid.*, pp. 340-41). But the similarity seems to be too farfetched.

300. Hultzsch, *ibid.*, pp. 4-5 ; and p. 5, note (5). Dr. Kane (*op. cit.*, III, p. 114), and Professor Mookerjee (*ibid.*, p. 331) have also noticed this.

301. *Kauṭilya*, Bk. II. Ch. IX. 70, p. 70 ; text, p. 70. See also Mookerjee, *ibid.*, p. 331.
302. Watters, *Yuan Chwang*, II. pp. 88-90 ; see also Kane, *ibid.*, III, pp. 406-07.
303. Hultzsch, *ibid.*, pp. 95-97.
304. Read Dikshitar's pertinent remarks on *parikeśa*. Dikshitar, *ibid.*, p. 165, note (4) as against Dr. Hultzsch's comments on the same term. (Hultzsch, *ibid.*, p. 96 note (2).
305. Lüders, Heinrich, *Sitz. Ber der Kön Preus Akad. der Wiss. für 1914*, p. 859, cited by Hultzsch, *op. cit.*, p. 96 n. (1).
306. Lüders, *op. cit.*, p. 855 ; Hultzsch, *ibid.*, p. 96, note (3). Professor Mookerjee also mentions these officials (Mookerjee, *Proceedings*, p. 331). If the interpretation of Professor Lüders is accepted, it seems as if the distinction between the Officer-in-Charge of the City (*paura*) and the Superintendent of Transactions (*vyavahārika*) made by Dr. Shama Sastry (*Kauṭilya*, p. 20) has to be given up, since the text clearly read—*sannidhātṛi-pradeṣṭri-nāyaka paura-vyavahārika*, etc. (text, p. 20). But we need not give up the interpretation of Dr. Sastry, since it is possible that the earlier offices of the *paura* and *vyavahārika* in the days of Kauṭilya, might have been amalgamated in the times of Aśoka.
307. *Kauṭilya*, Bk. V. Ch. III. 247, p. 276 ; text, p. 247.
308. *Ibid.*, pp. 255-60, *op. cit.*
309. Hultzsch, *ibid.*, pp. 124-25.
310. Hultzsch, *ibid.*, pp. 9-10, 32-33, 56-57 ; Mookerjee, *Aśoka*, p. 143, n. (2) ; *Proceedings*, p. 333 , Dikshitar, *op. cit.*, p. 165, and note (4) where there is a good discussion of the words *karman* and *parikeśa*, which is commendable. The meaning of *palibodha* as fetters was, however, first pointed out by Professor Lüders, *SPAW*, (*op. cit.*), p. 841. See also Hultzsch, *ibid.*, p. 33, note (8).
311. Hultzsch, *ibid.*, p. 97, *op. cit.*
312. Hultzsch, *ibid.*, p. 125, and its versions at Lauriya Araraj, Rāmpurvā, and Allahabad Kosam, pp. 143, 152, and 157, respectively.
313. *Kauṭilya*, Bk. IV. Ch. XI. pp. 256-58. Professor Dikshitar, while writing about the four kinds of punishment advocated by Kauṭilya,—fines, imprisonment, mutilation, and death—(Dikshitar, *op. cit.*, p. 165), refers to *Kauṭilya*, Bk. IV. Ch. II. But this is not correct, since Bk. IV. Ch. II. refers to Protection against Merchants.
314. *Kauṭilya*, Bk. II. Ch. V. 58, p. 56 ; text, p. 58.
315. *Ibid.*, Bk. IV. Ch. IX. 225, 226, p. 253 ; text, pp. 225-26.
316. *Ibid.*, Bk. II. Ch. XXXVI. 146-47, pp. 164-65 ; text, pp. 146-47. Professor Mookerjee also mentions this detail (*Proceedings*, p. 345). Professor Dikshitar finds fault with Dr. Shama Sastry for having translated the verse beginning with *divase* and ending with *hiraṇyānugraheṇa vā* (Dikshitar, *op. cit.*, pp. 175-76). It would have been possible to have agreed with Professor Dikshitar's interpretation of this passage but for the fact that one cannot understand what the prisoners could do with the money which, according to this learned scholar, was meant "perhaps for their personal up keep". Did the Mauryan Government give the prisoners money so that the latter might maintain their health or their hygiene or their looks? The idea is too ultra-modern even for our own enlightenend days! Dr. Sastry's translation is both reasonable and in accordance with the spirit of the verse.
317. Hultzsch, *op. cit.*, pp. 127-28.
318. *Ibid.*, pp. 32-33.
319. *Ibid.*, pp. 95-97, *op. cit.*
320. *Kauṭilya*, Bk. IV. Ch. IX. 223, 226, pp. 250, 254 ; text, pp. 223, 226.
321. *Ibid.*, Bk. IV. Ch. X, 228, pp. 255-56, *op. cit.*
322. Hultzsch, *ibid.*, pp. 164-65.
323. Thomas. *J.R.A.S. for 1909*, pp. 466 ff. Hultzsch, *ibid.*, p. 165, n. (2).
324. *Manu*, VII. 130, p. 237. See also Fleet, *J.R.A.S. for 1908*, p. 479 ff., Hultzsch, *ibid.*, p. 165, n. (3).

325. *Kauṭilya*, Bk. II. Ch. XIV. 94, p. 99 ; text, p. 94. Read Professor Dikshitar's remarks on *bhāga*. Dikshitar, *ibid.*, p. 143.
326. See note (251) above in this Part.
327. Hultzsch, *ibid.*, pp. 46, 49, etc.
328. *Kauṭilya*. Bk. XII. Ch. I. 382, p. 411 ; text, p. 382.
329. Cf. Mookerjee, *Proceedings*, p. 343.
330. Senart, *Ind. Ant.*, XX. p. 260 ; Hultzsch, *ibid.*, p. xlix.
331. Hultzsch, *ibid.*, pp. L., 175, 178. See also Rock Edicts III, IV, IX, XI, XIII, for further elucidation of this concept.
332. *Ibid.*, pp. xlvii-xlviii ; See Rock Edicts XIII and Pillar Edicts VII in their different versions.
333. Hultzsch, *ibid.*, pp. liii ; 25.
334. *Ibid.*, pp. 46, 48, 68, 70, etc.
335. *Ibid.*, pp. 98-99, 116-17.
336. Manohan, F. J., *Early History of Bengal*, p. 219 (Oxford, 1925).
337. Hultzsch, *ibid.*, pp. xl-xlii.
338. Hultzsch, *ibid.*, p. 134.
339. *Ibid.*, pp. 67, 68, 69.
340. Dikshitar, *op. cit.*, pp. 129-30.
341. Hultzsch, *ibid.*, p. XXXIX.
342. Saletore, *I.D.R. West*, pp. 140-61.
343. Professor Mookerjee also noticed the term *dharmavijaya* occurring in XIII Rock Edict, and the three kinds of conquerors mentioned by Kauṭilya (Mookerjee, *Proceedings*, p. 343). But he has nothing more to add by way of elucidating this comparison.
344. Cf. Aiyangar, *op. cit.*, p. 109.
345. Hultzsch, *ibid.*, p. xlviii.
346. *Ibid.*, pp. 13, 35, etc.
347. *Ibid.*, pp. xlviii-xlxix ; 13, 20-22, 95, 100, 117.
348. *Kauṭilya*, Bk. I. Ch. III. 8, p. 7 ; text, p. 8, *op. cit.*
349. *Ibid.*, Bk. I. Ch. V. 11, p. 10 ; text, p. 11. Cf. Bandopadhyaya, *op. cit. P.I.* p. 295 ff. ; see also Dikshitar, *ibid.*, p. 116.
350. *Kauṭilya*, Bk. I. Ch. I. 39, p. 38, *op. cit.*
351. Hultzsch, *ibid.*, p. l. See also Rock Edicts II, IV, VII, IX, XI, VIII ; see also Mookerjee, *ibid.*, p. 337.
352. Hultzsch, *ibid.*, pp. 134-35.
353. *Kauṭilya*, Bk. II. Ch. I. 47, p. 46, *op. cit.*
354. Saletore, *ibid.*, pp. 156-62.
355. *Kauṭilya*, Bk. II. Ch. XXI. 111, p. 122 ; text, p. 111.
356. *Ibid.*, Ch. XXII. 113, p. 124 ; text, p. 113. Professor Mookerjee, while referring to the previous chapter of Kauṭilya, writes that the latter "also encourages the import of seeds of unripe and medicinal plants by exempting such import from tolls" (Mookerjee, *ibid.*, p. 332). I cannot trace such exemption in the *Arthaśāstra*.
357. Hultzsch, *ibid.*, pp. 1-2, and note (4) on page 2 ; 27-28.
358. *Kauṭilya*, Bk. II, Ch. XXV. 121, p. 134 ; and *ibid.*, note (4) ; text, p. 121. See also Mookerjee, *Proceedings*, p. 332.
359. *Kauṭilya*, Bk. XIII. Ch. V. 409, p. 438 ; text, p. 409. See also Mookerjee, *ibid.*
360. Hultzsch, *op. cit.*, pp. 32-33. See also Mookerjee, *ibid.*, p. 333.
361. *Kauṭilya*, Bk. II. Ch. I. 47, p. 47 ; text, p. 47, *op. cit.*

INDEX